CALL & The Learning Community

Presented by Keith Cameron

Elm Bank Publications
Exeter
1999

First Published
in
1999
by
Elm Bank Publications
24 Velwell Road, Exeter, EX4 4LE, UK.

British Library Cataloguing in Publication Data Available

ISBN 1-902454-09-X

Printed and bound in Great Britain by Antony Rowe Ltd, Chippenham, Wiltshire.

CALL
&
The Learning Community

Elm Bank Modern Language Studies

General Editor: Keith Cameron

The Short Story: Structure and Statement, presented and edited by William F. Hunter.

As Mighty as the Sword. A Study of the Writings of Charles de Gaulle, by Alan Pedley.

Variability in Spoken French. A Socio-linguistic Study of Interrogation and Negation, by Aidan Coveney.

Translation: Here and There. Now and Then, edited by Jane Taylor, Edith McMorran & Guy Leclercq.

A Tragic Farce: The Fronde (1648—1653), by Wendy Gibson.

Multimedia CALL: Theory and Practice, edited and presented by Keith Cameron.

Dialogues 1: Ricochets, edited by Susan Bainbrigge.

Dialogues 2: Endings, edited by Ann Amherst & Katherine Astbury.

Marguerite de Navarre: The Coach and The Triumph of The Lamb, translated and introduced by Hilda Dale.

Francophone Voices, edited and presented by Kamal Salhi.

CONTENTS

FOREWORD

Keith Cameron
University of Exeter, UK

The Eighth Biennial Exeter CALL Conference adopted as its theme, CALL & The Learning Community. These Proceedings reflect the international nature of the assembly, with participants coming from all over the globe and from twenty different countries. They also provide us with an up-to-date glimpse of recent developments and practices in the construction and use of CALL materials.

As we all appreciate, the computer and computer-mediated access to information now form part of our daily life. The advent of the internet has revolutionised the dissemination of data and has been quickly recognised as an admirable teaching resource. Governments and education authorities see in the new technology a means of improving the education system and probably a way of effecting economies. Teachers at all levels are being encouraged to develop web pages, to make full use of the new teaching resource.

In the process of adapting to novel methods in the classroom. the former debate about whether computer-assisted teaching is more effective than the so called 'traditional' method seems to have lost its momentum. There is a growing universal awareness that the computer in teaching is here to stay; it has become a pedagogical reality. Teachers have had an appreciable stock of teaching resources for a long time in the form of the printed word, whether it be in the form of handouts or in printed books. OHPs have made it possible to bring illustrations and projected text within the possibility of all. Although a new resource has been made available, it has not necessarily followed that the learning outcome has improved in keeping with improvements in the transmission of knowledge.

It is to acknowledge the fact that development of information technology for teaching has to concentrate on its effectiveness as a learning resource that the theme of 'CALL & The Learning Community' was chosen. The creation of CD-ROMs, the availability of books in digital form and the presence of trillions of pages of data on the internet do not necessarily mean that people are going to learn more effectively from them.

What is encouraging when one reads the papers in this volume is the way in which language teachers reveal their commitment to learning — they also bear witness to their ingenuity in their ability to adapt a technological facility to a pedagogical task.

Many contributions deal, as is to be expected, with the use of the WWW in the classroom and with the subtleties of multimedia and hypermedia teaching programs. The effective incorporation of voice software, email, simulations, chat boards and MOOs into language learning is discussed as well as the benefits to be gained from tapping the resource that corpora and concordances provide. New technology can also assist with the learning of grammatical structures, with academic writing, with literary analysis, with listening comprehension, with reading, with helping the deprived and underprivileged, etc. Theoretical considerations are not overlooked and the relationship between design and didactic issues, the effective use of cyberspace, the integration of internet materials into language teaching, group dynamics, distance learning and the role of evaluation are all discussed.

The number of papers devoted to the learning of English as L2 illustrates the world-wide need for the development of an English Language program which will be flexible enough to allow it to be adopted, and adapted, to fit in with the respective culture, cultural needs and particularities of the indigenous L1. Such a program may seem impossible to realise, precisely because of the cultural and linguistic differences involved, but it would be worth a concerted effort to establish a pedagogical method.

It is obvious from the contents of these Proceedings that CALL is thriving and that it is a domain in which there still remains a great deal of research to be carried out to make it an even more effective learning tool.[1]

Acknowledgement: My thanks go to all those who have contributed towards the running of the colloquium; to Lindy Ayubi for her encouragement, hard organisationl work and good humour; to Nac Datta, Gary Stringer and the PALLAS team for their support and expertise.

---

[1] For a more detailed discussion of the areas of CALL which are deemed to be in need of more investigation, see K.C. Cameron (ed.) *CALL: Media, Design and Applications*. Lisse: Swets & Zeitlinger, 1999, and the editorials in *Computer Assisted Language Learning. An International Journal* (Swets & Zeitlinger).

CALL for BSL

Lynne Barnes, David Dorrington & Mark Heaton,
University of Central Lancashire, UK

Introduction

British Sign Language and the Deaf Community

The natural language of Deaf people in Britain is British Sign Language (BSL). This is a visual-gestural language used with ease and efficiency within the Deaf community. BSL is a language in its own right, with its own grammar, which differs to that of auditory-articulatory languages.

From data collected during an OPCS study in 1989, the British Deaf Association (BDA) has estimated that approximately 62,500 individuals in England, Wales and Northern Ireland and a further 7,000 in Scotland use British Sign Language as their first or preferred language (Davies: 1995).

These individuals are primarily Deaf, i.e. physically they have a (usually) profound hearing loss, but they also participate in a recognisable cultural grouping known as the Deaf community (Brennan, 1990). Within this community, the audiological construction, extent or nature of deafness is unimportant in comparison to the sharing of common heritage, language, life experiences and the sense of identity which is the context of this linguistic and cultural minority group (Brennan, 1992). Throughout this paper, these Deaf people will be referred to by use of an upper case 'D'. (This usage was proposed by James Woodward in 1982, and is discussed in Padden and Humphries *Deaf in America: Voices from a Culture,* Harvard University Press, 1988.)

Since the late 1950s, research into signed languages has developed in a number of countries around the world. In 1960, the American linguist William C Stokoe published the first paper 'Sign Language Structure: An outline of the visual communication systems of the American deaf' in which the basis for the linguistic analysis and recognition of signed languages was outlined. It represented the first major contribution to what is now the burgeoning field of sign language studies, and irrevocably changed the lives of Deaf people.

Research showed that the acquisition of spoken and signed languages occurs in much the same way, and at much the same age. The propositional power of both is identical. The formal properties of both are identical, even though they involve different types of signals, different kinds of information, different sensory systems, different memory structures, and perhaps different neural structures. The formal properties of sign and speech are identical, and so too is their communicational intent. (Sacks, 1989)

> Inspired by William C. Stokoe's work on American Sign Language, teams in Edinburgh and Bristol examined British Sign Language and found it was indeed a language, and one of greater complexity than had ever been suspected. By simply declaring that British Sign Language was a language, people's conceptions changed. Deaf people officially had something positive and attractive which made them equal with hearing people; deafness was not just viewed as being about the **loss** of something. (Ladd 1988)

At approximately the same time, an increasing number of Deaf clubs began to introduce sign language classes for members of the local community. Typically these classes were taught by the hearing Welfare Officer for Deaf People or by a hearing child of Deaf parents, often teaching basic signs in predominantly spoken English word-order. Classes were largely informal, tuition ad hoc and courses did not lead to qualification or certification. Nevertheless, these classes began to spring up around the country in response to increasing interest from hearing people.

In 1981 the Council for the Advancement of Communication for Deaf People (CACDP) was established, aiming to promote communication between deaf and hearing people by offering high quality nationally recognised assessments and accreditation in sign language and other forms of communication used by deaf people.

Nevertheless, it was still apparent that there was no formal teaching qualification for tutors of BSL and that Deaf people themselves were rarely involved in this tutition. During the 1980s, the issue of training BSL teachers became more prominent within the Deaf community and a number of papers, articles and books began to emerge from a range of sources (Heaton, 1998). The real progress in the training of BSL tutors began in 1985 when the first training programme for Deaf people was set up by the British Deaf Association (BDA). It was held at Durham University, which would, it was anticipated, enhance the status of BSL by placing it alongside other languages being studied and taught at university level (Denmark, 1990). This was the beginning of the British Sign Language Training Agency (BSLTA) and in 1986, the first Deaf students graduated from this course as qualified BSL tutors. Since this time over 142,000 hearing people have taken CACDP examinations, ranging from Introductory Level to Qualified Interpreter status, catering for a wide variety of requirements from those wishing to learn British Sign Language.

General deaf awareness, growing recognition of BSL as the true and vibrant language of the Deaf community, more familiarity with sign language interpreters in the media, FEFC funded courses in colleges, Deaf Studies courses in Universities, the implications of the Disability Discrimination Act have all led to a significant increase in the numbers of people who take sign language courses each year. In 1998 alone, 24,000 members of the community took CACDP examinations (CACDP Treasurer's Report, 1999). More recent developments have led CACDP to restructure their examinations in line with the National Vocational Qualification assessment system, and this, too, may increase the number of people wishing to learn sign language as an additional skill for their place of work.

The need for teaching and training in sign language skills has expanded rapidly and expert sign language tutors are in great demand. There is also a dearth of appropriate, well-developed, published resources for the teaching of BSL. Signed languages are quintessentially three-dimensional in nature. This presents a considerable challenge to the Deaf tutor faced with a learner-group of hearing students more attuned to oral-aural than visual-gestural language and dependant upon text-based materials, two-dimensional photographs or non-interactive video as the only choice of learning materials and teaching resource (Heaton, 1998). Ideas about teaching and learning in the context of signed language thus required particular reflection.

Why CAL?: The development of new technology has opened innumerable doors for the BSL tutor; the advantages of multimedia technology, in particular, seem 'obvious and dramatic' (Brien and Brennan, 1994). Multimedia computer assisted learning systems offer the opportunity to combine low-cost, high quality digital video (MPEG) with sound, text, and graphic images with the added advantage of interactivity. Applications developed using this technology offer the benefits of a training video — clear, high quality moving images — with the learner having the control and flexibility needed to work at their own pace, to view exactly what they want, when they want and having the opportunity to practice assessment exercises. Although advanced technology makes other options available to the field, CD-ROMs can store over one hour of MPEG 1 compressed digital video and has bandwidth capable of sustaining video quality. Furthermore, with the widespread availability of CD-ROM technology, members of the hearing community are better served to practice BSL in the comfort of their own homes.

The Project

The Team

With this in mind, the University of Central Lancashire began a project to produce a CD-ROM guided learning package to use initially with students on the university Deaf Studies course, and after a period of evaluation, to sell commercially to the under-resourced market.

The technological base for this project was quite unlike the developments happening in many other institutions at the time, where the design of CAL materials was the responsibility of specific departments. The University of Central Lancashire had deliberately set up an independent, specialist CAL development unit, which worked collaboratively producing materials with various academic departments. As such the CD-ROM was developed by the Centre for Learning Technologies and the Deaf Studies team. The benefits of this approach were manifold and obvious. The Centre was made up of application designers, video specialists, application authors, programmers, graphic designers all specialising in developing educational and training multimedia applications and websites, with a wealth of experience in many fields. Members of the Deaf Studies team brought specialist subject knowledge, awareness of teaching and learning outcomes, appropriate syllabus and assessment guidelines, a native use of BSL, an awareness of the proposed target audience and most importantly, first-hand Deaf community experience, which facilitated the formation of a network of consultants and colleagues from numerous Deaf Centres and organisations around the country.

Deaf and hearing working partnerships formed the basis of the day-to-day operations, the dynamics of which informed the project and inspired mutual respect. The fact that Deaf people were being actively involved in the production of these visual-based teaching materials, working in their own language, capturing live examples of Deaf culture and heritage, was of particular and intrinsic benefit.

The Subject

The aim of the CD-ROM was to illustrate how number is signed in British Sign Language. The focus on number was deliberate as this topic is quite complex for the student of Sign Language. Just as spoken English differs from region to region according to dialect and accent, so too BSL differs across regions. This regional variation is very clearly pronounced in the use of number systems in BSL (See Brien, 1992). This poses great problems for students who may be taught by one native BSL user from Manchester, but who may be assessed by someone from London and could meet a group of Yorkshire Deaf people within the context of their work. As regional variation is something that new learners need to be aware of, and more advanced BSL students need practice with, this focus allowed us to produce a CD-ROM of use to a wide range of learners. The programme was designed with this open access in mind; with users having options of using sign only, sign with full text, sign with captions, with or without voice-over. These options enabled students to learn at their own pace and level, provided for assessment of progress and gave free-reign to the BSL users themselves, who were filmed signing at their own pace, using their own native and regional sign. The result was a wealth of rich, natural signed narrative.

The Target Audience

In addition to learners across the sign language ability range being able to access the CD-ROM, we were particularly keen to allow access for both Deaf and hearing users.

Many BSL-users have English as a second or third language. In addition, there are cross-cultural implications for Deaf students faced with a barrage of written English text and innumerable icons and visual distracters. By making the written language and visual interface accessible to Deaf people, it would be possible to introduce the CD-ROM as a resource for deaf children in (particularly mainstream) schools, as a means of testing their own comprehension of BSL and English, introducing regional variation for those who do not attend Deaf clubs or socialise within the Deaf community, and creating a positive resource for children who seldom see Deaf people signing in the classroom.

The Design

Taking into consideration the target audience and the hardware platform available to run an application of this nature, several key requirements for the application were defined:

- The application to be delivered and executed entirely from CDROM
- The application to run with a 640 x 480 screen size with 16bit colour
- The application to run on a standard multimedia PC, be easy to use and accessible by the target audience
- Screen design to be uncluttered and visual noise limited
- All buttons, controls and interactive elements to be obvious and easy to use (no icons except for standard video controls)
- Users to have the option to view presentations in a variety of ways to suit their signing ability/learner level (options: sign only, sign with full text, sign with captions, with or without voice-over)
- Users must know where they are in the application and be able to access other elements easily
- Video (the main focus of information delivery) must be clear and controllable

Content

The programme was divided into five main topic areas:

- General numbers
- Age
- Money
- Clock time
- Calendar time

Each main topic area was sub-divided into 3 sections

- Tutorial — which provides information and tuition specific to the topic
- Practice Section — in which a different person signs a narrative, using a number of examples specific to the topic
- Test Section — in which students are able to watch five short sign clips and test their receptive skills. Four of the clips are accompanied by multiple- choice questions. The final clip requires a fully transcribed response and offers a model answer.

The programme ends with a

- Review Your Skills — a signed narrative incorporating many examples from the five topics including a MCQ exercise and an advanced piece of signing with no options of text, sound or captions.
- A glossary is provided with examples of regional number systems. Students may use this for reference.

The application navigation is controlled from a Menu screen, which gives access to all other sections contained within the application. This can be accessed from anywhere within in the application.

A Help Screen and the option to exit the programme are also available from anywhere in the application.

Screen Shots from the CDROM

Menu Screen

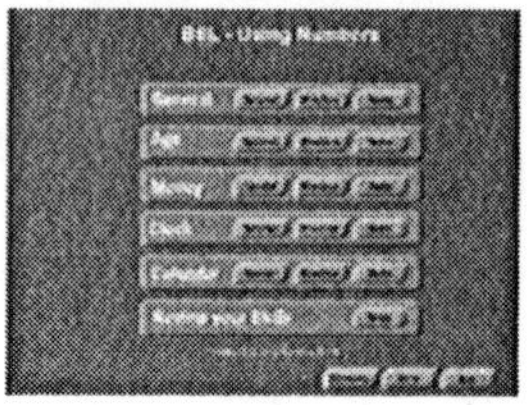

Tutorial Screen

MCQ Test Screen

Transcription Test Screen

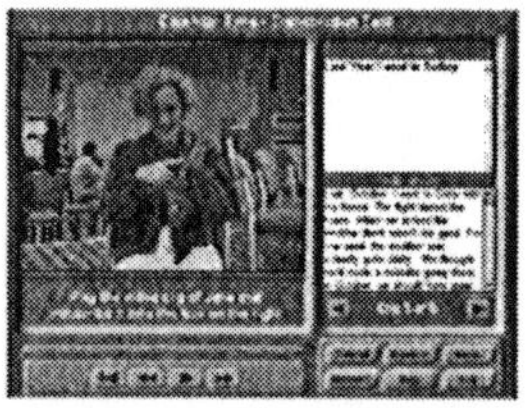

Evaluation

User Feedback: Evaluation of the CD-ROM has proved to be both interesting and informative. Thirty-nine respondents submitted evaluation forms and individual comments were also noted throughout the evaluation period. Amongst other responses, we were particularly interested in user-friendliness; if the programme was easy to access, use and control. In addition we needed to know how useful the CD-ROM was as a learning resource and ultimately if students would recommend this product to other users. During the evaluative exercise, a number of questions related to these concerns (See Appendix 1.)

The chosen subject of 'Using Number in BSL' was appropriate and achieved our specified aim of being at once engaging and challenging for all users of the CD-ROM. Students found that they were learning more than they had expected, by virtue of the regional variations, but also because of the wealth of rich language being presented by native BSL users.

As our sample of learners were university students, they were perhaps already computer-literate to some extent. However, comments do suggest that the CD-ROM was user-friendly and easy to navigate and manipulate. Students were aware of where they were in the programme, how to find their way around the sections and how to find information on specific topics:
'The simplicity of layout would enable even a technophobe to access the information easily'.

Students praised the layout, structure and accessibility of the material, believing it to be self-explanatory once in use. The screen was uncluttered, and key buttons were clearly labelled, kept to the same part of the screen and were colour-coded. Furthermore 'they did what they said they would do!'

The presentation, 'look and feel' all scored highly with users. The high-quality video resolution was recognised, especially by those who had seen other CD-ROMs incorporating video clips. Nevertheless, some of the footage was badly framed and poorly lit due to the way the video was sourced.

Above all, students appreciated the options of caption, text and/or sound as this enabled learners of different levels to complete the activities. Those at more advanced levels did not appear to use the voice option, whilst beginners found it an essential part of the package. Similarly, beginners did not attempt the more difficult transcript tasks, whilst more advanced learners were somewhat disappointed in the comparatively few test sections of this type.

Overall, users found the CD-ROM to be accessible, clearly presented, useful for their sign language study and in general could find activities appropriate for their current level of BSL learning; ninety-five percent would recommend the CD-ROM to other potential users.

Recommendations: As the aim of the project was to develop a teaching resource, it was necessary to explore recommendations for improvement and consider further developments which could be made in light of this experience. Students alerted us to a number of technical issues and practical considerations, some of which were resolved after the evaluation process. These included:

- Each video clip to indicate the level of BSL learning i.e. Stage 2, to facilitate speedier access, appropriate use and avoid beginners of the language losing confidence by working at too advanced a level.
- Ensure the glossary includes all number system variations, rather than a random selection.
- Possibility of user-activated questions rather than automatic application
- Possibility of a slow-down and/or repeat facility for beginners of BSL.

Conclusion: New technology has greatly advanced the field of BSL tuition, and opened up a whole series of possibilities and challenges for the Deaf tutor. There can be no mistaking the advantages of structured learning packages and interactive activities brought into the home. As learners of spoken languages have long had access to their target language at their fingertips (or headsets), so too, visual-gestural language learners can now appreciate a multi-dimensional representation of the living language rather than the text-based, still images recorded in sign dictionaries and phrasebooks. Whilst video resources give learners access to moving images, these do not have the breadth of function of the CD-ROM, nor do they allow for on-line student assessment, progression or development of receptive skills. The interaction and flexibility afforded students, who can enter and leave sections according to their aptitude and stage of learning is essential, whilst model answers and testing facilities are crucial feedback mechanisms for the language learner.

The possibilities for further developments are extensive. This 'Number' package contains specific subject material, which cuts across learner and assessment levels. However, the application has been developed in such a way that the basic 'shell' can be re-used with a different set of media. Future applications could continue in a similar style and structure across a whole range of topic areas. Whilst possibly limiting, this could greatly speed up the process of future projects, making extra time available for developing and refining the one core application shell, and cutting down on production costs.

In line with the new developments in Vocational Qualifications for Sign Language, CD-ROMs could easily be produced for learners in a wide variety of workplaces, such as hospitals, retail outlets, service industries and travel services, thus increasing the workforce's ability to communicate with Deaf people. Following implementation of the DDA (1995), employers might find CD-ROMs in Deaf Awareness a useful starting point for developing equal opportunities practice in their workplace; tailor-made resources being particularly economic and effective.

Education and training are changing as the government faces the immediate and immense challenge of equipping individuals, employers and the country to meet the demands of the 21st century (Blunkett, 1999). The BSL CAL package is an excellent example of how new technologies, communication and citizenship can be incorporated into lifelong and distance learning which will promote equality of access and opportunity for Deaf people and advance the field of sign language tuition.

References:

Blunkett, D. (1999) *A Summary; Learning to Succeed: A new framework for post-16 learning.* http://www.dfee.gov.uk/post16/summary.htm

Brennan, M. (1990) *Word Formation in British Sign Language.* University of Stockholm. 6.

Brennan, M (1992) The Visual World of British Sign Language: An Introduction in Brien, D. (ed) (1992) *Dictionary of British Sign Language/English.* Faber and Faber. London

Brien, D. (ed) (1992) *Dictionary of British Sign Language/English.* Faber and Faber. London. 823-848

Brien, D and Brennan, M. (1994) Sign Language Dictionaries: Issues and Developments in Bos, H. and Schermer, T (eds) *Sign Language Research 1994: Proceedings of the 4th European Congress on Sign Language Research; Munich, September 1-3, 1994.* Signum Press

Denmark, A. C. (1990) British Sign Language Tutor Training Course in Gregory, S. and Hartley, G. (eds) (1991) *Constructing Deafness.* Pinter Publishers in association with the Open University: Milton Keynes.

Davies, A. (1995) *Hearing in Adults.* Whurr. England.

Heaton, M. (1998) *Developments in Multimedia Technology: Numbers in BSL* Paper presented at First International Conference on Deafness Education and Technology: Tools for the 21st Century Nov 1998: Bermuda

Ladd, P. (1988) *The modern Deaf community* in Miles, D. *British Sign Language, A Beginner's Guide.* BBC Books. London

Miles, D. (1988) *British Sign Language, A Beginner's Guide.* BBC Books. London

Padden and Humphries (1988) *Deaf in America: Voices from a Culture,* Harvard University Press.

Sacks, O (1989) *Seeing Voices.* Pan Books. London. 120-121.

Appendix 1

The Content Structure Network for the 'Using Numbers in BSL' CD-ROM

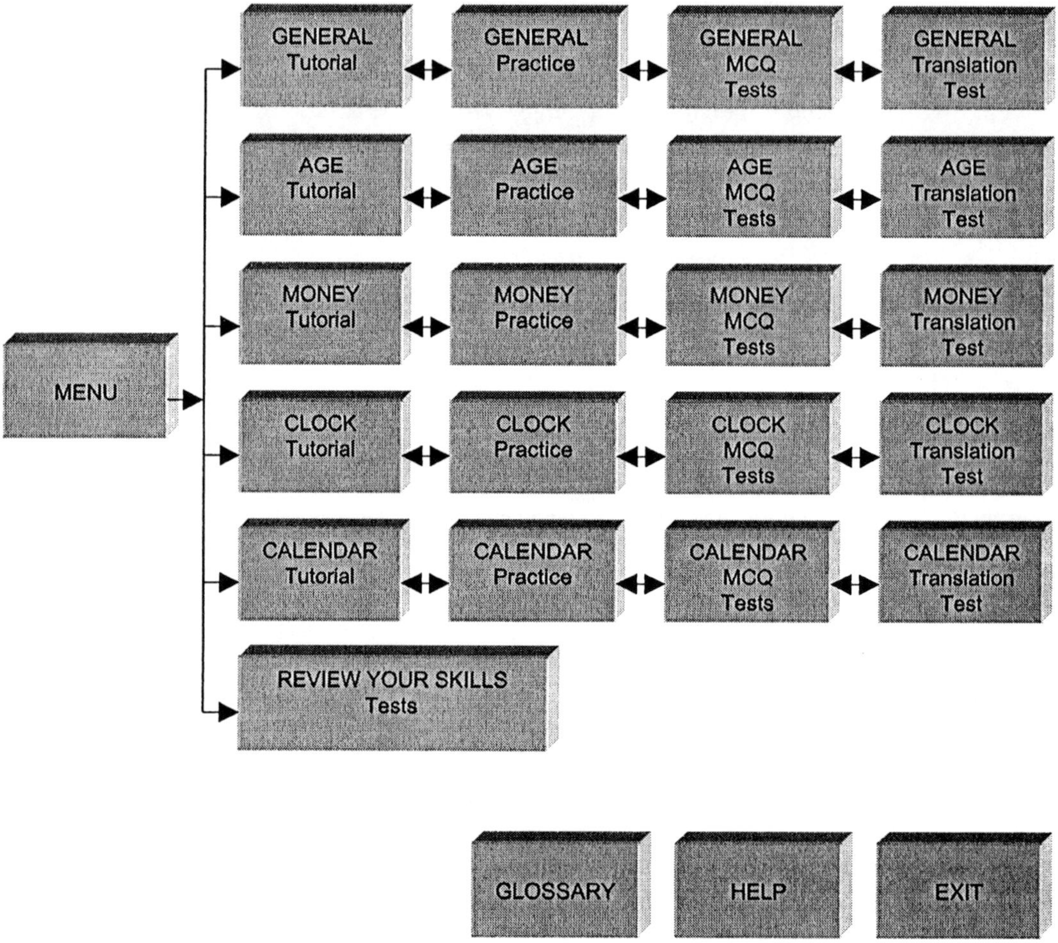

Appendix 2

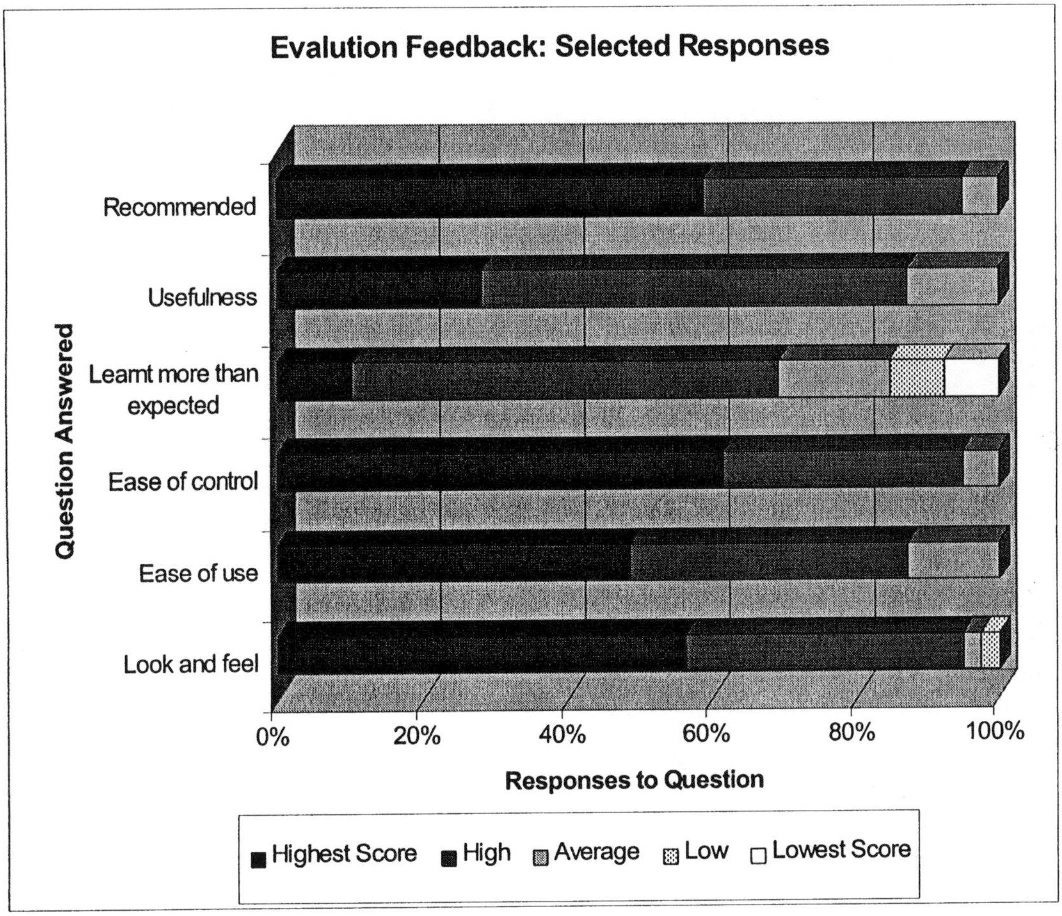
Evalution Feedback: Selected Responses
Question Answered
Recommended
Usefulness
Learnt more than expected
Ease of control
Ease of use
Look and feel
0%
20%
40%
60%
80%
100%
Responses to Question
Highest Score
High
Average
Low
Lowest Score

E-MAIL AND THE STUDENTS, THE SOCIAL PRICE OF ACCESS TO INNOVATION

Odile Blin
Université de Rouen, France

1. Introduction: The Study of Communication by E-mail as an Initiatory Course: The sociology of education is a source of definitive disenchantment for those who venture into it. According to the principles of the 'Declaration of Human Rights', the access to knowledge, culture and education, is the same for every individual. Men have equal rights and this equality is, in part, and in a theoretical way, transmitted through education. We are therefore completely in the domain of theory. Sociology demonstrated long ago that scholastic capital translates social differences and affects the academic career of the individual. Any approach to the students' world must deal with this sociological fatality. The works of Pierre Bourdieu and Jean-Claude Passeron have given rise to studies which oblige us to consider students' life as being something other than just a series of inculcation and training.

The choice of theme for our study, student communication through e-mail, brought us face to face from the outset with a somewhat vague set of questions tinted with ideologies that one could express in these terms:

Does the exercise of communication by e-mail perpetuate social differences and how? Does it require the possession of a personal computer?

So the use of some modern facilities, a category with which one can associate the PC (personal computer) develops according to a continuum resembling a pyramid from top to bottom.

Studying student use of e-mail introduces numerous questions that lack of research time prevents us from treating seriously. With which type of communication shall we associate communication by e-mail? Written, telephonic or 'cyber' communication and the culture which goes with it?

2. Methods and Hypotheses: Our study deals with the habits of the students in matters of communication, and more particularly with the different ways of using this new means of communication that is e-mail.

The choice of subject for our study reveals our theoretical presupposition. Some parents' economic resources play a part in the relationship of the student to communication by e-mail and this transcends the choice of the curriculum. So it is not necessary to study Sociology in order to know the registration fees in a Business School or a first-rate private school in France. One could assume that in one way or another the proximity with the computer and the Web will be favoured by the choice of such schools and also that the geographical mobility of the students will be more important and will encourage their affinities with e-mail.

Therefore, we chose three types of student:
1) Students from the Faculty of Arts (Rouen University).
2) Students from the Exact Sciences (Rouen University).
3) Students from the Business School in Rouen.

This choice is also governed by constraints of feasibility and theoretical presupposition.

The proximity of the institutions was considered, on the one hand, but again are not students of Science better acquainted with the techniques and the world of data processing than students of Arts and Human Sciences? Does not their own culture encourage them in terms of a larger subjective and objective familiarity with the computer and the network? Are not Business School students more destined to use professionally enhanced e-mail facilities for international communication?

In other words, to assimilate the students of Arts and Human Sciences amounts to constituting a category which, from the start, is at a disadvantage, this disadvantage translating our Bourdieu-type hypothesis made at the beginning: i.e. the social processes of social reproduction at work in the choice of curricula is made real and amplified in relation to the computer communication technologies that every specific student culture produces...

The less socially classifying curricula and the less discriminating ones in the field of employment are also those in which the relationship with the new communication technologies is less fundamental. This remains to be proved!

Another aspect of our investigation concerns the relationship that the students could maintain with electronic mail in terms of communication practices. So, comparing these practices with other more traditional ones, like letter writing, would give us (we supposed) some information on the meaning of the use of this new relational mode among young people. This aspect of our research is treated in publications elsewhere.

3. The Expected Results: A Meaningful Sample: We verified the representative value of our sample with regard to the whole student community (from every discipline) in Rouen. Then we made a number of flat and crossed sortings.

The population surveyed consisted of 191 people (62.8% women and 37.2% men). We carried out this investigation on the basis of the three adopted poles indicated above — the Sciences, the Arts + Psychology, Sociology and Business Studies. The level + 4 years was retained as it may indicate students concerned with initiation to research and thus users of e-mail. The 191 people surveyed were distributed as follows:

29.5% in Exact Sciences
22.1% in Business Studies
48.4% in Arts and Human Sciences

The gathered data enables us to know if there are any relationships in our sample, as well as at university level between sex, CSP and the choice of discipline studied.

3.1: Average Profile of the E-mail User: A typical profile of the Rouen student-user of electronic mail is that of a boy (the girls are lagging behind except in Arts where they are in the majority) studying Data Processing or Business with parents who are executives. He lives in a large city of over 100,000 inhabitants. He has stayed at least once in a foreign country. He is often a member of a sports club or a scientific society and is already connected to the Net. Considering this profile, one remains far from any democratisation of these new means of communication. The girls and the students in underrated curricula, from working class origins, are penalised in their access to e-mail. As a whole, our study made it possible to show that this new means of communication attracts the attention of most students.

Even if the students' opinion is positive, generally speaking, a difference exists between a widely favourable opinion — remarks often occur about the selective character of the Net and the Web — and the fact that there are many wrong practices in the field of picture broadcasting and economic monopolies.

But rather than hark back to the general data of the survey, which can be found in the report for Rouen University, we have chosen to concentrate on some specific aspects of student use of e-mail, which were uncovered by our study.

3.2: Cumulative Aspects of Web 'Snob' Practices: Is having a computer and other domestic means of communication such as a mobile phone the required condition in order to possess or use e-mail? If one combines the fact that possessing a computer and being connected encourages use of e-mail, we find that 56.9% of the students who have a computer have e-mail when 62.1% of the students who do not have a computer use e-mail. This also means that a significant proportion of students, (38.8%), use e-mail without possessing a PC.

The facilities offered by universities could, then, play a democratic role since they make it possible for those who have no computer to have, nevertheless, an electronic site, thanks to the departments of Computer Science in universities. But the more socially discriminating curricula and disciplines are by far the best equipped and vice versa. There, again, the democratic miracle goes to pieces. The university does not provide the same opportunities for access to the Net and to e-mail to all students. The distribution according to different curricula puts some of them at a disadvantage and favours others in so far as equipment is concerned.

Let us consider the relationship between the Net and e-mail once more. When one combines the variables: Net/possession of e-mail, 83.9% of the students who use the Net have e-mail while 97.3% of the students who are not on the Net do not have e-mail either. At first sight, it seems that the users of the Net are more likely to have e-mail than those who possess only a computer. So we see an ascending graph from the least e-mail concerned students to the most concerned as computer science equipment develops. The logic of use is in agreement with the technological logic of equipment.

As for owning a mobile phone, 61.2% of the students who possess one also have e-mail and only 38.8% of those who do not have a mobile phone have e-mail. The 'affilaires' ('wirelessers'), according to Julien Morel's phrase, (see the Master's Degree thesis, Rouen University: 'Mobile telephone and public places'). Users of mobile phones favour the combination of different modes of communication assisted by technology and different innovations in the field. On the other hand, 55.9% of surveyed students use neither mobile phones nor e-mail.

3.3: Community University Channels: Is there any relationship between curriculum and the use of e-mail? One notices that no less than 100% of the students in computer science at the Institute of Technology and at the Business School have e-mail. The Business School students are registered automatically at the beginning of the school year. For the Computer Science Institute, it seems normal to get access and to use the potentialities of the Net when the computer and its applications are at the heart of the discipline.

As for Arts curricula they are lagging far behind with up to 87.5% students without e-mail in sociology and even 92.2% in Applied Foreign Languages. This goes against the hypothesis according to which Applied Foreign Language students (because of their link with business) would be great users of e-mail, like the Business students. If one adds to this the PC variable which indicates that 54.4% of Business Schools students are workers' children and 70% of Business School students are executives' children, one understands more easily why language students use e-mail less than Business School students.

It can be accounted for by the combined action of cultural capital and economic capital. Language students cannot afford e-mail whereas e-mail is automatically made available at the beginning of the school year for students who could easily afford to pay for it.

3.4: A Toposociology of Communication: Does living in a large city encourage one to have e-mail? Considering the sortings we made, it appears that the students who live in a city of over 100,000 inhabitants (Rouen) are greater users of the electronic mail as 67.2% of them possess one, while among students living in towns of less than 2000 inhabitants only 38.5% have one. The inhabitants of large cities naturally have more information at their disposal in order to acquire new technologies. These results contradict our hypothesis according to which the inhabitants of small towns and of the country would be more likely to have e-mail in order to gain access to the world and not remain enclosed in their country, as hypothesis worked out from the very high percentage of farmers' sons who are equipped superior to that of workers' children who are townspeople. We also tried to discover whether the students who had lived in a foreign country were greater users of e-mails than the others. In our sample, only 9.5% of the students surveyed had lived abroad and among this group, 72.2% have e-mail while 48.4% of the students who had never lived abroad have it. Thus, living abroad would encourage students to have e-mails.

Are the correspondences national, local, or international?

It appears that between 41% to 42% of the students have essentially national exchanges. However, those who had lived at least once abroad have international exchanges in the proportion of 41.7%, while only 23% of those who had never lived abroad have them. Having stayed abroad then has some influence on the types of exchanges made.

3.5: Access to the Net: As for access facilities, 62.4% of students consult their e-mail at university, 10. 9% in their families and 13.9% at home. Paradoxically, none of them does so in a cyber-coffee house. This may be due to a bad circulation of information about cyber-coffee house addresses. The University colleges are not far behind since two-thirds of the students consult them at University. As the Business School students are automatically registered for e-mail at the beginning of the year, this partly explains why so many of them consult it at their University. We notice that electronic mail does not develop easily within the family circle.

60% of the students surveyed think that access to the Net is not easy at all at University. However, 78.4% of the students have free access to the Net because they are able to access it on University premises. Those who pay the highest price are those who use Internet the most often. This seems to be logical as they get access from home since they pay for it.

In so far as family habits are concerned, a lot of resistance persists: the style of the medium, the fear of the Web, the fear of the cost, apart from any objective acquaintance with the NTIC, are the most common reasons given.

Among those who use e-mail, 34.1% only use it for research work, studies, and 46.8% for private exchanges. This superiority of the private over research usage indicates some sort of friendly sociability that e-mail develops. Does it mean that electronic mail is going to replace letter writing? And what is the meaning of this practice? Electronic mail has a lot of advantages such as time saving and the simplicity of its use according to the different student populations. 61.5% of the students in IUP use electronic mail for their research work whereas Business School students, and those who study psychology or computer science use it up to 50% for private correspondence. This may be accounted for by the fact that these 'addicted' students communicate more with each other during their research than Arts students do.

Besides, one notices a correlation between the consulting frequency and the dispatching frequency. 45.5% of the students surveyed consult their e-mail at least once a week and 46.5% send at least one a week.

We get the same result if we combine the consulting frequency and the dispatching frequency month after month, day after day. This tends to show that exchanges are quite regular and it really establishes a form of pre-recorded interactive dialogue.

3.6: To Associate, to Communicate: Is there a link between belonging to an association and possessing e-mail? 31.6% of the students who answered our questions belong to an association, 33.8% to a cultural society and 35.3% to vague associations, most often sports clubs. One notices, in this field, that 15% of the students belonging to an association have an e-mail address, whereas 59.7% of the students who are not members of an association, do not. Therefore there is a link between belonging to an association and having an e-mail. We had theorised that individuals linked to the world of associations favour communication between people in all its aspects and thus favour e-mail. But the results can also be explained by the fact that associations need to communicate with one another to organise meetings, outings, etc.; to this end, e-mail seems to be an economical and simpler means of exchanging information and messages.

Which associations are the most frequent users of electric mail? 100% of Science-Club members have e-mail and 83.3% of the other categories essentially comprising sports clubs. These two types of association may need to send out more information than other associations and do so through the most sophisticated channels. On the contrary, 83.3% of the political associations' student members do not have e-mail. Is there a tradition and a preference for writing and speaking?

3.7: A Favourable Opinion: What are the reasons for not having e-mail? 32.9% of the people surveyed consider that they do not need it, and 39% of them think that it's too expensive. If we introduce the sex variable, we see that women think it's less useful than men, with 36.5% against 21.1% for men. Men are more conscious of expense when using e-mail with 52.6% of them, compared to 34.9% of women, thinking it too expensive. Similarly, women resist more than men (4.8% among women, 0% among men). In so far as new means of communication such as the Net are concerned, 19.7% think that their development depends on a choice directed as much by technical skill as by financial possibilities. 15.3% think that it can give an opening onto the world, 15.3% that their development is a matter of anarchy.

There is a correlation between each other's opinions about the NTIC (new technologies of information and communication) and specific student cultures. Thus, 32.1% of the Business School students think that the Net enables an opening onto the world compared to just 7.1% of the students in Sociology, who are far more sensitive to the discriminating aspect of the Net and have 42.9% who think that its development creates a selection, compared to only 10.1% of the Business students.

On the whole, the students view these new means of communication favourably since 11.4% of them regard them as positive.

4. Conclusion: Change and Continuity: Pierre Bourdieu's statement that there is not one class of young people but several, remains true. Some, thanks to their social origins, the choice of their curricula and their sex quickly make use of technological innovations because the most economically selective curricula are also those which, over-equipped, favour access to the Net. Therefore, the community of young students is not homogeneous and its relationship to cyberculture and e-mail testifies to this fact.

But beyond these first observations new questions appear:
Has electronic communication any influence on the social use of writing?
Has the use of e-mail enabled students to rediscover the tradition of letter writing?
Has the use of e-mail enabled students to get acquainted with electronic communication which is situated in between the telephone and the letter?

Is another student culture, perpendicular, interclass and international, emerging thanks to the possibilities of e-mail, among others?

Only careful research into the sociological determinates of the changes which are taking place will make it possible to appreciate their importance.

CULTURE, COMMUNICATION, NAVIGATION AND CALL: THE ROLE OF THE USER INTERFACE AND VIDEO MATERIAL IN A MULTIMEDIA PROGRAM FOR INTERMEDIATE ITALIAN LEARNERS.

Gabriella Brussino
University of Auckland, New Zealand

Abstract
For software designers, teaching language and culture through digital means presents particular challenges, some of which are closely related to the choice of design features to be used and others to the relationship between sociocultural context and communication. This paper focuses on two aspects of the design of 'Crescendo in Italia' a multimedia project for Italian learners developed to be an integral part of an intermediate-level language course. Firstly, it discusses the role of the navigational areas and video material in the contextualisation of language teaching. Then, it explores some of the practical considerations which accompanied the design of the user interface.

Description of the project: The interactive, multimedia project *Crescendo in Italia* was designed on the basis that multimedia development in the context of a language course must result from a close analysis of all factors involved: student needs, teachers' beliefs, the textbook adopted and the course methodology. The developers also believe that any CALL software which is an essential course component must be properly integrated in the course structure and must relate directly to the assessment aims of the course in order to be effective.

Intermediate learners of Italian need to expand lexical knowledge and be exposed to as many target language speakers as possible in order to contend with a variety of different regional idioms and accents. Notions of grammar and structures of the language also need to be developed and reinforced at this level. At the same time, the program aims at encouraging learners to take risks, become aware of their own learning style, take responsibility for their learning and become independent. Learners also need to sustain motivation, therefore factors related to interest, feedback, clear goals and ability to monitor progress need to be addressed. It is a firm belief of the project developers that multimedia has a significant role to play in the achievement of all of these aims.

The FLA method adopted by the textbook *Crescendo*, upon which the project was based, follows the communicative, functional approach and the course itself is taught within the communicative, functional, integrative parameters.

The project described comprises 6 CD Roms. Each of the CD Roms contains 2 or 3 language lessons which are closely linked to the lessons on the textbook *Crescendo*, both in terms of content and methodology of language teaching. However, all material was written by the developers who have maintained careful consideration of copyright regulations.

Each lesson has a setting in an Italian city. The host city was chosen according to its particular suitability to the theme of the lesson. Six cities play host to 14 lessons: Turin, Cortina, Venice, Bologna, Florence and Rome. The learner selects a lesson and is brought by an animation over the whole of Italy to his/her destination. The flight over Italy is symbolic of the learner's journey and places the theme of the lesson in a specific geographic context, much as the digital in-flight screens in a plane inform the passengers of their geographical whereabouts and flight progress. Notions of geography are thus introduced subtly and implicitly as other cities, mountains, lakes and rivers are bypassed in the flight to reach the learner's destination.

Upon arrival, the learner is introduced to some contextualised images of the city through an introductory video and commentary which presents the title and theme of the lesson. The learner is then required to click on a button to select language activities. The logic of the user interface, which simulates a visit to Italy, is to offer then four possibilities within each lesson:

- **video e attività** is a series of interviews purposefully filmed in Italy in order to let the learner hear Italians talk about the topic of each textbook unit. Through these, the learner meets native speakers of varying ages, gender and background (140 altogether) who talk about the topic found in the corresponding lesson of the textbook. The main language skill practised here is comprehension through a series of True/False contextualised statements.

- **giochi:** the next button gives access to games, which practice, reinforce and self-test vocabulary skills in context. The games (*parole crociate, minidialoghi, abbinamenti, concetti*) cover all of the vocabulary introduced in the corresponding lesson of the textbook. They are accompanied by music from the particular host city.

- **grammatica:** the grammar exercises presented in this part are of the fill-the-gap or drag-and-match type, respect the thematic context and are designed to offer variety and challenge. They self-test knowledge of linguistic input and language structures covered previously in class.

- **cosa diresti?** is a communicative game which encourages the learner to respond appropriately to some language challenges linked with the structures, theme and lexicon of the lesson. This video activity allows the learner to choose the appropriate one out of three video responses to a contextualised question. If the response chosen is inappropriate, the video interlocutor responds that she is confused and didn't understand what the learner meant.

Context and communication: The second year Italian program at A.U. assumes a basic knowledge of Italian and aims to assist the learner in developing the main language skills of listening, speaking, reading and writing as well as a more sophisticated understanding of Italian culture. The course is communicative in nature, encouraging learners to use language skills actively and creatively in meaningful communication. When the design specifications of the *Crescendo in Italia* project were drawn it was one of the designers' priorities to address what was perceived to be a major problem in developing competency in the Italian language in New Zealand: given the geographical distance, the lack of first-hand experience of the target culture, particularly and specifically in relation to the thematic approach of the textbook *Crescendo*. The textbook and program aim, in fact, at expanding on all important language structures focussing on language usage rather than abstract concepts. (Italiano, Marchegiani-Jones 1995)

This functional and thematic approach not only emphasises the importance of the relationship between language and culture, it places this relationship at the heart of language learning, stating that language structures acquire meaning when they are learnt in a specific sociocultural context and they are indissoluble from it. Learners need 'to negotiate the meaning of new words from the context, just as they would if they were living in an Italian-speaking environment.' (Italiano, Marchegiani-Jones 1995)

This approach is in line with an anthropological linguistic perspective, which views language structures as inextricable from the sociocultural context and embedded within it:

> ...(language structures) are but one system of signs among many that people use to give meaning to their environment. Other signs include not only gestures, facial expressions, body movements, verbal and non-verbal sounds, and proxemics, but also cultural artefacts such as traffic noise and folk music, pictures and billboards, and landscapes and city maps. Linguistic signs acquire their meaning because they point to other signs in the environment. When learners go abroad and interact with the members of the host culture, all these signs are there, live, to be recognised and decoded. (Kramsch, 1999)

When the natural interaction with the host culture is missing, or cannot be easily achieved, we risk jeopardising the aim of avoiding abstraction. One remedy may be substituting this natural interaction with interaction through multimedia. According to Hanks (1996) and Kramsh (1999), the focus for language teachers moves, with the use of multimedia, from teaching language structures only to 'communicative practice', an activity in which the often unspoken set of values and beliefs of a culture is reflected in its speech: language learning becomes language and culture learning and the two aspects are mutually strengthening and inclusive.

> ...Through multimedia in particular, language is no longer just a list of grammatical paradigms or lexical items. Rather, it is intimately associated with all kinds of verbal and paraverbal behaviours, an acoustic and visual context that is indissociable from the larger societal context in which the words are uttered. Language, in a sense, has become culture. Similarly, culture is no longer just the factual pieces of information that textbooks present in the form of culture capsules on foreign mores, but it is produced and reproduced under our very eyes, on the screen, through what people say and how they say it. In multimedia, culture is inscribed in language use. (Kramsch, 1999)

The designers of *Crescendo in Italia* believe that an appropriate design of the user interface and graphic component in CALL, as well as the use of contextualised video material, may provide an effective way of dealing with the potential lack of sociocultural context in the language classroom environment while supporting the natural role the indissoluble links between language and culture play in language acquisition.

The metaphor of a personal journey is central to the design of the CD Roms. When learners enter a lesson they are introduced to the theme by a video which contextualises the topic of the unit applying it to everyday life in a particular city. Thus, the unit on fascism opens with a panoramic of fascist architecture still existing in Rome and Mussolini's balcony in Piazza Venezia. The imposing, gigantic, stern, dominating nature of the buildings represents in itself a very effective culture lesson on the crushing nature of the dictatorship which adds the visual element and complements the discussions undertaken in class. Similarly, in other units the experience of entering factories and offices, shops, homes and restaurants, public and private spaces reinforces the cultural and thematic element while providing the natural environment within which language takes place: in other words, context.

Following this initial encounter with a particular theme within the city, language learning travellers are prepared to meet the people. The interviews in *video e attività* continue the metaphor while introducing the language component in its natural environment. The six CD Roms contain 140 interviews altogether. They were purposefully recorded in six different cities in order to expose learners to different intonation and regional accent. They are a useful lexical review and positive reinforcement in showing learners that they are able to understand the gist of a number of conversations by a cross-section of native speakers varying in class, age and gender. But the main language learning value of the interviews consists in their firmly embedding language in culture, as the lexicon used by the interviewees is inevitably linked with the thematic and cultural aspects they discuss, their facial expressions, their gestures and show of emotions, their surroundings.

The thematic approach of the course program was respected as the interviewees were asked to speak freely and spontaneously about the topic of a unit of the textbook relating it to their own thoughts or experience on the subject. In this activity, whilst 'apperceiving' lexical and linguistic input (Chapelle, 1998), learners absorb notions of culture naturally and effortlessly by listening to native speakers discuss their average day, their personal relationships, their work aspirations, their political views, their war experiences, their holiday preferences and their health concerns in their own environment. Each interview lasts between two and five minutes: in the case of the lesson on fascism, interviews with concentration camp prisoners and returned soldiers who recall their own experience are a chilling account and commentary of the historical times.

Learners in the intermediate course are asked to do follow-up projects in which they select four interviewees they find interesting and write a short expository piece on each. The video images stimulate the students to include both linguistic and extralingusitic information in their profiles highlighting such aspects as gestures, tone of voice, attitudes and environment. The assignments illustrate a level of comprehension that goes beyond that illustrated in the True/False comprehension exercise. The results exemplify the multi-dimensional nature of the knowledge acquired through this encounter with Italians.

The user interface: The concept of user interface represents the communication level between user and computer, and the navigational areas the steps along the path of human-computer interaction. The graphic design of screens and buttons which form the navigational areas thus represents the 'face' of a particular CALL product, or any multimedia product.

The role of screen design in this project deserves particular attention as the graphic design of screens and buttons within the navigational areas was conceived at the service of language and culture teaching, not as a mere item of added interest or colour. In this case, both practical and pedagogical considerations were the focus for the designer.

In a review of criteria for the design and evaluation of the user interface of foreign language multimedia software, Plass (1998) distinguishes between *Computer/*

Application-centred design and *User-centred* design, where the latter reduces as much as possible the added complications for the learner of understanding how the navigational system works. Too complex a navigational system is an added and unwanted distraction for the learner which often leads to frustration and encourages the user to abandon the software. Conducting usability tests is a practical and effective way of testing whether the user interface was designed to be user-friendly. When the first computer lesson was designed, the developers of this project conducted usability tests on the user interface and implemented changes suggested by users.

The navigational functions in *Crescendo in Italia* are presented on screens in which photographs of the six host cities form the background and buttons which allow the user to move to and from screens. The photographs which form the various screens were purposefully taken in Italy in order to highlight particular thematic aspects of each city thus adding extralinguistic signposts pointing at theme and context.

The buttons allow the user to move freely between screens containing various activities. They are always placed on the same position on the screen for consistency and ease of navigation and they indicate clearly the function of the activity and the direction they lead into, where and how to move on, how to come back. In this project, they represent cultural symbols or icons typical of that particular city and aim at attracting the learner's attention towards particular cultural themes. Thus, a city like Turin, best known for the Risorgimento period, its production of chocolate and cars and its Egyptian museum has King Carlo Alberto and Garibaldi, gianduiotti chocolates, vintage Fiat cars and Egyptian statues for buttons.

When the buttons are touched or clicked on, written messages appear and sounds are activated. They are all original sounds recorded on the streets of the host city, again with the purpose of providing culturally relevant context: the sounds of people walking and talking on the Ponte Vecchio, the horse hooves of the Florentine carts, the tolling bell in Venice's Piazza San Marco, the song of the street artists in Piazza Navona, the noise of the traffic in Torino are only some examples of the many genuine sounds which give this user interface its cultural value.

Evaluation summary: An evaluation plan was drawn up in the early stages of the project to identify:

- the available range of data sources and methods for continuous study of learning process and outcomes
- suitable means of assessing software related issues throughout the development and implementation phases

Evaluation procedures followed established practice for assessing the impact of teaching innovations as defined by Milne & Heath (1987). The Situated Evaluation of Computer Assisted Learning (SECAL) framework (Gunn 1997), provided the basis for all evaluation activities. The objectives of the evaluation were:

- to evaluate the degree of success achieved with implementation in multimedia of the principles of the communicative-functional teaching methodology
- to assess the quality of the multimedia programs from a usability perspective
- to assess the educational merit of the computer aided methods in the context of the intermediate level language course
- to reflect on how the evaluation findings relate to current theoretical understanding

All evaluation data sources suggest that the facilities offered by multimedia can support the principles of the methodology, i.e.

- students develop independence as learners so they can carry on alone at stage 3
- cultural understanding is extended
- basic skills, (reading, writing, comprehension, communication) are further developed at intermediate level
- learning of grammar structures and vocabulary is contextualised

Reactions to the inclusion of rich sources of cultural information were positive and the perceived high level of integration and relevance to course objectives indicates that motivation was well supported. Some reference to the literature on motivation, (Keller 1987), and the role of dual and multi-sensory channels in learning, (Paivio 1986), also underpins this development work. Finally, the emerging discipline of computer based learning provides the basis for the approach to integration, (Hodgson, McCartan et al. 1995), and evaluation, (Mitchell, 1996).

Integration of the programs into the course was favourably received by students who rated them as useful for a range of purposes, particularly grammar practice, reinforcing learning, revision and vocabulary. Figures 2 and 3 show questionnaire responses related to different usefulness and perceived benefits.

Only one area was identified as being in need of immediate improvement, and this related to the technical specification of multimedia lab computers rather than to program features or functionality. During the year, upgrades were installed and the problem of slow speed of operation was remedied. Other comments were more in the line of requests for inclusion of additional locations and extending existing activities.

Reactions to the inclusion of rich sources of cultural information were positive and the perceived high level of integration and relevance to course objectives indicates that motivation was well supported.

Although the evaluation planned for the development and implementation phase is nearing completion, ongoing study will be conducted to focus on finer points of how the multimedia programs support learning, how students make choices about what activities to pursue and the impact of particular multimedia features on memory.

References:

Brussino, G. (1996) *Developing a multimedia component for a foreign language course*, Occasional Papers, Institute of Language Teaching and Learning, Auckland University.

Buck, G. (1994) 'The appropriacy of psychometric measurement models for testing second language listening comprehension', Language Testing 11(2): 145-170

Chapelle C. (1998) 'Multimedia CALL: lessons to be learned from research on instructed SLA', *Language Learning and Technology* 2(1): 22-34.

Chapelle C. (1997) 'CALL in the year 2000: still in search of research paradigms?, *Language Learning and Technology* 1(1): 19-43.

Combs, A. W. (1982) 'Affective education or none at all', *Educational leadership*, 39 (7): 494-497

Ellis, N. C. (1995) 'The psychology of foreign language vocabulary acquisition: Implications for CALL', *Computer Assisted Language Learning* 8(2-3): 103-128.

Gunn, C. (1997). 'Future Directions for CAL Evaluation.' *Association of Learning Technology Journal (ALT-J)* 5(1): 40-47.

Gunn, C., Brussino, G. (1997) 'An evolutionary approach to CAL', *Active Learning* 6 (2).

Hodgson, M., A. McCartan, et al. (1995). 'Teaching and Learning in Higher Education : The Integrative Use of IT Within the Institutional Context', The University of Durham.

Italiano, F., Marchegiani Jones, I. (1995) *Crescendo*. Lexington Massachusetts: D. C. Heath and Company.

Keller, J. (1987). 'Strategies for Stimulating the Motivation to Learn' ,*Performance and Instruction* 26(8): 1-7.

Kramsch, C. (1999) 'Teaching Text and Context through Multimedia', *Language Learning and Technology* 2 (2): 31-42.

Milne, J. and S. Heath (1997). *Evaluation Handbook for Successful Courseware Development*. Centre for CBL in Land Use and Environmental Sciences, Aberdeen University, Scotland.

Mitchell, D. (1997). Evaluating the Impact of Technology on Education : A Radical Reappraisal of Education Technology Research, *Association of Learning Technology Journal (ALT-J)* 5(1).

Paivio, A. (1986). *Mental Representations : A Dual Coding Approach*. Oxford, Oxford University Press.

Plass, J. L. (1998) 'Design and evaluation of the user interface of foreign language multimedia software: a cognitive approach', *Language Learning and Technology* 2 (1): 35-45.

Powell, B. (1998) 'The use of computer assisted language learning', *Forum for Modern Language Studies* xxxiv (2):184-192.

Rogers, C. R, Freiberg, H. J. (1994) *Freedom to learn* (3rd Ed.), Columbus, OH: Merrill/Macmillan.

Stake, R. E. (1994). Case Studies, *Handbook of Qualiative Research*, N. K. Denzin and Y. S. Lincoln. Thousand Oaks, London & New Delhi, Sage Publications: 236-247.

LIFE AFTER ReLaTe: INTERNET VIDEOCONFERENCING'S GROWING PAINS

John Buckett, Gary Stringer & Nac K. J. Datta
University of Exeter, UK

Introduction: From small beginnings, the use of Internet videoconferencing for language teaching has now been part of the research landscape for approaching five years. The ReLaTe project (with funding from the UK's BT/JISC SuperJANET initiative and then the JISC JTAP programme) was one of the elements during the early years of this development. Since then, the collaborators in ReLaTe (Exeter and the Department of Computer Science at UCL) have carried on the work under a number of banners and there has been a steady, if not spectacular, take-up in its use across many academic disciplines including language teaching. This paper looks at some of the recent developments and discusses how far Internet videoconferencing has reached in its 'growing pains' and how far there remains to go before it becomes one of the language teacher's routinely-used tools.

Internet Videoconferencing: ReLaTe and Other Software: The ReLaTe project is a good example of the use of desktop videoconferencing, where each participant sits in front of a PC, sending video (via a camera) and audio (with a headset or microphone) to all the other participants.

Figure 1 Student participating in Internet videoconference

Probably the two key features of the software used in the ReLaTe project and its successors are its scalability and its robustness. It uses multicast network protocols, which means that multiway videoconferences become possible without the amount of network bandwidth required increasing too rapidly. Secondly, it uses an audio tool called RAT (Robust Audio Tool), written at UCL, which sends a second copy of each audio packet (RAT 1999). For a real-time application such as videoconferencing, the current generation of the Internet suffers from the defect that all applications compete on an equal footing, so that when a network becomes congested with e-mail, Web traffic etc, videoconferencing suffers. This is particularly critical for audio, where this can result in speech becoming broken or completely unintelligible. By sending a duplicate copy of all the audio information, RAT can to some extent reduce these problems, by using the second copy when the first gets lost or delayed. Together, these two key features mean that software such as ReLaTe is currently much more attractive for small-group work than other Internet videoconferencing tools such as Microsoft's NetMeeting.

ReLaTe has mainly been targeted towards small-group tutorial teaching, where a tutor is working with a relatively small number of students, but in a highly interactive manner, where the students are contributing as much as the tutor. For this style of teaching, ReLaTe has the important advantage that it can have video pictures of all the participants in the videoconference.

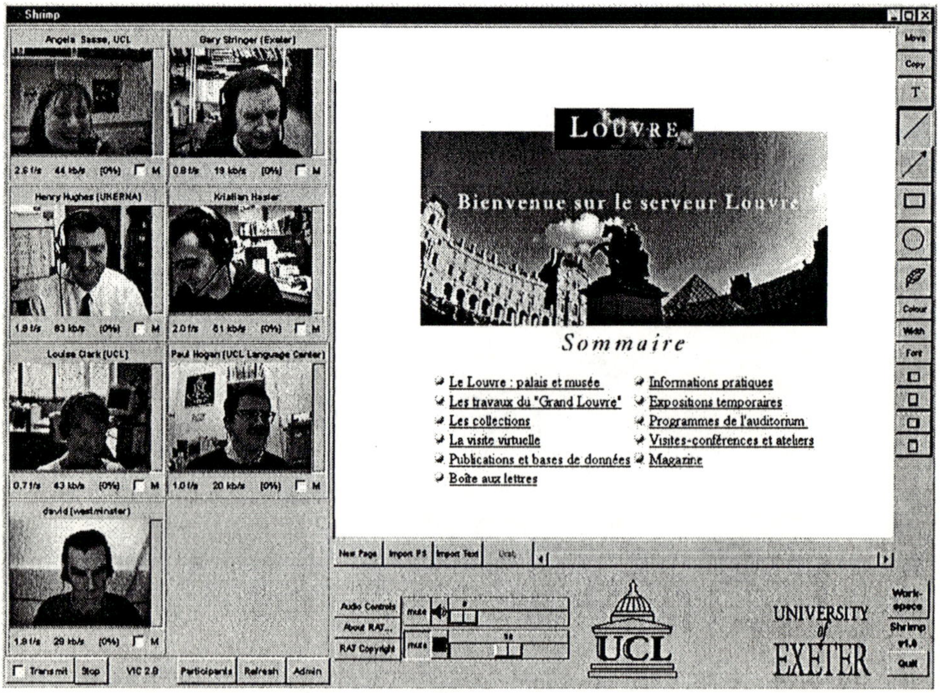

Figure 2 Screenshot of the ReLaTe interface

The ReLaTe interface shown in Figure 2 is very straightforward to use, even for those with little computing experience. The layout allows up to 8 video windows on the left of the screen, as shown (when the number of participants is 4 or less, one window can be enlarged by clicking on the title bar). A coloured vertical bar appears alongside the window of whoever is speaking, thus giving a visual confirmation of who is the current speaker. Audio controls for microphone and headset volume are at the bottom centre of the screen. The remainder of the interface is occupied by a shared workspace or whiteboard; anything drawn or typed here can be seen by all participants in the conference, or the material can be scanned in by the tutor prior to the session. Individual participants can each choose a different colour for their contributions, allowing them to be easily identified. Successful use of the shared workspace and other collaborative tools is often fundamental to many language teaching uses of videoconferencing and the topic will be returned to later in this paper.

Life after ReLaTe: Recent Developments: Much of the recent UK work on Internet videoconferencing in the academic world has been carried out under the auspices of the PIPVIC project (PIPVIC 1999). Led by the Dept. of Computer Science at UCL, with funding from UKERNA (who manage the UK academic network), the project has investigated the use of videoconferencing for a wide range of teaching and research applications. PIPVIC has grown to a total of 15 participating organisations, demonstrating that multicast videoconferencing is no longer such a 'minority sport'. Exeter's involvement in PIPVIC has remained mainly in the area of language teaching, including a series of Italian tutorials for Engineering students (with a tutor in Aberystwyth), but including a diversion into a short series of Art History seminars for students following a course on the Renaissance. One of the most recent sets of trials has involved a group of EFL students at Exeter taking a course discussing IT topics and terminology with a UCL tutor. This course made very heavy use of the NTE text editor (NTE 1999), which is a type of shared workspace tool that concentrates on text handling and does not have graphics capabilities. One of its strengths is that it has very good facilities for moving text around. It is therefore well suited to exercises such as gap-filling, where the tutor provides groups of words from which the students have the appropriate one; NTE can be used to drag and drop individual words in the correct space. It is clear that a shared text editor of this type makes possible collaborative work between students in a way that is not so easily possible in a normal face-to-face tutorial.

The experiences from this and other trials carried out as part of PIPVIC have in general showed that multicast Internet videoconferencing is well on its way to becoming a tool for routine teaching use. In the last couple of years, the power of PCs has increased to a point where a shortage of desktop computing power is no longer a major problem. In the same way, the advent of multimedia facilities on the standard office PC has meant that the only additional hardware needed for Internet videoconferencing is the camera and video capture card. Until recently, sound cards which handled full-duplex operation (where two participants can speak at once) adequately were a comparative rarity but this feature (crucial for highly interactive language tutorials) is now becoming available in commonly installed cards. The choice of operating system is also assuming a lesser importance. On the PC platform, Linux still has the edge in terms of performance on a given hardware base, but Windows 95 systems can now deliver very acceptable performance. The most noticeable drawback of Windows 95 is that its relatively poor multitasking and prioritisation performance can still give rise to problems if, for example, a user moves or re-sizes a window during a videoconference; if this happens, the audio and video is inclined to come to an abrupt halt until the window management is complete.

On the network front, things have also improved, within the UK at least. The multicast network (the MBone) is now a full user service on the UK's SuperJANET academic network and after a period of major problems whilst reconfiguration was carried out, it now seems encouragingly stable and reliable. Nevertheless, it is important not to overstate the case. MBone videoconferencing is still a long way from being as consistently reliable as, say, the telephone network and critically, if something does go wrong during a conference, tracking down the problem often remains difficult. A multiway videoconference with four participants has a considerable number of components, any of which could potentially fail. Problems could range from an overloaded LAN (local area network) to temporary congestion on the SuperJANET backbone or could even not be a network problem at all, but could be something as simple as a malfunctioning microphone or a badly-behaved background job running on a participant's PC. Because the causes of a problem can be so diverse, this type of videoconference will continue to need ready access to technical support, probably for the foreseeable future. Academic computing support services, whose Helpdesks are geared up to provide assistance with less time-critical queries such as 'How do I get accents in Word' are not necessarily going to find it easy to handle problems for real-time applications such as videoconferencing.

The other issue that remains is that in order to support multicast conferencing, an institution's local computer networking staff need to be capable of configuring and managing the underlying communications infrastructure, which can be a non-trivial task. Greater awareness of the issues involved is still needed amongst higher education's networking professionals.

Pedagogical Issues: Although the situation concerning the *technical* aspects underpinning Internet videoconferencing have considerably improved, the pedagogical validity of conducting language classes and tutorials by this method can still be questioned. Whilst there is good evidence from numerous trials to show that good learning outcomes can be achieved (PIPVIC 1998), most of these have been conducted with small numbers of concurrent users; typically a conference will still consist of a tutor and three or four students. In face-to-face small group tutorials, such low numbers would be considered very much a luxury; in UK universities, tutorial and seminar groups of up to 15 or 20 students are commonplace. Network bandwidth and processing power improvements mean that larger-scale trials should now be worth attempting. Certainly the PIPVIC project holds weekly project management meetings at which 15 or 20 participants take part, most of whom are transmitting video, albeit at low frame rates. However, it is by no means certain that tutorial style conferences would necessarily scale in the same way. Issues such as the need to shrink each video window to a 'thumbnail' in order to fit them all on the screen mean that the tutor might find it very difficult to gauge student feedback, body language etc. It is not clear that what works for a fairly structured management videoconference run by a chairperson will work as well for a more free-flowing, highly interactive language conversation class; more work is urgently required in this area.

Desktop vs. Seminar Room Systems: One interesting development in Internet videoconferencing has been a renewed interest in seminar-room systems. Instead of each student sitting at their own PC wearing a headset, greater attention is now being paid to the situation where groups of students are linked. Typically, this might involve perhaps groups of 10 or so students, each sitting in three different universities. Advances in audio-visual technology, rather than computing or networking *per se* have made this type of scenario much more attractive. High-resolution data projectors have now fallen in price so that large, readable video displays are now becoming common in seminar rooms. On the audio side, low-priced echo cancellers (WL Telecom 1999) are now coming onto the market which make it feasible to use speaker systems without suffering from audio feedback or howlround. The PIPVIC project has taken some tentative steps with this type of trial.

Figure 3 Tutor in Seminar Room Tutorial

Figure 3 illustrates a recent seminar given by Professor Trotter from Aberystwyth as a revision class for Exeter students on an early French text, the Strasbourg Oaths. In this instance, the students were at one site, using a data projector, but the lecturer was still using a desktop monitor, so that it was hard for the lecturer to distinguish the faces of the student audience. Even quite mundane audio-visual features can cause irritating problems; if the students are watching the tutor via a data projector display, this often involves turning down the seminar room lighting to a point where the tutor's view of the students becomes hopelessly dark.

In many cases, it would be desirable for a tutor to be able to teach a face-to-face class, *as well as* one or more groups of remote students. In this situation, a tutor will undoubtedly want to use the conventional teaching techniques of the face-to-face tutorial, using a whiteboard/blackboard to write notes, being able to walk about the room whilst talking and so on. Technology is now coming into existence that will enable a tutor to retain this flexibility whilst also teaching remote students at the same time; image-following video cameras can track the tutor, whilst electronic add-ons will soon enable a conventional whiteboard to also be interfaced to the videoconference's electronic version.

Collaborative Working: One of the key areas for further work in the future is the question of tools to support collaborative working. The shared workspace tools already available (such as NTE) have been shown to make possible a wide range of language teaching work. Nevertheless, more is still needed. Products such as Microsoft's NetMeeting have the ability to share PC applications (such as a word processor, PowerPoint or CALL software) between conference participants, but so far there has been few experiments in using the application-sharing capabilities of NetMeeting in combination with the multicast conferencing tools. One area where some initial trials have been carried out are in the use of collaborative Web browsing. In the Art History seminar series, for example, a collaborative version of Netscape (version 4.07) was used. Both sites ran Netscape alongside the conferencing software, but by using Netscape collaboratively, it meant that when the tutor switched their browser to display a new page (in this case, to discuss a Renaissance painting or a detail of one), then the Netscape running at the students' site automatically switched to the same page. This worked very well, albeit with some teething troubles (for example, scrolling around a page didn't make the remote page scroll in the same way), but with Netscape, the collaboration is limited to just two sites. Collaborative Web browsers which work with more than two sites do exist (Marratech 1999) and are undoubtedly worthy of further investigation. Further details in this area will be published as a report for the WELL project.

Where Next? Perhaps the most important short-term area for further work is in investigation of just how well larger tutorial groups can be handled by Internet videoconferencing; if they prove effective, the economics of language teaching using this technology will become much more attractive. In the slightly longer term, the possibilities of language teaching to the home using the ADSL (Asymmetric Digital

Subscriber Line) technology to give high bandwidths over telephone lines and the possibilities of connection to Europe using the TEN-155 research network (on which work is already underway) are more than enough to keep this group of researchers excited at the prospects for the future.

References:

NTE (1999)
http://www-mice.cs.ucl.ac.uk/multimedia/software/nte/
Marratech (1999)
http://www.marratech.com/
PIPVIC (1998)
http://www-mice.cs.ucl.ac.uk/multimedia/projects/pipvic/deliverables/d2.doc
PIPVIC (1999)
http://www-mice.cs.ucl.ac.uk/multimedia/projects/pipvic2/
RAT (1999)
http://www-mice.cs.ucl.ac.uk/multimedia/software/rat/
WL Telecom (1999)
http://www.wl-telecom.com/auduk5.htm

USING THE INTERNET IN ENGLISH INSTRUCTION AT THE CHINESE AIR FORCE ACADEMY

Der-li Chiao
Chinese Air Force Academy, Taiwan

Abstract
English is taught as a foreign language in Taiwan. It is especially important for the cadets of Chinese Air Force Academy (CAFA). Therefore, I think that I endeavor to create a supportive learning environment. Using recent developments in information technology, I try to use the network instruction to give more effective teaching and help my cadets to improve their abilities and furthermore, to enhance their comprehension in English learning. In addition, the Internet-based environment also provides a variety of tools and methods to help evaluate the learning process and assess cadets' ability. Afterwards, the network instruction is like knowledge treasure including multimedia and hypermedia; furthermore, it contains valuable resources under the World Wide Web. I teach the cadets how to use them and create the domain of knowledge.

Data collected from the questionnaires, pre-test on language acquisition and post-test on network instruction whether the Internet can enhance their abilities, interviews and classroom observations show that the cadets have positive attitudes toward the Computer Language Instruction Model (CLIM) through the World Wide Web (WWW). This paper attempts to highlight some significant applications and evaluation issues on network instruction. And the goal is to provide suggestions to improve the teaching. Hopefully, this innovative model will be advocated and integrated into English instruction in the future.

Introduction: The aim of this study is to investigate the improvement of the cadets' English ability via the language instruction site created for this study and related sites on the Internet in an EFL (English as a foreign language) classroom as well as to increase the cadets' achievement scores and language learning attitude in the process of language acquisition. The cadets' using the Internet as well as interacting between teacher and machine are the discussion and analysis based on classroom data collected by the writer. It briefly states the limitations of the observations and teaching procedures made in this study and proposes implications for improving classroom teaching on the World Wide Web (WWW). The results of this study will provide English teachers with a reference for future designs on the English curriculum incorporating the Internet materials; at the same time, I hopefully provide the findings to create new ideas for the conventional teaching and learning.

English is taught as a foreign language in Taiwan. It is especially important for the cadets of the Chinese Air Force Academy (CAFA). The Air Force is a high-tech service, so it requires its members to be not only intelligent but also scientific. Our nation is replacing old planes with new ones such as the Image 21 and other powerful fighter planes. The planes with technical directions completely are written English instructions such as those computer commands are on the operation console. So, the cadets should own more English abilities to compel the flight mission. Therefore, it is essential to create a supportive learning environment for them. I try to use language instruction on the Internet for more effective teaching and to help my cadets improve their language abilities. In addition, the Internet-based environment also provides a variety of tools and methods to help evaluate the learning process and assess cadets' abilities. Moreover, language instruction on the WWW (World Wide Web) is a learning treasure, which includes multimedia and hypermedia and other valuable resources. Especially, the multimedia and hypermedia are built through the Internet to integrate these four language skills — listening, speaking, reading and writing in English language instruction. That is to say, English teachers and students must grasp the gist that 'the four language skills are interlocked and interdependent' (Robinett, 1983, p. 173). In recent years, some studies have been done on the potential for English learning and teaching through web technology (Green, 1997; Sloane, 1997; Wei, 1997) which has attracted attention and interest of numerous computer users and teachers worldwide for learning English. I teach the cadets how to use them and create their own learning domain. So there is need for an effective tool to direct the cadets to explore and apply these treasures. This paper attempts to highlight some significant applications and evaluation issues on language instruction. And the goal is to provide suggestions to improve teaching.

However, current research has not provided sufficient evidence on whether student interests in learning English increase through the help of web technology or online materials. In order to improve students' motivation and make learning more effective, I shall integrate the Internet into English instruction. The purpose of this article is to find out (1) Are the effects of language acquisition on the test group different in influencing cadets in developing English reading and writing abilities? (2) Are the reading and writing abilities of the cadets in the test group influenced by the Computer Language Instruction Model (CLIM)? (3) Will student-student and teacher-student interaction be improved by using the Internet?

This study provides empirical evidence on the positive correlation between the cadets' attitude and the use of the Internet as a teaching tool. The results of this study will provide teachers with a reference for the future English designs incorporating the Internet English materials and hopefully compensating for the disadvantages of the conventional teaching.

Methodology

Background of the study and Subjects: Generally, the language proficiency of the majority of CAFA cadets is at the beginning level. I chose four sophomore classes, a total of 88 cadets, to train in the Computer Language Instruction Model (CLIM). Those subjects were divided into two groups: one group of 44 cadets represent the experiment group (G1); the other one of 44 cadets represents the control group (G2).

The purpose of the present study is to enhance the reading and writing ability of the cadets. To take control of the cadets' enhancement of the reading and writing abilities, I chose the ECL test which is held on the beginning of this semester by the authority of CAFA as their baseline of placement for their starting proficiency. When they graduate from the CAFA, they can have the opportunity to go abroad for the training of the maintenance and flight in the military or company in U.S.A. However, the examinees are required to pass the ECL test given by the American Institute in Taiwan. Even though the students have basic computer skills, they have to take extra basic computer and Internet training for eight hours.

Settings: The teaching activities for the experiment group (G1) are held in a language lab or a computer lab which is equipped with ninety Pentium II computers. The instructor taught the experiment group (G1) two hours per week during the spring semester in 1999. The control group (G2) stayed in a conventional classroom or a language lab for their studies. Outside the lab are computers available for the cadets to work on their projects or assignments in their free time. Moreover, many cadets of the G2 have personal computers with network connections. They can work on their projects either individually or in pairs. However, the teaching activities for the control group are held only in the language lab and in conventional classrooms.

Instrumentation: These data are collected by questionnaires, surveys, observations, and student records and comparisons between the experiments and the control groups with open-ended questions about the network teaching via the Internet. Questioners 'Language Learning Inventory' (Oxford, 1990a), 'Attitudes toward English Instruction' (Corbiy, 1979; Cox, 1979; Bushyager, 1981; Xenanko, 1996; Jacobs, 1996) are given to the two groups to compare the difference of their perceived attitudes and interest toward network English instruction before and after the experiment. The main approach of the experiment in this study is to integrate the WWW information into English instruction in the experiment group, but maintain the original and traditional approach of teaching in a classroom in the control group. The questionnaire — 'Attitudes toward English Instruction' consisted of thirty items on a 4-point preference-scale with four being the highest score to measure samples' general attitudes and interest toward English instruction. Another questionnaire — Strategy Inventory for Language Learning (SILL) consisted of six parts — cognitive, memory, compensation, metacognitive, affective and social strategies to integrate overall skills for learning language. Six of the questions in the survey are reverse coded in order to compensate for the possibility that those cadets might tend to answer positively on any survey. Furthermore, a Chinese version of the questions is given to assist with understanding and interpretation for the convenience of the cadets' answering (Appendix I). Additionally, an interview of open-ended questions (Appendix II) is consisted of ten items for the researcher to understand students' feelings and opinions toward English instruction through the WWW after this experiment is conducted in the experiment group. Classroom observations with the teaching in the experiment group are also included.

The cadets are assigned to experimental group and a control group. The post-test is application measures of achievement to be collected from the post-test with using a checklist for the application of visual literacy principled. Learner notebooks are collected immediately following treatment. Process efficiency is operationally defined as a measure of the efficiency of the process of learning in terms of learner note-taking strategies employed in learning. Learner notebooks are collected immediately following treatment, photocopied for the examination of learning process in terms of quantity of notes taken, and returned to the subject for studying purposes. These measures of English ability are used to compare the two types (G1 & G2) of cadets: the cadets' course grades, their scores on the departmental final examination and their acceptable-answer scores on a cloze test. Multivariate and discriminant analyses of these measures indicate that G1 is significantly better than the G2 on all these measures in this semester. Probable causes of this phenomenon are discussed, as well as a possible relationship between this ' new' variable and previous discouraging learning-gain (pre-test / post-test) findings.

Course Design: Computer Language Instruction Model (CLIM) and Resources: Two primary tools are used for this study: Computer Language Instruction Model (CLIM) and navigational tools (Netscape Communicator and Internet Explorer). Through CLIM, students exchanged ideas with peers and the instructor, and sent in homework as well. This created an opportunity for students to communicate in English (Savignon, 1983). In addition, two of the most popular navigational tools, Netscape Communicator and Internet Explorer, are used as browsing tools for cadets to access the web sites. The material uses network to examine the cadets' reading ability. First, the classmates browse the authentic text of *American Language Course* that I keyed in and converted to the 'html' format before uploading it to my web site — http://163.15.25.231). In order to decrease their anxiety and save time as well as acquiring good control over the Internet, cadets have been introduced to the different types of network instruction feedback which will allow them to keep track of their own learning process or review the front page on the hints. As with human communication (Robinson, 1991), network instruction may depend on factors related to the learner, e.g. learner perceptual processes, individual readiness and experience, and factors related to the feedback itself.
Furthermore, when cadets do not understand a meaning or know the pronunciation of a word or phrase, they can link to on-line teaching resource with the net address which I collected, e.g. the Webster Dictionary, Encyclopedia, Merriam Dictionary and the

Internet Thesaurus. Moreover, I set up useful web sites in the lab computers to make other search engines accessible. These are several pedagogical criteria for evaluating World Wide Web sites designed for computer instruction. According to Jeff Nelson (1986), the ideal ESL web site should be:

1. Interactive: Students can give input and the program utilizes that input; that is, students effect the machine.
2. Communicative: Students send or receive messages from real people.
3. Contextual: The site has a context or theme for the language which is presented.
4. Sensor: Information is presented in multiple formats — textual and visual.

Based on these pedagogical criteria, teachers can choose ideal Web sites which may help upgrade learners' proficiency in using the target language more effectively and appropriately.

Makulowsich (1994) offered some suggestions on how to teach the Internet, including introduction to the Internet, matching objectives to cadets interests, the importance of interactive sessions, conducting cadets evaluation, follow-up, keeping up with cadets, and renewal of teaching materials and teaching skills. These tips provide guidance for the instructor in selecting teaching materials through the Internet.

Therefore, the instructor selected some web sites from the World Wide Web (WWW) among the abundant Internet resources (Kitao, 1997; Leu & Len, 1997; Sperling, 1997) for English learning for this study based on these criteria. Sources available in the web site included the following:

(1) The 'Bulletin Board' and the 'News Sheet' which were created with the goal of increasing cadets' communicative ability. A medium such as computer-mediated conferencing can support two-way or multi-way dialogue very well.

(2) The Encyclopedia, Webster and Merriam dictionary which can be transferred to interactive multimedia in the form of multiply-linked teaching resources. The design is more successful in making the cadets active learners.

(3) The International Community Radio in Taipei (ICRT) site was made available since it was most popular radio stations and it is the only English radio station in Taiwan, which is easily accessed through the Web. Many cadets were already familiar with the radio programs and they are related to their real life experience which can promote their learning interests.

(4) Yahoo or Infoseek were incorporated since cadets already had basic computer skills and were easily trained to search for information and improve their independent reading ability.

(5) EFL/ESL web sites with clear and immediate applications to foreign-language teaching. Accordingly, students can learn English independently through EFL/ESL web sites in the future.

Data Collection and Analysis: All the required data for this study are collected before and after the experiment is conducted. The same survey is given at the beginning and the end of the spring semester in 1999. Additionally, the open-ended questions are given to ten randomly selected cadets. The survey includes a list of thirty questions as shown in Appendix I, and the open-ended questions included seven questions as shown in Appendix II. Those questions in the survey are randomly listed to sample interests and attitudes toward English learning. And the open-ended questions are related to sample attitudes and opinions toward English instruction through the WWW.

During data collection procedures, all participants understood their participation in this research to be confidential, and their responses to the survey to be used only for academic purposes. They are not asked to write their names or identification numbers on the questionnaire.

The information obtained by the questionnaire is coded in the SPSS for WINDOWS data sheet and then one-way ANOVA for pre and post-test analysis (Hatch & Lazaraton, 1991). The one-way ANOVA is used in the significant differences at the level of .05 in the effects between G1 and G2. The statistical procedures used for data analysis are based on the research questions, which are related to the sample interests and attitudes toward English instruction. Furthermore, the supplemental information gained from the open-ended questions complemented the explanation of the survey results. The latter data are analyzed with the assistance of the grounded theory techniques described by Strauss & Corbin (1990).

Limitation of the Study: The population of this study was limited to my teaching cadets at the CAFA. It would therefore be difficult to generalize the results of the study to the universal population of cadets at the CAFA. Also, the variable factor of the instructor's personality is not considered in the design of this study. Further, because of time constraint using the computer lab, on-line chat room is not designed in the course schedule of this study. Sometimes, the web activities are not keeping on the status because this study is limited to the equipment's speed and capacity. These factors result in the limitation of the study.

Results: The evidence collected in this study is categorized into three categories including the analysis of one-way ANOVA, responses of open-ended questions, and cadets' e-mail feedback.

Table of the Summary of ANOVA for Pre and Post-Test

Item No.	Pre-Test						Post-Test					
	Control		Experiment		F-test	p value	Control		Experiment		F-test	p value
	Mean	S.D.	Mean.	S.D.			Mean	S.D.	Mean	S.D.		
1	3.70	.90	4.00	.87	2.50	.118	3.48	.76	4.28	.66	28.97*	<.001
2	3.30	.85	3.15	.87	.62	.432	3.39	.68	3.55	.70	1.12	.292
3	2.39	.87	2.74	1.06	2.96	.089	2.84	.83	2.93	1.00	.23	.630
4	2.41	1.02	2.37	.88	.04	.844	2.48	1.01	2.16	.89	2.54	.115
5	2.50	.88	2.70	.79	1,25	.267	3.00	.78	3.85	.67	30.97	<.001
6	2.43	.85	2.35	.77	.24	.623	2.91	.88	3.87	.75	31.02	<.001
7	3.27	1.02	3.17	1.00	.22	.643	3.34	.89	3.07	.95	2.01	.159
8	4.43	.63	4.48	.66	.12	.732	4.57	.59	4.43	.78	4.43	.363
9	3.48	.51	3.52	.62	.14	.711	3.39	.78	4.02	.71	16.17*	<.001
10	2.82	1.21	2.93	1.16	.22	.642	2.75	1.24	2.54	3.02	.18	.675
11	2.36	1.28	2.24	1.10	.25	.621	1.72	.59	2.39	.93	16.25*	<.001
12	3.66	.91	3.89	1.06	.24	.269	3.91	.68	3.96	.96	.072	.788
13	3.45	1.00	3.76	0.99	2.13	.148	2.86	.82	3.50	.98	11.03*	<.001
14	3.00	.96	3.26	1.08	1.45	.232	2.73	.87	3.87	.91	36.92*	<.001
15	3.02	1.02	3.07	.77	.05	.824	2.98	.85	3.63	.91	13.26*	.148
16	1.50	.63	1.46	.62	.11	.742	1.78	.76	1.57	.63	2.13	.599
17	2.45	.93	2.67	.92	1.27	.263	2.37	.84	2.74	1.00	.28	.134
18	3.61	.75	3.46	.84	.87	.352	3.68	.88	3.37	1.06	2.29	.133
19	3.55	.90	3.65	.85	.33	.564	3.86	.82	3.67	1.01	.95	.333
20	2.18	.92	2.33	1.08	.46	.497	2.10	.83	2.02	.58	.21	.646
21	3.27	.97	2.91	.89	3.35	.071	3.32	.88	3.00	.99	2.58	.111
22	4.41	.62	4.61	.68	2.10	.151	4.55	.55	4.61	.65	.25	.620
23	3.64	.89	3.78	.99	.54	.463	3.77	.83	3.89	.90	.42	.518
24	3.07	1.04	3.02	1.18	.04	.844	2.95	1.08	2.93	1.10	.01	.932
25	3.86	.88	4.07	.77	1.34	.250	3.43	.85	3.89	.77	7.30*	.008
26	3.36	1.04	3.17	1.16	.67	.416	3.43	1.11	3.28	1.09	.42	.521
27	3.34	.91	3.43	.93	.23	.631	3.14	.90	2.70	.84	9.25*	.003
28	4.41	.58	4.54	.59	.19	.278	4.16	.65	4.30	.70	1.05	.308
29	3.45	.93	3.37	.88	.20	.656	3.27	.85	4.17	.68	31.31*	<.001
30	2.70	.85	2.91	.80	1.29	.260	2.93	.70	2.67	.84	2.49	.118

*p<.05

There is no significant difference between the control and the experiment group for pre-test; however, there were some items showing significant differences between the two groups after English instruction via the CLIM on the World Wide Web is conducted. Those items may be described in the following way:

Based on the table above, the Item 1 indicated significant difference between two groups, and G1 students thought learning English became more interesting via using the computer. Item 5, 6, 9 and 27 showing significant difference mean that G2 cadets liked to express their ideas and enjoyed communicating with their classmates in English class. Furthermore, they paid more attention to classmates' questions and discussions in English class and group discussion. Items 17 and 29 showed that students perceived English should be a required course, and they had a stronger desire to learn English. Furthermore, they thought that learning English would benefit their future career. Finally, Item 6 that G1 cadets would like to use the CLIM to help them to learn English.

Responses of Open-ended Questions: Generally speaking, cadets from the experiment group were satisfied with the teaching materials from the CLIM such as cloze tests, the usage of a dictionary, idioms and slang which attracted their attention more than other texts and materials. They thought that online materials were more practical and useful to their daily life, and that they were authentic. In addition, cadets thought that online materials could improve their English reading skills significantly. Moreover, there was the perception that ' Bulletin Board' could enhance teacher-cadet, cadet-cadet interaction, and cadets really enjoyed discussing and expressing some thoughts through the board. Furthermore, they post their interaction on the 'News Sheet' to share with the peers and teacher together.

According to the G1 cadets' opinions, they thought that the WWW applied in the English course would be appropriate; furthermore, they agreed that it will be necessary to offer another two-hour-period class of the English instruction through the CLIM besides their regular two-hour English class on campus. Meanwhile, students hoped that this course could be optimal for anyone who expressed interest.

Although G1 cadets believed that the learning resources from the WWW were tremendous, they did not feel free to use the equipment on campus because of the weakness of the settings. Most students did not spend extra time using the Internet outside the English class; they only searched for some English resources through the CLIM in class because they could not find the appropriate equipment otherwise. There is only one-computer lab open for the cadets, and it is frequently occupied. In addition, not every cadet owns a personal computer either in the dormitory or at home. They could not use the computer as much as they wished. When using the computer on campus, cadets often felt frustrated because of the slow speed of transmission. Furthermore, because the campus computers were not equipped with audio systems, cadets felt bored sometimes. Without audio capabilities, enhancement of interaction between the computers and cadets in listening and speaking was limited.

Conclusion: The purpose of this study was to investigate the cadets' attitudes and opinions toward the English instruction through CLIM on the Internet to find out whether cadets were interested in learning English through the Internet, if the cadet-cadet and teacher-cadet interactions were improve, and whether their perception of communicative ability was enhanced. The data for this study was collected through pre- and post-surveys, e-mail feedback, open-ended questions and classroom observations from two groups of students, 'the experiment group (G1) and the control group (G2). The following discussions of the cadets' attitudes and interests are toward online materials and English learning via the interactive function of the Internet. Also, some suggestions to English teaches are provided.

In sum, cadets involving the Computer Language Instruction Model (CLIM) through the World Wide Web (WWW) showed positive attitudes toward language learning, and had more opportunities to interact and communicate with each other. E-mail, especially provided cadets with in-class and out-of-class discussion and reduced their anxiety in front of the screen. Whether the lab equipment could be improved and technical problems eliminated and whether the instructor could get to know more about the cadets' interest and needs when selecting the online materials, use of the Internet will effectively facilitate learning. It is hoped that the results of this study will provide some perspective views of teaching English for the reference of English teachers. There is not only one wholly effective learning teaching approach. Instead of using only one approach or method, most successful English teacher use an eclectic approach, or a combination of several approaches which they have found form their past experiences to be most effective in promoting language learning for their cadets.

Another important goal of my research is to provide hypertext constructs with open hypermedia system. I propose an open hypermedia system framework to classify and evaluate hypermedia system and integration on the WWW. In the future, the WWW seems to be the major interface and development environment and all users will have access to it through the Internet, I have adopted the WWW as the backbone of our system architecture to combine the features of both the WWW and the hypermedia system and conforms the users' convenience. Those features include integration, distribution, across platforms, collaboration to enable us to adopt merits of both the WWW and the open hypermedia systems (Chiu, 1997).

Data gathered in this study included a wide range of formative evaluation and participant-observer accounts in the form of personal note, meeting notes, interviews, questionnaires and e-mail messages. The achievement measures for all treatment groups showed significantly higher levels of achievement when compared to the appended control group. Using multivariate ANOVA analyses of variance, the data is examined to determine what effect, whether any, the varying instructional strategies have on learning. Results indicates that there are statistically significant differences between any of the experimental groups. The significant effects are found in this study; results indicate further research will prove worthwhile in determining effects of instructional strategies on emerging technology-base instruction with designers' intelligence.

The possibility of replacing mainstream teaching and lectures by the use of the Internet has a number of implications for universities. According to Dr. Chuang's article, the four language skills interlocked the English Instruction via the Internet (Chaung, 1998). I have demonstrated, using a sophomore English course, and approach to making the transition from traditional teaching to lifelong learning. In particular, incremental construction makes the transition affordable, while at least maintaining the student learning experience, and perhaps improving it. I hope my experience encourages others to try using hypermedia technology as a central part of the cadets' learning experiences, rather than the peripheral role that it often plays today. Being English teachers, I believe that incorporating the Internet and multimedia into the integration of four skills (listening, speaking, reading, writing) in English instruction would be more effective and should be advocated (Chuang, 1998). In addition, I hope that the outcomes and suggestions of this study will be beneficial in the future curriculum design of English instruction.

References:

Al, Roger. 1990. Telecommunication in the classroom: Keys to succeed telecomputing. *The Computer Teacher,* Vol. 3 (8), p. 25-28.

Applebee, A. 1997. Rethinking curriculum in the English language arts. *English Journal, 86 (5),* 25-31.

Arishi, A & Yahya, A. 1994. An integrated approach to the use of technology in communicative language teaching. *Language quarterly, 3291-2,* 175-191.

Brownell, Gregg. 1992. *Computers and Teaching.* New York: West Publishing Company.

Bruce, C. B., Peyton, K. J., & Batsons 1993. *Network-based Classroom: Problems and Realities.* Cambridge: Uni. Press.

Chabay, Ruth W. & Sherwood Bruce A. 1992. A Practical Guide for the Creation of Educational Software. Edited by Larkin Jill H. & Chabay,

Ruth W. *Computer-assisted Instruction and Intelligent Tutoring Systems.* Lawrence Erlbaum Associates.

Chang Ye-ling. 1999. File Emanagement in an English Speech Community (http://140.127.40.7). *Conference on Advanced Joint English Teaching (AJET).* National Chung-shan Uni. Taiwan.

Chiu, Chao-min. 1997. Fusing the World Wide Web and the Open Hypermedia System Technologies (Hypertext, Dynamically Mapped Information System). Rutgers The State University of New Jersey. AAC 9806875 ProWuest — Dissertation Abstracts.

Chuang, Yuanshang. 1998. Modern teachers and multimedia instruction. *The Proceedings of the First International Conference on Multimedia Language Education.* Taipei: The Crane Publishing Co., Ltd.

Collins, A. S. 1993. Design issues and learning environments. New York, Northwester Uni. Center for Technique in Education. *ERIC No. ED 357733.*

Collins, Betty. 1988. *Computers, Curriculum, and Whole-class Instruction* (Issues and Ideas). Belmont, California: Wardwoth Publishing Company.

Harris, J. 1993. Using Internet know-how to plan how students will know. *Computing Teacher,* Vol. 20.

Harris, D. P. and L. A. Palmer. 1970. *A Comprehensive English Language Test for Speakers of English as a Second Language.* New York: McGraw-Hill.

Howie, Sherry Hill. 1989. *Reading, Writing and Computers.* London: Ally and Bacon.

Ko, Pei-yu Natalie. 1995. *Strategies Associated With Proficiency & Predicators of Strategy Choice: A Study on Language Learning Strategies of EFL Students At three Educational Levels in Taiwan.* Department of Language Education, Indiana University, Bloomington.

Krey, Cynthia Lucille. 1995. *A Study of Reflexive and Extensive Text Style in Instructional Materials Used in a Distance Learning Program.* UMI: Dissertation Services.
Laurillard, D. 1998. Multimedia and the learner' s experience of narrative. In *Computer & Education* 31, p. 229-242.
Levin, J. A., Rogers, A., Waugh, M. and Smith, K. 1989. Observations on educational electronic networks: Appropriate activities for learning. *The Computing Teacher,* in (8), 17-21.
Melanie Ward & David Bewkabds. 1998. Use of the Web in undergraduate teaching. In *Computer & Education.* 31 (1998) 171-184.
Oxford, R. L. 1986b. Development and psychometric testing of the strategy inventory for language learning (SILL). *ARI Tech. Rept. 728.* Alexandria, VA: Army Research Institute for the Behavioral and Social Sciences.
Phinney, Marianne. 1991. Computer-assisted writing and writing apprehension in ESL students. Edited by Dunkel, Particia. *Computer-assisted Language Learning and Testing.* New York: Newbury House, A Division of Harper Collins Publishers.
Reid, Joy M. 1995. *Learning Styles in the ESL/EFL Classroom.* New York: Heinle & Heinle Publishers.
Reid, Joy M. 1998. *Understanding Learning Styles in the Second Language Classroom.* New Jersey. Prentice Hall Regents.
Rogers, A. 1990. Telecommunication in the classroom: Keys to successful telecomputing. *The Computer Teacher,* Vol. 17 (8), p.25-28.
Scardamallia, M., Bereiter, C., Mclean, R. J., & Woodruff, E. 1989. Computer-supported intentional learning environments. *Journal of Education Computing Research,* 5 (1), 52-61.
Sun, Cecilia Shu-huei. *Directness in American Speech.* 1998. *The Proceedings of the Second International Conference on Multimedia Language Education.* Taipei, Taiwan: The Crane Publishing Co., Ltd.
Wang, Chih. Teaching and Learning Over the World Wide Web. 1998. *The Proceedings of the Second International Conference on Multimedia Language Education.* Taipei, Taiwan: The Crane Publishing Co., Ltd.
Warschauer, Mark., Turbee, L. & Roberts, B. 1996. Computer learning networks and student empowerment. *System,* Vol. 24(1), 1-14.
Waugh, M. L., Levin, J. A., & Smith, K. 1994. Organizing electronic network-based instructional interactions: Successful strategies and tactics. *The Computer Teacher,* 21 (5), 31-32.
Wu, Huei-fen Mary. 1997. *Use of Web-based Survey Instrument to Collect, Analyze and Present Course Evaluation Data (World Wide Web, Internet.* The George Washington University. AAC 9817201 ProQuest—Dissertation Abstracts.
Yan, Shu-chuan. 1998. The World Wide Web as an EFL Writing Tool. Edited By English Teachers' Association/ROC. *The Proceedings of the Seventh International Symposium on English Teaching, Vol. II.* Taipei: The Crane Publishing Co., Ltd.
Yan, Shu-chuan. 1998. Using the world Wide Web for Writing Instruction. *The Proceedings of the Second International Conference on Multimedia Language Education.* Taipei, Taiwan: The Crane Publishing Co., Ltd.

THE RESULTS OF ASSESSING LISTENING COMPREHENSION UNDER THREE LEARNING CONDITIONS AND THE APPLICATIONS OF COMPUTER-ASSISTED CLASSROOM DISCUSSION

Juei-ching Chung
Chinese Military Academy, Taiwan R.O.C.

Abstract
This study investigates the cognitive processes and outcomes of learning content-based materials delivered by different media as self-study. The subjects were 84 low-intermediate Chinese students of English in Taiwan. While audio and video groups practiced listening skills with the aid of media and workbook, and checked the answers with pen and pencil, CALL group worked and checked the answers at computer. In order to enhance the language use in authentic contexts, computer-assisted classroom discussion (CACD) was incorporated in CALL group. The test results showed that CALL group surpassed slightly the other two groups on listening and performed significant difference on reading. In addition, the theories, practices, and cognitive processes of each medium featured in this study, a qualitative analysis and applications of CACD were also discussed. Finally, some claims of feasible pedagogical integration of CACD into language learning and acquisition are put forward.

Introduction: The implementation of media in instructing the second language classroom has been a common practice for a long time. In the seventeenth century, teachers used pictures to teach Latin (Price, 1987). In recent decades, technological tools such as cassette recorders, OHPs, VCRs, satellite TV, and computers have been largely incorporated into language learning programs. The basic premise behind this technology was that if verbal behaviour was modeled, and then reinforced, students would quickly learn the language in question. Thus, the language lab activities based on audiocassettes were grounded in a stimulus-response behaviour pattern suggesting that more drill practice results rapid learning. Due to the lack of interaction, it was soon recognised that such activities in language labs were both tedious and boring for learners. Besides, the limited access to the target culture may not necessarily furnish a sufficiently rich environment for the acquisition of communicative competence, including many aspects of discourse activity, i.e. paralinguistic and extralinguistic behaviour. Many educators acknowledge the importance of the speech act and the cultural contexts of language and communication in the development of linguistic and pragmatic skills and competencies. Empirical studies also revealed that with exposure to authentic and dynamic video, such as the settings, accents, posture, gestures, etc. of native speakers relieve students from the boredom of the traditional class language drills. Whereas video viewing is still considered as passive learning, a shift to the interactive and communicative approach to second language education has been widely integrated into curriculum. Hypermedia/multimedia environments characterised by non-linear, random access and instant review or replay of any portion of the materials are proclaimed to provide a more appropriate setting for students to experience the target language in its cultural context.

In spite of some advantages beyond other media, computer programs may offer a very limited view if simply serve as grammar test and correction. Since listening as a co-operative participant involves interactive skills that cannot be developed by practising listening to recorded texts, the learner must experience 'intake' of language where holds the potential for developing the learners' linguistic system. The processes for using or holding the intake in short term memory influence the development of the linguistic system, which in turn affects the L2 output that the learner produces (Chapelle, 1998). Producing linguistic output forces learners to use the syntactic system and therefore to develop the aspect of their ability. Through the input from interlocutors, they notice aspects of the linguistic form and make necessary correction. This process, referred to as negotiation of meaning, is believed to facilitate L2 development. The use of e-mail, bulletin boards, teleconferencing, or discussion lists on worldwide networks such as the Internet enables learners and teachers to access and share information in a time- and space- independent fashion (Ortega, 1997). They place the technology more firmly under the control of the user. Most of these Cooperative learning activities constitute a development of the work of notable psychologists and philosophers like Vygotsky (cognitive functions are socially mediated or constructed) or Wittgenstein (linguistic knowledge is tied to 'language games'). Gay and Grosz-Ngate (1993) argue that working in small group promotes learning as an interactive process; thereby, developing critical thinking, social skills and the acquisition of specific knowledge (p. 420). In general these positions reflect a profound reappraisal of the social nature of language acquisition: situated cognition (Salaberry, 1994). For example, according to Vygotsky (1978), the mechanism of thought is the internalisation of external behaviours which occur while interacting with others. Doughty and Pica (1986) further argue that group and pair work are essential for increasing the amount of student practice time in classroom teaching.

Right after second and foreign language teachers began to integrate electronic communication into language teaching in the late 1980s, a number of researchers suggested that electronic communication differs linguistically from both traditional written and spoken discourse (Chun 1994; Ferrara, et. al. 1991; Kern 1995; Murray 1988; Wang 1993), and that these differences can be exploited for pedagogical advantage. Above all, Chun (1994) particularly contends that electronic discussion is similar to written texts in terms of language complexity, yet resembles face-to-face discussion in terms of functions performed, and thus can serve as an important bridge for transfer of communication skills from the written to spoken domain.

The researches mentioned above led to the purpose of this study: 1) to examine the outcomes of different media in acquiring listening comprehension and reading comprehension included lexical items, structures from content-based activities delivered by video, audiocassette with pictures, multimedia; 2) to explore the interaction and dynamics of group discussion in CMC; 3) to investigate the correlation between online discussion and the performances of reading and listening.

Using technology to aid listening comprehension: In the first half of the 20th century there was a shift in emphasis in foreign language teaching from written language to spoken language. Educators and researchers argued that language is in the first place spoken and that written language is therefore indirect, incomplete and an abstraction. The fact that in those days people had virtually no access to sound reproduction equipment such as tape recorders and cassettes made students very dependent of their teachers. The problem was partly resolved when language laboratories were introduced in the fifties. When audiocassettes appeared on the scene and sound reproduction equipment became cheaply available the problem was dispelled altogether. At the same time research was proving that in the initial stages it is more effective for the learner to listen to the foreign language he/she is learning than to speak it.

Most of today's language learning labs are centred around the delivery of materials through audio tape and video tape. However, the current trend has been focusing on delivering interactive multimedia with combination of video, audio, text and graphics to students. For listening activities, the computer is better than audio or video tape because students can listen as many times as he/she wants with just a click of the mouse-no clumsy rewinding and trying to find the same spot on the tape. Insofar as listening is the basis of oral language acquisition, CALL software can provide significantly more input than any other medium, with far more student control (Singhal).

One of the major factors that researchers believe enhance listening comprehension is visual support for texts. Carrell (1982) found out the provision of relevant context picture and title preceded the text facilitate reading comprehension, particularly for high intermediate ESL group. Video selected for listening strategy use also plays a critical role in information processing. Rubin (1990) found that the listening comprehension of high-beginning Spanish students who watched dramas on video improved significantly over students who received no video support for their listening training. While listening to recorded cassettes or radio programs is not visually rich as videotapes, a coherent organisation is still not devoid of context. For example, a radio program has an opening welcome, a list of the items to follow, a host who reappears in very program and whose style and voice become familiar to listeners. Nevertheless, pictures are necessarily provided with listening passage in narrowing down the listening topic since they not only facilitate comprehension, but also arouse attention and interest. Educators strongly believe that students, with context rich environment and proper instructional planning by the teacher, can be led to extract general and specific meaning from oral authentic texts while improving general listening comprehension skills (Herron, 1991).

Recently available interactive video technologies such as videodisc and DVD can efficiently serve as a learning unit in classes and in self-access centres. The computer technology allows the delivery of digital video and audio in the same interface as written text. This advance which provides listening tasks, language input and feedback on task success via the computer screen help develop listening skills. Due to the complexities of visual and verbal relationships in each media implemented in listening comprehension and related cognitive processes (Metallinos, 1994), research into the effectiveness of audio- and video-mediated instruments will present different gains in lexical items, structures or listening comprehension.

Co-operative learning: Current theory posits that language students can obtain opportunities to develop their cognition by actively communicating with others who are more proficient, and thereby expand each other's conceptual potential. It is assumed that while working alone, the less proficient learner needs help to comprehend the input both semantically and syntactically. Besides, they have better recall and internalised idea in the sociocultural realm if they actively engage in the cognitive process of assessing to meaning. In Vygostky's ZPD, more capable students can provide peers with new information and ways of thinking so that all parties can create new means of understanding. This mutually beneficial social process can also lead more experienced students to discover missing information, gain new insights through interactions, and develop a qualitatively different way of understanding (Hashimoto & Nyikos, 1997).

Bakhtin (1986), one of Vygotsky's Soviet contemporaries, and his circle further argues that the unique speech experience of each individual is shaped through constant interaction, and more focused interaction leads to higher forms of learning. 'Words, intonations, and inner-word gestures that have undergone the experience of outward expression' acquire 'a high social polish and luster by the effect of reactions and responses, resistance or support, on the part of a social audience' (Volosinov, 1973, p. 98). On the other hand, the text-mediational interpretation view texts as 'thinking devices' to generate new meanings collaboratively (Lotman, 1988; Wertsch & Bivenw, 1992). Chapelle (1998) claimed that when the tasks require a 'two way' interactant relationship, the quality of the interaction is superior.

Doughty and Pica (1986) and Long (1985) have proposed that the role of negotiation of meaning in normal conversation is the key factor in the overall process of SLA. Most important, group work generates the type of information exchange in which learners engage in conversational modification (clarification requests, confirmation and comprehension checks). This type of modified interaction is argued to be absolutely essential to make input comprehensible, and eventually to lead to successful acquisition of the target language (Salaberry, 1994). Collaborative learning has also been seen as the natural way for learners to become more autonomous or independent. Little (1994) also advances the idea that autonomy in language learning is inseparable from the 'development and internalisation of a capacity to participate fully and critically in social interactions'. Groups of learners are able through reflection externalised in discussion, to develop critical and independent attitudes towards learning processes and outcomes. For individuals working alone, language and language learning are more likely to remain fixed and immutable objects to which they can only accommodate themselves (Benson, 1997).

In the 1980s, with the advent of electronic communication integrated into the teaching of composition in the United States, the historical divide between speech and writing had been overcome. For the first time in history, human interaction now takes place in a text-based form with the features of easily transmission, storage, archive, revaluation, edition, and rewriting. Kroonenberg's (1994/1995) high school French students, who worked in pairs to discuss and debate ideas in a computer-mediated synchronous chat mode, experienced several benefits. They include rapid interaction of the synchronous communication, opportunity for reflection in the midst of interaction, and more expression in this mode than in ordinary written composition.

Warschauer (1996), in an experimental study comparing small-group ESL discussion online to discussion face-to-face, found that the online groups were twice as balanced, principally because the silent students increased their participation online. These data suggest important results for the possibilities of promoting collaborative learning in the classroom. With a class bulletin board or email discussion list, students can collaboratively work in pairs, small groups, or the whole class throughout the entire week. Chun (1994) claimed that electronic discussion appears to be a good bridge between writing and speaking skills, with the strengths of each domain apparently helping the other.

Cognitive process of each medium: The following review is the cognitive process or the strategy use of each media mentioned in this study while language learners engage in listening activity.

Audio cassette

Influenced by traditional translation, grammar-oriented teaching methods, my experiences of teaching cadets in Taiwan tended to emphasise on accuracy than on fluency, be more concerned with mastery of the forms of language word by word, work out its structure, and then to decide on its meaning. In other words, word recognition was a necessary prerequisite to perceive the listening content from their point of view. Thus, the insufficient word power was the most common answer when they explained the reasons for ineffective listening. In addition, they reported rare use of repair strategies when comprehension failed. They treated the audio as far as possible like a written text, constantly available for perusal. At intervals they would stop cassette the first time they listened and rarely tried to listen to the entire lesson to grasp a global understanding.

In regard to a dialogue delivered by audiocassette and its referent picture, the verification time is more critical than a verbal description and its imaginal description. Since the ESL beginners must rely on rigid grammar rules and follow a painstaking bottom-up, step-by-step deciphering process that goes counter to the immediacy of interpretation strategy, they fail to co-ordinate the pictures as comparison stimuli with words. Imaginal encoding would be favoured when the target audio is a concrete description of a subject, and when the subject is predisposed to use imagery (Paivio, 1986). A main idea of the dialogue might be inferred from the pictures, but the details of the story described on the audiocassette can certainly be difficult to be included in pictures.

Video tape

Video differs from audiocassette in that the former, as a multi-sensory medium, offers students more than listening comprehension; students have the opportunity to read visual as well as auditory messages. Danahy (1985) reminds his readers that 'from the colours, shapes, movements, and camera angles, as well as from voice and music, the L2 learner receives redundant messages and clues to decoding the foreign language (p. 58).

In the version of dual-coding theory adapted and modified from Paivio's theory (Paivio, 1971, 1986; Clark & Paivio, 1991) by Mayer and Sims (1994), a three-process account of how visually and verbally presented simultaneously constructs mental representations within working memory during cognitive process. The subtitles of video was also advocated in Danan's (1992) study that dual processing in the bimodal input condition gave positive results in the post-tests measuring vocabulary, sentence construction, and comprehension.

CALL

The advent of the CD-ROM and laser discs has really enabled students to learn interactively on their own initiative with hypertext links. Their ability to access information and to practice the target language in interactive settings goes far beyond what has been possible in the classroom. The multimedia software support the cognitive processes involved in the specific competency or skill. In the case of listening comprehension, the cognitive process of activating prior knowledge could be supported by the instructional activity of using an advance organiser. The level of support based on multimedia design is assessed for each of the relevant cognitive processes. These processes include:

a. Activating and processing prerequisite knowledge by pre-viewing or sound-off
b. Decoding the verbal representation with animation during viewing
c. Attending to familiar vocabulary and grammar to process a text with the aid of a checklist of comprehension questions
d. Forming a visual representation of what is being said in short term memory

e. Elaborating new information to process the existing knowledge
f. Monitoring the extent of understanding and repairing the inference while listening or in post-tasks

Methods

Subjects
The subjects in the study were originally 84 1st year male students enrolled in two different sections at the Chinese Military Academy in Taiwan. While 37 cadets receive two-year curricula at college level, 47 cadets receive four-year curricula at university level. Due to the availability of computer lab and class hour, 23 cadets from university level was assigned to CALL group, 24 at university level to audio group, and 37 at college level to audio group. However, only 79 students attended the entire study program when the post-test actually took place. 1 from audio group and 4 from CALL group were excluded from the statistical analysis.

Materials
The listening materials is *Family Album*, published in 1991 by Maxwell Macmillan, contain 26 episodes of story about a typical American family living in New York and the events happening around their daily lives. Learners are supposed to learn vocabularies, phrases, and expressions in the English language and its background culture through viewing of these videos. Each episode is a complete story and has its own title and theme. The episode chosen for this study was the first video from *Family Album, U.S.A.*, '*46 Linden Street*'. The reasons for choosing this particular video were because it was relatively easy, interesting and the availability of three different delivery modes: audiocassette, video and CD-ROM.

Electronic discussions were carried out using *Daedalus InterChange* (by Daedalus Inc., 1989) on a computer terminal and students are free to type in messages that can be sent by hitting 'enter'. Messages are instantaneously appear on the top half of their own screen, displayed in chronological order in which they were sent and automatically identified with the name of the sender. All class members can read each other's comments at their own pace by scrolling up and down the sent-messages window, and they can write messages at their own leisure without interfering effects (freezing, etc.) from incoming messages (Ortega, 1997). There were several questions relevant to the topic or language used in each Act. Appendix A shows the questions of Act II posited by the instructor.

Procedures
The study was conducted during a normal class period which lasted for two 50-minute class periods at a time. While the audio group studied the targeted audiocassettes with workbook and pictures of the story in it, video group also watch the video with English captions on individual screen with workbook. Likewise, CALL group worked at personal

computer in lab to listen to and watch multimedia delivered by LAN and for electronic communication.

At the second hour, the two groups were distributed a paper with correct answers on it. They checked the answers and discussed questions they proposed with the teacher. The CALL group, on the other hand, was working on their own to watch the video and check understanding at computer. In order to examine the effect of the integration of on-line discussion into CALL group, a listening and a reading test (Appendix B & C) held on the following week. The listening comprehension questions were recorded beforehand by a native speaker. The reading test contains a reading passage adapted from the *Teacher Resource Book*, 6 lexical items and 4 useful expressions translated from Chinese into English. In addition, a questionnaire (English edition, appendix D) was administered to explore the problems they met while attending each listening task delivered by different media.

Results: Table 1 presents subjects' listening mean scores under each group. A subject was given 10 point for each correct answer, with the highest possible score being 100 and lowest possible score being 0. In one-way ANOVA analysis reported in Table 2, the media which students chose to listen influenced the performance of listening comprehension. As a post hoc test shows in Table 5, CALL group gained better results comparing with the audio group. This confirmed that the cluster of dynamic visual and auditory elements created rich and primary source of understanding in the development of listening domain.

In regard of reading mean scores shown in Table 3, CALL group largely surpassed the other two groups while audio and video groups were almost identical in terms of mean scores. In one-way ANOVA analysis shown in Table 4, CALL group outperformed audio and video groups as a result of integrating CACD into classroom. Moreover, the standard deviation is small indicating that less proficient learners also benefited from CACD as exposed to a substantial amount of comprehensible input which is produced by peers of shared background through request and negotiation of meanings. In contrast, audio and video groups lacked the chance to read, write in a spoken form from which they could expand inherently competence in an authentic and interactive context.

Table 1
Group means and standard deviations of the listening test

Group	*Count*	*Mean*	*SD*	*Min.*	*Max.*
Audio	23	67.5783	14.5169	93.3	46.7
Video	37	75.0081	12.8198	96.7	43.3
CALL	19	83.8895	12.3629	100.0	53.3
Total	79	74.9810	14.3546	100.0	33.3

Table 2
Analysis of variance by groups on listening test

Source	df	SS	MS	F	Sig.
Between Ss	2	2768.297	1384.148	7.907*	.001
Within Ss	76	13304.0	175.052		
Total	78	16.72.3			

P<.05

Table 3
Group means and standard deviations of the reading test

Group	*Count*	*Mean*	*SD*	*Min.*	*Max.*
Audio	23	69.1565	14.9738	96.7	40.0
Video	37	65.9108	18.4801	90.0	33.3
CALL	19	87.3632	5.9612	96.7	70.0
Total	79	72.0152	17.5079	96.7	33.3

Table 4
Analysis of variance by groups on reading test

Source	df	SS	MS	F	Sig.
Between Ss	2	6042.345	3021.173	12.851*	.000
Within Ss	76	17866.9	235.090		
Total	78	23909.2			

P<.05

Table 5 Multiple comparison among three groups on listening

(I)groups (j)groups	MD	SE	Sig.
audio—video	-7.4298	3.513	.114
video—CALL	-8.8814	3.734	.065
CALL—audio	16.3112	4.102	.001*

P<.01

Table 6 Multiple comparison among three groups on reading

(I)groups (j)groups	MD	SE	Sig.
audio—video	-3.2457	4.071	.729
Video—CALL	-21.4523	4.327	.000*
CALL—audio	18.2066	4.753	.001*

P<.01

The qualitative analysis of the data from students' on-line discussion indicated some important features related to language formality, peer observation and negotiation of meaning. The electronic exchange will vary according to the task offered by the teacher. When expressing their own experience, they tended to defence for their own opinion as opposed to reduced interaction when facing the tasks concerning about grammar correction or peer co-operation on achieving a goal. The less proficient students quite often chose to show their agreement or just keep silent. They were likely to use solely the present tense to describe any event in terms of linguistic items. By observing their interaction from CACD, learner output showed a higher proportion of simple sentences over complex one. This analyses of syntactic complexity correlate with the findings of Chung (1994) and Kern (1995). Sometimes the level of interaction was direct, with people expressing their own ideas. Unlike the formal writing assignment, they do not care about the mistakes they made on computer-mediated communication. This seemed to be due in part to the fact that more than one person could be talking at the same time and they focused on meaning rather than on forms. The following is a typical electronic exchange:

S4: I think she left the bag on purpose.
S2: What is on purpose mean?
S4: It mean you do something not by accident.
S1: I know. The girl leave the bag because she want to give the chance to the boy. She must like him. So she want to know the boy deeply.

S4: The girl is smart.
S3: Smart? Why do you say 'smart'? I think she is stupid. She forget her bag because she has bad brain. She go home quickly, so she do not take her bag.

As in the simulation activity shown on the following electronic exchange, students took an active part in the development of the life situation and related it to what surrounded them. The interactive quality of discourse in CACD was similar to the flow of real conversation with the characteristics of 'nearly every computer comment ends with a direct question or a tag question to invite feedback' (Kern, 1995, P. 445). For Chinese culture, perhaps CACD is a substitute for language learners to alleviate their anxiety while practising language due to its concrete advantages of more democratic and equitable participation in terms of potential learner development in discoursal, interactional, and functional competence.

S4 (being a father): Do you have good score on the exam?
S2 (being a son): Yes. Of course. I am a good son. ^^
S3 (being a mother): Do you have good time in school?
S2: No. The schoolmate (in Chinese) told me to do a lot of works. This make me no time to play to have fun.
S1 (being a visitor): Hello, hello. Anyone home? I want to look for your son.

Conclusion

The potential pedagogical effect of the technological tools used in L2 instruction is inherently dependent on the particular theoretical or methodological approach that guides its application. The outcomes of listening and reading tests do not represent necessarily the successful application of media and online discussion. Other variables might result different outcomes, i.e. students' motivation, learning styles, language aptitude, task features...etc. It is not the medium itself that determines the pedagogical outcome, but the specific focus of the theoretical approach on the language learning phenomena. On the other hand, instruction which is well designed and rightfully targeted can be extremely successful even if the nature of the technology itself is not in accordance with the major tenets of the prevalent methodological approach (Salaberry, 1997). Thus, educators should be knowledgeable the educational theory and practice, and the process of instructional design and use of different technologies (Bates, p. 246). By constantly check students' perception of listening task, students can find out the mistakes and track language progress as a diary (is not discussed in this study). Most of the students defined the listening task as a difficult due to lack of lexical items and idiomatic expression. However, they found the task interesting and useful.

Although we could not directly proposed that on-line discussion facilitate the comprehension, it maximise opportunities of using language in a communicative and a Co-operative way. This study only examined the impact of CACD on the reading and listening comprehension, further studies can explore the development of other language skills such as paper writing and oral speaking.

References

Ak-Ansari S and Wigzell R., (1996) The influence of the tape-recorder on attainment in EFL, *System*, Vol. 24, No. 2, pp. 233-243.

Bakhtm., M. M. (1986). *Speech genres and other late essays.* Austin: University of Texts Press

Bates, A. W. (1995). Technology, Open Learning, and Distance Education. London, UK: Routledge. Brown G., Investigating listening comprehension in context, *Applied Linguistics*, Vol. 7, No. 3, pp. 284-302

Benson, P. (1997). Self-access and collaborative learning. *SIG Selections 1997.* Special Interests in ELT, edited by Alan C McLean.

Carrell, P. L., (1982), Three components of background knowledge in reading comprehension, *Language Learning*, Vol. 33, No. 2.

Clark, J.M., & Paivio, A., (1991). Dual coding theory and education. Educational *Psychology Review*, 3, pp. 149-210.

Chapelle, C. A. (1998). Multimedia CALL: Lessons to be learned from research on instructed SLA. *Language Learning & Technology,* Vol. 2, No. 1, July 1998 pp. 22-34.

Chun, D. (1994). Using computer networking to facilitate the acquisition of interactive competence. *System*, 22, pp. 17-31.Danan, M., (1992). Reversed subtitling and dual coding theory: new directions for foreign language instruction, Language Learning 42: 4, pp. 497-527

Doughty, C. & Pica, (1986). Information gap tasks: Do they facilitate second language acquisition? *TESOL Quarterly* 20, 2, pp. 305-325.

Ferra, K., Brunner, H., & Whittemore G. (1991). 'Interactive Written Discourse as an emergent register'. *Written Communication* 8, 1, pp. 9-33.

Herron, C A. & Seay I., (1991). The effect of authentic aural texts on student listening comprehension in the foreign language classroom. *Foreign Language Annals* 24, pp. 487-95.

Gay, G. & Mazur, J. (1993). The utility of computer tracking tools for user centered design. *Educational Technology*, April, pp. 45-59.

Kern., R. (1995). Restructuring classroom interaction with networked computers: Effects on quantity and quality of language production. *Modern Language Journal* 79, 4.

Kroonenberg, N. (1994/95). Developing communicative and thinking skills via electronic mail. *TESOL Journal,* 4(2), 24-27.

Little, D. (1994). *Freedom to lean and compulsion to interact: Promoting learner autonomy through the use of information systems and information technologies.* Paper presented at the Conference on Autonomy in Language Learning. Hong Kong University of Science & Technology, June 1994.

Long, M. (1985). 'Input and second language acquisition theory. Input in Second Language Acquisition', edited by S. Gass and C. Madden. Rowley, Mass.: Newbury House.Lotman, Y. M. (1988). *Text within a text.* Soviet Psychology, 26, pp. 32-51.

Mayer, R. E. & Sims, V. K. (1994). For whom is a picture with a thousand words? Extensions of a dual-coding theory of multimedia learning. *Journal of Educational Psychology*, Vol. 86, No. 3, pp. 389-401.

Mettalinos, N., (1994). Physiological and cognitive factors in the study of visual images. *In Visual Literacy*, eds D. M. Moore and F. M. Dwyer, pp. 53-64. Educational Technology Publications, Englewood Cliffs, NJ.

Murry, D. (1988). Computer-mediated communication: Implications for ESP. *English for Specific Purposes* 7, pp. 3-18.

Nyikos, M. & Hashimoto, R. (1997). Constructivist theory applied to collaborative learning in teacher education: In search of ZPD. *Modern Language Journal*, 81, iv, pp. 506-517.

Ortega, L., (1997). Processes and outcomes in networked classroom interaction: defining the research agenda for L2 computer-assisted classroom discussion, *Language Learning & Technology,* Vol. 1, No. 1, pp. 82-93

Rubin, J., (1990). How learner strategies can inform language teaching. Language Use, *Language Teaching and the Curriculum.* Ed. Verner Bickley. Hong Kong: Institute of Language in Education, Education Department.
Paivio, A., (1986). *Mental representation: A dual-coding approach.* New York, New York: Oxford University Press.
Savage W., *Learner-directed video, Asian Institute of Technology*, Bangkok, Proceeding for the 1993 ECTall symposium on the Occasion of the 10th AILA World Congress in Amsterdam. 135-147
Paivio, A. (1971). *Imagery and Verbal Processes.* New York: Holt, Rinehart, and Winston.
Salaberry, M. R.(1994). A theoretical foundation for the development of pedagogical tasks in computer mediated communication, *CALICO Journal* 14 No.1, pp. 5-34
Price, K. (1987). *The Use of Technology: Varying the Medium in Language teaching. Interactive Language teaching*, edited by W. Rivers. New York, NY: Cambridge University Press.
Singhal M., The internet and foreign language education: Benefits and Challenges, The Internet TESL Journal http://www.aitech.ac.jp/~iteslj/Articles/Singhal-Internet.html
Volosinov, V.N. (1973). *Marxism and the philosophy of language* (L. Matejka & I. R. Titunik, Trans.). New York: Seminar.
Vygotsky, L. S. (1978). Mind in Society. Cambridge, Mass: Harvard University Press.
Wang, Y. M. (1993). E-mail Dialogue Journaling in an ESL Reading and Writing Classroom. Unpublished Ph.D. dissertation, University of Oregon at Eugene.
Warschauer. M., (1996). Comparing face-to-face and electronic communication in the second language classroom. *CALICO Journal*, 13, pp. 7-26.
Warschauer, M., (1997). Computer-mediated collaborative learning theory and practice. *Modern Language Journal,* 81, iv. pp. 470-481.
Wertsch, J., & Bivens., J. A. (1992). The social origins of individual mental functioning: Alternatives and perspectives. *The Quarterly Newsletter of the Laboratory of Cooperative Human Cognition*, 14, pp. 35-44.

Appendix

(A) 1. Did Alexandra leave her bag by accident or on purpose? What do you think?
2. Do you have a girl friend? How did you meet your girl friend?
3. With your group, imagine that you are sitting around a dinner table with other members of your family. Talk about the day's events. While you are talking, the doorbell rings. Who is at the door?
4. If you were Robbie, what would you do next without any clue to Alexandra's apartment?

(B) I. Listening comprehension:
1. Who cooked dinner? A)Bobbie B)Marilyn C)Susan D)Ellen
2. What was the dinner? A)Noodles B)Japanese food C)Pasta D)Hamburger
3. What was forgotten in the dinner? A)appetizer B)soup C)bread D)dessert
4. Alexandra said 'Richard showed me your photo' to A)Philip B)Ellen C)Marilyn D)Susan
5. While they were having ice cream, who answered the door? A)Bobbie B)Marilyn C)Susan D)Richard
6. What happened to Alexandra on her way to the Stewards? A)Traffic jam B)She took the wrong train C)She lost something. D)Someone talked to her
7. What did Alexandra drink? A)iced coffee B)iced tea C)iced water D)iced coke
8. Why didn't Alexandra stay for dinner? A)She has a date. B)She has classes. C) She will go home for dinner. D)She has to work
9. What does Alexandra's father do? A)a pediatrician B)an accountant C)a lawyer D)a vice-president at a toy company
10. What are Alexandra's favorite subjects? A)biology and math B)English and history C)geography and math D)trigonometry and algebra

(C) I. Reading comprehension:

U.S. LIFE

When Richard Steward introduced his family to Alexandra Pappas, he said, 'This is my wife Marilyn…And this is my mother, Ellen Stewart…and my father, 'Dr. Philip Stewart'.

American usually make introductions with first names and last names. They usually don't use *Mr., Mrs., Ms.*, or *Miss* in an introduction because they feel that these titles are very formal. In fact, if someone calls an American *Mr., Mrs., Ms.,* or *Miss*, he or she usually says 'Please call me Dave (or Jane or Sandra)'. Americans usually call you by your first name right away, too. When they use first names, they are being friendly, not impolite.

But if you are not comfortable with calling someone by his or her first name, especially an older person, Alexandra says, 'Thanks, Mrs. Stewart'.

Medical doctors, judges, college officials, military officers, and clergy are usually addressed with an *occupational* title, however. Examples of occupational titles are *Dr.* Stewart, *Judge* Brown, *Dean* Rafer, *Captain* Snyder, and *Father* O'Hara.

Of course you can always be very polite and call a man *Sir* or a woman *Ma'am* if you are not sure of his or her name.

1. How do Americans usually make introductions?
2. How do they feel when someone calls them with titles?
3. What do they use, first name or last name if Americans feel uncomfortable, with your calling by his or her titles?
4. Is it impolite for Americans to use first names?
5. How do you call Paul Sullivan who works as a public officer with authority to decide cases in a law court?

6. According to the passage, what should people call you when you serve in the military right after graduation?
7. Do we usually call older people by their first name in Taiwan?
8. How do you call a man when you don't know his name and you want to show your politeness to him?
9. How do you call a woman when you don't know her name and you want to show your politeness to her?
10. Comparing Stewart family, how are they different from your own family?

II. Vocabulary

1. delicious	2. dessert	3. scoop
4. vanilla	5. take it easy	6. pediatrician

III. Translation:

1. How do you do? It's nice to meet you.
2. Would you like something to eat?
3. Can I drive you home?
4. I am so glad you took the time and trouble to return the bag.

(D)Thinking about listening

1 Today I found the listening...

Easy (go to 2a) about right (go to 3) difficult (go to 2b)

2a I found it easy because...

There weren't many words I didn't know
The speaker(s) was/were talking about something I know about
The speakers spoke very clearly
The CD-ROM helped me understand better the listening.
I could easily predict and guess the content by watching the video
The listening was short
There wasn't much to remember
The listening task/questions was/were easy
Other reasons...

2b I found it difficult because...

There were a lot of words I didn't know
The speaker(s) was/were speaking about something I don't know much about
There were a lot of speakers, I didn't know who was talking
The speaker(s) spoke very fast/unclearly
The listening was too long-I couldn't keep concentrating
I still think listening by CD-ROM is as difficult as an audiocassette
There was too much to remember
I listened word by word, so never got access to the main idea.
The listening asks/questions were difficult
Other reasons...

3 Today I found the CALL listening activity...

Interesting boring useful not useful
Because ....

4 **I could help myself understand better if I..**

5 **My teacher could help me understand better if she ....**

6. Have you ever tried on-line discussion? Do you like it or not? Why?

THE ROLE OF DIDACTIC FUNCTIONS IN CALL DESIGN

Jozef Colpaert and Wilfried Decoo
University of Antwerp, Belgium

1. Introduction: According to recent figures from the Flemish Ministry of Education,[1] DIDASCALIA represents more than 85% of language courseware use in Flanders (25% of Flemish students are using language courseware). This position has never been an explicit goal in our research and development, but it has been reached after thirteen years of specification, development, implementation and evaluation of more than fifty applications, building new working hypotheses at each step. Since the publication of *Verbapuces*, we have continuously been receiving all kinds of suggestions and requests from our users.[2] One of the major challenges was to adopt a middle course between developing what users want to use and developing what they should use according to research findings.

Our focus has always been on learning-from-developing: 'No aspect of CALL can be viewed in isolation, but rather as a part of a total instructional system with many variables. The user and the content are two variables which have attracted our particular attention given the context of our research'.(Decoo & Colpaert 1999, p. 57).

What we have learned, however, is that it is very difficult to extrapolate our findings to other language learning situations and environments. Hence the need for a reflective moment on the role of the computer in the language learning process and on how to conceptualise solutions. In this paper we want to confront our findings with recent literature on the subject and to formulate some useful, and hopefully reusable, concepts.

2. A growing concern. What strikes us most in recent publications is the growing concern for CALL design, defined as a pre-development stage during which the role of the computer, the modes of using the software and the interaction with the learner are to be specified. In 1980 Taylor wrote: 'For the foreseeable future, computing will play an increasingly important role in human learning. However, no one yet knows exactly how great that role will eventually be, or precisely what form it will finally take'. (Taylor 1980, p. 1). Taylor's own framework is based on the Tutor, the Tool and the Tutee as three 'modes' of using computing in education.

While in many publications a lot of emphasis was put on interface design, Decoo in 1984 already insisted on applying didactic principles to courseware evaluation. He stressed the

[1] Inquiry carried out in 1999 with 11,187 students and 1,183 teachers.
[2] This evolution is described in detail in Decoo & Colpaert (1999).

need for 'more language and education specialists able to use these sound didactic principles that will make courseware better embedded in actual curricula, more precise and cost-efficient'. Decoo regretted in some courseware the 'lack of basic conceptualisation as to the actual educational process in a normal classroom setting where the learning of a foreign language follows a well-defined, linear or concentric build-up and where the confident progress of the students is based on the thorough integration of outlined pieces of subject-matter'. (Decoo 1984, p. 45-46).

In the nineties findings in Second Language Acquisition, Human-Computer Interaction, Natural Language Interfacing, Intelligent Tutoring, Courseware Engineering, Learning Psychology, Instructional Design and other domains, nourished a scientific discussion which is still going on today.

Hubbard presented a comprehensive methodological framework for CALL. 'A methodological framework here means a framework for the description and analysis of methods, which are ultimately nothing more than a set of procedures applied in a consistent and reasoned fashion in the pursuit of a given goal, such as learning to speak and understand a foreign language'. (Hubbard 1992, p. 41). The three main components of the framework for courseware development are Design, Approach and Procedure, with special attention for content and learner.

In 1996 we tried to establish a framework of criteria which have an impact on added value, based on our own experience in language courseware development. 'The introduction of new technologies in the language learning process should entail more didactic efficiency, educational effectiveness and pedagogical efficacy'. (Colpaert 96, p. 309). This principle puts in a broader context the concern about design, which 'should be based on both actors or role players involved and factors that may have an influence on research, development and implementation'. (Colpaert 1996, p. 312). Hubbard insists on the role of four players: the learner, the developer, the evaluator and the classroom teacher. His development framework is inserted as a development module next to an implementation and evaluation module (Hubbard 1996).

Chapelle a.o. argue that 'Examining CALL research from the perspective of other classroom researchers brings into focus a number of important research questions that might be investigated in a CALL context as well as the methods CALL researchers might use to investigate them. It is clear that the uncharted territory in CALL research lies in the process-oriented domain, a domain investigated through interaction analysis, discourse analysis, and ethnographic methods. The range of process-oriented research questions in CALL becomes more interesting as our understanding of second language acquisition increases and as technological developments expand the range of potential computer uses in second language classrooms. Through continued CALL research, we may begin to understand how software can be developed and used to best facilitate second language acquisition'. (Chapelle a.o.1996).

Chapelle states later that 'CALL software designers look to research and principles from a variety of cross-disciplinary sources. Despite the potential value of diverse perspectives, SLA theory and research might also be consulted to suggest CALL design and to guide research on effectiveness'.(Chapelle 1998, p. 22). Chapelle formulates seven relevant hypotheses about SLA and exemplifies each hypothesis for multimedia CALL design and evaluation.

Both through a review of literature and through a survey, Levy analyses how CALL practitioners have conceptualised CALL. His tutor-tool framework 'has implications for program design, methodology, teacher and learner expectations, the teacher's role and the relationship of work completed at the computer with work completed away from it'. (Levy 1997, p. 193) Hémard presents a detailed set of guidelines that 'was intended to fulfil two crucial functions: its main role was to provide clear and concise guidance throughout the various stages of the process whilst, similarly, it was also conceived as a potential checklist providing authors with a valuable evaluation tool for existing and newly developed applications'. (Hémard 1997, p. 25).

3. CALL design guidelines and principles. The number of publications on the subject is increasing rapidly. It is rumoured that this evolution might be a symptom of a deeper process where the whole 'raison d'être' of CALL is being questioned: if CALL applications would already have proven their usefulness and effectiveness (cfr. computers, cars or bridges), would we still be discussing its conceptualisation and design to that extent?

The concern seems to be genuine. Approaches are diverse and complement each other in a remarkable way. Some aspects however need more clarification or reorientation:

- 'In the literature on design in CALL so far, the emphasis has tended to be on providing principles or guidelines for the potential developer (...)'. (Levy 1999, p. 83). These guidelines and principles could however also be very useful for all involved actors or players in the language learning process (learners, teachers, parents, publishers, evaluators ...), both from a 'how-to-use' point of view as from a 'how-to-evaluate' point of view.

- What do we mean by design, specification, conceptualisation, rules, procedures, principles, criteria, guidelines, techniques, models, parameters, tactics, processes, strategies, approaches, suggestions, workable concepts, building blocks, frameworks, checklists, ...? How can we build a serious theory on terminology that is often still too vague?

- According to Levy (1999), developers should pay attention to the design space, to levels of conceptualisation and the link between theory and design. In our view, these principles are perhaps 'manageable', but not immediately 'workable'. More work should be done in translating them into tools for decision making that take into account the specific working situation of developers.

- From a software-engineering point of view, interface design is not the key issue. 'Too often appearance alone seems to provide sufficient justification for a design, and the 'look' of a program or learning environment is given too high a priority' (Levy 1999, p. 85). Distributed programming, multi-tier software architecture, remote data access seem to be neglected areas in CALL design research.

- Software engineering is one thing, content engineering another. '*Content* is a problem area not just for a software developer, but for any language learning materials developer'. (Hubbard 1992, p. 54). Situational and linguistic realism are mentioned as factors that are of significant importance to the learner. Problems of content selection, formatting, exploitation and reuse on the other hand also impact heavily on program design, as is shown in projects like MALTED (Paul Bangs, University College London), which focuses on *templates* for courseware production, in the DISSEMINATE project (Philippe Delcloque, University of Abertay Dundee) on enhanced authorability, and in current DIDASCALIA research on generic models for in-depth content structuring.

- Many guidelines focus on 'tasks' to be performed by the learner, and insist on the fact that learning environment and interaction should reflect natural communicative situations. Besides the facts that not enough knowledge seems to be available and that didactic strategies (exercises and scenarios) in CALL remain rather poor, a more realistic description of the role of the computer from a didactic point of view is needed.

- We have to 'know our audience'. 'Key elements derived from the educational setting, and the nature and goals of the learner are often overlooked, or their influence understated'. (Levy 1999, p. 91). We have to establish learner profiles, but when do we know enough? What information is relevant? And even when we have a lot of knowledge about the learner at our disposal, do we have the know-how to implement this information into the system?

4. About goals and scenarios

4.1. Identifying user goals: Most CALL developers don't (have to) use the programs they design. Instead, developers of software tools, text processors, ... are users of the same systems at the same time. Is this the reason why there is a CALL design problem?

In his latest book, Alan Cooper[3] states that a good design starts with the definition of user personas and their goals. He makes a clear distinction between tasks and goals. Goals are the reason why we perform tasks:

> (...) we were asked to design a classroom management system for elementary school teachers. The engineers had provided facilities for testing students, tracking performance, and accessing a database of lesson plans. From a task point of view, things seemed adequate. We looked — metaphorically speaking — deep into the teacher's eyes to determine what the typical primary school teacher really wanted and came up with a surprising answer. We learned that teachers feel isolated in their classrooms, and they crave feedback on how they are doing. In order to improve, a teacher needs a way to measure her own performance. This simple need is not obvious when you decompose the teaching process into its component tasks. That human need is easily visible when you examine goals. In our design, we provided a facility that tracked the teacher's achievements from semester to semester and also from room to room. With this tool, the teachers had a better sense of continuity and progress, and their confidence in their work grew. (Cooper 1999 p. 153-154)

Identifying user goals is a first conceptual step in design. 'The real interaction designer makes her decisions based on what the user is trying to achieve. The ersatz designers make their decisions based on any number of rationales'. (Cooper 1999, p. 23).

4.2. Pre-development stages: 'To deliver both power and pleasure to users, you need to think first conceptually, then in terms of behaviour, and last in terms of interface'. (Cooper 1999 p. 24). We applied this principle to our pre-development work and we have been using the following table ever since:

design stage	**design type**	**applies to**
conceptualisation	interaction	user's goals
specification	behaviour	system functions
creation	interface	component tasks

As far as user goals are concerned, traditional long-term, medium-term and short term goals can be distinguished (Cooper even makes a further distinction between personal goals, corporate goals, practical goals and false goals). Goals also vary according to the identity of the user. Parents may want to have a more detailed view of their child's performance. Teachers may want to spend more time on conversation and culture; they may want to have more homogeneous groups. Students may want to gain self-confidence or simply a lot of time.

System functions are groups of tasks, bundled in a software component according to a meaningful and functional criterion (e.g. didactic functions for monitoring the learning

---

[3] Alan Cooper's book is not academic, but it is a state-of-the-art plea for interaction design by the 'father of Visual Basic'.

process, linguistic functions for form generation and recognition,…). Component tasks are simple procedures that execute a command (e.g. print, count, send, …).

Some CALL conceptualisation efforts focus on the user before development ('know your audience') and after development (testing and evaluating with users). Levy insists on checking with theory while designing and adapting continuously the design space; different levels of conceptualisation are to be linked with theory.

Our experience rather points at the opposite: be sure you know your theory before development and check it after development, but check your user goal scenarios continuously. 'As the design work becomes more detailed, scenarios become more and more effective. We play our personas through these scenarios, like actors reading a script, to test the validity of our design and our assumptions'.(Cooper 1999 p. 179).

5. Design and added value. 'Though many CALL programs and learning environments have now been created, the extent to which we are able to recognise successful design elements is questionable. Equally, the degree to which we can support or defend the use of a particular design element, backed up by empirical evidence, is limited'. (Levy 1999 p. 84-85). We cannot deny this, but we have to stress the fact that it is sometimes difficult for developers to communicate what they have learned.

First of all, there is too much Dancing Bearware.[4] Speech technology and the web create false expectations as far as didactic efficiency is concerned. When developers respect user's goals, applications might loose the 'it's magic!' effect. From a scientific point of view, useful applications are typecast as 'drill and practice' too easily if they do not include some kind of innovative feature. It takes courage to present an interactive textbook with 'traditional' strategies at conferences. Secondly, if you are successful and you have a large group of demanding users, you do not have to wonder about conceptualisation, but about how to make more effective products with less effort. Thirdly, it takes days to switch from programming or content engineering to 'reflective' scientific activities like reading, thinking and writing.

Research carried out within the scope of the PEDAGORA project (Flemish Government, IWT-Medialab) and the DIDASCALIA experience in courseware engineering confirm the need for an elaborate, accurate and operational framework, based on empirical research. Previously developed frameworks, which originated from different perspectives

---

[4] Alan Cooper uses the image of the dancing bear on the town square to describe the effect of some new technologies on people. 'The bear is really a terrible dancer, and the wonder isn't that the bear dances well but that the bear dances at all.' (Cooper 1999, p.26). 'The sad thing about dancing bearware is that most people are quite satisfied with the lumbering beast. Only when they see some real dancing do they begin to suspect that there is a world beyond ursine shuffling. So few software-based products have exhibited any real dancing ability that most people are honestly unaware that things could be better — a lot better.' (ib., p. 59).

and which range from CALL typology to added value analysis, should be taken into account.

The contribution of DIDASCALIA in this respect is situated on the level of a checklist of criteria. Potential CALL systems, applications and services which emerge from available technologies are first checked against needs, goals, expectations and background of all actors (learner, teacher, parent, content provider, ...) in the field. Subsequently they are screened on feasibility, added value and cost-effectiveness.

Feasibility analysis focuses on decisive specification factors such as:

- actor compatibility;
- availability of multidisciplinary know-how;
- interactivity as measurable exchange of Information;
- content authoring and formatting;
- prototyping, engineering and implementation.

Added value is defined as an overall quality resulting from four components:

- role, involvement and impact of actors;
- quantity, quality, flexibility and reusability of content;
- authenticity and practicality of tasks, skills, strategies, exercises, ...;
- didactic functions.

6. Didactic Functions in Interaction Design: We have conceived didactic functions from the specific working situation of the developer, who makes important decisions at each step of the design, development and implementation phases. They allow to take into account user goals as much as possible.

CALL systems, applications and services can always be designed as incorporating one or more of the following didactic functions (in order of increasing system initiative and decreasing learner initiative):

Tool:
Under 'tool' we can classify tasks that are merely instrumental to the learner. Examples of such instrumental tasks are: printing content or session reports, sending and receiving updates or corrections, displaying authentic reading material, playing music or video... The system simply executes the user's command. These features, although very useful, should not be overexposed.

Monitor:
The 'monitor' function on the contrary gives advice on demand. Like with the F7-key in Word, we can ask for spelling and grammar checking, we can ask for translation, for pronunciation.
The reaction of the system is content-related and relevant to the situation of the user. It is supposed to help the user from a linguistic-didactic point of view.

Mentor:
This function takes care of the follow-up of the learning process. This follow-up is built in, without the user asking for it. The system does not take any other initiative than to follow the learning process and to make a report (for parents or teacher). It includes tasks like answer analysis, feedback, evaluation and reporting.

Tutor:
The tutor, in a more narrow meaning than the one given by Taylor and Levy (evaluator), is organising the learning process in one way or another. The system takes over the initiative in the learning process. This is rather clear in cases of (intelligent) tutoring, (adaptive) language testing and remediation. The Tutor function can also play an important role in content selection and presentation, in offering relevant strategies, in designing learning scenarios or in determining paths for navigation relevant to the user.

Lector:
The Lector function is the classical one-way instructor, which can be a recorded lesson, a course on hyperlinked web pages, etc. The learner does not take any other initiative than to follow the course.

These functions do not exist separately as applications, but they should be considered properties that each contribute in a unique but concerted way to the eventual overall added value. They can easily be translated into software classes and objects for components in a three-tier architecture. The traditional three-tier architecture consists of a user interface layer, business rules and data layer. For CALL, DIDASCALIA is currently elaborating a structure, which consists of the user interface, the didactic-linguistic engine and the data engine. The goal is not only to increase productivity, but also to enhance didactic efficiency for both teacher and learner. This model is totally independent of any didactic approach, theory on SLA or specific software development tool. The way didactic functions are being implemented mainly depends on the user goals.

Didactic functions are not only useful in design and development, but also for implementation and evaluation. Users and evaluators find in didactic functions another way of typologising CALL applications and systems.

7. Implementation. The DidaLink prototype, developed by DIDASCALIA, shows the possibilities of an environment for remote language learning that can integrate an (intelligent) tutor, an online teacher, dictionaries, grammars, textbooks, video, web pages and applications in a scalable manner. The environment is built on a learner-centred approach. The teacher is 'polymorphous' (live online, playback video, broadcast or built-in tutor).

DidaLink shows that through an elaborate conceptualisation, development time can be reduced and didactic efficiency increased considerably. Conceptualisation of content authoring, exploitation and reuse, together with more authentic tasks based on natural language interfacing will be the next challenges.

Conclusion and recommendations: Didactic functions appear to be very useful for developers as they allow to take into account user goals, new software architectures and didactic requirements. The two main problems in CALL however remain the same: the in-depth structuring of contents for more efficient selection, formatting, exploitation and reuse of content (Decoo & Colpaert 1999) on the one hand and the specification of adequate didactic strategies and scenarios on the other.

Design and conceptualisation theory is necessary, but it should start from a more accurate profile of both developer and user in order to deliver more workable concepts. The danger with frameworks is that developers might think to obtain automatic results when applying them. Even when applying frameworks and models, which should be regarded as 'working hypotheses', important decisions still have to be made at each step.

The danger with citing, quoting and referring in publications is that something might be considered true because a particular author says so. Our suggestion is that authors should try to apply concepts, models and guidelines to concrete projects in practice, and to describe this process. In this way, the main concern of Michael Levy might come true: theory must have a more important role in CALL design, but in our view it has to be tested thoroughly before publishing it.

It is also impossible to integrate the latest findings of all related sciences involved. 'What we have learned is that in order to obtain more and better results, we should aim at overall satisfaction, meeting a large number of criteria, rather than excellence on one point' (Colpaert 1996, p. 311).

Feedback from developers to theory must be communicated: a first step could be that applications developed by researchers should be regarded as scientific publications. Learning from real-world CALL development and implementation should be recognised as scholarly research. Dancing Bears have to be exposed and reduced to their real value.

References:

COLPAERT, J., 'Learning from the past, building new working hypotheses: the DIDASCALIA criteria framework for more added value in CALL', *Computer Assisted Language Learning*, 1996, Vol. 9, N° 4, pp. 309-318.

CHAPELLE, C., JOAN JAMIESON, YUHSOON PARK, 'Second Language Classroom Research Traditions: How does CALL Fit?', *The Power of CALL* (ed. Martha C. Pennington), Athelstan, 1996, pp. 33-53.

CHAPELLE, C., 'Multimedia CALL: lessons to be learned from research on instructed SLA', *Language Learning & Technology*, Vol. 2, N° 1, July 1998, pp. 22-34.

COOPER, A., *The Inmates are Running the Asylum. Why High-Tech Products Drive us Crazy and How to Restore the Sanity*, SAMS, 1999.

DECOO, W., 'An application of didactic criteria to courseware evaluation', *Calico Journal*, II, 2 (December 1984), pp. 42-46.

DECOO, W., JOZEF COLPAERT, 'User-driven Development and Content-driven Research', *CALL: Media, Design and Applications* (ed. K. Cameron), Swets & Zeitlinger, 1999, pp. 35-58.

HEMARD, D. 'Design Principles and Guidelines for Authoring Hypermedia Language Learning Applications', *System 25* (1):9-27, 1997.

HUBBARD, Ph., 'A methodological framework for CALL courseware development', Computers in applied linguistics: An international perspective (ed. M. Pennington & V. Stevens), 1992, pp. 39-65.

HUBBARD, Ph., 'Elements of CALL Methodology: Development, Evaluation and Implementation', *The Power of CALL* (ed. Martha C. Pennington), Athelstan, 1996, pp. 15-32.

LEVY, M., *Computer-Assisted Language Learning: Context and Conceptualisation*, OUP, 1997.

LEVY, M., 'Design Processes in CALL: Integrating Theory, Research and Evaluation', *CALL: Media, Design and Applications* (ed. K. Cameron), Swets & Zeitlinger, 1999, pp. 83-107.

TAYLOR, R. P. (ed.), *The Computer in the School: Tutor, Tool, Tutee*, Teacher's College Press, 1980, pp. 1-11.

INTEGRATING INTERNET-BASED CALL MATERIALS INTO MAINSTREAM LANGUAGE TEACHING

P. M. Crompton
Manchester Metropolitan University, UK

Many if not most Language Departments are feeling the strains of current dichotomies imposed on the University system as this millennium draws to a close. On the one hand there is the ever-present institutional striving for good for research ratings, which pushes academic staff in the direction of publishable research outputs, to be counted for the Research Assessment Exercise. On the other, there is the recurrent incidence of the Quality Assurance Exercise, which evaluates and grades the teaching process, including the quality of the materials deployed in that process. Yet in the design of those materials, a labour-intensive process, there is little scope for work that may be included within the RAE.

Increasingly language departments find themselves obliged, even forced, however reluctantly, to resolve this dichotomy by means of a variety of solutions. The first and most drastic, is to do away altogether with language teaching below a certain level of attainment. Thus at least in one University two of its language departments have no language teaching below 'A' level, preferring to hand this labour-intensive task to outside agencies, such as the Goethe Institut or the Instituto Cervantes, in the case of German and Spanish. Other Universities have established Language Centres for internal and often external language work, and especially for the non-advanced work required by other sectors of their institution. Typically these Language Centres may be wholly responsible for the Institution-Wide Language Provision (IWLP), service work to other Departments, or even lower levels of language work within their own languages departments.

For those universities that have adopted neither approach, a third possibility seems to be emerging; that of the increasing use of distance learning or self-access materials in language teaching. Much time and effort seems to have been devoted to this area in recent times, to judge by the amount of funding made available.[1] Indeed, some of the most exciting areas of development in Modern Languages seem to be the application of the new technologies to language teaching. It is perhaps a step in the right direction to halt the drift away from language teaching, which under the new pressures is in many institutions often assigned to part-time or temporary staff, since with rare exceptions it cannot be considered part of the RAE submission.

---

[1] See for example the various strands of funding under the FDTL (Funds for the Development of Teaching Languages): WELL, CIEL, Tandem, etc.

It is this area of language development that will be addressed in this paper. It is not the intention to argue whether language teaching is or should be developing in this direction: the paper takes for granted the fact that existing pressures are sufficient to push inexorably this way, not the least being the overall growth in the undergraduate populations in recent years which for the most part has not been accompanied by a corresponding growth in academic staff. New forms of language teaching have had to emerge in a labour-intensive discipline, and what will be explored in this paper are the techniques by which the new developments and the new technologies can and should be incorporated into a language teaching strategy.

The new materials, as we have called them, are with some exceptions new means of delivering existing materials. The new medium is in essence the computer. True, language laboratories have been around a long time; radio and latterly television transmissions (via satellite) have been available; and foreign language newspapers, magazines, periodicals are available as never before. In addition, many if not most universities will have their quotas of Erasmus or Socrates students, even students of the target language countries studying full-time courses in the UK. The opportunities for language practice have multiplied enormously, offering facilities unheard of a generation ago.

Yet it is the computer that offers perhaps the greatest possibilities for change in the new media, and this for a variety of reasons. First of all, it can support a range of resources that other modes cannot hope to emulate. For modern language teaching, there is the use of CALL materials, invariably by computer. Usually in the form of a CD-ROM, there is already a great deal available commercially and from developmental organisations such as the TELL Consortium.[2] CD-ROM has many advantages over other forms of educational technology, not the least because it can combine interactive text, sound and vision, to broadcast quality. This form of CALL has some disadvantages, which we shall discuss later; it is however usually the first form of the new technologies that most language teachers encounter.

The advent of the Internet and its ready availability in Universities has meant that undergraduates have at their disposable if not an infinite resource, then one that is immeasurably large, and growing by some 100 gigabytes of information per day. It is virtually inexhaustible. At the time of writing, there are over three hundred *thousand* language journals of every description — newspapers, magazines, periodicals — available *in Spanish* on the Internet.[3] The total number of printed sources available electronically in foreign languages must run to many millions; even the most comprehensive search engines can only give a fraction of the sources available. To have

---

[2] TELL: Technology Enhanced Language Learning, run by a consortium of British Universities with its lead organisation at the University of Hull.

[3] There are for example over five hundred daily newspapers published on-line in Spanish alone, from Spanish speaking and other countries (e.g. the USA).

at one's fingertips the national newspapers of every country in the world as they are published is a priceless resource.[4]

In addition to the printed word, there are now increasing numbers of web sites that include diagrams, visual materials, photo archives, 'virtual' museums, city guides, and so on, all of which can be immensely useful as additional realia in teaching. And as if this were not sufficient, many countries now transmit their national and independent radio stations over the internet, so that as the student completes a task, he or she can enjoy that most elusive of all factors, *immersion.* I cannot prove this, but I am convinced that daily exposure to a foreign language as it is meant to be heard contributes in no small measure to the absorption of that language.

Some universities, including my own, have now begun to put some of their teaching materials on the internet, as a means of ease of student access, and as a net saving in terms of distribution and duplicating costs. Although technically accessible to external users,[5] the materials are often designed for internal consumption, complementing or even replacing areas of the taught courses.[6] The results can mean considerable savings in administrative time and even tutor time, by systematically 'culling' from class contact time those elements of the coursework that do not require the presence of a tutor, or which can be best completed in the students' own time. We shall return to this point in a moment.

This is just one aspect of foreign language resources which has changed out of all recognition over the last decade, even over the last five years. Useful as it is, this resource is less than useful if it is not incorporated into the learning process; if the student at whatever level does not consistently make use of, and benefit from, this resource. The best equipped Language Centre in the world is useless if no-one actually uses it. This is a factor we have learned to our cost in Manchester, and what follows is an analysis of the problems that have arisen in internet teaching, and the remedies that have been attempted.

The primary reason for using the Internet was not one of innovative technology, but the simpler motives of economy and environmental concern. A complete grammar course

---

4 Compare the situation some fourteen years ago, when even a limited archive of article *titles* was considered useful. (See: P. Gummery and P. M. Crompton: 'A newspaper archive retrieval system for students of Spanish', in K. Cameron, (ed.) *Computers and Foreign Languages,* Harvester Press, 1986.)

5 The Spanish materials developed at Manchester Metropolitan University have been undergoing trials with Coventry University since November 1998, and are due for full-scale trials from September 1999.

6 There are a number of indications that increasing amounts of materials packages will be franchised to other institutions via the Internet, and these developments may well herald the advent of the 'virtual university'.

had been developed over a number of years in Spanish, to cater for students from ab initio to Post 'A' level standard. A similar course is also being prepared in French, in the first instance for Post 'A' level students. This course was in hard copy, and came complete with grammar explanations, grammar exercises and a self-check section, so that students could complete the exercises in their own time. The course is divided into a number of levels from one to six, each level corresponding to approximately two hours of self-access work per week for one academic year. Originally designed for the Institution-Wide Language Provision (IWLP) of two taught hours per week, we found that the materials could be used on the major language degrees, but accelerating progress to four levels per year. This meant that we had a standard grammar course to form the core of our language teaching. Students were required to complete the grammar work, and to hand in a Student Progress Log, charting their scores on each exercise and logging the audio and other work they had completed. Perhaps the single most useful innovative step we have taken has been the Progress Log.

Given then that we had a tried and tested method, and materials with which to work, it seemed a logical step to move to an electronic form of these materials. This, as I have already stated, was not a move to indulge in technology for its own sake, but simply to save the one and a half *tons* of paper required to ensure that all students had hard copies of the grammar exercises. It was environmentally motivated, on the one hand; on the other, it was initiated simply to save the sheer logistics of distribution.

The Internet was chosen for a number of reasons, rather than say CD-ROM. First, with the Internet there are no distribution costs, and certainly for a University student within the institution, there is no cost to gain access. Even externally, a student may have access for relatively low cost. Second, the system via the Internet is capable of registering and storing student scores; each log-in is recorded by the system and performance recorded. And amongst a host of other reasons, the Internet version can be changed and updated instantaneously. The various advantages have been discussed by this author elsewhere.[7]

The disadvantages of CD-ROM, even though this medium offers superior technological facilities, are by and large precisely because it is a fixed and finite corpus of material; it is published, and to be changed has to be re-issued. Furthermore, it does not offer feedback of results and performances to a central database for tutor access. And of fundamental importance to the success of self-access materials is direct or indirect interaction with a tutor, at whatever remove in time or space. A CD-ROM is a self-contained exercise; it is done alone (or in pairs) by the student, who does not have access to interactive feedback offered by the Internet. Unless this type of work is the subject of close integrated monitoring, there is a 'take-it-or leave-it' approach to its use.

---

[7] See P. M. Crompton: 'Interactive Spanish on the Internet: integrating technology and tradition', in *International Journal of Iberian Studies,* Summer 1999. (Forthcoming).

What is sometimes conveniently ignored in University teaching is the fact that undergraduates face a similar intensity of pressure to that borne by tutors. Workloads are such that completed assignments tend to be those that are absolutely essential if course marks are to be obtained. It is perhaps the case that the extremely able student will make time to explore what is merely desirable rather than essential to know: rarely will even the best have time to visit the simply optional. To put it another way, the majority of even well motivated students have little time for other than the work which contributes directly to their course outcomes. In this respect, self-access work, which includes the use of the Internet, has to become essential, part of the core tasks, unless it is to remain forever a Cinderella of the syllabus, desirable but largely ignored.

For us, and I suspect for many tutors, the problem of non-use of facilities is one which has bedevilled teaching of foreign languages for some considerable time. No matter what the resources available, undergraduates for the most part tend only to do the work they can be seen to be doing, and which carries some direct benefit to their course profiles. In moving the materials onto the Internet, a key part was to incorporate a monitoring system which showed how often the student logged in, what exercises were attempted, and how long the log-in lasted. It was thought that in this way student progress would be logged automatically, and the mere fact of being thus logged would bring the perception of these materials into the 'essential' rather than 'desirable' category, at least as far as students were concerned. This turned out to be true, but in a way in which was least expected. The first and most lasting lesson of this exercise has been that the teaching and learning process is an extremely complex *anthropological* activity, and the simple monitoring of results does not constitute a satisfactory means of checking on progress.

The first aspect we discovered was that although in general students liked the move to the Internet from the printed materials, with little exception they preferred and in fact insisted on handing in their hard-copy Progress Logs, with their scores meticulously recorded. It was not sufficient to know that their access to the grammar exercises had been logged and their scores recorded: they needed some sort of transaction in the process, a ritual of handing something in. The handing in could have been electronic; the point was the transaction, and via that transaction, the contact with a tutor.

Second, the student needs to have a visibly record of his or her progress. There were constant enquiries from students to be reminded of their previous scores. It was in fact these requests, which prompted the move back to Progress Log hard copy. Much of this transaction was via e-mail, since we had incorporated a direct e-mail link to the tutor into the materials. This facility was immensely successful: students seem to be much more forthcoming about problems, glitches, queries, simple requests for help, when the medium is both personal, that is one-to-one (no-one else can see the nature of the request), and yet at one remove from a direct face-to-face encounter.

Third, as well as incorporating their scores in the Progress Log, students seem anxious to record all other activities: once the idea has taken hold that someone will actually see what they have done, they tend to do more. But most fascinating are the comments they include. Given the facility to *evaluate* the materials they have been given, the vast majority offer some of the most constructive comments we have received. It is as if participation — not only by doing the exercises — but by suggesting ways they can be improved or changed is an important part of the Internet process. The fact of the exercises being two-way has greatly contributed to the success.

The fourth great learning curve was one, which came from monitoring activity via the master file which records log-on times and scores. By comparing the times on the net and the exercises completed, it appears that there is an inverse ratio between the length of the exercise to be completed and the amount of time the student spends doing the exercises. That is to say, the longer the exercise, the shorter the time the student is logged on, and vice-versa: the shorter the exercises the more time the student devotes to them. It is this factor alone which has been most instructive in generating the Mark II version of the material we have begun.

When the log-on times were examined more closely, what appeared to be happening was that students log-on for a certain period of time, disappear for up to half an hour, sometimes more, sometimes less, then log on again to repeat the cycle. What apparently they do is go off 'surfing' the Internet to look at other sites and then return to the exercises. In other words, as well as short exercises, there has to be a variety of activities within the units to keep the attention. The Internet is not electronic text; it is a much more exciting place, and any materials placed on it have to reflect that excitement, above all in the range and variety of activities offered. Just as no-one would think of producing a videotape consisting entirely of a scrolled text, so the Internet has to match the professionalism and variety of other web sites. It has to be *interesting.* Seasoned practitioners in the techniques of CALL production will know this already; and that is, for the first time possibly in the production of teaching materials (outside the commercial world) the design, layout, shape, colour of the materials is at least as important as the content, as is the number of hyperlinks to related or varied materials.[8]

The question of professionalism in the design of materials is directly relevant to the degree in which the materials have to 'stand alone', that is, the extent to which they are to be incorporated into the weekly teaching of language. It can be correctly surmised from the previous discussion that a second version — Mark II — of these materials is nearing completion, which incorporate many of the lessons learned in the trial runs of Mark I.

The original materials — Mark I — are still running, but require a fairly high degree of integration in class progression. To ensure constant student practice, all beginners groups

[8] Numerous sources have reported that IBM has engaged Walt Disney Productions to design their major web sites.

work from the same texts, to which the grammar exercises are closely linked. Classroom teaching reinforces the materials, which are specifically designed in units to be completed each week, with each unit containing its own self-contained grammar explanation. In this way the learning 'bands' of *essential*, *desirable* and *optional* are reversed, in that these apply to the tutor, not the student. The core grammar is essential and must be done; successful assimilation allows the tutor to include additional desirable elements in the class.

As my colleague Chris Dawson has indicated in his paper, much of the communicative elements of language teaching are reserved for the most valued element still in language acquisition: the tutor. More formal structured elements are assigned increasingly to self-access work, but reinforced in class.[9] To a great extent therefore, the success of this type of internet material is first, to make it an essential part of course work; second, to ensure that it is emphatically integrated into the mainstream of the course. In this way the Internet becomes another way of delivering part of the course. For work, which is inordinately time-consuming, as much language work can be, it is a boon. Unlimited numbers of students can have work automatically checked and corrected without the intervention of a tutor, and yet if the system is sympathetically constructed, can have the support that traditional teaching gives. The economies of scale are enormous: the economies of effort even more so, since the 'mechanical' elements are mechanised, and only the 'interesting' queries dealt with on a one-to-one basis.

The mark II version we have developed from the experience of running our mark I grammar course is a more sophisticated beast, and has been designed to be as self-contained as possible. It still has an e-mail link for immediate contact with a support tutor, but contact is now much more pro-active on the part of the student: he/she chooses when test information is to be sent to a central file, and when the electronic students Progress Log is to be submitted. The main features incorporated in this new model are:

- *Shorter exercises*

Exercises are now no more than seven questions, with a simplified screen layout. The rule of thumb seems to be to treat the screen as an OHP slide with a minimum amount of 'clutter'.

- *A variety of hyperlinks with each exercise*

Each exercise has its own vocabulary page, as well as the click-on grammar page constantly present and which covers the whole unit of ten exercises. In addition there are two *desirable* exercises based around the grammar learned, and two *optional* links to relevant or interesting sites to stimulate curiosity.

---

[9] C. Dawson: 'The communicative versus the grammatical approach to language teaching'. July 1999. (Forthcoming).

- *Inclusion of realia from first exercise*

To build confidence, the student is encouraged via the hyperlinks to do exercises on 'real' links, for example through a built-in hyperlink to that day's Spanish (or Bolivian, Argentinian, etc) newspaper, and perhaps in the very early stages, say pick out a word or two from a headline which they recognise. Other 'real' links include Spanish (or Latin American) radio stations.

- *The whole module can be downloaded*

This feature is especially useful for external or home use, when the student is actually paying for on-line time. The Internet link is activated only when external hyperlinks are required, or when submitting the test or Progress Log.

- *Discrete test*

The scores are not recorded for each exercise, but rather a test is set at the end of the unit (each unit has ten exercises) which the student completes and chooses when to submit. The student also submits his/her Progress Log in which the scores of each exercise are manually entered by the student, as well as details of each of the additional desirable/optional bits of work completed. Progress can only be made to the next unit when an optimal score has been achieved.

- *External accreditation*

This is being negotiated with an external body, and will give the student the additional motivation of additional certificates etc. to stimulate his/her interest.

It can be seen that the design and degree of independence of the mark II version of these materials is quite a different type of Internet activity. It is designed to be free-standing, and also available to external users. It can be run alongside the mark I version, although our intention is to extend the mark II so that it will cover the range of materials in mark I. Monitoring of student progress can still take place, above all with the Progress Log, now much more sophisticated and in electronic form — but still with the option if the student so wishes of submitting an additional hard-copy version. This mark II version is undergoing extensive trials during the summer of 1999 and it is hoped to run fully accredited modules by the autumn term.

To conclude: integrating internet materials into the mainstream of language teaching has been achieved by ensuring a close monitoring of student progress and development, and by building into the system a means of electronic contact between tutor and tutee. Although in the case described in this article the integration has been based on our own materials, the monitoring procedures that have been developed are applicable to a wide range of activities, exercises and resources available on the internet. Knowing that any work completed will be monitored and *appreciated*, students can be highly motivated to achieve an astonishing degree of independence in their acquisition of knowledge. For once more, with the use of the Internet, we can incorporate in the learning process two vital elements that are sometimes forgotten: curiosity, and wonder.

BUILDING ON-LINE COMMUNITIES FOR LANGUAGE LEARNERS

Paul Daniels
Tokai University, Japan

David Brooks
Kitasato University, Japan

I. Rationale and Vision for building on-line communities: A community is a group who shares a common territory. The members possess bonds of purpose and practice and they are usually interdependent. They pass on knowledge of acceptable behaviour and jointly look after the good of the whole group. It is not every classroom of learners that can reach the stage of becoming a community of learners (Williams and Burden, 1997 pp. 192-202).

It is the purpose of this paper to offer a rationale for and to inspire a vision of how computer assisted language learning through communication media over the Internet can provide both the tools and the virtual environment for building learning communities. Furthermore, this paper serves to suggest important activities that enhance an on-line learning community's functioning and which can directly benefit its members — both language learners and language teachers.

Why introduce students to computer-mediated communication?

1) Building a communicative environment: Connecting students with their teacher, classmates or similar learners around the block or across the globe is a way to increase opportunities for communication, to broaden the variety of language usage, and to enhance the quality of involvement in using the target language (Warschauer, 1997). Furthermore, more students can be participating simultaneously in meaningful communication so that the amount of practice and positive feedback multiplies. Because electronic communication can be saved for later review, there are greater chances for students to engage in self-evaluation and self-correction, while the possibility for teacher monitoring and feedback is also increased (Kern, 1995). As direct person-to-person communication is not always feasible, the use of web tools to place language learners in meaningful, personalised contexts for communicative tasks serves to heighten the sense of purpose (Ortega, 1997). Students have more of a reason to engage in practice and review since they are motivated to improve language skills in order to increase the effectiveness of their communication with real people.

While on-line communities and discussions are certainty not a replacement for face-to-face interaction, there are definitely some advantages with on-line interaction. The most widely documented advantage is that students remain anonymous, therefore, reducing their fear of mistakes. Another advantage is that an on-line discussion gives students an equal chance to respond. In a typical classroom discussion, the answers will usually come from the same few students who dominate the discussion (Sproull and Kiesler, 1991). If a questions is sent out to each student who must respond to the question before viewing his or her classmates answer, all students given a more equal chance to respond. The responses are more likely to be unique since students can not give the simple answer of 'me too'.

2) Creating a sense of community: Schools should be perceived as learning communities and the classroom is the central unit of this community. (Sergiovani, 1992) Not only do students register for a class, but they also become part of a more complete learning experience when they are asked to participate in on-line communication. When students know that they can reach their teacher and classmates outside of the scheduled class times, they begin to feel they are part of a larger entity. In many traditional classrooms, the isolation of the students from one another is a barrier to improving language skills because they often fail to make good use of their classmates as communication partners.

Adding computer-mediated communication activities can give students a sense of belonging because they begin to know and communicate with classmates both inside and outside of class. They start to learn the names, interests and opinions of people outside of the small circle of 'classroom' friends they usually associate with. They realise that the members of the community care about them (Noddings, 1986). Each learner's identification with the larger group helps to build the sense of a learning community, where each member is valued for his or her differences and respected for his/her contributions. As members add their own work and energy to building a more extensive on-line environment, a sense of pride in collective achievement works to reward continued efforts.

3) Addressing students' learning styles and accessing their multiple intelligences: There has been a growing body of research evidence based on the learning styles models from the work of Keefe, Gregoric, Dunn & Dunn and McCarthy that suggests every unit of study that a second language student encounters should provide some dissonance and consonance for each individual's learning style (Reid, 1998).

The pioneer work on the psychological, social and cultural aspects of the intellect by Howard Gardner has illuminated the responsibility that classroom teachers and educational institutions have for adequately supporting the multiple intellectual development of students (Armstrong, 1994). Gardner (1993) espoused the notion that all individuals possess at last seven types of intelligence and that it is the interaction among these culturally-defined intellectual competencies that figure prominently in the person's contribution to a society. CALL, CAI, and computer-mediated communication offer promise for extending the range and modalities of learning (Dryden, 1998).

4) Enhancing teacher growth and fostering educational change: When teachers share with other educators their ideas, frustrations, plans and resources, the walls of isolation that have long barricaded lone teachers into single classrooms start to break down. The Internet and its collaborative nature have encouraged a renaissance in teacher development opportunities by offering a vehicle for professional interaction (Serim and Koch, 1996). Similarly, over the last decade years, there has been a broadening of the active research endeavours that embrace the collaborative involvement of the teachers themselves (Nunan, 1986). Consequently, the advent of classroom action research has put many teachers into a in-depth relationship with CALL in their own classroom, as informant, participant-observer, practitioner, and researcher (Richards and Lockhart, 1994).

5) Assisting and implementing course management: Putting parts of a regular course and its classroom procedures on-line can be useful in increasing teacher effectiveness in managing paperwork, clerical tasks, and organising information for students. Keeping up with the syllabus, passing out handouts, explaining assignments and reminding of homework, administering forms and surveys, assessing students' needs, marking calendars, keeping absent students informed are just a sample of the kinds of daily classroom teacher tasks that can be improved by using computer-mediated communication tools.

Similarly, instructional management can be facilitated through use of computers in the classroom environment. By employing positive independence, individual accountability, face-to-face positive interaction, social skill development and group processing, co-operative work can be made an active and central focus of classroom instruction (Johnson and Johnson, 1989). Co-operative learning activities can be integrated into CALL and computer-mediated communication instruction.

6) Aiding in the presentation, distribution, collection of course content and evaluation: Similarly, computers can be helpful in getting important information to students about what is being taught and what is expected for the students to master. Summaries of daily activities, lists of important skills, expressions, or vocabulary can be created by the teacher and distributed on-line. The students themselves can also be made responsible for consolidating notes from several classmates to share via the on-line course. Content-based courses can include such information as lecture notes, additional readings, places for submission of opinions or reactions, and a message board for on-going discussion of important points or issues from the course content.

Moreover, use of CALL and computer-mediated communication can be helpful in collecting data for teacher and student self-evaluation. Portfolio assessment is an systematic alternative to traditional forms of evaluation that continually changes as learner grow and develop their skills and conceptualisations. Portfolios are collections of a student's work for demonstrating progress (Sulzby, 1990) are easily facilitated using computers and interactive multimedia. (De Fina, 1992).

School sites can easily be tailored to their own students' needs and help direct them to relevant and useful information. A simple example would be a site containing links that help direct students to sites with information related to the teacher's course content. Links made to outside resources along with a simple explanation of the site that can help increase student productivity as he or she navigates the World Wide Web for the first time. A more elaborate on-line community may provide in-house resources, such as, teacher prepared lectures with accompanying images, sound files or even video clips demonstrating difficult concepts. Interactive database that allow students to check on their progress in class or a vault containing a collection of past and present student projects and discussion sessions are a few other examples that can be part of an on-line community. An interesting concept could include a collection of on-line lectures created by several teachers or even by the students themselves. Students would be able to select an activity of interest to them and complete an accompanying assignment.

7) Increasing learning autonomy: All classroom teachers, who have groups of students whom we guide toward language acquisition, search for effective ways for helping these learners become greater shareholders in their own learning (Williams and Burden, 1997 pp. 127-133). Because on-line communication tools and information media can be self-accessed both within and beyond the classroom, there are increased chances for students to take initiative to empower themselves as language learners. Through learner training of strategy in contexts (Tudor, 1996), the students can be guided through the experience of using on-line learning resources to realise themselves that they are masters of their own language acquisition. Instead of waiting for the teacher to instruct them, they can begin to experience the positive rewards of taking steps on their own to increase their opportunities to communicate and to improve their language competence beyond the walls and apart from the scheduled time of the language class.

On-line learning communities brought about by computer-mediated communication can enhance the individual's capacity to meet goals for motivated learners and may be helpful in encouraging unmotivated language learners through variety and teacher monitoring of effective feedback (Wilhelm, 1998). They are particularly effective if integrated into a full range of learning activities, such as group projects, small tutorials, individual modules, multimedia creation, games, role-plays, pair activities, video, listening activities, oral presentations, simulations, language learning software, e-mail communication, and voice mail exchanges.

8) Reflecting transition to a digital society in the information age: Inevitably, today's students will live and work, in the not too distance future, in a technology-enhanced, information-driven society, where computers and digital media will be of primary importance for work, play and learning. Giving students the skills to navigate the seas of information and multiplexed channels of communication in this kind of technocratic environment is a clear responsibility for educational institutions today. We owe it to our students, no matter what discipline we teach, to provide them with the knowledge and experience in using computer-mediated communication technology. On-line communication using the computer terminal will become the most popular means of communication and information exchange by the time today's learners enter the working world.

9) Transforming the local into a global community of learners: Finally, computer-mediated communication can shift the bounds of communication territory beyond the doors, hallways and buildings of a single institution and into the far reaches of the world. New and valuable perspectives on real people, whose native language is the one trying to be learned, can be more easily gained by not only observing them via the broadcast media, but by actually engaging in dialogue with them on a person-to-person level through computer telecommunications (Kramsch and Andersen, 1999). These perspectives, whether or not they are derived from computer-mediated communication, offer authentic journeys into the sometimes tricky current of cross-cultural communication, validating our students' perceptions of their own culture and offering a basis for comparing customs, beliefs, values, styles of social interaction, and patterns of communicative behaviour (Kramsch, 1993).

II. Using On-line communities with student project work: An on-line community's success relies heavily on the type of activities that students are expected to complete. A variety of activities are possible to implement on-line including reading passages, interactive writing seminars, grammar exercises, and even listening comprehension activities with integrated sound and video clips. One type of activity that integrates well with on-line communities is project-based activity work. Project work involves students working both in and out of the classroom, working both alone and in a group, and ideally working with learners from outside the classroom, whether it be in the learner's community or with students from a distant classroom. Working in an on-line community accommodates these student needs nicely. Motivation can increase as students work together on a project and realise they are becoming part of a larger learning community. Project based learning allows students to develop and apply their background knowledge, acquire higher order thinking skills, and connect learning with real-life situations (Vilmi, 1995). Through the use of on-line communities and project-based work, learners use language as a tool to learn (Bayer, 1990).

On-line Community based Projects: The advantages of a classroom community have been spelled out but implementing these ideas and developing and organising classroom activities is where the actual teaching process begins. The following section is an overview as well as a guideline for establishing effective classroom community projects.

Listed below are some ideas to keep in mind when developing student projects that encourage a global community.

Suggestions for a successful on-line community project:

- The project is completed with the help of students from distance classrooms.
- The project can be a way for students to voice their opinion or to improve a situation in their community. *e.g. an environmental concern.*
- The project is incorporated with other aspects of the course. *e.g. used in conjunction with class discussion or oral presentations.*
- Projects combine various skills that involve accessing information, communicating thoughts, collaborating on shared topics and displaying knowledge.
- The finished project contributes something of value to the public.
- The project allows for students to express their creativity. (art work, poems, drawings).

The first step in creating a sense of community within a classroom project would be to establish a common shared space where learners can get to know each other, share ideas and access relevant course information. This 'common space' could be in the form of a mailing list or a bulletin board accessible to all students via a network. Setting up your own digital classroom space no longer requires technical knowledge thanks to the many free services, such as discussion boards and mailing lists, that already exist on the Internet. Students should even be encouraged to become participants in on-line communities outside the language learning community. Although many language classes take place using the target language, many learners are never exposed to authentic native language outside the classroom, let alone native speaker interaction. Visiting a discussion board such as the ones offered by Yahoo.com or CNN.com can bring native English speaking content into the language learning arena.

Once students have their 'communication space' established, they are ready to launch an on-line project. One simple but effective example is a culture comparison between groups of students from different countries. A learning community involving more than one culture can improve cross-cultural communication skills, enhance knowledge of specific cultures and increase cultural awareness (Cohen and Miyake, 1986). A list of specific tasks can be posted on a shared web-page for classmates to refer to and information from participating cultures can be collected and shared via a discussion board, a listserv, or by personal email. Once information is collected, it can be organised and presented on-line or orally in class. A student from one culture working together with a student from another culture would be able to create a web page jointly that includes a simple comparison of their likes/dislikes, daily activities and views on selected issues. An activity such as this encourages students to see the common similarities held by different cultures and can help to break down stereotypes. Intercultural interaction on-line urges students to re-examine their own beliefs as well as their community beliefs.

An example that can help to foster student autonomy emerges from the students' extensive use of their background knowledge. A 'student teach' project reverses the role of the teacher being the expert to the student being the expert. The student becomes the teacher on a topic that he or she is an expert on. Every student holds a vast amount of background knowledge and is often motivated to share their special knowledge with classmates or students from another culture. This type of activity can work well in a single classroom, although, teaching a distant classroom 'how to' do something adds to the excitement of the project. An example of this type of project may involve a step by step illustration of how to prepare a local dish; something that is representative of the student's culture and something which the student has considerable background knowledge in.

Students must not only be exposed to language literally, but they must be able to interpret and criticise language. Collecting, analysing and interpreting data is one such activity that encourages these skills. Surveys have traditionally been a common activity in the language class since students are able to collect authentic data and present findings that give a real purpose to a language learning task. On-line communities are an optimal setting for collecting a large number of responses from people with varying backgrounds. Questions and responses can easily be distributed and collected on-line and shared among classmates. Results can also be presented on-line in the form of a chart or graph. Authentic survey results can act as a basis for discussion both on-line and in face-to-face classroom interaction since students have the authentic data to use to support their comments and opinions.

A final example of an on-line community activity involves databases. Databases are excellent tools for organising and making sense of language even for the beginning language learner. Databases can include simple information such as world price comparisons or more advanced data describing regional dialects. Databases even serve as useful information for other readers around the world and, most importantly, they can be constantly added to and expanded upon with each incoming class. Databases can be constructed by collecting data on almost any topic of interest to the students. A number of student produced databases can be found on-line ranging from city restaurant guides to regional consumer good costs to weather data.

Summary: As extensive research is being conducted on usefulness of computer aided communication in the language classroom, educators are realising that today's digital information exchange has become a useful tool to increase student motivation, develop learner autonomy, and streamline the process of delivering information to students. Although most on-line communities lack certain important communicative elements such as the ability to visualise facial expressions or body language, their benefits are clearly recognised by educators who want to improve upon their time-limited physical classroom. A traditional classroom can be enhanced by allowing student interaction to extend 24 hours a day via an on-line learning community. Whether educators are comfortable with computer aided communication or whether computer aided communication has been proved to be an effective means of interaction, one thing seems to be sure, it is here to stay and will continue to progress as one of the leading venues of communication in the next millennium. Language is an important part of communication and we as language teachers cannot ignore this rapidly expanding communication technology that is evolving. Educators will have to continue to investigate this new communication and information retrieval service that we call the Internet and implement on-line learning communities that process, retrieve, and distribute information, ideas, and feelings.

References:

Armstrong, T. (1994). Multiple intelligence in the classroom. Alexandria, VA: Association for Supervision and Curriculum Development. p. 86.

Cohen, M., & Miyake, N. (1986). A worldwide intercultural network: exploring electronic messaging for instruction. Instructional Science, 15, 257-273.

Dryden, L. M. (1998). *What does multiple intelligence theory tell us about CALL?* In P. N. D. Lewis (Ed.) Teachers, learners, and computers: Exploring relationships in CALL. Nagoya: Japan Association for Language Teaching, pp. 95-102.

Gardner, H. (1983, 1985). Frames of mind: The theory of multiple intelligences. New York, BasicBooks. pp. 316-320.

Johnson, D. W. and R. T. Johnson. (1989). Co-operation and competition: theory and research. Edina, MN: Interaction.

Kern, R. G. (1995). Restructuring classroom interaction with network computers: Effects on quantity and characteristics of language production. Modern Language Journal, 79, 457-476.

Kramsch, C. Context and culture in language teaching. Oxford University Press, pp. 205-210.

Kramsch, C. and R. W. Andersen. (1999) Teaching text and context through multimedia. Language Learning & Technology v. 2, no. 2, January. pp. 31-42

Ortega, L. (1997). Processes and outcomes in networked classroom interaction: Defining the research agenda for L2 computer-assisted classroom discussion. Language Learning & Technology, 1 (1) 82-93. Retrieved November 22, 1998 from the World Wide Web: http://polyglot.cal.msu.edu/llt/vol1num1/ortega/default.html.

Noddings, N. (1986). 'Fidelity in teaching, teacher education, and research for teaching', Teacher Education and Research for Teaching, vol. 56, p. 503, Nov.4.

Nunan, D. (1986). Research methods in language learning. Cambridge University Press, pp. xi

Reid, J. M. (1998). Understanding learning styles in the second language classroom. Upper Saddle River, NJ: Prentice Hall Regents.

Richards, J. and C. Lockhart. (1994). Reflective teaching in second language classrooms. Cambridge University Press, pp. 1-5.

Sergiovanni, T. (1992). The moral dimension in leadership. San Francisco: Jossey-Bass, pp. 47-48.

Serim, F. and M. Koch. (1996). NetLearning: Why Teachers Use the Internet. Sebastopol, CA, Songline Studios, pp. 150-182.

Sproull, L., & Kiesler, S. (1991). Connections: New ways of working in the networked organization. Cambridge, MA: MIT Press.

Sulzby, E. (1990, April). *Writing and reading instruction and assessment for young children: Issues and implications.* Paper commissioned by the Forum on the Future of Children and Families of the National Academy of Sciences and the National Association of State Boards of Education. Ann Arbor, MI.

Tudor, I. (1996). Learner-centredness as language education. Cambridge University Press, pp. 35-37.

Vilmi, R. (1995). HUT e-mail writing project: An ongoing experiment. In T. Orr (Ed.), English for science and technology: Profiles and perspectives (pp. 47-59). Aizuwakamatsu, Japan: University of Aizu, Center for Language Research.
Warschauer, M. (1997). Computer-mediated collaborative learning: Theory and practice. Modern Language Journal, 81, 470-481.
Wilhelm, J. & P. Friedemann. (1998). Hyperlearning: Where Projects, Inquiry, and Technology Meet. York, Maine: Stenhouse Publishers.
Williams, M. and R. L. Burden. (1997) Psychology for language teachers: A social constructivist approach. Cambridge University Press.

TURNING HALF CIRCLE — CALL AND THE DEBATE BETWEEN COMMUNICATIVE AND STRUCTURAL GRAMMAR TEACHING

Chris Dawson
Manchester Metropolitan University, UK

Abstract
In the past five years or so it has become apparent that the communicative language teaching revolution, for all the benefits it has brought about, has been accompanied by a decline in grammatical awareness and standards at all levels of language learning. Indeed, the extent of this decline is born out by the fact that CILT, one of the leading arbiters of good practice in the area of second language teaching, has produced various publications on grammar, such as Grammar! A Conference Report *edited by Lid King and Peter Boaks,* Grammar Matters *by Susan Halliwell,* Teaching Grammar: Perspectives in Higher Education, *edited by Dulcie Engel and Florence Myles, and* Teaching Grammar Communicatively *by Sue Purcell, advocating a renewed emphasis on grammar teaching although within a communicative context. In this paper I will assess the effect that CALL technology might have on grammar teaching in schools in the years to come. In the future can we expect that most grammar teaching in schools will be carried out within a communicative framework? Or will we be talking of a more integrated approach, comprising communicative or implicit methods of grammar teaching during class time reinforced by 'traditional' or explicit methods outside of class using CALL programs?*

1. Introduction: During the late 1970s the teaching of Modern Foreign Languages (MFL) in Britain underwent a transformation. Teaching strategies moved away from the so-called 'grammar-translation' approach, which placed a strong emphasis on the learning and accurate application of grammatical structures, and towards the 'communicative approach', whereby emphasis was given to communication and fluency. In this article I assess the effect that CALL might have on strategies for MFL grammar teaching in schools in the years to come. I will begin by offering a brief outline of the principal characteristics of Communicative Language Teaching (CLT) and of the way in which it has evolved in response to concerns about falling standards of reading and writing among MFL students. I will then attempt to gauge the possible role of CALL on MFL grammar teaching in schools by outlining those areas of the secondary syllabus where active grammatical knowledge is most needed. Following this I will outline some of the characteristics that are likely to give CALL materials an increased profile in MFL grammar teaching strategies before finally offering my conclusions. Where it has been necessary to refer to language-specific sources such as syllabuses or reference books, such references have been made to French teaching sources. However, in all cases the underlying point made is generic.

2. The origins and characteristics of Communicative Language Teaching: There are various factors which might be said to have influenced the development of Communicative Language Teaching:

Linguistic factors

- *Chomsky's Universal Grammar.* According to Chomsky, children have an innate knowledge of the characteristics and structures of language (which he called a Language Acquisition Device or LAD), a knowledge which develops through exposure to L1.
- *Krashen's Monitor Model.* This includes his Acquisition-learning hypothesis, according to which L2 acquisition, like L1 acquisition, results from exposure to language via meaningful interaction. And his Natural order hypothesis, according to which L2 grammar develops along similar lines, whether or not explicit grammatical instruction has taken place.
- *Hymes and Communicative Competence.* This involved the notion that grammatical competence is a subset of Communicative Competence which contains previously neglected socio-linguistic competences such as such as register, appropriateness, and so on.
- *Corder.* Corder viewed errors as natural symptoms of progression from 'interlanguage' to full proficiency.
- *Notional / functional approach.* (Austin, Searle, van Ek, Halliday, Wilkins) — This embodied the view that where the L2 curriculum is arranged in terms of function rather than form it is more motivating and more relevant to learner's needs.

Sociological factors

- The huge post-war expansion of education and the development of comprehensive education led to much greater demands for language teaching.
- The 1970s saw a significant increase in the opportunities for European travel.
- Developments in media technology made it easier to gain access to authentic materials for classroom use.

Educationalist factors

- Broader trends in education, such as student-centered learning, differentiation, and pair and group work were adopted in language teaching.

The basic characteristics of Communicative language teaching (henceforth known as CLT) are as follows:

- Language use in class to involve meaningful communication where possible — where language has a practical purpose there is greater motivation for learning.
- Broadening of teaching objectives to included sociolinguistic and strategic aspects. The whole united in new notion of 'communicative competence'.
- Syllabuses to be organised according to notions and functions rather than structures.
- Use of 'authentic' language materials where possible — hold more interest credibility for students and better preparation for when students visit the FL country.
- Teaching to remain student-centered where possible: takes learners' needs and interests as starting point.
- Teaching to involve as much exposure to the FL as possible — increases learner confidence.
- Emphasis away from accuracy and towards fluency. Correction kept to a minimum.
- Greater emphasis on speaking and listening
- Implicit rather than explicit teaching — emphasis on enabling students to work out rules for themselves from exposure to language

It can be seen from the above that CLT is not a tight defined teaching method, but a loose amalgam of ideas with diverse origins, which have come to constitute good practice. Its principal achievements as far as school education is concerned might be listed as follows:

- Giving access to MFL teaching to the broad population of schoolchildren rather than simply to the academically gifted.
- Increased motivation of all students in the classroom, thereby increasing learning possibilities, attracting more students to study languages and encouraging more students to carry on to higher levels.
- Increasing oral and aural proficiency, and a broader communicative competence among all students. This has led to the development of more practical communicative skills more relevant to the needs of most students: e.g. French for holidays / short visits, rather than for reading literature, broadsheet newspapers etc.
- Encouraging an increase cultural awareness of the foreign countries.

During the 1990s, as CLT entered its second decade, there has been an increasing questioning of some aspects of the CLT methodology, especially by those teaching at a post-GCSE level. For example, lack of knowledge of grammatical structures made 'bridging the gap' between GCSE and A-Level, a problem at the best of times, all the more difficult, given the increased emphasis on written language and more complex linguistic structures. This in turn was feeding into HE teaching where lack of grammatical proficiency was causing an impediment to the acquisition of the advanced linguistic skills required of professional linguists.

Furthermore, some of the theoretical grounding on which CLT was based began to be called into question or challenged by alternative theoretical findings. For example researchers have challenged Krashen's view that language learned by conscious means cannot become as spontaneous as language acquired, while other of Krashen's hypotheses (such as the Monitor Hypothesis, the Natural Order Hypothesis and the Input Hypothesis) have been criticised for being vague and difficult to verify.[1] Meanwhile, Hawkins and Towell have suggested that L2 acquisition is subject to a critical period beyond which learners become 'physiologically incapable of acquiring full L2 grammatical competence on the basis of mere exposure'.[2] This criticism from researchers has been reinforced by more general criticisms from teachers, especially those teaching A Level and post-A Level, regarding low grammatical standards and awareness in their students.[3]

As a result of this questioning a new notion was born, Communicative Grammar Teaching (or CGT), constituting a marrying of the basic principles of CLT with the newly rehabilitated notion that active grammar teaching **can** facilitate language acquisition.[4] The question was not *whether* but *how* to teach grammar. The two basic characteristics of CGT are:

- A renewed emphasis on and development of ways of teaching grammatical structures and paradigms *implicitly* (sometimes called the *inductive approach*).
- A more overt acceptance that this may on occasions need to be backed up by explicit grammar teaching (sometimes referred to as the *deductive approach*).[5]

These two characteristics are accompanied by an acceptance of the need for greater flexibility on some of the original principals of CLT within the context of active grammar teaching. For example, a more flexible approach to the notions of functionality and authenticity was needed, as the new grammatical input into classes required the creation of examples of usage not necessarily related to the immediate classroom context, and not necessarily derived from 'authentic' sources. Flexibility was also

---

[1] Rosamund Mitchell and Florence Myles, *Second Language Learning Theories*, London: Arnold, 1998, pp. 35-39.

[2] Roger Hawkins and Richard Towell, 'Why Teach Grammar?', in *Teaching Grammar: Perspectives in Higher Education* ed. Dulcie Engel and Florence Myles, London: CILT / AFLS, 1996, p. 201.

[3] See Dulcie Engels and Florence Myles, *Grammar Teaching: The Major Concerns*, in *Teaching Grammar: Perspectives in Higher Education* ed. Dulcie Engel and Florence Myles, London: CILT / AFLS, 1996, p. 9

[4] For a justification of this idea, see Hawkins and Towell, 'Why Teach Grammar?', p. 207.

[5] See Norbert Pachler and Kit Field, *Learning to Teach Modern Foreign Languages in the Secondary School*, London: Routledge, 1997, p. 148 & ff. For a introduction to Communicative Grammar Teaching, see Sue Purcell, *Teaching Grammar Communicatively*, London: CILT, 1997.

required in the area of L1 speaking, in order to allow the explanation of grammar points by the teacher, and student response to this.

3. The role of CALL grammar-teaching materials in schools

As more and more schools become equipped with multi-media computers, develop internal networks and gain access to the Internet, CALL will unquestionably play an increasing role secondary MFL teaching. CALL is particularly suited to the teaching of grammatical structures. This is because computer systems, in the current state of technology, are better suited to mechanical data processing such as displaying text or matching user input against a predefined 'right' answer, than to handling the more unpredictable and nuanced responses required in communicative activities (e.g. teacher interaction activities, role play in pairs / groups etc.). To what extent then might CALL grammar teaching materials be used in schools in the years to come?

3.1. GCSE teaching: When endeavouring to gauge how CALL grammar-teaching materials might be used GCSE teaching, it is necessary to establish how much grammatical knowledge is needed for a given grade. Although such information is not wholly explicit in Exam Board GCSE syllabuses, it is possible on the basis of lists of linguistic structures and grade descriptions, to gain a reasonably clear picture of the structures that need to be covered at which levels at GCSE. It is true to say that up to and including grade C GCSE very little active grammatical knowledge is needed. Although students will be exposed to a wide variety of structures[6], error tolerance is such as to make ability to use them subservient to communication. As such, knowledge of these structures is either for purposes of recognition (in listening or reading) or else is embodied as part of lexical items (for speaking and writing). As about three-quarters of MFL students obtain grade C or below in French, it follows that communicative teaching in its original CLT form is likely to remain the dominant pedagogical approach to use with the great majority of GCSE students, with little need for CGT or other forms of active grammatical input save for the most basic of structures.

Grade B constitutes something of a threshold with regard to grammar knowledge, not surprisingly as it is from this level that students can realistically proceed to A Level. Although grade descriptions tend to cover only grades F, C and A, it is possible to infer from the criteria of assessment that some evidence of active grammatical knowledge is required. It remains true, however, that it is possible to achieve a B grade with only a superficial or partial knowledge of the structures listed in Exam Board syllabuses, and for this reason many teachers would provide only periodical active grammar teaching to students expecting a B, especially those in the B minus band. In general it is only in classes with a majority of students expecting an A grade that sustained active grammar

[6] See NEAB Syllabus for GCSE French 1999, (1211, Manchester: NEAB, 1999, pp. 32-5).

teaching takes place, in response to Exam Board grade descriptions such as that of the NEAB exam board:

> [Candidates] produce longer sequences using a range of vocabulary, structure and time references. Their spelling and grammar are generally accurate, and the style is appropriate to the purpose.[7]

CALL grammar materials, then, are liable to have a increasing influence in the following areas of MFL teaching at Key Stage 4:

- In classes with a majority of students expecting an A grade. This could involve whole-class teaching, mixed activity teaching or self-access work.
- In classes with a substantial number of students expecting a B grade or (in schools without setting) in classes with pockets of students expecting an A or B grade. This could involve mixed activity teaching or self-access work.

3.2. Bridging the gap

Another area of teaching where CALL grammar materials are liable to have an increasing influence is in teaching specifically aimed at bridging the gap between GCSE and A Level. Some MFL Departments offer specially designed courses in the summer after GCSEs have been taken, or else set prospective students preparatory work. In the future these might take the form of on-line exercises, possibly backed up by workshops or study days.

More commonly Schools and Sixth-Form Colleges have strategies for reinforcing grammatical knowledge during the Lower Sixth. CALL, especially when used as a self-access tool, is well suited to assisting with this task for the two following reasons:

- One of the difficulties inherent in bridging the gap is the amount of time, and especially class time, that needs to be invested in bringing students up to speed before real progress towards A Level standards can be made. CALL self-access materials, if properly used, could greatly increase the speed of this progress.
- According to Pachler and Field 'Approaches to the study of MFL at 'A'/'AS' level are much less teacher-centered and demand a higher level of motivation from the student. The transition from dependence on the teacher to independence is a big challenge for students and MFL teachers alike.'[8] CALL materials might be able to counter this shortfall in student motivation better than hard-copy materials through

---

[7] NEAB Syllabus for GCSE French 1999, p. 126.

[8] Pachler and Field, *Learning to Teach Modern Foreign Languages in the Secondary School*, p. 334.

greater availability (they can be accessed from anywhere) and accessibility (easier navigation, self-marking etc.).

3.3. A level teaching: The final area where CALL grammar materials could have an increasing influence at secondary level will be in A Level teaching. The difference between the grammatical knowledge required at higher grade GCSE and A Level lies not so much in the nature of structures themselves as in the depth of knowledge students are expected to have of them. For as Pachler and Field write, whilst grammatical knowledge at GCSE is essentially passive, at A Level 'all knowledge is assumed to be active to enable the generation and manipulation of language forms'.[9] For this reason specific grammatical structures are prescribed at A Level whereas at GCSE grammatical requirements need to be inferred by teachers from syllabuses and past papers.[10] It thus becomes important for teachers to adopt a systematic, whole-class approach to grammar teaching as opposed to the fragmentary and student-centered approaches possible at GCSE.

An obvious aspect that favours the use of CALL grammar-teaching materials at A Level is time. Compared with GCSE students, Sixth Formers have a considerable amount time outside of class but in school to devote to self-study (according to Pachler and Field, A Level students have up to 6 hours of independent study time per week).[11] This does not mean to say that use by GCSE students is not possible, but is very restricted to before or after the school day, or during the lunch hour, a factor which works against student motivation.

The need for a more systematic approach to grammar teaching at A Level has given rise to a new generation of grammar books aimed at intermediate and advanced learners of French and suitable both for class work and self-access work. These could be said to divide into two basic types: grammar course books (e.g. Jubb & Rouxeville, Ribière & Marriot, Turk and García Vandaele[12]) and grammar reference books backed up by workbooks (Lang and Perez, Hawkins and Towell[13]). CALL grammar-teaching

---

[9] Pachler and Field, *Learning to Teach Modern Foreign Languages in the Secondary School*, p. 331.

[10] The grammar structures required for a Level are listed in the A Level subject cores.

[11] Pachler and Field, *Learning to Teach Modern Foreign Languages in the Secondary School*, p. 342.

[12] Margaret Jubb and Annie Rouxeville, *French Grammar in Context*, London: Arnold, 1998; Thalia Marriot and Mireille Ribière, *Help Yourself to Advanced French Grammar*, Harlow: Longman, 1998, Phil Turk and Geneviève García Vandaele, *Action Grammaire*, London: Hodder and Stoughton, 1996.

[13] Margaret Lang and Isabelle Perez, *Modern French Grammar — A Practical Guide*, London: Routledge, 1996; Margaret Lang and Isabelle Perez, *Modern French Grammar — Workbook*, London: Routledge, 1997. Roger Hawkins and Richard Towell, *French Grammar and Usage*,

materials would constitute a transferal of this development to an on-line teaching environment, with all the advantages that this would present (e.g. self-marking, logging of marks and so on).

There are two further factors making CALL materials particularly useful at A Level:

- Because GCSE is so based on CLT, it is important for reasons of continuity that A-Level class teaching maintains a strong emphasis on such communicative factors as fluency, confidence and motivation. With CALL, it is possible to move much of the more formal, structured forms of teaching to self-access work.
- MFL Sixth-Form groups are often shared by teachers: as such, CALL materials could help provide a consistency that is sometimes compromised in a team-teaching context.

4. The characteristics of CALL grammar-teaching materials

If computer systems are better suited to the mechanical data processing involved in testing grammatical structures than to contributing to the more interactive and nuanced activities of communicative teaching, it follows that CALL grammar-teaching materials are most likely to be used in self-access work outside of the classroom, in much the same way as hard-copy grammar reference and workbooks. This would leave class-contact time for the more communicative and interactive activities which computer systems are less able to emulate. CALL materials would differ from hard-copy equivalents in two fundamental ways. First is the capacity for self-marking. This presents a number of advantages:

- Where CALL work replaces hard-copy homework, there is an obvious saving of teacher marking time, time which can be reinvested in more interactive / communicative activities.
- Where CALL work replaces self-access work undertaken at the student's own initiative, the time and effort saved in having to look up answers and self-mark can serve to increase student motivation.
- Automatic feedback — A computer can offer an explanation of a correct answer by either cross-referencing to the relevant section of an on-line grammar reference, or else by offering brief explanations of each answer in the style of a Help facility. As with the above point, the time and effort saved in having to retrieve this information can serve to increase student motivation.
- Immediacy — As a given topic is still fresh in student's mind when the answer is given (unlike in teacher-marked homework), there is an increased learning potential.

London: Arnold, 1996; Roger Hawkins, Marie-Noëlle Lamy and Richard Towell, *Practising French Grammar*, London: Arnold, 1997.

The second difference lies in the computer's ability to keep an automatic record of student marks. The advantages that this presents are as follows:

- Saving of teacher administration time.
- Permits teachers to see what self-access work a student has covered, and with what success.
- Guarantee of teacher supervision and resultant feedback and encouragement increases student motivation.
- Future, more intelligent CALL grammar teaching programs will be able to produce customised learning paths / revision packages, based on the analysis of a student's performance in a given set of exercises.

Whilst CALL grammar-teaching materials are likely to be fundamentally deductive in approach, this is not to say that there are not possibilities for including elements of CGT in a CALL package:

- Elements could be arranged in terms of notions and functions (as in Lang & Perez), or else in terms of structure whilst maintaining a close link with communicative function (as in Nott).[14]
- On a language level, texts can include or even privilege spoken language as opposed to written language. This might involve the use of familiar terminology or usage, transcriptional orthography of some oral contractions (e.g. *Y'a* in French), and privileging the first person over the third person.
- Chapters can be introduced by short texts illustrating a given structure in use (as in Jubb & Rouxeville), begin with a diagnostic test (as in Ribière & Marriot) or else begin with an inductive exercise.[15]
- Exercise instructions, or possibly even grammatical explanations might be written in the target language (as in the *GramEx* package).[16]
- Standard deductive exercises could be complemented by exercises designed for pair or group work in class (as in Turk and García Vandaele, Nott).
- Illustrative examples and text questions could be taken where possible from authentic sources (as in Lang & Perez).
- Hint functions can help keep the student actively engaged in the learning process, rather than a passive recipient of information.

---

[14] Davis Nott, *French Grammar Explained*, London: Hodder and Stoughton, 1998.

[15] For an example of an inductive exercise, see Pachler and Field, *Learning to Teach Modern Foreign Languages in the Secondary School*, pp. 149-151.

[16] Paul Hickman, *GramEx*, Hull: TELL Consortium, University of Hull / Hodder & Stoughton Educational, Version 2.3, 1995.

None of these elements, of course, are without their drawbacks. For example reading grammatical explanations in L2 poses great difficulties for students; it is difficult to find from authentic sources sentences that are self-standing (i.e. not relying on context) and thematically generic; and notional / functional organisation of material can at times become overly lexical and data heavy. However, if well thought out, the inclusion of CGT elements in CALL can mean that they benefit from recent developments in MFL teaching and ensure that they tie in directly with topics covered during class teaching.

One significant factor, however, affecting CALL's chances of success in the future lies in the domain of student motivation. For all the media attention that computers and the Internet receive, it is nevertheless certain that for many students the prospect of using computers as part of their learning remains a daunting and thereby unattractive proposition. If CALL is to become a significant tool for grammar teaching in the future, programs need to be made that are accessible and motivating:

- Login, access and use needs to be easy.
- Programs must run smoothly and speedily. Programs delivered by Internet are best down-loaded in advance (this also reduces costs).
- Programs need to be backed up by written materials, and be supported in the school / college by a low cost printing facility.

This is, of course, in addition to the appropriate use of formatting, graphics, and audio-visual and other design elements. However, against these factors needs to be considered the factor of cost. Budgets for MFL Heads of Department are small, and priority will of needs go to shareware and cheaper programs. Furthermore, it will be a long time before it can be assumed that most schools are in possession of high-specification multimedia PCs with advanced Internet navigator software. As such, programs containing high levels of graphics, audio-visual material and other elements requiring high levels of data processing are less likely to succeed on a general level.

5. Conclusion: It is clear that CALL materials have the potential to play a significant role in MFL grammar teaching in the future. But if in some areas teaching grammar were increasingly to become a dual strategy between teacher-led communicative grammar teaching and computer-based structural grammar teaching, what implications would this have for the ethos of grammar teaching in our schools? Can one really talk of grammar teaching as being 'within a communicative context' if the context of language teaching has been extended to include active grammar teaching through the medium of CALL?

Although much of the information contained in CALL grammar-teaching materials is essentially the same as that presented in hard-copy materials, CALL grammar-teaching materials differ significantly in terms of their pedagogical status. With their capacity for self-marking, automatic feedback, logging and so on, CALL grammar-teaching materials can no longer be considered as support materials, as with optional or loosely structured programmes of extra work, but as an essential and integral strand in an overall MFL teaching strategy, more akin to supervised classroom work. This will have important consequences on the methodological ethos of some MFL teaching. For if CALL grammar-teaching materials are by their very nature explicit or deductive, any return of such active grammar teaching as a major strand of overall teaching strategies would serve to involve a further shift away from CLT and towards a greater balance between the acquisition and learning of grammatical structures.

As has been mentioned, the amount of active grammatical input into a given course is very much dependent on the level and ability of a given class: most classes at Key Stage 3, and lower ability classes at Key Stage 4, these making the majority of students learning French in schools today, are likely to be taught primarily with the context of CLT. To this extent CLT is likely to remain the dominant methodological force in MFL in the years to come. However, for more advanced classes and levels CLT and CGT practices are likely to become increasingly supplemented by CALL grammar-teaching materials. In this way the CALL revolution might be said to be leading to a less unitary, more integrated style of language-teaching methodology, involving a symbiosis of contrasting, but essentially complementary approaches to grammar teaching.

It would be argued by some that CLT never sought to exclude active grammar teaching, but merely privileged other aspects of language acquisition. As CLT was a broad set of guidelines rather than a defined teaching method, it has always had the capacity to accommodate active teaching of grammatical structures where teachers considered this to be appropriate. As such, the consideration of CALL-based self-access materials as part of the diet of more advanced level MFL curricula could be seen not to make any significant change to the communicative structure and objectives of CLT.

Others, however, would argue that some interpretations of CLT did indeed seek to exclude active grammar teaching from the classroom, on the grounds that there was no evidence that it had any effect on language acquisition.[17] And even if these constituted a minority, the way in which CLT pedagogy has been translated into practice (in terms of curriculum design, examination assessment and teaching practice) and the standards it is producing (in terms of accuracy and linguistic awareness), would tend to indicate that there has been an excessive downplaying of active grammatical knowledge, especially at more advanced levels. As such a CALL-inspired increase in active grammar teaching input would involve a significant shift in MFL pedagogical strategy.

---

[17] See Hawkins and Towell, 'Why Teach Grammar?', p. 197.

Such a shift, though significant, would not — indeed **could** not — involve a return to the 'grammar-translation' methodology of the past: save for IT correspondence courses, CALL grammar teaching packages of the future will only constitute one of many varying ingredients in the overall diet of MFL teaching. Rather things have turned half circle. In the future, teaching methodologies at advanced levels seem set to achieve a greater balance between language acquisition and language learning, between fluency and accuracy, between meaning and form, and between teacher-led and student-centred education. Furthermore, in a situation where many secondary teachers find themselves overstretched in terms of teaching, marking and administration, the time savings that CALL promises to offer in all three of these areas can only serve to make teachers better equipped to turn methodological theory into good teaching practice.

ARE WE STILL READING OR JUST FOLLOWING LINKS? HOW THE HIGHLIGHTING OF HYPERLINKS CAN INFLUENCE INCIDENTAL VOCABULARY LEARNING

Isabelle De Ridder
University of Antwerp (UIA), Belgium

1. Introduction

The incidental learning of new words: Most literature on first and second language acquisition research agrees that (extensive) reading is one of the main ways of learning new words (Nagy, Anderson & Herman, 1987; Sternberg, 1987; West & Stanovich, 1991; Nation, 1990; Grabe, 1991). In first language acquisition for instance, it has been shown that children add approximately 3,000 words annually to their reading vocabularies (Nagy, Anderson & Herman, 1987). A study in the Netherlands has established that second language learners, upon entering university, have an average second language receptive vocabulary knowledge of 11,000 words (Hazenberg & Hulstijn, 1996). Words — or word growth — in such large quantities simply cannot have been learned only by means of vocabulary instruction. The default hypothesis must therefore be that many words must have been 'picked up' during listening and reading activities, while the primary goal was to attempt overall comprehension (Hulstijn, Hollander & Greidanus, 1996; Nagy, Anderson & Herman, 1987). This type of vocabulary learning is called 'incidental': it is a 'secondary product', not the goal of the main cognitive activity (Huckin & Coady, 1996). Hulstijn (1989) and Schmidt (1994) have therefore defined incidental vocabulary learning as 'the accidental learning of information without the intention of remembering that information'.

The powerful notion of context: Within the process of (incidental) vocabulary learning, the notion of 'context' is obviously fundamental. When encountering an unknown word, the reader can rely on the context to 'reconstruct', 'guess' (Huckin & Coady, 1996) or derive — and therefore using specific techniques[1] — the meaning of that particular word (Sternberg, 1987; Sternberg & Powell, 1983).[2]

---

[1] According to Sternberg & Powell (1983), three processes are involved in learning new words from context: selective encoding, selective combination, selective comparison .

[2] The theory of Sternberg & Powell (1983) has been refined over the years (Elshout-Mohr, van Daalen-Kapteijns & van Oostendorp,1999) but contextual clues of different nature (temporal, spatial, functional,..., see Sternberg & Powell, 1983) and value remain important for the acquisition of new words.

However, contextual clues are often ignored or overlooked by the reader: s/he might not possess the adequate world, cultural or domain knowledge (Drum & Konopak, 1987) to appreciate the treasures of the context. But a context could just as well contain too many unknown words, thus preventing the reader to derive (correct) word meanings from the context. At this particular point, dictionaries and/or marginal glosses could come at a rescue. Research has indeed shown that the well-determined use of a dictionary (Knight, 1994) and/or the provision of marginal glosses (Hulstijn, 1992; Ellis, Tanaka & Yamazaki, 1994) seem to promote pick-up rates.[3] When context fails, dictionaries can provide a worthy alternative (Knight, 1994; Davies, 1989).

What does CALL do to dictionary definitions and marginal glosses?: While reading a book, a magazine or a newspaper — and this we all know from experience —, readers are often reluctant to interrupt their reading for a trip to the dictionary.[4] With the advent of new technologies in language learning, translations and definitions have become available at the click of a mouse. Consulting a dictionary or marginal glosses can now be handled quickly and efficiently and is no longer a major interruption of the reading. The time consuming searches in dictionaries and the endless turning of pages have come to an end. Text comprehension is indeed only but a mouse click away...

However, should we not raise the question on how to present these glosses to the user/language learner? It could, for instance, be a choice in reading software material to highlight 'difficult' words, thus indicating a link towards dictionary definitions and/or translations. Nevertheless, little is known about the effect of these highlights on the readers or the reading process. Nor has it been established how the randomly highlighting of words in texts on screen affects the incidental learning of vocabulary. It is this question which the present study addresses.

2. Research Question: We have attempted to explore whether the highlighting of words in a hypertextual setting — on a sole basis that the word is presumed to be 'unknown' to the reader — influences the amount of incidental vocabulary learned. Could it not be indeed that the randomly highlighting of words disturbs the natural structure or

---

[3] Other factors seem to have a positive influence on incidental vocabulary learning. Hulstijn, Hollander & Greidanus (1996) give a full overview of these factors with full bibliographical references. Meanings relevant for the understanding of the text for instance, are likely to be rembered better (Hulstijn, 1992). Frequent appearances and high verbal ability favorably affect incidental vocabulary learning (Krantz, 1991). Moreover, Hulstijn, Hollander and Greidanus (1996) have proven that the combined influence of frequency of occurrence and provision of word meanings on incidental vocabulary learning is a positive one.

[4] The study of Hulstijn, Hollander & Greidanus (1996) suggests that 'intermediate and advanced learners, when reading a fictional or non-fictional text of more than one page in order to understand the main idea, seldom use a dictionary. Only when they read a short text (Knight, 1994) or when dictionary consultation has been made extremely easy by a simple click of the mouse in a computer presentation (Hulstijn, 1993), do some readers look up the meanings of unknown words'. (p.336)

organisation of the text in such a radical way that it prevents the learners from inferring word meanings from context? Could it not be that since attention is drawn towards the unknown word, learners might ignore contextual clues and be incited to click too quickly? Dictionary use, in such a setting, would no longer be 'well-determined', but would become indiscriminate. We have stated above that incidental vocabulary learning is closely related to the notion of context and therefore to the reading process. Could it not be that the at random marking of words in texts, actually prevents readers from reading and that what started as 'reading' evolves towards 'clicking'?

We have thus investigated the influence of highlighted hyperlinks on incidental vocabulary learning, replicating two fundamental characteristics of many real-life reading situations:

(a) advanced learners read an authentic text on screen with the purpose of gaining overall understanding of it;
(b) the text contained a number of words which the readers were not familiar with.

The L2 learners involved in this study read two texts under two conditions:

(1) marginal glosses are provided; links towards them are highlighted;
(2) marginal glosses are provided; links towards them are not highlighted.

We entertained the following hypotheses:

a) The amount of vocabulary — receptive or active — 'picked up' from the text will be lower in the highlighted condition because the reading process in itself will be fundamentally disturbed, preventing the context from being beneficial. Dictionary use will thus no longer be well-determined, will no longer be just a tool in case of failing contextual clues, but a purpose in itself.
b) Consequently, we postulated that in the condition using highlights, students would spend significantly more time on 'clicking' (i.e. looking up words).

3. Method

Design: Advanced learners of French second language read two economic texts in French under two conditions: a marked or highlighted condition and an unmarked or not highlighted condition. The students were instructed to read the text they were given and prepare to answer comprehension questions. After reading, the students took a comprehension test and a receptive and active vocabulary test. The vocabulary tests where repeated one week later, in order to evaluate retention of the incidentally learned words.

Subjects: 17 second-year students of economics (19-20 years of age) voluntarily participated in this experiment. They all had Dutch as their native language, had a fairly advanced, more or less equal level of French (8 years of French second language or more) and were finishing a course of economic French, incorporated in their curriculum.

The subjects individually read the two French economic texts on screen in two separated sessions within a time span of two weeks.

Reading materials: The two economic texts presented to the students were selected through a pilot study held with a comparable group of 28 subjects. The students of the pilot study were asked to evaluate four texts — selected in close consultation with the staff of French — on their relevancy and degree of interest.[5] The texts were comparable in length (approximately 2000 words), grammatical difficulty and vocabulary load. While reading, the students of the pilot study indicated words that were unknown to them. Afterwards, they took an unexpected vocabulary test in which they were requested to translate approximatively 130 (isolated) words from the text into Dutch. Out of the four submitted texts, the two texts that were most valued by the students and that contained the largest number of unknown words were chosen. The selected texts concerned the diamant industry in Antwerp (T1) and the human capital in business (T2).

Glossed words: In T1, 109 words were glossed; T2 contained 116 dictionary definitions. These words were unknown to at least one of the students of the pilot study or were specifically indicated by at least one of the students while reading the text. Most of these words appeared more than once in the texts.

Conditions: Each one of the texts was molded into two different conditions: one that we qualified as 'marked' (M1) and another one that we referred to as 'unmarked' (M2). In the marked condition, glossed words were highlighted. While the overall text was presented in black, these words took a blue colour and were underlined in blue. In the unmarked condition, explained words were not highlighted in any particular way. In this condition, glossed words were retained black and were not underlined. Throughout the experiment, a Latin square design was used:

group 1 (4 students): T1C1 + T2C2
group 2 (5 students): T1C2 + T2C1
group 3 (4 students): T2C2 + T1C1
group 4 (4 students): T2C1 + T1C2

No time limits were imposed on the students. Eventually, every session took about one hour. Furthermore, the students were allowed to take notes on paper while reading (in order not to disturb their individual, normal reading process).

Technical settings: The students were asked to read the texts on screen (15 inch, 800x600 resolution). The texts were accessed through Internet Explorer 4.0, running on

---

[5] On the importance of the reader's interest and the pleasure s/he takes in reading for incidental vocabulary learning, see Coady (1997). In the additional questionnaire after the main experiment, 76 % of the students rated the texts on a scale of interest (7 points) higher than 'just ok'. Not any one rated the texts lower than 'just ok'.

an intranet supported by a personal webserver. A black text was presented on a white background. In both conditions, the translations and dictionary explanations were available by a simple mouse click on the unknown word. A small pop-up window (javascript) would appear, containing the primitive word (in blue), a Dutch translation and a French dictionary explanation, separated by a horizontal line.[6] The context-bound explanations were given first, more general translations were given at the end, between brackets.

Testing materials: After reading the text, the students were unexpectedly presented with a vocabulary test, containing two parts. The first part focused on more receptive word knowledge; the second part dealt with actively using a word in a given context. In order to examine the possible receptive acquisition of new words, we designed a multiple-choice vocabulary test with 4 choices per item: one key, two distractors and one choice 'I don't know'. The correct choice was randomly allocated to one of the first three positions.[7] This first part focused on 27 items, chosen out of the respective 109 and 116 glossed words. For the selection of these 27 words, the pilot vocabulary test was taken into account. Only words that appeared more than once where included into the test. In the second part of the submitted vocabulary test, the students were asked to complete five French sentences with a word from the text.[8]

For each item tested in both the vocabulary tests, the students were asked to reflect on where having learned the given word. Did s/he think to know this word a) already before reading the text? or b) from reading the text? An 'I don't know this word'- option was included.[9]

After having completed the vocabulary test, the students concentrated on a multiple-choice test focusing on text comprehension. For each part of the text, a question was prepared (which statement is in/correct, concerning a specific theme of the text).

---

6 We have chosen to provide L1 and L2 cues, since research has indicated that preferences in this matter are highly individual (Jacobs, Dufon & Fong, 1994).

7 This design was based upon a vocabulary test that was used by Dupuy and Krashen (1993) to confirm incidental vocabulary learning in French as a foreign language. The 'I don't know'-option is included to discourage guessing. In the results, however, we have only taken those words into account that the students declared to have learned from the text and had correctly translated (see *Scoring procedures*).

8 In experiments on incidental vocabulary learning, active vocabulary tests were — to our knowledge — not included. The small test concentrating on the use of a word in context was a personal choice, and based on the concern of being exhaustive. We did not expect the students to score particularly high on this part, for indeed we are aware of the fact that it is extremely difficult to use a word in context, when only encountered once. For an overview of the literature on what it is to 'know' a word, we refer to Beck & McKeown (1991).

9 Hulstijn, Hollander & Greidanus (1996) applied this same technique in their study on the combined influence of frequent occurrences and the use of dictionaries/marginal glosses on incidental vocabulary learning.

The entire vocabulary test was repeated one week later. The same items were tested, only the order of the words was scrambled.

Further data collection: During the sessions, data were collected through logfiles (java-script), indicating where the students clicked and at what specific time. In this way, it was possible to establish how long it took the students to read the text, which links they followed and how long they consulted the provided glosses. The activities on the screen were registrated with a Microsoft Camcorder. After having read the text and having completed the tests, the students answered some general questions concerning their reading and surfing-on-the-Internet habits. A small interview concluded each session, allowing the students to reflect on each session and formulate their overall impressions.

4. Results

Scoring procedures: In the correction of the vocabulary test we only took into account those words

(a) that the students declared to have learned from the text,[10] and
(b) that the students answered correctly in the multiple-choice test or used correctly in the given sentences.

Vocabulary and comprehension: Table 1 presents the results on the receptive vocabulary test (percentage of words that the students declared to have learned from the text and answered correctly) immediately after reading [(1) & (2)] and one week later [(3) & (4)]. As can be seen in Table 1, the marked condition scores higher than the unmarked condition in both moments of measurement [(1) versus (2) and (3) versus (4)]. The marked condition, however, has a greater relapse when both moments of measurement are compared [(1) versus (3), compared to (2) versus (4)].

	N	*M*	*SD*
Immediately after reading			
Marked (1)	17	41.17	13.15
Unmarked (2)	17	34.41	10.03
One week later			
Marked (3)	17	34.85	13.29
Unmarked (4)	17	30.71	10.29

Table 1 — Results of the receptive vocabulary test in percentage

[10] This to exclude pre-knowledge, which — despite the homogeneity of the group — can be different, due to individual differences.

Table 2 presents the results of the test where students were asked to use words of the text in context (percentage of words that the students declared to have learned from the text and answered correctly). The results of the tests taken immediately after reading in both conditions [(1) versus (2)] seem to be identical. If the second moment of measurement is taken into account (one week later) however, a higher score for the unmarked condition [(3) versus (4)] is indicated, which implicates that the regression for the marked condition is again greater [(1) versus (3), compared to (2) versus (4)].

	N	*M*	*SD*
Immediately after reading			
Marked (1)	17	15.29	19.40
Unmarked (2)	17	15.29	18.06
One week later			
Marked (3)	17	4.70	8.74
Unmarked (4)	17	7.05	12.12

Table 2 — Results of the active vocabulary test in percentage

Table 3 presents the results of the comprehension test, taken immediately after reading. The marked condition seems to score higher [(1) versus (2)].

	N	*M*	*SD*
Marked (1)	17	82.35	19.85
Unmarked (2)	17	72.94	19.92

Table 3 — Results of the comprehension test in percentage

Are these differences — if differences there are — statistically different? Given the limited number of subjects ($N = 17$) involved in this experiment, our expectations of significance were very low indeed. The MANOVA, looking for an overall effect among the dependent variables, yielded no significant overall effect (Hotelling's value = .58; p = .30). However, this result is strongly influenced by the weak differences in the two vocabulary tests of the second session. A MANOVA on these two tests yielded a Hoteling's value of .09; p = .53. A MANOVA on the three tests immediately after reading yielded a Hoteling's of .49; p = .12. The differences in these three tests are not significant, but nevertheless a clear indication in favour of the marked condition is — given the extremely limited number of subjects involved — worth mentioning. These outcomes could become significant when involving more students.

'Clicking'-behaviour: Table 4 presents the total amount of time spent on clicking (thus looking up words) in seconds per text and condition (normalised). The results were submitted to a chi-square test with a .05 level of significance necessary to reject the null hypothesis, being in this case that there would be no statistical difference between marked and unmarked condition in 'clicking-behaviour' .

	Estimate	*S. Error*	*Prev. Estimate*	*Chi-square (1 df)*
Text 1 — marked condition (1)	243.5	55.55	243.5	
Text 1 — unmarked condition (2)	188.8	52.38	188.8	
Text 2 — marked condition (3)	332.9	52.38	332.9	
Text 2 — unmarked condition (4)	156.0	55.55	156.0	
				5.92

Table 4 — Total time spent clicking, in seconds per text and condition

Looking at table 4, we see that in the marked condition, clicking takes up more time than in the unmarked condition. The chi-square tests shows that this difference is significantly at greater than 3.84, so the null hypothesis must be rejected. Even with the limited number of subjects involved, it could be established that the students click (significantly) more and therefore look up (significantly) more words in the marked condition.

Table 5 presents the total time spent reading in seconds per text and condition (normalised). Looking at table 5, one can see that readers seem to spend slightly more time on the marked texts than on the unmarked. The chi-square test with a .05 level of significance however, did not reveal this difference to be statistically different.

	Estimate	*S. Error*	*Prev. Estimate*	*Chi-square (1 df)*
Text 1 — marked condition (1)	2118	169.8	2118	
Text 1 — unmarked condition (2)	2096	160.1	2096	
Text 2 — marked condition (3)	2229	160.1	2229	
Text 2 — unmarked condition (4)	2136	169.8	2136	
				0.24

Table 5 — Total time spent on reading, in seconds per text and condition

It can be noticed that if looking at the real time spent reading (total reading time — total clicking-time), the unmarked condition scores slightly higher. This difference however, is not statistically different.

Summary and Discussion: Summarising the analysis of the results, one could formulate the following:

a) On the receptive vocabulary test, students score higher on the marked condition. When tested one week later, however, the results of the marked condition seem to have suffered a greater regression than the results of the unmarked.
b) The active vocabulary test, taken immediately after reading, seems to reveal no difference between the results of the marked or unmarked condition. When tested one week later, however, the marked condition again seems to have suffered a greater relapse than the unmarked.
c) Students seem to score higher on the comprehension test of the marked condition.
d) Students spend slightly more time on real reading in the unmarked condition (total reading time — total clicking-time).
e) Students click considerably more in the marked condition.

None of the differences from a) to d) are statistically different, but this is — more than probably — due to the limited number of subjects that was involved. Nevertheless, in our view, it seems interesting to examine more closely the direction these results seem to take. Moreover, we think that more than likely, the differences revealed would become statistically significant with a larger group of students. However, even with the group of 17 students that were involved in this experiment, it could be established with statistical certainty that students clicked considerably more in the marked condition e) — which confirms a part of the hypothesis that we formulated (hypothesis b), see above).

As for hypothesis a), we had postulated that the amount of vocabulary learned would be lower in the marked condition, starting from the idea that the reader would be incited to click too quickly. Therefore, the reader would pay less attention to contextual clues and the dictionary would no longer be a well-determined tool, but would become a goal in itself. Quite unexpectedly, the results of the tests seemed to be in favour of the marked condition. Can this phenomenon be explained?

Given the fact that the students click considerably more in the marked condition, we believe that the highlights of the texts must have drawn the attention in such a striking way, that students went from one clickable word to another (the logfiles also confirm this). What started as 'reading' has more than probably become 'clicking'. Consequently, one could ask whether in this condition the vocabulary learned is still 'incidental', a 'co-product' of the reading process. Instead of closely reading the text, students seem to have been incited to constantly look up the highlighted words and study them, almost as if they were listed and out of context. When going over the notes some students took, we also remark that when reading a marked text, the students write down more vocabulary than in the unmarked condition.[11] When these considerations are taken into account, it seems logical that students perform better on a vocabulary test taken right after reading.

The second test, however, brings on additional information that seems to be in favour of our hypothesis. These results in fact indicate that words out of the marked condition are less thoroughly retained than the ones distilled out of the unmarked text. The regression of the results of the marked condition is indeed greater for both vocabulary tests. In the unmarked condition, students only seem to consult words when contextual clues fail, and retention here seems to be more thorough. When reading an unmarked text, the students still seem to actually concentrate on 'reading'.

How did the students themselves experience both conditions? In the interviews, 15 out of 17 students actually affirmed that the blue highlights disturbed their reading in a very fundamental way. 15 out of 17 students declared to prefer the unmarked condition for reading but the marked one for vocabulary learning. One student even stated that 'for quickly learning some vocabulary, the marked condition was definitely better'.

Students themselves also delivered the answer on the question why scores on the comprehension test seem to be higher for the marked condition. Indeed, if there was more reading going on in the unmarked condition, it would be logical to deduce that comprehension would be lower in the marked condition. Considering the results, one can see that this was not the case. One student said that 'overlooking the blue highlights you could get a fairly good impression of the content of the text and therefore perform well on the comprehension test'. It is indeed so that in the comprehension test, only overall comprehension questions were taken into account. The results presented above are also overall results. An in-depth analysis of the results of the comprehension test is certainly in order. Looked at each question separately, and correlated to the clicking-behaviour, the results of the comprehension test could be put in perspective.

Conclusion: We have asked ourselves the question whether the at random highlighting of words — on the sole basis that these words are unknown to the learner — have an influence on incidental vocabulary learning during reading. We postulated the hypothesis that vocabulary learning would be lower in the marked condition, since students would fail to identify contextual clues. We also expected the students to click considerably more in the marked condition. An experiment was conducted with 17 students. This very limited number of subjects was expected to have its reflection on the statistical outcomes. This was indeed the case, but nevertheless, the results — more than probably significant with more students involved — do seem to indicate that reading in the marked condition is fundamentally different from reading an unmarked text.

---

[11] 5 out of 17 students took notes in both conditions.

The marked condition seems to draw attention to the unknown words and clearly incites students to consult every link presented. Within this condition, clicking almost seems to prime on reading and the vocabulary learned does not seem to be 'incidental' any more but almost 'intentional'.

The unmarked condition seems to incite students to concentrate more on reading. Words are only looked up when the context fails to deliver the correct meaning of unknown words. This seems to relate much more to reading as we know it and as it was involved in other experiments of incidental vocabulary learning and dictionary use. The vocabulary learned in this condition seems to be retained in a more thorough way.

Given the limited amount of students involved, further investigation is undoubtedly needed. A closer analysis of the present results is also a point to be put on the agenda. Further research can hopefully look into the cognitive processes that are behind this kind of reading in hypertext. Involvement of think-aloud protocols for instance, could be a plausible option.

In conclusion, we would like to draw the attention to the fact that when CALL introduces new technical possibilities, these should in fact be evaluated closely. Marking a text randomly for instance, might indeed, instead of helping the foreign language learners as it was intended, disturb their reading process in a fundamental way. What started as reading, might just as well become 'just following links'.

References:

Beck, I. & McKeown, M. (1991) 'Conditions of vocabulary acquisition', in R. Barr, M. L. Kamil & P. B. Mosenthal (eds), *Handbook of Reading Research. Volume II.* New York: Longman, pp.789-814.

Coady, J. (1997) 'L2 vocabulary acquisition through extensive reading', in J. Coady & Th. Huckin (eds), *Second Language Vocabulary Acquisition.* Cambridge: University Press, pp. 225-237

Davies, J. N. (1989) 'Facilitating effects of marginal glosses on foreign language reading', *Modern Language Journal* 73: 41-48.

Drum, P. A. & Konopak, B. C. (1987) 'Learning word meanings from written context', in M. G. McKeown & M. E. Curtis (eds.), *The nature of vocabulary acquisition.* Hillsdale, NJ: Erlbaum, pp. 73-87.

Dupuy, B. & Krashen, S. (1993) 'Incidental Vocabulary Acquisition in French as a Foreign Language', *Applied Language Learning* 4 (1&2): 55-63.

Ellis, R., Tanaka, Y. & Yamazaki, A. (1994) 'Classroom interaction, comprehension, and the acquisition of word meanings', *Language Learning*, 44 (3): 449-491.

Elshout-Mohr, M., van Daalen-Kapteijns, M. & van Oostendorp, H. (1999). 'A theoretical framework to synthesize research on cognitive processes in vocabulary acquisition', *Reading Research Quarterly* (in press).

Grabe, W. (1991) 'Current developments in second language reading research', *TESOL Quarterly,* 25: 375-406.

Hazenberg, S. & Hulstijn, J. H. (1996). 'Defining a minimal receptive second language vocabulary for non-native university students: An empirical investigation', *Applied linguistics,* 17: 145-163.

Huckin, Th. & Coady, J. (1996). 'Incidental vocabulary learning in a second language', paper given at the world conference on applied linguistics of 1996. Summary and translation into Dutch made by M. Goethals. Available: http://fuzzy.arts.kuleuven.ac.be/wvt/incident.htm.

Hulstijn, J. H. (1989). 'Implicit and incidental second language learning: Experiments in the processing of natural and partly artificial input', in H. W. Dechert & M. Rauchpack (eds), *Interlingual processess*, Tübingen: Gunter Narr, pp. 49-73

Hulstijn, J. H. (1992). 'Retention of inferred and given meanings: Experiments in incidental vocabulary learning', in P.J.L. Arnaud & H. Béjoint (eds), *Vocabulary and applied linguistics.* London: Macmillan, pp. 113-125

Hulstijn, J. H., Hollander, M. & Greidanus, T. (1996). 'Incidental vocabulary learning by advanced foreign language students: the influence of marginal glosses, dictionary use and reoccurence of unknown words', *Modern Language Journal,* 80 (3): 327-339.

Jacobs, G. M., Dufon, P. & Fong, C. H. (1994) 'L1 and L2 vocabulary glosses in L2 reading passages: Their effectiveness for increasing comprehension and vocabulary knowledge', *Journal of Research in Reading*, 17: 19-28.

Knight, S. (1994) 'Dictionary: the tool of last resort in foreign language reading? A new perspective', *The Modern Language Journal,* 78: 285-299.

Krantz, G. (1991) *Learning vocabulary in a foreign language: a study of reading strategies.* Göteborg: Acta Universitas Goteburghensis.

Nagy, W. E., Herman, P. A. & Anderson, R. C. (1985) 'Learning words from context', *Reading Research Quarterly*, 20: 233-253.

Nation, I.S.P. (1990) *Teaching and learning vocabulary.* New York: Newbury house.

Schmidt, R. (1994) 'Deconstructing consciousness in search of useful definitions for applied linguistics', *AILA Review*, 11: 11-26.

Sternberg, R. J & Powell, J. S. (1983) 'Comprehending verbal comprehension', *American Psychologist,* 38: 878-893.

Sternberg, R. J. (1987) 'Most vocabulary is learned from context', in M. G. McKeown & M. E. Curtis (eds.), *The nature of vocabulary acquisition.* Hillsdale, NJ: Erlbaum, pp. 89-105

West, R.F. & Stanovich, K.E. (1991) 'The incidental acquisition of information from reading', *Psychological science,* 2 (5): 325-329.

INITIATING LEARNER AUTONOMY WITH CALL

Joseph Dias
Kitasato University, Japan

Introduction: This paper reports on an on-going action research project in which ICT (Information and communication technology) was introduced into selected oral English classes (approx. 300 students in total). The students, attending a Japanese university specialising in health and animal sciences, were enrolled in a required English B course that has speaking and listening skills as its primary focus. A colleague, David Brooks, and I cooperated to develop a program that integrates email, internet-based activities and authoring software into a course that covers the functional language usually neglected during the first six years of formal English study in Japan. At the beginning and close of the academic year, students in classes that were exposed to ICT, and those in English B classes where teachers made no use of computers, were surveyed to determine their pervious experience with — and attitudes toward — ICT and language learning. Some of the results of the two surveys will be presented here.

We embarked on this project knowing that the time demands of the computer activities might prevent us from dealing with the range of functions and conversational strategies that we had covered in previous years. However, we felt that the ICT would allow us to deal with this narrower range at greater depth, in still higher levels of motivation, engage students in real world tasks, provide them with some additional useful skills, and, most importantly, help free them from a dependence on teachers for achieving language learning goals. The surveys showed mixed results, but participants in the ICT classes made greater effort to speak English with their classmates and teacher. They were also more likely to anticipate a need for English in their future lives.

How ICT was used: We chose computer activities partly on the basis of available software, which included, a web browser, HyperStudio (an authoring package similar to HyperCard but easier to use and capable of producing a more attractive final product) and word processing software. We wanted the computer activities to be useful for students in continuing their English study after the course ended and in their speciality-related courses. Goals for the CALL element of the course included:

* register for a web-based email account
* become comfortable using email
* join a class mailing list that would later be opened to students in other countries
* learn how to use the Internet to gather information

* employ the information in tasks — to be accomplished on the mailing list — that reinforce functions covered in the course book (inviting, negotiating plans, giving directions, etc.)
* create a HyperStudio Stack that integrates email experiences, personal information and a presentation of what interests them most in their major area of study [See Wachman (1999) for a comprehensive treatment of the use of authoring software to foster learner autonomy.]

Computers in Japanese education — still lagging but catching up: Holmes (1998) has noted the paradox that although Japan is a technologically advanced country it has been much slower than the West in introducing ICT into schools (p. 184). Computers were brought into schools as part of reforms proposed in the early 1980s that were intended to nurture a freer and more flexible educational system. Deep structural change proved impossible to achieve. The much criticised and demoralising system of entrance examinations has remained in place, however, the reforms calling for the education system to enter the information age and to internationalise received enough support to lead (then Prime Minister) Nakasone to create an advisory council that played a key role in introducing computers into schools (Sakamoto & Gardener, 1995).

The reforms have had a negligible effect on preparing university students for effectively using computers as tools. In our survey we found that 26.9 percent of freshmen respondents (out of 942 asked) had not used a computer for functions other than games before entering university. Few of those who had previous exposure to computers in schools had adequate typing skills or experience dealing with email or the Internet. So, in leaving it up to insufficiently trained teachers in individual schools to implement specific programmes, the policies of the Ministry of Education have led to an uneven and scanty introduction of ICT skills.

Cultural factors affecting Japanese students' reception of self-directed learning: In her article on autonomy and language learning, Healey (1999) notes:

> As teachers of individuals from a variety of cultures ... it behoves ESL/EFL professionals to keep in mind that learner self-direction and autonomous learning are Western concepts that fit smoothly into U.S. culture in particular. These concepts may not be as logical to others … . (p. 391)

In his groundbreaking work on the Japanese psyche (Doi, 1971), the psychiatrist Takeo Doi, relates an experience he had soon after he arrived in America to study psychiatry. Although he knew that Americans used the expression 'please help yourself' as a matter of kindness, it left an unpleasant ring in his ears. He understood that it meant 'please take what you want without hesitation', but he couldn't help but feel that the phrase implied 'if you don't help yourself, nobody else will'. He could not see how it came to be an expression of good will.

Instead of completely going against the cultural grain, we tried to channel classroom behaviour that many Western teachers (and quite a few Japanese) see as antithetical to autonomy, into constructive directions. For example, when asked a question by a teacher it is common for Japanese students — from elementary to university level — to turn to classmates sitting nearby and engage in a sometimes lengthy and animated discussion in Japanese about how the question can best be answered. This is not seen as abnormal behaviour and in my fifteen years of teaching in Japan I have never observed classmates chastise such students for wasting their time. It is seen as a natural part of the classroom experience. When this behaviour is suppressed by teachers who believe that students 'should stand on their own two feet', the result is frequently a standing statue, as silent as the Buddha.

In a computer classroom, the same behaviour that teachers have considered annoying, rude and counterproductive, can become efficient cooperative learning. For instance, if a student asks the teacher what might be preventing his email account application from being processed, the teacher might ask 'Did you fill out the zip code field?' (the most common reason for failure). If the student then engages classmates on either side of him with the questions 'Where is that field located?' and 'What does 'zip code' mean?' (which most students eventually are able to infer from the context) and 'Should I use my home or the university zip code?', the teacher is free to respond to other questions and students have, in a sense, helped themselves.

Structuring the ICT environment: Being aware that students might interpret our efforts to help them become more autonomous learners as an abandonment of our responsibilities as teachers and as a way to minimise contact with them, we carefully thought out how we would structure the ICT aspect of our course to minimise misunderstanding and the loss of motivation that might ensue. We fully concurred with Dickinson's (1987, p. 15) view that 'the promotion of self-direction encourages learners to make free choices, including the choice to follow a highly directed course'. We tried to accommodate various approaches to learning with the goal of bringing all students farther along the autonomy continuum. We did this by providing a variety of channels which students could attend to when accomplishing tasks. For example, when engaging in the rather complex processes of registering for an email account and joining a class mailing list, students were supported in the following ways:

* Detailed directions were handed out. [For Japanese students, accustomed to being hand fed knowledge that they are not expected to translate into action, it takes a great deal of self-direction to carry out instructions, particularly if they are written in English.]

* Teachers were present initially and students could freely ask them for assistance. [This mode was preferred by the majority of students and, as the focus of the course was speaking and listening skills, we didn't discourage it as long an attempt was made to use English.]
* Teachers identified areas that caused students most difficulty and instructed students in a jigsaw manner so they would have complementary knowledge they could share with others. [Students were not left to voluntarily teach classmates; they were told to stand up and go around the room teaching everyone else what they had just been taught.]

To someone unfamiliar with teaching environments in Japan, it might appear that this approach has little to do with encouraging self-direction and autonomy. It can even be argued that some of the procedures promote greater dependence on the teacher and classmates. Depending on the efforts of others to understand what we mean, and the responsibility for determining what we need to ask (or tell) in order to understand (or be understood), are taken for granted in the first language, but, when L2 is taught with little regard to its communicative qualities — as it is in Japan — these skills do not become established. As language learning and use is a social activity, and Japanese students have had little experience learning/using English for social purposes, it is necessary to set up situations in which communicating in the target language is perceived as being possible and even desirable. This was a necessary step in structuring the self-directed learning we hoped would follow.

Effects of the ICT environment on attitudes and behaviour: Referring to the results of our surveys, we will describe and try to account for changes we measured and observed in students' attitudes and behaviour. The survey was intended to determine students' preparedness for using computers and the effect of their use on attitudes, motivation and English usage.

Two surveys were administered; the first one, five or six weeks into the spring term (but before ICT was introduced), and the other at the end of the second term of the year-long course. Both surveys, which were translated into Japanese, offered 50 multiple choice items that could be answered on a computer mark card. Some of the items (those that used a four-point Likert Scale) were identical in the two surveys to help us examine whether measurable changes could be detected. The second survey mainly dealt with previous language learning experiences and computer use before and during the academic year. Three categories of students enrolled in the English B course were surveyed: those taught by Japanese teachers (without ICT — labelled 'Japanese Ts'), those taught by the present writer and an American colleague employing ICT (D/B — Dias and Brooks), and students taught by another American teacher who used a functional, conversational strategy-based text similar to the one we were using but made no use of ICT. The number of students surveyed in each of the categories and the average number of students per/class who responded are noted below:

	Japanese Ts (w/out ICT)	D/B(using ICT)	Other NS teacher(w/out ICT)
Total:	552	311	252
Ave # of Ss per/class:	34.5	38.88	31.5

[Total surveyed in the first survey: 1115 students]

The number of students in the three groups who completed the second survey were as follows:

	Japanese Ts (w/out ICT)	D/B(using ICT)	Other NS teacher(w/out ICT)
Total:	532	280	135
Ave # of Ss per/class:	33.25	35	33.75

[Total surveyed in the second survey 942 students]

One interesting finding was that whether students used ICT in their English class or not, those who used the Internet in the two groups showed similar usage patterns. 'Studying English' was dead last (or tied for last) in both groups. The results are summarised below:

Q) If you use the Internet, for what purpose do you use it? (multiple answers are possible)

	ICT Classes	Non ICT classes
private interest related	54.5	46.8
surfing (without purpose)	34.4	32.9
have not used the internet	20.1	30
class-related research	12.2	11.2
chatting	11.8	7.9
shopping or travel info	7.6	5.3
to study English	7.6	0.8

After going to great lengths to make it possible for students to have more contact with English by searching English web sites and using the language meaningfully in email exchanges, we were, at first, rather disheartened to find that our students ranked 'studying English' as low as students in classes where ICT was not used. How can this be explained? One optimistic possibility is that students were so unaccustomed to studying English in this way that they were reluctant to label it as 'English study'. As one of our stated goals was to increase learner autonomy, we are pleased that almost 9 percent more of our students used the Internet to pursue private interests. Of course, we would be more pleased if this was done in English. We plan to add an item to the next version of the survey to find out which of the activities were done in English. The finding that 20.1 percent of our students reported never having used the Internet is perplexing since we know that virtually all of them DID make use of it, at least, to sign up for an email account, join a mailing list and do various web-based activities. It is possible that these students did not realise they were on the Internet.

The most surprising and encouraging findings were that students in the ICT-supported classes reported making more effort to speak English with both classmates and their teacher. A summary of the data showing the frequency of English use with classmates in English B is as follows:

Q) In English B class I made an effort to speak English with *classmates.*

	D/B	Jpn	Other
always	17	1.5	1.5
sometimes	33	1.9	3
rarely	33	7.9	34.1
above 3 categories combined	83	11.3	38.6

The extraordinarily large difference in reported English usage between our students and those taught by Japanese teachers, can partially be explained by the tendency for Japanese teachers to rely on the grammar translation method even when teaching courses ostensibly concerned with oral/aural skills. They are also less likely to use English to conduct classroom business or in giving directions. However, the large difference between our students' reported use of English with classmates and that of students taught by the other foreign teacher cannot be explained in this way. The foreign teacher who did not employ ICT did pair and group work, and evaluated students' development of oral skills in private interviews more frequently than we did. One explanation for the striking differences is that they are partially the result of our 'jigsaw teaching', in which we taught individual students how to accomplish a task on the computer and then they were asked to teach it to the others in the class. Students were able to put the modelled English explanation to immediate use. This may have had the auxiliary effect of making them comfortable and confident enough in using English to make more of an effort to speak with classmates during pair and group activities in our classes that took place outside the computer lab.

In the case of speaking English with *the teacher,* the differences are even more striking between the ICT group and those taught without ICT by Japanese teachers, but there is a narrower difference between the ICT group and those taught by the other foreign teacher.

Q) In English B class I made an effort to speak English with my *teacher.*

	D/B	Jpn	Other
always	24.3	0.6	14.8
sometimes	38.5	2.1	31.9
rarely	32.6	11.1	40.7
above 3 categories combined	95.4	13.8	87.4

The larger percentages in the 'D/B' and 'Other' categories (compared with the 'speaking English with classmates' item) can be explained partly by the fact that students feel a greater need to speak English with an English native speaker teacher than with their Japanese counterparts. Although the difference in combined frequency levels between 'D/B' and 'Other' is only 8 percent, almost 10 percent more of the ICT-supported students report *always* using English with their teacher. We believe this is due to increased need created by the ICT tasks to seek clarification and receive help when things went wrong.

Another difference between the ICT-supported and non ICT-supported groups was that higher percentages of the former saw a need for English for a variety of purposes in their future life. The results are summarised as follows:

Q) In your future life and work in what situations do you think English will be necessary?

	D/B	Jpn	Other
to understand & communicate w/ foreigners	62.8	53.2	45.2
for travel	55.6	40.8	37
to write reports and theses in English	42	39.7	33.3
to read newspapers, magazines, etc.	41.3	36.1	29.6
to use the Internet	28.8	20.3	19.3
to be able to understand films & other media	27.1	19.9	13.3
to write email in English	23.6	14.7	13.3

Interestingly, the *order* of perceived importance of English uses is constant in the three groups; they differ only in *magnitude*. We were pleased with this result in that we felt that perceived need would be tied to motivation and lead to a greater likelihood that English study will be continued after the completion of required courses (one of our principal project goals).

A behaviour that we may have inadvertently encouraged with our ICT-supported students was the teaching of students from *other* classes how to sign up for web-based email accounts and use the Internet. Outside of class time we frequently observed our students in the computer lab giving impromptu 'lessons' to friends from other classes.

This may explain an odd anomaly in our data. When asked what they thought about the statement: 'Computers cannot help to improve one's ability to communicate in English?' percentages of those who 'disagreed' or 'disagreed strongly' are noted below.

First semester results
(before ICT activities)
% of Ss who *dis*agreed

D/B	Jpn	Other NS T
61.6	49.8	52.8

Second semester results
(after ICT activities)
% of Ss who *dis*agreed

D/B	Jpn	Other NS T
75.4	67.4	74.8

Jump from First to Second survey	
D/B:	13.8
Jpn:	17.6
Other NS T:	22

A higher percentage of our students felt that computers could help in improving English communication skills both before and after the ICT activities were introduced. The most striking feature of the results, however, is the fact that non-ICT classes made more dramatic gains from the first to the second semester in positively regarding the role of computers in English education. Why should students who had no exposure to computers for language learning purposes show so much greater gains? The only explanation that is consistent with our observations is that the unprompted teaching our students gave to their friends in the non-ICT classes gave the recipients a feeling for the potential for ICT in language learning. So much so that they came to (at least in the case of the students taught by the other NS) value it nearly as highly as our students. Another possibility, which is not mutually exclusive with the first, is that students in non-ICT classes who did not receive exposure to computers through friends, may have been influenced into thinking that ICT might have a lot to offer language learners by hearing about the experiences of those doing the CALL activities. The 'grass is greener' phenomenon might have been at work.

Conclusion: It is not possible to say that the ICT-supported course led students to be autonomous learners in any absolute way. However, these students did report greater amounts of English usage with classmates and teachers. From our observations, we speculate that the jigsaw presentation of ICT tasks and the necessity for students to acquire skills and knowledge to complete tasks led to more English being spoken. In addition to teaching their newly acquired skills to classmates some of the ICT students shared their knowledge with students from other classes. We hope to measure and more closely observe this unprompted teaching in our on-going study. To be a teacher is perhaps the ultimate in autonomy and we hope to encourage such behaviour as much as possible.

References:

Dickinson, L. (1987). *Self-instruction in Language Learning.* Cambridge: Cambridge University Press.
Doi, T. (1971). *The Anatomy of Dependence.* (translated by John Bester) Tokyo: Kodansha International Ltd.
Good, T. L., & Brophy, J. E. (1987) *Looking in Classrooms.* New York: Harper & Row.
Healey, D. (1999). Theory and Research: Autonomy in Language Learning. In J. Egbert & E. Hanson-Smith. (eds), *CALL Environments: Research, Practice, and Critical Issues.* Alexandria (Virginia): Teachers of English to Speakers of Other Languages, Inc., pp. 391-402.
Holmes, B. (1998). From Black Ships to Microchips: The Arrival of ICT in Japan. In P. Lewis (ed.), *Teachers, Learners, and Computers: Exploring Relationships in CALL.* Nagoya: The Japan Association for Language Teaching Computer-Assisted Language Learning National Special Interest Group, pp. 181-187.
Sakamoto, T., & Gardener, J. (1995). Informatics in teacher education in Japan. *Journal of Computer Assisted Learning* 11: 35-39.
Wachman, R. (1999). Classroom Practice: Autonomy Through Authoring Software. In J. Egbert & E. Hanson-Smith. (eds), *CALL Environments: Research, Practice, and Critical Issues.* Alexandria (Virginia): Teachers of English to Speakers of Other Languages, Inc., pp. 403-426.

LEARNING ENGLISH ON THE WEB WITHIN A GLOBAL EAP COMMUNITY

Marina Dodigovic and Piphawin Suphawat
Macquarie University

Abstract:

With the advent of Internet, the concept of community began undergoing a radical change. Whereas in pre-Internet times a community was usually defined as a group of people pursuing common interests in a geographically restricted area, nowadays this restraint is being lifted. Thus the whole world seems to be amalgamating into the global village. At Macquarie University there used to be an EAP community, restricted to the first year Macquarie University on-campus students. With the development of the new Web tutor of EAP (English for Academic Purposes) this concept will grow to include off-campus, very often also off-shore students, whose learning purposes will not always be the same either. Some of them will be full time or part time students of institutions overseas, bringing in their very special needs into the learning environment. It is hoped that the flexibility of the Web as a medium will allow for successful learning in a heterogeneous EAP community. This paper will discuss the process of curriculum development and evaluation under the above circumstances.

Introduction: The Macquarie Dictionary defines *community* as 'a social group of any size whose members reside in a specific locality, share government and have a cultural heritage'. A new type of locality is increasingly emerging as a defining criterion for a new type of community. The locality is called cyberspace. It is governed more or less by its own rules, successfully defying in particular the trade barriers otherwise effective in the actual space. It may be still somewhat early to talk about the cultural heritage of the Internet, but it is easily foreseeable that this invention is likely to have a global impact on every aspect of human lives. To name just one, the Internet has already given rise to a new breed of language learners who might be living in Hong Kong, studying in Sydney per email, conversing with dozens of people around the globe in virtual space and learning German off the Web. Such is a representative of a new community of learners being generated by the new technologies.

This change will have a lasting effect on the way courses are designed and developed in general. In most instances of needs analysis, it is assumed that the learning population will live within reasonable distance of the provider, and will therefore be able to attend the classes. Thus, a large number of courses are developed relying on the audio-visual potential of the venue itself and the participants. It is true that the notion of programmed learning, and later CALL, brought about an increased awareness of the need to create the learning context rather than taking it for granted. However, CALL and traditional classroom learning went their separate ways. It was not until the advent of the Internet (Geoghegan 1997) that the boundaries between the two started to blur.

Recently, many courses have become offered both on campus and on the Web. When developing such courses, the author suddenly starts facing restraints which were not there when the courses were offered in the on-campus mode only. Thus, new copyright laws for electronic media will strongly restrict the range of documents to be available on the web. Furthermore, the potential variety of client machines will impose restrictions on Web page design. In addition, a discussion component needs to be added to make room for human-human interaction on the Web. On the other hand, the type of interactivity characteristic for CALL will influence the course materials even when delivered in the classroom. To begin with, the needs analysis becomes a more difficult task, simply for the fact that it is not easy to define the target population. Also, computer literacy and motivation to use the computer for learning purposes have to be investigated, no matter what subject the course is in. Accordingly, this paper will explore the effects of the Web-induced learner community on the development of a course in English for Academic Purposes (EAP) to be offered both on-campus and on the Web. It will focus on the stages of needs analysis, document selection, interactive tasks and Web page design.

Needs analysis: Research in CALL can both precede and follow software development (Dodigovic 1998). When it happens before the development, it is mostly some form of needs analysis. Unfortunately, this kind of research is slightly looked down upon by the CALL establishment. The publishers will often call it 'unfinished', which is very unfortunate. In a community as diversified as the Internet users, it is extremely important to understand the needs of potential program users.

Preceding the development of the EAP tutor, a survey was conducted with the aim to find out more about students' needs for a computerised EAP classroom. The questions asked of students were about their needs in terms of communicative skills (reading, writing, listening, speaking), preferred academic genres, acceptable learning styles and computer literacy as well as motivation for learning EAP with computers. The survey included all NESB (Non-English speaking background) students enrolled in EAP in the second half of 1998 and was conducted by Piphawin Suphawat, a postgraduate student in Linguistics. Some of the research goals were to find out whether the students would be interested in pursuing this subject on the Web, and if so, how their computer skills and preferred learning styles could be matched.

It is important that the development of CALL materials provides an adequate response to the students' learning styles. It is clear from the survey that the students' preferred learning style is communicative (Nunan 1991). Communicative language teaching specifically focuses on enhancing students' autonomy and control over the language learning process. Therefore, obviously this particular group of students is more likely to employ the computer integrated into English language class successfully because computers provide students with an excellent opportunity for control and initiative. For instance email seems to free the students from time and distance restraints. By using it, they are able to initiate discussions with teachers or other students any time from a number of places, thus bringing about a greatly increased student-teacher interaction (Warschuaer, Turbee & Roberts 1994). The result is greater student enthusiasm, initiative, and personal communication (Paramskas 1993).

The students' learning strategies were investigated first. It was revealing to identify the communicative learning style as the preferred one.

Table 1: Communicative learning style

Question	Percentage
Q4. I like to learn by conversations.	57.78%
Q12. I like to learn by talking to friends in English.	55.56%
Q11. At home, I like to learn by watching TV in English.	37.78%

Table 2: Concrete learning style

Question	Percentage
Q5. I like to learn English by talking in pairs.	24.44%
Q3. I like to learn by playing games.	15.56%
Q2. I like to listen and use cassettes.	13.33%

Table 3: Authority-oriented learning style

Question	Percentage
Q1. I like to learn by reading.	22.22%
Q6. I like to have my own textbooks.	20.00%
Q7. I like the teacher to explain everything to us.	13.33%

Table 4: Analytical learning style

Question	Percentage
Q9. I like the teacher to let me find my mistakes.	40.00%
Q10. I like to study grammar.	20.00%
Q8. I like the teacher to give us problems to work on.	17.78%

From the above it is clear that communicative learning style was the generally preferred one, 50.37%, and there was quite a large gap between this one and the second rated, analytical style, 25.93%.

Table 5: Learning styles preferred by EAP students

Question	Percentage
Communicative style	50.37%
Analytic style	25.93%
Authority-oriented style	18.52%
Concrete style	17.78%

All students seemed to be highly motivated to use the computer to learn EAP. The length of exposure to CALL or even general computer literacy did not seem to be a major factor in their motivation. Thus it was to be expected that a computer based tutor of academic English, especially the one delivered on the Web, for which the students had a high preference, would provide the best answer to their communicative needs and indicated learning styles.

Computer literacy
Students were asked to indicate at what level their computer literacy and their typing skills are. Both categories were rated as good, 44.44%. In addition, 84.44% of the students used computer before attending this university course and the majority of students used it for their studies, 63.64%. Interestingly, 75.56% of the students had their own computers and 41.94% of them had computers for more than three years.

Computer activities
Table 6: Computer activities that students had previously engaged in

Activities	Percentage
Word Processing	75.56%
Email	68.89%
World Wide Web	62.22%
Spreadsheets	22.22%
Computer Games	22.22%
On-line Chat	22.22%
Graphics	15.56%
Database	11.11%
VDO Conferencing	2.22%

From the above it appears that the largest proportion of computer activities that the students had engaged in were Word Processing, Email, and then World Wide Web, 75.56%, 68.89% and 62.22% consecutively. This is consistent with some previous surveys (Geoghegan 1997)

Computer-assisted language learning
It was obvious from the survey that 42.22% of the students knew how to use a computer to help them learn English. 45.45% of them revealed that using the computer makes

learning English more interesting, and computer programs are useful, 56.25%, and useful to their studies, 36.67%. In addition, 54.54% of them indicated that they would enjoy learning a language by using computer.

35.56% of the respondents indicated that they used computer help learning a language before and the activities which were used often were 'Word Processing' 23.63%, 'Spelling Exercises' 21.81% and 'Multiple-choice Exercises' 10.91%. The reasons that the students used Word processing were:

- It gives a neat and tidy result. Indeed, there is spell and grammar check.
- Because I can edit my essay much more freely by using word processing.

For Spelling Exercises, the respondents commented that it was:

- Necessary for job purposes. If a person has poor spelling or vocabulary skills, these exercises will help learning.
- Very useful to help us to correct our writing or write in a proper way.
- Help me to revise the spelling which I maybe often spell it wrong.

Additionally, for Multiple-choice Exercises the respondents pointed out that 'it is a relaxing activity which does not take too much time', and 'more practical than solely reading, more participation and active'.

CALL approaches

According to the survey questions, 67.74% of the respondents indicated that they preferred to choose their own computer activities, practise something they have learned, and write English by using computers. When they do not understand a computer activity, 42.86 % of the students want teachers to help, 26.19 % need help from friends, and 21.43% stated that the computer is the only thing they need. Moreover, 61.54% of them preferred to work alone on the computer, 17.95% want to work with teachers, and 10.26% want to work in pairs or in a group.

Motivation

Motivation to use computers was the next variable examined. It appears that all students were highly motivated to use computers to learn EAP.

Table 7: Questions with highest mean scores

	Mean
Learning how to use computers is important for my career.	4.461
An advantage of email is you can contact people any time you want.	4.316
I learn much better when I have fun.	4.131
I enjoy using the computer to communicate with people around the world.	4.079
I enjoy seeing the things I write printed out.	4.051
Revising my papers is a lot easier when I write them on the computer.	4.026

As can be seen from Table 7, the most significant positive response, at a mean of 4.461, was 'Learning how to use computers is important for my career'. The second most popular option was 'An advantage of email is you can contact people any time you want', at a mean of 4.316.

From the survey, the mean motivation for all students for 22 questions of motivation was 3.707, which was significantly higher than a hypothetical neutral score. Moreover, 21 out of 22 questions were considerably higher than neutral.

Subsequently, motivation was gauged according to gender and access to computer at home.

Table 8: Mean motivation score by gender and access to computer at home

Group	Number	Percent	Motivation
Females			
With computer at home	18	90%	3.466
Without computer at home	2	10%	3.377
Total	20	100%	3.422
Males			
With computer at home	8	61.54%	3.472
Without computer at home	5	38.46%	3.327
Total	13	100%	3.399

Although not significant, Table 8 shows the students with access to computer at home had a more positive attitude toward CALL than the students without a computer at home. Moreover, it is interesting that the female students had a more positive view of CALL than the male students. However, all students, both female and male, with and without a computer at home, scored considerably higher than expected.

Table 9: Mean motivation score by major course of study

Major course study	Number	Percent	Motivation
Science	6	16.22%	3.468
Business	20	54.05%	3.363

Arts	11	29.73%	3.453
Total	37	100%	3.428

It is obvious that Science students, including Computer, Biological and Behavioural sciences, were somewhat better motivated than the students from other majors. In addition, it is a surprise to discover that Arts students, including Modern Languages, Linguistics, Education and Media, had higher motivation than Business students.

The following section presents the analysis of three personal background aspects in order to evaluate the differences. It includes computer literacy, length of owning a computer, and typing skills.

Surprisingly, there were hardly any significant results that would lend themselves to the conclusion that if computer literacy, length of owning a computer and typing skills were rated high, then the students' attitudes in using the computer in learning a language would be positive.

It would be reasonable to suppose that the small number of subjects caused such inconclusive results. However, as the sampling subjects were EAP students who normally have learning expectations different from other students. These students rarely have time away from their study, therefore even if the research survey had been received from a greater number of students, the results may have still been the same. This may also imply that the students are uncertain of the outcomes of the use of computers in language learning, or simply their lack of knowledge in this regard.

Document selection: While the needs analysis shows that using a computer is a popular way to learn EAP, which is very encouraging, the document selection process for a Web course development can drive the author to despair. The copyrights for electronic media are even stricter than those for photocopying. While it was possible to photocopy one chapter or 10% of a book for educational purposes without the explicit permission of the copyrights owner, on the Web nothing of the sort is allowed. Thus, the developer has the following options: a) write his or her own texts, which is not always profitable in terms of trying to teach the student a variety of styles; b) purchase the right to reproduce the original, which can be costly, especially for educational institutions; c) embedding a link to the texts already published on the Web. The latter, of course, has to be done without bypassing the home page for the target site.

Some of the challenges of embedding interactive links to other Web sites are a constant need to update the links due to the flexible and ever changing nature of the Web and the writing style on the Web which has its own distinctive features. It appears relatively easy to search the Web for appropriate topics, much more so than it is to search the periodicals in a library. However, it is not always easy to find texts at an appropriate level of difficulty. Very often, the level would be one of the extremes — either too popular or too scholarly. In academic English, needless to say, popular texts are to be avoided. Believing that the subject of flexible learning would be interesting to our students, we searched the Web and found an abundance of really scholarly materials on the subject. However, the students later complained that the texts were too difficult. This was confirmed in their own essays on the topic, from which it was obvious that the sources were far from understood. Another problem with Web based texts is that they can be removed any time. This has happened once or twice in the middle of a class, and can be a very humiliating experience to go through.

Finding authors, possibly friends, who would make their texts available at little or no cost is an ideal solution. Thus the text becomes a part of the Web sites it goes with. Parts of it can be copied for analysis, without having to count words every time. Such texts do not disappear at unexpected times, they are always there.

Interactive tasks: Communicative language learning, which is particularly promoted within the constructivist theory of leaning, will place a great emphasis on communication and interactive tasks. Indeed, the communicative learning style seemed to be preferred by the learning population as well. Email and various types of conferencing programs provide ample opportunities for communication. However, with a global community in mind, where local time differences can impair synchronous chats, email and bulletin boards will prevail. This type of interaction, which is actually computer facilitated human-human interaction, though serving an excellent purpose, can be very demanding on the teacher and rather labour intensive. Another type of interaction is human-computer interaction. It is the type of activity that would allow the teacher to become a coach encouraging the student to engage in the process of autonomous learning.

The former is rather structure free and can rely on ready-made email and conferencing packages, which nowadays come at low cost. It however places a demand on the teacher to plan, initiate discussion, reply to most individual messages. Considering the fact that every reply made by the teacher will remain documented in writing, the need for accuracy and objectivity is higher than ever.

The latter interactivity, which develops between the student and the computer, requires careful planning only in the development phase. Once the program has been coded, it is just a matter of making the student aware of its existence. It can tirelessly provide feedback to any attempt of the student to use language or make decisions about the correct use of language. The limitations are, of course, set by the scope of the program, but the advantage, especially with the Web, lies in the large number of interactive programs covering a wide range of topics available on the Web. Links to such sites can be easily embedded in one's own program. These links do not constitute a breech of copyright laws.

Logically, the above demands called for the following materials structure: 1) hypertext course notes which would allow the student both free browsing and guided progress, 2) interactive tasks, 3) grammar and vocabulary tests 4) electronic essay marking aid involving e-mail and word processing, combined with routines for semi-automatic comment and exercise generation, and finally 5) access to language corpora to learn, hypothesise about language and verify one's own hypotheses.

1. The hypertext course notes are mainly text, including graphics, animation and audio, with hypertext links between the lecture notes and a number of external resources, including CD-ROM multimedia dictionaries, concordancing software, pronunciation aids or simply external Web sites.
2. The interactive tasks are closely related to concepts explained in the notes, thus providing individualised feedback within a learner centered approach. This module contains some added value: a parser, an intelligent interface capable of analysing student sentences for grammatical correctness.
3. Grammar and vocabulary tests are automatic assessment tools designed to free up the lecturer for more creative tasks, like research or a more individualised approach to teaching.
4. Essay marking aid provides the means for delivering feedback in a more efficient way. Based on previous research, student errors will be classified into several distinctive groups. Providing comment on them is possible by choosing an appropriate sentence from the database on the click of a button. It is also possible to associate exercises in the areas where individual students seem to have problems.
5. The academic language research tool enables the user to search for examples of use of a particular word in a body of academic writing (concordancing). The search results in a list of occurrences of that word in different types of linguistic context, which gives the user an idea of many different ways to use this vocabulary item or even a grammar category.

All modules are interconnected via hypertext links and can be used for tutorial or exploratory learning. The teaching methods implemented are what is known in the theory of computer assisted language learning (CALL) as *tutorial* and *non-tutorial.* The *tutorial* method involves the provision of explicit guidance, as if the students were working under the close supervision of a tutor. *Non-tutorial* refers to the exploratory mode of learning where the students are free to browse through the materials at their own pace as well as in the order of their preference (Higgins 1988).

This facility is designed to serve a number of students on campus or in the distance mode. To have their 'grammar checked', the students won't have to wait until their assignments are corrected and even then see the tutor for more feedback. Instead, they will be able to parse their sentences for grammatical correctness before putting them on paper. The program will, on repeated failure to construct grammatical sentence, offer a tutorial on relevant grammar categories. This makes the Macquarie University EAP courses extremely flexible and easily integrated into the distance program of any university worldwide.

Conclusion: The effects of the above design will inevitably affect the structure of the activities in the classroom, whereby the objective is to keep the classroom and the Web based tutorials similar. As the activities on the Web will mostly constitute objectively assessable tasks like ordering sentences, slightly paraphrasing texts, identifying stages in text development etc., the same will be done in the classroom as a group activity, where the feedback will come both from peers and the teacher. This will not exclude the much favoured discussion from the classroom. It will rather focus it on linguistic and textlinguistic issues.

Thus, the global community will influence and change the way teaching and learning is done in the classroom. As publishing on the Web becomes more prominent, the source texts will also increasingly come from the Web. As a result of greater sophistication, individual learner needs will be much better catered for, provided that bad practices from the classroom do not infest software design, but rather the opposite happens.

References:

Dodigovic, M. (1998) 'Elements of Research in CALL Development Projects', *CALICO Journal*, 15 (4), 25-38.
Geoghegan, W. (1997) 'Instructional technology and the mainstream: The risk of success'. In Oblinger, D. & Rush, C. (eds.) *The Future compatible campus*, Bolton: Anker Publishing.
Higgins, J. (1988) *Language, Learners and Computers*, London: Longman.
Nunan, D. (1991) *Language Technology Mehodology: A Textbook for Teachers, Prentice Hall*, London
Paramskas, D (1993) 'Computer Assisted Language Learning (CALL): Increasingly into even more Electronic World', The Canadian Modern Language Review, (50)1, p.124-143.
Warschauer, M., Turbee, M. Roberts, M. (1994) *Computer Learning Networks and Student Empowerment*, National Foreign Language Resource Centre, Second Language Teaching and Curriculum Centre.

EMPOWERING STUDENT LEARNING IN CYBERSPACE THROUGH CALL

Randall P. Donaldson
Loyola College, Maryland, USA

I. Introduction: In recent years there has been growing recognition of the importance of a four-skills approach to language learning in combination with an integrated approach to the culture of the area(s) in which the target language is spoken. In the States at least this shift in emphasis has given rise to the communicative approach, which takes its place in the pantheon of acceptable methods of foreign language teaching methodologies, supplanting — at least theoretically — the explicit teaching of grammar. Nonetheless, most of us find it difficult, if not impossible, to orchestrate classroom sessions which are both culturally and linguistically authentic yet pedagogically effective. Promoting natural communication is a laudable goal but not one easily achieved in the fifty-minute time frame which is typical in an American college or university. The result is too often a kind of low-grade Berlitz, where saying anything is emphasised over saying something meaningful.

Those of us interested in and/or fascinated by the computer have, of course, been exploring ways in which that technology can be employed to make language learning more effective and motivating for students. Some of us have dared to hope that CALL might compensate for the time deficit by extending both instructional — and learning — activities beyond the normal class period. As technology has improved, the possibility of making any encounter with a machine or a machine-driven exercise a truly authentic and communicative experience seems both real and realistic even as it hovers just beyond our grasp. But the instructor dedicated to employing the latest technology in a truly effective fashion must find a way to realise the potential of recent innovations in a way which makes their relevance immediately apparent to the learner and encourages further exploration.

Unfortunately despite the very real promise of computer technology in language teaching the hype surrounding CALL understates the difficulty of implementing CALL in a fashion which is both time- and cost-effective. Particularly in a small to medium-sized liberal-arts college such as mine one needs to recognise the constraints. We are finally paid to teach, and hours spent on program development may not even be recognised in an annual review of performance. Moreover, the monies for large-scale projects are just not there. We need to fall back on pre-packaged programs. Yet even most authoring programs require a considerable investment of time upfront. And, if one is willing to spend the time, the result is more likely to be a very good ten-minute exercise rather than a well-articulated course. We need a middle ground — a technical device with a gentle and short learning curve which promotes authentic communication in a relatively natural setting and which can be incorporated into the regular syllabus with a minimum of fuss.

II. The Experiment: From January to May 1998, a colleague and I undertook a joint project in teaching intermediate language which from my vantage point held great promise as a potential answer to some of the problems I've just posed. The details of that undertaking are available in two separate articles, one in the June issue of the *CALICO Journal* and one in the April issue of *Linguistic and Literary Computing* so I won't expound upon the project at any length here. Rather I want to examine a few of the insights which grew out of the initial project and suggest possible ways of capitalising on the lessons learned. As to the project, let me simply say that we had several objectives in mind. We wanted to provide a framework within which a learner could practice his or her foreign language skills in conversation with native speakers of the target language, thereby creating an opportunity for communication in the target language which was at once both authentic and realistic. We wanted those conversations to be freewheeling, unstructured conversations in which the participants have the ability to set the agenda. Nonetheless, we hoped to provide the impetus to advance the conversation beyond simple chatting to purposeful communication leading to the completion of specific tasks.

The venue for the initial experiment was a MOO. I'm going to assume that I need not preach to the choir with this group and that hence MOOs need little introduction. I will note, however, the importance of MOOs as the location of choice for our venture. Whatever else they might offer MOOs are fundamentally textual space. As Turkle has suggested, words constitute the reality which one inhabits in a MOO, 'it is landscape, and it is momentarily frozen speech' (x). Additionally, encounters in a MOO take place in real time, and a MOO advances the concept of a chat program.[1] One does not have to wait an hour or a day for a response to an inquiry as can happen with electronic mail. Moreover, the user can personalise the virtual space in which encounters take place, thus establishing a more intimate relationship to MOO-space than one would have to a chat room.

We were struck as well by the fact that although MOOs have certainly been the focus of any number of teaching enterprises, the potential of a MOO to reform our paradigms for teaching and learning has been largely untested.[2] Yet instruction in a MOO is perforce different from instruction in a traditional classroom if for no other reason than that a

---

[1] For a complete 'history' of the MOO, see, for example, Curtis (1998).

[2] Tari Fanderclai noted with disappointment in 1995, there have been few, if any, attempts to realise the potential of text-based, object-oriented virtual realities such as MUDs and MOOs in liberating the learner from the 'classic' conception of a classroom and hence reformulating the normal paradigms for student-teacher interaction. Of particular interest here is Fanderclai's complaint that most, if not all, of the instruction in MOOs which has been documented does little more than transfer the paradigms of normal teacher/pupil interaction in the classroom into cyberspace, which of course fails to recognise or capitalise on the unique possibilities which the MOO holds in store as a learning environment.

MOO, for all its capabilities, is a textual space. Its very nature is determined by text. Langham (1994) has a particularly interesting discussion on the verisimilitude of a virtual reality, noting that '…the 'realism' of virtual reality systems is not a product of how well they mirror the 'real' world, but rather the extent to which they create structures that allow for a sense of a routinised existence, a sense of fixity we generally associate with ordinary, repeated, commonplace behaviour'. In the context of the current discussion the degree to which a given virtual reality emulates everyday reality in its effect on participants will have a decided effect on the sense of community which develops and hence the level of authenticity in any exchange. That fact alone demands that an instructor rethink the paradigms of student/teacher interaction and that learners readjust their perceptions of classroom participation.

The project consisted of two groups: one a class of American college students in their fourth semester of German language study; the other adults in Germany ranging in age from early twenties to mid-sixties who were enrolled in a evening-school class for intermediate English. The groups met in a MOO for two hours once a week. After a few initial sessions, the larger groups were broken down into pairs, with one partner on each side of the Atlantic. Each partner team was asked to pick a topic of general interest from a list which was available to all participants or to generate a topic of common interest to the team members. In general the topics were meant to inspire discussion about the stereotypes or misconceptions which the home culture of one team member might have about that of the other and visa-versa. One example might be the prevalence of smoking in each culture or its status as a socially acceptable behaviour. Over the course of several meetings each team was to discuss the topics previously agreed upon and develop a series of conclusions and observations to present to the entire group in the final session. The events as they unfolded were fascinating, and the implications for language learning many; but I want to focus on one in particular.

III. The Results: The most tangible result of the regular meetings in the MOO was a growing sense of commitment to and responsibility for the agenda for each successive meeting on the part of the participants. Relationships developed between partners in the various pairs, and a genuine sense of community arose within and among the various groups. Partners summarised the activities of the current session, planned for the next meeting, and generally assumed responsibility for the on-going process. Despite often rather notable differences in age, background, or language ability, partners showed real concern for the learning of their counterparts. The conversations in the various groups were very natural and animated. Language learning in the MOO took on the flavour of an authentic everyday experience.

Most significantly, participants reported (and evinced) a marked increase in interest and, hence, motivation as a result of having a weekly appointment with their counterpart across the Atlantic. Almost everyone was excited by the prospect of becoming acquainted with the genuine 'expert' in the everyday usage of the language he or she was studying. The opportunity for relatively spontaneous, 'real-time' conversation with a native informant had undeniable appeal. It seemed as well that the ability to create personal spaces to which a given team could withdraw influenced both the nature and the intensity of the relationship which each team established. It was manifestly clear that motivation and commitment to the task increased in the course of the undertaking, and no pedagogue could gainsay the beneficial influence such elements exercise in a successful learning experience. Yet the very success of the undertaking in developing strong, supportive partnerships had a somewhat more problematic aspect.

IV. The Implications: The success of the tandem partnerships was so pronounced that the presence of a 'teacher' in the weekly on-line discussion, even in the role of consultant or mentor, was seen as an unwelcome intrusion. We therefore sought ways to influence the on-going process without disrupting the natural flow of conversation. In large part those techniques, such as communicating by e-mail between sessions, allowed us to guide the process without interrupting successful dialogues in the MOO. However, when it became apparent that most participants were not always capable on their own of capturing, organising, and retaining the advice and information which a partner offered in a useful and effective fashion, it proved more difficult to provide guidance without diminishing the positive effects of the spontaneous and natural conversations which the MOO has fostered. And yet the groups did need guidance. There were other goals to be achieved beyond simple conversation, as gratifying as the success of those efforts might have been. As instructors (and teachers even though closeted) we wondered to what degree the participants were making measurable progress in language learning or deepening their cultural awareness and whether the MOO experience would enhance retention of any items learned. It became apparent that any guidance would have to be subtle and would have to take place outside the group sessions.

Fortunately, the initial list of possible projects was well-crafted and provided guidelines for conversation without forcing a given strand of conversation unnecessarily. But the move from conversation to a 'project', a summary or set of conclusions drawn from the weekly discussions, proved difficult. Of course, the fault did not lie with the MOO or even necessarily with the ability of the participants to learn another language. Even in L1 many had difficulty organising the often random observations and comments of a conversation into a coherent and logical whole. But in L2 those difficulties were magnified many times over, and lack of vocabulary was a particular concern. Given these problems, we finally dispensed with the requirement of presenting a finished project. Rather, the American students had to select, annotate and submit a certain number of logs as part of their grade while the German students had the chance to highlight and to discuss specific linguistic pitfalls amongst themselves and with their teacher in two more sessions after the end of the joint project. That experience made it clear, however, that even if the teacher qua teacher was superannuated in conversations within the MOO there was an urgent need for a trained pedagogue to help the learner solidify and retain the knowledge gained during encounters in the MOO.

V. A Final Suggestion: Tari Fanderclai (1995) notes in the paper I have already cited that 'a MUD[3] is not an environment that can be controlled; to use MUDs effectively, educators must replace control with structure'. Our experience bears out those remarks emphatically. The role for the teacher has changed drastically in the context of the new media, yet the need for someone to structure the learning situation so that the learners derive maximum benefit from the experience is, if anything, even greater. In retrospect we were largely successful in guiding the participants through a rewarding learning experience. The primary aim of proving the efficacy of a MOO as a venue for language learning in tandem was accomplished. Yet it was obvious that there was a need to structure the whole by adding assignments outside the MOO after each session which would provide the learners with the opportunity to reflect on the learning process which had just taken place. As Rosanne Potter notes in commenting on the issues raised by a special number of Computers and the Humanities on computers and the teaching of literature (1996:187): 'My own practice in the computer lab convinces me that there should always be time for and a requirement that students sum up their computer-mediated learning experience right after they have it'.

In conclusion I would like to suggest but one possible untapped possibility. The client which we used to connect to the MOO allowed the user to log each session in the MOO and save it to a text file. Working with and revising the logs, perhaps even editing them into finished essays in an extension of the methods I have already noted is an attractive option, but one immediately encounters many of the difficulties implicit in everything I've been discussing. On the one hand, a MOO demands structure of a new type which allows the learner a certain level of autonomy and creativity in the learning process yet permits the teacher/mentor to shape and encourage the insights which promote the acquisition of knowledge which endures. On the other hand, an instructor is often faced with the difficulties I noted in my introduction. There is not enough time or resources to develop a program from scratch, and authoring programs may not be flexible enough for all situations. I have, however, found a solution which I believe will work. In a blatant paraphrase of one of the earlier scenes of The Graduate, let me say that I have just one word for you — not 'plastics' but 'Storyspace'. Storyspace bills itself as a 'hypertext writing environment'. It is available from Eastgate in Cambridge, Massachusetts, in both PC and Mac versions and has been used in certain instructional contexts, particularly writing classes, extensively. To my knowledge, however, it has not been used in language instruction. Yet the potential is there. I envision a student dumping the text of a session logged in a MOO into Storyspace, where it can then be parsed, linked, broken down, formed and reformed. The instructor facilitates the creative process by providing written or electronic instructions which are independent of the individual conversations logged in the MOO yet help the learner shape his or her spontaneous thoughts into a finished presentation, thus organising the whole in a fashion which may encourage retention of the information.

---

[3] Throughout her article Fanderclai uses MUD generically to indicate both MUDs and MOOs.

References:

Curtis, Pavel (1998) 'Not just a game: How LambdaMOO came to exist and what it did to get back at me. In C. Haynes, & J. R. Holmevik (eds.), High Wired. On the Design, Use and Theory of Educational MOOs. Ann Arbor: University of Michigan Press. 25-42.

Donaldson, Randall P. & Markus Kötter (1999) 'Language learning in a MOO: creating a transoceanic bilingual virtual community', Literary and Linguistic Computing, 14:1 (April 1999), 67-76.

—— 'Language Learning and Cyberspace: Teleporting the Classroom into the Target Culture', CALICO Journal,16:4 (June 1999), 531-557.

Langham, Don (1994) 'The Common Place MOO: Orality and Literacy in Virtual Reality', Computer-Mediated Communication Magazine, 1:3 (1 July 1994), 7.
Available: http://sunsite.unc.edu/cmc/mag/1994/jul/moo.html

Potter, Rosanne (1996) 'What Computers Are Good for in the Literature Classroom', Computers and the Humanities, 30:181-190.

Turkle, Sherry (1998) 'All MOOs are educational — the experience of 'Walking through the self''. In C. Haynes, & J. R. Holmevik (eds.), High Wired. On the Design, Use and Theory of Educational MOOs. Ann Arbor: University of Michigan Press. ix-xix.

BRINGING THE WWW INTO THE ESL CLASSROOM

Christina Gitsaki and Richard Paul Taylor
Nagoya University of Commerce, Japan

Abstract
Access to the Internet provides language teachers and learners with an abundance of English resources for classroom use. Through the large number of English web sites students are exposed to authentic English language use and culture. There are a number of ways for using the different web sites for language teaching purposes. This paper outlines three classroom projects aiming to integrate ESL learning and the use of computers and the Internet. Each project is presented in terms of its structure, the teaching materials used, and the outcomes achieved.

1. Introduction: Web-Assisted Language Learning (WALL), i.e. using the World Wide Web as a classroom resource, is a new approach to ESL teaching that has many advantages:

- **Motivation**

The web offers a variety of topics to satisfy a diverse audience, it is versatile in its use, and it is motivating. A successful web search leaves students with a sense of achievement, personal fulfillment and increased self-confidence (Shneiderman, 1998).

- **Updated and Current Information**

The Internet provides students with opportunities for exposure to authentic language use and natural language that is current and frequently updated (Frizler, 1995).

- **Enhancing learner autonomy**

Using the Internet enhances student autonomy (Warschauer, Turbee & Roberts, 1994). Students choose the information *they* want to read and find information that is pertinent to their particular preferences and interests. Students do not limit themselves to the information included in their textbooks, while they discover that coping with authentic English is not impossible.

- **English outside the classroom**

Students can continue using the Internet and be exposed to English even outside the classroom, making learning English an on-going process (Berge & Collins, 1995).

- **4-Skills practice opportunities**

The web offers ample opportunities for project-driven language learning (Debski, Elder, Lynch & Gassin, 1998). Using the web in the classroom gives students the chance to practice reading English, skimming and scanning, synthesising information and formatting text, learn new words and collocations, be involved in writing projects, as well as speaking-oriented tasks sharing the information they found on the web orally with their classmates.

- **English and Computer Skills**

The Internet has become a part of our life and learning how to use it is an essential skill for students, so through the use of computers and the Internet students develop basic computer skills and learn English at the same time (Black, Klingenstien & Songer, 1995).

- **Fun! Fun! Fun!**

Using the Internet is fun. Websites are full of pictures, sounds, animation, interactive pages and video clips transforming learning into a joyful, enriching and memorable experience (Shneiderman, 1998).

For a more detailed account of the advantages of using the Internet for ESL teaching see Frizler (1995) and Muehleisen (1997).

Despite the advantages of the www-based approach to ESL, 'the World Wide Web cannot be a solution to educational needs unless the creative component is included' (Shneiderman, 1995: 28). Technology alone is inadequate as an educational tool in the absence of specifically designed educational tasks. Similar concerns have been expressed by first and second language educators alike (see Trickel & Liljegren, 1998; Yang, 1998; Dodge, 1997; Frizler, 1995). WWW-based materials for ESL students need to integrate computers and tasks with a language focus. There are four basic keys to successful www-based projects:

- There is a clear and specific task to be accomplished.
- The task is based on a topic that is relevant to the specific group of students.
- There are plenty of English resources on the Internet to cover the topic.
- Students are given direction and guidance to perform specific tasks (e.g. searching the web, retrieving information, downloading information, etc.).

The next part of this project describes three different ways of implementing www-based project driven language learning. These are projects that we have designed and used with our ESL students: web-search project, homepage project, and newspaper project. All three projects have been used with Japanese College students at pre-intermediate to advanced level of English. The projects are described in terms of their difficulty, both in English language and computer skills. The web-search and homepage projects are suitable for learners who are at least at a pre-intermediate level of English, while the newspaper project is suitable for post-intermediate students. All three projects make use of computers, so they should be taught in a computer lab or, if they are taught in a traditional classroom, they should allow time for learners to complete their computer tasks outside class time (e.g. as homework). The time for the completion of each project can vary according to class size and the learners' proficiency level. The minimum time for the completion of a web-search project is three hours, the homepage project can take more time, but a lot of it can be assigned as homework to be completed outside the classroom. The newspaper project requires at least 4 hours of group work, while the actual information gathering and writing can be assigned as homework.

2. Web-Search Project

2.1 Introduction: Web-search projects can be designed around a number of different topics (e.g. famous people, movies, restaurants, shopping, job hunting, etc.)(see also Dodge, 1997; Harrison & Shimada, 1999; Gitsaki & Taylor, 1999). There are a number of features that each web-search project exhibits. It provides learners with a clear task, it uses the Internet as a tool for accessing information, it gives learners steps to complete the task, it helps learners practice their English and produce something that they can share with their classmates. There are four basic parts in a web-search project:

- Introduction to the topic: Informs learners of the project topic and outlines the sequence of tasks that the learners will have to perform.
- Formulation of a research question: Helps learners narrow down their focus and formulate a research question.
- Completion of a web search: Learners search the web for specific information.
- Information sharing: Learners share the results of their search with the rest of their classmates.

2.2 Description of a Sample Web-Search Project: This part describes one of the web-search projects we designed and carried out with our students. The project is called 'Vacation Abroad' (see Appendix A). There are five parts in this project: *Identify*, *Prepare Your Search*, *Search the Web*, *WebTalk*, and *Computer Writing Project*.

Part 1: Identify

This part introduces the topic to the students and outlines the sequence of activities: students will plan a vacation abroad on the Internet. First they will talk about different vacation destinations around the world, then they will choose a vacation destination and activities to do, next they will search the Web for information and put together a vacation plan, and finally they will share their vacation plan with their classmates. For the warm up, students have a look at pictures of famous monuments around the world (e.g. Statue of Liberty, Golden Gate Bridge, Sydney Opera House, etc.), and write down the city and/or country these monuments are in. Students then can check their answers with their partners using a model dialogue for guidance.

Part 2: Prepare Your Search

In this part, students review a list of vocabulary items (e.g. different activities to do while on vacation- scuba diving, safari, mountain climbing, surfing, skiing, etc.) and then they have to write a vacation destination for each activity. After that, students have to write down three vacation destinations they would like to visit and one activity for each. Finally, students have to choose one vacation destination they would like to find information about and one activity they would like to do there. At the end of this part, students can discuss their choices with a classmate using a model dialogue as a guide.

Part 3: Search the Web
Now that students have decided where to go for their vacation, it is time for the web search. Students have to write down the keywords for their search (e.g. Australia diving). Students may need to do more than one search in order to find information about activities in the destination they have chosen and accommodation information. Students can also try the travel information available in any of the popular web directories. Before students start searching the web, they get a chart that they will have to complete using the information they find on the web (e.g. dates, accommodation, activities, weather information, special attractions, cost, etc.). Then students open their browser, go to their favorite search engine, type their keywords and then search the web. Students browse through the search results and choose a website that they like the best. Then, they complete the chart with the information from the website they chose.

Part 4: Web Talk
In this part, students interview two of their classmates about their vacation plans. Students can use a set of sample questions and answers provided as a guide for their interviews. They also have to write down their classmate's answers. When students finish their interviews, they look at their classmate's answers they wrote down and decide which vacation plan is better, theirs or their classmates'.

Part 5: Computer Writing Project
For the computer writing section, students create a brochure for the vacation they planned using their word processor and the information the found on the web. They download pictures and text from the web to a word processing document, they edit the information they copied and add their own ideas and opinions, arrange the pictures and text in their document, and check the spelling. At the end of the document, students list the URL(s) of the website(s) they used to get the pictures and information about their vacation. In order to chare their computer project with their classmates, students can make a printout of their vacation brochure and post it on a noticeboard, and/or they can E-mail their brochure as an attachment to three or four of their classmates. Finally, students have a look at their classmates' vacation brochures and choose the best one.

2.3 Outcomes: By completing web-search projects, students get a lot of opportunities to practice their English. They practice scanning and skimming English information on the web, they encounter new vocabulary in context, they practice their conversation skills through model dialogues and speaking tasks, and they practice their writing skills, synthesizing information and presenting information. The web contains authentic and current English, so students are exposed to real life and contemporary English. Finally, students develop confidence that they find almost everything on the Internet, and they are happy to search for information that they are interested in.

3. Homepage Project

3.1 Introduction: As students complete web-search projects, they gather URLs of their favorite web sites. In order to utilise their web searching experience, students can create a basic web page in English. Creating a homepage can be very rewarding: students get to publish a web page that people from other parts of the world can see and read, they can be creative and practice their English at the same time. Using basic HTML tags for creating a homepage has many advantages: there is no special software required (just a text editor and a web browser), students become aware of the way web-pages are constructed and they can utilise the format of other web pages by viewing the HTML source of those pages, students can continue working on their homepage and using English outside the classroom, and finally, there are a lot of resources on the Internet teaching basic HTML tags and homepage construction.

3.2 Structure of the Homepage Project: There are three stages to this project: sorting out the HTML tags, training students to use the tags, creating the web page.

Part 1: Basic HTML Tags

For the creation of a homepage, a small set of basic HTML tags is sufficient (see Appendix B). These tags cover the setting up of a HTML document, text formatting (using different fonts, bold, italic, etc.), arranging text in paragraphs, making lists, creating tables, drawing lines, and adding links and pictures. There are many sites on the web offering basic HTML tutoring and instructions on to how to create a basic homepage. Here is a list of useful sites that we have used:

http://apk.net/~jbarta/tutor/makapage/
http://www.baus.hypermart.net/html1.html
http://www.edb.utexas.edu/resta97/aisd/students/turnbull/HTMLtutr/index.html
http://www.charlesriver.com/demos/htmltm/MACFILES/enough
http://www-ssg.sr.unh.edu/tof/WebLesson/web_lesson.html
http://204.98.1.2/high/awest/learnhtml/00conten.htm
http://www.hollandcomputers.com/Internet_services/html.htm

Part 2: Using HTML tags

Once the HTML tags are sorted out, the next step is to teach these tags to the students. Preparing handouts that show students exactly what to do is very helpful (see Appendix C for a sample handout or access http://opinion.nucba.ac.jp/~gitsaki/ for printing a set of three lessons for teaching basic HTML to ESL students). Tags are introduced sequentially: first students start the HTML document using the basic tags, then they type some text and they learn how to format the text and how to arrange text into paragraphs, then they learn how to display information using different formats (lists and tables), how to separate the different sections of their homepage using lines, and finally they learn how to add links to their favorite websites and how to add images and pictures to their page. During the training stage, students do not create their homepage, but rather they practice the different tags by performing small tasks. For example, they can practice using the different font sizes by creating a rollercoaster, or they can create lists by writing what presents they would like for their birthday (for more ideas on different tasks for HTML training see Joe Barta's site http://apk.net/~jbarta/tutor/makapage/).

Part 3: Creating a Homepage
After students have practiced using the HTML tags, they can start creating their homepage. Depending on their level of English and their web searching experience, students can include a number of different things in their homepage. Table 1 gives a list of contents for a basic homepage for pre-intermediate or intermediate learners.

Table 1. What to include in a homepage

Contents	Outcome
Self-Introduction	students practice introducing themselves, describing their family and hometown, using simple present to describe their daily routine, etc.
School and Course information	students explain what they are studying and give information about their school
Web surfing experience	students write about their favorite movie star, movie, food recipe, holiday destination, on-line shopping mall, etc., and provide links to their favorite web sites for each of them
Past experiences	students practice using past tense to talk about places they visited, things they liked, movies they saw, etc.
Plans for the future	students use future tense to talk about their plans for the future (dream job, house, car, travelling, etc.)

Students should also add a link to their e-mail address for prospective keypals. After students have completed their homepages, the teacher should proofread them and then publish them on the web. If the teacher maintains a homepage, it is easy to add a link to the students' homepages. If, however, the teacher does not have a homepage, or the school does not have a server, then the teacher and/or the students can find a website on the Internet that offers free server space for publishing web pages.

3.3 Outcomes: Creating a homepage helps students practice their English. During the training session, they have to read English instructions and they have to write English text. When they write their homepage they utilise the language they were taught in their English language course. The topics dealt with in their textbooks can be used as a guide for what to include in their homepage. Furthermore, students get a chance to be creative. Even though all students receive training for the same set of HTML tags, they use them in quite different ways. Their creativity and individuality is reflected in the homepage they create. Composing a homepage in basic HTML makes students aware of formatting issues. Students have to decide when to use bold or italics, when to start a new paragraph, how to sort information and how to display information (in lists, tables, etc.).

Finally, publishing a homepage is very motivational for the students. All students, irrespective of their level of English proficiency, can create a basic English homepage and publish it on the web. Students with a higher level of proficiency create longer homepages, they write larger paragraphs and include a lot more information. Students of a lower proficiency level create shorter homepages, with a lot of images and most of the information displayed in tables or lists.

4. Newspaper Project

4.1 Introduction: The last project described in this paper is writing a newspaper. This project requires a higher level of English proficiency (upper-intermediate to advanced). It combines a number of different skills: writing English, searching the web for specific information, downloading information from the web, manipulating text and images, formatting text.

4.2 Structure of the Newspaper Project: There are four basic parts in the newspaper project: introducing students to the different parts of a newspaper, assigning working teams, searching the web for information, putting the newspaper together.

Part 1: Parts of a Newspaper

At the start of this project, students familiarise themselves with the different parts of a newspaper. They have a look at different newspapers (printed and/or on-line), and they classify the different articles into the following major categories:

- News Stories (a story about something that happened recently)
  National News, Local News, International News
- Feature articles (a story about a place or person, or an interview)
- Sports (National, Local or International)
- Fashion
- Cooking (recipes)
- Music Groups & CD reviews
- Entertainment Guide: Movie Previews, Cinema guide, Where to eat, What to see....
- Book reviews
- Advertisements
- Comic strips (cartoons)
- Classified Advertisements: Jobs, things students want to sell or buy, etc.
- Horoscope
- Crosswords, Word Games, Puzzles
- Traveling
- Weather Information

In this part, students are also informed about the inverted pyramid style of writing news stories. News stories answer six basic questions: who did what? when? where? why? and how? Stories begin with the most important facts in the first paragraph (lead) and then they give some other important details. The less important details are towards the end of the story.

Part 2: Assigning Working Teams
In this stage the working teams are assigned and the role of each person in a team is defined. Depending on the class size, students can form groups of 5-6. Each group assigns an editor and a chief-of-staff. The editor makes decisions on what to include in the newspaper and where to put each piece. The chief-of-staff makes sure that all 'reporters' cover all areas of news and they are progressing well. Then the team has to decide on a preliminary title for their newspaper, which parts to include in the newspaper, which parts each student will write about, and setting deadlines for first drafts, final drafts, and for putting the newspaper together.

Part 3: Surfing the Web
Now that each student knows what articles they need to write about, it is time to search the web for information. Students should have some previous experience on using keywords and searching the web. They can use the information they find on the web to write their stories. They can download information and pictures from different sites and then they can edit the text, synthesise information and add their own ideas and opinions. It is important that students list all URLs of every site they used to collect information. Depending on the level of the students, additional practice in paraphrasing and referencing may be required.

Part 4: Printing the Newspaper
After all pieces of the newspaper have been written, each team has to put together the different pieces (merge the different files), choose interesting and informative headlines, and finally print the newspaper.

4.3 Outcomes: Writing a newspaper gives students the opportunity to practice and improve their writing skills, practice searching the web for specific information, and write about something that they are interested in. Students can find almost everything on the web, so there is no limit as to what they can write about. They also learn to work in teams, they develop skills for project management and efficient use of time, and they practice speaking English as they negotiate who writes what, when to submit drafts, what headlines to use, etc. As with the other two projects, students can work outside class time to complete their stories and achieve their goals. Reading news stories on the web is challenging (the news stories are written for native speakers and they contain a lot of specialised vocabulary), so this project requires a post-intermediate level of English. However, in classes with students in varying language proficiency levels, even the less proficient students can contribute to the newspaper. For example, less proficient students can create the advertisements, the cartoon strips, or create a restaurant or a cinema guide. In the end, each team will create a newspaper that they can show to their classmates, or even publish on the web.

5. Conclusion: 'Successful students create to learn and learn to create' (Shneiderman, 1998:26). The use of web-based projects in the ESL classroom enhances active learning. Learners are involved in activities that require them to search for specific information on the web, find useful resources and collect information, synthesise information and transform it in some way, and finally share the information and produce reports. Students do not need special computer skills, but an initial introduction to basic computer skills is required (i.e. how to open, save and print a word-processing document, how to use a web browser, how to copy text and pictures from the web to a word-processing document, how to send and reply to e-mail). Each project can be expanded to include additional and more challenging components such as having students evaluate each other's homepages and put together a list of features that make a good homepage, or having students present their report/ homepage/ newspaper in class. By undertaking real-world tasks and exposing themselves to authentic English, students will ultimately improve both their computer skills and language skills (Neu & Scarcella, 1991; Falsetti, 1995), and learn how to use the web as a tool for practicing English, not only inside but outside the classroom too. Finally, the web as a resource of authentic language use and project-based learning is far too valuable not to be exploited.

References:

Berge, Z. & Collins, M. (1995) *Computer-mediated communication and the on-line classroom in distance learning.* Cresskill, NJ: Hampton Press.

Black, L., Klingenstien, K., & Songer, N. (1995) 'Observations from the Boulder Valley Internet project', *Technological Horizons in Education (THE) Journal 22* (10-11), 75-80 & 54-57.

Debski, R., Elder, C., Lynch, B. & Gassin, J. (1998). *Integrating multimedia tools into project-driven foreign language learning.* <http://www.hlc.unimelb.edu.au/projects.htm#research1>

Dodge, B. (1997). Some thoughts about webquests. *The Distance Educator, 1*(3), 12-15.

Falsetti, J. (1995) 'What the heck is a MOO and what's the story with all those cows?', Paper Presented at *TESOL '95*, Long Beach, CA.

Frizler, K. (1995) 'The Internet as an Educational Tool in ESOL Writing Instruction.' Unpublished Master's Thesis, San Francisco State University [WWW document]. URL http://thecity.sfsu.edu/~funweb/thesis.htm

Gitsaki, C. & Taylor, R. (1999). *Internet English: WWW-based communication activities.* New York: Oxford University Press.

Harrison, R. & Shimada, N. (1999). *WebQuests: A model for implementing WWW-based CALL.* Paper presented at CALLing Asia'99, Kyoto Sangyo University, Kyoto, Japan, May 21-24.

Muehleisen, V. (1997) 'Projects using the Internet in College English classes', Paper Presentation, *CALL: Basics and Beyond*, Chubu University, Nagoya, Japan, May 31.

Neu, J. & Scarcella, R. (1991) 'Word processing in the ESL writing classroom: A survey of student attitudes'. In P. Dunkel (ed.), *Computer-assisted language learning and testing: Research issues and practice* , New York: Newbury House Publishers, 170-187.

Shneiderman, B. (1998). Relate-Create-Donate: A teaching/learning philosophy for the cyber-generation. *Computers & Education, 31*(1), 25-39.

Trickel, K. & Liljegren, K. (1998) 'Using multimedia computers effectively in the ESL classroom: Use the computers. Don't let them use you.' Paper Presented at the *1998 Southeast Regional TESOL Conference*, Louisville, Kentucky.

Warschauer, M., Turbee, L. & Roberts, B. (1994) 'Computer learning networks and student empowerment.' (Research note #10), Honolulu, HI: University of Hawaii, Second Language Teaching & Curriculum Center.

Yang, P. J. (1998) 'Networked multimedia and foreign language education', *CALICO Journal* 15 (1-3), 75-88.

Appendix A. Sample web-search project.

Vacation Abroad

Your Mission

- **Identify your classmates vacation preferences**
- **Prepare your vacation**
- **Search the Web and collect information about activities, hotels, and plan your vacation**
- **Talk about your holiday plans with other students**

Identify

1. Look at the pictures. Write down the monuments you recognise. Then write the city/country where these monuments are.

	Monument	City/Country
1.	____________	____________
2.	____________	____________
3.	____________	____________
4.	____________	____________

2. Check your answers with a partner.

Example

A: What's that?
B: That's *the Statue of Liberty.*
A: Where is it?
B: It's in *New York, U.S.A.*

Prepare your Search

1. Work with your partner. Write a vacation destination for each activity. Add two more activities to the list.

Vacation Destinations	Activities
Australia, Great Barrier Reef	scuba diving
	safari
	mountain climbing
	surfing
	skiing / snowboarding

2. Write down your three favorite vacation destinations and an activity for each one.

Vacation Destinations	Activities
1.	1. ....
2.	2. ....
3.	3. ....

3. Choose a vacation destination to research and the activities you would like to do.

Destination ________________________ Activities ________________________

4. Now talk about your choice with a classmate.

A: Where would you like to go for your vacation?
B: I'd like to go to *Australia*.
A: That sounds great. What will you do there?
B: I'd like to go *scuba diving* on the *Great Barrier Reef.*

Search the Web

1. Look for vacation information on the web. Do a search using the *destination* you have chosen and *vacation* or the *type of activity* as keywords. Write your keywords in the box. Then do a search about *hotels* and the *country* you have chosen.

Your Keywords

Example
Australia diving

2. Explore the holiday websites you found.

Search Tip!
You can also try
the travel information and
package tours
in your favorite search engine.

3. Now choose the most interesting vacation websites and write the URLs below. You may have to explore several different websites in order to collect all the information you need.

URL ____

URL ____

4. Plan your vacation. Find information about accommodations, activities, costs, etc.. Look up unfamiliar words in a dictionary.

Destination: .... Dates: from................ to.................
Accommodation: B& B, hotel, hostel, camping, other..............................
Number of nights............................ Cost............................
hotel facilities...
Other Information: best food to eat ....
tours...
weather ....
Activities: ....
....Cost............................

Web Talk

1. Interview two students in your class about the vacation they have chosen and write their answers.

Questions				*Answers*
Where	will	you go?		I'll go to Cairns in Australia.
How long		you stay there?		One week.
What		you do there?		I'll go diving on the Great Barrier Reef.
How much		it cost?		Diving will cost about AU$560.
Where		you stay?		I'll stay at a holiday resort.
What		you eat there?		I'd like to try crocodile steaks.
What	is	the weather like?		It's hot and humid.
Why	did	you choose this holiday?		Because I want to try diving and ......

	Student A:	*Student B:*
destination		
duration		
accommodation		
cost		
activities		
cost		
best food		
weather		
special attractions, tours		
other information		
reason for choosing this vacation		

2. Have a look at your classmates' answers. Answer these questions.

Which holiday is the most interesting? ________________________________

Why? ________________________________

Language Window

1. These are some ways to talk about holiday plans.

I'd like to visit Australia ***I would really like to*** go diving on the Great Barrier Reef ***I'd enjoy*** try***ing*** the local food ***I'd prefer*** a beach holiday ***to*** an adventure holiday ***I'd rather*** stay at a cheap hotel

2. Now write a few sentences about your holiday plans.

I'd like to.. I would really like to.. I'd enjoy.. I'd rather..

Computer Writing

1. Use your word processor and follow the steps below to produce a brochure about the vacation you planned.

a. Open a **new text file.**

b. Use the information you found on the **Internet** and your ideas.

c. At the end of your document write the **URLs** of the homepages you used.

d. Save the **file** as *YourName.*Vacation

E-mail Activity

1. E-mail the vacation brochure to your classmates as an attachment.
On the Subject line write the vacation destination.

2. Have a look at the other students' brochures. Answer the following questions.

1. What are some of the vacation destinations that the other students have chosen?

....

2. Which other vacations would you like to have? ....

....

Appendix B. Basic HTML Tags

Basic Tags	Heading	<HEAD>….</HEAD>
	Title	<TITLE>….</TITLE>
	Body of the Web page	<BODY>….</BODY>
	BackGround Color	<BGCOLOR>
Formatting Text	**BOLD**	<B>….</B>
	Italics	<I>….</I>
	Underline	<U>….</U>
	Font	<FONT>….</FONT>
	Specifying font Size (1-7)	<FONT SIZE=7>...</FONT>
	Specifying a special font	<FONT FACE=ARIAL>...</FONT>
Breaks	Break line	
	Paragraph break	<P>
	Extra space	
Lists	Ordered List (1, 2, 3, ….)	<OL>….</OL>
	Unordered List	<UL>….</UL>
	List Item	<LI>
Tables	Table	<TABLE>….</TABLE>
	Table Header	<TH>….</TH>
	Table Rows	<TR>….</TR>
	Contents of each Cell in the Table	<TD>….</TD>
Lines	Horizontal Rule	<HR>
	Line Width	<HR WIDTH=50>
	Line alignment	<HR ALIGN=CENTER>
	Line thickness	<HR SIZE=15>
Links	Anchoring	<A>….</A>
	Specifying the location of the link	<A HREF=‘http://www.yahoo.com/‘> Yahoo!</A>
Pictures	Specifying an Image location	<IMG SRC=‘picture1.gif’>

Appendix C: Sample handout for introducing HTML tags.

Introduction to HTML

PART 1

In this part you will learn some of the basic **HTML** tags that will help you put together a homepage in English. To create the HTML files you will need to use a text editor **(SimpleText or Notepad)** and to view your files you will use your web browser (e.g. **Netscape or Internet Explorer**).

- Turn on your computer
- Open **SimpleText or Notepad**
- Now you are ready to start typing your **HTML code**.
- Type

```
<HTML>
</HTML>
```

Each one of those is called a **<TAG>**. There is a *starting* <TAG> and a *closing* </TAG>. To make a closing tag just add a / to the starting tag. With tags you give instructions to the computer.
What you have just told the computer is 'this is the start of a HTML document' (<HTML>) and 'this is the end of a HTML document' (</HTML>).

Now you can add some more things to the homepage. Every HTML document needs a pair of HEAD tags, TITLE tags and BODY tags. The rest of your homepage is going to be within the BODY tags.

- Type

```
<HTML>
<HEAD>
<TITLE> </TITLE>
</HEAD>
<BODY>
</BODY>
</HTML>
```

- Now you can give your document a title

```
<HTML>
<HEAD>
<TITLE>Rick's Homepage</TITLE>
</HEAD>
<BODY>
</BODY>
</HTML>
```

- Now you need to **Save** your file **As**: **index.html**

To view your homepage:

- Open **Netscape or Internet Explorer**
- From the File menu select **Open File**
- In the new window find your **index.html** file and click **Open**

PART 2

In this part you will learn how to use **Bold**, *Italics*, Underline, as well as different Fonts, and Sizes.

- Open your **index.html** document
- Between the <BODY> tags type a sentence (for example: This is my Homepage)
- Use the <B> tags to make the word 'my' **bold**.

  <BODY>
  This is **<B>my</B>** homepage.
  </BODY>

- Now use the <I> tags for *italics*

  <BODY>
  This **<I>is</I>** <B>my</B> homepage.
  </BODY>

- Use the <U> tags for underlining

  <BODY>
  <U>This </U><I>is </I><B>my</B> homepage.
  </BODY>

- You can use tags in combination if you want to.

  <BODY>
  This is **<I><B>my</B></I>** homepage.
  </BODY>

- Now you can use different fonts and sizes
- First add the <FONT> tags...

  <BODY>
  This is my **<FONT>homepage</FONT>**
  </BODY>

- Then specify a SIZE attribute.

  <BODY>
  This is my **<FONT SIZE=6>homepage</FONT>**
  </BODY>

A <TAG> tells the browser to do something.
An ATTRIBUTE goes inside the <TAG> and tells the browser how to do it.
So <FONT> is a TAG and SIZE is an ATTRIBUTE.

- Fonts come in 7 sizes
- Now try and make a rollercoaster!

THE WELL PROJECT: LOCAL PARTICIPATION AND NATIONAL EVALUATION

William Haworth
Liverpool John Moores University, UK

David Cowling
University of Exeter, UK

Abstract
The WELL (Web-Enhanced Language Learning) project, funded over a three-year period by HEFCE's Fund for the Development of Teaching and Learning, has a simple but demanding brief: to encourage teachers in Higher Education institutions to make use of Internet resources in the language curriculum, and to equip them with the skills necessary to exploit and create such resources. To this end, WELL is funding a number of pilot projects at each of the four consortium universities (Liverpool John Moores, Brighton, Exeter and Teesside) with the aim of demonstrating the pedagogical benefits to be derived from the appropriate use of the World Wide Web either as source of authentic foreign-language material or as delivery medium for online courses or course elements. Languages covered include French, German, Italian, Spanish and Russian.

This paper will consider the different ways in which Web-based resources may be used for foreign language teaching, and the metaphorical models underpinning these strategies. These range from a model of the Web as library of authentic material ready to be harvested by the language teacher (media and government sites) to a more dynamic model of the Internet as interactive medium permitting (virtual) contact with native speakers of the target language (e-mail penfriend projects, such as Tandem). The paper will be supported by a demonstration of successfully completed and ongoing pilot projects from consortium institutions, and by discussion of the set of tools developed by WELL in order to enable teachers and learners to evaluate their online experience.

Introduction: The WELL Project is an initiative across the HE language teaching sector to promote good practice in the use of telematic resources. The WELL acronym stands for **W**eb **E**nhanced **L**anguage **L**earning. It is one of 10 language-related projects supported by the Fund for the Development of Teaching and Learning (FDTL) under the Higher Education Funding Council for England. The geographical constituency of the project is therefore circumscribed; nevertheless a number of centres in Wales have been included. Project duration is 3 years, from October 1997 until September 2000. The project is run by a consortium of four universities — Brighton, Exeter, Teesside, and Liverpool John Moores — with the latter acting as overall co-ordinator.

Background: The FDTL followed the TQA visits held, in the case of languages, in 1995 and 1996. Institutions were invited to bid for funding to disseminate aspects of their provision identified as 'excellent' with a grade 4. Some early work on the use of the Web to support language teaching and learning had been done at Liverpool John Moores, where the World Language Pages ***http://www.livjm.ac.uk/language/*** had been developed within the School of Modern Languages. This site was the first in Europe to offer audited and documented Web resources for language teachers and learners, providing pointers to resources in 14 languages and pedagogical, methodological and technical guidance on their use. Learning resources at JMU received a grade 4, and it was decided to seek consortium partners to put forward a bid to the FDTL. The three partner institutions identified represent centres of particular experience or interest in language learning applications of the World Wide Web.

The University of Brighton Language Centre has a long tradition in the exploitation of educational technology in the teaching and learning of languages. The Department has investigated and used a variety of technologies with educational potential, including satellite television, interactive video and multimedia; in particular the use of hypermedia has been extensively investigated and promoted, and staff within the Department have authored a number of commercial language learning CD-ROMs. It had already established a substantial on-line guide to resources for Spanish studies on the World Wide Web — Recursos.

The School of Modern Languages at Exeter had worked closely with the Pallas Project at the University. Housed in the same building as the departments, the Pallas Project was set up in 1984 under the Computers in Teaching Initiative. A good deal of interesting work had already been done — of particular note is the 'Reportage' course taught jointly by the department and Pallas to second-year French students. This is a multimedia course in which students are encouraged to use the WWW to secure information for their own 'newspapers' which are delivered and assessed on-line.

The Language Centre at Teesside has taken part in projects such as CAMILLE, a European Consortium funded by the European Union. CAMILLE produced Computer Assisted Language Learning packages such as 'FranceInteractive' and 'À la Recherche d'un Emploi'. With the project ©ALICE, the Language Section, and a team of computing research students, was working on transferring 'FranceInteractive' onto the established WebSite ©ALICE. The University of Teesside has also received European funding to build a state-of-the-art Virtual Reality Centre.

Telematics in support of language teaching and learning: It is significant that of the ten FDTL language projects launched, only the WELL Project has an explicit technology element. Were the process to run again now, it is likely that this number would be greater, as the Web has achieved a much higher profile in a very short time. The reasons put forward on submission are as valid in 1999 as they were in 1996, and more widely recognised as such.

The explosive development of the World Wide Web presents a range of opportunities and challenges to HE and other sectors. A number of issues were identified at the outset of the project.

- low levels of awareness amongst language academics
- low levels of competence in C&IT amongst language academics
- inefficient search tools and strategies; despite the existence of substantial amounts of materials of direct relevance to teaching and learning, time may be wasted searching for them
- poor validation of resources — once material has been located, users cannot be sure that they have found the best example of that particular class of resource. Newcomers are not even aware of what they should be looking for.
- the scale of the impact the new technology will have on practice -traditional pedagogical models no longer serve, and the roles of teacher and learner will need to be radically redefined. In addition to resources there are many forms of on-line interactive communication which are of particular and direct interest to language learners and which offer potentially new paradigms for learning and teaching.
- the need for guidelines and examples of good practice — it is essential that clear guidelines be laid down in order to maximise the potential of the resource and to begin the process of definition of viable pedagogical models. Whilst the rapid evolution of the medium means that these cannot be exhaustive, it is nevertheless feasible to present teachers with examples of good practice.

While all of these issues are still relevant in 1999 and there is a greater urgency about many of them, substantial progress has been made. For example, in 1996 the lack of maps for this new territory was identified as problematic; today the proliferation of maps has solved one problem while the very diversity and unevenness of these same maps has created another.

In the face of the problems and opportunities identified, the Project seeks to promote a coherent approach to defining and exploiting the potential of the World Wide Web and associated technologies for teaching and learning languages. The benefits are multiple:

- ♦ a vast quantity of resources (multilingual, multimedia) already in place
- ♦ new forms of accessible, high-quality and cost-effective modes of teaching and learning
- ♦ promotion of student-centred, independent learning
- ♦ development of transferable skills
- ♦ potential benefits to a wider user public than traditional media, because of the unique accessibility of Web-based resources;

- developments are relevant beyond HE to the entire educational sector;
- the avoidance of expensive, inefficient and uncoordinated parallel developments which are currently emerging at random across the sector.

In the recent past, the opportunities presented by new language teaching resources and technologies have not been fully exploited. This is commented on in the HEFCE Subject Overview Reports for Languages. For example:

- 'optimum use of language laboratories was not always achieved; in such cases, these resources were not fully integrated into the curriculum and were under-utilised' *(QO 4/96 — Iberian Languages.Conclusions)*
- 'less than 20% of institutions are making consistent use of IT in the delivery of the language curriculum' *(QO 3/96 — German Languages. Section 17)*
- 'the majority of providers do not yet have a coherent strategy for IT at the subject level' *(QO 4/96 — Iberian Languages.Conclusions)*
- 'in nearly one third of institutions, the assessors noted a failure to exploit the facilities of (language resource) centres largely because the resources they offer are not fully integrated within an overall learning strategy' *(QO 3/96 — German Languages. Summary)*

This last point — identifying a lack of integration of valuable resources in the curriculum — is the most vital and difficult issue to address. In the case of web-enhanced learning, the issue goes beyond integration of resources to include integration of new practice.
Aims of the project: The project does not purport to disseminate advanced techniques for exploiting state-of-the-art technology. The emphasis is predominantly on disseminating established basic good practice in order to improve the effectiveness of language teachers who are still largely uncertain of what the Web has to offer, or where to start using it to good effect for the improvement of student learning. There is clearly a developmental aspect to the work, as it is not realistic to talk in terms of disseminating an established model of good practice in an area which is still evolving.

The WELL Project does not seek to promote unconditional use of the new technologies, but rather to develop a critical awareness of when and where they might most appropriately be used. It is also essential to inform academics on the impact that the technology is likely to make on their working conditions — issues such as intellectual property rights and copyright are going to take on a new prominence in the near future.

In brief, the project aims are as follows:

- dissemination of good practice and critical awareness in using the World Wide Web for teaching Modern Languages in HE and beyond
- embedding of good practice in individual institutions through funded remission
- avoidance of duplication of effort across the sector.

- continued evaluation of innovative communication technologies for authentic language practice
- definition of a model of Web-based teaching and learning relevant to other subject areas

Project activities: The Project is committed to delivering a number of specific outcomes during its 3-year course. The core elements of this are workshops and a web site, and these are being delivered as planned. In quantitative terms, the targets are relatively straight forward, but it is only by including some qualitative evaluation that some meaningful measurement of effectiveness can be derived.
Qualitative evaluation is being carried out by June Thompson from the CTICML in Hull.

Workshops: The WELL Project aims to promote wider awareness and more effective use of Web resources for language teaching across the HE sector through a programme of workshops. The aim is to provide training for 900 academics in total. The target group for these sessions is made up of academics who are complete or relative newcomers to the exploitation of telematics to support their teaching — that is to say, the majority of academics in the sector.
In Year 1 each consortium member ran 3 workshops at his own institution. The take-up of places offered was good, but the problem which soon emerged was that, despite the sessions being publicised as for the inexperienced, the people coming to these sessions were not predominantly within this target group of 'beginners' or 'post-beginners' but rather they had good levels of competence and experience.
In Year 2 we have come nearer addressing the target group by running workshops at other institutions. In the first half of 1999 there were 24 such workshops organised around the country and a further 20 are planned for 1999-2000.

The content of the workshop varies according to local circumstances. Allowing for some variation, it provides a mix of presentation, hands-on and discussion. There has been a significant maturing in demand — greater emphasis is now placed on authoring, for example, than at the start of the project.

The materials used for these workshops are all on-line, and are freely accessible.

Web site: It was considered to be essential to set up a server with a non-institutional domain name to minimise the 'not-invented-here syndrome' which has emerged as a barrier to effective adoption within the sector of otherwise useful materials, so the well.ac.uk domain was registered with UKERNA. Physically it is located on the JMU web server, but there is no explicit identification with any institutions.

The web site holds validated resources for language teaching and learning in the major languages taught in the UK. The development of the resource links has taken time to develop. It is not a simple list of resources, but is a searchable database. Each resource is categorised in terms of type and suitability for learners at specific levels, and a description provided. Users may propose new resources for addition by clicking on the Add New button and completing the form that appears. Each suggested resource is moderated prior to inclusion in the database by a team of language-specific specialists to whom each suggestion is e-mailed automatically. A moderator accepts or declines the resource, editing the category, learner level and/or description as appropriate.

Under the section 'WELL in the Classroom', there is a growing body of pedagogical guidelines for delivery and use of Web-based learning materials and exploitation of new communicative potential, and on-line procedural instructions for use of Web resources and activities relevant to language teaching and learning.

Case studies: At the start of the project, funding was allocated to support remission for a number of academics at different institutions around the country, in order to generate a series of case studies This policy was then revised as it would only provide limited funding for a small number of academics. HEFCE approved the redefinition of this funding as small (typically £250) direct payments to academics who run a small-scale project exploiting some aspect of telematics and then submitting a case study in a standard format. These will be made accessible on the WELL site.

Survey: A questionnaire was distributed across the entire HE sector in the UK in October 1997 to provide a snapshot view of the current use of C&IT — with particular emphasis on the WWW — by staff and students.
The resulting picture is based on 104 responses and may be taken as broadly representative of current use. It will be repeated in 2000 to determine to what extent the situation has changed. Hence the main significance of the survey lies in its comparative and not its absolute value. The responses has been analysed and a summary of the results is shown on the WELL web site.
The most significant findings which the questionnaire has brought to light are

- Most institutions have as yet made little use of telematic resources to support learning and teaching, despite a high level of investment in hardware and infrastructure.
- The commonest use of Web resources is as a source of materials which are downloaded by the lecturer and distributed to students. Instances of interactive use or exploitation of communicative potential are very limited.
- Most training in Web use has been carried out through individual initiative rather than institutional policy.
- The major obstacle to more effective use of telematic resources is identified as lack of staff training.

Newsletters: A WELL newsletter is produced twice a year and distributed with the ReCALL Newsletter, with a print run of 4,000. It is considered worthwhile to use a paper-based medium to attempt to draw in some of the academics who are still not accustomed to electronic access to information.

Mailbase — well@mailbase.ac.uk: The WELL mailbase list has over 400 members, of who around 60% are in the UK. In the coming year, a series of invited 'speakers' will lead discussion on specified topics. These topics will be announced in September.
The majority of academics who use this list are not strictly within the Project's main target group of (post) beginners; many of them are expert developers and innovators. The discussion of issues such as copyright and the transfer of materials from traditional media to the web is nevertheless of potential interest to all academics.

Conclusion: The experience of traditional Computer Assisted Language Learning provides a valuable object lesson. CALL has been exploited since the 1970s but progress has been slow, uneven, and expensive. Despite examples of excellent practice and large-scale initiatives to publicise the potential benefits, adoption has been only partial, so that instead of becoming an integral part of the language curriculum, CALL has remained an add-on across a large part of the sector. In the near future, it is unlikely that telematics will retain this optional character, as it has generated an impetus which goes far beyond purely pedagogical applications. For better or for worse, telematics is going to make a huge impact on education and training. For the sake of learners, teachers and institutions, this process needs to be managed in as coherent and focused a manner as possible. The WELL Project aims to contribute to this process by increasing awareness of where the potential gains lie, how they may be realised, and how the possible dangers may be minimised.

DESIGNING A WEB-BASED CALL ENVIRONMENT: FROM ACCESS TO ACCEPTABILITY

Dominique Hémard & Steve Cushion
London Guildhall University, UK

Abstract
This paper focuses on an on-going CALL project in the Language Studies Department at London Guildhall University, combining Human Computer Interaction (HCI), web-based JAVA programming, CALL authoring and language teaching expertise, designed to generate new CALL-enhanced curriculum developments within the broader confines of the existing language learning environment. Based on HCI data derived from summative evaluations and student requirements, it attempts to redefine the role and function of CALL with a view to improving its usability and, ultimately, its general acceptability amongst a disenfranchised student population. On this premise, this paper endeavours to highlight the transition from design theory to practice as well as present and contextualise the adopted aims and objectives, placing particular emphasis on the conceptual basis supporting this web-based language learning approach.

1. Introduction: The aim of this paper is to present a CALL project through its design process placing particular emphasis on theoretical design considerations as evidence of good practice and illustration of the important articulation between theory and practice. In so doing, it attempts to shed some light on the structured nature of the design process itself and theoretical underpinning from an HCI perspective whilst highlighting adopted high level points of departure (Levy, 1997). Thus, the approach purposefully combines a theoretical basis with a specific emphasis on pre-design considerations, relevant to the presented web-based CALL project, establishing important links between HCI and CALL as two distinct but overlapping and inter-dependent disciplines.

1.1 Design Expertise: It is now widely accepted that advanced interactive systems, capitalising on new computer technology, are potentially more usable than earlier, more basic, versions. By the same token, it is also acknowledged that the greater versatility and related impact of new computer systems coupled with web-based delivery have noticeably improved the breadth of human-computer interaction at the user interface. Paradigms for interaction are indeed conditioned by technological advances (Dix *et al.*, 1993) but technologically driven improvements, though capable of producing more usable systems, do not necessarily design and deliver the expected interface with enhanced usability and greater depth. This last point is particularly relevant to the design minefield of hypermedia and web-based CALL design.

Notwithstanding the above considerations, it is generally agreed that the success of a good interface design will initially lie in the proper composition of the design team. To stand a greater chance, it should reflect, on the one hand, the need to appreciate, consider and master the range and scope of the available technology and, on the other, the need to understand the human dimension and adaptability to changes. This approach, as suggested by Dix *et al* (1993), should enable system developers and evaluators to combine creativity, usability and ultimately performance in conjunction with the purpose and functions of the system to be designed. However, it ought to be stressed that much of the shortcomings of user-interface design initially lie in the very nature of its multi-discipline approach and process. Not only the all too convenient 'problem formulation to solution implementation' (Jens Rasmussen, 1992) cannot apply in an area which, despite its own evolution, is fundamentally empirical and hypothetical but, above all, the ideal designer combining technological know-how, HCI expertise and deep contextual knowledge is hard to find. Moreover, user interface design is still handicapped by a lack of collaboration and, therefore, cross-fertilisation between these inter-dependent disciplines, be they from the field of HCI, CALL or the computer technologist community, which, in turn, help explain the relatively few in-roads and benefits achieved in CALL design. Acknowledging these new trends in the context of existing practices and the need to adjust to new changes, it was felt that the necessary expertise to support the CALL project needed to be internal and team-based to promote and encourage knowledge sharing and cross-pollination. As a result, this expertise encapsulated and combined deep contextual knowledge of the language, language teaching and learning experience, HCI and programming specialisation and thrived on a close co-operation between the small design team and colleagues, as would-be authors, within the language Department. Thus, the breadth and depth of expert knowledge meant that the design process itself was covered and attention could focus on closing the gap between functionality and usability.

1.2 Methodology: A crucial issue to be considered at the conceptual stage of the design context is to define the most relevant and appropriate approach to interface design in conjunction with its objectives. In other words, how to exploit the design expertise combining technological, HCI expertise and language learning theories with a view to conceiving the best possible design. In the context of the CALL project, a broad, three-fold approach to methodology was adopted.

Firstly, it was determined by the main design prerogatives and conditions attached to the project. On the strength of previous design experience and through a process of weighing and assessing the existing HCI and technological input, it was agreed that the design method would rest on a user- centred approach instead of the more rigid and coercive technology-based approach relying on automated development and directed by programming constraints. As a result, a customised craft method (Wallace & Anderson, 1993) facilitating iterative design based on direct feedback and systematic evaluation was felt to be particularly adapted to the given design context and language environment to be designed.

Secondly, it was equally crucial, once the targeted user groups and the broad parameters, within which the project operated, were identified, to select the most appropriate evaluation methods to yield accurate and reliable HCI data on as wide a range of user-interaction variables as possible. Indeed a fast and positive response to feedback and reactions was seen as an important aspect and characteristic of the adopted approach and rated high amongst design considerations. This continuous feedback was undertaken by staff and student volunteers either through the authoring mode or class-based interactive sessions.

Thirdly and most importantly, this CALL project needed to be seen as an integral if not central part of an on-going curriculum development process, if it stood any chance of meeting its design objectives and be granted a crucial seal of approval from future CALL users. Thus, language learning strategies, highlighting grammatical competence, were discussed alongside appropriate learning approaches and theories with a view to identifying as clearly as possible what Jacobson (1994: 141) called the 'modalities for conveying knowledge with interactive multimedia and hypermedia technology'. In turn, these pre-design considerations played a critical role in involving a greater number of colleagues in the language teaching community, at secondary school, FE and HE levels, in order to elaborate different views and needs on the learning environment to be conceived. Design approaches, which were discussed, ranged from the more prescriptive and structured, instructional design approach to the more minimalist, constructivist position. The CALL project was also instrumental in generating ideas and raising concerns related to distance learning, learner autonomy and access and, more generally, the relationship between language teaching and independent study.

1.3 The Design Process

1.3.1 A Principled Approach: The process of designing human-computer interfaces often differs and adopts cycles tailor-made to the particularities of given requirements or adapted to generate better user-oriented design practices (see for example: Foley, 1983; Henderson, 1991; Pylyshyn, 1991). However, consensus is generally reached on the need for greater collaboration between designers and users to achieve more accurately defined designs, best suited to their respective end-user groups. Whilst this might be a prerogative in the field of HCI, it is often lacking in CALL. In this respect, Pylyshyn's (1991) comment criticising designers who are too often driven to design solutions by their own requirements and technological innovations is still particularly pertinent. Interestingly, this last point emphasises the basic and fundamental difficulty, which arises out of the inherent discrepancy between 'the language of the requirements and the language of the design' (Dix *et al.*, 1993). It is for this reason that a structured and principled approach to design was adopted in order to best match the information input in the form of design considerations and specifications, and the interactive output to satisfy student requirements.

1.3.2 Model of the Adopted Design Cycle: Based on Foley's (1983) model, the chosen design process progressed from the pre-design information gathering stage, followed by the design stage of the prototype with its formative evaluation to the design implementation stage and its summative evaluation. The process itself, though naturally structured from one phase to the next, was intrinsically iterative at any point in the proceedings. It is summarised as follows:

Phase 1: Pre-Design Information Gathering:
This initial phase, and the main focus of attention of this paper, was concerned with a study of the system to be performed. Its main activity revolved round the task analysis, itself predicated upon the identification of design objectives, user requirements and design constraints. Therefore, the pre-design stage consisted in determining and circumscribing the required functionality of the product to be designed on the strength of the users' characteristics in addition to assessing and analysing the tasks involved in achieving the proposed design goals. The early identification of functional specifications provided a useful point of evaluative reference as well as a basis for the setting of usability goals and the subsequent recognition of identifiable design constraints (Christie and Gardiner, 1990).

Phase 2: Design of prototype and early formative evaluation:
The design phase was concerned with the conceptual development and formative evaluation of design scenarios and alternatives on the strength of the task analysis, functional requirements, user characteristics and design constraints. Therefore, the application was conceived during this stage within well-defined conceptual parameters linked to the information output from the pre-design stage. This phase also ensured that the system to be designed was acceptable and realisable. Therefore, design decisions related to the quality of the resulting design were made at this stage.

Phase 3: Design implementation:
The implementation phase consisted in designing the system through a process of modifications and improvements. Existing software engineering tools and object-oriented programs, providing fast, efficient and integrated design outputs, have now greatly

facilitated such iterative design implementations of the prototype. In this particular case, the presented project was written in Java for web-based implementation.

Phase 4: Summative evaluation:
This last phase was concerned with the evaluation of the designed system and its corrections. The summative evaluation stage was entered when the designed application had reached an acceptable state and only when minor modifications have to be made.

Whilst conveniently establishing a meeting point between both conceptual and design phases, it must be emphasised that the design process is neither structurally static nor coercive in its approach. Indeed, the process itself is iterative and 'transformational' (Shneiderman, 1997) in its pursuit of a greater match between requirements and design towards an appropriate 'design fit' (Levy, 1997:163) as it gathers its own design momentum. Ultimately, the design process is a balancing act between theory and practice, highlighting two important dimensions, which could be tagged the metaphysical gap and the physical gap. Firstly, the metaphysical dimension implies that user characteristics and requirements have to come into the design equation if the designed actions are to map intentions and expectations (Norman, 1988). Secondly, the physical gap suggests that designing can be compared to a balancing act between theories and technologies but also between theories and design solutions, encapsulating the concept of moving usability goal posts allowing for regular repositioning and design improvements.

2. Pre-Design Considerations

2.1 Student Requirements: Although the emergence of graphical interfaces and advanced object-oriented tools have generally improved software development and its adjacent human computer interaction, much remains to be done at the user-interface level. Paradoxically, the greater the success of computers, the more undetermined their impact seems to be on end-user groups. This observation is all the more applicable to CALL where the wide spectrum of different design agendas, be it from authors, researchers and administrators, have blurred or simply ignored the issue of student requirements. Globally, design prerogatives and objectives affecting CALL development are very much rooted in the area of language teaching and learning strategies and are particularly concerned with levels of attainment, approaches and deliveries. Whilst the most commonly shared objective is, undoubtedly, to improve the students' learning process and experience, there is still too little hard evidence to suggest that this is so. Indeed, findings from an HCI research into hypermedia CALL (Hémard, 1998, 1999) surprisingly show that the majority of students of French at London Guildhall University, irrespective of levels, lacked in ICT experience, confidence and interest. Moreover, summative evaluations of existing hypermedia CALL packages yielded interesting data in the form of student requirements.

Overwhelmingly, students opted for greater usability and learnability rather than complex, technology-driven functionality. At the level of screen design, the CALL interface was too often perceived as being amateurish and students wanted a clear, uncluttered, robust and professionally designed interface which would adhere to existing standards and protocols and adopt known interface designs. When considering the interactive potential of the evaluated software, students demanded full navigational facilities and control over their interaction. They requested clear commands and functions and, generally, a more intuitive interaction to generate a more authentic language environment within which multimedia representations would be put to better use. On the question of applicability for language learning, students needed to be convinced of CALL's added value. Indeed, the presupposed attractiveness of the computer-based approach simply was not enough to justify its use. In fact, students expressed the need for more appropriately stated learning objectives suggesting that CALL's learning potential should be more clearly identified as a complementary resource, in terms of input and access, whilst indicating that the student interaction was not sufficiently meaningful or goal-oriented. Furthermore, they disliked profoundly, if not physically, the artificiality and unreliability of the computer when used in a tutorial and evaluative role, providing patronising feedback and misleading assessment by scoring. Finally, of particular interest, students wanted the computer to provide a greater interactive combination of the grammatical structures of the language, with its machine-based drills and individual practice, as well as multimedia applications and representations. These student requirements, summarised albeit succinctly, formed the original conceptual basis from which key design considerations were drawn.

2.2 CALL Authoring Requirements

2.2.1 Characteristics of Authoring: The expression 'author' and, by extension, the process of 'authoring', which came to encapsulate design perceptions and positions in terms of traditions, idiosyncrasies and characteristics is ambiguous at best if not misleading in CALL development. Even if the image is rather *cliché* and prone to exceptions, evidence from surveys (Hémard, 1997; Levy, 1997) suggests that CALL design is still, largely, undervalued, marginalised and poorly supported by academic institutions. Consequently, the language specialist-turned-author still is to an extent, by default or necessity, the archetypal self-taught and enthusiastic stakhanovist driven by the attractive potential of technology but also by technology itself. Thus, viewed from a design perspective, the CALL author hardy fits the profile of the practitioner, *a fortiori* that of the designer, whose respective roles are more often linked to a recognised, professional and sustained practice in an income-generating field. In effect, CALL authoring developments, at the institutional level, have been piecemeal and under funded, whilst, at departmental level, they have been empirical and task-based in approach. Last but not least, the rationale for using authored material by the language teaching community varies considerably from experimentation, imposition to expediency with little concern for the subsequent impact it might have on learners.

On such a premise, the concept of authoring was held as an important pre-design consideration for this project inasmuch as it was felt that the language teaching profession, as potential authors, represented an hitherto neglected user group, on a par with the targeted learners. Critically, therefore, the term 'author' needed to be precisely redefined in terms of characteristics and requirements in order to design an interface tailor-made for language teachers as well as language learners.

2.2.2 Author Requirements: Although misleading in its interpretation, the term 'author' was originally used to evoke the notion of originator, founder and creator. By extension, authoring tools were designed to empower the author to become a creative instigator and designer in charge of the whole design process and, in so doing, leave a personal mark or signature on the finished product, like some film directors or *auteurs*. However, and ironically perhaps, the term 'author' is still generally associated with or even synonymous with 'writer'. This latter, reductionist authoring dimension is particularly pertinent to CALL authors, more naturally drawn towards the text and its manipulation than interface design, judging by existing metaphors such as the book form or conventional text-based or text-driven tasks. However, whilst the vast majority of language teachers appreciate that they do not have the expertise, time and resources to develop new courseware, the fact remains that a real authoring need exists fuelled by the difficulty to integrate and exploit existing CALL applications, perceived as too rigid or too static. Thus, author requirements essentially focus on the need for a readily designed but customisable language environment, a creative language input facility, an easily recognisable and learnable authoring tool and a wide range of flexible interactive scenarios and modes.

3. Design Objectives: The chosen methodology pre-empted, in many ways, the aims and objectives of the design project in the form of usability features. Indeed, such an approach enabled the early identification of the overriding rationale for the project, the main characteristics of the user group and the required learning strategy to be supported by the system.. The initial investigative phase of the design context yielded, through an emphasis on human factors, a reasonably accurate assessment of student and author requirements and achievable user tasks measured against the possible system functionality within identified constraints such as technological possibilities and known or projected resources.

3.1 Usability Features: On the strength of pre-design considerations, three crucial usability features were to become the hallmarks of the new language environment.

3.1.1 Web-based Interactivity: Firstly, the prevalent need to provide easy access and interactivity led to the adoption of a web browser as the chosen platform for the project supported by a Java-written environment for enhanced interaction. As opposed to existing authoring platforms, the web-based language environment was seen as offering a number of advantages, which seemed to meet student requirements. It meant capitalising on the popularity and increased accessibility enjoyed by the Web amongst students. On this basis, it was felt that such a Java-written environment would be:

- intuitive therefore easy to learn due to its widely adopted design protocols and recognisable interface,
- comprehensive, as it could combine a constructive approach providing communicative competence as well as embedded grammar competence within the same language navigational space,
- versatile, as it could generate relational and support links necessary for a multimedia language learning resource at the macro, navigational level, but, similarly, sequential links at the micro level for a more hierarchical approach favoured for a grammar-oriented interaction,
- resourceful and strategic, as an environment capable of accommodating both language acquisition and learned knowledge as well as language structures and content,
- appealing, as a platform harnessing cutting edge technology and further exploiting the interactive potential of the computer as a tool.
- realistic and manageable within existing financial constraints and the current availability of hardware and software.

3.1.2 Authoring Input: The second main usability feature concerned the authoring input. In order to solve the design problem created by authoring needs, it was agreed that the new CALL environment would provide flexibility with a built-in, teacher-centred authoring tool. In design terms, what seemed to be fundamentally important was to separate the language input interface from its CALL output as clearly and purposefully as possible. Conscious of the fact that the tool authoring wheel did not need to be re-invented but, similarly, aware of existing authoring shortcomings, it was agreed that the inputting tool for language specialists would work in a familiar word processing environment thus greatly facilitating the user interaction between teacher and computer. Equally, additional gains were considered enormous. Firstly, new members of staff could be encouraged to key in their own language material without having to go into a programmer's model of an authoring facility, which often meant an unknown and technically threatening piece of software. Secondly, setting up a collective approach to large scale inputting was considered a necessity if the CALL project was to be successful. Thirdly, it was seen as the best way of capitalising on the existing technology instead of being subservient to it. Finally, by winning over new staff, it would bring back CALL onto the language teaching agenda and into the curriculum in a meaningful way.

3.1.3 Learning Strategy: Finally, the design of a language learning environment was supported by the adoption of an appropriate learning strategy. The main thrust at this stage was to combine both communicative and grammar competence as 'equally important and complementary partners in the acquisition of linguistic competence' (McBride & Seago, 1997:19). By extension, such a teaching approach embedding grammar into a communicative environment (see for instance Rogers, 1996) meant supporting the contextualisation of the language input to strengthen the relationship between language as linguistic vehicle and language as meaningful content. Increasingly, the interactive web browser, providing hierarchical and hypertextual links, was seen as an ideal environment to develop a discourse-based approach to language learning (McCarthy & Carter, 1994) prioritising a text-based dynamic process. It was also seen as being instrumental in developing better-integrated CALL interaction as well as more sustained and purposeful access.

4. Task Analysis: The task analysis, at this level of conceptualisation, was limited to providing a broad task decomposition and appropriate task hierarchies. This analysis, based on structure chart notations (Preece *et al.*, 1994) and sketches, was concerned with the initial mapping of high-level tasks and functions within the agreed parameters of the conceptual model. It identified interactive nodes on the basis of their relevant tasks as well as structural and navigational links. On the basis of sampled sentences and relevant texts, it highlighted the degree of potential exploitation and interaction, which could be designed and programmed. For example, a text related to a relevant content unit would be shown in different interactive forms according to the required exploitation, within a projected interface and in different representations to benefit from the potential of multimedia deliveries.

5. From Access to Accessibility: By providing a large amount of HCI data, previous research findings (Hémard, 1998, 1999) showed the extent to which students had become disenchanted with, if not alienated from the CALL interface. Moreover, if a majority of students had little expertise, consideration, time and interest in CALL and indicated that they seldom and artificially interacted with such an environment, so too were a number of colleagues for precisely the same reasons. Above all, in addition to known technological deficiencies, which had been largely identified by students, this negative assessment of CALL was pointing at the poor integration and inadequate use of CALL in language teaching. Worse still, observed attitudes corroborated that this apparent status quo was maintained by a tacit acceptance from staff and apathy from students as if CALL was conveniently or by default kept on an institutional life support machine justifying the existence of computers and playing lip service to staff development.

Against this negative or nihilistic culture, the ultimate aim of this project, conveyed by pre-design considerations, was to reverse such a trend. Indeed, it was strongly felt that, at this critical stage, improving and facilitating access to CALL was key to generating renewed acceptability. Reasons supporting this view can be identified in the following areas:

- Learning environment: The process of language learning involves students in acquiring the language within the confines of the university environment which can be seen according to Barrett (1994), as a *hypercontext* with its real-virtual presence generated by its various sites such as, for example, the library, the classroom and the language laboratory. In many respects, this hypercontext could be likened to some forms of exploratory and associative learning under learners' control. Therefore, by adopting web-based, hypertext links, access to learning material in CALL becomes more easily recognised and appreciated.
- Learning experience: Within this hypercontextual educational structure offering modularised units, the use of CALL must be perceived and developed as a necessary linking device between teaching and learning, but also, fundamentally, between language and content units. By providing access to a contextualised language environment CALL becomes both an extension of classroom-based language teaching as well as a useful and accessible satellite mechanism removing some of the artificiality of the institutionally organised learning experience.
- Open access experience: By the same token, the open access experience can only gain from greater recognition and direction if additional learning material and references are provided by the CALL interface. The teaching process would be less artificial whilst students would be encouraged to access, process and digest knowledge more appropriately.
- CALL interaction: Exposure to CALL applications in terms of contact hours and interaction is limited by existing resources and further hampered by a ratio of students per computer, which can be as high as three to one. Conversely, the CALL interface, by adopting a mixed communicative approach and contextual links can easily redesign and develop fruitful types of user interaction accommodating and capitalising on different combinations of interaction within the triangular parameter formed by teaching staff, students and computer.
- Authoring access: All language teaching staff are potential authors in the more traditional and generic sense of the term. Disenchantment and non-co-operation on the part of the teaching profession in CALL stem from a lack of appreciation or conviction of its learning capability, a lack of understanding of its functionality as an electronic environment and a subsequent lack of involvement in its creation and meaningful implementation. By allowing an authoring input to be accessed from within a known word processing environment, the main technological stumbling block is largely eradicated, thus enabling all teachers, in schools and colleges, to be implicated and creative at their level of linguistic specialisation.

- Access to technology: CALL development is often negatively tagged amateurish, experimental as well as technologically led, which, in turn, impact on a design process conditioned by task-oriented solutions and imposed design scenarios. For once, CALL interface design can claim to have caught up with and harnessed cutting edge technology in its exploitation of the web in conjunction with Java applets. Such an access to state-of-the -art technology can only help staff and students alike feel more motivated or simply reconciled with an interface worthy of consideration.

6. Conclusion: Whilst this paper only attempted to concentrate on pre-design considerations within a more conceptual presentation of the overriding design methodology and process, it is worth noting that the project itself is progressing successfully and about to deliver a number of language units, once the current summative evaluation session is completed and processed. But beyond the project itself and its own progression, the clearly stated aim was to demonstrate that a new approach to CALL design could facilitate access as well as generate greater acceptability on the part of its users from the wider language teaching and learning community. In turn, it is to be hoped that the need for a structured design process and approach can generate further applications and emulation with a view to supporting a new and better-adapted learning environment commensurate with current views on language learning and acquisition.

References:

Barrett, E. (Ed.) (1994). *Sociomedia: Multimedia, Hypermedia, and the Social Construction of Knowledge.* MIT Press.

Christie, B. and Gardiner, M. M. (1990). Evaluation of the human-computer interface. In J. R. Wilson and E. Nigel Corlett (Eds.) (1990) *Evaluation of the Human Work: A Practical Ergonomics Methodology.* London: Taylor and Francis: 271-320.

Dix, A., Finlay, J., Abowd, G. and Beale, R. (1993). *Human-Computer Interaction*, Hemel Hempstead: Prentice-Hall International.

Foley, J. D. (1983). Managing the Design of User-Computer Interfaces. *Computer Graphics World*, 12: 47-54.

Hémard, D. (1997). Design Principles and Guidelines for Authoring Hypermedia Language Learning Applications. *System* 25 (1): 9-27.

Hémard, D. (1998). Knowledge Representations in Hypermedia CALL Authoring: Conception and Evaluation. *Computer Assisted Language Learning*, 11, (3): 247-264.

Hémard, D. (1999). A Methodology for Designing Student-Centred Hypermedia CALL. In R. Debski and M. Levy (Eds.) *WorldCALL (provisional title)*, Swets & Zeitlinger Publishers (to be published).

Henderson, A. (1991). A Development Perspective on Interface, Design and Theory. In J. Carroll (Ed.) *Designing Interaction: Psychology at the Human-Computer Interface.* Cambridge University Press.

Jacobson, M. (1994). Issues in Hypertext and Hypermedia Research: Toward a Framework for Linking Theory-to-Design. *Journal of Educational Multimedia and Hypermedia* 3 (2): 141-154.

Levy, M. (1997). *Computer-Assisted Language Learning — Context and Conceptualization*, Clarendon Press, Oxford.

McCarthy, M. & Carter, R. (1994*). Language as Discourse: Perspectives for Language Teaching*. London: Longman.

McBride, N. & Seago, K. (1997). Bridging the Gap: Grammar as Hypertext. *ReCALL* 9 (2): 17-25.

Norman, D. A. (1988). *The Psychology of Everyday Things*. Basic Books, New York.

Preece, J., Rogers, Y., Sharp, H., Benyon, D., Holland, S., Carey, T., (1994). *Human-Computer Interaction*. Addison-Wesley Publishing Company, Wokingham, England.

Pylyshyn, Z. W. (1991). Some Remarks on the Theory-Practice Gap. In J. Carroll (Ed.) *Designing Interaction: Psychology at the Human-Computer Interface*. Cambridge University Press.

Rasmussen, J. (1992). The Ecology of Work and Interface Design. In: A. Monk, D. Diaper, M. D. Harrison (Eds.) (1992) *People and Computers VII*, Cambridge University Press.

Rogers, M. (1996). What's theory got to do with it? Grammar and Communication in L2 Acquisition. In D. Engel and F. Myles (Eds.) *Teaching Grammar: Perspective in Higher Education*, London: CILT, 21-33

Shneiderman, B. (1998). *Designing the User Interface; Strategies for Effective Human-Computer Interaction*, Addison-Wesley Publishing Company.

Wallace, M. D. and Anderson, T. J. (1993). Approaches to Interface Design. *Interacting with Computers, journal of the British HCI Group*.

SIGNALLING STRUCTURE IN WEB DOCUMENTS: SUPPORT FOR THE NON-NATIVE READER

Lawrie Hunter
Kochi University of Technology, Japan

Many of the long-standing techniques for signalling text structure in continuous text documents such as books are not appropriate for hypertext documents such as World Wide Web (www) pages. As a result, text structure in web pages is relatively difficult to identify. This increases the load placed upon the reader, in particular the non-native (NN) reader of the language in which the document is written.
This paper identifies text structure issues relating to accessibility of text and proposes a comprehensive strategy for supporting the NN reader's reading for structure.

Background: The author teaches a two year foundation English program at a new Japanese engineering university in rural southern Shikoku. In high school, the students studied English in a print based, examination driven program. Most Japanese undergraduate programs may be, have been, characterised as 'a four-year vacation' where university entrance is the most important prerequisite for university graduation. There the nature of the (committed) English teacher's task is to a large extent remotivating the students and shifting their approach to language learning towards self-directed learner strategies.

As far as reading English, most students have found little that they want to read, and when they do want to read a piece of text, they have few skills with which to unravel the information encoded there. 'Considerate text' (Kantor *et al.*, 1983) has proven to be helpful to these NN readers, but even more helpful is the provision of multiple versions of a text which in various ways throw light on content and/or text structure.
In terms of theoretical grounding, this paper leans heavily on one resource. From a teaching point of view this is pragmatic: in the psychosocial complex of the classroom, simple frameworks are preferable, if not essential.

Definitions / limitations: 'Reading' refers to reading a piece of text in order to garner overall comprehension of the content of the text (as opposed to searching, reading to locate specific information or the answers to specific questions).

'Hypertext' refers to all electronic documents (such as computer files, multimedia products and web pages) which contain live links to other sections of the same text or to other documents.

1. Text and the non-native reader

Linear text is accessible for those who are familiar with its systems of signalling structure. It is more accessible for those with background knowledge of the topic within. The non-native reader is not so familiar with structure signals in the second language, and background knowledge may be lacking too.

When it comes to hypertext such as web text, which is not linear like continuous text, there are fewer within-text signals, since terms like 'above' and even 'therefore' are often rendered useless when they span web pages rather than bound pages.

But hypertext, web pages, here is a medium where empty space is inexpensive, virtually free. We are at the beginning of the development of this medium and we need to learn how to give structure signal support to the reader, especially the non-native reader.

1.1 Models of reading: Current reading research offers two somewhat overlapping approaches to characterising the process of reading:

1. A metaphoric approach and
2. A 'reading components' model.

Chun and Plass (1997) list the three most common metaphors for describing the reading process as

1. Bottom-up processing,
2. Top-down processing and
3. Interactive processing.

The bottom-up metaphor emphasises the decoding of text. Reading models based on this metaphor see text type input as first and foremost, and focus on low level processes such as word recognition.

The top-down metaphor emphasises the reader's interpretation of text and, consequently, related reader background knowledge. Reading models based on this metaphor see knowledge (both syntactic and semantic knowledge) as most important; the focus is on the reader sampling the text content and predicting ensuing content or structure.

The reading components approach views reading as a composite of discrete subskills. Grabe (1991) summarises five general component skills and knowledge areas:

1. automatic recognition skills,
2. vocabulary and background knowledge,
3. formal discourse structure knowledge,
4. content/world background knowledge,

5. synthesis and evaluation skills/strategies, and
6. metacognitive knowledge and skills monitoring.

Regardless of which view of the reading process one adopts, or which form of reading is prevalent in a given instance, it remains fair to say that reading (understanding) a text consists in the building of mental representations of the information presented in the text. The understanding which a reader achieves in reading a passage is then a function of two variables:

1. nature (accessibility) of the text and
2. reader resources.

Simply put, then, reader resources for understanding text may be characterised as being of three types:

1. Background knowledge related to the information presented in a text.
2. Knowledge of the structure of different writing genres.
3. Knowledge of the various knowledge structures

1.2 The non-native reader: The NN reader reads differently from the native reader. NN readers pay more attention to low-level processes such as word identification, whereas L1 readers use much of their attention for higher level processes such as generation of inferences and general knowledge associations (Chun and Plass, 1997). This points to a need to support the NN reader in identifying the structure and background knowledge references in text.

A skilled native reader of English can hold the construction of a paragraph, a chapter, a book in conscious mind while reading. A NN reader can do that too, but cognitive load is increased by tentative (guessed, vague, half-forgotten) meanings of words, complex grammatical structures, and rhetorical devices perhaps unknown to the reader. As a result the NN reader more readily jumps from dense text to titles, lists, graphics, numbers, italics, bold fonts and other visual signals embedded in the text. And if such signals are absent, as they often are in hypertext, the NN reader is at a greater disadvantage than the native.

1.3 Structure of text, structure of knowledge: It is a truism (but nonetheless important) that the organisation of text does not necessarily reflect the structure of the information in the text. Text structure which does not reflect knowledge structure is an obstacle to reading. Goldman and Rakestraw (1998) summarise research on the importance of structure in reading as follows:

A. In text-driven (bottom-up) processing:
1. Structural cues improve identification of main or important ideas and their memorability.
2. Parallelisms between the surface structure text and the underlying conceptual structures of the information facilitate comprehension, i.e. comprehension is hampered when the two are not aligned.
3. Making the structure of a text more salient improves comprehension and learning.

B. In knowledge-driven processing (top-down):
1. Readers use their knowledge of structure in processing text. When an expected structure is violated, comprehension is impaired.
2. Knowledge of structural forms of text develops with experiences with different genre, and is correlated with age/time in school.
3. Making readers more aware of genre structure improves learning.

2. Reading support for the non-native reader of hypertext: Providing the kinds of reader support suggested above assumes the reader's ability and readiness to take advantage of that support. In discussing communication strategy in L2 reading support, Goldman and Rakestraw (1998) identify the following as key considerations:

1. The effects of structural aspects of the text depend on whether or not the readers can supply the structure themselves (and thus do not need the cues in the text).
2. If readers cannot supply the structure themselves, they need to have sufficient knowledge of structure cues in text to allow them to interpret and use information to construct coherent and appropriately structured mental representations of the information.
3. Readers in low knowledge circumstances need assistance in constructing a representation of the information in the knowledge domain.
4. Surface text clues should be aligned with the underlying conceptual or situational models.
5. Surface structural cues to organisation and main idea identification can assist readers in learning a new domain if readers know how to interpret these cues.

2.1 Strategies for NN reader support in hypertext reading : Support for the NN reader may be divided into two categories:
1. Support for the reading of a specific document.
2. Support for the acquisition of reading skill.

From a process point of view, acquisition of reading skill may be seen as a process wherein a person who does not have sufficient background knowledge or knowledge of structure in text is transformed into one who has sufficient background knowledge and knowledge of text structure.

From a systems point of view, NN hypertext reading support may be seen as coupling a software component to a (human) learner component in light of a learning theory complex. It is useful to consider two interacting components in a reading support scenario:

1. Human component. In reader support, the reader should be a witting user of the documents/software provided, and also a self-assessing processor of text. The witting user should be the driver of the reader support system; this is the implicit goal of reader support.
2. Machine component. The software/documents which the reader confronts ought to provide the reader with an array of 'lenses' through which to view the documents, these lenses providing views of text structure and concept structure in both text and graphic forms. As well, the reader should be guided towards selecting one of a number of 'attack styles', based on the reader's self assessment.

A review of recent literature in Hunter (1998) listed the following ways in which NN reading may be supported by document design:

1. Assure that conceptual structures are arranged for rhetorical transparency.
2. Assure that text surface structure clearly parallels conceptual structures.
3. Provide 'structural glossing' where structures may be new to the reader or so complex as to be challenging to the reader.
4. Do not overstructure hypertext; it is essential that the reader bring something to the meaning construction process.

Balance between (3) and (4) is crucial, and both require a high degree of tailoring to the background and skill of the individual. In the case of authoring of materials for EFL learners at the college level in Japan, this balance is often not so difficult to achieve, given the relative uniformity of learner background and skill, but even in that extreme case, learner differences point to the need for the strategy outlined in (7) below.

5. If the reader is well-informed about the content of a text, do not provide overly explicit signalling of local coherence in text, so as not to impede deeper processing of underlying conceptual coherence (or the taking of more than one intellectual perspective on the content).
6. Support the reader's active involvement in creating representations of text. This calls for a trade-off between what is explicit in the text and what the reader has to infer.
7. Provide multiple versions of a text, and guide the reader in choosing the appropriate version (hypertext is eminently suitable for this):

(a) Original, found text. Original versions may well be poorly structured, structure poorly signalled, and text structure may not be parallel to conceptual structure.
(b) Structurally rearranged version. This version presents the same material, only rearranged so that text structure is parallel to conceptual structure.
(c) Fully rhetorically signalled version. Unlike much found text, this version provides rhetorical signals for all intertextual relations; the demand for reader inference about structure is much reduced.
(d) Fully rhetorically signalled version with highlighted signals. As in (c), this version provides rhetorical signals for all intertextual relations and those signals are highlighted (by underlining or coloured font) so that readers may check their perception of what signals are present.
(e) Glossed version. Here concepts and vocabulary essential to understanding of the text are provided in a gloss, in footnotes or in sidebars.
(f) Outline version. A text outline shows the essential conceptual elements of the text structure, in the order in which they occur.
(g) Minimal summarising statements version. This version comprises one sentence for each of the fundamental meaning elements of the text.
(h) Structure diagram version. A diagram shows the elements in the outline version and the relationships between the elements.

The mention in (7) of guiding the user suggests the provision of some kind of 'users' guide' which suggests strategies (sequences) for reading combinations of the various versions of a text. See section 2.6 for a brief description of the author's curriculum design in this area.

2.2 Reader training in text patterns and their cues: Reading may be characterised as an isolated and internal task. Document based support for the task of reading may be available; structure may be articulated, key words may be highlighted, glosses may be made available, outlines or summaries may be provided as navigation aids.

Nevertheless, it is the reader who must monitor the degree of comprehension with which the reading is proceeding, who must decide when to make use of any of the support available. In this sense the reader may be said to be 'active'; the reader must be monitoring the reading, and must decide on an acceptable degree of understanding, must take action when understanding flags.

Signalling knowledge structure by means such as those listed in section 2.1 presupposes reader knowledge of the writing structures (genres) being signalled, or presupposes that, by being exposed to mention of structure and signalling of structure, the reader will develop awareness of the variety and use of knowledge structures.

2.3 Knowledge structures: Then, what are the structures of knowledge (and the structures of text, the genres, which reflect them)? And to what depth need the NN reader know these structures (or know of them)?

A wide variety of knowledge frameworks (typologies of knowledge structures) have been proposed in recent research. A few provocative examples are described briefly below; each is suitable for some combination of reader background, reader maturity and the kinds of text the reader is learning to read. The balance of manageable simplicity and sufficient detail of typology varies greatly among these frameworks.

Meyer (1985) proposes a set of five 'top-level' rhetorical structures in order to systematise the structure of the major expository text genres:

1. Collection or list
2. Description
3. Causal
4. Comparative
5. Problem/solution

In his extended discussion of the use of 'key graphics' to support reading comprehension, Mohan (1986) proposed a knowledge structure (reflecting a parallel structure necessarily found in language) composed of three theoretical structures paired with three practical structures:

Description — Classification
Sequence — Principles
Choice — Evaluation

Critics of this knowledge structure point to its lack of comprehensivity. Proponents speak highly of the theoretical-practical pairing as useful for verification of completeness in language learning materials.

Jonassen (1996), in his chapter on semantic networking (also known as concept mapping), uses a more open, visual approach to knowledge structuring: knowledge representations identify concepts and describe relationships between them. This approach does not include a method for mapping language structure onto knowledge structure, and may well lead away from doing so. This opens the Pandora's box topic of the evolution of literacy, which is outside the scope of this paper, but is not to be ignored.

Systemic functional linguistics, for example Butt (1995), identifies 'text types' by function:

Narrative
Recount
Information report
Discussion
Explanation
Exposition
Procedure.

Each text type has certain obligatory or common language structure and knowledge structure elements, and as such constitutes a genre. The systemic functional linguistics approach has been widely implemented into language education in Australia.

Grow (1996) identifies as useful this writing typology:

> ... three generic types of organisation which occur widely in writing of all kinds:
> 1. Texts containing one major element, plus supporting information...
> 2. Texts describing a sequence...
> 3. Texts comparing two or more elements...
> Each type of text organisation embodies a different kind of thought process and reveals that thought process through the use of 'signal' words.

A number of such structure systems have been proposed, but the important points are that there are such rhetorical structures, and that knowledge structure and language structure recognition are fundamental to text comprehension. How structures/genres are named and categorised is not as important as the reader's awareness of ability to recognise various genre and anticipate the knowledge structure represented by each.

2.4 Signalling structure in documents: Structure signalling in text documents leans heavily on the fact that text is linear in structure. For example, a cause-effect relation between two sentences, two paragraphs or two adjacent sections is easily signalled in text. In hypertext there is no easy way to signal the same relationship between two 'pages'. This is often seen in web sites which are cut and paste versions of an original linear text.

This weakness in much of hypertext is temporary, reflecting the embryonic nature of design for the medium. Moreover, with web page frames and the ease of incorporation of navigation aids and visual and textual links into web documents, hypertext can be designed so that the reader is supported to the point where she/he is always informed of a page's position in the overall structure of the text, and of the page's information relationship to other pages in the document.

For any local piece of text (the text on one web page), there are four kinds of structure signals which afford structure-related support to the reader:

1. Signalling the text's position in the overall document structure
2. Signalling the text's position in the local knowledge structure
3. Signalling the text's internal text structure
4. Signalling the text's internal knowledge structure

Not all of these signallings are appropriate or necessary all of the time; rather each type of signalling should be used when there is some clarifying benefit.

2.5 Examples of structure signalling: A number of structure signal types are necessary for maximum reader support in identifying text and knowledge structure in hypertext. Text structure in hypertext is familiarly signalled in the same ways as linear text: indexing, outlining, glossing, section numbering, use of titles and text styles.

Reference links from the text should not immediately take the reader outside the document. Exemplary in this is the web site version of Wakefield (1997) (see fig.1), which is designed so that one may click on references within the main text and view those references, annotated, in a sidebar without leaving the main text, in fact without leaving one's place in the main text. Unfortunately, in this site the references and the main text do not move independently, so by clicking on a reference in the main text, the reader is taken to the reference, but taken away from the spot in the text being read.

Berners-Lee (1998) should be a good example of signalling text structure in hypertext, given that it is a piece of a broad proposal for standards in web text format. This is not the case however. The index page of the site is a hot-linked table of contents, but the individual pages (see fig. 2) of the site give no information as to their position in the overall document. Another example of this limbo type of pages is Mobil Oil's web site (www.mobil.com), which contains a useful, well illustrated multi-page discussion of greenhouse gases and global warming, unnecessarily difficult for the NN reader in particular because of lack of structure signalling.

Good examples of text structure signalling can be found in a not so surprising web site. ThinkQuest is a student web site construction competition, and many of the examples of student work have good structure signalling. For example, one site devoted to philosophy (see fig. 3) is Stilman *et al.* (1998). When the user selects a topic, a new window opens, showing the directory. Selection of a topic from the directory opens a content window; the user can rearrange the desktop to place these two small windows so that both content and index are visible.

There are numerous web sites which do in various ways signal text structure. As for signalling knowledge structures, no good examples were found. In general the knowledge structure of the material on each page, or of a page and its neighbours, is only signalled by means of textual devices, which puts the burden on the reader to know the structure of the information already, or to slowly intuit it.

Signals of knowledge structure in a web page may be divided into two types, those which portray the structure of knowledge within the page, and those which portray the page's place in a larger structure, in a group of informationally adjacent pages. Figures 6 and 7 show the author's prototype for visual signals of hypertext document knowledge structure; the symbols used are drawn from the author's set of semantic mapping symbols (fig. 4).

This presents a fruitful area for materials development. An inroad to the teaching of structure signalling issues is seen in the following section.

2.6 An unfolding curriculum: structure in writing: The author has been creating and teaching a college EFL curriculum for some years now, and an emerging focus in this work has been in three areas:

1. Increasing learner awareness of structure and its signals through the use of structure signalling visuals in listening, speaking and writing tasks.
2. Increasing learner awareness of structure through semantic mapping in reading tasks.
3. Encouraging learner use of semantic mapping for reading, for organising data, and for the planning of writing.

The knowledge structure symbols used in task groups 2 and 3 provide an inroad into signalling knowledge structure in hypertext (see fig. 4). As well, the student 'textbook' introduction to semantic mapping is available on line at http://www.info.kochi-tech.ac.jp/lawrie/semanticmapindex.htm

Extension: As for supportive document design, the approach described here provides the reader with an array of structure-revealing signals and document versions. This points to the need for reader training in recognising rhetorical structures.

Visually signalling within page and inter-page knowledge structures appears to be a fruitful area for exploration and materials development. Foltz (1996:7) envisions an eventual state of the art in structure signalling technique: '... as hypertexts become more accepted and widespread, writers of hypertext may develop standard rhetorical styles. Readers who are then familiar with those rhetorical styles can use that knowledge to help in their structuring of the information in an effective manner'.

Many of the recent developments in hypertext authoring are paralleled in text authoring. In his section on considerate text in journalism, Grow (1996) says that the recent success of the redesign of major publications defies older psychological concepts such as stimulus-response and can only be explained in terms of cognitive theory. Now, Grow claims, '... practitioners of journalism can do far more than they can explain. Practice has outrun theory'. But this is surely just another swing of the practice-theory pendulum.

References:

Anderson, Richard C., & Armbruster, B.B. 1985. Studying. In P. D. Pearson (Ed.), Handbook of Reading Research. New York: Longman, pp. 657-680. *Style guide for online hypertext* http://www.w3.org/Provider/Style/Overview.html

Berners-Lee, T. 1998. *Style guide for online hypertext.* Part of the World Wide Web (W3) Consortium's Style sheets recommendations. http://www.w3.org/Provider/Style/

Bolter, Jay David. 1998. In Reinking, D., McKenna, M. C., Labbo, L. D., & Kieffer, R. D. (Eds.) *Literacy and technology* (pp. 3-13). Mahwah, NJ: Erlbaum.

Butt, D., Fahey, R., Spinks, S., and Yallop, Colin. 1995. *Using functional grammar.* Sydney: Macquarie University, National Centre for English Language Teaching and Research.

Chun, D. M. and Plass, J. L. 1997. Research on text comprehension in multimedia environments. *Language learning and technology* 1(1): 60-81.

Foltz, P.W. 1996. Comprehension, coherence and strategies in hypertext and linear text. In Rouet, J.-F., Levonen, J. J., Dillon, A. P. & Spiro, R. J. (Eds.) *Hypertext and cognition.* Hillsdale, NJ: Erlbaum.

Fulkerson, Richard. 1996. *Teaching the argument in writing.* Urbana, IL: National Council of Teachers of English. ISBN 0-8141-0190-9

Gillingham, M. G. 1996. Comprehending electronic text. In van Oostendorp, H. and de Mul, S. (Eds.) *Cognitive Aspects of Electronic Text Processing.* New Jersey: Ablex.

Goldman, S. R., & Rakestraw, Jr., J. A. (in press). *Structural aspects of constructing meaning from text.* In M. L. Kamil, P. Mosenthal, P. D. Pearson, & R. Barr (Eds.), Handbook of reading research (Vol. 3, pp. xx-xx). Mahwah, NJ: Erlbaum.

Grabe, W. 1991. Current developments in second language reading research. *TESOL Quarterly, 25(3)*, 375-406.

Grow, Gerald O. 1996. *Serving the Strategic Reader: Reader Response Theory and Its Implications for the Teaching of Writing*, an expanded version of a paper presented to the Qualitative Division of the Association for Educators in Journalism and Mass Communication. Atlanta, August, 1994. Available on-line at: <http://www.famu.edu/sjmga/ggrow>. Original paper available as Eric Documentation Reproduction Service No. ED 406 644.

Hunter, L. 1998. Text nouveau, visible structure in text presentation. *Computer Assisted Language Learning* 11 (4) October 1998.

Johnson, Steven. 1997. *Interface culture.* New York: Harper Collins.

Jonassen, David H. 1996. *Computers in the classroom: mindtools for critical thinking.* Englewood Cliffs, NJ: Prentice-Hall.

Kantor, R. N., T. H.Anderson and B. B.Armbruster. 1983 (not seen). How inconsiderate are children's textbooks? *Journal of Curriculum Studies* 15(1): 61-72.

Keep, Christopher and McLaughlin, Tim. 1995. *The electronic labyrinth.* http://jefferson.village.virginia.edu/elab/hfl0006.html

Lawrence, Mary S. 1996. *Writing as a thinking process.* Ann Arbor: University of Michigan Press.

Lynch, Patrick J. and Horton, Sarah. 1998. Refining web pages: effective design strategies for educators. *Syllabus*: February 1998: 39-43.

Mohan, B.A. 1986. *Language and content.* Reading, MA: Addison-Wesley.

Morkes, John and Nielsen, Jakob. 1997. *Concise, scannable and objective: How to write for the web.* Sun Microsystems. http://www.useit.com/papers/webwriting/writing.html

Morris, Charles. 1938. *Foundations of the theory of signs.* Chicago: University of Chicago Press.
Muter, Paul. (in press) Interface design and optimization of reading of continous text. In van Oostendorp, H., and de Mul. S. (eds.) *Cognitive aspects of electronic text processing.* Norwood, NJ: Ablex. http://psych.utoronto.ca/~muter/pmuter1.htm
Norman, Donald A. 1988. *The design of everyday things.* New York: Doubleday.
O'Donnell, James. 1998. *The avatar and the word: from papyrus to cyberspace.* Cambridge, MASS: Harvard University Press.
Peterson, Mark. 1997. Creating hypermedia learning environments: guidelines for designers. *Computer Assisted Language Learning* 11(2) 1998.
Purves, Alan. 1998. Flies in the web of hypertext. In Reinking, D., McKenna, M. C., Labbo, L. D., & Kieffer, R. D. (Eds.) *Literacy and technology* (pp. 235-251). Mahwah, NJ: Erlbaum.
Reinking, D., McKenna, M. C., Labbo, L. D., & Kieffer, R. D. 1998. *Literacy and technology.* Mahwah, NJ: Erlbaum.
Schank, R.C. and Cleary, C. 1995. *Engines for education.* Hillsdale, NJ: Lawrence Erlbaum Associates.
Scheiderman, B. 1997. *Designing the user interface: strategies for effective human-computer interaction.* Reading, MASS: Addison-Wesley.
Shrum, Judith L. and Glisan, Eileen W. 1994. *Teacher's handbook: contextualized language instruction.* Boston: Heinle and Heinle.
Spiro, R., Feltovich, P., Jacobson, M. & Coulson, R. 1992. Cognitive flexibility, constructivism and hypertext: random access instruction for advanced knowledge in ill-structured domains. In T. Duffy and D. Jonassen (eds) *Constructivism and the technology of instruction.* Hillsdale, NJ: Erlbaum, pp.112-48.
Stilman, M., Bender, M., & Gay, K. 1998. *Philosophia* web site. http://library.advanced.org/17934/
ThinkQuest web site http://www.thinkquest.org/
Tufte, E. R. (1990) *Envisioning information.* Cheshire, CONN: Graphics Press.
Wakefield, John. 1997. *A problem-solving model of textbook design.* Paper presented at the Text and Academic Authors national convention, Las Vegas, NE, June 18 1997. Available on the web at http://www.winonanet.com/taa/ARTICLES/9706jun/970618wakefieldtext.html
Williams, Robin. 1997. *The non-designer's design book.* Berkeley, CA: Peachpit Press.
Wurman, R. S. 1996. *Information architects.* Zurich: Graphis

Appendix 1
A structure signal strand in a college EFL curriculum

A. Writing tasks which increase student awareness of structure and its signals
  1. My Past, Present and Future (HyperCard stack):
    -student task: create a document
    -navigation with structure signals only on Directory card (signals are section names)
  2. My Hometown (HyperCard stack):
    -navigation menu in background
    -navigation order linear (links show text structure only)
  3. Sequence stack:
    -background menu has the same text and knowledge structure
  4. Group research:
    -background menu uses Hunter's semantic mapping symbols*

B. Oral group tasks using structure symbol graphics to increase student awareness of structure signals
  1. Listening comprehension tasks involving placement of words or phrases in a structure symbol diagram.
  2. Student oral presentations using visual incorporating structure symbols.

C. Increasing awareness of structure signals through semantic mapping tasks using a supplied set of structure symbols*
  1. Mapping single sentences
  2. Mapping sets of sentences (one or two paragraphs)
    -discovering that structure signal words help (e.g. cooking)
  3. Mapping found text (short articles)
    -discovering that professional text often has few structure signals
    -discovering that not all sentences are central to topic (background information)
  4. Mapping with limitation on number of nodes
    -selecting key information bits is easier after mapping

*Hunter's semantic mapping symbols: see figure 4

SYNCHRONOUS COMPUTER MEDIATED COMMUNICATION. CHAT AND MOO: WHERE DO WE STAND?

Sophie Ioannou-Georgiou
Cyprus Pedagogical Institute, Cyprus

Computer Mediated Communication: Susan Herring (1996) has defined CMC as '...communication that takes place between human beings via the instrumentality of computers'. This communication is distinguished between synchronous (real-time) communication and asynchronous communication. Synchronous communication includes such modes as IRC, MOOs and videoconferencing whereas asynchronous includes e-mail and Newsgroups. Web publishing and interacting with published material on the web is often considered as a form of CMC. John December (1997 and Ferris (1997) make clear that CMC would encompass such communications as well. For the sake of this paper, though, we will exclude it from the discussion and we will focus on human-to-human interaction and especially on Chat and MOO.

Computer Mediated Communication: Types and applications[1] or Foreign and Second language learning

Asynchronous Communication: Asynchronous communication seems to be preferred by language teachers at least at their beginning stages of CMC experience. It is considered to be easier since it is simple to use, does not depend on the whims of the network and offers communication with native speakers without requiring special time co-ordinations with students from other countries.

E-mail: E-mail projects have been one of the first ways in which CMC was incorporated into language learning. These projects vary from simple key pal projects to complicated collaborative projects that result in excellent work such as published enzines or web pages. E-mail is also used as a way to facilitate tandem learning[2] since it helps satisfy its main prerequisite which is to bring together two students from different countries native speakers of each other's target language.

---

[1] Given the many ways CMC can be used in language learning, I hope to be excused if I do not mention interesting and fruitful projects.

[2] For more details on tandem learning see the Tandem Server Bochum of the University of Bochum at http://www.slf.ruhr-uni-bochum.de/ .

Discussion lists: E-mail has also been used in the form of discussion or mailing lists. Often, it is a solution to the problems of unresponsiveness and dropouts facing individual key-pal projects. Sometimes they are used in the form of an open class journal promoting community building and open communication within a class. On other occasions, they are used in projects that realise all the principles of process writing[3] and/or intercultural awareness with students working in groups to find out about each other's country and culture.

Newsgroups: Newsgroups have been used by language teachers especially as a means of providing authentic communication in a subject of interest to the students. If, for example, the students are football fanatics they might join a football newsgroup where they can join other football fans in authentic, heated discussions. In other cases, the teacher might create a Newsgroup based on a class discussion in order to promote a type of communication similar to that of e-mail mailing lists without the problem of cluttering private e-mail accounts.

Newsgroups have, however, been recently spoiled by foul language, spam mail and flaming which have, at least for now, made Newsgroups unsuitable for many groups of learners (Eastment, 1999)

Synchronous Communication: Synchronous communication is increasing in popularity as teachers get access to the technology, acquire familiarity with it and the processes involved in using synchronous CMC in language learning.

Videoconferencing: In the past few years audio and visual cues would not co-ordinate, the software needed were very expensive and the communication pace was very slow. Things have got better now although they are not perfect. It is still much more expensive if you compare it to other modes of communication such as MOOs and Chat. Videoconferencing still faces problems. Sometimes it is again a problem of dealing with audio and video.[4] Other problems may be network overload and breakdown of the system if one joins after the session starts as mentioned by Butler and Fawkes (1999). They also mention that the costs for the school, even though they used comparatively inexpensive products, were £2.700 for the initial kit, £4000 for their first year and £5000 for the second year when more classes joined in the programme. This amount of money might well be beyond the budget limitations of many schools.

Audioconferencing: This is another way of communication that has recently grown in use due to the better quality of audio provided by faster connections, larger bandwidth

---

[3] See, for example, the highly successful International Writing Exchange project at http://www.hut.fi/~rvilmi/Project/ .

[4] iVisit, for example, has problems with video which is transmitted in a jerky fashion.

and stream audio. Voice Chat, as it is also known, is becoming as easily available as ordinary text Chat programme.[5] One example of audioconferencing in learning was presented by Shield et. al. at the 1999 BALEAP conference (April '99). With the help of an audioconferencing client, students were brought together and collaborated on three projects each lasting between 2-4 weeks.

IRC/ Chat programmes: IRC and other Chat programmes have recently seen a wider use by language teachers. There are different Chat programmes available. Some you can run off the web without having to download any particular software (e.g. Dave Sperling's café, yahoo chat) while others need special software to be downloaded into your computer (IRC, Global chat, etc.) Many programmes include facilities such as automatic messages, buddy lists and paging (AOL messenger, ICQ etc.).

Some recent additions to IRC are facilities such as the ability to include graphics in the messages, ability to share files (DCC File Server), user-friendly interface with toolbars to access frequently used commands, ability to open websites in special windows as they are mentioned (Track Urls), ability to add colour or sound, excellent help functions and even ability to support text extensions such as various fonts, bold and underline. All users of such Chat programmes are, however, still relying on the web and the servers they subscribe to. If the server is down no communication can take place.

A very interesting example of Chat in language learning was presented at the 33rd International IATEFL conference in Edinburgh by Laurent Borgmann (1999). In this case, Chat was used in a European Union project among students of three countries. The students were to meet in a fourth country and it was decided that particular students would be assigned responsibilities such as travel arrangements, etc. So that the right person to undertake the assigned responsibilities would be chosen, the interested students had to be interviewed by a committee. Each country's student-candidates had their 'job' interviews by another country's committee through a chat programme.[6]

CACD: Problems to do with web reliability can be avoided by installing commercial Chat programmes on a computer network. In cases where such a programme is used for educational purposes, Chat has been given the term CACD (Computer Assisted Classroom Discussion). These programmes are usually expensive and not many institutions can afford them. Such a programme is the well-known Daedalus InterChange

---

5 See Excite Voice Chat (http://www.excite.com) which has very little requirements and allows up to ten people to chat at the same time.

6 The project was co-ordinated by the University of Fulda, Germany. Although the website might not be very detailed it might give you some idea about the project — http://www.fh-fulda.de/language/borgmann/borgmann/pro_cont.htm .

that has been successfully implemented in foreign and second language learning as well as native language composition classes.

There are also other in-house versions of CACD that have been produced by other institutions to suit their budgets and their needs. The programme is most often used as an aid to writing through brainstorming sessions and peer editing, as a general conversation aid or as help towards in-depth understanding of reading passages.

MOOs: MOOs (Multi-User Domain Object Oriented) are mainly text-based virtual reality programmes. MOO environments take the form of existing places. Some are, for example, programmed to resemble Universities and Colleges while others resemble houses or towns. The basic differences between a MOO and a CHAT programme are:

a) A MOO is always there even when there is nobody logged on.
b) A user/player can interact with the environment as well as with the participants, e.g. order a pizza, go for a swim, read a book.
c) A user/player can create his own space in a MOO or create objects including himself e.g. personal description (clothing, physical appearance, personality).
d) A MOO offers other means of communication within its programme (MOOmail, mailing lists, bulletin boards, paging).

MOOs have until now been described as strictly text-based virtual reality environments. There are, however, recently quite a few MOOs which although mainly text-based incorporate three-dimensional additions and advanced graphics such as movable avatars and rooms that you can move around in or allow for the transfer of audio files.[7] These MOOs, impressive as they may be, are not as user-friendly as they claim to be and usually one has to wait a long time for an avatar to move from one room to another or avatars might not move at all, in real time. In addition, they usually require the latest computer models and various computer software or other equipment.
An interesting fact is that many MOO users are refusing to adapt to this new generation of graphical and 3-Dimensional MOOs and go on using text-based MOOs instead (Sempsey, 1998). Purely text-based MOOs seem to be the ones the learning community prefers for I have not heard of many implementing new generation MOOs into their teaching. Instead, it is SchMOOze University,[8] MOO Francais,[9] Pueblo Lindo,[10] (MOOs prepared especially for language learning)[11] and Diversity University,[12] which seem to

---

[7] The Palace (http://www.thepalace.com) and Active Worlds (http://www.activeworlds.com)are such examples.

[8] http://www.cc.rim.or.jp/~awaji/schMOOze/

[9] http://www.umsl.edu/~moosproj/moofrancais.html

[10] http://pueblolindo.heinle.com

[11] These are not the only MOOs for language learning. There are others (e.g. Mundo Hispano) and the number of MOOs is steadily growing.

be mostly used for language learning. Developments, however, have happened in text-based MOOs as well with the introduction of Java clients, hypertext and web page editors.

Recently, a very promising new text-based MOO has made its appearance. It's called TAPPED IN[13] and it is run by the Teacher Professional Development Institute. It is a virtual conference centre and has about 5000 members. It incorporates a web interface and pull down menus of commands, help topics and suggestions. Learners, therefore, who cannot remember the commands needn't face that problem any more. Other interesting features of this new MOO is a script editor and a facility which enables all the players of a particular room to share the same web site. Another factor worth considering is the enthusiasm of the members and especially the volunteer assistants. As soon as you enter the door you are greeted with 'May I help you?' Later on in your stay 'Have you seen this feature?', 'Shall I project it for you?'.

MOOs are used as another way to facilitate tandem learning, to get students involved in conversations with native speakers or other learners from other countries and as a tool to allow collaborative learning projects between learners either from the same class or from various classes around the world. Examples of projects carried out in a MOO are the creation of objects or spaces in the MOO such as the creation of Virtual Versailles (Sanchez, 1996), using the MOO to peer edit writing projects (frequently happens between teacher players at SchMOOze) or collaborating for the creation of a common Web page as has recently been done by Shield and Weiniger (1999).

Pedagogy to support CMC use: We are lucky to have these 'phenomenal' (Higgins, 1997) tools available to us. Use of CMC, however, is more than just showing off our high tech knowledge or a way to boost our school's entrance rates. There is sound pedagogy to support CMC use. To analyse the supporting pedagogical theories in detail I would need to exceed my word limit by far so I will limit myself to briefly touch on each of them.

Collaborative learning: Vygotsky's (1978) theory of social learning and the Zone of Proximal Development has recently given an extra incentive to the teaching world for the promotion of collaborative learning. Through the process of collaboration, the learners are guided/helped by other learners to achieve their potential. Vygotsky's theory of the Zone of Proximal Development makes collaboration seem as a necessity (Renie & Chanier, 1995). One way of such social learning is through social interaction, which is the simplest form of a CMC activity. Another advantage of CMC environments for collaborative learning is the feeling of community that CMC and especially Chat and

---

[12] http://www.duets.org

[13] http://www.tappedin.org/

MOO environments have been found to foster (Reid, 1991; Bruckman, 1995). MOOs, in particular, have been found to have an even friendlier atmosphere than Chat (Serpentelli, 1995). A strong sense of community and a caring atmosphere will promote collaboration and the help offered by the 'caregivers' — in this case more advanced learners or native speakers.

Motivation: Motivation has been claimed to be the one most important factor in influencing a learner's success or failure in the language learning task (Pulvermuller and Schumann 1994). Even if we do not accept this particular opinion, however, I do not think there is anyone who can question the fact that motivation is a very influential factor in language learning as well as any other kind of learning for that matter. CMC has been repeatedly reported to increase learners' motivation and promote positive attitude development towards language learning. This is especially so if it is used as an integral part of the language programme rather than as an extra add-on activity that students do now and then (Warschauer 1995, 1996b).

Communicative learning: Most of the teaching world still adheres to the basic principles of communicative learning although it is accepted that we are now in the postcommunicative era. CMC provides a unique tool with which to satisfy most of the principles of communicative learning. The language used in CMC activities is authentic and communication is authentic in itself without the teacher needing to invent all kinds of imaginary situations. CMC activities usually provide the learner with a purpose, an audience, feedback, choice of language and an info-gap - fundamental characteristics of any communicative activity. They also satisfy the communicative activity criteria set by Richards & Rodgers, 1986:

> ...engage learners in communication, and require the use of such communication processes as information sharing, negotiation of meaning and interaction.
>
> (Richards & Rodgers, 1986)

Interactionist theories: If the aim is communication, then what takes place during a communication, i.e. the interactions, should be very significant. A strong theory of second and foreign language learning is based on Interaction. The theory supports that comprehensible input is fundamental for language learning (Krashen 1982, 1985), even more so when the learner has been involved in bringing the input to a level where it is comprehensible to him/her. This is achieved by the learners' contributions in negotiating the meaning of the interaction (Long 1981, Pica 1981). In addition, the learner's production of output promotes the development of his/her interlanguage by forcing the learner test and develop his/her grammatical and syntactical competence (Swain 1985). CMC, therefore, seems to provide a perfect environment for 'optimal' interactions. There is a lot of communication going on, most of the time between learners, therefore a lot of it is bound to be at the right level (i+1) so as to be comprehensible. When input is not comprehensible, the misunderstandings or non-understandings will have to be resolved otherwise there will be no communication. In this way, we achieve negotiations of meaning and finally there is plenty of production since that is the only way communication can take place. One could say that CMC was tailor-made for language learning.

Learner Autonomy: Learner autonomy is one of the main aims of teaching since it helps satisfy the goal of lifelong learning. By helping the learner develop learning strategies such as using the dictionary we help him/her take control of their learning and offer them the ability to continue learning outside class and well after they have finished their language course. CMC activities help promote learner autonomy by teaching the learner how to use the technology and access opportunities for communication and learning. He/she may, therefore, continue to do so after class and/or after the end of the language course thus promoting his/her own personal development. Also the nature of CMC environments is such that once used in class they give the learner another edge on gaining autonomy. Once on Chat or in a MOO there is no direct control by the teacher. The learner has the power to initiate new topics of conversation and he/she can choose whether or not he/she would like to participate in the discussion at all or whether he/she will follow the teacher's suggestions or propose their own instead.

Empirical findings about CMC use: The strong pedagogy supporting CMC use is not by itself enough to argue the case of CMC validity to Headteachers, Directors of Studies, Heads of Parents' Associations, Ministry officials or language teachers. It is very often that we hear high-ranking all-powerful Ministry officials say things like 'Yes, it is fashionable now, isn't it?' or 'It is the latest trend, is it?'. It is not unusual to hear language teachers talk in the same way about the latest 'fad'. This could be explained partly by their disbelief that CALL in general and the Internet and CMC in particular, could be of any real help to language learning and anything more than frills. These feelings might be caused by a partial fear of the Internet or by a disappointment with what CALL has achieved until now.

There is a need, therefore, to prove that CMC activities are indeed useful in promoting our goals. I believe this can be done through the provision of hard data and empirical research, which will unquestionably prove whether or not CMC does indeed deliver the goods we hope it does.

There are some empirical findings already available and I will here focus on the research that has already been done in the area of Chat and MOOs. The existing research for Chat is summarised in Tables 1 and 2. It has mainly been carried out on LANs and most of it while the learners were using Daedalus InterChange.

Research Results	Researcher/s
greater student motivation	Beauvois 1992,1994 Kelm 1992 Kern 1995 Warschauer 1996b
greater student participation	Bump 1990 Pratt & Sullivan 1994 Kelm 1992 Kern 1995 Warschauer 1996a
learners experience less anxiety	Beauvois 1992, 1994 Kelm 1992 Kern 1995
CMC helped both introverts and extroverts	Beauvois & Eledge 1996
CMC led to more production in the TL (as opposed to oral discussion)	Beauvois 1992, 1994 Kelm 1992 Kern 1995 Pratt & Sullivan 1994 Warschauer 1996a
students had favourable attitudes towards CMC	Warschauer 1996b Meunier 1997

Table 1: Research that has been carried out on Chat in LANs and resulted in positive findings.

Research Results	Researcher/s
CMC caused learners to develop computer anxiety	Bump 1990 Meunier 1997 Sabatelli 1997 Pinto 1996
learners had problems keeping up with the content of the discussions	Meunier 1997
a lot of flaming occurred during CMC	Meunier 1997
CMC was time consuming	Kelm 1992 Freiermuth 1998
learners were exposed to untraditional language (Cyber English)	Lundstrom 1995
gender differences in CMC were exposed	Meunier 1997

personality differences in CMC were exposed	Meunier 1997
slow speed of interaction	Bump 1990
loss of coherence when discussing a topic	Bump 1990
Increased literal translation from L1	Kelm 1992

Table 2: Research that has been carried out on Chat in LANs and resulted in negative findings.

As far as MOOs are concerned, there is even less empirical research available. Apart from a number of ethnographic studies that have been carried out by academics from other disciplines, we know very little about what actually happens in a MOO or about the effects it has on language learners and their language development.

Pinto (1996) found that her students developed positive attitudes to interacting in a MOO and that they gradually felt more and more comfortable, more successful and more active in the MOO[14]. The language they used was, however, limited to short interactions (interview style) and had a low level of cohesion.

Sanchez (1996) reported that the majority of the students enjoyed interacting in a MOO and they felt more secure than in oral interactions. It is also reported that the students believed their language had improved and that the researcher noticed higher grammatical accuracy in the language produced by the students.

Although there is a lot of movement in the area of MOOs and a lot of interesting projects going on, I am not aware of any other empirical studies in the area. Luckily, this is about to change. At present, there is a group of researchers investigating various aspects of language learning in a MOO and we should soon be able to have a more in depth understanding of this area when their results are published.[15]

Is it all a fad? Can we make a decision?: For an area that seems to be attracting so much enthusiasm, so much attention and so much money there doesn't seem to be adequate research available. There also seems to be evidence of many problems during these activities as well as evidence of contradictory results (e.g. anxiety). It seems it is not clear if the benefits outweigh the problems and in which cases the problems override the benefits. I want to remind us all of Peter Lidell and his question: 'Are we on the right

---

[14] Two of Pinto's students, however, remained disoriented throughout the study.

[15] I, personally, am aware of three PhD research projects: James Backer studying at Nova Southeastern University, Florida, USA deals mainly with factors of motivation and anxiety. Jerry Bicknell at West Virginia University, Morgantown, USA deals with learning styles and field dependence/ field independence and myself studying at the University of Portsmouth, UK dealing with negotiations of meaning and transferability of language development to oral proficiency.

track or are we letting ourselves be seduced by an appealing fad?' (Lidell, 1994). I do not want to be a pessimist and I am aware that a lot of progress has been done since 1994. For one, I believe, the theory and practice in SLA have integrated but unfortunately this is not the case with research in SLA. Research has not until now given us an insight into what I believe is the most important aspect of CMC: the linguistic quality of the interactions it fosters. For CMC activities to be worthwhile according to the communicative approach and according to the interactionist theory, there must be real interaction (and not mere production of unrelated utterances) and instances of negotiation of meaning. A common sense approach would tell us that there must not only be use of the target language but it should be appropriate use as well. Until now, we know very little, if any, of what actually goes on when learners are interacting in CMC. Most of the research available is quantitative and the quality of interactions is not clear. Although, for example, there is data on greater participation and greater production we are not aware of the nature of the learners' participation and production. Is it true interaction or are these utterances low in interactivity as was the case in Warschauer's study (1996a)? What we do know about the linguistic quality of CMC interactions is also contradictory as Table 3 illustrates.

Research Findings	**Researcher**
Higher proportion of simple sentences rather then complex ones.	Chun 1994
More advanced morphosyntactic features than in oral discussion	Kern 1995
Higher proportion of simple sentences rather then complex ones.	Kern 1995
Low interactivity of utterances	Warschauer 1996a
Higher syntactic complexity and higher lexical range.	Warschauer 1996a
Low level of cohesion and short utterances (interview style interactions)	Pinto 1996

Table 3: Research on the linguistic quality of CMC interactions.

Chun's study had shown an increasing rate of complex sentences that might have eventually become higher than the rate of simple sentences. Chun's is also the only longitudinal study. We could suppose, therefore, that had the other studies been longitudinal we might have had evidence of an improving quality of language — in terms of interactivity as well as in terms of syntactic and lexical features.

Finally, there is another problem that has not been adequately addressed - that of the skills we are teaching when using CMC activities. Which skills are benefited, if any? Is it reading, writing or speaking that is developed when we spent time in the computer labs?[16] We have many suggestions of a possible transfer of development to oral skills (Chun, 1994; Kern 1995; Schweinhorst, 1998). There are also anecdotal reports of improvement in writing (Bump, 1990; Kern, 1995) and suggestions that it can help improve reading skills (Kelm, 1992). There is, however, no evidence of any such results. Even when Chun (1994) maintains that CACD offers excellent opportunities for students to develop their discourse skills and their interactive competence, we do not know to which environment she is referring. Is it their discourse skills for traditional face-to-face interactions or their skills for interacting in a chat room? There is no evidence that what we are teaching is transferable to any other environment other than the electronic environment. Krause's (1995) study[17] on discussion lists aimed to find out whether the high degree of interactivity in students' online writing transferred to interactivity (in the sense of audience awareness) in their writing off-line. The results were negative. It is advisable then, that until there are other studies to deal with this issue we must be wary about what we are actually teaching and what goals we think we are working towards.

Concluding Remarks: Based on the empirical research we have available to us, it seems that we cannot clearly say that the affective benefits of CMC are overwhelming or describe the interactions fostered during CMC activities or how they affect the learners' language development. In addition, if it is particular types of activities that produce the higher performance that others testify too, then research should be carried out so that every practitioner can know what activities should be used as well as how and when they should be used.

It is clear that we cannot, at this stage, define the nature of CMC interactions and consequently the nature of CMC activities. We are unable to assert whether they are Interlanguage stretching and under what conditions they would be beneficial to language learners. Based on the knowledge we now have, two years after Chapelle's (1997) and Ortega's (1997) calls for further research, we still lack important knowledge. We can only renew our call for more research in the area and especially a call of longitudinal, qualitative studies based on interaction and discourse analysis.

---

16 Beauvois (1992) did point out the question of which skills are promoted by CACD.

17 Even though this study has serious limitations, it is the only one I am aware of in the area of skill transferability and it is, therefore, worth mentioning.

References:

Beauvois, M. H. (1992) 'Computer-assisted classroom discussion in the foreign classroom: Conversation in slow motion', *Foreign Language Annals*, 25 (5)

Beauvois, M. H. (1994) 'E-talk: attitudes and motivation in computer-assisted classroom discussion', *Computers and the Humanities*, 28

Beauvois, M. H. & Eledge, J. (1996) 'Personality Types and Megabytes: Student Attitudes Toward Computer-Mediated Communication (CMC) in the Language Classroom', *CALICO Journal*, 13 (2&3)

Borgmann, L. (1999) *International Internet Simulations*, Paper presented at the 33rd International IATEFL Conference

Bruckman, A. (1995) 'The MediaMOO Project: Constructionism and Professional Community', *Convergence*, 1 (1), Spring

Bump, J. (1990) 'Radical changes in class discussion using networked computers', *Computers and the Humanities*, 24

Butler, M & Fawkes, S. (1999) 'Videoconferencing for language learners' *Language Learning Journal*, 19

Chapelle, C. A. (1997) 'CALL in the year 2000: Still in search of research paradigms?', *Language learning and Technology*, Vol.1 (1)

Chun, D. M. (1994) 'Using computer networking to facilitate the acquisition of interactive competence', *System*, 22. (1)

December, J (1997) 'Notes on Defining of Computer-Mediated Communication', *CMC Magazine,* January

Eastment, D. (1999) *The Internet and ELT*, Summertown Publishing

Ferris, P. (1997) 'What is CMC? An Overview of Scholarly Definitions' *CMC Magazine*, January

Freiermuth, M. R.(1998) 'Using a chat program to promote group equity' *CAELL Journal*, 8 (2)

Herring, S. (1996) *Computer-mediated Communication: Linguistic, Social and Cross-Cultural Perspectives*, Amsterdam: John Benjamins

Higgins, R. (1997) *'Milking the MOO COW: Combining Interim Technologies for Learning in Cyberspace*', Paper presented at the TCC Conference, University of Hawaii

Kelm, O. R. (1992) 'The use of synchronous computer networks in second language instruction: A preliminary report', *Foreign language Annals*, 25 (5)

Kern, R. G. (1995) 'Restructuring Classroom Interaction with Networked Computers: Effects on quality and characteristics of language production', *The Modern Language Journal*, 79 (4)

Krashen, S. (1982) *Principles and practice in second language acquisition*, Oxford: Pergamon

Krashen, S. (1985) *The Input Hypothesis: Input and Implications*, Longman

Krause, S. (1995) 'How will this improve student writing?' Reflections on an Exploratory Study of Online and Off-line Texts' *CMC Magazine*, May

Lidell, P. (1994) 'Learners and second language acquisition: A union blessed by CALL?', *Computer-Assisted Language Learning*, 7 (2)

Long, M. H. (1981) Input, interaction and second language acquisition, in Winitz, H. (ed) *Native Language and Foreign Language Acquisition*, Annals of the New York Academy of Sciences 379

Lundstrom, P. (1995) *Synchronous Computer-Mediated Communication: Will Internet Talkers Improve the Communicative Competence of ESL/EFL Students?* Unpublished Master's thesis, The University of Hawaii, Manoa.

Meunier, L. (1997) *Affective factors and cyberteaching: Implications for a postmodern pedagogy,* CALICO Monograph Series, 4

Ortega, L. (1997) 'Processes and outcomes in networked classroom interactions: Defining the research agenda for L2 computer-assisted classroom discussion', *Language Learning and Technology*, Vol. 1 (1)

Pica, T. (1981) 'Second language acquisition, social interaction and the classroom', *Applied Linguistics*, Vol 8 (1)

Pinto, D. (1996) What does 'schMOOze' mean?: Non-native speaker interactions on the Internet, In Warschauer, M (ed.), *Telecollaboration in Foreign Language Learning*: Proceedings of the Hawaii Symposium, Honolulu, University of Hawaii, Second Language Teaching and Curriculum Center

Pratt, E. and Sullivan, N. (1994) *Comparisons of ESL writers in networked and regular classrooms*, Paper presented at the 28th Annual TESOL Convention, Baltimore, MD

Pulvermuller, F. & Schumann, J. (1994) 'Neurobiological mechanisms of language acquisition', *Language Learning*, 44

Reid, E (1991) *Electropolis: Communication and Community on Internet Relay Chat*, Bachelors Thesis, University of Melbourne

Renie, D. and Chanier, T. (1995) 'Collaboration and Computer Assisted Acquisition of a Second Language', *Computer Assisted Language Learning*, Vol. 8 (1)

Richards, C. J. and Rodgers, S. T. (1986) *Approaches and Methods in Language Teaching*, Cambridge: Cambridge University Press.

Sabatelli, A. (1997) Of Mice and Pens [Online] Available: http://home.microsoft.com/reading/archives/voices9-15.asp

Sanchez, B. A. (1996) *Le MOO Francais: Text-Based Virtual Reality in the High School Foreign Language Classroom*, Unpublished master's thesis, The University of Texas at Austin, Austin: Texas.

Schwienhorst, K. (1998) *Co-constructing learning environments and learner identities — language learning in virtual reality,* Paper presented at the ED-Media/ED-Telecom, Freiburg

Sempsey, J. (1998) 'When is the MUD too Gooey?', *MUD Journal* Vo.3 (2)

Serpentelli, J. (1995) *Conversational Structure and Personality Correlation of Electronic Communication*, Bachelors Thesis, Haverford College

Shield, L. & Weiniger, J. M. (1998) '*Collaboration in a virtual world — groupwork and the distance language learner'* in Debski, R. and Levy, M. (eds) forthcoming

Shield, L., Kotter, M & Hauck, M. (1999) *Taking the distance out of distance learning,* Paper presented at the 1999 BALEAP conference

Swain, M. (1985) Communicative competence: Some roles of comprehensible input and comprehensible output in its development, in Gass, S.M. & Madden, C.G. (eds), *Input in second language acquisition*, Rowley, Mass: Newbury House

Vygotsky, L. (1978) *Mind in Society: the Development of Higher Psychological Processes*, Cambridge, MA: Harvard University Press

Warschauer, M. (1995) *E-Mail for English Teaching*, TESOL Inc.

Warschauer, M. (1996a) 'Comparing Face-To-Face and Electronic Discussion in the Second Language Classroom' *CALICO Journal*, 13, (2&3)

Warschauer, M. (1996b) Motivational aspects of using computers for writing and communication, in Warschauer, M. (ed) *Telecommunications in Foreign Language Learning: Proceedings of the Hawaii Symposium*, Honolulu, University of Hawaii, Second Language Teaching and Curriculum Center.

Warschauer, M., Turbee, L. and Roberts, B. (1996c) 'Computer Learning Networks and Student Empowerment', *System*, 24

E4E — A NEW PROGRAM FOR TERTIARY SUPPORT IN ENGLISH

Beth Jeffery
Vista University, South Africa

If Ficino believed that our music is composed by our lives, the contemporary Czech Milan Kundera thinks, contrariwise, that our lives are composed like music. 'Without realising it, the individual composes his life according to the laws of beauty, even in times of the greatest distress'. To stand the old principle of good design on its elegant head: in our functioning we follow the dictates of our need for form.

Salman Rushdie *The Ground Beneath Her Feet* 380.

You don't have to be working with language problems in order to learn a language

(Hutchinson and Waters 1987,128)

English for Everyone, icon **E4E**, is a language support program for all students at tertiary or late high school level. It is about to be marketed by Prentice-Hall as a CD-Rom and on their web sites.

The two quotations above sum up what I found most fascinating about making the program: in this paper I intend to look what determined design choices and also what determines the kinds of language and language theories one uses when creating support programs.

E4E was created by myself and my colleague Jano Jonker who is a lecturer in physics. It was designed as a multi-purpose support for students and teachers at tertiary level, and as a self -access program, as a teaching tool with materials which can be downloaded, and as an aid in distance learning. We called it E4E, not because we feel that everyone must learn English, but rather with reference to the program's multi-purpose nature.

The title raises controversial issues. It is generally accepted that each discipline has different language needs. The program was designed in response to the multiplicity of needs, but also in response to the instability of resources and to the diversity of ideological positions about the role of English and the models by which support English should be taught. To a large extent, the diversity of needs and of ideologies has until recently made it difficult to create workable courses acceptable to all the interested parties. Many useful courses have bitten the dust for political reasons. The power vacuum, which followed the phase of transformation after 1994, led to a new Scramble for Africa, with academics competing in the time-honoured way — ruthlessly — for courses and resources. The fields of English for Academic and for Special Purposes have for the second time therefore become highly contested sites in South African Universities.

And from the two quotations with which I have chosen to begin this paper, it will be clear that I am interested in the tension between practical design parameters and theoretical ideas about 'how a language program should be'.

I approached language support teaching from a base of systemic functional linguistics, and a belief that one teaches through content and not the metalanguage of linguistics. But design parameters, whether of course syllabuses or of software begin for me with what I am required to do. I had always imagined, as Rushdie's character Rai suggest above, that our innate feeling for 'form' should shape design, but in practice it has been brought home to me that physical constraints, such as time, numbers, costs, or the potential and power of the software one is using, have a more profound and in the end enhancing effect than the abstract theories however elegant which one drags along with one to the task in hand.

One of the nicest results of pragmatism is that one learns an awful lot by doing the task.

A minor side effect of the diversity which faces lecturers in Southern Africa is that academic papers, whatever the topic, and whether written under the old regime or the new, tend to begin in an irritatingly personal and experiential way, with disquisitions on the state of learning under the current dispensation, and / or disclaimers as to the writer's complicity with the current orthodoxies. This paper is no different from the others — but of course in this case the experiential and the personal do have a bearing on the shape of the program E4E, because it evolved initially in response to the needs and parameters of the environment out of which it grew. In a later phase the program took a second evolutionary leap, in response to the potential — and the seduction — of the software.

The Environment out of which the Program E4E Grew: Vista University is made up of seven campuses for full time students, one each in Port Elizabeth, Bloemfontein, Welkom, East Rand, Mamelodi, Soweto, and there is also a distance learning campus in Pretoria. The administration — academic and financial — of the whole University is managed from a head office effectively cushioned from the murmurs of the academic staff who are dispersed all over the country. Members of academic departments who work together on courses have often never met except by e-mail.

The student population is mainly black. Each campus serves a local region, with a different language — isiXhosa, siZulu, siSotha, Setwana, etc. So there is no one-to-one correlation between one home language and English. This factor complicates the teaching of support English.

Many students come from economically deprived backgrounds and are also products of the schools boycotts of the 70s and 80s. 'Poor English' is therefore in our context often a misdiagnosis for cognitive or information disabilities, which can be remedied.

English departments in South Africa are faced with a many-faceted brief and an acute cash flow problem. Staff are expected (not necessarily in this order) to:

- raise the research capacity of the institution
- produce Masters and PhD students
- teach the regular undergraduate and postgraduate mainstream courses in English with emphasis on postcolonial Englishes
- be sensitive to the home languages and backgrounds of our students
- create new programs which reflect and build on 'where our students are coming from'
- teach support courses for other disciplines, although what they want and what we offer diverge
- accommodate part-time learners who are already professional teachers, and others with 'educational equivalents'
- contribute to 'staff development within the institution'
- contribute to schools outreach programs to 'uplift the community'
- revise courses to fit outcomes-based formats in time to meet government deadlines
- be available in the office for consultation for 40 hours per week
- raise funds through project proposals from business and industry to support innovations.

In this context it is difficult to set up any course which can please everyone, find funding, and be taught well by someone who has the time and qualification(s) to do it.

For those reasons, and because for most students the discourse of their discipline is like a pane of glass through which they look without observing it, a program like E4E is essential.

The Idea of a 'Core Course': One of the tasks of an English support program is to sensitise students to the discourses of their disciplines without resorting to the metalanguage of linguistics — otherwise the support course turns into a course in grammar or linguistics instead of a course in English for physics students.

The idea of a core course was from my point of view born of necessity and justified after the event. In the late 1980s, what M. H. Orr has called 'coerced conscripts'[1] ended up teaching 'communication' to large, non-homogeneous groups of physics, maths, geography, statistics, chemistry, computer science, business, economics and / or law students. As one of them, I resorted to dividing up 'good English' into its component parts and teaching what I isolated as 'core' needs which applied to the members of all of the groups. I then, again for practical reasons, treated the areas in which they differed as material for specific assignments, for which each group had different specific instructions.

- *In this way I embarked on a way of thinking about English in which practical considerations and pragmatic conditions were allowed to modify or even shape both linguistic and pedagogical theory.*
- *In the same way, for more pleasurable reasons, this time the potential of the new medium itself, practical parameters helped to determine the design of the program E4E. In this area I'm indebted to my colleague for his insight and perception, scientific and linguistic, as well as his expertise.*

The idea of a core course is based on the observation that all varieties of academic English present students with the same requirements and problems, whatever the discipline in which they specialise.

> The distinctive quality of scientific language lies in the lexico-grammar (the 'wording') as a whole, and any response it engenders in the reader is a response to the total patterns of the discourse.
> Naturally it would engender no response at all unless it was a variety of the parent language. Scientific English may be distinctive, but it is still a kind of English ... It is English with special probabilities attached: a form of English in which certain words, and more significantly, certain grammatical constructions, stand out as more highly favoured, while others correspondingly recede and become less highly favoured, than in other varieties of the language... . (Halliday and Martin *Writing Science* 1993, 4)

and further

> Scientific language is merely foregrounding the constructive potential of language as a whole. The grammar of every natural language ... is already a theory of human experience ... It transforms our experience into meaning ... The fact that language is used for a specific purpose does not imply that it is a special form of the language, different in kind from other forms. Certainly there are some features which can be identified as 'typical' of a particular context of use and which, therefore, the learner is more likely to

---

[1] Orr *Scrutiny 2* 'It's a dirty job, but someone's got to do it: skills teaching in departments of English' in *Scrutiny 2* Vol. 1 no.½.

> meet in the target situation. But these differences should not be allowed to obscure the far larger area of common ground that underlies all English use, and indeed, all language use ... ESP is an approach not a product. (Hutchinson and Waters 1987, 18-19)

The core needs of 'good English' are clear — cognitive abilities, planning and structuring writing, formats and information searches.

At tertiary level the impact of 'grammar mistakes' on an essay or report is minimal in comparison with that of cognitive inadequacies. 'Good English is sooner achieved by improving structure and planning than by fixing points of grammar. In the case of second language students whose ears have been attuned to spoken not written English, for every concord error fixed, another one pops up. It is quicker to get a friend to read the work over than to try to teach the complex rules which govern English grammar.

> Though the content of learning may vary there is no reason to suppose that the processes of learning should be any different for the ESP learner than for the general English learner. There is, in other words, no such thing as an ESP methodology, merely methodologies that have been applied in ESP classrooms, but could just as well have been used in the learning of any kind of English. (Hutchinson and Waters 1987, 19).

In addition, it's clear that new styles of academic writing are developing to accommodate new Englishes, hands-on and experiential approaches, post-colonial reactions to perceived tyrannies of genre, authority, and empiricism, and thinking processes which do not try to universalise or generalise from the premises available, but try to add another facet to the web(s) of experience.

There are many reasons for the trend towards 'more democratic forms of discourse' (Ib.21), not least among them the development of information technology. E-mail has introduced a whole new register with its own netiquette. At the same time shifts in educational philosophy towards the concept of the student as a client paying for a service, the right of all to education, the opening up of formerly arcane subjects through the world wide web and the removal therefore of the need for entrance qualifications in order to advance through the portals of academe, have all contributed to the development of a more experiential style of writing. The new, originally American, non-discriminatory style is gradually finding favour in academic writing in the rest of the world, at least in the humanities.

It follows that programs using new media to facilitate communication in English should not engender linear lists of facts and points of grammar.

Students and learners have their own ideas of what they want to get out of a course — what, in fact, they are paying for. There is no essential connection between necessities as perceived by the sponsor or ESP teacher and what the learners want or feel they need. It is also quite likely that the views of the sponsor and teacher will similarly be at odds!

Hutchinson and Waters (1987,51) again:

> We should like to make two points:
> (a) We still do not know very much about learning. It is important, therefore, not to base any approach too narrowly on one theory. As with language descriptions, it is wise to take an **eclectic** approach, taking what is useful from each theory, and trusting also in the evidence of your own experience as a teacher...
> (b) Theories of learning and language description are not causally linked. As Corder (1973) says: 'There is no logical connection between a particular psychological theory of how grammar is learned and any particular theory of language structure ... there is, however, an undoubted *historical* connection between them'.

Against this loosening-up process, as Halliday and Martin point out,

> linguists often notice how, when highly sophisticated thinkers from other sciences turn their attention to language, they often ignore altogether the findings of linguists and regress to treating language at the level at which it is presented in the early years of secondary school. (1994, 17)

A quick survey of marking comments and expectations from lecturers in departments other than English, and who want their students to be given language help, showed that they supported a prescriptive and proscriptive approach to English, in contrast with the more permissive approach of those in the language business. And even teachers trained in language sometimes forget that

> describing a language for the purposes of linguistic analysis does not necessarily carry any implications for language learning. The purposes of the linguist and of the language teacher are not the same ... we must not confuse how people *use* a language with how people *learn* it. (Hutchinson and Waters 1987, 37-8)

No one system is the only possible one. A linear course has to opt for a choice of one system moving to defined goals.

But the great virtue of the size and the navigability of software programs for language support is that one can build in to a program the potential for users from different theoretical backgrounds to go to what they want, just as in the world of the real we can each seek out the interpretations or models we choose to live our lives by. Choice is a useful cognitive model.

The idea of a core course for all ESP students is more in tune with 'connectionist' language acquisition theories and systemic functional linguistics, than with 'learnability' theories and generative grammar. In a learnability framework, all language use diverges progressively from the ideal model. In a connectionist framework, all language use selects from the same bank of options. Situation and context determine the choices that are made. Connectionist theories enable teachers and students to focus on the contingencies of English usage in particular contexts, and to substitute examples of what is done for explanations of rightness or error.

Connectionist language acquisition theory lends itself to computer software programs for language support in a way that learnability theories do not. Connectionist theories predict a web of structured and organised learning. Learnability theories famously predict trees, where the navigation possibilities are difficult to envisage. This is for the good reason that

> connectionist models have their origin in the computer modelling of behaviour and are almost always implemented as computer programs. They are built up out of simple processing units ... Connectionist models can carry out a wide variety of tasks, not just language processing The trick is to come up with a scheme for coding the input as a set of activation levels of the input units, and another scheme for interpreting activation in the output units as the result of processing the input. The network then has to be 'set up' ... so that with the same configuration of the network, a wide variety of inputs can be transformed into the appropriate outputs. (Garnham, 1994, 101-2)

There are therefore input units, hidden units, and output units.

Since I find practical and empirical approaches to language learning attractive, I tend to prefer 'connectionist' theories of language acquisition, where language structure is determined by the linguistic environment that exists outside the learner. In the context of creating software for language support, connectionist theories are also attractive, perhaps because they tend to rely on the same bank of explanatory metaphors: in describing one particular connectionist theory [the competition model], Bialystok for example says

> It is based on associations perceived in linguistic input. It is more functionalist than other models, in that it also depends on competitions between form-function mappings in the underlying networks. As the competitions are resolved, a network emerges that strives for the most parsimonious and efficient solution to the form-function problem. (Bialystok, 1994, 124)

> The connectionist approach ... assumes that linguistic symbols and rules are not represented directly in the brain, but are categories invented to describe the complex structure of the 'fall-out' from processes which are themselves much simpler and more basic. These fundamental processes are conceived of in terms of neural networks, where

> the suggestion is that these resemble, or at least symbolise, what is known about the physical behaviour of the brain. These neural networks have to be modelled on computers since there are far too many simple operations happening at once for a human being to be able to calculate them ... From the point of view of modelling human learning and human understanding, the connectionist approach has many attractive features ... [One of those features is] the explicit appeal to **context** at all levels of language teaching, not only because different levels of skills appear to need to be integrated during language comprehension, but also because the learner can use information from one level to compensate for lack of competence at another. (Brown et al. 1994, 97-98)

The connectionist approach informs the model of language help provided by E4E. The DNA strand image is an appropriate model for an integrated system, and the windows with navigation guides allow students to move from information to background in several directions.

According to Gardham, however

> Connectionist models are unable to represent the systematicity of mental representations. For example, if a person can understand the sentence 'John loves Mary', they will be able to understand the sentence 'Mary loves John'. A connectionist model in which this link is broken is just as easy to set up as one in which it holds. Related to this problem is the suspicion that connectionist models are unable to learn highly structured tasks. In language, structure and systematicity tend to go hand in hand, so connectionist machines may be unable to carry out many of the complex processes which comprise language understanding. (Garnham, 1994, 104)

The question is what is meant by 'understand'. In science, and in systemic functional linguistics, understanding seems to mean doing, following a real process step by step, falsification theory, empirical thinking. There need not be a 'vision' or image to go with the understanding, but all of us 'know' that 'John loves Mary' is not the same as 'Mary loves John' in any 'real' sense. Mary and John are quite different people. In generative grammar and in learnability theory, it may be that models are unconsciously assumed to be Platonic in the sense that there is a vision or even a cosmology which the ***model*** represents analogically or metaphorically, and in that sense 'understanding' one = 'understanding' the other. And that sort of meta-thinking about language is immaterial to getting a feel for the sorts of language which are and are not appropriate to the context or discourse of the discipline the learner is studying.

From the point of view of teaching English for science or maths or law to students from a variety of home language backgrounds, J. S. Bruner, Watts Professor of Experimental psychology, University of Oxford says:

> In the era when cultural relativity was a dominant theme, it was hoped that one could find a *weltanschauung* contained in each particular language that would give a unique cultural cast to the thought of members of that linguistic community. Today the emphasis has shifted more toward language (and cultural) universals and how, in general, they impart a universally human character to all information processing, whatever the culture. The ***concept*** of the psychic unity of mankind has replaced the ***doctrine*** of cultural relativism. (Bruner in Davies 1976, 60-81)

— again reinforcing the idea that learners hold more in common than not. The frontiers between L1 and L2 are more illusory than actual; it is perhaps more realistic to see a continuum of registers and situations and contexts — a huge web in which some areas correspond very closely and others diverge. In the area marked academic writing, teaching needs are probably more homogeneous than those in other areas.

Interactivity. Program users and language theorists tend to rank 'interactivity' very high on the list of what makes a good CALL program. R. Last (in Butler 1992, 233) suggests that the complexity and cost-effectiveness of programming in interactive solutions and intelligent responses makes the project impractical. Now, however, technology, in the form of wizards and templates, makes it easy to set up discussion groups with the tutor. Students can respond to materials, ask questions of the tutor or of each other using an internal distribution list or using the software associated with the program which was used to create the materials.

But a program produced for a CD-Rom can include only simplistic question and answer drills, or cloze exercises, which don't translate well from country to country or language group to language group. South African Xhosa speaking students find British cloze exercises mystifying because they make cultural assumptions. In a revised version I will include a bigger exercise and practical component.

In E4E we have introduced, however, a concept of interactivity which moves inside and outside the program. Students bring their work to the program, and apply their current questions about corrections, approaching problems, language use, information-searching to the program. It is possible in a windows environment to keep consulting the program while writing a report or assignment in another window.

Last also introduced the idea of complexity.

> The humanities programmer rapidly discovered [1992] that there appeared to be an inverse relationship between the complexity of a program and its efficacy and robustness. Very straightforward programs deliver reliable and effective results, whereas attempts to move into more challenging areas offer marginal and often dubious gains at the expense of a disproportionate amount of programming effort. This is particularly true

> when the programmer attempts to move from the lexical to the semantic level. (Last 1992, 233)

Last (232) claims that the program should not be too complex, because of the ration of cost-effectiveness to usefulness. But that sort of complexity has been made easier and quicker since he wrote, because of packages and internet and e-mail facilities.

We have to distinguish between the real complexity of the underlying programming, and the great necessity for simplicity in the interface between program and user. Keeping it clear and simple, with well-mapped navigation paths and return paths, good design, minimal blurb, and few opportunities to get lost, is a very complex and demanding business for the maker of the program.

The interface must be simple and clear: hyper-links make it possible to prune sentences and show structure while at the same time allowing infinite expansion to a very large program which is invisible to the users until they need to explore any bit of it.

The Role of Questions in Shaping the Program. There were three different ways in which questions played a part in shaping E4E.

(1) We asked questions of ourselves in relation to the needs of learners, similar to those suggested by Hutchinson and Waters 1987, 21-2:

> Why does the student need to learn?
> Who is going to be involved... (stakeholders)
> Where is the learning going to take place (important — mechanics of the course)
> When? How much time, how distributed?
> What will students need to learn?
> What are the goals, outcomes, content of courses?
> What learning theories?
> What methodologies?

(2) We formulated the program in the shape of asking questions on behalf of the students — How do I...? What is...? In this way we built in a new kind of interactivity in terms of choice — students have to work out what they need to know.

(3) We asked questions constantly of ourselves about how to design and rank the information we wanted to include. We chose to rank our input in terms of sets and subsets; what do students need to know to understand this? What are the related ideas / concepts? What counts as background knowledge in this case? And we ranked the output in terms of; Where should students go next? Where should they be able to get back to? Where should they be free to explore? How do we prevent them from getting lost?

> *For me this was the most exciting part of the making of the program, because for the first time, I saw what I understood to be, in Aitchison's terms, a language web full of many choices and many paths, turn before my eyes into a structured navigation view of language. For me, a new sort of hierarchy of usefulness and needs, relevance and marginality took shape before my eyes, and it seemed to transcend the paradigms of systemic functional linguistics or generative grammar or syllabus design. Both linearity and weblikeness were replaced in my mind by a mass of potential trajectories which intersected at chosen points (that is, where we chose to place hyperlinks). Wow! I like it!*

As Johnson says, 'The translation of text into digital form can produce extraordinary — and unpredictable — secondary effects' (145).

The computer is not just a tool, but a new medium, which can change thought patterns — and where linear thinking is replaced by spatial geometry

The greater the illusion that students are manipulating the material for themselves, the greater the complexity of the behind-the-scenes part of the program. The illusion of depth in the creation of the program has repercussions for language learning support based on lists of dos and don'ts and ad hoc exercises. In the windows environment, the program itself can become a space to enter and explore, and the arrow of the mouse pointer becomes a doppelganger (Mitchell, William J. 1996 *City of Bits* Cambridge, MIT Press, 24).

In this context links are carefully chosen and limited to direct learners. They are not about 'surfing' or about random information-gathering like bees going for pollen. They needn't fragment or dissolve knowledge, but rather guide the acquisition process. As Johnson (133) points out, hypertext serves to condense prose, not expand it. Links aren't the optional extras on the menu 'further reading' and they aren't constructing an 'environment' — ' hypertext is an opportunity to withhold information, to keep the reader at bay' — you can move faster, leave trails to do the work, point to allusions and leave it to the reader to choose or not choose to follow. 'Links like modifiers, like punctuation, something hardwired into the sentence' 'the grammar of links' (Johnson 133) 'the more you know about the site on the other end of the link, the more meaningful the sentence becomes' (144).

This is truly interactive learning in place of the over-determinism of cloze exercises which masquerade as interactivity — do this exercise, click on the answer, get none of the steps of the process, and get stuck because you can't move forward till you get it right.

Hypertext follows a centrifugal path, forcing its readers outwards (Johnson, 133) along structured paths, where students analyse their own needs, and the program anticipates their analysis by showing them where to go next and also showing them the way back. Choice is built in, but informed, guided choice.

This sort of program allows for asynchronous learning, and economises on personnel.

> It is important to allow the learner the opportunity to interact with the package in a variety of different ways, at different levels of difficulty, and in different modes, from intensely active, to passive observation. (Last 1992, 235)

Despite the seduction of graphics — and here I was influenced by my colleague who has matured past those things while I still love colours and pictures — we have kept those to a minimum, for practical reasons, and because text in interface design ***is*** the design.

> 'The textual revolution may be the Great Leap Forward of interface design circa 2000'. (Johnson 149).

How to Use the Program. In theory it has many uses:
(1) individuals can use it at home;
(2) it can be loaded on a network;
(3) teachers or lecturers in any discipline can use it to create own courses, by using a slate, or making overhead slides;
(4) it helps overburdened English departments or writing centres;
(5) it can be used for accelerated learning, distance learning, outreach programs;
(6) it provides asynchronous learning.

In practice, it is hard work!

It is easy to use the program. And if the institution has labs, supervisors, student access to PCs, IT support, the right software ... and if the lab is not at the other end of the campus from the supervisor's office, it can be done.

This month I've 'processed' 150 first-time users in my 'spare' time, and they have progressed from finding the on button to writing poems in Xhosa and saving them in fonts of their choice on disk, and accessing CALL programs and the internet in two 1 hour lessons. But I have spent two weeks of full time work making the system go!

Evaluation: The program allows for self-evaluation by students, in the sense that they will seek to answer their own questions.
It can be formally evaluated:

- in client courses, by improvement in performance over a period
- by course evaluation forms and feedback (quantification needed)
- testing if it is used as part of an ESP course, along with films and information sessions and group projects
- matching of outcomes to needs

Program Specifications. Resolution: 800 x 600 Hi-color (16 bit) or better. The screens will look the BEST at this resolution; at a lower resolution the typeface will simply look bigger and bulkier, but it will still be completely readable and fully functional. We wanted to make the program as 'with it' as possible.

The CD will have a built-in browser. It caters for Windows 95 and above and Pentium processor.

We have made a demo disk, and I will show either the demo or the whole program.

References:

Aitchison, J., 1994 'Understanding Words', in Brown et al., *Language and Understanding*, 83-95.
_______, 1997, *The language Web* Cambridge: Cambridge University Press.
Brown, G., K. Malmkjær, A Pollitt, and J. Williams (eds.) 1994. *Language and Understanding*; *Research Centre for English and Applied Linguistics, University of Cambridge.* Oxford: Oxford University Press.
Bruner, J. S., 'Language as an instrument of Thought' in A. Davies (ed) 1976 *Problems of Language and Learning*. London: Heinemann., 60-81.
Bialystok, E., 'Towards an explanation of second language acquisition' Cambridge Language Teaching Library 1987- Series, Cambridge University Press
Butler, C. S., (ed) 1992 *Computers and Written Texts* Oxford, Blackwell
Cameron, K., (ed) 1989 *Computer Assisted Language Learning: program structure and principles.* Oxford. Blackwell Scientific.
Garnham, A., 'Psychological Processes and Understanding' in Brown et al. (eds) 1994, 99-114.
Halliday, M.A.K., and Martin, J. R., 1996 *Writing Science: Literacy and Discursive Power* The Falmer Press, London.
Hutchinson, T. and Waters, A., 1995 *English for Specific Purposes: a learning centred approach* Cambridge Language Teaching Library, Cambridge University Press.
Johnson *Interface design*
Last, R., 1992 'Computers and language learning, past, present and future' in Butler, C. S., (ed.) 1992, 227-246.
Orr, M. H., 1996 'It's a dirty job, but someone's got to do it: skills teaching in departments of English' in *Scrutiny 2* Vol. 1 no. ½.
Sutton, C., 1992 *Words, Science and Learning* Open University Press. University Press, London, reprinted Vintage Books, 1990.

THE DEVELOPMENT OF CALL MATERIAL FOR JAPANESE IN A COMMUNITY COLLEGE SETTING

Sachie Karasawa
Community College of Southern Nevada / University of Arizona, USA

Abstract
This paper discusses issues involved in the development and the implementation of hypermedia — particularly digitised audio and video — instructional material for enhancing the learning of Japanese as a foreign language in a community college setting.
The two main discussion points for the use of hypermedia in this paper are (1) contextualisation of language use by presenting cultural information and (2) the accommodation of individual learner differences.
The description of a community college as a specific language learning environment is followed by discussions of the processes taken for the development of the courseware, and finally a suggestion is made for future research.

Introduction: An increasing number of studies in computer assisted language learning (CALL) discuss the computer as a useful medium for teaching/learning language (e.g. Blake, 1998; Bush & Terry, 1997; Herring, 1996; Pennington, 1996; Smith, 1987). When viewed as a medium, the computer presents a number of options for language instructors, depending on their teaching philosophy or beliefs. It can be used for drill practice or the instruction of grammar, pronunciation, reading and writing. It can also be used for obtaining real-life information or can be used as a communication tool.

This paper discusses an application of hypermedia to the teaching of beginner level Japanese courses in a community college setting in the U.S. The main focus of the project is to put language use in context by providing cultural information through computer technology.

Background

Facilities Available. Like many other community colleges in the nation, the Community College of Southern Nevada is a multi-campus institution. In addition to the main campus, the college has two other campuses where the degrees of availability of and accessibility to the computer facilities vary.

The computerised language laboratory at the main campus of the community college opened in 1996. When it first opened, it was a Mac lab equipped with 36 Power Macintosh computers, one at each student workstation. Each station was also equipped with one video player, one video recorder, and an audio cassette player. All of the equipment could be centrally controlled by a console located in front. Since then, all the Macintosh computers have been replaced by networked PCs. All the other equipment that came with the original lab is still in use.

One of the other two campuses has a smaller scale lab which houses 23 computers and a limited number of audio and video players that are used separately.

Administrative and Departmental Support for the Language Lab: Until recently, both labs at the main campus and the other campus were mainly used as drop-in labs where students worked individually on their own time. The rate of lab use by individual students, however, stayed relatively low, and the college administration decided to urge the department to increase its lab use. In response to the administrative decision, the department is currently working on the integration of lab components into the existing foreign language and ESL curricula. From the Fall 1999 semester, the main campus lab will be mostly used as a classroom where computer-based activities are expected to be performed regularly as a part of the foreign language or ESL courses taught.

The administration is supportive of the expansion of the lab facilities on at least one of the other two campuses. Some funding has also been made available for faculty members who are involved in computer-related projects.

Student Population: 'Diverse' is the most appropriate word to describe the student population at the community college. In addition to the regular college population coming out of high schools, people of all ages attend classes. They are engaged in various occupations with varying degrees of education and previous exposure to foreign languages. The number of foreign students with different ethnic backgrounds has also increased dramatically in the past few years as the college rigorously recruits them to expand its international student program. The purpose of taking a particular language course also varies among individual students.

Another important factor is that not all the students have easy access to computers. Although the price of computers keeps dropping, not all the students own a personal computer. The language lab and other computer facilities in the computer centre available at college do not necessarily solve this problem, because many of the community college students have full-time jobs and cannot always find time to use the facilities. The low rate of lab use mentioned above is the case in point. Thus, the accommodation of the diverse student population is the primary concern for the development of CALL material in this setting.

The project

Rationale for Developing Japanese Courseware for In-class Use: The main difficulty in integrating a CALL element into the existing curriculum lies in the fact that most of the commercially packaged courseware programs are designed for individual use rather than in-class use. Each program has its own specific sequence of introducing grammatical/functional features of the language with its own set of vocabulary. Unless the courseware is specifically created to accompany a particular textbook, it is hard to co-ordinate it with other components of the course.

The scarcity of good quality Japanese courseware for PCs adds to the difficulty. The few good Japanese tutorial programs for Mac available at the main campus lab are no longer in use after its transition to a PC lab. The project of developing customised Japanese courseware for in-class use, therefore, started as a solution to the problem of lack of suitable CALL material.

Rationale for Developing Hypermedia Courseware for Providing Cultural Information and Contextualising Language Use: Once the focus was made on the development of Japanese courseware for in-class use, the project was set out with two questions in mind:

> (1) How can the teaching/learning of beginner level Japanese as a foreign language course for community college students be enhanced by the use of computer technology?
>
> (2) How can individual learner differences be accommodated?

The first question is closely related to another more general question which is often asked by CALL researchers: What aspects of the language can be taught effectively by the use of computer technology? As was stated in the introduction, there are many ways in which computer technology can be used for language instruction. Much CALL literature to date has addressed the question and discussed various possibilities as well as limitations of its use. Discussing what *can* be taught is certainly a good starting point, but it does not address all the specific needs of a particular teaching/learning environment. Thus, the much more specific question stated above was formed.

The second question not only addresses the diverse student population at the community college mentioned in the previous section, but also involves how to accommodate students' different learning styles. This question is discussed further in the next section. The remainder of this section will focus on the discussion concerning the first question.

Use of Hypermedia. One outstanding characteristic of the computer as a medium is that various media can be linked and integrated into one program by the use of hypermedia. Text, graphics, digitised audio, and video are the types of media that can be linked. A text-based approach to hypermedia, however, is of very limited use for beginner level Japanese courses because the Japanese language has a rather complex writing system, acquisition of which typically requires many years. In addition to two sets of syllabic writing systems called *hiragana* and *katakana*, somewhere between 1500 – 2000 *kanji* characters are used regularly in authentic written texts. It is, therefore, not practical to design courseware that involves extensive reading and writing of Japanese texts for the students enrolled in the beginner level Japanese courses. The text feature of hypermedia at this level can be marginally utilised in the descriptions of cultural objects and the annotations in English.

The biggest attraction of hypermedia for beginner level Japanese, then, is its capability of integrating graphic, audio, and visual presentations of course material. In a foreign language learning environment, in particular, this capability serves as a valuable tool for presenting authentic cultural material to the learner. As Conrad (1996) points out, CALL research in general does not make a clear distinction between second language (SL) and foreign language (FL) settings. In an FL setting where learners are studying the language outside the target language (TL) culture, however, creating opportunities for exposure to authentic cultural material is an important strategy for making connections between what they learn in classroom and how it is used in natural context. It could also enhance the learners' interest in TL culture and contribute to increasing their motivation to learn the language.

Types of Cultural Information Presented: Although culture is not merely different customs, food, and some other readily observable phenomena, these are often what confront people from other cultures and affect their perception of the TL culture and people on the surface level. Not knowing customs of another culture, for example, could be a cause of embarrassment, and more seriously, of miscommunication. Hypermedia could be used for constructing fun activities for introducing FL learners to some visible and outstanding features of TL culture. Targeting visually and aurally presentable cultural information is particularly suitable for beginner level learners since the vocabulary in earlier lessons tends to be dominated by words concerning tangible objects.

Contextualisation of Language Use: The meaning of 'context' in language use has been interpreted in many different ways. Various perspectives emphasise external, linguistic, social/socio-linguistic, cognitive, and/or pragmatic factors of context to varying degrees (e.g. Olson, 1977; Halliday & Hasan, 1985; Sperber & Wilson, 1986). In this project, a cognitive perspective of context is adopted and the definition of 'context' includes both the physical context of communication and the cognitive environments of the participants in communication.

In this perspective, presenting cultural information via visual and auditory media, or more precisely via digitised video, can facilitate the contextualisation of language use in at least two ways. First, video can present context as external physical situations of communication without any textual explanations. Second, visual images and sounds on the video can provide additional information for various lexical items to form better mental representations which can be retrieved from the learner's memory as contextual information for language use.

Courseware Design

Structure of the Program. Until recently, including video segments in a computer program was problematic due to the limitation of memory space. Thanks to the development in the area of CD writing, and more extensive use of DVD on the horizon, use of digitised video is no longer a big problem.

Each lesson of the courseware opens with a short video segment which shows a particular scene in Japan. Some practice activities that are thematically related to each scene are clustered around each video segment.

Contents

Video Segments. All of the video segments used in the program were filmed in Kyoto, Japan. There are two reasons for filming original video segments for the program. The primary reason is to control the comprehensibility of input to the learner by scaffolding the speech to an adequate level. The other reason is to eliminate the problem of copyright.

The main mode of presentation used in each video segment is the narrating/reporting of an event. This means that the person who is filming the scene narrates or reports what is shown on the screen most of the time.

The following five scenarios have been created for the video segments:

(1) Visiting a friend's house;
(2) Going on a trip by *Shinkansen* (Bullet Train);
(3) Visiting a shopping district;
(4) Walking in the neighbourhood, which includes some popular sightseeing spots;
(5) Visiting a university campus.

Each scenario has a very specific setting, but its actual content is adaptable to the topics learned in multiple lessons. The 'Visiting a friend's house' scenario, for example, includes: (1) greetings used in visiting someone's house (a situation introduced in Lesson

18 in Jorden's *Japanese: The Spoken Language*), (2) ritual expressions for offering and receiving food and drinks (Lessons 1, 3, and 5), (3) visual information of unique features of a floor plan of a typical Japanese house and how each room looks and functions (related to the topic of Lesson 24).

In other words, these video segments are recyclable and can be used repeatedly in introducing different lessons. Different practice activities can be linked to the same video segment in different lessons to reinforce the use of new material learned. Even when the learners view the same video segments repeatedly for multiple lessons, the main topic of a particular target lesson will direct their attention to different parts of the segment and make some features that are related to the topic more salient than others. As a result, the students will find themselves understanding the content of the video better each time they view it and will be able to feel that they are actually making progress.

Practice Activities: Creation of practice activities to accompany each scenario is still in progress and far from being completed. The following is a sample activity for the 'Visiting a friend's house' scenario.

When the activity is opened, the main menu is displayed as a floor plan of a Japanese house. The learners can click on any of the rooms to get to the room of their choice. Each room comes with a picture of the room. Some of the rooms also comc with a sample conversation that is likely to take place there.

If, for example, the living-room is clicked, the picture of the room appears with a set of conversation between the host/ess and the guest. The conversation is presented with a still picture of the two participants plus audio. The learners are given an option to go to a practice section after they learn the model conversation. The practice section presents a few sets of short conversation that follow the model conversation with a little variation. The learners can click on the answer option to hear the feedback.

Accommodating Individual Learner Differences: This hypermedia program can accommodate individual learner differences in the following ways.

(1) Those who do not have time to use the lab other than the regular class time will get opportunities to use CALL material.

(2) Those who do not normally use a computer for studying Japanese, whether it is because they do not feel confident or comfortable in using it, will get to learn how to use it.

(3) Since the cultural information contained in each video segment goes beyond the learning material of a single lesson, those who are more advanced

learners of Japanese or those with some previous experience in Japanese will be able to keep interested by having a peek at the topics of later lessons.

(4) Different types of practice activities will accommodate visual, auditory, analytic, and experiential learners.

In addition, presenting visual images via video could promote incidental learning. The viewers, for example, may notice some signs written in Japanese and try to read them. They may pick up some speech uttered by a passer-by. They may also listen to a public announcement in the background of a scene at the station or at the department store. It is very likely that each learner will pick up additional pieces of information to those originally intended to be picked up, one way or the other.

Hardware and Software Used: Hardware equipment used for this project consists of: (1) a PC with 64MB RAM and 6 GB HD, (2) a CD writer, and (3) a digital camcorder. Since the editing of digital video captured on a digital camcorder is much easier than the editing of analogue video, the use of a digital camcorder eliminates the need for separate video editing software. Macromedia's *Authorware 4* is used as the authoring tool for creating the hypermedia program.

Conclusion. Once the program is developed, the next step is to test its effectiveness and validity. The current situation at the community college provides an ideal setting for implementing classroom research in that only the main campus has a full-size language lab to be used as a classroom although one of each of the first semester Japanese course is offered regularly at the main campus and at one of the other campuses. It means that this situation justifies the use of different ways of instruction, one with a CALL component and the other without it. In the event that experimental classroom research is actually implemented, however, the research design will have to take careful consideration of possible confounding factors caused by the diverse student population.

References

Blake, R. J. (1998). The role of technology in second language learning. In H. Byrnes (Ed.). *Learning foreign and second languages: Perspectives in research and scholarship*, (pp. 209-237). New York: The Modern Language Association of America.

Bush, M. D. & Terry, R. M. (Eds.). (1007). *Technology-enhanced language learning.* Lincolnwood, IL: National Textbook Company.

Conrad, K. B. (1996). CALL — Non-English L2 instruction. *Annual Review of Applied Linguistics, 16,* 158-181.

Halliday, M. A. K. & Hasan, R. (1985). *Language, context, and text: Aspects of language in a Social-semiotic perspective.* Victoria: Deakin University.

Herring, S. C. (Ed.). (1996). *Computer-mediated communication.* Amsterdam: John Benjamins.

Jorden, E. & Noda, M. (1987). *Japanese: The spoken language, part 1.* New Haven: Yale University Press.

___________. (1988). *Japanese: The spoken language, part 2.* New Haven: Yale University Press.

Olson, D. R. (1977). From utterance to text: the bias of language in speech and writing. *Harvard Educational Review, 47,* 257-281.
Pennington, M.C. (Ed.). (1996). *The power of CALL.* Houston: Athelstan.
Smith, W. F. (Ed.). (1987). *Modern media in foreign language education: Theory and Implementation.* Lincolnwood, IL: National Textbook Company.
Sperber, D. & Wilson, D. (1986). *Relevance: Communication and cognition.* Oxford: Blackwell.

THE TEACHER IN THE MACHINE: MAKING WWW TECHNOLOGY SERVE PEDAGOGY

Ken Keobke
City University of Hong Kong

Abstract
Developments in educational technology have tended to govern associated pedagogy, rather than good pedagogy influencing technology. In many cases, this has had negative impacts as constraints, for example, in computer-assisted language learning, have often ignored areas of whole language development such as speaking and writing simply because they were technologically difficult and pedagogically challenging for a machine to teach and assess.

Despite its communicative and interactive aspects (particularly within the area of computer mediated communication), the World Wide Web (WWW) is the latest in a long list of technologies which have generally been used to support discredited behaviourist models of learning. In such behaviourist models, learners are usually faced with pre-determined choices leading to increasing levels of difficulty and token extrinsic rewards. Based on research and in reference to an educational WWW site, this paper explores ways in which the WWW can support less behaviourist approaches. Specifically, it looks at ways by which learners might have greater control over their own learning and use the resources of the WWW to determine their own learning paths in more reflective ways. This paper also offers guidelines for what good pedagogy might ask for in future WWW technology.

Developments in technology: Developments in educational technology are certainly not restricted to the computer or even to technologies of the past fifty years. Rather, video cameras, tape recorders, overhead projectors, chalk and blackboard and even books are all innovations beyond the basic educational necessities of a teacher and a pupil. These technological innovations have certainly changed the ways in which we teach and learn and we generally agree that these changes have been, for the most part, positive and have lead to increased productivity in our teaching and better learning in our students.

However, there are also drawbacks to any innovation in teaching and learning technology. Socrates, for example, decried the use of books for learning, claiming that they would reduce the scholar's discipline in memorisation. The first books of the printing pioneer Aldus Manutius, often with limited monotone illustrations if illustrated at all, must have seemed at the time an enormous step backwards from the rich beauty of illuminated manuscripts. Still, the new books offered different advantages for the average person: affordability and increased access.

Ideals of scientific progress have made replacing books a 20th century fixation. Cuban (1986) writes of Thomas Edison's 1913 prediction, 'Books will soon be obsolete in the schools. Scholars will soon be instructed through the eye. It is possible to touch every branch of human knowledge with motion picture' (p.11, cited in Ravitch 1989). Clearly this has not come to pass and Cuban notes that neither radio nor television have replaced books or the traditional schools although both have had influence as supplementary learning materials.

A general problem with all such innovations in educational technology is that they have tended to govern associated pedagogy, rather than good pedagogy influencing technology. That is, administrators and teachers have tended to stand in awe of the machine and think that they must conform to it, rather than having it adapt to and serve their needs and the needs of their students. Proclamations about computers in general and the World Wide Web (WWW) in particular have been heard as the latest resonance of Edison's death-knell for book-based learning and schools. But how effectively computers are being used is open to question; although computers appeal because of their aura of the modern, in fact, most computer-based learning materials favour, or are limited to, traditional behaviourist models of learning. Rozycki (1996), for example, notes that '... behaviourist theory has provided the rationale for a variety of marketable although short-lived teaching devices. Educational budgets have long proven to be easy prey for scientific-sounding entrepreneurs' (p. 54). Nowhere is this truer than in the field of Computer-assisted Language Learning (CALL) where the technology has often ignored areas of whole language development

Behaviourism and CALL: A central defining characteristic of many CALL materials is their heavy reliance on a behaviourist model of instruction, using behaviour modification principles in their design. These principles include features that are so ingrained in standard classroom practice that many teachers may assume there is no alternative. In general, these principles include beliefs that lessons must proceed along strictly sequenced lines, that learners need incentives such as grades to motivate them to learn and that these grades must be measured against standardised tests.

Within the area of CALL, behaviourist aspects generally include stating the purpose of the program or task, offering reinforcement through text, images, audio, animations or video and providing a marks system for each task summarised at the end with grades or some other statement of progress. Much of this is endemic to the nature of the computer and the limited ways in which it can simulate interactions with the learner.

Theories of behaviourism: Theories of learning do not appear in a vacuum. They are influenced by earlier practices (e.g., observations of classroom behaviour) and theories from other disciplines (e.g., mathematics, philosophy, psychology). In the case of behaviourism, there is a great deal of earlier practice in teaching methods dating back to the ancient Greeks. More recent and empirical influences include Ivan Pavlov (1849-

1936) whose well-known experiments observing dogs salivating as a *conditioned reflex* (response) to the ringing of a dinner bell, the bell being considered a *conditioned stimulus*. Pavlov's ideas are now called *classical conditioning*, as opposed to *operant conditioning* (explained below). Ideas of stimuli and responses working to modify behaviour were expanded upon by several other researchers, but the figure to be most associated with the place of behaviourism in the classroom is B. F. Skinner (1904-1990).

Like those of his predecessors, the behaviourist theories of Skinner are based upon the idea that learning is a function of change in overt behaviour. Changes in behaviour are the result of an individual's response to events (stimuli) that occur in the environment. Skinner advanced previous behaviourist theories by showing how a response produces a consequence such as defining a word, hitting a ball, or solving a math problem. When a particular stimulus and response pattern is reinforced through token extrinsic rewards, the individual has been *conditioned* to respond. Skinner called this approach *operant conditioning* and it differs from earlier forms of behaviourism (now called *classical conditioning*) in that it recognises that an organism can *emit* responses and not only *elicit* responses in reaction to a stimulus.

Another important feature of Skinner's theory is the role of reinforcement: things or actions that strengthen a desired response by making the learners feel better about themselves. He also suggested a role for *negative reinforcers* or reduced rewards for inappropriate responses; Skinner did not believe in punishment, which he suggested only reduced responses (Skinner 1968 pp. 57-58). Fosnot (1996) suggests that the assumptions of behaviourism for educators using it in the classroom include the following:

> Pre-planning a curriculum by breaking a content area (usually seen as a finite body of predetermined knowledge) into assumed component parts — 'skills' — and then sequencing these parts into a hierarchy ranging from simple to more complex. It is assumed (1) that observations, listening to explanations from teachers who communicate clearly, or engaging in experiences, activities, or practice sessions with feedback will result in learning and (2) that proficient skills will quantify to produce the whole, or more encompassing concept (Bloom 1956; Gagne 1965). Further, learners are viewed as passive, in need of external motivation, and affected by reinforcement (Skinner 1953, pp. 8-9).

Many recognise Fosnot's behaviourist assumptions as an accurate description of much classroom experience over the past few decades.

Programmed Instruction: One of the practical applications of the behaviourist approach was the design of *programmed instruction* or *programmed learning*, on which Skinner's behaviourist contributions to CALL centre. This approach suggests that learners can be taught a wide variety of subjects if presented with information in small steps, each step requiring appropriate responses (e.g. correct answers to questions) from the learner before going on to a more difficult or advanced step. Thorndike put the idea forward in 1912 when he wrote:

> If, by a miracle of mechanical ingenuity, a book could be so arranged so that only to him who had done what was directed on page one would page two become visible, and so on, much that now requires personal instruction could be accomplished by print (cited in Merrill *et al* 1996, p. 54).

Thorndike was thinking within a paper metaphor long before the invention of computers, but Merrill *et al* (1996) note that such a machine was constructed as early as 1926 by Sidney L. Pressey (1888-1969) and explain that Pressey's machine:

> ... presented multiple-choice questions on a rotating cylindrical drum. Students responded by pressing one of four keys, each of which represented one of the answer choices. In the drill mode, all keys except the one representing the correct answer were locked; in the test mode, no clues of correctness were given. The machine recorded all responses and was capable of giving the user a piece of candy when a programmable number of correct responses had been made (p. 54).

Skinner (1968) describes Pressey's work, suggesting that it was ahead of its time, but supports the idea of machine instruction as a way of increasing learner autonomy to avoid an essential problem in classroom instruction, the pace of instruction in a group of non-homogenous learners:

> Even in a small classroom the teacher usually knows that he is going too slowly for some students and too fast for others. Those who could go faster are penalised, and those who should go slower are poorly taught and unnecessarily punished by criticism and failure. Machine instruction would permit each student to proceed at his own rate (p. 30).

This advantage crosses the boundaries of different models of instruction. Skinner and others designed more mechanical and electrical machines that tried to put these ideas into practice but the computer presented an ideal technology for such lockstep learning. McArthur (1983) notes that behaviourism:

> ... has been linked with a number of aids such as programmed learning, teaching machines and language 'laboratories' by means of which purposeful students could steadily train themselves or be trained in the right kind of language behaviour (p. 76).

He goes on to explain two variations on programmed instruction:

> Programs can be linear, in which all students go through the same sequence of frames, or branching, in which a variety of paths through the program is provided. Linear programs tend to use constructed responses, while branching programs conventionally use a multiple choice format. These structures were closely followed in the first CAL

> (Computer-Assisted Learning) programs, and, as has been said, both types are still in use today (pp. 76-77).

Fox (1991) notes, '...a number of features of programmed instruction still characterise CAL today, such as the use of multiple choice questions and of constructed response answers, and the extensive use of branching techniques' (p. 73). But programmed instruction has its faults and Stevens (1992) notes its downfall:

> Eventually, as Brown puts it (1980: 242), 'language teachers were discovering that the ALM actually was not working! People were not learning the communicative functions of the language'. A similar impression of programmed instruction is conveyed by Rivers (1981: 119), who notes that its tendency to 'preoccupation with the teaching of innumerable details about the language ... can distract from the real 'terminal behaviour', that is, the whole of language as it operates in an act of communication'. The problem with early CALL, as with the teaching practices it emulated, was that while both might have succeeded in teaching the surface forms of the language, neither promoted carry-over to spontaneously communicative contexts (p. 12).

Despite these criticisms, programmed instruction continues to be pervasive in CALL, sometimes combined with other, less behaviourist approaches.

Mastery Learning: These aspects of programmed learning are also seen in the Mastery Learning method summarised by Fosnot (1996):

> This model assumes that wholes can be broken into parts, that skills can be broken into subskills. Learners are diagnosed in terms of deficiencies, called 'needs', then taught until 'mastery' — defined as behavioural competence — is achieved at each level. Further, it is assumed that if mastery is achieved at each level, then the more general concept, defined by the accumulation of the skills, has also been taught (p. 9).

Lai and Biggs (1994) add to this explanation and summarise mastery learning as:

> ... a strategy that is based on the assumption that learning is a function of time (Bloom, Hastings & Madaus 1971; Carroll 1963). In theory, by varying time for learning, nearly all students are able to learn a subject to the point of 'mastery' (Guskey 1985). In implementing mastery learning, it is thus necessary to establish a criterion, and to provide corrective instruction in the event of failure. Learners failing to reach the objectives initially are given more time in which to pass in subsequent attempts. The content to be learned is divided into units, with a formative test on each unit (p. 13).

The challenge of mastery learning in CALL is the necessity of providing new material or new approaches when a learner fails to accomplish the initial goals. It is important that in a restricted time frame, learners do not abrogate the task of thinking and take advantage of a software program's willingness to supply default answers. Motivation is a key consideration in the creation of CALL materials, many of which are set up as adventure games or include positive reinforcement in the form of points, including items to be collected by the player. In many cases, learners learn more about how to acquire points than the knowledge intended to be imparted by the game's creator. For example, learners quickly discover that in some programs, repeatedly selecting random answers prompts a default sub-routine giving the correct answers. Learners can proceed through a program making numerous errors then try the program again, apparently showing remarkable progress. In fact, they have learned, but only how to manipulate the *system*, not to understand the *content*.

Despite these problems, it is easy to understand the attraction of the computer as a vehicle for a mastery learning model. The computer's principal defining characteristics are *consistency* and *patience* (see Keobke 1994); the computer can provide uniform repetitive lessons to the same learner or a group of learners and test indefinitely. But this requires a behaviourist/mechanistic view of the learner quite at odds with current humanistic thinking. So-called *Mastery Learning* also tends to assume that once a learner has demonstrated the ability to answer a question or complete a task, he or she knows it forever. But, in reality, something may be only stored in a learner's short term memory; learners not only learn, they also forget.

An educational WWW site: *The Secret Diaries of Lotus & Rose*: *The Secret Diaries of Lotus & Rose* (www.cityu.edu.hk/ls/lotus&rose) attempts to foster language learning through a non-behaviourist approach. The website of sixteen episodes and various resources makes use of extensive literary references and explanations woven into a story of two young women having a series of small adventures. Language learners engage in learning by looking at resources within the program, including reading the two women's contrasting diary entries (one of the women is a naive innocent, the other a pathological liar). Understanding the subtleties of the plot requires that learners use critical thinking skills, in particular analysis and synthesis, to construct a clear narrative and interpretation of the events, although many hints and explanations are available. In the course of this, learners learn more about language and literature as well as how to express concepts and language common to Hong Kong, the local setting for the virtual soap opera aimed at Hong Kong learners.

Literature in language learning: The use of literature in language learning is sometimes debated as it is considered too advanced to be of practical use to learners. However, learners often acquire language through activities peripheral to the study of literature and other disciplines. Collie and Slater (1987) offer four main justifications for the use of literature in the language classroom: valuable authentic material, cultural enrichment, language enrichment and personal involvement. They recognise the place of non-fictional authentic materials, such as bus schedules, but suggest:

> Literature is a valuable complement to such materials, especially once the initial 'survival' level has been passed. In reading literary texts, students have also to cope with language intended for native speakers and thus they gain additional familiarity with many

> different linguistic uses, forms and conventions, and so on. And, although it may not be confined within a specific social network in the same way that a bus ticket or an advertisement might be, literature can nonetheless incorporate a great deal of cultural information (p. 4).

By cultural enrichment, Collie and Slater refer to the wealth of insights about other cultures (particularly the target language culture) that literature offers. In discussing language enrichment, they note that:

> While there is little doubt that extensive reading increases a learner's receptive vocabulary and facilitates transfer to a more active form of knowledge ... literature provides a rich context in which individual lexical or syntactical items are made more memorable. Reading a substantial and contextualised body of text, students gain familiarity with many features of the written language — the formation and function of sentences, the variety of possible structures, the different ways of connecting ideas — which broaden their own writing skills. The extensive reading required in tackling a novel or long play develops the students ability to make inferences from linguistic clues, and to deduce meaning from context, both useful tools in reading other sorts of material as well (pp. 4-5).

And by personal involvement, they suggest:

> Core language teaching materials must concentrate on how a language operates both as a rule-based system and as a socio-semantic system. Very often, the process of learning is essentially analytic, piecemeal, and, at the level of the personality, fairly superficial. Engaging imaginatively with literature enables learners to shift the focus of their attention beyond the more mechanical aspects of the foreign language system (p. 5).

In addition to the arguments raised above, there is also the fact that a simple love of literature supports autonomous language learning (see Montali and Lewandowski 1996). Learners who are exposed to literature in the classroom and enjoy it are likely to expand their exposure to literature in various forms and provide themselves with associated opportunities for language learning outside of the classroom.

This approach to language teaching and learning is not behaviourist as it assumes experience on the part of the learners and their need to construct meaning from disparate ideas. This approach can be classified as *constructivist*, and further characterised as *subversive* in the sense that learning takes place as an act peripheral to the learner's perception of the program's intention, in the case of *The Secret Diaries of Lotus & Rose*, through having to decode multiple narratives.

The advantage of multiple narratives is that they provide a rich language resource similar to group experiences and discussion. One sees an object not from a single point of view, as is too common in teacher-centred activities or with one right answer, as is common in behaviourist tasks. Instead, learners see ideas from more than one point of view thus encouraging upper-level skills of analysis and synthesis. Also, within the website, learning opportunities are structured to provide several opportunities for entry to learners of different ability levels. An inspiration for this multiple-perspective approach are the traditional *Rupert* cartoon stories which feature a parallel page title, four pictures, rhyming couplets for each picture and a story with quoted speech (for an example, see Robinson & Harrold, 1993). Such a structure presents learners at lower levels with opportunities for both comprehension and challenge, encouraging them to improve their language proficiency through natural curiosity.

CALL and literature: Collie and Slater described the relationship of literature to language learning in the context of the book and traditional classroom. But their same points also hold true for computer-based learning materials. A principal difference, however, is that computer-based learning materials easily bridge the gap between fictional and non-fictional materials by routinely offering multimedia links from fictional passages to non-fictional resources as is sometimes found to a lesser degree in annotated editions of literary works. Multimedia also allows convenient tools for the study of literature such as search mechanisms, on-line dictionaries, thesauruses and concordancing tools.

A wish-list: a model learning program: What good pedagogy might ask for in future WWW technology includes guidelines likely to be offered in a multimedia CALL environment summarised by Murray, Morgenstern and Furstenberg (1989). The guidelines (paraphrased below) also serve to suggest how narrative-driven multimedia learning environments might be evaluated:

1. Multiplicity of protagonists: allows for the story to be told from different points of view creating learning gaps necessitating the learners to fill in information.
2. Multiplicity of plot events: creates variety based on learner choices that influence the development of the narrative.
3. Knowledge-based choice points: allow for learning tasks that are necessary to the continuation of the narrative.
4. Choice-points based on temperament of the learner: allow learners to pursue the narrative according to the depth of their own interest or to complete more practical or narrative tasks which, nonetheless, cover the same materials.
5. Whimsy in the form of momentary diversion that encourages exploration. In many programs, this is encapsulated in programs called *Easter Eggs* that, like the elegant jewelled Fabergé eggs created for the Russian aristocracy, contain unexpected surprises.
6. Multiple media for presentation: offers different methods of input (aural, textual) but also in different realistic contexts, such as a radio, telephone or newspaper.
7. Intrinsic rather than extrinsic rewards: motivates learners to progress through the program because completing the tasks and acquiring language are the same objective.

Murray, Morgnstern and Furstenberg contrast this to embedded quizzes that must be completed as an irrelevant test before the learner progresses through the narrative.

There are many narrative and non-narrative multimedia materials that do not accommodate some of the above points but the list is a useful starting point for deciding what is possible and desirable within a multimedia context. Another aspect of an ideal WWW program would be a concern for all four language skills. At the present time, reading takes precedence over the other skills in most WWW applications. Speech synthesis and speech recognition programs are beginning to make learning listening and speaking more possible, but most speech synthesis still sounds wooden in comparison to a human voice and effective speech recognition requires hours spent training the computer for each individual's voice.

Several researchers have done work in the area of intelligent computer-assisted language learning (ICALL). Many of these programs rely upon Eliza-type programs (See Weizenbaum 1966; A killer app for computer chat, *The Economist,* April, 1999) that use psychology-based subroutines and large databases of information to create so-called intelligent responses to learner questions and directions. This is a promising area, but still in it infancy. As Murray (1995) notes:

> Such pattern matching programs have severe limitations. For machines to understand and produce language, they must be able to process natural language at the morpho-syntactic, semantic and discourse levels. For spoken language, the system also needs to process language at the phonetic and phonological level (p. 146).

Clearly, these are great challenges that will require systematic and concerted research to overcome. Such research is all the more difficult in working with a medium that seems to be in constant flux. Studies in CALL conducted a decade ago are often worthless as computing power and technology has advanced and solved any problems that have been identified or taken the direction of CALL away from previous standards, for example, the abandonment of DOS-based educational computing. Kenning and Kenning's book *Computers and language learning: current theory and practice* provides an excellent caution to anyone hoping to draw conclusions on quickly-evolving technologies. So much has changed that a great many of their conclusions are now quite out of date. For example, they conclude that the computer's display of information is severely limited in the printed page because of the lack of right ragged edge and paragraph indentations and problems with typography (see pp. 96-98). They little realised that within five years the computer would all but replace and revolutionise traditional typography and provide far more flexible display options than the printed page.

Conclusion: The problem of ensuring that technology adapts to pedagogy rather than the other way round, remains a problem of both the model of learning and limitations in the technology. Innovations in these areas may eventually point to a replacement of books and schools as the principal means of education but the search for solutions may also simply serve to affirm the singular value of the traditional teacher.

References:

_______ (1999). A killer app for computer chat. *The Economist,* April, 1999. 79-80.
Collie, J., & Slater, S. (1987). *Literature in the language classroom.* Cambridge: Cambridge University Press.
Fosnot, C. T. (1996). Constructivism: a psychological theory of learning. In C. T. Fosnot (Ed.), *Constructivism: theory, perspectives and practice* (pp. 8-33). New York: Teachers College Press.
Fox, J. (1991). *Learning languages with computers: a history of computer assisted language learning from 1960 to 1990 in relation to education, linguistics and applied linguistics.* Unpublished Ph.D., University of East Anglia.
Kenning, M. M., & Kenning, M. J. (1990). *Computers and language learning: current theory and practice.* New York: Ellis Horwood.
Keobke, K. (1994). The Patient but Stupid Teacher: Computers in the Classroom. *CAELL Journal, 5*(2), 2-9
Lai, P., & Biggs, J. (1994). Who benefits from mastery learning? *Contemporary Educational Psychology, 19,* 13-23.
McArthur, T. (1983). *A foundation course for language teachers.* Cambridge: Cambridge University Press.
Merrill, P. F., Hammons, K., Vincent, B., Reynolds, P., Christensen, L., & Tolman, M. (1996). *Computers in education.* (3rd Edition ed.). Boston: Allyn and Bacon.
Montali, J., & Lewandowski, L. (1996). Bimodal reading: benefits of a talking computer for average and less skilled readers. *Journal of Learning Disabilities, 29*(3), 271-279.
Murray, D. E. (1995). *Knowledge machines: language and information in a technological society.* Harlow, Essex: Longman.
Murray, J. (1995b). Lessons learned from the Athena Language Learning Project: using natural language processing, graphics, speech processing, and interactive video for communication-based language learning. In V. M. Holland, J. D. Kaplan, & M. R. Sams (Eds.), *Intelligent language tutors: theory shaping technology* (pp. 243-256). Mahwah, New Jersey: Lawrence Erlbaum Associates Publishers
Murray, J. H., Morgenstern, D., & Furstenberg, G. (1991). The Athena Language Learning Project: design issues for the next generation of computer based language-learning tools. In W. F. Smith (Ed.), *Modern Technology in Foreign Language Education: applications and projects* (pp. 97-118). Lincolnwood, Illinois: National Textbook Company.
Ravitch, D. (1989). Technology and the curriculum: promise and peril. In M. A. White (Ed.), *What Curriculum for the Information Age?* (pp. 25-39). New York: Lawrence Erlbaum Associates Publishers.
Robinson, I., & Harrold, J. (1993). *Rupert, The Daily Express Annual.* (Vol. 58). Exeter: Pedigree Books.
Rozycki, E. G. (1996). Behaviourism. In J. J. Chambliss (Ed.), *Philosophy of education: an encyclopedia* (pp. 52-54).
Skinner, B. F. (1954). The science of learning and the art of teaching. *Harvard Educational Review, 24,* 86-97.
Skinner, B. F. (1968). *The technology of teaching.* Englewood Cliffs, New Jersey: Prentice Hall.
Stevens, V. (1992). Humanism and CALL: a coming of age. In M. Pennington & V. Stevens (Eds.), *Computers in applied linguistics: an international perspective* (pp. 11-38). Clevdon, Avon: Multilingula Matters.
Weizenbaum, J. (1966). ELIZA — a computer program for the study of natural language communication between man and machine. *Communications of the ACM, 9*(1), 36-45.

GROUP DYNAMICS AND THE ONLINE PROFESSOR

Kathleen King, Ph.D.
Idaho State University, U.S.A.

Abstract
Much has been written about online groups, but the writings are fragmented into technical information or advice about teaching methods. No overall theory of why online groups work or fail has been developed. Psychoanalysts W. H. Bion and I. D. Yalom shaped contemporary thinking about group process, and the theories of Bion and Yalom can be used to organise online educational groups. My goal in this paper is to use their theories to provide a framework for thinking about online groups. I will create a structure for understanding group process in the new online groups and provide a context which can contain and place more specialised contributions.

The Tradition of Educational Groups. Educational groups are as old as wisdom, perhaps originating in storytelling and in the preservation of myths which held the first humans together. Instinctively, it seems, we humans know that individual knowledge is somehow less than group knowledge. Remember the NASA Test? Perhaps you participated in this role-play as an undergraduate in a sociology class. Stranded on the moon with basic supplies necessary to travel 200 miles to base camp, you could only carry so much. Students were asked to take the test first as individuals, and then in groups. Individuals died miserably (in make-believe) of cold or thirst, but almost all the groups survived because the pooled knowledge and discussion of alternatives enabled them to choose the necessary supplies successfully.

Now we have been overtaken by a new sort of group: the online communities of mailing lists and realtime chats. The workings of groups in this new environment seem mysterious, but theories derived from observation of psychotherapeutic groups can explain the interpersonal dynamics of online groups. At first, it may seem that psychotherapy groups cannot be compared to online groups of university students. But members of both types of groups have a task, whether getting well, getting an A, or just getting through English 201. Each group also has a process, a method of interaction, and if the process fails, the group's work will be completed poorly or not at all.

Much has been written about online groups, but the writings are fragmented into technical information or advice about teaching methods. No overall theory of why online groups work or fail has been developed. Roger Clarke (1996) noted this lack in calling for a 'means of developing ... control mechanisms over dysfunctional behaviour'. Peter Kollock (1998) points out that 'As the online world is a wholly constructed environment, it is worth considering what features, constraints, and challenges of the physical world might be profitably introduced into virtual worlds'. Psychoanalyst W. H. Bion (Grinberg, Sor, & Bianchi, 1975) and psychiatrist I. D. Yalom (1975) have shaped contemporary thinking about group process, and the theories of Bion and Yalom can be used to understand and solve problems in online educational groups. My goal in this paper is to use their theories to provide a framework for thinking about online groups. I will create a structure for understanding group process in the new online groups and provide a context which can contain and place more specialised contributions.

Two Theories of Group Dynamics. W. R. Bion was a psychoanalytic theorist who wrote on group dynamics. Among his important ideas are the container and the contained; mental processes as influenced by trauma; and the role of leader, saviour and genius in group dynamics. He created an abstract model of psychic functioning (the grid) based on algebraic concepts and notation, and studied the behaviour of individuals in groups and the emotions which resulted from their interactions. During World War II, Bion organised the rehabilitation of soldiers in a psychiatric hospital by treating getting well as a group project. Later he worked as a group psychotherapist.

According to Bion, a group mentality arises as the group becomes a unit. At any given moment, a group holds one of three basic assumptions, which may differ from the beliefs of the individual members. The basic assumption of dependence arises from the group's anxious need to depend absolutely on someone who ought to protect the members and satisfy all their desires. Collective belief in an enemy who can be dealt with only by attack or retreat forms the basic assumption of fight-flight. The basic assumption of pairing defines the notion that some future event or person will come from outside to solve all problems.

Bion envisioned two basic types of groups: the basic assumption group and the work group. The basic assumption group is shaped by the unconscious of each group member, and the assumptions play out without the co-operation or even knowledge of individuals. The dependent group seeks an all-powerful leader, the fight-flight group needs an enemy and wants the leader to formulate a defence, and the pairing group looks forward to some promised perfect state in the future. The concept of a pairing group needs some explanation. The metaphor here is that the group allows two of its members to become a couple; these two create a child who becomes saviour of the group. New ideas (the contained) always carry the power to disrupt a basic assumption group (the container) in the process Bion called catastrophic change. Primitive and hostile, basic assumption groups resist learning. Members of this type of group use language as a weapon rather than as a tool for exploring ideas.

On the other hand, the work group depends upon a certain maturity in members, manifested by co-operation, tolerance of frustration, and rational thought. Although the task may be difficult, group members experience growth as they are guided in their work by a leader. The basic assumption group evades or disposes of new ideas without considering them, but the work group focuses on the task at hand instead of drowning in fear. However, it is important to remember that every work group contains an unseen and irrational basic assumption group which may erupt at any time.

Irvin D. Yalom, a psychiatrist who wrote an important textbook on group therapy and studied encounter groups, stresses the importance of group cohesiveness, defined as the attraction of members to one another and the group. According to Yalom, twice-weekly meetings of not more than two hours keep group members involved without overwhelming them. A group size of seven is ideal, with fewer group members if the meeting is shorter, and more members to fill up a longer time period. Face-to-face contact is important, whether the group sits around a table or in a circle with an empty middle. The second arrangement allows better observation of nonverbal responses. Group members always have two jobs: the assigned task and the social interactions necessary for completion of the task.

Groups go through an initial honeymoon phase, followed by disenchantment, which then leads to cohesiveness. Members Yalom calls 'early provocateurs' challenge the group leader and then depart, and normally 10 to 35 percent of psychotherapy group members drop out by the twentieth session. Lateness and missed sessions signal resistance to group cohesiveness. Subgroups which set themselves apart from the main group by forming outside alliances also endanger cohesiveness. For instance, a romance or close friendship between two members of a larger group may make others feel excluded. Yalom believes that conflict may not be a negative factor for groups; disagreement can foster excitement and learning. Too much aggression by one member results in the assertion of group norms by the others, teaching individuals how to work together.

Online Groups Differ From Face-to-face Groups. Online groups are different from traditional groups because they lack the face-to-face contact so important to us as human beings. Humans use visual, auditory, olfactory, and pheromone (via the vomero-nasal organ) cues to divine the emotions of others in the group. Computer-mediated communication strips these important emotional cues from the conversation, leaving only the typed words on a computer screen. This creates an anonymity which at once invites quick intimacy and weakens the power of group norms. Even a telephone conversation allows some transmission of emotion via voice modulation, but words on the computer screen carry no emotion beyond their dictionary definitions. Yet people share their inmost secrets and strongest beliefs with strangers on the Internet.

Two types of online groups used frequently in educational settings are mailing lists and realtime chats. The mailing list, essentially an elaborated email system which forwards to all members messages sent to a central processor, creates a slow and unwieldy conversation, with response times measured in hours or days. Nevertheless, people become intensely bonded in mailing lists. Collins and Berge (1996) point out that asynchronous mailing lists create 'a constant stream of reminders that the conference is proceeding ... students ... have time to think and reflect on their responses'. Regular contact creates the sense of an ongoing relationship. Realtime chats increase the rate of information exchange to nearly the speed of in-person dialogue, but the participants remain faceless and voiceless, known only through ephemeral lines of type moving across an inanimate screen. However, the pace of synchronous computer chats resembles that of face-to-face conversation. According to Collins and Berge, 'the text on the screen can scroll along at a furious pace'. Another advantage is the potential to download a transcript of the conversation for study at a later time. In this regard, it resembles a book, which the reader can stop to reflect upon at any time.

Owston (1997) points out that some faculty members believe a high quality of learning can be achieved with online interaction. Rheingold (Electropolis) reminds his readers about the substantial effect of health-related information and support groups on the lives of the chronically ill. Rheingold believes that we're not yet sure what virtual communities are, but we're learning more about them all the time. Pointing out disadvantages, Mark Slouka (Electropolis) calls virtual communities 'a world of enormous silence' where 'language grows strained and awkward'.

Collins and Berge (1996) offer hope for 'a virtual community ... that provides support and encouragement and promotes sharing ... and can help overcome the isolation of remote areas'. Karaliotas (1997) agrees, comparing the Internet to an 'agora ... in which knowledge is not only shared, but created and recreated'. In the late 1970s, the author of this paper was privileged to use PLATO, the source of an accidental online community which arose from an early email and newsgroup system developed by David R. Woolley (1994). The PLATO community brought together academics, first in Illinois and later throughout the world, and Woolley believes that PLATO showed how online communities can flower. Rheingold (1992) agrees, calling a deliberately constructed online community, the WELL, 'a bit like a neighbourhood pub or coffee shop ... a salon ... a groupmind', where 'we do everything people do when people get together, but we do it with words on computer screens, leaving our bodies behind'.

Relevant Literature: The first task in setting up a work group is to think about the characteristics outlined by Bion and Yalom. What is the task of the group? And how will the group interact to accomplish this task? Paulsen (1995) suggests that instructors 'identify their preferred pedagogical styles, based on their philosophical orientation, their chosen moderator roles, and their preferred facilitation techniques'. Attitudes about learner-centred classes, including teaching, assessment, and tone, can help a moderator develop his or her teaching style. According to Berge (1996), the online instructor has four roles: pedagogical, social, managerial, and technical. The leader contributes knowledge, keeps the discussion on track, weaves together various discussion threads, and maintains group harmony.

The role of the leader is to organise the group, to set the goals and agenda, and to build cohesiveness by focusing attention on group process. Rohfeld and Hiemstra (1995) point out that 'the moderator must attend to two types of group processes ... group building relates to the task the group is undertaking ... maintenance refers to the function of the group as a group'. Their terminology is a bit confusing here, but group building is equivalent to the group task, and maintenance refers to the interaction necessary to accomplish that task. Although the leader sets up basic group norms, he or she should not forget that the group acting together can overpower the leader. Kollock (1998) believes that each group should build customised norms for behaviour.

Students and teachers who participate in online groups must be comfortable with technology. Karaliotis (1997) points out that three levels of technology use are available. The simplest use is as an aid to instruction, but technology may be added on to conventional classes, or used to produce technology-driven courses on the Internet, classes beyond the ordinary limits of place and time. A dozen years ago, 10% of students at Idaho State University had used computers on campus or off. Now 90% are familiar with the basics of word processing and the Internet. Rohfeld and Hiemstra (1995) suggest that educators pay attention to the need for 'appropriate technical support materials and well-designed course study guides'.

Co-operation, tolerance of frustration, and rational thought characterise the work group, creating an atmosphere in which members experience growth. Although the work group is a safe container for new ideas, a basic assumption group always lurks just beneath the surface. Clarke (1997) writes that 'Communities in cyberspace need means of achieving cohesion and maintaining relationships, while avoiding unduly dysfunctional behaviour by community members and outsiders'. Kollock (1998) agrees, noting that 'group boundaries must be clearly defined so that there is a clear sense of who might make use of collective resources and in order to prevent individuals from entering the group, making use of its resources, and then departing without ever contributing to the group'.

Special Characteristics of Online Groups. The online instructor preparing to use work groups is able to use the group dynamics theories of Bion and Yalom to enhance group cohesiveness. The instructor must be willing to serve as a strong leader and facilitator, someone who will construct and direct the group, but will remain an impartial observer of group process. The chart below compares the characteristics of therapy groups to those of online groups. Although the work and structure of the group may differ, the group process remains the same. The table below compares therapy and online groups in terms of leader role, structure, contact, and cohesiveness.

Table 1. Comparison of Therapy Groups and Online Groups

Therapy Group	Online Groups	
	Synchronous: Chat	Asynchronous: Mailing List
Leader as facilitator	Attends meetings of groups, keeps discussion on track, summarises threads of discussion, helps group interpret Basic Assumption Group behaviour	Reads messages, summarises and focuses discussion, interprets Basic Assumption Group behaviour
Meet twice per week Not more than 2 hours Ideal size seven, plus or minus according to time	Twice-weekly meetings – Split online time between groups of smaller size, like reading groups in grade school: Bluebirds, Robins	Read collected email messages and write a long reply at least twice each week
Face-to-face contact	Individual home pages for group members with biography, interests, photographs, links to papers Insert photograph from student ID card into email messages	
Resistance to Cohesiveness	Leader fosters meta-discussion of group process Brings up for discussion lateness, missed sessions, lack of contribution to work of group Early provocateurs will challenge leader and leave group Subgroups or outside alliances may form	

The leader directs attention to group process through a technique known as meta-talk or meta-discussion. Meta-discussion is talk about the talk, a chance to understand and improve group process and group norms. According to Holeton (1997), 'metadiscussion can be a valuable exercise in negotiating norms and conventions'. Collins and Berge (1996) agree, suggesting that 'metacomments ... be used to remedy problems in context, norms or agenda, clarity, irrelevance'. Rheingold (1992) describes the '"MetaWELL," a conference ... about the WELL itself, its nature, its situation (often dire), its future'.

In a poetry class, the professor received two messages in one week. The first writer, sensitive to criticism, had hurt feelings over a rather gentle critique of his poem by other students during a face-to-face class. The second wondered if she was talking too much. Both of these students need counselling on their relationship to the group, one about viewing a critique as hostile criticism, and the other on ways to involve more bashful group members who lurk at the edge of the discussion. In addition, the leader must increase group cohesiveness by fostering discussion on ways of talking about writing and the responsibility of shy persons to participate fully in the work of the class.

In most classes, the online group will have more than the seven members suggested by Yalom, and the leader may want to design exercises which allow students to work in smaller, more intimate groups. Synchronous chat groups should meet twice a week, and asynchronous mailing list members should read the collected messages and write a long reply at least twice per week. According to Yalom, disagreement is valuable because it 'fosters excitement and learning' while 'too much aggression leads to assertion of group norms'. The instructor should expect the group to go through honeymoon and disenchantment phases on the way to cohesiveness. Lateness or missed sessions should be discussed by the entire group. 'How do members of the group feel about X's lateness?' might be a good starting question. The early provocateurs will challenge the leader and may leave. Subgroups or outside alliances between group members may form.

Lack of face-to-face contact is a major drawback of online groups. Group cohesiveness is enhanced when members can see, hear, and smell each other. The group leader can use simple techniques to increase cohesiveness. According to Rohfeld and Hiemstra (1995), bringing the group together for 'an initial get acquainted and orientation session' allows students to visualise their classmates. Another useful technique is to require each group member to construct a home page which contains a biography, a list of interests, photographs, and links to papers or other class materials. Each student at Idaho State University has access to his or her digital photo, used on the student ID card stored in the mainframe computer. Professors can print out a class roster containing these photographs, and students can copy their photos into email messages. Inserting a photo, as I have done here, instantly brings personality to the document.

The group leader has access to many simple techniques to increase participation and cohesiveness. Giving each group member a set task brings everyone to the table. A question of the week — How does sensitivity to criticism help or hinder the poet? — can focus on both the subject matter and the interaction between group members. Cross-fertilisation occurs when students begin to respond to each other's comments as they would in a classroom. Techniques which increase participation tend to enhance

group cohesiveness, a vital factor according to Yalom. Rohfeld and Hiemstra (1995) suggest debates, polling activities, and learning partnerships. Journal writing can stimulate critical and reflective thinking, and a guest lecturer or student-moderated discussion can pick up the pace. The moderator should open each discussion by providing background and describing the issues to be explored, ending this opening statement with a question designed to stimulate conversation.

Participants must have a stake in the group. When asked about the purpose of their class mailing list, students responded that the group was good for asking and answering questions, communicating with each other, and communicating with the professor. A graduate student wrote that 'I think this part of the class, the news group, is our own little coffee and steamed milk shop ... I like to think of each of you pulling up class email with your feet propped on a bean bag and a bit of improv playing in the background' (Ovard 1998).

Conclusion: Educators using online discussion groups and realtime chats have a unique opportunity to shape an emerging culture. At the beginning of any group, the members look toward the leader expectantly. The leader's response determines how the group will operate and what will be accomplished. Using the theoretical framework of group dynamics, the instructor can set up work groups and maintain group cohesiveness. The group dynamics theories of Bion and Yalom, allow leaders of online groups understand group process and to act in a way that creates a context in which the initiative and creativity of the group can emerge.

References

Berge, Z. (1996). The role of the online instructor/facilitator. [Online]. Available: http://star.ucc.nau.edu/~mauri/moderate/teach_online.html [1998, November 30].
Clarke, R. (1996). Cyberculture: Towards the analysis that internet participants need. [Online]. Available: http://www.anu.edu.au/people/Roger.Clarke/II/CyberCulture.html [1999, February 26].
Clarke, R. (1997). Encouraging cyberculture. [Online]. Available://www.anu.edu.au/people/Roger.Clarke/II/EncoCyberCulture.html [1998, November 30].
Collins, M., & Berge, Z. (1996). Facilitating interaction in computer mediated online courses. [Online]. Available: http://star.ucc.nau.edu/~mauri/moderate/flcc.html [1998, November 30].
Grinberg, L., D. Sor and E. T. de Bianchedi. (1975). Introduction to the Work of Bion. Scotland: The Roland Harris Educational Trust.
Holeton, R. (1997). A case study of electronic community building in a freshman dorm. [Online]. Available: http://www.stanford.edu/~holeton/wired-pages/wired-main.html [1998, November 30].
Karaliotas, Y. (1997). Learning on and over the internet: dynamics and limitations. [Online]. Available: http://users.otenet.gr/kar1125/education.htm [1998, November 30].
Kollock, P. (1998) Design principles for online communities. [Online]. Available: http://www.sscnet.ucla.edu/soc/faculty/kollock/papers/design.htm [1998, November 30].
Ovard, Leslie (1999, February 17). Re: Question of the Week. Email to Kathleen King.
Owston, R. (1997). The world wide web: a technology to enhance teaching and learning?

[Online]. Available: http://www.edu.yorku.ca/~rowston/article.html [1999, February 27].
Paulsen, M. (1995). Moderating educational computer conferences. [Online]. Available: http://www.nettskolen.com/alle/forskning/20/moderating.html [1999, February 26].
Rheingold, H. (1992). A slice of life in my virtual community. [Online]. Available: gopher://gopher.well.sf.ca.us/00/Community/virtual_communities92 [1998, November 30].
Rheingold, H. Public life in the electropolis. [Online]. Available: http://www.feedmag.com/95.08dialog/95.08dialog1.html [1998, November 30].
Rohfeld, R., & Hiemstra, R. (1995). Moderating discussions in the electronic classroom. [Online]. Available: http://star.ucc.nau.edu/~mauri/moderate/rohfeld.html [1998, November 30].
Slouka, M. Public life in the electropolis. [Online]. Available: http://www.feedmag.com/95.08dialog/95.08dialog1.html [1998, November 30].
Woolley, D. (1994). PLATO: the emergence of online community. [Online]. Available: http://thinkofit.com/plato/dwplato.htm [1998, November 30].
Yalom, I. D. (1975). The Theory and Practice of Group Psychotherapy. New York: Basic Books.

USING ON-LINE CHAT IN LANGUAGE TEACHING

S. Kathleen Kitao
Doshisha Women's College, Kyoto, Japan

Kenji Kitao,
Doshisha University, Japan

As the Internet grows, there are more and more opportunities to students to study English using a wide variety of types of Internet resources. (For a discussion of on-line resources, as well as links to these resources, see Kitao and Kitao [1995].) Especially for English language students in countries where English is a foreign language — that is, where English is not used in everyday life — these resources are important, because they greatly increase the opportunities for using English.

One potentially useful Internet activity for language students is 'chatting', that is, communicating in real time by typing a message into a computer, so that it can immediately be read on other computer screens, even computer screens in another part of the world. Some sites on the Internet are specifically intended for non-native English speakers, and they provide opportunities for non- native English speakers to communicate in English. (For the purpose of this paper, I will be discussing mainly with the use of chat to teach English. However, there are chat-related sites for other languages. Some of these are found in the last section.)

In this paper, we will discuss the role that communication in general interaction in particular plays in language learning will introduce two specific Internet sites, SchMOOze University and Dave's ESL Cafe Chat Central. We will also provide a list of sites on the Internet that are useful for teachers and students interested in chat.

The Role of Interaction and Communication in Language Learning

Interaction: While Krashen (1981) asserted that comprehensible input was both a necessary and a sufficient condition for the acquisition of language, Ellis (1985, p. 161) conducted an analysis of various studies and theoretical treatments of the subject and concluded that both input and interaction influence second language acquisition. He listed eight characteristics of input and interaction which seem to facilitate rapid acquisition, based on this analysis. They are:

1. A high quantity of input directed at the learner.
2. The learner's perceived need to communicate in the L2.
3. Independent control of the propositional content by the learner (e.g., control over the

topic choice).
4. Adherence to the 'here and now' principle, at least initially.
5. The performance of a range of speech acts by both the native speaker/teacher and the learner (i.e., the learner needs the opportunity to listen to and to produce language used to perform different language functions).
6. Exposure to a high quantity of directives.
7. Exposure to a high quantity of 'extending' utterances, (e.g., requests for clarification and confirmation, paraphrases and expansions).
8. Opportunities for uninhibited 'practice' (which may provide opportunities to experiment using 'new' forms).

Of these factors in language acquisition, most are either facilitated by interaction or require interaction, as opposed to input alone. Interaction can be used to elicit input, increasing its quantity. Making friends through interaction is one perceived need for communication. Interaction helps the learner control the propositional content. Interaction can involve a range of speech acts, a high quantity of directives and extending utterances, and opportunities to practice.

Using Interaction to Learn Language: As Ellis concluded, the opportunity to use language in interaction plays an important part of language learning. Klein (1986, pp. 146-167) points out that the more the learner interacts, the more language he/she has an opportunity to learn, and the more language he/she learns, the more input he/she can solicit in order to learn more language. At first, the learner uses whatever non-verbal means and small amount of verbal language he/she already knows. This elicits language, which the learner can use to confirm or contradict his/her hypotheses about the language. The learner can use the newly acquired language to elicit more language and confirm or contradict new hypotheses.

However, many language students, particularly those in foreign language situations, do not have the opportunity to use English extensively outside of the classroom. In addition, language learners in a foreign language situation may have difficulty even seeing English as a means of communication. In Japan, for example, English is generally necessary for college entrance exams, and students may think of English mainly as something that they learn about in order to take a test. The purpose of the language that they produce is mainly for the teacher to evaluate, not for the purpose of expressing their ideas. As Muehleisen (1998: 69) wrote,

> In the case of EFL in Japan, the challenge for teachers often lies in moving students away from a mindset in which English is something learned through rote memorisation for entrance exams, towards a view of English as a living language they can use to communicate with and learn about the world around them.

Even non-native English speakers who live in an English-speaking country may feel that they do not have enough opportunity to use English, or may prefer chatting on the

Internet because it is less stressful than using English face-to-face.

For language students who wish to be able to communicate in English on line, the Internet provides an important opportunity to learn English. As Fritzler (1995) pointed out,

> In general, to use the Internet is to communicate (Anderson, 1995). The main purpose of the Internet is to connect people all over the world to share information, experiences, and opinions. Because the Internet is a natural resource (i.e. not a textbook created for the purpose of teaching a language), it contains real language. As students navigate their way around the primarily text-based Internet, they must read and write in English, which helps them acquire the language...

On-Line Interaction for English Language Students: As mentioned above, there are many resources for language learning on the Internet. However, synchronous communication in a MOO or chat room offers opportunities for interaction. This interaction, even though it is written and not face-to-face, can be more authentic that the type of face-to-face interaction that many language learners where English is a foreign language have access to. Davies, Shield, and Weininger (1998, pp. 17-18) asserted that

> There is a real possibility to interact 'naturally' with native speakers — comMOOnication is real, despite the virtual interlocutors, whereas the target language interaction in the classroom is quite often unreal, despite the real interlocutors. Perhaps most importantly, though, is that the target language switches focus within any MOOing activity: language is no longer a goal but an instrument to pursue other (real) goals; integrating into the MOO's Community is socialising in the target language, one of the highest ranking activities in foreign language learning.

Weininger, Shield, and Davies (1998: 90) agreed, saying

> ...very basic textbook activities, such as talking about the weather or introducing oneself, become authentic by virtue of the fact that learners constantly meet new participants, perhaps based on the other side of the globe, whereas the same, classroom-based exchange could never be authentic. In other words, MOO users have easy access to authentic communication partners and actually want to know the answer to a simple question rather than asking it as a formulaic classroom activity...

As Michael Guest pointed out in an interview with Elin Melchior (Melchior 1997, p. 14), although MOOs involve reading and writing, their structure is like conversation, and they have the advantage for students that because they are not face-to-face conversation, and though the conversations take place in real time, there is not as much time pressure or stress as with face-to-face conversations.

Chat can be used either among students in the same class or between students in the class (either as individuals or in pairs or groups) and outsiders from other parts of the world.

Freiermuth (1998: 85) argues that it is better to have students chat with other students in the same class for a number of reasons, including that native speakers become disinterested in chatting with non-native speakers of low proficiency, that the language used may be too difficult, that there is not topic, and that the non-native speakers may be confronted with harsh language, insults, etc. However, using chat rooms, MOOs or other sites that are specifically intended for non-native speakers seems to solve some of these problems. Native speakers who come to such sites are interested in chatting with non-native speakers, and they are likely to be patient with their difficulties in expressing themselves in the target language. In addition, the teacher may give the students certain tasks to fulfil during their time chatting, for example, certain information to ask for.

Two Internet Sites for Synchronous Communication: There are a number of sites and types of sites for chatting. In general, they fall into two categories — virtual worlds, either text-based or graphic, and chat rooms. In this section, we will describe one example of each. The first is SchMOOze University, which is a MOO for non-native English speakers and those interested in communicating with people of other cultures. The second is Chat Central at Dave's ESL Cafe.

Descriptions of the Sites:
SchMOOze University. One site intended for non-native English speakers which allows synchronous communication is SchMOOze University. (See http://ilc2.doshisha.ac.jp/users/kkitao/class/schmooze.htm for a handout to orient students to SchMOOze University.) A MOO is a text-based virtual world, which means that as a user moves around, he/she will see written descriptions of places in the MOO, including descriptions of rooms, furniture, open spaces, and exits into other places. SchMOOze University is a virtual college campus, with a dormitory, offices, classrooms, malls, and an off-campus bar.

SchMOOze University can be accessed through telnet (schmooze.hunter.cuny.edu 8888), the World Wide Web (http://schmooze.hunter.cuny.edu/test.html) or a dedicated program which can be downloaded from the World Wide Web (http://www.chaco.com for PCs).

SchMOOze University is specifically intended for non-native English speakers to practice their English as well as for native English speakers interested in intercultural communication. A total of approximately 550 people are registered at SchMOOze University, and guests can log on as well. Users are divided into four levels — players, builders, programmers, and wizards. Wizards are the administrators of the site, and there are ten of them. The vast majority of the users of the site are players, who can chat, play games, and sign up for and decorate a dormitory room. Builders and programmers are allowed to do increasingly more programming of various structures in the MOO.

SchMOOze University, like any other MOO, requires participants to communicate with others, in order to find out how to do something they want to be able to do, and to figure out how to use the commands (Rosenberg, 1992).

Some teachers may be hesitant to allow students to use the Internet due to stories of sexual harassment or other inappropriate behaviour. Such incidents are rare at SchMOOze University (personal communication, Yoshimasu Awaji, April 1998), and if a problem is reported to the wizards (there is almost always a wizard logged on), the wizard can speak to the person causing the problem, and if necessary, ban the person from the site. (In many hours spent at SchMOOze University, I have very rarely encountered anything inappropriate.)

Dave's ESL Cafe Chat Central. Dave's ESL Cafe (http://www.eslcafe.com) is a World Wide Web site that has various resources for English language learners. Among these is Chat Central (http://www.eslcafe.com/chat/chatpro.cgi), which is a web page where users can chat. Users go to the Chat Central page, where they log in. (The first time, it is necessary to register, by choosing a name and a password and providing an e-mail address to confirm the registration.) After entering Chat Central, the user can enter messages in one box and see a list of their own and others' messages. Chat Central has several 'rooms', and messages can either be directed to the entire room or to any individual logged on at Chat Central.

Chat-Related Sites on the Internet: There are a number of sites on the Internet where language students can chat. (There are probably thousands of sites on the Internet where it is possible to chat, but this discussion will be limited to sites that are most useful to language learners.) In addition, there are many sites where teachers can learn about chat and get practical suggestions for introducing chat to students.

The following is a selection of some of the more useful chat-related sites on the Internet, including lists of links; FAQs, explanations, etc.; individual chat sites for English language students and teachers; and sites for students of languages other than English. It is adapted from a links page found at http://ilc2.doshisha.ac.jp/users/kkitao/online/www/chat.htm. Comments that follow each site that are marked with ** are by the authors. Descriptions and comments that are unmarked are from the original page.

Lists of Links:

http://edvista.com/claire/internet-esl.html#moo
The Internet for ESL Teachers: MOOs

http://www.primenet.com/~ctallis/moopapers.html
MOOing
**A list of links to papers, explanations, etc., with emphasis on Diversity University.

http://www.linguistic-funland.com/language.muds.html
MUD's, MOO's, and other Virtual Environments

http://www.tcom.ohiou.edu/OU_Language/english/eMail.html

Online learning for English Language
**Links to various types of Internet resources, including chat and e-mail sites.

http://www.yahoo.com/Recreation/Games/Internet_Games/MUDs__MUSHes__MOOs__etc_/
Recreation : Games : Internet Games : MUDs, MUSHes, MOOs, etc.
**Lists of links.

Explanations, FAQs, Resources, Etc.
http://www.psychology.nottingham.ac.uk/staff/Jenifer.Tennison/MOO/basics.htm l
Basic Concepts in MOOs

http://www.itc.virginia.edu/virginia.edu/winter97/moos/
Constructing the Virtual Campus: Instructional Use of MOOs
**List of MOO commands, with explanations.

http://www.eslplanet.com/
ESL Planet
**Site for teachers interested in using MOOs and the Internet for language teaching.

http://home.earthlink.net/~lonnieturbee/PCI_9.html
Integrating virtual communities into the language class
**Outline of a TESOL '99 Pre-Conference Workshop given by Lonnie Turbee and Greg Younger. Includes information about MOOs and other uses for the Internet in language teaching.

http://langue.hyper.chubu.ac.jp/ozeki/saMOOraiIntro.html
Introduction to SaMOOrai
**Mostly in Japanese

http://elicos.qut.edu.au/moo/
An Introduction to Text Based Virtual Reality
**A very useful site, with explanations of MOOs, teachers' notes, etc.

http://spot.colorado.edu/~youngerg/how2moo.html
MOOing made Easy by Greg Younger
**Explanation of using SchMOOze University, by one of the 'wizards'. Includes links.

http://www.primenet.com/~ctallis/MOO_Commands.html
MOO QUICK START
**List of MOO commands, with explanations.

http://www.primenet.com/~ctallis/how_teach.html
MOO Teacher's Tip Sheet
**Good advice for teachers on using MOOs.

http://www.boker.org.il/eng/etni/jimmy/front.htm
Multi-User Domain Object Oriented (MOO) as a High School Procedure for Foreign Language Acquisition

**Doctoral dissertation.

http://www.cc.rim.or.jp/~awaji/schMOOze/
SchMOOze University
**Information about how to use SchMOOze University, along with a chart of commands that would be useful at any MOO.

http://samoorai.hyper.chubu.ac.jp:8080/
Welcome to SaMOOrai
**Information about SaMOOrai and links to MOO-related and Japan-related links

Links to Individual Chat Sites
DaedalusMOO
telnet to moo.daedalus.com 7777

http://moo.du.org:8888/
Diversity University
**Web-based entry portal to Diversity University.

http://www.englishlearner.com/chatstudents.html
Englishlearner.com Chatroom
**Chat site for learners of English.

http://www.englishtown.com/English/chat/wavepool.asp
Englishtown
**Chat site for learners of English.

http://www.epals.com
E-Pals
**Site which allows individual 'room' to be set up for chatting.

http://www.eslcafe.com/chat/chatpro.cgi
Dave's ESL Café Chat Central

http://www.talkcity.com/chat.htmpl?room=TheESLHubChat
TheESLHubChat
**A chat site for ESL students. The same site also has chat rooms for many other interests.

http://www.globalstudy.com/cgi-bin/chatpro.cgi
GlobalStudy Chat
**A chat room specifically to discuss study in English-speaking countries

http://www.planetenglish.com/chat/index.html
Planet English Chat

http://www.esl-lab.com/chat/
Randall's ESL Chat Centre
This site is designed for both ESL/EFL students and teachers around the world.

Registered members can chat in several different rooms, create their own unique profiles for others to look at, find pen friends via the WebBoard, and more.
**A chat site with links to other chat sites as well as information on using chat.

http://www.ramat-negev.org.il/~greenelt/newchat1.htm
Ronald Green's EFL On-Line Chat
**A chat site for English language teachers.

SaMOOrai
telnet to samoorai.hyper.chubu.ac.jp:8888
**SaMOOrai is a MOO intended for English language classes to use. It is organised as a cyber replica of Japan.

Schmooze University
http://schmooze.hunter.cuny.edu/test.html
telnet to schmooze.hunter.cuny.edu 8888

http://studentcenter.infomall.org/studentchat.html
Student Centre Chat
**A chat centre for high school and university students, not limited to non-native speakers. This site also has other resources for students.

Non-English MOOs
http://little.usr.dsi.unimi.it:4444/
Daedalus French-speaking MOO
telnet to moo.daedalus.com 8888

http://little.usr.dsi.unimi.it:4444/
Little Italy
telnet to little.usr.dsi.unimi.it:4444
**A MOO for Italian, which is not specifically intended for non-native speakers

MOO Francais (French) telnet to moo.syr.edu:7777

MOOsaico (Portuguese) telnet to moo.di.uminho.pt:7777

http://web.syr.edu/~lmturbee/mundo.html
Mundo Hispano
telnet to moo.syr.edu 8888
the Spanish language learning MOO

Conclusion: Interaction is an important part of key to developing proficiency in a second language, and chatting on the Internet is one way for students to find opportunities for interaction in the target language. Language teachers can use chat in the classroom or can introduce students to chat so that they can go on the Internet and chat individually.

References:

Davies, L. B., Shield, L., & Weininger, M. J. (1998). Godzilla can MOO, can you? MOOs for construction, collaboration and community and research. The Language Teacher, 22(2), 16-21.
Ellis, R. (1985). Understanding second language acquisition. Oxford: Oxford University Press.
Freiermuth, M. R. (1998). Small group on-line chat: The great equalizer. In P. Lewis (Ed.), Teachers, learners, and computers: Exploring relationships in CALL (pp. 81-86). Nagoya: The Japan Association for Language Teaching Computer-Assisted Language Learning Special Interest Group.
Fritzler, K. (1995). The Internet as an Educational Tool in ESOL Writing Instruction. MA Thesis. http://thecity.sfsu.edu/~funweb/thesis.htm
Fillmore, W. (1982). Instructional language as linguistic input: Second language learning in classrooms. In L. Wilkinson (Ed.), Communicating in the Classroom. New York: Academic Press. Cited in Ellis (1986).
Galloway, I., & O'Brien, D. (1998). Learning Online: Choosing the best computer-mediated communication activities. The Language Teacher, 22(2), 7-15.
Kitao, K., & Kitao, S. K. (1995). Internet Resources for linguistics, language teaching, and communication. http://ilc2.doshisha.ac.jp/users/kkitao/online
Klein, W. (1986). Second language acquisition. Cambridge: Cambridge University Press.
Krashen, S. D. (1981). Second language acquisition and second language learning. Oxford: Pergamon.
Melchior, E. (1997). Students and schMOOze. C@lling Japan, 6(3), 9-14.
Muehleisen, V. (1998). Motivating language learning through email exchange. In P. Lewis (Ed.), Teachers, learners, and computers: Exploring relationships in CALL (pp. 69-74). Nagoya: The Japan Association for Language Teaching Computer-Assisted Language Learning Special Interest Group.
Rosenberg, M. S. (1992). Virtual reality: Reflections of life, dreams, and technology, An ethnography of a computer society. http://www.oise.on.ca/~jnolan/muds/about_muds/ethnography.txt
Snow, C., & Hoefnagel-Hohle, M. (1982). School-age second language learners' access to simplified linguistic input, Language Learning, 32, 411-430.
Weininger, M. J., Shield, L., & Davies, L. B. (1998). A MOOving Experience. In P. Lewis (Ed.), Teachers, learners, and computers: Exploring relationships in CALL (pp. 87-94). Nagoya: The Japan Association for Language Teaching Computer-Assisted Language Learning Special Interest Group.

THE SELECT PROJECT: LANGUAGE ENGINEERING IN CALL FOR LEARNERS IN THE BUSINESS COMMUNITY

Ramesh Krishnamurthy, Stephen Hagen, Paul Brett, Ruslan Mitkov
University of Wolverhampton, UK

Abstract:
The SELECT project (Strategies for European LE-Enhanced Communication Training: EC Project LE4-8304, http://www.wlv.ac.uk/select/) offers new learning opportunities for European managers, equipping them with the cultural competence, language skills and language engineering tools necessary to communicate and operate effectively in a multilingual business environment, assisted by interactive multimedia courseware.

This paper will argue that European business managers, as a learning community, have been inadequately serviced in the past in terms of both language and cross-cultural materials. The consequence has been a high rate of failure in cross-border ventures. The SELECT project is a response to the demands of rapid internationalisation.

The paper will examine the existing and potential role of electronic language and cultural resources in the learning process, and discuss the re-use of existing resources and the creation of new user-specific resources. In the past, many of these resources have been designed and tailored for language engineers and researchers, rather than for non-specialists in the business community. By outlining the Language Learner's Workbench, an integral part of SELECT, we will show how such resources can be associated both with learning elements and practical business tasks, and combined in a single, user-friendly software environment.

The pedagogic approach which underpins the courseware, and aims at increasing users' cross -cultural awareness of business practices, will also be described. Some of the resulting multimedia materials, which exemplify culturally bound business practices and also aim to develop language competence, will be demonstrated.

1. Introduction

1.1 The Aim of the SELECT Project: The aim of SELECT is to develop an intelligent tutor for managing self-directed cross-cultural communication training in an interactive learning environment. It is aimed at international managers who are involved in cross-border activity, largely resulting from mergers, acquisitions or joint ventures, and who require intercultural communicative competence for a clear business purpose. For this reason the syllabus is contextualised within finance and banking — the sector which provides significant business information and advice to SMEs engaged in mergers or take-overs. It also has the added advantage of being a sector which is itself the object of mergers and acquisitions across Europe (see below). The SELECT learning model is designed to provide the user with access to additional 'select' (hence the project title) linguistic resources and cultural information in the Language and Culture Learning Workbench (LLW). The intelligent tutor will assist the user to navigate pathways into other Language-Engineering (LE) programs and relevant commercial products, so as to provide a more individualised learning programme. The project supports the development of competence in three European languages (English, French and Portuguese), each of which was chosen for its relevance in the global market beyond Europe.

1.2 The SELECT Consortium: The SELECT consortium combines a range of major European organisations: a hardware producer and software developer (IBM); publishers and educational learnware producers (Klett, Giunti); developers of multimedia language learning software and authoring tools (Wolverhampton University); representatives of groups of SMEs with an additional training interest (Augsburg and Schwaben IHK; CONFAPI); universities interested in syllabus development and ODL delivery (Open University, Portugal and Wolverhampton University); and Language Engineering Research Institutes (IAI, Saarbrucken and OFAI, Vienna) who are subcontractors.

1.3 The Specific Objectives of SELECT

The Project's specific objectives are:
1.3.1 To enable managers in small and medium-sized European companies undergoing internationalisation to overcome cross-cultural communication barriers more effectively.
1.3.2 To define and develop an agent-based 'intelligent tutor' to enhance the acquisition of cultural and linguistic competence through ODL methods.
1.3.3 To define and implement an electronically-delivered learning model suitable for use in European companies with access to intranets, the internet, and/or CD-ROM drives.
1.3.4 To prepare a model syllabus for French, English and Portuguese.
1.3.5 To design and implement gateways and interfaces within the LLW which support the genericity and re-usability of existing LE products, programs and other commercial(isable) programs with a view to constructing a customised holistic learning experience for users.
1.3.6 To map learning outcomes to the Council of Europe framework in order to ensure a common European standard.

1.4 SELECT and the European Commission's aims: SELECT's aims are also in line with the aims of the European Commission's *White Paper on Education and Training* insofar as it:

1.4.1 Addresses the second 'factor of upheaval' — the internationalisation of the economy (p.1).

1.4.2 Fosters the acquisition of new knowledge — in this case, cross-cultural competence (*Towards the Knowledge Based Society*, p.1).

1.4.3 Implements a possible model of lifelong learning in the context of global technology and the internationalisation of trade.

1.4.4 Fosters the principle of proficiency in three languages (focusing on English, French and Portuguese).

1.4.5 Recognises the importance of understanding other cultures to the achievement of social cohesiveness and mobility in Europe (when faced with 'an increasing variety of...cultural contexts', p.8).

1.4.6 Supports collaboration between universities and industry in pursuit of bringing education and the business sector closer together.

2. Learners In The Business Community

2.1 The Market Situation: The Business User

2.1.1 The Internationalisation of Business: The internationalisation of companies has accelerated over the last decade, with the need to increase competitiveness and mobility within the European and global marketplace. As V. K. Jolly expressed it in his *Global Strategies in the 1990s* (Strategic Management and Implementation, Part 16: p.6): 'Global competition today is about a lot more than cross-border competition... It is equally about building and managing a multinational infrastructure... (which) means internationalising all of the competencies and functions of a company — its R&D, procurement, production, logistics, marketing as well as human resources and finance.' Empirical studies carried out in the Berlitz European Division (1995) stated that: 'More than ever, managers in Europe need to become cosmopolitan, international communicators and negotiators, and generate cultural synergy'. SELECT focuses on developing cultural synergy in European managers in order to fit them for globalisation. The SELECT package is designed as a response to their needs in a climate of rapid cross-border mergers and acquisitions.

2.1.2 Individual SELECT Users: SELECT primarily addresses the needs of individual, mobile European managers who, in order to operate effectively across European borders need 'a good knowledge of the language, culture, business environment and the kind of detailed knowledge that only emerges after a long period of familiarisation' (Tyson, Cranfield University study 1991).

2.1.3 Companies Recognise the Need for Training: Many of the larger companies have recognised the need for action. In their study *Skills for Graduates in the 21st Century*, the 500-member Association of Graduate Recruiters confirmed that globalisation of organisations was `leading to a growing need for managers with international skills as well as mobility'. Moreover, the Harvard/Amrop International survey of nearly 1000 senior executives world-wide showed that 94% felt that the development of international executives is of `vital future importance' to their company. `Early identification and development of global executives is the only way we're going to be able to compete in the future'.

2.1.4 Managers Need Language *and* Cultural Training: Management today cannot be separated from its cultural context (Lorbiecki, 1993). Managers in international organisations increasingly need linguistic skills within a culture-specific context. This applies equally to cross-border trade, as well as to inward investment. There is a particular need for European companies in the small and medium-sized sector to improve their linguistic and intercultural capability. It is now becoming clear from an emerging body of knowledge from European studies that appropriate use of the customer's language and knowledge of the local culture can influence companies' export performance (Schegelmilch & Ross, 1987; Bjarnarson, 1992; Weiss, 1992; Castro, 1992; Dicht *et al.*, 1990, Hagen, 1993).

2.1.5 Needs Confirmed by Research: Qualitative research findings have indicated, for example, that foreign language acquisition is viewed by business people to be important for understanding linguistic nuances in the target language, and as a gateway to understanding another culture. Linguistic competence is perceived to be particularly important to a number of areas of management: sales, marketing, negotiation, after-sales service and establishing rapport. Findings from the ELUCIDATE project (the most recent Europe-wide *Leonardo da Vinci*-funded survey of the foreign language needs of comparable samples of English, French, German and Spanish SMEs) suggest that language and cultural barriers are a major hurdle to successful cross-border activity (Hagen, 1999). Other studies confirm that communication barriers are a major cause of difficulty to both sides (Olie, 1990; Hagen, 1993). Such a problem is likely to increase in future (Tollgerdt-Anderson, 1996) and current evidence suggests that this is already happening.

2.2 Cultural Barriers

2.2.1 The Severity of the Problems: It is clear that the linguistic interface is multifaceted, involving misunderstandings over behaviour, as well as simple communication. Cultural aspects of communication are often embedded within, and inseparable from, the linguistic aspects. In the UK, almost one in five companies claim to have experienced cultural barriers, which is similar to Western Spain but considerably greater than SE Germany (8%) and Central France (8%) (see Fig. 2). Many more companies face barriers without realising it.

2.2.2 The Nature of the Problems: As for the cultural barriers cited in ELUCIDATE, there is a wide range of societal, behavioural and interpersonal causes, which can be culture-specific (e.g. `awareness of local business environment') or generic (e.g. `etiquette'). A sample of the comments is given below:

Country	**Comment Cited in ELUCIDATE**
France	*Misunderstandings occurred through misinterpretation of cultural differences*
Germany	*Rigid approach to most operational procedures*

Other Comments cited in ELUCIDATE (country not specified):

Lack of confidence
Misunderstandings leads to wrong actions, leads to poor reputation, thus no business
We cannot follow the other sides confidential talk and we guessed wrong
Slow progress — prevents you going forward
Unable to follow-up mailshots etc. by telephone
Overseas exhibitions: when interpreters are busy — potential customers leave stand and do not return.

2.3 Language Barriers

SELECT bases its syllabus on the analysis of business needs described below. The main languages causing barriers are English and French. English is the main language barrier in France (17%) and Spain (30%). French is the main language barrier in the UK (20%) and Germany (25%). The third target language for the SELECT project is Portuguese, which causes barriers for 3% of Spanish SMEs and 2% of French and German SMEs in the ELUCIDATE sample.

Fig. 1 Languages causing Barriers in European Companies

UK Average		SE Germany		Central France		Western Spain	
French	20%	**French**	25%	**English**	17%	**English**	30%
German	19%	**English**	21%	German	16%	**French**	15%
Spanish	11%	Italian	15%	Spanish	10%	German	14%
Italian	8%	Spanish	9%	Italian	6%	**Portuguese**	3%
Chinese	5%	Russian	5%	Japanese	2%	Chinese	2%
East Europe	5%	Japanese	3%	Chinese	2%	Arabic	2%
Japanese	5%	Czech	3%	**Portuguese**	2%	Italian	2%
Russian	4%	Portuguese	2%				

(as % of sample)

Fig. 2 Table of Causes of Lost Business in ELUCIDATE sample

	UK Average	Central France	SE Germany	Western Spain
Inability to communicate effectively	33%	27%	18%	26%
Misunderstandings	14%	3%	-	9%
Lack of confidence	9%	6%	-	-
Exhibitions and trade fairs	9%	9%	18%	13%
Problems with agents and distributors	9%	-	6%	4%
Enquiries not followed-up	7%	12%	18%	4%
Cannot capitalise on opportunities	7%	12%	24%	9%
Lack of cultural affinity	7%	-	-	-
Phone and switchboard problems	2%	3%	-	4%
Errors in translations/interpreting	2%	-	6%	9%

(as % of companies that lost business)

2.4 Future Training Demand

In the UK, 56% of the sample indicated that they would require training in the next three years but a high proportion of these did not state which languages. The two languages in most demand are German and French, with 20% of companies requiring training in French. Portuguese is cited by 2% of companies as a requirement for the future.

In Germany, although only 38% of the sample state that they will need language training, the vast majority of these (29%) require training in English, with less than half requiring training in French.

English is the language in most demand in France (36%) with Portuguese in the top five.

Spanish companies are clearly aware of their needs with 67% of the sample indicating they need training — almost 90% of these (59%) quoted English as a language requirement and almost 50% (32%) quoted French. A significant proportion of the Spanish companies (6% of sample) will need training in Portuguese due to the proximity to that country.

TOTAL/EU		UK		GERMANY		FRANCE		SPAIN	
English	22%	German	24%	**English**	29%	**English**	36%	**English**	59%
German	17%	**French**	20%	**French**	15%	German	16%	**French**	32%
French	16%	Spanish	12%	Italian	9%	Spanish	11%	German	18%
Spanish	9%	Italian	5%	Spanish	6%	Italian	6%	**Port.**	6%
Italian	6%	Chinese	4%	Russian	1%	**Port.**	1%	Italian	4%
Portuguese	2%	Japanese	4%			Russian	1%	Russian	1%

3. SELECT: Design, Specification, Functionality and Components

The SELECT package is based on the unique combination of the design and functionality of the Learner Manager and the Language Learner's Workbench. The former is generis able, the latter is devoted to accessing reusable resources and converting resources into reusable resources, all of which can run on the SELECT model. Innovation is achieved through the development of the particular Language Engineering concepts:

- The **Learner Manager** — or intelligent, adaptive tutor — has a strong theoretical base (see below) and practical base
- The **Language Learner's Workbench** — adapts reusable resources to provide individualised learning pathways for the user.

3.1 The Learner Manager ('Intelligent Tutor'): components

The Learner Manager integrates four interacting components:
3.1.1 A pre-study **Learner Profiler,** identifying learner-type, learner preferences and learning style against known models (e.g. *inductive/deductive learner; grammar/structure vs. communicative tendency* etc.) and pre-defines learning pathways for the user to follow in order to reach his/her predefined goals.

3.1.2 A software-driven **Adaptive Tutor** derived from the Learning Model which helps users/learners organise and manage their own learning and navigate within a multimedia environment. The self-selected navigation routes, tagged to the above profiler, leading to optional linguistic diagnosis and self-evaluation tools for *self-monitoring* enabling evaluation and progress-charting against own pre-defined learning goals within the

Council of Europe framework with options for self and on-line assessment, self-correction exercises and learner feedback.

3.1.3 A Learning Measurement loop embedded within the Learner Manager system which supports the learner's activities by providing model answers, charting his/her progress with graphs and diagrams (which can also be used for assessment by a remote tutor) and measuring specific needs.

3.1.4 A Language Learner's Workbench (LLW), which acts as an Interface management operator for incorporating access to (a) *support resources* (b) gateway search modules and links to on-line support facilities (including WWW linguistic tools) and Intranet assets.

3.2 Concept of the Learner Manager

3.2.1 Learner-centred: In terms of functionality, there is little evidence of business users wishing or knowing how to devise, select and convert material into their own learning package. Users prefer simply to navigate their way through a series of set exercises and activities, skipping unwanted activities and moving to preferred ones. They increasingly expect the system to think for them by offering them customised choices, so they can *select* the most suitable learning options (hence the project title) e.g. activities or resources, based on their individual needs (e.g. grammar, additional revision activities and/or spellchecks). This more controlled and user-focused approach distinguishes SELECT from similar projects in the language acquisition domain, such as TELOS and SPEAK, which place greater emphasis on the user either as author of his/her own learning materials as he/she progresses, or the user as professional materials producer.

3.2.2 Flexible: The main goal of the LM is to develop an appealing intelligent learning environment, which meets the requirements mentioned above. Interaction should be varied and flexible, i.e. highly adaptive to the student's performance. The kernel of the SELECT system is the intelligent or 'adaptive' tutor. The LM system is designed in a modular way. The instruction network contains the course material. Its structure provides information about the relative level of difficulty of the various lessons and exercises. The student history contains a history of the student's performance. The dialogue with the student is designed by the teaching expert.

3.2.3 Domain-independent: We believe that the LM is independent of the chosen domain (hence its genericity), and that it can be used in various teaching applications in disciplines ranging from languages to mathematics. The domain expert, on the basis of information from the teaching expert, generates exercises and examples, and evaluates the student's answers. This component represents the domain-specific side of teaching. The interface manager provides the interface of the system to the student.

3.3 Theoretical Basis for the Learner Manager

3.3.1 Computer Aided Instruction (CAI): The main problem with traditional computer aided instruction (CAI) systems is that they are unable to provide adaptation or individualisation. In response to this and other problems CAI faced, Self (1974) argued that an interactive learning program should contain knowledge of how to teach, knowledge of what is being taught, and the knowledge of who is being taught. Carbonell (1970) also argued that the CAI problem could not be solved without the use of A1 techniques.

3.3.2 Intelligent Tutoring Systems (ITS): Consequently, CAI systems have evolved into what are now usually called 'Intelligent Tutoring Systems' (ITS). SELECT adopts this model for its intelligent tutor. A central assumption of an ITS is that the cognitive diagnosis of a learner's errors is an essential step towards meaningful individualised tutoring: the student model is mandatory to the goal of cognitive diagnosis, and consequently to the goal of adaptation. More specifically it is assumed that:

1. Student modelling allows feedback adequate to correct any misconceptions or missteps that result in error.
2. Beyond error correction, a dynamic representation of the developing knowledge of each student determines what to teach next and how to teach it (Snow & Swanson, 1992).

In ITS the student is modelled in terms of the domain expert, either in terms student does not (overlay model) or in terms of what knowledge units the expert has but the student does not (overlay model) or in terms of what knowledge units (i.e. buggy rules) the student has and the expert not (process model). In line with the expert systems approach, it is assumed that both types of student model can be used with an inference engine.

O'Shea (1979) has argued that one of the most important aspects of any CAI program is its response-sensitivity: an interactive learning program is more response -sensitive than another when it is more adaptive to the individual learning needs of the student than the other system. In a classical ITS system the performance is interpreted within the representation model of the expert. Hence the degree of response-sensitivity of the ITS is determined by the extent to which the set of all possible behaviours of the students fits within the representation framework of the ITS. As the student's performance is rarely consistent and it is in fact impossible to predict the full range of student behaviours, the response-sensitivity or adaptivity of an ITS is limited, (see, e.g. empirical research:

Payne & Squibb, 1990). In other words, a classical ITS is not robust as it cannot cope with any unexpected (i.e. not predefined) behaviour by the student. Moreover, as further instruction is based on the hypothesised knowledge state of the student and not on the student's behaviour itself, problems can arise because the student's performance was misinterpreted within the expert module.

To determine which new topic or exercise to address, or to which to return, information from the instruction network and student history is used. In the instruction network, information can be found about which topics or kinds of exercise are considered beforehand to be the more difficult. The student history (as maintained by the student model agent) provides information about which topics and exercises a student has already encountered, and his or her performance on these.

3.4 Practice Agent

The navigation agent determines which topic and kind of exercise will be addressed. In most cases, however, the topic to be taught will consist of a number of items of which the relative difficulty level is not necessarily known beforehand. For instance, with the conjugation of the verb 'to be' as topic, there could be an item for each grammatical person. The practice agent decides at any time which item will be presented in an exercise or example.

The most efficient way of teaching seems to be to confront a student with those items he/she does not know yet. The difficulty is that it is not always obvious what a student knows. As a basis for the behaviour of the practice agent we took quite trivial hypotheses. In the first place, we are convinced that performance of the student in the past predicts future performance.

3.5 Instruction Agent

The instruction agent is an important agent in the system as it determines not only the adaptivity, but also the interactivity level of the system. The behaviour of the instruction agent is determined by the rule 'If the student succeeds, when next intervening offer less help. If the student fails, when next intervening take over more control.' (Wood, Wood, & Middleton, 1978, p. 133). Furthermore, the instruction agent is based on a layered model of intervention, varying between the 'general verbal encouragement' level and the 'demonstration' level, whereby each layer represents a different level of control from the side of the teacher agent. This implies that the behaviour of the instruction agent is contingent on the performance of the student (cf. the situatedness principle); the most appropriate intervention is chosen on the basis of the student's success.

3.6 Feedback Agent

Our first rule is that feedback should be immediate. For instance, in the before-mentioned jigsaw exercise the student gets immediate feedback when he or she tries to put a word where it does not belong. The word bounces back and a sound is produced.

3.7 Presentation Agent

The behaviour of the presentation agent can be compared with the task of the director of a television broadcast of a soccer game. The default rule of the director is that as long as the game goes up and down the field, the television viewer gets a general overview of the whole soccer field. However, when a goal is scored, the director focuses in on the goal-scorer and replays the goal-scoring in slow motion. As in the case of the broadcast director, the presentation agent tries to choose at each moment in the learning session the optimal representation for the student. The presentation agent is based on a layered model, whereby each layer represents a different level of abstraction. The general rule determining the behaviour of the presentation agent is that information is presented at the abstract level (cf. the default rule of the director). However, when a student is having difficulties with a particular exercise, or is asking for more explanation, the presentation agent can decide to focus in on the problem in a more concrete representation format. It is obvious that efficient behaviour of the presentation agent will depend on the collaboration with the other agents, especially the student model agent (for information on the performance level of the student) and the feedback and instruction agents (those are the agents requesting a specific representation format).

3.8 Student Model Agent

All the agents mentioned so far need some information about the history of the student's performance. The student model agent maintains this kind of information. We decided exactly what to record by looking at which information the other agents needed. So student modelling did not become a goal per se, but is used only to supply the other agents with the information they need.

In the first place, the student model agent maintains the good and bad set needed by the practice agent. The following rules are used for this purpose:

If the student answered incorrectly to the item presented, it is added to the bad set and removed from the good set.

If the student answered correctly, the item is added to the good set and removed from the bad set.

For the navigation agent, information regarding which topics and exercises the student has encountered and his or her performance on these is maintained. This means that a good set and bad set is kept not only for the current exercise, but for all the exercises the student has done so far. The expression 'the student performs well', in the precondition of the rules of the navigation agent, has been formalised as 'at least 95% of the items is contained in the good set'. Whether the student's performance is improving is determined by comparing the size of the current good set with the size of that set before a certain number of items has been presented. For this purpose, a history of the number of items in the good set is maintained for the current exercise.

4. The Language Learner's Workbench (LLW)

4.1 Introduction to the LLW: The LLW is a typical example of the use of Language Engineering tools in Computer-aided Language Learning (CALL): the concept of the LLW is based on developing/re-using a host of practical Natural Language Processing (NLP) resources with proven efficiency of use in CALL, and integrating them into a user-friendly interface. The modular workbench will be adaptable to meet the needs of language students with particular requirements (e.g. for business language) or more generally, the needs of anyone who has to read or to write in a language in which she or he is not fluent. The multilingual workbench will, to begin with, contain language resources and reference materials in English, French and Portuguese; it will initially be geared up for users and learners of those three languages. It will offer real-life texts or situations written/produced by native speakers in each of the languages involved.

With a view to achieving feasible results in the foreseeable future, we have decided to combine various corpus and statistical techniques thus circumventing deep (and not necessarily always correct) natural language (e.g. semantic or pragmatic) analysis. Therefore, our contribution will be practically orientated and of a typical Language Engineering (LE) nature as opposed to the (usually) more theoretical developments in Computational Linguistics which are of less practical value.

One of the main advantages of the workbench is that it will draw on the experience of existing LE (e.g. use of corpora, on-line dictionaries, speech databases, translator's workstation, etc) integrating them for the first time into a single, uniform and powerful architecture. We regard the use of real life textual and speech (and possibly visual) repositories as a big step towards achieving a more natural and 'high fidelity' learning environment. The large scale language resources backed up by rapid search capacities and a whole host of additional language aids, together with the potential to incorporate interactive multimedia facilities and to include the workbench in a distance learning network, make the implementation envisaged highly practical and attractive.

4.2 LLW: Functional Specification: The principal feature of the LLW is its access to reusable linguistic resources. The LLW permits the learner to call down relevant aids to assist him/her with knowledge gaps. This includes interfaces to other LE reference tools which have undergone a critical review to test their feasibility for incorporation and which, as a result, are considered suitable for inclusion in the SELECT platform. The LLW can be used not only as a writing but as a learning environment — by reinforcing the knowledge acquired by looking at numerous real-life examples, and also for self-learning. Consider the following scenario. A business-user with a limited knowledge of the language he/she is learning has received a letter from his foreign counterpart. He uses the Machine-Aided Translation component to get the gist of the letter and on-line dictionaries to read it. He would like to reply, but has no experience in writing letters in the foreign language. The 'Formats and templates' module provides an appropriate template which the business-person has to complete. Now he/she can turn not only to the bilingual dictionaries, reference materials, grammar, style and spell checkers, but also to the corpora to see how certain words (expressions) can be used. Thus the LLW potentially offers on-line access (gateways) to selected language resources available on other nets (e.g. Internet) to support learners; asynchronous on-line tuition will be tested with members of user groups in order to monitor learning progress with and without tutors. In terms of the distinction between LLW architecture and design and actual development of the workbench, we shall instigate a smaller-scale application rather than a huge repository of resources and tools, especially as far as the corpora are concerned. We shall aim at implementing a core of modules (e.g. modules such as corpus, dictionary look up, spell checkers, MAT, formats and templates) which will serve as a basis upon which the system will be further extended.

4.3 LLW: Market Survey of Reusable Materials: The general approach for LE components of SELECT (i.e. combining corpus and statistical techniques) means that in the LLW the keyword extraction component, for example, will use a termbank backed up by statistical techniques (e.g. frequency, collocation etc.). Likewise, the multilingual abstracting component will not attempt to analyse the document — it will extract a summary on the basis of various clues for identifying important sentences (Mitkov et al. 94) or corpus-based techniques (Mitkov 96), enhanced by statistical techniques for extracting whole paragraphs (Fukumoto et al. 97). A similarly 'surface' approach will be adopted in the other typical LE architecture in SELECT, the automatic generator of achievement tests for the purpose of measuring the student's progress. Heuristical sentence splitting, followed by part-of-speech tagging and possibly robust parsing will be used in order to identify the constituents / lexical categories of the sentence. A small transformational grammar will be developed to transform declarative sentences into wh-questions or incomplete sentences. The selection of test distracters will be based on WordNet.

The LE components will be linked so that they can be called upon interactively. For instance, if dictionary look-up is performed, this could be enhanced by part-of-speech disambiguation using another component, or could be further enhanced by retrieving relevant real-life examples from the corpus component. We envisage the employment of QUECON — a tool under development which supports the author during the production of a document in the source language with. linguistic and terminological correctness (Haller 96). It helps the user to navigate more easily through the text by indicating additional possibilities for the combination of expressions or text macros.

The source language text has to fulfil certain linguistic criteria: it would not make sense to support the production of a text version in a foreign language, if it is done on the basis of a defective source language version. These criteria include orthographic, terminological and syntactic correctness, the avoidance of long sentences and of meaning ambiguities etc. They are important for a better understanding of the source language text. This type of monitoring function in text production is already available with existing text systems which are endowed with spellcheckers as well as programs checking syntax and style, which are mainly available for English and French. As far as spelling and syntax checking is concerned, we aim to re-use and adapt the DIMACHECK tool developed by IAI in co-operation with Gruppo DIMA, Torino (Bolioli et al. 92, Chambers et al. 95). Morphological components will be re-used as well (Mass 96).

4.4 LLW: Reusability / Genericity: Reusability (and genericity) in LLW is in evidence in the integration of various existing resources and in the modular architecture of the system which, in turn, will make it easy for it to incorporate, if necessary, additional modules in the future or to use some of its modules for other relevant applications. Among the resources to be used are corpora such as BNC and ECI, Machine-aided translation packages such as Power Translator Professional or Language Assistant; intelligent dictionary look up (including part-of-speech disambiguation) such as *Locolex* (Bauer et al. 95); business letter support programs such as EuroBrief/WorldLetter, MABLE etc. Indeed, we think that one of the main advantages of the workbench is that it will draw on the experience of existing LE and multimedia technologies integrating them for the first time into a single, uniform and powerful architecture. Reusability of the test generator is in evidence in the adoption of existing sentence splitters and part of speech taggers (e.g. the GATE modules (Cunningham et al. 96) could be taken over directly — their POS tagger is based on E. Brill's tagger) as well as by adopting WordNet (the EuroWordNet project envisages developing Wordnet in French (Asterias et al. 97).

The Language Learner's Workbench (LLW) is innovative in that even though there are already different programs which address most of the functions to be performed by the modules of the LLW, there is no integrated platform which could enable the user to navigate through / call upon different language learner's aids thus making the support as comprehensive as possible. Also new is the use of key-word extraction, automatic abstracting and even of machine-aided translation for the purpose of supporting the learner. Another clear advance to the state-of-the-art of CALL is the development for the first time of a knowledge-poor automatic generator of achievement tests on the basis of instructional texts. This was possible previously only by relying heavily on semantic and world knowledge (Mitkov 94).

4.5 LLW: Components

4.5.1 Corpora: The use of corpora in CALL is extensively documented (see, for example, http://web.bham.ac.uk/johnstf/biblio.htm for an excellent, comprehensive bibliography of Classroom Concordancing/Data-driven learning literature; see also http://web.bham.ac.uk/johnstf/ddl_lib.htm for a Virtual DDL Library containing samples of concordance-based teaching and learning materials). The LLW will be supplied with large corpora of texts in each of the languages involved. We regard the availability of corpora as crucially important to the efficiency of the learning process and of the workbench in general because it is the corpus of texts (produced by native speakers) which provides the numerous examples of how a certain word, collocation, idiom or phrase is used. For locating words and collocations in real texts, for instance, Key Words In Context (or KWIC) concordance programs will be used. The concordance gives access to many language patterns in texts and provides evidence about a language that is superior in quality to any other method. The learner will be able simply to input a word, phrase, or idiom to obtain hundreds of illustrative examples of its use. Standard corpus processing tools will accompany the corpora to allow their access/processing. Finally, the corpora will serve as reservoirs not only of examples of lexical usage, but also of usage of moods and tenses, appropriate performance of speech acts in various situations, and of the cultural background of the foreign language. For English, general corpora such as the British National Corpus and the Collins COBUILD Bank of English, as well as domain-specific business language data from the Financial Times, Economist and Wall Street Journal are under scrutiny. Similar corpora are under investigation for French and Portuguese. Corpus tools such as Wordsmith and Qwick are also being examined.

4.5.2 Bilingual Corpora: The workbench will offer aligned bilingual corpora (such as MLCC, Crater, or ECI/MCI) for each pair of languages which will help the learner/user to examine a text in the foreign language and its equivalent in his/her native language, or vice-versa. This will be particularly helpful in understanding the different meanings/uses of a certain word or expression in the language learned. Special bilingual concordance programs (such as Multiconcord or Paraconc) will extract words and collocations in the user's native language and their translations in the foreign language (and vice-versa).

4.5.3 Speech Databases and Text-to-Speech Systems: Speech databases will be an ideal counterpart to the corpora when it comes to listening practice and, when integrated in a multimedia environment, can provide invaluable help. For example, if the language learner needs to hear how a certain word or expression should be pronounced, she/he could type it in and select a recorded piece of speech featuring this word or expression. The audio feedback will not only demonstrate pronunciation but will also give useful insights into intonation, formality of expression etc. In addition, a text-to-speech system can be incorporated and used to read aloud all possible texts.

An important aspect of language learning is mastering correct pronunciation. Speech databases can be of invaluable help in learning pronunciation. In traditional settings this is covered mainly by conversation with the teacher and/or listening to pre-recorded speech samples. At every point, the language learner will be able to highlight a certain word or phrase and ask for spoken examples. The LLW will then search through its speech databases to come up with a number of sound examples containing that word/phrase. The obvious advantage is that these examples will be spoken by different speakers in a number of different (but realistic) contexts. As a fall-back position for words/phrases not contained in the databases, the LLW could make use of text-to-speech systems; another possibility is the additional use of video material including sound.

For the successful operation of this application, properly tagged (monolingual) speech corpora will be needed. If transcripts were available, the alignment between speech and text could be made automatically. Finally, search algorithms will be used to identify fitting sentences.

4.5.4 Repository of Video Materials: This database will provide similar help to that offered by the speech databases. In addition, it will illustrate gestural and emotional aspects of conversation, capturing typical social/cultural differences. The multimedia discs will contain a wide range of language learning scenarios in each of the languages involved.

4.5.5 On-line Dictionaries: The on-line dictionaries will provide speedy access to each of the extensive vocabularies (3 monolingual and 3 bi-directional bilingual). If, however, the learner wants to check the usage of a particular word in the corpus, the concordance program will be activated. The dictionary support module will have a large number of navigational capacities. For each word in the display window these will include (but will be not limited to) easy access to its synonyms, antonyms, hyperonyms, hyponyms, semantically related words, and translation examples from corpora of available translations.

4.5.6 Termbanks: A multilingual termbank will also be available which would dramatically cut the time required for terminology search, and would make sure terms are consistently used/translated.

4.5.7 Spellcheckers, Grammar and Style Checkers: Standard spellcheckers will be built into the Language Learner's Workbench to support writing texts in each of the working languages. Grammar checkers will check for syntactic agreement, acceptable phrase-structure etc. To this end we plan to use statistically-based taggers and parsers and to adapt/integrate them to this task. Standard style checkers will be included as well.

4.5.8 Machine-aided Translation: The Machine-aided Translation (MAT) component will be of particular interest to teach-yourself beginners. Looking at a sentence in the foreign language, the student may wish to have it translated crudely by a MAT program. The translation may not be exact but could help the student to work out certain words, combinations of words and syntax rules.

4.5.9 Formats and Templates: Special formats and templates will be provided for business users (e.g. templates for writing business letters and other standard documents). In addition, when using the bilingual corpora (or memory-based translation databases), the user will be able to copy chunks of previously translated documents that are similar to the one currently being translated (written).

4.5.10 Reference Materials: The reference materials will consist mainly of reference grammars for each language which will have pointers to the corpora so that the learner can benefit from naturally occurring examples. 'Bookmark' facilities will also be available to the users.

4.5.11 Keyword/Term Extraction: Keyword and term extraction will be a very useful feature for students reading foreign language texts. Keywords and terms in a given document will be extracted by statistical techniques enhanced by termbanks and will be displayed upon request by the student (usually before his familiarising with the text). We believe that a list keywords and terms will make the document easier to follow.

4.5.12 Multilingual Abstracting: The workbench will feature for the first time a multilingual automatic abstractor which will be developed specially for the purpose. The role of the abstractor will be to produce a preliminary (possibly rough) abstract of a longer document which the student intends to read. We believe that reading in advance the concise summary of a long foreign language document makes its understanding easier.

4.5.13 Design Tools: The LLW will offer editing tools which will be very helpful in extending and/or adapting the existing repositories, in creating new formats and templates, reference materials etc. Our objective is to produce the workbench initially for Windows platforms, thus making it possible for more users to benefit from it. The interface will be configurable for various applications.

4.6 LLW: Implementation and Development Phases: The development of the Language Learner's Workbench (LLW) will be addressed as a 3-stage process:

1. the design and implementation of a 'minimal, core configuration' of the LLW,
2. the enhancement of the LLW into an 'extended configuration' and
3. the definition and future implementation of the 'ideal configuration'.

The inclusion of resources will depend on various factors, such as their availability, their cost, our evaluation of them during the resources review, and the ease of adapting their interfaces to the common LLW interface. Many of the types of resources mentioned above are available from distribution organisations such as the LDC (Linguistic Data Consortium) based at the University of Pennsylvania in the USA, and ELRA (European Language Resources Association) in Paris. However, some domain-specific resources and project-specific software may not yet exist, and may need to be created within the SELECT project.

5. The SELECT Courseware

The SELECT courseware aims to provide multimedia-based learning opportunities for the target group to develop self-directed inter-cultural training in cross-cultural business environments. The courseware has both cultural strands and linguistic strands. This brief description of the design and the implementation of the SELECT courseware covers two areas. Firstly some of the themes from research into intercultural differences and from training Second Language Acquisition (SLA) theory are described. These ideas frame the development of the courseware. The second section describes the elements included in the training courseware.

5.1 The Theoretical Background to the Courseware

5.1.1 Cross-cultural Training and Multimedia: The aim was to develop multimedia courseware which increases intercultural-awareness in the business context and also develops linguistic competence. These two components have been seen by scholars as inextricably linked aspects of becoming communicatively competent in host cultures (Kramsch, 1993). Early investigations of cultural differences which manifest themselves in business environments include work by Hofstede (1980) and Trompenaars (1993). These studies extracted defining characteristics and commonalties of different cultures and indicate the ways in which these may impinge on and hinder the pursuit of business between cultures. These studies characterised cultures according to variety of concepts such as 'individualist' or 'collectivist', 'strong uncertainty avoidance' or 'weak uncertainty avoidance', 'monochronic' or 'polychronic', 'specific' or 'diffuse', 'universalist' or 'particularist' and 'neutral' or 'command'. A brief illustration of how the characterisation of cultures using such concepts shows where cross-cultural differences may occur in business contexts and is provided through the concepts of 'individualist' and 'collectivist'. In 'collectivist' cultures company representation is likely to be manifested through groups, as unaccompanied people may be thought to lack status, individuals will not generally have the authority to make decisions on behalf of the company, these need to be decided collectively and thus perhaps the decision making process will take longer. In 'collectivist' cultures personal relationships may be thought more important than the business tasks themselves but the reverse in 'individualist' cultures. The aim of a 'collectivist' business philosophy might be to build relationships but in 'individualist' cultures to do quick deals. Trompenaars (1994) categorises British business culture as one of individualist with weak uncertainty avoidance and Portuguese as collectivist with strong uncertainty avoidance. Readers though are referred to the texts above for a full understanding of the concepts, arguments and evidence for such assertions. This body of knowledge, alluding though to tendencies in cross-cultural differences rather than reinforcing stereotypes, was one of the rationales which underpinned the project. The important role which multimedia applications might be able to play in the development of cross-cultural training has also been noted in the literature e.g., Kramsch (1993. pp 196-203). She notes five ways in which multimedia environments may provide new ways of learning and teaching about the contexts in which cross-cultural phenomena are embedded. These are that it is non-linear, context-bound, recursive, constructivist, and learner-directed.

5.1.2 Second Language Acquisition Theory and Multimedia: The rationale for applying multimedia technology to language learning is framed by the negotiated interaction model of SLA (Doughty, 1991; Pica, 1994; Chapelle, 1997, Chapelle, 1998). Language input for SLA is essential and debate has centred on what type of input may best facilitate acquisition. Krashen (1985) with the Input Hypothesis put forward that comprehensible input 'i + 1' was the key to SLA. Discourse analyses of native speaker (NS) / non-native speaker (NNS) communication examined the kinds of interactional moves which mended communication breakdown (e.g. Pica and Doughty, 1986) and found that strategies such as requests for clarification, confirmation checks and comprehension checks seemed to promote comprehension. The proposal is that it is the interactional modifications made upon raw input to make it comprehensible which serve to facilitate acquisition.

Multimedia can be designed to provide resources which will enable learners to retrieve meaning from the input. These might provide the same types of information as would be available from a NS i.e., to clarify meanings of words or grammar. By augmenting input with a variety of learning support resources, e.g.; on-line dictionaries, subtitles, and comprehension tasks with corrective feedback, learners may have the necessary resources with which to make non-comprehensible input comprehensible. The strong version of such a connection is articulated by Chapelle as:

These interactional modifications initiated by the learner on input from the computer should yield similar psycholinguistic effects as those in oral face-to-face linguistic exchanges in which they were first investigated. (Chapelle 1997, p. 27)

Furthermore, multimedia allows learners to control and determine their use of such features. The place, extent, length and type of learner / computer exchange, together with the choice of support feature, can be determined by learners according to their own pace, needs and preferred learning style, thus personalising the negotiation. Learners can engage in individualised clarification of meaning by exploiting available multimedia resources, where, when, and if, their own comprehension breaks down.

Lastly, multimedia is able to provide interactive tasks. Comprehension tasks may be written to guide learners towards comprehension of texts, written or spoken. Previously, real-time listening comprehension tasks with instant feedback have been technically impossible to provide. Such listening comprehension tasks, coupled with feedback may help learners to 'notice the gap' in their comprehension (Swain and Lapkin, 1995). Furthermore, the multimedia environment may provide access to the linguistic phenomena which have caused comprehension breakdown and the resources to facilitate a negotiated understanding of these problematic linguistic items.

5.1.3 Research into the Effects of Video, Subtitles and Computer Feedback on Comprehension: This section provides a brief overview of studies of these features when used outside of the multimedia environment.

5.1.3.1 The Effects of the Use of Video on Aspects of Language Learning: Video enables learners to experience the dynamics of communicative interaction and all the paralinguistic features present in face-to-face communication such as the speaker's age, appearance, dress, cultural behaviour, gestures etc. Comprehension may be facilitated by the presence of lip synch (Kellerman, 1990) and may add interest and motivation to the listening classroom. Studies show that video generally enhances aural comprehension. Rubin (1990) found that the listening comprehension of late-beginner students of Spanish improved significantly compared to students who received no video support for their listening comprehension work. Ramsey (1991) investigated the impact of video on the learning of grammar and found positive effects. Secules et al. (1992) investigated the use of video for listening comprehension over a term, finding that the group which had experienced video scored higher on listening comprehension in the three areas of main ideas, understanding details and of inference. Baltova (1994) used three conditions: video, video with sound, and sound only, finding that the visual clues aided comprehension and had added affective and attentional advantages. Herron et al. (1995) compared the effects of video-based instruction with that of the traditional text and audio syllabus over the period of a year. Results showed no significant differences between the groups on speaking, reading, writing or grammar. Only in one particular test of listening comprehension did the video-based group score significantly higher. Video is common place in many second language classrooms and it appears from the studies described above that it can have a positive and cumulative effect on the language and comprehension skills of FL learners, although the degree of this effect may depend on how the visual image supports the aural text, how consistent the visual imagery is with the aural text (Grimes, 1990, 1991) and how proficient the learners are.

5.1.3.2 The Effect of Subtitles on Second Language Comprehension: The provision of subtitles raises the question as to whether learners are reading, listening, or doing both either simultaneously or alternatively. If they are just reading then such a provision could be argued to be detracting from any development of the listening skill (Guillory, 1998). Comprehension researchers such as Lund (1991) view the L2 reading process to be more developed than listening and to lead to more efficient comprehension of ideas. Price (1983) found significant comprehension gains with groups who used subtitled video. Garza (1991) demonstrated that subtitles increased scores on comprehension tests and additionally learners showed increased use of the original lexicon of the aural text when they retold the story. D'Ydewalle et al. (1991) found that the attraction of subtitles to the eye, even with L1 sound track and subtitles, was automatic and occurred due to cognitive priority of visual processing rather than aural processing. Danan (1992) studied various types of subtitling and their effect on vocabulary recall, finding that reversed subtitling (L2 written subtitles with L1 sound) was most beneficial, but that L2 sound and L2 subtitles also yielded comprehension gains. Vanderplank (1988, 1990) demonstrated that subtitles were valued by learners, increased comprehension, unlocked accents, dialects and humour and drew learners' attention to unfamiliar phrases and words. Borràs and Lafayette (1994) found that the use of subtitled multimedia had positive effects on later spoken performances and argued that subtitles are useful in bridging the gap between reading and listening skills. Guillory (1998) examined the effects of : no captions, full verbatim captions and keyword captions. She found that the highest levels of comprehension were achieved by the full subtitles group, followed by keyword and lastly, the no captions group. There was, though, no statistically significant difference in comprehension between the keyword and full-subtitles group. She concluded that full subtitles may be detrimental in that 'full text second language captions to authentic video encourage the learner to read the text, to the detriment of processing the linguistic message' (1998: 104) and that the use of keyword captions may assist listening comprehension more than full subtitles. These studies show that the inclusion of subtitles significantly increases comprehension of aural texts.

5.1.3.3 The Effects of Computer Feedback: In the context of instructed second language learning Ellis (1990) sees a crucial role for feedback in learning as that it 'raises learners' consciousness about the lack of correlation between the target language and her own interlanguage' (1990: 93). Bationo (1992) showed positive effects for the combination of computer-delivered written and spoken feedback for learning future verb forms. Brandl (1995) investigated learner preferences for four types of feedback options within a CALL activity to transforming German sentences from active to passive. Overwhelmingly learners preferred the right/wrong form of feedback, the type used here, which allowed them to think over and attempt to correct their own errors. Brett (1997) attributed learners' greater success with multimedia to the role of the on-line feedback in guiding and re-aligning the learners' on-going interpretations of the meanings within the oral texts. In summary it appears that the use of video, of subtitles, and of feedback when used outside of the multimedia environment increase second language comprehension.

5.1.3.4 The Effectiveness of Multimedia Applications in Language Learning: The majority of investigations of learning success through use of multimedia or Interactive Video Disc (IVD) report learning gains. Gale (1989) worked using three IVD programs for Spanish and compared linear classroom instruction using the same materials, with that delivered by IVDs. The IVD groups scored higher on post-use achievement measures and reported more favourable attitudes to the learning experience. Watts (1989) used IVD with French beginners and found positive effects for the translation of words and short sentences into and out of French and for the understanding of short spoken sentences. A second study compared learners using IVD with those using identical material delivered by video tapes and worksheets. Both groups showed increases in understanding but the IVD group made more significant gains. She notes particular gains in pronunciation for the IVD users. Borrás and Lafayette (1994) investigated the use of subtitled multimedia courseware on the spoken performance of students of French. They found significant effects on spoken performance, that those viewing with subtitles spent less time watching the video sequence than those without and had more positive reactions to the application. Johnstone and Milne (1995) in a year-long study showed that the use of a teacher-controlled multimedia tool increased the use of communicative discourse in the classroom by both teachers and pupils. Chun and Plass (1996) found positive effects for the learning of German vocabulary through a multimedia program with hypertext annotations combining pictures and text more effective than those with video and text. In summary studies of various aspects of language learning using multimedia all seem to indicate it has a beneficial role.

5.1.3.5 The Effectiveness of Multimedia Applications in Listening Comprehension: There have been a few studies of the use of multimedia for developing listening comprehension. Grezel and Sciarone (1994) investigated the effects of daily computer testing of listening comprehension versus computer-delivered cloze test both over a period of 3 weeks. Learners were then measured for the effects of the two instructional modes on general language proficiency via a cloze test. Significant effects were found for the computer-based listening group. Greifnieder (1995) used computer delivered audio to support learning of vocabulary in a CALL environment with 70 children. He found however that the aural input did not add anything extra to the learning which is not supplied by just seeing the word. Brett (1996) found carried out investigations into the affective domain of multimedia for listening skills. Results showed strongly favourable attitudes, that learners believed they could learn effectively from multimedia and believed that it delivered a high quality independent learning experience. Brett (1997) found more successful comprehension and recall while using multimedia than either audio or video plus pen and paper even though none of the additional supports of multimedia (definitions, subtitles etc) were used. The reasons proposed for the greater success rates were: efficiency of delivery with all the media for input and learning tasks in one place, the incisive and supportive nature of the on-going on-line feedback in guiding learners to correct interpretations of the message, and the effect of these in enabling learners to monitor their interpretations of the message. Liou (1997) investigated learners' exploitation of such on-line help resources such as control of video, translations, gist summaries, definitions etc. in a video-based multimedia listening programme. Surprisingly, she found that 'the frequency of students' use of the help devices did not have an impact on their understanding of the video' (1997: 91). It appeared that subjects rarely used some of the on-line help features and that use of these did not significantly increase comprehension. Englesberg (1997) evaluated the integration of a multimedia package into a university course by focusing on learner attitudes. She found that initial satisfaction was high, but that after 5 weeks learners became increasingly dissatisfied with the application. In summary applications of multimedia technology to listening skills generally report increased comprehension and initially favourable attitudes.

5.2 Description of the Courseware

5.2.1 A Cross-cultural Syllabus

5.2.1.1 Training Materials: Three different countries have been involved in the preparation of cross-cultural training materials, Britain, France and Portugal. The description provided here is based on the work of the British side of the project. Each country has created multimedia-based learning materials which aim to illustrate, and thus increase understanding of aspects of its business culture. Rather than focus on the differences which there tend to be between two or more particular cultures the more holistic approach of modelling and exemplifying pertinent features of the host countries business culture was adopted. This approach enables learners from any culture to have access to the materials and to be form their own interpretations of how and where cultural differences may manifest themselves. The approach also avoids the danger of invoking stereotypes.

5.2.1.2 Questionnaire on Cross-cultural Differences: Taking the work of cross-cultural investigators (Hofstede 1980, Trompenaars 1994) as the theoretical basis, the project approached more than fifty companies who had successful experience of cross-cultural training. A questionnaire was designed and subsequently administered aiming to elicit contemporary and experienced areas of cross-cultural differences. The results of these were analysed and the significant defining features of the British business context were listed as the building blocks of a syllabus for cross-cultural training. The aim of the syllabus was primarily development of cultural competence with embedded language competence and thus specific linguistic items e.g., functions or grammatical components were seen as secondary to, and supportive of, the cross-cultural component. The syllabus was also determined by the limitations of the means of delivery (computer-based and Internet-based) hence the main focus is on receptive skills. It would be a relatively simple matter, however, for others to add a productive dimension to the syllabus. This might be envisaged if the syllabus was delivered by a trainer in a classroom context or there were fundamental advances in speech recognition technology.

5.2.1.3 Syllabus Levels: The syllabus is divided up into seven levels and two are described above. Because the focus of each unit is to develop incrementally the cross-cultural competence of the learner, the language functions and knowledge itemised in each unit have been selected according to their degree of relevance to cross-cultural factors. In addition the syllabus can be used as basis for cross-cultural training aimed at groups working in specific business sectors i.e., *Engineering, Media, Medicine* but would need to be supplemented with profession related learning tasks and vocabulary. No attempt has been made to specify the learning time needed for each level as this will be situation specific.

Fig. 3 An example of the cross-cultural syllabus items at Levels A1 and B2

LEVEL A1	**TITLE: The Business Day**
DESCRIPTOR	Can compare and contrast the daily business framework in the target and the source cultures.
CULTURAL FACTORS	Working hours; Breaks; Lunch
READING TASKS	Understanding the key content in:menus, business diaries, company information

LISTENING TASKS	Identifying times; Distinguishing between foods and meals; Identifying daily work patterns
FUNCTIONAL LANGUAGE	Talking about daily routines and habits; Time; Holidays; Ordering meals; Expressing non-comprehension (e.g.: *I'm sorry I didn't understand*)
GRAMMATICAL ISSUES	Present Simple; Adverbs of frequency (often, sometimes, etc); Like + -ing; Questions; Numbers

LEVEL B1	**TITLE: Business Presentations**
DESCRIPTOR	Can follow a presentation on a familiar topic from his/her own field provided it is well structured and clearly delivered.
CULTURAL FACTORS	Protocol to be followed at the event (including dress); Body language; Introductions; Design of the discourse; Degree of linguistic formality required by the situation; Question time
LISTENING TASKS	Identifying functions; Distinguishing signpost and bridges; Distinguishing between main points; Distinguishing between opinion and fact
READING TASKS	A paper connected to the topic of the presentation; Bullet points from a Powerpoint
FUNCTIONAL LANGUAGE	Openings; Stating objectives; Moving on; Handling interruptions; Referring to visual aids; Discourse signposts; Discourse bridges; Closings
GRAMMATICAL ISSUES	Present tense: simple and continuous; Present Perfect; Relative clauses; Linking expressions; Indirect questions

5.2.2. Video Materials: The core learning resource is authentic (Sinclair and Renouf, 1988) video of business interactions within the target culture. It time-consuming and not easy to persuade companies to allow cameras in to film authentic business interactions. However the project eventually had considerable success with the co-operation of companies such as British Telecom, Rover and VideoLogic. The project aimed to create materials to illustrate one section of the syllabus and Level B, covering business presentations, meetings, negotiations and lunches and a variety of such interactions were filmed. It was assumed that this section of the syllabus would have the widest target audience. A selection of six clips for each of these topics was made according to the richness of cultural features which were on show. So, for example, the titles of each of the six clips selected in the category of business meetings for exemplification of the British approach to business meetings serves to illustrate this. These were: *Fitting in to British business meetings*; *Agendas*; *Deadlines*; *Participation*; *The boss is part of the team*; and *Procedures in British business meetings*.

5.2.3 Courseware Design

5.2.3.1 Knowledge Types: Learning material was then written for each of these video clips. Each video clip and topic was provided with learning tasks aimed at six different types of knowledge, culture, reception, grammar, vocabulary, functions and reading and writing.

5.2.3.2 Three Types of Subtitles: The subtitles to the video clips are available in three learner chosen forms. These are full subtitles where each word is available, keyword subtitles (Guillory, 1998) where the key word from each 10 second element is provided and finally simplified subtitles where a simple version of the authentic dialogue is available.

5.2.3.3 Learning Tasks: The pedagogic sequence of learning tasks (Willis and Willis, 1996) was a three stage one and this applies to all six knowledge types. Learning material was written at two levels of difficulty. Tasks were written to prepare learners for the video (or written) input by raising schematic and linguistic awareness, a pre-watching stage (e.g., Underwood, 1990). Tasks which also accompany the video and written texts were also written. The aims of these were to extract either the important cultural features, the communicative messages or to focus on specific linguistic items. These were designed to be completed whilst watching the video. The final task stage of post-watching further exploited and extended the content or language of the video clips.

Fig. 4 The learning material to accompany the *Culture — Business meetings Deadlines — Level A* video

(1) Before watching

Deadlines and timescales for most businesses tasks are important in British business. Look at these statements and predict if you think they are true or false for British business.

Projects will have deadlines
Deadlines are agreed in advance
Nobody keeps to the deadlines
Items on agendas will usually have a time limit even if this is unwritten
Deadlines are more important for top-management
A large project will have several deadlines for small tasks
It is usual to explain why deadlines are not kept
Deadlines can be negotiated about
Meetings will have time limits

(2) While watching

Watch Sue talk about to a meeting about her idea for analysing the training needs of new staff. A key part of her description is the timetable she proposes. Click on the one item which is not discussed.

They did not know what skills new people had.
Sue proposes a timetable.
Sue proposes deadlines for two stages of the project.
The second deadline is the next team meeting.
Sue asks for opinions about the timescale
The timescale is discussed before the approach.
Sue asks for agreement on the timescale

(3) After watching

1. A gap-fill exercise based upon verbs used in the video
2. Watch and look at the subtitles — all the phrases connected to deadlines are highlighted
3. Who said what? An exercise allocating phrases connected to deadlines to the participants in the meeting

[NB Only three of the learner-controlled choices are shown here (abbreviated for the purpose of this paper)]

5.2.3.3 Feedback: The courseware allows learners to choose the type of feedback to the tasks which is made available to them. The choices are feedback only, hints or full explanations. Feedback only is through ticks and crosses, the hints option gives information as to what the answer might and the explanations gives the answer and a full reason for why this is the answer.

5.2.3.4 Error Collection: In addition, each of the task elements is hard coded with up to four error codes. These are based on the material writers best guesses as to why an incorrect answer might have been given. There are more than 100 code types which can be allocated. The computer records the errors and is able to provide feedback on repeated errors when error patterns become clear.

This section has provided the theoretical justification for the use of multimedia for harnessing cross-cultural training and described, briefly how such features were realised in the design of the courseware.

6. Conclusion: The first phase of the SELECT project is due for completion in December 1999. The initial ideas and the core modules are in place and are currently being tested at various academic and commercial institutions in Europe. As well as the three target languages (English, French and Portuguese), three additional access languages (German, Spanish, and Italian) are also being incorporated into the design. Once feedback from the test sites has been received, final modifications will be made to the demonstration package. Assuming that further funding is obtained, the courseware and the LLW can be extended, and the Learner Manager enhanced and refined. At some stage, a commercial product could follow. The success of the project so far ensures that the ideas and methodologies will impact on the future development of applications of LE in CALL. There is also the obvious possibility of creating similar packages for other domains such as automobile engineering or health care, or for other groups of users such as the sight-impaired. The package is currently intended to be delivered on CD-ROM to a desktop machine which may be networked, but a future project could easily take advantage of recent technological advances, and satellite delivery of a constantly-updated package to a hand-held device might be considered.

References:

Agre, P.E., and Chapman, D. 1987. Pengi: An implementation of a theory of activity. *Proceedings of the AI Conference* (pp.268-272). Seattle, Washington.

Atserias, J., Climent, S., Farreres, X., Rigau, G., Rodriguez, H. 1997. Combining Multiple Methods for the Automatic Construction of Multilingual Wordnets. *Proceedings of the international conference 'Recent Advances in Natural Language Processing' (RANLP'97)*, Tzigov Chark.

Balatova, I. 1994. The impact of video on the comprehension skills of core French students. *The Canadian Modern Language Review* 50: 507-23.

Bationo, B.D. 1992. The effects of three feedback forms on learning through a computer-based tutorial. *CALICO Journal* 10: 45-52.

Bauer, D., Segond, F., and Zaenen, A. 1995. Locolex: the translation rolls off your tongue. *Proceedings of ACH/ALLC'95*. University of California.

Berlitz European Division. 1995. *An Investigation into how Managers handle the different cultures in Europe* (27.3.95, 62pp)

Borrás, I. and Lafayette, R.C. 1994. Effects of multimedia courseware subtitling on the speaking performance of college students of French. *The Modern Language Journal* 78: 61-75.

Bouwhuis, D., and Bunt, H. (in press). Interactive instructional systems as dialogue systems. In Verhoeven, L. (Ed.), *Training for literacy*. Dordrecht: Foris.

Brandl, K.K. 1995. Strong and weak students' preferences for error feedback options and responses. *The Modern Language Journal* 79: 194-211.

Brett, P. 1996. Using multimedia:- an investigation of learners' attitudes. *Computer Assisted Language Learning Journal* 9: 191-212.

Brett, P. 1997. A comparative study of the effects of the use of multimedia on listening comprehension. *System*, 25: 39-53.

Chapelle, C.A. 1997. CALL in the year 2000: Still in search of research paradigms? *Language learning and Technology* 1: 19 — 43. <http://polygot.cal.msu.edu/llt/vol1num1/chapelle.htm> (accessed 20th November 1997).

Chapelle, C. 1998. Multimedia CALL: Lessons to be learned from research on instructed SLA. *Language Learning and Technology* 2: 22-34. <http://polyglot.cal.msu.edu/llt/vol2num1.html> (accessed 10th August 1998).

Chun, D.M. and Plass, J.L. 1996. Effects of multimedia annotations on vocabulary acquisition. *Modern Language Journal* 80: 183-98.

Chun, D.M. and Plass, J.L. 1997. Research on text comprehension in multimedia environments. *Language Learning and Technology* 1: 60-81. <http://polyglot.msu.edu/llt/vol1num1/chun_plass/default/html> (accessed 24th August, 1997).

Connah, D.M. 1993. The design of interacting agents for use in interfaces. In Brouwer-Janse, M.D. and Hagen, S. (Eds.) 1999: *Business Communication Across Borders*. London: CILT.

Cunningham, H., Wilks, Y., Gaizauskas, R. 1996. Software infrastructure for Language Engineering. *Proceedings of the workshop on Language Engineering for Document Analysis and Recognition*, Brighton.

Danan, M. 1992. Reversed subtitling and dual coding theory: New directions for foreign language instruction. *Language Learning* 42: 497-527.

Doughty, C. 1991. Theoretical motivations for IVD software research and development. In Bush, M., Slaton, A., Verano, M. and Slayden, M.E. (eds.) 1991: *Interactive videodisc: the 'why' and the 'how'*. CALICO Monograph Volume 2: Provo, Utah: Brigham Young University.

d'Ydewalle, G., Praet, C., Verfaille, K., and Van Rensbergen, C. 1991. Watching subtitled television — Automatic reading behaviour. *Communication Research* 18: 650-66.

Ellis, R. 1990. *Instructed Second Language Acquisition*. Oxford: Blackwell.

Englesberg, R. 1997. An evaluation study of a multimedia package for learning English. *CAELL Journal* 8: 15-20.

Fukumoto, F., Suzuki, Y., Fukumoto, J. 1997. An automatic extraction of key paragraphs based on context dependency. *Proceedings of the 5th International Conference on Applied Natural Language Processing (ANLP'97)*, Washington.

Gale, L.E. 1989. Macario, Montevideodisco and Interactive Dígame: Developing interactive video for Language instruction. In Flint Smith, W. (ed.): *Modern Technology in Foreign Language Education: Applications and Projects:* 235-248. Lincolnwood, IL: National Textbook Company.

Garza, T.J. 1991. Evaluating the use of captioned video materials in advanced foreign language learning. *Foreign Language Annals* 24: 239-58.

Greifnieder, U. 1995. The influence of audio support on the effectiveness of CALL. *ReCALL* 7: 29-35.

Grezel, J.E.D. and Sciarone, A.G. 1994. Computer testing of listening comprehension. *Computers in Education* 23: 125-32.

Grimes, T. 1990. Audio-video correspondence and its role in attention and memory. *Educational Technology Research and Development* 38: 15-25.

Grimes, T. 1991. Mild auditory-visual dissonance in television news may exceed viewer attentional capacity. *Human Communication Research,* 18: 268-98.

Guillory, H.G. 1998. The effects of keyword captions to authentic French video on learner comprehension. *CALICO Journal* 15: 89-109.

Harrington, T.L. (Ed.), Human-machine communication for educational systems design (pp. 197-206). Berlin: Springer-Verlag.

Herron, C., Morris, M., Secules, T., and Curtis, L. 1995. A comparison of the effects of video-based versus text-based instruction in the foreign language classroom. *The French Review* 68: 775-96.

Hofstede, G. 1994. *Cultures and organisations: software of the mind.* HarperCollins.

Johnstone, J. and Milne, L. 1995. Scaffolding second language communicative discourse with teacher controlled multimedia. *Foreign Language Annals* 28: 315-29.

Kellerman, S. 1990. Lip service: The contribution of the visual modality to speech perception and its relevance to the teaching and testing of foreign language listening comprehension. *Applied Linguistics* 11: 272-80.
Kramsch, C. 1993. *Context and culture in language teaching.* Oxford: Oxford University Press.
Krashen, S. 1985. *The input hypothesis.* London: Longman.
Liou, H.C. 1997. Research of on-line help as learner strategies for multimedia CALL evaluation. *CALICO Journal* 14: 81-96.
Liu, M. and Reed, W. M. 1995. The effect of hypermedia-assisted instruction on second language learning. *Journal of Educational Computing Research* 12 :159-75.
Lund, R.J. 1991. A comparison of second language listening and reading comprehension. *The Modern Language Journal* 75: 196-204.
Mitkov, R. 1994. Computer-assisted language testing: new opportunities offered by Artificial Intelligence. *Computers in Applied Linguistics* conference, Ames, Iowa, USA.
Mitkov, R., Le Roux, D., Descles, J.P. 1994. Knowledge-based automatic abstracting: experiments in the sublanguage of elementary geometry. In Carlos Martin-Víde (Ed) *Mathematical linguistics*, North-Holland.
Mitkov, R. 1996. A corpus-based approach to automatic abstracting. *Proceedings of the AISB Workshop on Language Engineering for contents analysis and information retrieval*, Brighton.
Mitkov, R. 1998. Language Engineering in CALL: The concept of the Language Learner's Workbench. Paper given at *NLP in CALL* conference, May 1998, UMIST, Manchester.
O'Shea, T. 1979. A self-improving quadratic tutor. *International Journal of Man-Machine studies* 11: 97-124.
Pica, T. and Doughty, C. 1986. Making input comprehensible: Do interactional modifications help? *ITL Review of Applied Linguistics* 72: 1-25.
Pica, T. 1994. Research on negotiation: What does it tell us about second-language learning conditions, processes and outcomes? *Language Learning* 44: 493-527.
Price, K. 1983. Closed-captioned TV: An untapped resource. *MATESOL Newsletter* 1-8.
Ramsey, R. 1991. French in action and the grammar question. *French Review* 65: 255-66.
Rubin, J. 1990. Improving foreign language listening comprehension. In Alatis, J.E. (Ed.) *Georgetown University Round Table.* Washington D.C.: Georgetown University Press. 309-316.
Secules, T., Herron, C., and Tomessello, M. 1992. The effect of video context on foreign language learning. *The Modern Language Journal* 76: 480-90.
Shoham, Y. (1993). Agent-orientated programming. *Artificial Intelligence* 60: 51-92.
Sinclair, J. and Renouf, A. 1988. A lexical syllabus for language teaching. In Carter, R. and McCarthy, M. 1988 *Vocabulary in language teaching.* Oxford: Oxford University Press.
Swain, M. and Lapkin, S. 1995. Problems in output and the cognitive processes they generate: a step towards second language learning. *Applied Linguistics* 16: 371-91.
Trompenaars, F. 1993. *Riding the waves of culture: Understanding cultural diversity in business.* UK: The Economist Books.
Underwood M. 1989. *Teaching Listening*. Harlow: Longman .
Vanderplank, R. 1988. The value of teletext sub-titles in language learning. *English Language Teaching Journal* 42: 272-81.
Vanderplank, R. 1990. Paying attention to the words: Practical and theoretical problems in watching television programmes with uni-lingual ceefax subtitles. Sy*stem* 18: 221-34.
Watts, C. 1989. Interactive video: what the students say. *CALICO Journal,* 7: 17-20.
Wavish, P.R. and Connah, D.M. 1990. *Representing multi- agent worlds in ABLE.* Technical Note, Philips Research Laboratories.
Willis, D. and Willis, J. 1996. *Challenge and change in language teaching.* London: Heinemann.
Zhao, Y. 1997. The effects of listeners' control of speech rate on second language comprehension. *Applied Linguistics* 18: 49-68.

E-MAIL AS A LEARNING TOOL: CONSTRUCTION OF KNOWLEDGE ONLINE

Christine Leahy
Nottingham Trent University, UK

Abstract
This paper will look at some of the results of an international e-mail project between vocational language learners (business) in England and Germany. The project will be briefly introduced and some of the results considered.

I. The Study in Context

Several studies about computer-mediated communication have been conducted, often focusing on beginners or intermediate learners of a foreign languages, e.g. Beauvois (1998), Chun (1998), St. John/Cash (1995), Sullivan (1998), Warschauer (1999), Vilmi (1995) or on learners who were not matched according to language proficiency (Brammerts/ Little,1996).

Computer-mediated communication via a computer-assisted class discussion can improve communicative language proficiency (Chun, 1998; Sullivan, 1998; Vilmi, 1995; Woodin/Ojanguren, 1995; Warschauer, 1997; 1999)

Building on the results of previous studies like those mentioned above, the international e-mail project introduced here combines the following elements: Computer-mediated communication via e-mail, a subject specific task, internet use for primary source materials and a written as well as oral *modified* output. Therefore it makes use of the four skills of reading, writing, speaking and listening, and does not focus on reading and writing alone.

The project's two main objectives were to acquire language as well as content.

1. Introduction to Project: The students are advanced second language learners of German,[1] doing a combined degree course of Business studies and German. Their e-mail partners are German native speakers also studying business who take English as a supplementary option.

---

[1] All British students entered their main degree course with an A-level in German.

2. Outer Framework of Project: E-mail was introduced here as a learning *not* a teaching tool. Students worked on the project as part of their directed/independent learning. Twenty-eight business students completed the project. Only in one country (England) was the project formally assessed. Students were supported during the whole time, mainly via e-mail. The initial introduction took place face-to-face. The British students also had the opportunity to meet the project leader during office hours.

3. Inner Framework of Project: Students agreed to write at least 1 message to their partner per week. The exchanges were mainly asynchronous, e-mail based and were to be written approximately 50% in the target language and 50% in the mother tongue. The native speaker was to administer some corrections of the partner's foreign language passages. Participants were encouraged to observe their partners' language style and register.

II. Task development in context

1. Computer-Mediated Communication (CMC). Computer-mediated communication can become a powerful learning tool, not only in foreign language learning, but also in other learning situations.[2] It allows students to interact with their partners beyond traditional restrictions of time (in the case of asynchronous communication) and place. Asynchronous, and to a certain degree synchronous,[3] communication enables students to set their own pace, provides time to comprehend, reflect and to compose several drafts. It also provides the opportunity to check facts and, in the case of SLA, to analyse and/or copy native speaker style.

There are different forms of CMC of which e-mail is one. E-mail is usually asynchronous communication which combines the advantages of computer-assisted text production with the possibility of rapid exchanges of ideas over potentially vast distances. Furthermore, text production does not need to be an entirely linear process anymore. Additional information can be fed in at any time, the structure and content can be rearranged before sending the message off. These qualities can aid language learning considerably.

2. General considerations regarding the framework of e-mail exchanges: One obvious advantage of native speaker — non-native speaker communication is the relative equality between partners (facing similar difficulties). Partners share equal opportunities for growth and learning.

---

[2] E.g. Katz/Lesgold, 1993; Sherlock II, problem-solving tasks, i.e., electronic fault diagnosis.
[3] Compare Warschauer, 1999, example of studying Hawaiian through CACD.

Language correction
Within foreign language acquisition, error correction plays an important role. Students were asked to correct each other, but not every error, and to help the partner improving her/his foreign language within a subject specific context. Since this was a reciprocal approach, it was hoped to minimise the possibility of feeling offended or intimidated by the partner's corrections.

4. Specific Task (content). In order to supply a suitable challenge for these advanced learners, the task developed was designed to include reading skills which incorporated top-down as well as bottom-up processing, and led to individual composition (writing) and modified output (writing and oral). The following tasks were constructed for the students:

- *reading and e-mail exchange with partner abroad*

Students collected material about an existing company from the internet and through their own market research (the company has branches in Germany as well as GB) and through e-mail exchanges.

- *e-mail exchange with partner abroad*

Students discussed the company's marketing strategies and target groups in both countries.

- *writing*

The assessed group (British students) wrote an evaluation of the company's strategy for an imagined British competitor (Does the new company represent a threat to established ones?)

- *oral*

The written recommendation served as a basis for a short oral test, in which questions were asked by the tutor.

III. Result

1. E-mail Example: Collaborative Construction of Knowledge

During the project, Alex and Claudia showed progress on various levels: They both gained confidence using L2 and improved linguistically. They learned expressions and idioms from one another and developed together a concept of X' sales philosophy and strategy, a supermarket Alex had hardly heard of before the project. They compared their findings with other supermarkets they had known before.
Furthermore, they developed a personal relationship and became friends. They exchanged photographs and personal information, they talked about their weekend activities. They will also meet during the following year which Alex will spent in Germany.
Alex proved his understanding in his written report and oral examination.

The following describes the process of the first phase of the construction of knowledge as it developed in the case of Claudia and Alex.

Date	Alex Approx. 70% L2	Date	Claudia Approx. 50% L2
10/3	personal introduction		
11/3	ditto		
		13/3	X: cheap; no brand products; simple interior; always full of customers; one day a week: special products on offer; *was* perceived as cheap, for low income families; *now*: customers of all incomes; has still reputation of cheap, inferior products; Claudia buys there occasionally; private information
15/3	X only recently joined the Brit. market while GB in recession, which increased X's profits; sells food+drink; agrees: cheap products; but better quality products can be bought in other shops; no special offers like computers; simple interior; Alex visited X once or twice; pers.: sends home address to C. for her to send photograph to.		
16/3	He visited X's website (URL); suspected target group: low income, large families; hourly rate more than double the rate A. receives at p/t job; little advertisement; enquiry: when synchronous discussion?		
19/3	3 weeks holidays		1.5
		21/3	pages on X: history, discount concept, purchasing policy, location, product quality, logistics, type of product, sales strategy, 'no frills': simple and practical interior
25/3	Did she receive his recent mails?	25/3	No
12/4	Holiday impressions; lang. corrections; offers encouragement to Claudia re. L2	12/4	Holiday impressions; synchronous mailing (offers convenient times); asks for clarification re. idiom; sends private address for photograph to be sent to; failed an exam — no 'Leistungsschein', but

			'Teilnahmeschein' — explains terms briefly; lang. corrections
14/4 1.30 pm	Encouragement re. disappointing exam result; Asks back about distinction between 'Leistungsschein/Teilnahmeschein' clarifies question about idiom 'pass with flying colours'; -describes British customer		
		14/4 9.03	She looked up recom' URL re. Z; is competitor to X (low prices); thoughts on clubcard; difference between X North and South; special promotion days: sometimes electrical goods like computers; Germans spend less on food; timing of synchronous disc.; explains again: 'Leistungsschein+Teilnahmeschein'
16/4	Pleasantries; priv. com'; thanks for explanation re. division X North+South; do G's eat out more? Why do they spend less on food?; lang. corrections; looking forward to synchron. discussion; plans for week end; offers more idioms		
		17/4	Priv.; translation for 'programme crashed'; back to clubcards: (Germany:) only in big stores for office equipment etc.; job after graduation?; more proverbs please; what are plans for weekend?; asks for translation of 'bitte' as in 'you are welcome'.
19/3	Mainly priv.; answers to question re. translation of 'bitte';		
Session 1, 'synchronous' (webboard) Mainly private example: person. description, exams, complaint about the time it takes to transmit messages			

The e-mail exchanges between Claudia and Alex show a clear development of understanding of X's sales strategy and target groups in both countries. Both participants acquired knowledge not only about X abroad, but also in their home country. Claudia, a regular shopper at X, also visited X's web sites and sent her newly gained knowledge to Alex. Differences and similarities between the two countries were discovered, but the underlying reasons for these phenomena were not questioned.

Furthermore differences between the accreditation systems at universities in GB and Germany surfaced and were explained. Idioms were explained and used in context. The students recognised and acknowledged their personal development through the e-mail project in their feed back.

Early feedback[4] from Alex:

> I think that the e-mail tandem program has been very successful for me, writing German in a less formal style has given me confidence and has enabled me to type and think in German faster.
> I have really enjoyed writing to Claudia, she's very good and she replies to all my messages.
> Mit diesem Projekt bin ich sehr imponiert und ich habe ganz viel gelernt.[5] (28/4/99)

Final Feedback from Alex:

> The project was useful and different. Through it I have made new friends and have learnt a substantial amount about Germany and its universities.
> I feel that I have learnt plenty and have had plenty of fun in doing so.

Early feedback from Claudia:

> I am not sure if I really have improved, but I am enjoying writing e-mails to Alex! [...] I think it was a very good idea to practice this project! (28/4/99)

Final Feedback from Claudia:

> I really enjoyed very much writing to my partner. At first I thought the topic X would be very boring, but I really thought it was interesting. Also, I was very lucky with my partner. We got on well right from the start and we will keep in touch. I am not quite sure whether my English improved, but my confidence to use English has improved!

---

[4] Student messages are printed verbatim, omissions are indicated by square brackets [...].
[5] I am very impressed [?] with this project and have learned a lot.

IV. Summary

Objectives achieved?

Overall, students produced good to very good results at the end of the project. Learning progress regarding content and language was made. Students started with varying L2 proficiencies and progressed from there. More subtle learning objectives e.g. time management, autonomous learning via computer-mediated communication, and improving negotiation skills were not always achieved. Other secondary objectives e.g. developing or improving electronic literacy skills, increasing vocabulary and reading subject specific material in the target language were successfully achieved. This is documented in the written report as well as the oral examination.
In the students' self-perception, learning was acknowledged: 87% agreed to have improved their L2 generally. Broken down into skills, 83% felt they had improved their writing as well as their reading skills. 43% gained confidence using e-mail and 35% gained confidence using the computer generally. The British business students already had advanced IT skills at the beginning of the project and therefore a lesser-perceived gain had been expected.

Individual student comments

The majority of comments volunteered were positive. The students enjoyed the project and in several cases made friends. Plans were made to meet partners during their stay abroad. Several German students indicated that they would like to participate in another e-mail project next year.

Conclusion: In the future the writing of e-mail messages and webboard discussions will be incorporated more into class time.

Recommendations

Except with very autonomous learners, clear 'scaffolding' (Warschauer, 1997) or a guiding framework will prove helpful. The framework should stipulate frequent exchanges of messages and frequent deadlines. It is helpful if the project continues over several weeks. This allows the participants to build up a personal relationship as well as venturing into the subject specific task. Without some kind of personal relationship between partners, the likelihood of higher drop-out rates will increase.

References:

Beauvois, M., 1998. E-Talk: Computer-Assisted Classroom Discussion - Attitudes and Motivation. In: J. Swaffar, et al., eds., *Language Learning Online. Theory and Practice in the ESL and L2 Computer Classroom.* Austin. Texas: Labyrinth Publication, 1998, pp. 99-120.

Brammerts, H., 1996. Language learning in tandem using the Internet. In: Warschauer, M., ed., *Telecollaboration in foreign language learning: Proceedings of the Hawaii Symposium. Honolulu, HI: University of Hawaii Second Language Teaching and Curriculum Center.*
Chun, D., 1998. Using Computer-Assisted Class Discussion to Facilitate the Acquisition of Interactive Competence. In: J. Swaffar, et al., eds., *Language Learning Online. Theory and Practice in the ESL and L2 Computer Classroom.* Austin. Texas: Labyrinth Publication, 1998, pp. 57-80.
Clément, R., Dörnyei, Z., Noels, K., 1994. Motivation, Self-Confidence, and Group Cohesion in the Foreign Language Classroom. *Language Learning* 44:3, pp. 417-448.
Coleman, J., 1996. *Studying languages. A survey of British and European students.* London: CiLT.
Crook, C., 1994. *Computers and the Collaborative Experience of Learning.* London/New York: Routledge.
Fischer, G., 1998. *E-mail in Foreign Language Teaching. Toward the Creation of Virtual Classrooms.* Tübingen: Stauffenburg.
Jaeglin, C., 1998. Learners' and Instructors' Attitudes towards Computer-Assisted Class Discussion. In: J. Swaffar, et al., eds., *Language Learning Online. Theory and Practice in the ESL and L2 Computer Classroom.* Austin. Texas: Labyrinth Publication, 1998, pp. 121-138.
Katz, S., Lesgold, A., 1993. The Role of the Tutor in Computer-Based Collaborative Learning Situations. In: P. Lajoie, S. Derry, eds., 1993. *Computers as Cognitive Tools.* Hillsdale, New Jersey: Lawrence Erlbaum Associates, pp. 289-317 .
Leahy, C., 1999 (a). Motivational Factors and Student Attitudes in Language Specific Classes with Advanced Learners of German (forthcoming).
Levy, M., 1997. *Computer-Assisted Language Learning: Context and Conceptualization.* Oxford: Clarendon Press.
Little, D., Brammerts, H., eds., 1996. A guide to language learning via the internet. *CLCS Occasional Paper* No. 46.
Little, D., Ushioda, E., 1997. International E-Mail Tandem Network, Telematics for Autonomous and Intercultural Tandem Learning. A report on the pilot phase of the sub-project to evaluate tandem language learning via e-mail and MOOs (1996-7), August 1997; [then unpublished paper].
Little, D., Ushioda, E. 1997. Designing, implementing and evaluating a project in tandem language learning via e-mail; then unpublished paper of contribution to *EuroCall conference in Dublin, September 1997.*
Nattinger, J. R., DeCarrico, J. S., 1992. *Lexical Phrases and Language Teaching.* Oxford: Oxford University Press.
Oxford, R., Nyikos, M., 1997. Interaction, Collaboration, and Cooperation: Learning Languages and Preparing Language Teachers, Introduction to a Special Issue. *The Modern Language Journal,* 81: iv. pp. 440-442.
Oxford, R., 1997. Cooperative Learning, Collaborative Learning, and Interaction: Three Communicative Strands in the Language Classroom . *The Modern Language Journal,* 81: iv., pp. 443-456.
St. John, E., Cash, D., 1995. German Language Learning via e-mail: A Case Study. *ReCall* 7 (2), pp. 47-51.
Schinke-Llano, L., 1993. On the Value of a Vygotskian Framework for SLA Theory and Research. *Language Learning* 43:1, pp. 121-129.
Sullivan, N., 1998. Developing critical reading and writing skills: Empowering minority students in a networked computer classroom. In: J. Swaffar, et al., eds., *Language Learning Online. Theory and Practice in the ESL and L2 Computer Classroom.* Austin. Texas: Labyrinth Publication, 1998, pp. 41-55.
Swaffar, J., 1988. Readers, Texts, and Second Languages: The Interactive Processes. *The Modern Language Journal*, 72:ii, pp. 123- 149.
Vilmi, R., Helsinki University of Technology E-Mail Writing Project. Ana Gimeno ed., *EuroCall '95 Proceedings, Sept. 1995*, pp.469-486.
Warschauer, M., Ortega, L., 1997. CALL Research - Investigating Network-Based Language Teaching at *TESOL '97, Orlando, Florida, USA [recording of conference paper].*
Warschauer, M., 1997. Computer-Mediated Collaborative Learning: Theory and Practice. *The Modern Language Journal*, 81, pp.470-481.

Warschauer, M., 1999. *Electronic Literacies. Language, Culture and Power in Online Education.* Lawrence Erlbaum Associates.
Warschauer, M., ed., 1996. Telecollaboration in Foreign Language Learning. Proceedings of the Hawaii Symposium at Manoa. Second Language Teaching & Curriculum Center. University of Hawaii at Manoa.
Warschauer, M., ed., 1995. Virtual Connections. Online Activities & Projects for Networking Language Learners. Second Language Teaching & Curriculum Center. University of Hawaii at Manoa.
Woodin, J., Ojanguren, A., 1995. E-mail Tandem Work for Learning Languages. In: Gimeno, A., ed., *EuroCall Proceedings , Universidad Politécnica de Valencia, Spain, 1995*, pp. 487-507.
Woodin, J., 1997. E-mail Tandem Learning and the communicative curriculum. *ReCall* 9:1, pp. 22-33.

'Urlography'

Brammerts, H. 1999. International Tandem Network, homepage
http://www.slf.ruhr-uni-bochum.de/email/idxeng00.html [accessed 22/7/99]
Brammerts, H. 1999. International Tandem Network, Select Bibliography
http://www.slf.ruhr-uni-bochum.de/email/biblio.html [accessed 22/7/99]
Brammerts, H. 1999. Language Learning Tandem Bibliography
http://www.slf.ruhr-uni-bochum.de/learning/idxeng11.html [accessed 22/7/99]
Chapelle, C. 1997. CALL in the year 2000: Still in search of research paradigms? Language Learning & Technology, 1 (1), pp. 19-43.
http://polyglot.cal.msu.edu/llt [accessed 7/99]
Grotjahn, R. 1995. The electronic C-test bibliography: WWW version Dec. 1995
http://www.slf.ruhr-uni-bochum.de/biblio/ctbib.html [accessed 27/7/99]

L2 FRENCH LEXICAL CREATIVITY IN CONTEXT

Greg Lessard & Michael Levison
Queen' s University

Background: One of the defining characteristics of knowledge of a language is access to linguistic creativity. On the one hand, as every linguist knows, native speakers can produce and understand new forms and structures at the syntactic and lexical levels. On the other, although this has received less attention, they can also evaluate the relative acceptability of creations. Consider, for example, the following pair:

Irresolvable
Unresolvable

Both are possible (and both are attested by the Concise Oxford, 9th Edition). Yet many native speakers, even if they are not sure that they have previously seen both forms, will have the sense that the second is more general in meaning, or more usual, or more acceptable than the first. While their interpretations of the difference may vary, they tend to agree on the difference itself. More generally, as a variety of researchers have shown (Aronoff 1976 and Marchand 1969 for example) *un-* is more productive than *in-* and its morphological variants. The ability to perceive this difference, both in general and in its instantiations in various lexical forms, forms part of the knowledge of English.

In principle, coming to learn a second language (L2) involves acquiring similar skills. In this paper, we will be concerned with the study of L2 linguistic creativity as it manifests itself on the lexical level, particularly with respect to word formation. More specifically, we are concerned with measuring the extent to which anglophone learners of French of varying degrees of experience are capable of judging the relative productivity of different word-formation devices in French, and how this performance compares to that of native speakers of French. In particular, we are interested in how these intuitions with respect to productivity can be tested, and ultimately, how they can be taught.

We will attempt to demonstrate that a computational environment offers advantages unavailable in other media, such as oral or paper testing, while at the same time discussing some of the challenges inherent in testing of the sort. Before describing the environment itself, we make a short detour through some basic aspects of productivity and productivity testing.

Productivity and Productivity Testing: At the lexical level, productivity is a measure of the relative capacity of different word-formation devices to produce new and acceptable forms at a given point in time. One approach to its measurement consists in observing the entry of new lexical items into a language in a given period, and comparing the relative frequency of each derivational mechanism. This is the technique adopted by Dubois (1962), for example, who compares two successive editions of the *Petit Larousse* dictionary. Unfortunately, inclusion in a dictionary is at best an imperfect measure of productivity, given the effects of lexicographical techniques and practices: for example, dictionaries tend not to store regular derived forms, such as all verbs with the prefix *re-*. A promising alternative method is provided by Baayen' s work, which (to greatly simplify the issue) associates productivity with the occurrence of hapax legomena (single occurrence) forms. (See Baayen and Renouf 1996, Baayen and Lieber 1991.) However, such an approach lends itself less well to the study of L2 productivity, given the absence of many large corpora of L2 productions. In any case, as we point out in Lessard, Levison, Maher and Tomek (1994), the study of a corpus of advanced learner French shows relatively little evidence of word-formation. This is due, no doubt, in part to the influence of the educational context, which tends to discourage wordplay in academic essays, but other researchers on L2 have also observed a low level of derivational devices in their corpus data. See for example Broeder et alii 1993 who base themselves on a large multilingual European corpus of L2 adult speech. It would appear, then, that the study of productivity in L2 learners must use other instruments. We will argue below that, although it has been relatively little used to date, elicitation provides an excellent means of observing L2 lexical productivity.

In a nutshell, elicitation tests involve presenting a subject with some stimulus and requesting some response. This response can be *linguistic* in nature (for example, the response to the question: *tell me about your summer vacation*) or *metalinguistic*, that is, involving evaluation of a form, but not the production of a form (for example: *which is more acceptable, oxen or oxes?*).

The use of elicitation as a means of accessing L2 lexical creativity raises a number of theoretical issues. The first of these has to do with the status and reliability of metalinguistic performance, particularly in the case of L2 learners (for discussion, see Birdsong (1989) and Gass (1994) among others). As Gass points out, the level of indeterminacy among L2 learners is higher than in native speakers. With specific reference to L2 French, Coppetiers (1987), using a series of grammaticality judgements elicited from native and near-native speakers, argues that even those near-native speakers whose production is (almost) indistinguishable from native speaker speech show metalinguistic judgements which differ substantially from those of native speakers. (We will return to this point later.) A further problem from our perspective is that most discussions of grammaticality (or more precisely, acceptability) judgements have hinged on the evaluation of sentences rather than complex lexical forms. To our knowledge, little research has been done on elicitation to test lexical productivity in French, particularly among L2 learners. Hawkins (1985) forms one exception, but he was concerned primarily with the class of past participle markers, which are at the borderline of affixation and derivation.

Despite these potential difficulties, some work has been done, particularly with respect to L1 judgements. For example, Aronoff and Schvaneveldt (1978), Gorska (1982), and Anshen and Aronoff (1991) used a lexical decision task (providing a new form and asking subjects whether it is a possible word) to study judgements of English suffixation, with promising results. More recently, Levison and Lessard (1995a) emulated this approach using a computational environment to study several competing English prefixes (*non-, semi-, super-*) and suffixes (*-less, -ish, -like*). In a related vein, Fowler and Liberman (1995) used a morphological production task (*Four. The big racehorse came in* _____.) to elicit lexical creation in children, while Keane and Costello (1997) used a similar approach to examine elicited compounding in adults.

Computational Environment. In what follows, we will describe work done using the VINCI natural language generation environment. Over the years, the VINCI generation environment has increased substantially in power, and now permits the following operations:

1) specification of context-free phrase structure rules;

2) attachment and inheritance of attributes to tree nodes to represent morphological (number, gender, etc.), functional (subject, object), and semantic (human, agent, physical_object, etc.) information;

3) partial ordering of attributes, to capture class inclusion (for example, *book* as a subset of both physical object and reading matter);

4) dynamic construction of attribute combinations (such as *human.subj.p1.sing* indicating a first-person singular human subject) as well as their dynamic deconstruction, such that various nodes of a tree may each select parts of a complex attribute specification;

5) guarded syntax rules which ensure that the development of a tree is sensitive to the attributes present on parent nodes (so that, for example, a parent node containing a first or second person will give rise to a child node consisting of a pronoun, but not a full noun phrase);

6) a transformational mechanism which allows the construction of an in principle unlimited number of simultaneous transforms of an initial tree (such as a stimulus question and a set of variant answers, in the area of subject testing);

7) lexical selection constraints based on a variety of factors including attribute information (human nouns), formal specifications (regular conjugation verbs, adverbs ending in *-amment*), frequency, and so on;

8) a lexical pointer mechanism which permits any given lexical item to point at related lexical items such as synonyms, antonyms, hyperonyms, homonyms, etc.;

9) a rich set of context-free and context-sensitive morphology operations;

10) a lexical transformation mechanism in which one or more word formation rules may be exhaustively applied to a base lexicon in order to exhaustively generate all possible new forms while taking account of a wide range of formal and semantic constraints (for example, all compound nouns based on a verb implying a transformation of its object applied to a physical object direct object: *coupe-papier, déchire-papier, écrase-papier*);

11) an inverted lexical transformation mechanism which allows the specification of a formula for the real-time creation of a new lexical item in the course of the generation of an utterance. For example, let us suppose that the generation of a particular utterance requires the insertion of an adjective which means the opposite of *saved* (in the sense of *a saved document*) and that the base lexicon contains both the adjective *saved* and a rule which specifies that the opposite of an adjective may

be formed by prefixing it by *un-*. Then, an inverted lexical transformation is just that rule which states that if one needs the opposite of a base form, then one obtains it by looking for the appropriate base form and performing the appropriate operation.

12) a formalism for efficiently determining differences between subject input and the expected result, and analysing the reasons for the differences.

Earlier Studies and Results. In Lessard and Levison (in press) we describe a computer-based elicitation experiment designed to measure native and non-native judgements with respect to knowledge of verb forms and acceptability of derived forms based on the suffixes *–able, -age, -ment, -tion, -ure.* (The forms in *–able* were used as a test of reliability, in that *–able* is appropriately attached to all *–er* transitive verbs.) In order to perform the experiment, we started with a base lexicon of verbs drawn from a 2000 item lexicon of frequent French verbs (according to the *Dictionnaire des fréquences du Trésor de la langue française).* All verbs were from the *–er* conjugation. Word formation rules were applied to the lexicon to obtain a set of candidate derived forms. These forms were then randomized by suffix and base verb, with each suffix appearing 20 times. No derived form appeared more than once. In each case, subjects were asked whether they knew the base verb, and then whether they would accept a particular derived form.

Connaissez-vous le verbe suivant?
Fraterniser
Répondez y (oui) ou n (non) : ?

Pourrait-on en faire le mot suivant?
Fraternisement
Répondez y (oui) ou n (non) : ?
Appuyez sur ESC puis 1 pour avancer.

Initially, the test was applied to six native speakers of French, who were subsequently used as a point of comparison. Their mean results are shown below, along with the range of variation from subject to subject.

Suffix	% of accepted derived forms	% range (max – min)
-able	77	30
-age	52	76
-ment	39	53
-tion	30	55
-ure	10	25

Despite the large range of variations, judgements define a continuum from *–able* to *–ure* which is in general agreement with other measures such as corpus data. The particularly large range of variation in the case of *–age* stems from the fact that for speakers of Québec French, this suffix is highly productive, while for speakers of France French, it is less so.

Subsequently, the test was applied to 19 anglophone L2 learners of French. Linguistic backgrounds varied from some with high school training in French to some with significant university level studies in French. A comparison with native speaker results showed that as knowledge of verb bases decreased, non-native speakers showed increasing discrepancy in their judgements. In particular, subjects with less than a 70% success rate in recognizing the base verb showed significant deviation in their judgements of productivity. For example, subject a26 ranked *–ure* at 64%, above *–age* (45%), *-tion* (53%), *-able* (62%), and behind only *–ment* (79%). As the following table shows, these results are far off the average of the L1 speakers tested.

Suffix	**% of accepted forms (average of native speakers)**	**% of accepted forms (subject a26 – L2 French)**	**Difference (L1 – L2)**
-able	77	62	**+15**
-age	52	45	**+ 7**
-ment	39	79	**- 40**
-tion	30	53	**- 23**
-ure	10	64	**-54**

Later, the experiment was reproduced using students in oral French classes at Queen's University. Five levels were represented, ranging from 016 to 320, where 016 represented those with essentially no previous knowledge of French, while 320 represented those with near-native proficiency. Placement in these classes had been done on the basis of an oral interview. Similar results were found, as well as a good correlation between placement by interview and test results. (For details, see Lessard and Levison 1999.)

Improving the test environment. Despite the positive results discussed above, the test environment in its basic form had a number of weaknesses. In particular, (1) acceptability judgements were binary, (2) word forms were tested in isolation, not in context, and (3) there was no provision for real-time diagnosis and adaptation. The remainder of this paper will discuss these points in turn and show how the environment has been modified to deal with the shortcomings and the sorts of results now being obtained.

Binary versus multi-valued judgements. The earlier versions of the test environment required students to evaluate forms as known or acceptable using a two-valued system (yes or no). While this had the advantage of making statistical work easier, it failed to capture the fact that metalinguistic judgements are often not binary, but scaled. (See Bard, Robertson and Sorace (1996) for discussion of the advantages of magnitude estimation as a device for measuring metalinguistic judgements. See also Hug (1995) who uses a five point scale to allow L1 speakers of French to evaluate the relative acceptability of low-frequency French words.) As a result, we have now modified the test environment to require numeric responses. These can be used in one of two ways.

In the first format, subjects are given a form or utterance to evaluate and asked to assign an integer value indicating the degree to which they find the form acceptable, with 0 indicating rejection and some value indicating acceptance. In our research to date, we have used a scale from 0 to 5. The following example is taken from a test sequence generated by VINCI.

> Connaissez-vous le verbe suivant?   rattacher(5 = oui, 0 = non):5Peut-on dire en français?rattachement(5 = oui, 0 = non):5

Preliminary results from using the multi-point scale with L2 speakers suggest a hypothesis which we are currently exploring. Consider the following results provided by a very advanced anglophone L2 speaker of French:

Derived form	Acceptance score
Abandonnage	0
Coûtage	0
Vérifiage	0
Déchiration	0
Comptation	0
Adorement	0
Causement	0
Chassement	0

None of these forms are attested by the *Petit Robert*, so in a strict sense, the subject is correct. Note however that forms are rejected outright. Yet in a number of cases, it would appear that native speaker judgements would be more nuanced.

In the second format, subjects are presented with a series of simultaneous possible forms and asked to rank them by assigning an integer value. Earlier work on subjective evaluation of frequency (see Oléron 1966, for example) suggests that humans have a finely developed capacity for relative evaluations of the sort.

Connaissez-vous le verbe suivant? rattacher(5 = oui, 0 = non):5Classez les exemples suivants selon leur acceptabilité.(5 = le plus acceptable, 0 = le moins acceptable):
rattachement : 5
rattachage : 3
rattachation : 1
rattachure : 0

The order of presentation of forms can be either fixed or variable.

Contextualisation of Examples. We have already noted that previous results involved measuring word forms in isolation. Apart from the difficulties which this poses for subjects and the high degree of variability it leaves for their responses, there is also the problem that uncontextualised responses can be quite ambiguous. Consider the following example:

Connaissez-vous le verbe suivant?
serrer(5 = oui, 0 = non):5Peut-on dire en français?serrure(5 = oui, 0 = non):
5

Given the fact that the subject in question rejected with a score of 0 all other potential forms in *–ure* such as *annulure, mêlure, rapporture*, the positive score here is more likely due to the influence of the noun *serrure*. However, in the absence of context, this is impossible to determine.

One solution to this problem consists in hand-constructing contexts for each example to be tested. This has the advantage of allowing the researcher to exercise a fine degree of control over the product, but runs the risk of introducing unwanted and uncontrolled variables based on the researcher' s own linguistic biases. For example, it is exceedingly difficult to control for factors such as the relative frequency and phonological structure of words, syntactic structure, semantics and pragmatics. To take just one of these dimensions, Plenat (1997) uses corpus data from written French to show that the specific form of derived adjectives in *–esque* is conditioned by a series of phonological constraints on the base form, some of which are in competition with one another (length versus the tendency to avoid the repetition of similar phonetic sequences, for example). It seems clear that ideally we should use a computer to generate contextualised examples on the fly.

To show how this is done, it is necessary to take a short detour through a description of utterance generation by means of VINCI. Consider the following utterance specification expressed in the VINCI formalism. (Some elements have been removed for simplicity of the presentation.)

```
ROOT = choose Ge : Genre;

        N[prp]
        V[humain.suj, influencer, événement.objd, p3, sing, prés]
        DET[déf, Ge, sing]
        N[événement, Ge, sing]
```

In essence, this states that the system should produce an utterance with a proper noun subject (N[prp]) followed by a present tense third person singular verb (V) about which we require that it be transitive, that it take a human subject and an event direct object. In turn, these are followed by a determiner (DET) and a noun (N), with the latter two agreeing in gender (Ge) and both being singular (sing).

Each part of speech element of this tree represents a lexical search pattern (LSP) which is applied to the lexicon. The lexicon itself is a series of records. Two typical (somewhat simplified) lexical records are shown below:

```
"annuler"|V|humain.suj, influencer, événement.objd, Personne, Nombre, …
Temps|512|$12|…

"réunion"|V|événement, fém, Nombre|3093|$3|…|syn: "rencontre";|…
```

Each record is divided into fields by vertical bars. The first field gives the headword, the second the part of speech, the third the attribute specifications, either values (like *fém*) or classes (like *Nombre*, which means that either number is acceptable). The fourth field contains the relative frequency calculated on the basis of the *Dictionnaire des fréquences du TLF*; within a given lexicon, once all words matching an LSP have been found, one of them is selected at random, with the choice weighted by the relative frequency. The fifth field contains a call to a morphological rule responsible for inflecting the word. For example, rule $12 specifies regular *–er* verbs, while rule $3 specifies nouns which form their plural by the addition of a final *–s*. (Morphological rules are contained in a separate file.) Later fields contain lexical pointers to synonyms, antonyms, derived forms, etc.

A typical product of such a ROOT rule might be *Marie annule le rendez-vous.*

Specification of entries in the ROOT file may also be based on formal characteristics or word relations, as the following example illustrates:

```
ROOT = choose Ge : Genre;

        N[prp]
        V[humain.suj, influencer, événement.objd, p3, sing, rés]/"a*"/5=$12/
        DET[déf, Ge, sing]
        N[événement, Ge, sing]/"*ion"/14=syn
```

In this case, the verb must begin with the letter *a* and be conjugated according to the *–er* paradigm, while the noun must end in *–ion* and possess a synonym in the 14th field of the lexicon. (A typical sentence meeting this constraint would be *Marie annule la réunion.* In this way, quite finely detailed specifications are possible.

The VINCI transformation mechanism manipulates trees to produce variously modified copies. Consider, for example, the following (somewhat simplified) transformations.

```
MAKE_INFINITIVE = TRANSFORMATION
* V * : 2[inf] ;

MAKE_PASSIVE = TRANSFORMATION
N V DET N : 3 4 V[vcop, 2!Temps, 4!Nombre, p3] 2[pp, 4!Genre, 4!Nombre]
PREP[par] 1 ;
```

The first transformation (MAKE_INFINITIVE) simply looks for a syntax tree which contains any sequence of nodes, including none (*) followed by a verb (V) and possibly another sequence of nodes (*). If one is found, the verb (element 2 in the sequence) is given the trait *inf* which causes the morphology to inflect it as an infinitive. The other parts of the tree are thrown away.

The second transformation (MAKE_PASSIVE) looks for the sequence N V DET N and reorders the elements. The DET and N are placed first, a copula verb (*vcop*) is inserted which takes its tense from the verb of the ROOT and its number from the original object noun. These are followed by the original verb (item 2) which is made into a past participle (*pp*) and made to agree in number and gender with the original noun object. Finally, a preposition is added, plus the original subject.

The products of transformations can be called to the screen in any order by an overall specification. For example, the following specification may be applied to a ROOT specification such as that described above.

```
R_1 = Q[connaissez] %
R_2 = MAKE_INFINITIVE : ROOT%
R_3 = Q[rangée] %
R_4 = Q[voici_phrase] %
R_5 = ROOT %
R_6 = Q[passif] %
R_7 = MAKE_PASSIVE : ROOT %
```

If so, one result is as follows :

Connaissez-vous le verbe suivant?
annuler
(5 = oui, 0 = non) :
<student types answer here>

Voici une phrase.
Marie annule la réunion.

Mettez la phrase au passif.
<student types answer here>

Note that the rubrics (*Connaissez-vous le verbe suivant?,* etc.*)* are themselves generated by the system in the same way as the linguistic forms to be analysed. The precise placement of items on the screen is controlled by a further set of specifications. So, for example, the correct answer (R_7) may be hidden away for comparison with the student answer.

Standard Lexical Transformations: Let us now return to the problem of testing derivational mechanisms. Let us assume that, to continue the series of experiments described in the early part of the paper, we wish to examine in context deverbal nouns using the suffixes *age, -ment, -tion* and *–ure*. One option is to use the VINCI lexical transformation mechanism to generate new lexical records for all possible derived forms.

```
rule 1

?|V|vtd,humain.suj|?|$12|

_makes_

[#7.1+"+ement"]|N|masc, sing, action||$3||||||||vrb:V/[#1];|...

%
```

The rule specifies that it will be matched by any word (the initial ?) which is a verb (V) with the traits *vtd, humain.suj* and that the verb must be of the *–er* paradigm ($12). For each one of these found, the lexical transformation produces a new word which adds –*ement* to the base form of the verb, and specifies that the new item is a noun (N) with the traits *masc, sing,* and *action*, that it is inflected by adding *–s* and that it is linked to a the base verb which gave rise to it. A complementary transformation adds to the verbal entry itself a link to the new derived noun.

```
rule 2

?|V|vtd,humain.suj|?|$12|

_makes_

#1|#2|#3|... |ment:N/[#7.1 + “ement”];|...

%
```

Applied to one of the VINCI verbal lexicons which contains 432 high frequency French verbs, rule 1 generates 142 new nouns: *abandonnement, acceptement, accompagnement, accusement, admirement, adorement, affirmement, aidement, aimement, ajoutement, améliorement, annulement...* These new words may then be added to the base lexicon and used by ROOT and TRANSFORMATION specifications to produce examples. Consider, for example, the following transformations:

MAKE_DERIVED_WORD = TRANSFORMATION
* V * : /@14:ment ;

MAKE_DERIVED_NP = TRANSFORMATION
N V DET N : DET[déf, masc, sing] 2/@14:ment PREP[de] 3 4 ;

The first looks for a verb and follows its lexical pointer to the derived noun in *–ment.* The second generates a noun phrase which uses the derived noun. Typical output of this system is as follows:

Connaissez-vous le verbe suivant?
annuler
(5 = oui, 0 = non) :
<student types answer here>

Peut-on dire en français?
Marie annule la réunion.
(5=oui, 0 = non) :
<student types answer here>

Peut-on dire en français?
L' annulement de la réunion par Marie
(5=oui, 0 = non) :
<student types answer here>

Inverted Lexical Transformations: The standard lexical transformation mechanism is quite powerful. However, it has two weaknesses, one practical and the other more theoretical. First, if we assume that there exist many possible derived forms for any given base, then we are faced with the prospect of an explosion in the size of the lexicon. This may be overcome by selective loading of lexicons and by the use of machines with large resources of memory and disk space. The theoretical difficulty is more serious. By pre-storing the products of a derivational rule, we essentially limit ourselves to a single framework in any given testing sequence. However, as Brown (1997) points out, there is significant potential to be explored in the area of adaptive testing. In essence, this uses previous test results to determine the succeeding questions to be asked. In particular, it allows the researcher to focus in on problem areas. This is particularly important for teaching L2 word formation.

The possibility of adaptive testing is opened up by the use of an additional feature of VINCI: inverted lexical transformations (ILTs). In a nutshell, rather than generating all possible products of a word-formation rule and adding them to the lexicon, this mechanism constructs in real time a required derived product. For example, let us assume that we have a base verb and need a derived noun. An inverted transformation asks the question: what must I have and what must I do to obtain a derived noun. It searches the lexicon for candidate forms and performs the operation.

The following example shows a simplified inverted lexical transformation. Note that such a transformation takes the form of a specialised lexical item which, for legibility, we have divided into three lines.

```
_ilt_|N|masc, sing, action||
_lsp_|V|vtd, influencer||$12|
_rhs_[#7.1 + "ement"]|N|||$lt1||[#7.1 + "er"]|
```

The first part of the inverted transformation, preceded by the keyword _ilt_ , specifies that the hoped-for product is a noun with the traits *masc, sing,* and *action*. The second part, preceded by _lsp_ (lexical specification) states that such a noun may be formed on the basis of a verb having the traits *vtd* and *influencer* and which is part of the *–er* paradigm. Finally, the last part, preceded by _rhs_ (right hand side) shows how the noun in question is to be formed. One form is made by adding the string *–ement* to the base of the verb (for example, *annul-*), while another is formed by adding *–er* to the base of the verb. Additional morphological specifications are provided by morphology rule $lt1, which uses the same formalism as regular morphology rules. (Additional information on inverted lexical transformations may be found in Levison and Lessard 1995b.)

Inverted lexical transformations produce output which is in all respects indistinguishable from that of regular lexical transformations, as the following example shows:

Connaissez-vous le verbe suivant?
chauffer
(5 = oui, 0 = non):

Peut-on dire en français?
chauffement
(5 = oui, 0 = non):

On the other hand, they make it possible to deal with phenomena having a high degree of productivity such as the prefix *re-*, as the following example illustrates:

Connaissez-vous le verbe suivant?
(5 = oui, 0 = non):
laver :

Peut-on dire en français?
(5 = oui, 0 = non):
Marie lave la religieuse. :

Peut-on dire en français?
(5 = oui, 0 = non):
Marie re-lave la religieuse. :

There is a cost. Because products are generated in real time, hand-editing becomes impossible. Consequently, any specification must be formulated in terms of rules. Consider for example the problem that new creations tend to be blocked by previously existing forms. If we are to take account of such blocking phenomena, we must build the tissue of links which allows them to be captured. Take the case of *annulation*. As a lexicalised form, we should assume that it has a built-in advantage over potential competitors such as *annulement* and *annulage* which are formed by rule from the verbal base. So in a testing environment, we must incorporate into the lexical entry for the base verb the link to the lexicalised derived form:

"annuler"|V|... |deverbal:"annulation"|

Then, when any new deverbal form is created, the information on the lexicalised form can be carried over and used in the generation and analysis of new items.

"annulement"|N|... |deverbal:"annulation"|

In order for these elements to be usable in an adaptive testing environment, several additional features are required.

First, an error analysis environment is needed. In the current system, it is possible to specify a series of transformations which predict anticipated errors and to use a match between these and subject input to provide targeted feedback. We are currently working on an extension of this research which will automatically generate possible alternative responses at the orthographic, morphological, lexical and syntactic levels. An initial prototype is now being tested.

The results of this error analysis environment provide in essence a collection of symptoms: a subject (or a language learner) tends to do X, Y and Z, but not A, B and C. For these to be useful, they must be interpreted over time, just as a language teacher will read a series of essays and come to diagnose a particular learner' s areas of difficulty. We are in the early stages of developing this component.

Finally, for testing (and teaching) to be purely adaptive, the results of a diagnosis must be capable of directing further generation. This element remains for the future.

Other Testing Frameworks. All the examples discussed to date have been based on metalinguistic judgements. However, the mechanisms shown here lend themselves equally to other sorts of tests. (See Feldman (1995) for discussion). We will show two examples here.

In the first case, instead of producing a metalinguistic judgement, we wish a subject to produce a new form. Using a simple ROOT form, some basic transformations and an inverted lexical transformation, we can generate a fill-in-the blanks test, illustrated by a typical example below:

Connaissez-vous le verbe suivant?
chasser
(5 = oui, 0 = non):

Peut-on dire en français?
Marie chasse l' artiste encore.
(5 = oui, 0 = non):

Reformulez la phrase précédente.
Remplissez la lacune avec un seul mot.
Marie <student input goes here> l' artiste.

If the correct derived form is also generated by transformation and kept in the background, it can then be used to verify subject input and generate an appropriate reaction.

The second case is based on the use of non-linguistic stimuli. For example, in their study of experimentally elicited English deverbal compounds (*toe-painter*, etc.) by native speakers of Spanish, Lardiere and Schwartz (1997) used basic drawings as their starting point. VINCI is capable of producing analogous material in that the output of trees need not be orthographic strings, but image files, sound files or in principle any other multimedia event. We have only done initial work on this, but the area does appear promising.

Conclusions: Testing of both L1 and L2 French subjects is still underway. More detailed results of this testing will be presented at the conference. However, results to date demonstrate clearly the advantages of a computational as opposed to a paper-based format and point the way toward a teaching tool for word-formation.

Notes: Research described here was made possible by a grant from the Social Science and Humanities Research Council of Canada.

References:

Anshen, F., Aronoff, M. (1981) Morphological Productivity and Phonological Transparency. *Canadian Journal of Linguistics* 26/1: 63-72.
Aronoff, M. (1976) *Word Formation in Generative Grammar*. Cambridge, MA: MIT Press.
Aronoff, M., R. Schvaneveldt (1978), Testing morphological productivity, *Annals of the New York Academy of Sciences* 318: 106-114.
Baayen, H., Lieber, R. (1991) Productivity and English derivation: a corpus-based study. *Linguistics* 29/4: 801-844.
Baayen, H., Renouf, A. (1996) Chronicling the Times: Productive Lexical Innovations in an English Newspaper. *Language* 72/1: 69-96.
Bard, E., Robertson, D., Sorace, A. (1996) Magnitude Estimation of Linguistic Acceptability. *Language* 72/1: 32-67.
Birdsong, D. (1989) *Metalinguistic Performance and Interlinguistic Competence*. Berlin: Springer Verlag.
Broeder, P., Extra, G., van Hout, R., Voionmaa, K. (1993) Word formation processes in talking about entities. In (C. Perdue, ed.) *Adult language acquisition: cross-linguistic perspectives*, Cambridge: Cambridge University Press, vol. 2, pp. 41-72.
Brown, J.D. (1997) Computers in Language Testing: Present Research and Some Future Directions. *Language Learning and Technology*, 1/1:44-59.
Coppetiers, R. (1987) Competence Differences between Native and Near-Native Speakers. *Language* 63/3: 544-573.
Dubois, J. (1962) *Étude sur la dérivation suffixale en francais moderne et contemporain; essai d' interprétation des mouvements observés dans le domaine de la morphologie des mots construits*. Paris: Larousse.
Feldman, L.B. (ed.) (1995) *Morphological aspects of language processing*. Hillsdale, NJ: Lawrence Erlbaum.
Fowler, A., Liberman, I. (1995) The Role of Phonology and Orthography in Morphological Awareness. In Feldman, L., ed. *Morphological Aspects of Language Processing*, Hillsdale, NJ: Lawrence Erlbaum, pp. 157-188.
Gass, S. (1994) The Reliability of Second-Language Grammaticality Judgements. In (Tarone, E., Gass, S., Cohen, A., eds.) *Research Methodology in Second-Language Acquisition*. Hillsdale, NJ: Lawrence Erlbaum, pp. 303-322.
Gorska, Elzbieta (1982) A way of testing the productivity of word formation rules (WFRs)?, *Studia Anglica Posaniensa* 14/1: 169-174.

Hawkins, R. (1985) Errors in the Use of French Past Participles By Foreign Speakers and Their Implications for a Model of Morphology, *Lingua* 67:171-188.
Hug, M. (1995) Frequency and Acceptability of Infrequent French words. *Journal of Quantitative Linguistics* 2/1:53-66.
Imbs, P, Martin, R. (eds.) (1971) *Dictionnaire des fréquences : vocabulaire littéraire des XIXe et Xxe siècles*. Paris: Klincksieck.
Keane, M., Costello, F. (1997) Where Do "Soccer Moms" Come From? Cognitive Constraints on Noun-Noun Compounding in English. Proceedings, Computational Models of Creative Cognition Conference, Dublin, 5 pp.
Lardiere, D., Schwartz, B. (1997) Feature-marking in the L2 development of deverbal compounds. *Journal of Linguistics* 33:327-353.
Lessard, G., Levison, M. (1999) Beyond Corpora: Elicitation as a Tool in Second Language Word Formation Studies. *ACH/ALLC 99*, Virginia.
Lessard, G., Levison, M. (in press) Lexical Creativity in L2 French. To appear in *Internation Review of Applied Linguistics.*
Lessard, G., Levison, M., Maher, D., Tomek, I. (1994) Modelling Second Language Learner Creativity. *Journal of Artificial Intelligence in Education* 5/4:455-480.
Levison, M., Lessard, G. (1995a) Experiments in Word Creation, *ACH/ALLC 95*, Santa Barbara. (Conference abstracts, pp. 74-77.)
Levison, M., Lessard, G. (1995b) New Words from Old: A Formalism for Word Formation. *Computers and the Humanities* 29:463-479.
Marchand, H. (1969) *The Categories and Types of Present-Day English Word-Formation: a Synchronic-Diachronic Approach. Munchen: Beck.*
Oléron, P. (1966) Estimation de mots français sur des échelles de fréquence et d' abstraction. *Bulletin de psychologie* 247, XIX, pp. 603-610.
Plenat, M. (1997) Analyse morpho-phonologique d' un corpus d' adjectifs dérivés en *–esque. French Language Studies* 7: 163-179.

INVESTIGATING FEATURES OF AN INTERNATIONAL E-MAIL COMMUNITY

Linda Mak and Stella Yeung
Hong Kong University of Science and Technology

Abstract
While recent research is moving in the direction of investigating the effects of synchronous computer-assisted classroom discussion on language learning, few studies have analysed the community features exhibited in international e-mail discussion groups of ESL students.

This paper investigates the community features that characterise the CMC among a group of tertiary students who took part in an international e-mail discussion. Data gleaned from a large international collaborative project will be examined to establish how cultural and ideological exchanges, collaboration in learning, and interactive competence have been fostered through the use of CMC among international students in this project.

Introduction: The last decade has seen a phenomenal expansion in the use of computer technology in language education, and its interactive capability has opened up new ways and opportunities for language learners not only to learn on their own but also to collaborate in their learning. Whereas in the past the phrase 'learning community' referred to a school or classroom setting, today, thanks to the increased use of the Internet and electronic mail in education, it can have a much wider, even an international, application.

A spate of literature has been published documenting different projects using computer technology in the foreign language (FL) classrooms as well as in TESL settings. Innovative collaborative projects using computer networks both within the classroom and across countries or even continents have reported different degrees of success not only in raising student interest and motivation in learning, but also in actual improvements in language learning (See Warchauer, 1995). However, in spite of a resurgence of interest in collaborative learning and learning communities and the fact that groups of learners interacting online have been described as 'online communities' (McGee, n.d.), to date there has been a lack of published research on how networked students actually collaborate in their learning and what features they exhibit as learning communities.

Our paper focuses on a qualitative analysis of the sociocultural features of one of the international ESL e-mail discussion groups in a large-scale international collaborative e-mail project involving tertiary students from different countries.

Previous Research: A learning community has been characterised by shared goals and objectives (Wilson, 1998), partnerships, interaction, and collaboration (Maring, et al. 1997; DeMulder & Eby, 1999). Tierney and O'Flahaven (1989) describe members of a learning community as people who 'facilitate their own and each others' learning by sharing, offering support, suggesting possibilities, and evaluating ideas in a social context' (p. 301). The application of the term 'learning community' has traditionally been very much restricted to a school or classroom context (Cooper & Boyd, 1999; Rousculp & Maring, 1992). Increasing use of computer technology, however, has revolutionised ways in which learners communicate and is now providing a new scenario by extending the boundaries of learning communities (Watkins & Marsick, 1999; Yungbluth & Bertino, 1996).

Computer-mediated communication (CMC), now a 'ubiquitous medium' (Lawley, 1994; Paramskas, 1993), is changing the way people communicate and learn. It has expanded the horizons of learners and brought learners together over distances, transforming them from classroom learners into 'world communicators' (Gonzalez-Bueno, 1998, p. 51). Classroom learning is taking on new meaning with CMC 'declassrooming the classroom' (Sharrock & Watson, 1985), or turning the traditional classroom into a 'global classroom' (Baugh & Baugh, 1997; Harris 1994, Repman & Logan, 1996; Soh & Soon, 1991). CMC, with its powerful potential for collaborative learning and cross-cultural communication (Warschauer, 1997), has ushered in new possibilities of interaction (Ortega, 1997) and new forms of learning communities — virtual learning communities (Furlong, 1997; Parson, 1997; Warschauer, 1998; Yungbluth & Bertino, 1996).

A virtual (or online) learning community — also known as a 'networked community' (Sherry, 1996) — resembles the traditional learning communities in many ways. It is a group of people who share common interests and goals (McGee, n.d.). It is highly participatory (McLellan, 1998), with members expecting to interact with one another (McGee, n.d.), working closely to construct knowledge together (Scardamalia & Bereiter, 1994; Warschauer, 1997), and using different strategies for 'expressing, interpreting, and negotiating information' (Lee, 1997). The chief difference between a traditional learning community and a computer-mediated learning community has been aptly summarised by McLellan (1998):

> the model of an Internet-based virtual learning community, with students interacting dynamically with the content, the technology, and most importantly, each other, offers a powerful and convivial approach to providing education at a distance (p. 92).

Learners now have new ways of communicating and collaborating with each other electronically: in real time (synchronous communication) or at their convenience (asynchronous communication). A number of studies have been conducted to ascertain the benefits of using computer technology in FL and ESL/EFL teaching and learning to help students attain communicative competence and proficiency in the target language. In the context of foreign language learning, Barson et al. (1993) conducted six e-mail projects (which they called 'experiments') involving intermediate students of French in Stanford, Harvard, and the University of Pittsburgh between the period of 1988-1993, and reported positive results in terms of the students' target language competence, interactive competence as well as sociolinguistic competence. Gonzalez-Bueno (1998), using asynchronous CMC with her Spanish class in a longitudinal study, affirms the effectiveness of using CMC as a tool to promote linguistic and interactive proficiency in and out of the classroom.

Several other FL studies explored the software *InterChange* which allows for synchronous computer-assisted class discussion (CACD) on a local area network (LAN), and all reported favourable results. Kelm (1992), working with a group of intermediate Portuguese students, noted improvements in reading skills as well as increased participation and interaction among them. Beauvois (1992) reported progress both on the linguistic and attitudinal levels in her case study of a French student. Chun's (1994) longitudinal study of the syntactic development of her first-year learners of German led her to conclude that CACD provides 'excellent opportunities' for foreign language learners to enhance their sociolinguistic and interactive competence (p. 28). Kern (1995)'s French classes likewise saw overall improvements on motivational, affective, and discourse levels.

In the ESL/EFL field, there are a few studies on the use of both CACD and asynchronous e-mail discussion lists. Warschauer (1996), also using *InterChange*, compared student participation and interaction in the use of CACD with face-to-face discussion in an ESL class in Hawaii, and reported an improvement in his subjects' writing skills as well as heightened participation. Other studies involving cross-country communication and collaboration also reported positive results. Soh & Soon (1991) conducted an e-mail project involving students from two schools, one in Singapore and one in France. These teenage students studied literature texts together, and gains in both writing skills and cultural insights were reported. Davis and Chang (1994/1995) linked their classes in North Carolina and Taiwan to one another to help their students expand their reading and writing skills and enhance their cultural awareness, and they noted positive results in these areas. Liaw (1996) reported a yearlong e-mail project involving EFL students in Taiwan and pre-service ESL teachers in Texas, and witnessed increase in the EFL students' confidence in using English and a greater repertoire of communicative strategies.

CMC projects involving students at multiple sites have also been undertaken. One of these involved EFL Finnish students at 3 secondary schools communicating with native speakers of English in Britain and the United States (Tella, 1992). In another project (Goodwin et al., 1993), staff at the English Programs for Internationals at the University of South Carolina used e-mail to provide distance training in language/ academic skills and cultural information to 8 students in 7 Latin American countries to help these students prepare for intensive English study in the United States. Positive results were noted in both of these projects, and students were found to have benefited in enrichment of their linguistic and cultural knowledge.

Overall, language researchers and pedagogues have affirmed the value of CMC as a tool to foster learner competence at the linguistic, sociocultural, communicative, interactive, and even cross-cultural levels, and many collaborative online projects between individuals, classes and schools have been carried out. However, as pointed out by Liaw (1996), 'very little do we know … what exactly happens in this new communication territory' (p. 20). To date, not much research has been reported to document the community features of an online learning community of ESL learners. Given the meteoric expansion of the use of computer technology in language education, it can be foreseen that in the coming years learners will have more and more opportunities to be engaged in electronic forms of long distance and cross-cultural communication and collaboration. How these learners interact in the dynamics of such learning communities remains to be explored. This pilot study seeks to examine the community features of an online community and to establish how cultural and ideological exchanges, collaboration in learning, and interactive competence have been fostered in this international ESL virtual learning community.

Data and Methodology: The following analysis is a pilot study on the data collected from the Helsinki University of Technology (HUT) e-mail writing project in Spring 1994. It involved 256 college students (mainly ESL learners) and 9 teachers from 8 universities in 4 continents communicating in 20 e-mail groups for one semester. The students chose and joined a topic group they were interested in and took part in electronic discussion for about 3 months. In most classes, students were required to write a research paper or a report, and to present the result of their discussion or research in class at the end of the semester.

All e-mail messages first went to the server in Finland and were then redistributed to the participants. To provide support and to monitor the progress, the project co-ordinator was on all the e-mail lists, while other teachers chose to be present in some or all of the lists that their students joined.

To investigate the features of an online community, a pilot study was conducted on one of the discussion groups that satisfied the following criteria: (i) the group was active, with around 100 messages; (ii) the group involved participants from three or more universities and a number of countries, so as to reflect the cultural diversity. Four groups satisfied the above criteria, and Group 33 (Suicide) was selected at random. Nine people took part in the discussion of this group (3 male and 6 female; 3 teachers and 6 students).[1] Totally 98 messages were sent, only 8 of which were by the teachers.

---

[1]Originally 13 people signed up for this group. However, 4 of them (3 students and 1 teacher) who also signed up for another group never posted any message in this group, so they are not counted in this study.

This paper is a report on the pilot study. Three major areas of the electronic data were examined: strategies in rapport building, collaboration in learning and evidence of interactive or communicative competence.

Analysis and Discussion

A. Rapport/Community Building: Our investigation shows that the online community of our study shares many common characteristics with a traditional community, while at the same time it has features that are specific to an online community. This section will examine these community features.

In all communities, rapport is an important aspect of community building. According to Yungbluth & Bertino (1996), messages pertaining to well-wishing, teasing, social support, and agreement without elaboration are all instances of rapport building (p. 12).

In the data of the present study, examples of **well-wishing** abound, including 'Hi, nice knowing you'[2] (Student R, Feb. 3), 'Hi! Nice to communicate with all of you!' (Student S, Feb. 8), 'With all best wishes to you' (Student G, Feb. 8). It was interesting to find that in their greetings/salutations, in addition to 'hi', 'hello, I am…', they used phrases that create a sense of community. For example:

- Dear student penpals (Teacher L, Feb. 13)
- Dear members of the project 'suicide' (Student S, Feb. 8, 19:49:42)
- Dear project-family members (Student S, Feb. 8, 20:39:56)

Teasing is not found in the exchanges of this group of students. This could be due to the fact that our subjects, unlike those of Yungbluth & Bertino's who were members of a class, did not really know one another well enough and so did not share the common understanding on which teasing can be done in a safe and non-offensive way. Instead of teasing, **jokes** were used as rapport-building tactics. An example is one student writing '[at your university]... if there is a student from INDONESIA I would be interested to know! Specially a female student!… (just kidding….)' (Student R, Feb. 2). The same student had also made an earlier onomatopoeic attempt to mimic laughter by writing 'HE… HE… HE…' (Student R, Feb. 8). The element of humour could also be an attempt to lighten up the serious academic atmosphere in the online community

In terms of **social support**, numerous examples can be found. For example, one student wrote, 'I am excited to have this wonderful opportunity to start working on E-Mail as well as YOU' (Student F, Feb. 21). Sometimes, students expressed empathy with one another to show support for one another, e.g. 'I also feel the same way as you did.' Apart from content-related discussions, these students also shared personal feelings/likings and showed appreciation for help/support and encouragement. Messages expressing agreement were frequent. Yungbluth & Bertino (1996: 23) point out that affirmation and

---

[2] All quotes are reproduced without editorial emendations.

agreement without elaboration show a sincere affirmation instead of a transition in the dialogue, and there are numerous examples of this in the e-mail exchanges among our subjects, e.g.

- I agree with you, xx. (Student N, Mar. 9)
- I agree with what you are saying. (Student A, Feb.18)
- I agree with you/ X that .... (Teacher C, Feb. 23; Student N, Mar. 30)
- I'm agree about narowing the topic to teenage suicide. (Student R, Feb. 8)

There was also the other kind of affirmation which was used as a transition, as in the following example:

- I agree with you to a certain extent. I understand that family do play a very important role .... However, teenages are also affected by their peer group. (Student G, Feb. 18)

We find a small number of disagreements and even conflicts in this community. In investigating **disagreements** in this online community, we discovered that in spite of concerns raised in CACD data (Warschauer, 1997; 1998), there was no flaming in this group of subjects. This could be explained by the fact that the e-mail interchanges were the only connection among this group of students, and they were careful not to destroy rapport. Disagreements were always expressed politely; conflicts were resolved or toned down. Here are some examples that show participants acknowledging some points in previous messages and then expressing opposing opinions in a mild way:

- I know that someone must disagree with the above approach because .... But it is just for fun. (Student N, Feb. 23)
- To a certain extent, they are selfish as X said, but have we consider ...? (Student N, Feb. 24)
- It is quite interesting that we value life in economic term. I would like to talk about my opinion ... My point is that how you define the term 'benefit'. ... (Student P, Mar. 26. See Appendix B for the whole message.)
- I do not think that a person who feels suicide is the only solution to their problems has rational first thoughts nor could even give second thoughts to the matter. It seems to me that the level of desperation must be so great in order to consider suicide. (Teacher R, Feb. 25)

Another interesting finding is that our subjects' written utterances adhered to Lakoff's (1973) **politeness principle** for conversations.[3] The linguist Lakoff (1973, cited in Cook 1990: 32-33) points out that in conversations, people are guided by a 'politeness principle' and they assume that certain maxims, such as 'Don't impose', 'Give options, and 'Make your receiver feel good', are being followed in the utterances of others. As

---

[3] It might be worth noting here that a lot of studies have found e-mail discourse to be a hybrid between speaking and writing (e.g., Kathleen et al. 1990; Maynor 1994; Spitzer 1986; Yeats 1994).

evidenced in the examples above, the students sounded very polite and helpful even in disagreements. It can be said that on the whole, these students tended to adopt a courteous tone in their effort to maintain goodwill in the learning community.

An examination of our data shows other community building features not mentioned by Yungbluth & Bertino (1996). For example, we would also include **self-introduction** as a significant rapport- and community-building device. An online community, like all communities, is a social construction (Riel, 1996). It is important for the members of the community to establish their own identities before they can develop acceptance and trust and cultivate their relationship within the community. Our subjects, however, unlike members of the traditional communities in the classroom, had never met one another before and did not have any other means (e.g. face-to face, telephone) to get to know one another. Their only way to interact with one another was through the text-based e-mail messages. Their self-introductions were therefore an important way for them to establish their own identities in the virtual learning community. Our data show that our subjects took the self-introduction seriously, sharing with one another who they were and providing information about their countries, their universities, their courses and the like.

One more interesting feature that characterises this particular online learning community is their tacit understanding of their own and each other's **commitment** to the group. No doubt, for an asynchronous e-mail project to work, such commitment is necessary. Riel & Levin (1990) refer to this commitment as 'response obligations' in network participant structures. In our data, there are numerous examples of promises that one would write back (and keeping the promise), anticipation or invitations to the others to write back or to continue the discussion, and apologies given for not having written back sooner. Some examples include:

- Last time, I said that there is an interesting in Hong Kong. The story is as follows… (Student N, 24 Feb. 24).
- I'm sorry to reply so late because I am really busy last week (Student N, Mar. 10).
-

All these bear out McGee's (n.d.) point that anticipation of future interactions is 'a necessary attribute for a[n online] community' (p. 2).

B. Collaboration in learning: Rapport building alone is not enough to build a learning community. The members need to establish *collaboration in learning*. In our study, the students had to fulfil their academic requirements, that is, to write up a research paper or a report and give an oral presentation. This is similar to the 'work' interaction in a learning community that Yungbluth and Bertino (1996) proposed. In our data, members of the community tried to provide academic support to one another. They went through the normal stages of working on a class project. After exchanging self-introductions, they brainstormed ideas in the first week. Then they narrowed down the topic and exchanged information. Afterwards, they drafted questionnaires or papers and posted them to the whole group to collect data or receive peer feedback. At the end of the semester, they presented their findings orally in class, or submitted their papers to their class teachers.

In sharing with one another their knowledge of the societies they were living in, and summarising materials they had read or the results of their library search, these students acted as *experts* in the eyes of the rest of the community. In reading about the situation in other countries, they were able to expand their understanding of other cultures and develop *multi-perspectives* of the issue under discussion. More importantly, this sharing and discussion formed part of their effort to *construct knowledge* together. All these in turn helped community building.

Let us examine some examples of collaborative acts found in the community discussing 'Suicide' in detail. First, cultural exchanges were provided and expected. Students were interested in finding out whether the values or the situations in their own countries also existed in other cultures. For example:

In response to xx's case, I think that the school should not bear ALL the responsibility. *It a popular phenomenon in HK* that good schools and students are with high discipline and conformity.

So, it is rather that *cultural and tradition view of Chinese* that intellectual should be highly respected are to be blame. ...

But social value are not easy to change in a time. ... *I wonder if countries outside Asia has such a social value.* (Student N, Mar. 9)
(emphasis ours)

They exchanged information on comparable social systems or phenomena with one another, thus providing multi-cultural perspectives to the whole group. For instance, ESL learners in the US referred to practices in both their home countries (Japan, Columbia, etc.) and in the US:

Date: Fri, 25 Feb 94 16:10:30 +0800
Subject: about social workers

> I think the social workers do can help the students to solve their
> problems. ... However, there are actually not enough social workers in HK.
> On average, one social worker has to deal with 3000 students. And the class
> size in HK is very large, about 38 students in a class. Teachers can hardly
> build up relationship with the students, let alone care about them. ...
> How about the situation in your countries?
> What is the ratio of social worker to students?
> What is the class size?

> > Student N
>
> Dear Nxx,
> I don't quite understand what you wrote about. In the United States and Japan, there are many social worker and there are so many kind of social worker. I think you are talking about social worker and volunteer who advice for people who are in trouble In the U.S. maybe they are called psycothelapist or something like that. I am not sure. Do they have a class like teachers. In the United states and Japan there are many hot line for people in trouble. But I don't know if many people use that line. please tell me specifically about social worker.
> (Student I, Mar. 9)

The above exchanges show clearly how collaboration offered an opportunity for the students to widen their knowledge of a foreign culture. This is especially valuable for students from a homogenous cultural background. Such kind of exchanges also enabled all the participants to reflect on their preconceptions and to discover that even such a mundane term as 'social worker' could be loaded with cultural implications which might lead to misunderstandings in communication.

Ideological exchanges are a necessary part of collaboration in learning. The following message is a good example of ideological exchange that took place:

> Date: March 23, 1994
> To: 33@hut.fi
> From: Student N
> Subject: how much value does a life possess? (in economic view)
>
> It is quite interesting to apply some economic concept to this question. Let's take an example. Although lifeguards are employed in beaches to save life, people are drown and died every year. However, the lives can be saved if there are MANY MANY lifeguards in EACH beach. That is, one lifeguard target on one person. However, this is not practiced because to employ so many lifeguard cost too much. That is to say, the cost (salaries of lifeguard) outweight the benefit (value of life). So we can get a rough idea of the value of life.
>
> There is another approach to estimate the value of life by adding the present value of one's lifetime income and wealth. That is to calculate the amount of income one can generate.
>
> I know that someone must disagree with the above approach
> because the value of life not only consist of money but also love, feelings and the happiness etc. But it is just for fun.
>
> (See appendix A for the whole message.)

In this message, Student N raised a philosophical question: what is the cost/value of life? She shared an extreme approach, an economic perspective. Anticipating disagreement from other members of the community, she acknowledged the value of love, feelings and happiness. This message by Student N generated a lot of discussion. For example, Student P disagreed with Student N, and responded strongly in her reply: 'I would like to talk about my opinion referring the two concepts.' She went on to query the definition of value and cost, and questioned the understanding of the term 'benefit'. She pointed out this was dangerous to 'regard life as goods', to equate one's value in life with one's contribution, and that the disabled or the mentally-ill might be at a disadvantage. She also challenged this economic view by listing a series of questions. (See appendix B for the whole message.)

It can be seen that these students were deeply engaged in a debate on the value of life. As members of an online community, they were not hindered by differences in time, culture, or geographical location.

In this online community, students also played the role of **experts**: they did not only share their personal knowledge, opinions and experience, they also supplied source and cultural information with one another. Their sharing included *statistics* (Student I, Feb. 24, statistics of 1990 U.S. teenage suicide rate; Student N, Feb. 25, statistics of suicide rate in Hong Kong between 1971-91), *library information* (Student F, Mar. 24, a library leaflet) and *local cases* (Student N, Feb. 24, the story of how and why a local student threatened to kill himself at the end of an examination). In doing so, these students played the role of both information-providers as well as informants.

The students sometimes sent out pleas for help to other members of the community — they sought information in general, comments on assignments/questionnaires/paper drafts, and help in filling out questionnaires. In asking for help and trying to help one another, these students again played the dual role of both learners and teachers. The following is an extract from an e-mail in which a student commented on another student's paper draft (see appendix C). It shows the student adopting the tone of a teacher in giving feedback:

> 1. I think it is good to have an introduction and conclusion,
> 2. There are spelling and typing mistakes.
> 3. You can give some statistics to support your argument.
> 4. Actually, there are many other points to add such as the peaceful environment give little opportunities for children to tackle problems and the teens become weaker. The society's attitude toward the committed teens. And love affairs also plays a role.
> 5. What we/society can do to tackle the problem?
>
> (Student N to Student A, Mar. 30)

Like a teacher, Student N commented globally on the organisation, language and content of the paper. She pointed out areas which required improvement and expansion, using a direct and almost authoritative tone. Much collaboration of this kind went on in this learning community.

We would also like to examine evidence showing that the e-mail discussion was in fact a **co-construction of knowledge** in this online community, and affected/developed individual learners' views on the issue of 'suicide'. An analysis of all the e-mail messages Student A wrote and other participants' responses to her supported this. It was observed that at the beginning of the discussion, Student A thought *family* was the major cause of suicide, and in her message quoted below, the word 'family' appeared three times:

- The reason I choose suicide is because I think is very sad to see people that are in between 13-20 years are killing themselves. I can't believe that a person who has a life ahead decides to die. I think that there are many reasons for this, but for me, the bottom line is the *family*. If you analyse the different cases of suicide, most of them are from people that came from a broken *family*, or a *family* that only gave him/her material things. Also, because they have problems and there is nobody there to help them. (Student A, Feb. 14) [emphasis ours]

In her draft of paper sent on Mar 25, she mentioned several reasons for suicide, namely, feeling of loneliness, support, pregnancy, problems and pressure in their schools. Then she concluded by saying: 'This are only a few reasons of suicide. For me the main point is the lack of support, not having where to go.' Interestingly, there was absolutely no mention of 'family' at all. The only related term used is 'parents': 'Sometimes they don't find support among their boyfriend, friends or parents. ... they are disappointing their parents.' (Please refer to appendix C for the whole draft.)

To uncover why there was such a change in her thought, a search on the key words 'pregnancy', 'pressure' and 'support' in all the e-mail messages was conducted. The result strongly indicated that she had picked up the ideas through her discussion with the other community members, and expanded and integrated them into her paper. First, Student R suggested five reasons why teenagers committed suicide — one of which was 'pregnant' (Feb. 8). Then Student N suggested 'studying pressure from schools, fellows, society etc.' as one of the other major reasons (Feb. 17). Student N also pointed out that family was the source of financial support to the teenagers. Another student agreed: 'The parents will be the financial support of their children (Student G, Feb. 18). All these ideas found their ways into Student A's draft. However, it can also be seen that Student A did not uncritically incorporate everything other people mentioned. She chose to discuss 'support' in a broad sense on Feb. 18: 'What I also learnt was, teenagers don't have any support from their parents.' Following this direction, Student G expanded her idea of (financial) 'support' to 'no support for family... they may also find no support from friends' (Feb. 22). Then, Student A concluded the discussion in her paper draft by writing: 'When you are a teenager you need a lot of support, because you go through a lot of crisis. ...' (Mar. 25). In her conclusion, she also stated: 'In many schools there are advisors that can help, but not many go there, because they don't like to express their feeling to extrangers.' This shows a possible evaluation and subsequent repudiation of a point raised by Student G who, in an earlier discussion, said that advisors could help teenagers contemplating suicide. All of the above show how an enriched understanding of the topic being discussed can result when members of an online community work together to construct knowledge.

We can conclude that their online collaboration was successful. One of the reasons may be that their communication, although online, adhered to the co-operative principles of conversation proposed by Grice (1975). These students provided one another with a lot of information relevant to the topic suicide, thus satisfying Grice's *maxim of relevance*. Their messages were clear and their communication was effective despite a number of grammatical errors. So Grice's *maxim of manner* was observed. Their exchanges were mainly based on supported facts (e.g. statistics, library search), thus complying with Grice's *maxim of quality*. The length of their messages sometimes did not follow Grice's *maxim of quantity* (brevity). However, this is understandable as writing gives students more time to think, reflect and draft, and thus is generally much longer than the turns in face-to-face conversation. This finding may imply that observing the general principles of face-to-face communication can contribute to the success of online collaboration.

Content and language use are inseparable. Collaboration was enhanced by effective use of language, and vigorous interaction among the members. So in the next section, we will examine the language use in this online community.

C. Interactive/communicative competence: Collaboration of learning is achieved through interaction among the members of a learning community. In explaining the centrality of interaction in language learning, Rivers (1987) points out that '[t]hrough interaction, students can increase their language store as they listen to or read authentic linguistic material, or even the output of their fellow students' (p. 4), and that '[s]tudents achieve facility in *using* a language when their attention is focused on conveying and receiving authentic messages' (p. 4, emphasis original). One of the distinguishing features of CMC is its capability to enable many-to-many interaction (Warschauer, 1997), thus providing an ideal context for L2 learners to develop a wide range of target language skills and a high degree of interactive competence. Chun (1994) affirms that CACD facilitates the acquisition of interactive competence, noting that the computer-assisted discussions of her first-year German students showed evidence of many of the 10 types of interactive competence listed by Kramsch (1983).

- Can create, express, interpret and negotiate meaning
- Can take turns
- Can open and close conversations

• Can take the initiative, capture attention • Can construct and expand on a topic • Can elaborate on others' ideas • Can show and check understanding • Can ask for clarification • Gives feedback to others • Can steer or avoid topics

Table 1. Kramsch (1983): Interactive Competence (cited in Chun, 1994)

Although we can find plenty of examples that match Kramsch's functional types of interactive competence, we will not strictly follow these functional types in analysing our data for several reasons. Firstly, types such as 'can take turns' and 'can open and close conversations' are more relevant to face-to-face discussions than e-mail exchanges. Secondly, the type 'can create, express, interpret and negotiate meaning' in fact includes other types such as 'can construct and expand on a topic', 'can ask for clarification', and 'gives feedback to others'. Also, different from the synchronous exchanges of Chun's (1994) CACD, the e-mail discussion of our study was asynchronous and so a great number of the entries in our data are extended and complex, covering different functions simultaneously. For the purpose of this paper, we will concentrate on two areas that we believe are of special interest to our study of computer-mediated asynchronous communication in a learning community.

Attention-getting: In a many-to-many asynchronous interactive situation in which messages come from different participants at different times, it is important to have the attention of your audience to make sure your message will not be overlooked or even has an impact on the audience. Several attention-getting devices are found in our data, and these were placed at different parts of the messages. For example, there was the innovative use of subject lines, ranging from a dramatic 'HHEEELLLLOO!!!', to a subject line that creates suspense: 'such a mysterious case!', and something more philosophical and thought-provoking: 'how much value does a life possess? (in economics view)'. There were also other attempts to draw attention to the message. For example, one student alerted other people to her (public) reply to another student: 'Hello, I've just sent a mail to Rxx talking about the reasons for the teen committing suicide. It's 'Re: questionnaire'. Please refer to it.' (Student G, Mar. 31). Another used eye-catching capital letters with a series of exclamation marks and even onomatopoeia to draw attention to her message:

- BOMB!!!! BOMB!!!! BOMB!!!! BOMB!!!!
  So, they commit suicide. (Student N, Feb. 22)

Maintaining coherence: In an online community there may often be different strands of discussion going on at the same time, and there may be multiple viewpoints on the same issue. According to Warschauer (1997), this could lead to 'information overload', which is one of the barriers to computer-mediated collaboration. Citing Moran (1991), he states that 'discussants can be so overwhelmed with messages that they ignore what others write and the conversation devolves into monologues' (p. 473). Undoubtedly, for an asynchronous online learning community to work, it is of paramount importance for its members to be able to pick up the different threads of discussion and weave them into a meaningful and coherent whole. In our data, we do not see any evidence of information overload. (This could be because of a prior agreement on the members' part to focus on a particular aspect of the self-selected topic). Instead of monologues, we find a wide range of strategies our online community members used to build or maintain coherence in their dialogue. These strategies could be classified into the following categories:

1. Using anaphoric references to previous messages to provide a context for further discussion:

Naming the topic in a previous mail before giving new input:	• Hi this is rxx again, I'm agree about narowing the topic to teenage suicide. I think teenager commite suicide because they are... (Student R, Feb. 8)
Referring to a particular addressee and the topic:	• Hello is me again. First i want to answer Axx about the advisor. (Student A, Feb. 22)
Referring to a previous mail:	• In reply to your case, I want to tell you that I also have a friend who… (Student F, Mar. 24) • Have you read the case and my feelings that I've sent you this morning? Now, I suddenly think of something about the question that I've mentioned in my feeling about the case. (Student G, Feb. 26)
Referring to and paraphrasing an earlier message before replying:	• I want to reply the message from Axx and Txx. Axx says that … I understand that … However, … (Student G, Feb. 18)
Acknowledging others' opinions:	• I'm glad to receive those reply. What I mean is that … (Student G, Feb. 22)
Clarifying an earlier point:	• Tank you all for writing back. I agree with what you are saing. But, what I meant also was … (Student A, Feb. 18) • Thank you for replying to my letter. But, don't confuse! I said that that the suicide rate among Japnese older woman is very high, not the U.S. (Student I, Feb. 24)

2. Managing the discourse:

Chun's (1994) classification of discourse management includes requests for clarification, giving feedback to others (agreement, apologies) and social formulas such as greetings and farewells. Similar functions are found in our data. Greetings and patterns showing agreement and disagreement have been discussed earlier. In addition, we find our students performing a greater variety of interactional speech acts which are specific to online collaborative projects outside the classroom. These include:

a) Paving the way for further discussion:

Asking for information:	• I would like to ask whether the situation in your countries will have any differences. If any, why? Would it be due to the difference in culture or anything else? (Student G, Feb. 26) • In Hong Kong, there is a pheonmeon of copycat suicides among teenages. Is there such a phenomeon in your countries? (Student N, Feb. 24)
Asking follow-up questions on an earlier mail:	• I have heard from Ixxx that there is many hotline in the US. What is the aims of the hotline? Are they focus on teenagers problems? (Student N, Mar. 10)
Promising to give information in a subsequent message:	Recently in Hk, there is an quite interesting case. I would tell you next time … (Student N, Feb. 17)
Keeping promise/Refreshing readers' memory before giving details:	• Last time, I said that there is an interesting in Hong Kong. The story is as follows …(Student N, Feb. 24)

b) Asking for/Giving/Acknowledging help:

Inviting peer comments on one's writing:	• Hello this is a rough draft, can you please read it and give me some suggestions? (Student A, Mar. 25)
Giving advice:	• I advice you to help your friend to learn 'learn from failures'. (Student P, Mar. 26)
Showing appreciation for help:	• Thanks for responding to my questionnaire, it can really help me for doing my paper. (Student N, Mar. 31)

The above examples from our data show that the online community members were carefully processing incoming information and actively engaged in purposeful interaction with one another. They showed awareness of the need to make their ideas lucid to their audience and made conscious attempts to do so. Questions posed were always answered, and everyone stayed on task. There was plenty of lively language practice through their communicative interaction. Thus we can conclude that Computer-Assisted Discussion *outside* the Classroom (CADoC) also provides students with plenty of opportunities to enhance communicative proficiency.

Conclusion: Innovative use of CMC is bringing in new paradigms in teaching, but it is being developed at such a fast pace that much of what is being done in this field still remains unreported (Bailey & Cotlar, 1994; Warschauer, 1997), and there is also 'a lack of extensive theoretical research' (Gonzalez-Bueno, 1998: 51). Studies of different aspects of what is happening online when learners work together as a community are needed to fill the gap and inform further research, and it is hoped that the present study makes a contribution to that effect. From our analysis of the interchanges among this specific group of international ESL students collaborating in an asynchronous CMC project, we can affirm that a virtual language learning community brings about manifold benefits. As the students used the target language in authentic communication with each other across national boundaries, not only were they actively involved in communicating with one another in a wide range of discourse, but they also had a chance to examine the speech styles of other members in the online community (both teachers and students) as they interacted with one another. All these provided them with opportunities for expanding their linguistic, communicative and interactive competence while at the same time widening their cultural perspectives. Engaged in collaborative learning and playing the multiple roles of learners/teachers/experts, these students took part in a powerful learning experience of constructing knowledge together through thrashing out ideas and sharing, hypothesising, questioning, testing, evaluating, clarifying, affirming, supporting, and assimilating others' viewpoints.

The findings discussed in this paper, though based on a small group, show positive results of involving students in online learning communities. The next stage of our research is to examine whether the characteristics identified in this study are also found in other communities in our project. At the same time, several other areas of the use of CMC in language teaching and learning require further investigation. Firstly, it has been found that students are playing the multiple roles of learners, teachers and experts in online learning communities. What role(s), then, should the language teacher play in a collaborative online learning community? Secondly, our study is based on data collected in early 1994. Since then, online communication has flourished. How is the discourse in our study different from the discourse used in communication such as ICQ which is rampant today? Thirdly, apart from positive results noted in CMC, does it have negative effects on the verbal and writing skills of the online community members?

Using computer technology in language teaching and learning was still relatively new at the beginning of the nineties, but now its use has mushroomed. In the near future, as technology continues to advance, teaching and learning will continue to expand beyond the classroom and school settings. As Warschauer (1997) points out, 'the ability to access and interpret information gained through communication and collaboration with people from a variety of cultures will be a critical skill for success in the 21st century' (p. 477). In the context of language education, more cross-cultural collaboration and interaction can be predicted, resulting in new kinds of communal relationships and enriched language learning environments.

References:

Bailey, E. K. & Cotlar, M. (1994) Teaching via the internet. *Communication Education, 43,* 2, 184ff.

Barson, J., Frommer, J., & Schwartz, M. (1993) Foreign language learning using e-mail in a task-oriented perspective: Interuniversity experiments in communication and collaboration. *Journal of Science Education and Technology, 2,* 4, 565-584.

Baugh, I. W. & Baugh, J. (1997) Global classrooms — E-mail learning communities. *Learning and Leading with Technology*, 25, 3, 38-41.

Beauvois, M. H. (1992) Computer-assisted classroom discussion in the foreign language classroom: Conversation in slow motion. *Foreign Language Annals, 25,* 455-464.

Chun, D. M. (1994) Using computer networking to facilitate the acquisition of I interactive competence. *System, 22*, 1. 17-31.

Cook, G. (1989) *Discourse*. Oxford: Oxford University Press.

Cooper, C. & Boyd, J. (1999) Schools as collaborative learning communities. Online document: http://www.vision.net.au/~globallearning/services/CLC.html [1999, June 4]

Davis, B. & Chang, Y. L. (1994/1995) Long-distance collaboration with on-line conferencing. *TESOL Journal, 4*, 2, 28-31.

DeMulder, E. K. & Eby, K. K. (1999) Bridging troubled waters: Learning communities for the 21st century. *The American Behavioral Scientist, 42*, 5, 892-898.

Furlong, M. (1997) Creating online community for older adults. *Aging and Information Technology, Fall Issue*, 33-35.

Gonzalez-Bueno, M. (1998) The effects of electronic mail on Spanish L2 discourse. *Language Learning & Technology, 1*, 2, 50-65.

Goodwin, A. A., Hamrick, J. & Steward, T. C. (1993) Instructional delivery via electronic mail. *TESOL Journal, 3*, 1, 24-25.

Harris, J. (1994) People-to-people projects on the Internet. Online document: http://lrs.ed.uiuc.edu/Mining/February94-TCT.html. [1999, June 23].

Kathleen, F., Brunner, H. & Whittemore, G. (1991) Interactive Written Discourse: An Emergent Register. *Journal of Written Communication 8*, 1, 8-34.

Kelm, O. R. (1992) The use of synchronous computer networks in second language instruction: A preliminary report. *Foreign Language Annals, 25,* 441-454.

Kern, R. G. (1995) Restructuring classroom interaction with network computers: Effects on quantity and characteristics of language production. *The Modern Language Journal,* 79, 457-476.

Kramsch, C. J. (1983) Interaction in the classroom: Learning to negotiate roles and meanings. *Die Unterrichtspraxis* 16, 2, 175-190.

Lawley, E. L. (1994) The sociology of culture in computer-mediated communication: An initial Exploration. Online document: http://www/itcs.com/elawley/bourdieu.html. [1999, June 16].

Liaw, M. L. (1996) Communicative devices used by EFL students in e-mail writing. EDRS. ED 401 752.

Lee, L. (1997) Using Internet tools as an enhancement of C2 teaching and learning. *Foreign Language Annals, 30*, 3. 411-427.

Maring, G. H., Wiseman, B. J., & Myers, K.S. (1997) Using the World Wide Web to build learning communicties: Writing for genuine purposes. *Journal of Adolescent & Literacy, 41*: 3, 196-207.

Maynor, N. (1994) The Language of Electronic Mail: Written Speech? In Little, G. & Montogomery (Eds.*),* *Centennial Usage Studies* (pp. 48-54). Tuscaloosa, AL: Alabama University Press.
McGee, P. (n.d.) Building an on-line community for learning. Online document: http://www.gsn.org/wce/archives/MCGEE.htm. [1999, June 4].
McLellan, H. (1998) The Internet as a virtual learning community. *Journal of Computer in Higher Education*, *9*, 2, 92-112.
Moran, C. (1991) We write, but do we read? *Computers and Composition, 8*, 56-61.
Ortega, L. (1997) Processes and outcomes in networked classroom interaction: Defining the research agenda for L2 computer-assisted classroom discussion. *Language Learning & Technology, 1*, 1, 82-93.
Paramskas, D. (1993) Computer-assisted language learning (CALL): Increasingly integrated into an ever more electronic world. *The Canadian Modern Language Review, 50*, 1, 124-143.
Repman, J. & Logan, S. (1996) Interactions at a distance: Possible barriers and collaborative solutions. *Techtrends, 41*, 6, 35-38.
Riel, M. (Winter, 1996) The Internet: A land to settle rather than an ocean to surf and a new 'place' for school reform through community development. In *ISTE SIG/TEL Technology in Education Newsletter.*
Riel, M. & Levin, A. (1990) Building electronic communities: successes and failures in computer networking. *Instructional Science,* 19, 145-149.
Rivers, W. M. (1987) Interaction as the key to teaching language for communication. In W. M. Rivers (Ed.) *Interactive language Teaching*. London: CUP.
Rousculp, E. E. & Maring, G. H. (1992) Portfolios for a community of learners. *Journal of Reading, 35,* 5, 378-385.
Scardamalia, M. & Bereiter, C. (1994) Computer support for knowledge-building communities. *The Journal of the Learning Sciences*, 3, 3, 265-283.
Sharrock, W. W. & Watson, D. R. (1985) 'Reality construction' in L2 simulations, in D. Crookall (Ed.) *Simulation Applications in L2 Education and Research* (pp. 195-206). Oxford: Pergamon. (Special issue of *System, 13*, 3.)
Sherry, L. and the Internet Task Force, University of Colorado at Denver (1996) Supporting a networked community of learners. *Techtrends, 41*, 5, 28-32.
Soh, B. & Soon, Y. (1991) *English by E-mail: Creating a global classroom via the medium*. Paper archived at LISTSERV@CUNYVM.CUNY.EDU.
Spitzer, M. (1986) Writing style in computer conferences. *IEEE Transactions on Professional Communications*, PC29 (1), March 1986, 19-22.
Tella, S. (1992) The adoption of international communications networks and electronic mail into foreign language education. *Scandinavian Journal of Educational Research, 36*, 4, 303-312.
Tierney, R, & O'Flahaven, I. (1989) Literacy, learning, and students' decision-making: Establishing classrooms in which reading and writing work together. In D. Lapp, J. Flood, & N. Farnan (Eds.), *Content Area Reading and Learning*, (297-303). NJ: Prenctice Hall.
Warschauer, M. (Ed.) (1995) *Virtual Connections: Online Activities & Projects for Networking Language Learners*. Honolulu, HI: University of Hawaii, Second Language Teaching & Curriculum Center.
Warschauer, M. (1996) Comparing face-to-face and electronic discussion in the second language classroom. *CALICO Journal*, 13, 7-25.
Warschauer, M. (1997) Computer-mediated collaborative learning: Theory and practice. *The Modern Language Journal, 81*, iv, 470-481.
Warschauer, M. (1998) Online learning in sociocultural context. *Anthropology & Education Quarterly, 29*, 1, 68-88.
Watkins, K. E. & Marsick, V. J. (February 1999) Sculpting the learning community: New forms of working and organizing. *NASSP Bulletin*, 78-87.
Wilson, B. G. (1998) Creating technology-supported learning communities. [Online document: http://www.cudenver.edu/~bwilson/learncomm.html [1999, June 4].
Willson, M. (1997) Community in the abstract: A political and ethical dilemma. In D. Holmes (Ed.) *Virtual Politics: Identity & Community in Cyberspace*. London: SAGE Publications.
Yates, S. (1992) Speech, Writing and Computer Conferencing. In R. Mason
(Ed.) 1993. *Computer Conferencing: The Last Word*. Victoria: Beach Holme.

Yungbluth, S. C. & Bertino, S. (1996) Extending the borders of community and learning with electronic mail discussion lists. Paper presented at the Annual Meeting of the Speech Communication Association. (82nd, San Diego, CA, November 23-26. EDRS. CS 509 461.

Appendices: Sample E-mail Messages

Appendix A: Ideological exchange

Date: Wed, 23 Mar 1994 15:55:18 +0500
To: 33@hut.fi
From: student N
Subject: how much value does a life possess? (in economics view)

Hi! I have just read something quite interesting---How much value does a life possess?

It is quite interesting to apply some economic concept to this question. Let's take an example. Although lifeguards are employed in beaches to save life, people are drown and died every year. However, the lives can be saved if there are MANY MANY lifeguards in EACH beach. That is, one lifeguard target on one person. However, this is not practiced because to employ so many lifeguard cost too much. That is to say, the cost
(salaries of lifeguard) outweight the benefit (value of life). So we can get a rough idea of the value of life.

There is another approach to estimate the value of life by adding the present value of one's lifetime income and wealth. That is to calculate the amount of income one can generate.

I know that someone must disagree with the above approach
because the value of life not only consist of money but also love, feelings and the happiness etc. But it is just for fun.

Children is the future of the society. The more the no. of children commit suicide, the more the society loss. So, the government should do something to avoid the lossing of lives. Now that the HK gov't have done something to improve the situation of teenages suicide. But suicidal cases continue reporting. It shows that the affort is not effective. Maybe, it is because that the cost of avoiding teenage suicide is too high or that the benefit from saving their lives is too low.

Student N

Appendix B: Conflicts

Date: Wed, 23 Mar 1994 15:55:18 +0500
To: student N
From: Student A
Subject: Re: how much value does a life possess? (an economics view)
Cc: 33@hut.fi

> Nxx,

It is quite interesting that we value life in economic term. I would like to talk about my opinion refering the two concepts.

First: lifeguards-- the cost to save life is higher than the benefit.

My point is that how you define the term 'benefit'. Is it we call a lif which is beneficial when he/she contributes a lots to the socity or they are talent and capable people? Is it a life value of the disabled or mental-diseased people are lower than that of a professor?

Actually, we can help or concern all those who want to kill
himself/herself. It is due to the limit of resources ,not the cost is
greater than the benefit. I think such a concept is danger that it regard life as goods.
Second: estimate the value of life by adding the present of one's
Lifetime income and wealth;

I think such an idea is acceptable in academic level, but if we use this concept in daily-life, it is poor! Who can caculate other's value?
Who know the value of life? Who defines? etc. If we cannot answer the
Questions then we cannot value the value of life.

Pxx

Appendix C: A paper draft

Date: Fri, 25 Mar 1994 09:57:49 -0500 (EST)
From: Student A
Subject: suicide
To: 33@hut.fi

Hello this is a rough draft, can you please read it and give me some suggestions?

Suicide Among Teenagers..

Day by day the rate of suicide among teenagers increases. It is shocking to think that people with their whole lives in front of them decide to give it an end. And this is not only happening in a few countries, is happening all over the world.

Why does someone decide to kill him/her self? This is a question who's answer is very wide. There are many reasons for this to happen. One of them is the feeling of loneliness that some people has. When you are a teenager you need a lot of support, because you go through a lot of crisis. You need to feel that someone is there to help you. Teenage are the years were you built your personality, and were you start to realise how life really is. That is why you need someone to help you go through this years.

Another reason is pregnancy in early years. This is a normal problem today. Today people are starting to have sex been very young. Some of them are not taking the precaussions necessary for this. Therefor many young girls get pregnant and they don't know what to do. They feel trapped, like if they don't know where to go. Sometimes they don't find support among their boyfriend, friends or parents. In other occasions they are afraid to tell. They feel rejected, so they decide that life is not worth any more.

Another reason is when they get rejected, or have problems in their schools. They feel that they can't do anything right. Also, that they are disappointing their parents. They get preasured, and they don't know what to do. So, in some cases they decide to kill themselves because for them this id the only solution.

This are only a few reasons of suicide. For me the main point is the lack of support, not having where to go. In many schools there are advisors that can help, but not many go there , because they don't like to express their feeling to extrangers. We have to do something to end this. It is sad to see how people is loosing interest on life. So, we better find solutions, because we need to built a better place for our children.

[The Student's name]

IN THE SHADOW OF AN INFORMATION SOCIETY: A COLLABORATIVE INTERNET TEACHING PROJECT

Maire Mäkinen and Donald Smart
Helsinki University Language Centre, Finland

Abstract
This paper describes the impact of moves towards an information society at the national level in Finland on the work of two teachers who work at the Language Centre of Helsinki University. We examine the background to, and what we have done so far in our attempts to move from the shadows to the mainstream of the information society. We also highlight the problems we have faced, and try to predict a way forward.

Introduction

Description of our Situation: We both work at the Language Centre of Helsinki University in Finland. The Centre was founded in 1978 and in 1998 it employed 55 full-time and 69 part-time language teachers, who taught 18 languages. We teach English for Specific Purposes (ESP) to students who mostly study in the Faculty of Science. Unlike all the other language groups at the Language Centre, English teaching is done by two distinct groups of teachers. These are the oral skills teachers, and the reading comprehension teachers. The oral skill teachers are all native speakers of English and the reading comprehension teachers are all native Finns.

The Concept of an Information Society: It is difficult to define what is currently meant by the term 'information society' as it means many different things to different people. Problems with this term are well illustrated by the following statement by Lievrouw quoted in Tella (1998):

> In recent decades the term information society has become a widely used shorthand for complex social, economic, and institutional changes related to the proliferation of information and communication technologies. Researchers continue to debate whether the term stands for fundamental social change or merely the extension of the principles of industrial capitalism into new areas of society. (Lievrouw 1998, 83)

The emergence of the World Wide Web as part of the Internet in the early 1990s has made the information society even more visible to the layman.

There have been attempts to plan and guide the incorporation of the information society into the daily lives of the citizens of many countries. Some of the earliest attempts to formalise and incorporate the essence of the information society were undertaken at the level of the European Union, and these early efforts have influenced the form in which European Union member states, including Finland, have approached their information society initiatives. When we speak of the information society we must be careful to make a distinction between information, data and knowledge. Such a distinction is made by the European Union High-level Expert Group in their report 'Building the European Information Society for us all' (1997), in the following manner:

> First and foremost it is essential to make a clear distinction between data, information and knowledge. From our perspective, the generation of unstructured data does not automatically lead to the creation of information, nor can all information be equated with knowledge. All information can be classified, analysed and reflected upon and otherwise processed to generate knowledge. Both data and information, in this sense, are comparable to the raw materials industry processes into commodities.

This observation of the High-level Expert Group should be borne in mind especially when we come to teaching using the WWW. Are we really teaching, if our Internet classes just involve getting our pupils to surf the Web?

The Finnish Government's Information Society Initiatives: The Finnish Government has implemented information society strategies in many sectors, such as in the industrial and commerce sectors. We will concentrate here on its information society initiatives in education.

The National Strategy on Education, Training and Research has the following central goals:

1. moving from once-and-for-all training to lifelong learning
2. basic information society skills for all
3. high level of vocational skills
4. high level of teachers' professional skills
5. securing the development of information products and services
6. support for multidisciplinary research on the information society
7. building education and research networks into an open global network.

These goals are very similar to those of other European Union countries.

We at the Language Centre have come into contact with this policy, as the collaborative project which will be described in this paper is financed through the Finnish Government's information society educational (OPM) funds. We shall later look at how the work we have done in the shadows conforms with some of these seven central goals.

The Computing Facilities Available to Us: Like any modern well equipped university, we have a wide range of computing facilities available to us at Helsinki University. Each

University Department has its own computer co-ordinator, computers and intranet. There is also a central computer department which provides the following:
A university intranet
Links to the Internet
Computing expertise
Computer workstations
Computer peripherals, e.g. printers, scanners etc.
When it comes to the types of computers available to students and staff, the computing service offers both PCs and Macintoshes. They also provide a variety of operating systems. It is up to the user to decide what s/he prefers. It should, however, be noted that the most popular operating systems used by computer literate personnel at the University is the Linux system, which was written in 1991 by an ex-student of Computer Science at Helsinki, Linus Torvalds.

What Has Been Done Before: Even before we became part of the National Information Society project we had been involved in various computing projects at the Language Centre. We will now take a brief look at the projects which the authors have been actively connected with:

Reading while listening

This was a project undertaken by Mäkinen with some assistance from Smart in 1991, and it was part of her M.A. dissertation for Birmingham University. It involved students listening to texts displayed on a computer screen while they listened to the same text read on a audio cassette. The PC synchronised the text on the screen with the audio tape.

Icons

The ICONS (International Communication and Negotiation Simulations) project has been used at various Finnish universities since the middle 1980s. It is organised and directed by the University of Maryland, and for two years, Smart assisted Leena Koskinen of the Language Centre with the simulation. Briefly, the simulation involves groups of students in different universities representing various nationals in negotiations concerning various issues. The negotiations take place over several weeks, and they are mostly asynchronous. However, there are two or three synchronous sessions with a moderator in Maryland. The system used to run on the POLNET II UNIX based system, but it has been moved to a WWW system.

Various multimedia projects

Smart has been involved in various projects which involved the delivery of computerised language learning materials using, Authorware, Director, SuperCard, and Hypercard on the Macintosh. Most of these projects were limited in their application in the Language Centre which is very PC-centric. However, he is now taking a hybrid approach to development, and is writing applications for both platforms. The project he is now working on is a virtual language laboratory authored in Authorware, to be delivered on CD-ROM.

The Internet project

Our first project under the auspices of the OPM started in 1997, when various teachers at the Helsinki University Language Centre worked on an Internet project together with language teachers from Helsinki University of Economics and Business Administration and Tampere University. The project was co-ordinated by The Media Centre of Tampere University. The Helsinki University teams produced Web pages for English and Swedish language instruction and the Swedish team won a prize for the best implementation of computer assisted teaching at Helsinki University in 1997. Our participation in this project provided many insights into what was desirable in WWW-delivered materials, and we have attempted to apply these lessons to our collaborative project.

The Current Collaborative Project

Aims and Objectives of Study

An attempt to apply standard methods of evaluation to Internet materials: Evaluation plays a crucial role in the writing of traditional English language courses, as can be seen in Weir and Roberts (1994). Evaluation of the use and efficiency of materials enables a course writer to fine-tune his materials to a particular group of users. As we move from materials delivered on paper to materials disseminated on the Internet, there is no reason why evaluation should not still be an important aspect of materials design. The World Wide Web is an imminently interactive environment, and with a little know-how it is possible to build transparent feedback mechanisms into materials which can aid the designer in his/her quest for better and more efficient courses. With this in mind, we decided that we should make evaluation central to our WWW-delivered materials.

Collaboration between an English reading comprehension teacher and an oral skills teaching using Internet technology: The system of having reading comprehension and oral skills English teachers at the Language Centre means that it is possible to live in the world of either one of the two groups. However, as members of one group may have skills which members of the other group may not possess, it is always worth our while to sometimes put out heads together and pool our skills, to the benefit of both groups and the Language Centre.

An attempt to give teachers full control over the technology they use: One of the most striking aspects of the Tampere Internet project was that the design and implementation of the Web materials were totally outside the control of the teachers. These decisions were made by technology experts at the Hypermedia Laboratory. This meant that the final product was constrained by the following:

- The amount of time one expert could devote to a group of some 20 teachers
- How well the teachers could convey their perceptions of the materials to the expert

- How the expert perceived the use of the materials

We thought it might be better if the course designers and the course implementers were one and the same i.e., the teachers. We decided to use commercially available equipment to attempt to have full control of the process ourselves. Commercial Web course programs come in two types, integrated programs, which try to incorporate all the features that the course builder may need such as e-mail, discussion groups, tracking features etc., and Web component programs which only provide one or two features, so the course builder has to stitch many of these components together to obtain a suitable application, for more on this dichotomy see Kaplan (1999)

Materials and Methods

The European Union Terminology Course: The course we decided to use was a European Union Terminology Course. The aim of the course is to introduce students to the specialised Finnish and English terminology of the European Union. It is based on official European Union documents which cover all the institutions of the EU, and which are not copyrighted. The course had been first taught without any CALL component to it by Mäkinen in autumn 1997. We decided to teach the course both through the WWW and 26 hours of classroom sessions.

The Students: The students on this course come from all the faculties of the University. On the autumn 1998 course, we had eight students from the following faculties:
The Humanities
Law
Science
Social Science
Dentistry

TopClass: The Internet authoring program we use is TopClass, a product of WBT Systems, a Dublin based firm. The reason why we use TopClass is simple, when we first started looking for a simple Web authoring teaching program in 1997, TopClass was the only one available. TopClass works within the metaphor of a classroom. There is one administrator of the system who assigns passwords to instructors. The instructors can then assign their students to courses in various 'classes'. The course material is placed in the system in HTML form. TopClass imposes a modular structure on course designers. The program has eight predefined question types which the course designer can use to test his/her students' understanding of his materials. Some of the question types can be marked by the computer. Others, have to be sent back for the course instructor to mark. The system assigns unique homepages to each user. There are 3 types of users, administrators, instructors and users, and thus there are 3 types of homepages. The administrator has the most features and the students the least on his home page.

TopClass has a built-in comprehensive tracking system, which depends on the users' unique usernames and passwords. The tracking features allow an instructor to evaluate all aspects of his/her Internet course.

The system also has a built-in discussion group feature, so that members of the class can communicate with each other. It also has a bulletin board feature, which instructors can use to send messages to their classes. The program is sold in various configurations depending on the number of concurrent users. Our license allows 50 concurrent users.

The hardware: We initially used Smart's desktop computer, a Macintosh Internet Server, to host TopClass. The program now runs on an iMac, housed in our Language Centre's computer administrator's room. Our Internet server program is Webstar, a product of Starnine.

Results

The actual conversion of the materials to the Internet: The conversion process of Mäkinen's course materials to the TopClass system, and hence to the WWW was accomplished within 70 hours and it proved relatively straightforward. However, we had problems with the actual course. Prior to the course, we updated TopClass from version 1.0 to 2.0. We unfortunately found that our 120 MHz Macintosh was not powerful enough to meet the demands of the new version, as it needed at least a 200 MHz computer. This meant that accessing the system was very slow. Much to our surprise some of our eight students regularly used the system, and provided us with invaluable feedback on the course content.

Discussion

We have now solved the problems we had in autumn 98 with our TopClass server by buying an iMac, and we will rerun the experiment this autumn. We now both feel quite comfortable using the system and we intend to make this year's course WWW more collaborative for the students taking part by getting them to use the discussion features of the program, and encouraging them to generate new materials from the Internet, by sharing relevant links with other course members within the system. We are aware of the opportunities that Internet courses offer for collaborative learning and have discussed them in an earlier paper (Mäkinen and Smart (1999).

There are other authoring programs available for teaching over the Internet. Atkinson (1999) has reviewed some of these programs, including the very popular Learning Space by Lotus, and WebCT written at the University of British Columbia. Neither of these programs run on the Macintosh. As we already have a huge investment in equipment and expertise in the Macintosh, and one of the aims of our project is to make the entire system, including the server, user-friendly, TopClass is for the time being our best choice.

The future for Web-based courses: Web based courses are at present especially suitable for courses which mainly involve text and graphics, such as the courses taught by the reading comprehension teachers at Helsinki University. Attempts to teach courses which involve speech on the Web, usually run into bandwidth and storage limitations. The bandwidth problem is only found with slow Internet connections. Fast connections such as the T1 ones within the University can transmit audio without any problems. But, as many of our students prefer to work on Net courses from home using their own computers, they would be subject to the 'World Wide Wait' if we offered them Web-based oral skills courses and they tried to do them at home. Anyone who has used streaming sound such as a Real Audio mediated radio broadcast with a 33.6 modem connected to a telephone line, would be conversant with these problems. Sound files are also quite large even when they are compressed, so it would be impractical to teach oral skills lessons over the Web with our present set up.

These limitations with Web based sounds are bound to be overcome in the future, with faster, cheaper, bigger, computer storage devices, and faster Internet home connections. We intend to extend our TopClass courses to students of Pharmacy this autumn, and we hope our colleagues who teach other languages will use TopClass to deliver their courses.

The future for other courses: We intend to tackle the oral skills component of our courses using CD-ROM based materials written in Authorware. The CD-ROMs will be available for the students to use at any of the University's numerous workstations. Their progress through the courses will be sent over the Internet to be recorded in a central database.

How we have conformed with the goals of the official Information Society: Our collaborative project is in line with the government's first goal : moving from once-and-for-all training to lifelong learning. Using a language involves life long learning, this is true for both native and non-native language users. As language teachers we always impress this fact on our students. Our language courses last for a fixed amount of weeks, but the language learning process is life long. We assume that the Internet is here to stay in all our lives, and that it will expand to provide more and more of an individual's educational needs in the future. So, our fledgling work with TopClass will serve help familiarise our students with one more method for lifelong learning.

Our work with TopClass and our other attempts to get to grips with writing computerised materials mean that we have been conforming with the governments fourth and fifth goals, which are respectively: a high level of teachers' professional skills and securing the development of information products and services.

As far as the government's last goal, building education and research networks into an open global network, is concerned we see ourselves and our work as small cogs in the big machine.

Our work continues, but we now feel that we are slowly emerging from the shadows to the full glare of an Information Society.

References:

Atkinson, Roger (1999) *Putting your unit on the web... Course server software for online teaching* http://cleo.murdoch.edu.au/teach/guide/res/examples/course-servers.html

High Level Group of Experts on the Social and Societal Aspects of the Information Society (1997) *Building the European Information Society for us all* http://www.ispo.cec.be/hleg/hleg.html

ICONS International Communication and Negotiation Simulation (n.d.) http://www.icons.umd.edu/

Kaplan, Howard (1999) *Building your own web course: The case for off the shelf component software.* http://howard.uml.edu/buildingweb/buildingweb.htm

Mäkinen, Maire (1992) *Reading while Listening and its Possible Applications in Self-access at Helsinki University Language Centre* unpublished M. A. dissertation for the University of Birmingham

Mäkinen, M, and Smart, D. (1999) *From a Tape to the Net: Two collaborative CALL Teaching Projects* Paper given at the conference of Collaboration and Learning in Virtual Environments in Jyväkylä, Finland

OPM The Information Strategies of the Ministry of Education and their Implementation (n.d.) http://www.minedu.fi/eopm/strategi/2_2.html

Tella, Seppo (1998) *The Concept of Media Education Revisited: From a Classificatory Analysis to a Rhizomatic Overview.* http://www.helsinki.fi/~tella/mep8tella.html

WBT Systems (n.d.) TopClass. http://www.wbtsystems.com/

Weir, C. J. and Roberts, J. R. (1994) *Evaluation in ELT* Blackwell: Oxford

CA-EAP: A MULTI-TASK SOFTWARE PACKAGE FOR THE TEACHING OF ACADEMIC WRITING

Jon Mills
University of Luton, UK

1. Introduction: This paper describes CA-EAP software, which has been developed, and continues to be developed by Jon Mills at the University of Luton. The purpose of CA-EAP is to provide online teaching materials for the *Academic English and Study Skills* module for first year undergraduate students who are studying for a degree at Luton University and whose first language is not English. This module attracts approximately 150 students who are taught by three teachers in classes of up to 20 students. Foreign students who are studying in what is not their first language need help with their English. However since they already have the difficulty of studying in what is not their first language, it was decided that English language support should not increase their workload. These modules, therefore, form part of the modular credit scheme which means that students who attend them obtain credit towards their degree. Students attend one 3-hour session per week, which takes place in a computer lab. CA-EAP provides all the materials for the writing component for this module. In all, CA-EAP provides approximately 40 hours of writing activities.

The syllabus is functional. CA-EAP aims to explain and provide practice in a number of language functions that are employed in academic discourse: definition, classification, cause and effect, comparison and contrast, illustration and exemplification, generalisation and qualification, analogy, evidence, interpretation of data, argument and thesis.

2. The Virtual Classroom: Mills (1997) describes the management of the computer mediated communication that takes place in the virtual classroom. Through a system of networked computers, students and their teacher are able to communicate in cyberspace. The virtual classroom is the area in which this computer mediated discourse takes place between class members. Virtual classroom management involves, amongst other things, the maintenance of links not only between human participants but also between human participants and androids. Androids include such automata as the on-line library catalogue, help files and on-line dictionaries (See Figure 1). CA-EAP provides seamless integration with the word-processor and a concordancer, and permits student's scripts to be exchanged via the server for peer critiquing.

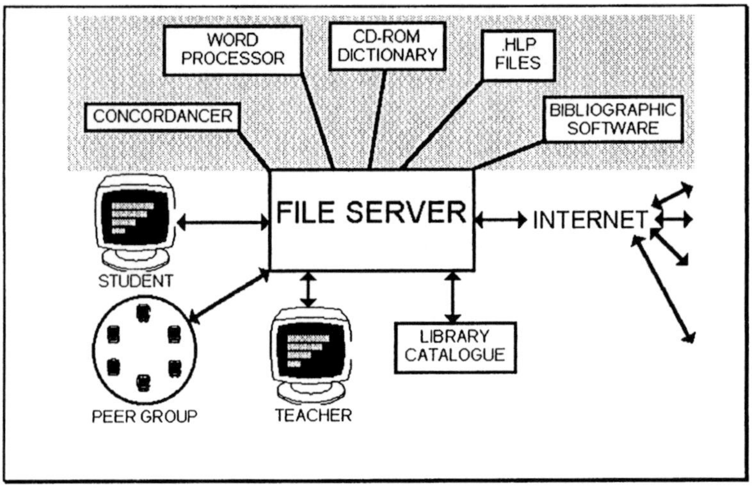

Figure 1

On-line communication in cyberspace focuses on the written form. Discussion is still possible; use of shared first language is still possible. However extra-linguistic and paralinguistic features are not communicated via the digital word. In class, facial expression, body language and tone of voice all contribute to the act of communication. On-line the only message is the text. This narrow expressive range brings about a focus on simple, clear and effective writing. The medium can foster a surprisingly close relationship between teacher and student. A detailed written comment somehow carries more authority and impact than spoken words. Students, eager to initiate a real dialogue, sharpen their writing skills still further as they argue their points. Successful computer communication demands a great deal of empathy between writer and reader. The writer is forced to put her/himself in the reader's place and anticipate what s/he needs.

The medium is particularly adapted to the teaching of argumentation. Students post a claim plus three reasons, each backed by evidence, plus a brief rebuttal of major counter-arguments. This elicits a powerful response from their peers, who pound the keyboards to argue specific points. The resulting position papers benefit from these on-line arguments by demonstrating far more rhetorical sensitivity, fewer broad generalities and a strong sense of arguing with reasons plus proof. One might argue that this experience could be duplicated by class discussion. Only partially so. Not only is the on-line debate a writing experience, but the entire discussion can be printed out or saved onto disk.

3. **Activity Typology:** Each lesson incorporates a variety of tasks and task types including pages of exposition, drills, short essay writing, peer critiquing and use of a concordancer.

Expository pages explain and exemplify the functions and their exponents for the lesson in question. This involves the passive intake of knowledge by the student. Figure 2 shows an expository page which forms part of a lesson to teach the rhetoric of comparison and contrast. This particular page shows the exponent, ‘X is virtually as long as ...’ or ‘X is almost as cheap as ....’

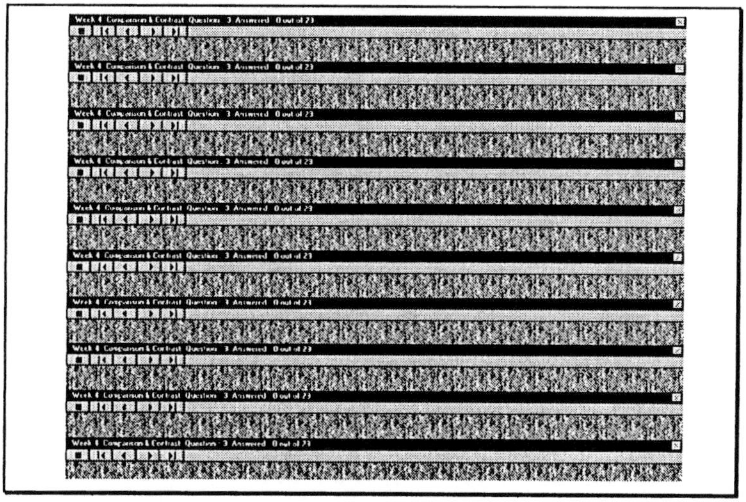

Figure 2

Drill type activities provide the student with the opportunity to practise the structures and vocabulary that have been encountered in the expository pages for the lesson that is being undertaken. Drill exercises are marked automatically by the computer and the student can work at their own pace. Three types of drill have been employed in CA-EAP: gap-fill, multiple choice and hot spot.

In the case of a gap-fill exercise, the student is required to fill the spaces in a given sentence in order to practise use of the exponent that is being taught. So for example in the exercise shown in Figure 3, the student is practising the comparison and contrast exponent that we saw in Figure 2. The answer is, of course, ‘The Thames is **nearly as** long **as** the Severn’.

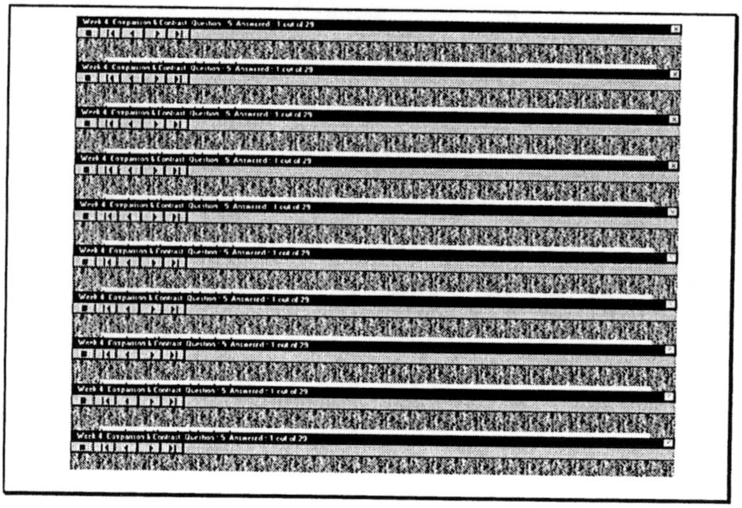

Figure 3

The multiple-choice exercise requires the student to distinguish the correct answer from a number of distracters. The example in Figure 4 is from a lesson on the rhetoric of definition and classification. A poor definition of the word 'lecturer' has been given and the student has to identify the reason why it is a poor definition.

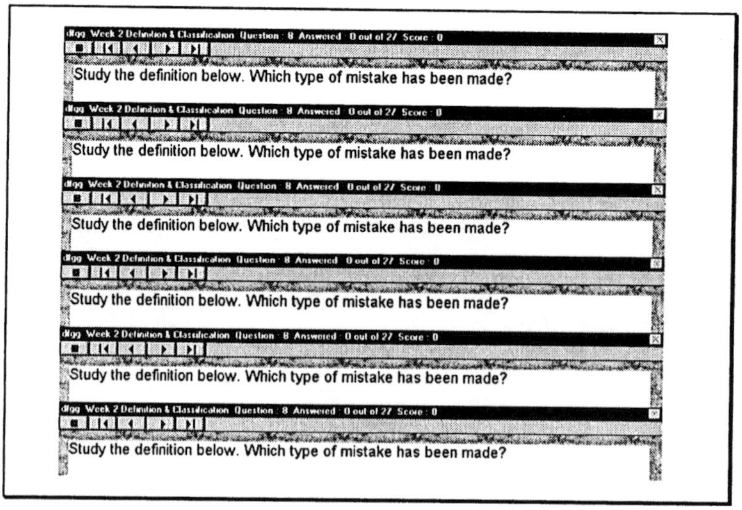

Figure 4

The hot spot exercise requires the user to answer the question by using the mouse to point at a specific location on the screen. In the exercise in Figure 5, this involves pointing at a specific sentence in a short text extract.

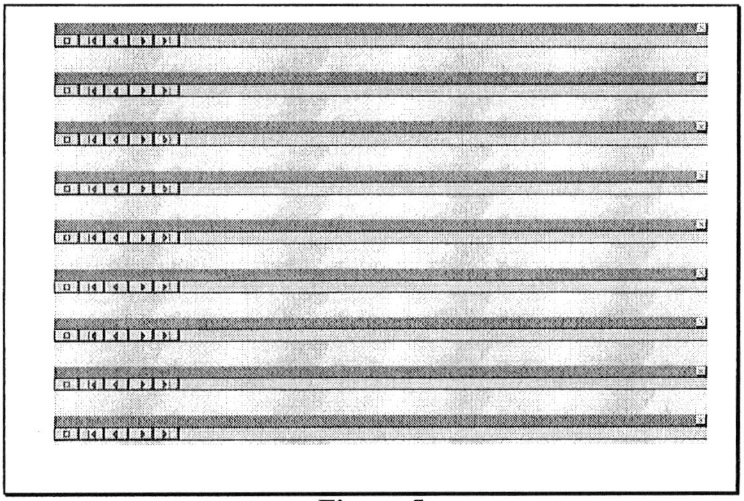

Figure 5

Drill activities are followed by writing tasks. In the example shown in Figure 6, the rubric for the task is given, then the student clicks on a button to start the word processor. CA-EAP makes a multi-media call to *MS-Word*. The rubric is given again in the word processor.

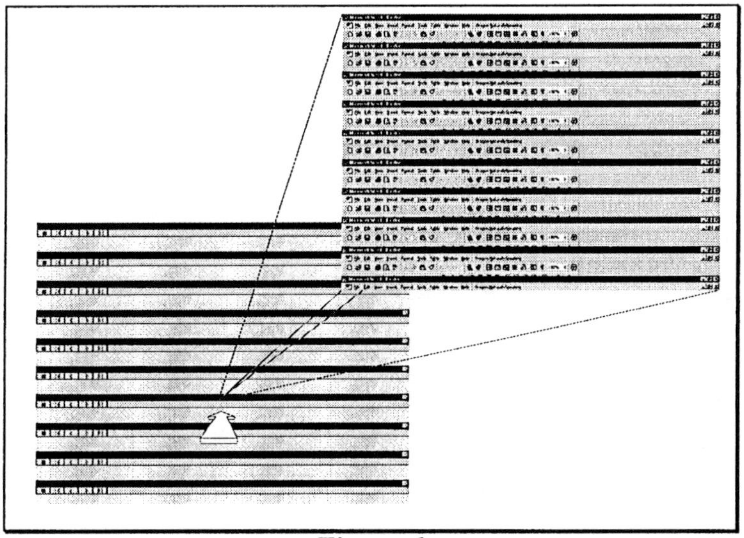

Figure 6

Peer critiquing helps students to develop their rhetorical skills by making the whole critiquing process active rather than passive. It brings about awareness of writing as process. One approach is to have students critique each other's first draft for content and organisation, and later proof read each other's second or third draft for form and mechanics.

The method works like this (see Figure 7). Students save their texts on the central fileserver using a pseudonym given to them by the teacher. Students are then allotted another student's text to download from the server. Working from a feedback sheet prepared by the teacher, students write the answer to the questions about the text on screen in front of them by inserting revision annotations into that text. When all the students have finished critiquing, the files are saved and the students retrieve their original files from the server. The original author reviews the revision marks in his/her text and accepts, rejects or ignores each change.

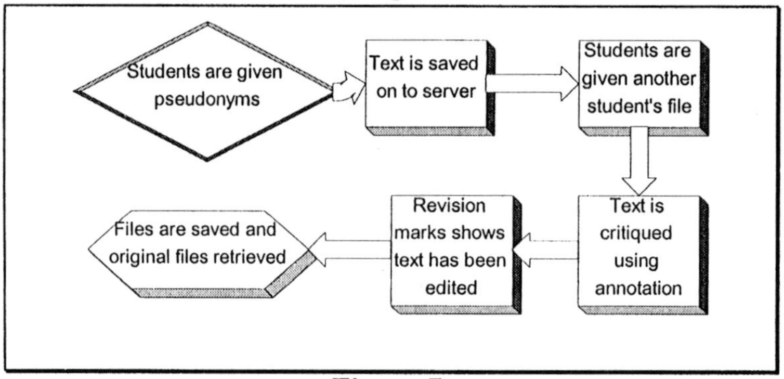

Figure 7

Recent research in America has shown that when students peer critique each other's work, less credibility is given to the work of female students even by other female students. For this reason, we have adopted a system whereby students are given pseudonyms, such as 'Chris' or 'Nic', which can refer to either sex. Students save their texts under their allotted pseudonyms (see Figure 8) and the texts are then exchanged in cyberspace for critiquing. The virtual classroom thus provides anonymity by which students not only become androgynous but also have their race, creed colour, etc. hidden. Shyer, more introverted students lose their inhibitions as they take on their new personas.

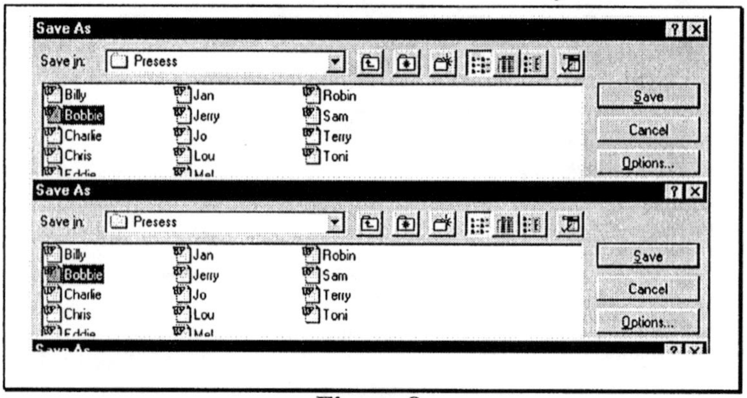

Figure 8

Next the students are given another student's text to critique. They do this by using *MS-Word*'s special revision marking facility. Revision marks help the critiquing process by showing the changes that have been made to a text since the last version. *MS-Word* uses special formatting, such as underlining, strikethrough characters and different colour to show edited text. In the example that we see in Figure 9, the student who is critiquing has decided that they think that 'It is **in** the south of Spain' should be 'It is **on** the south of Spain'. Of course the students who critique do not always get it right.

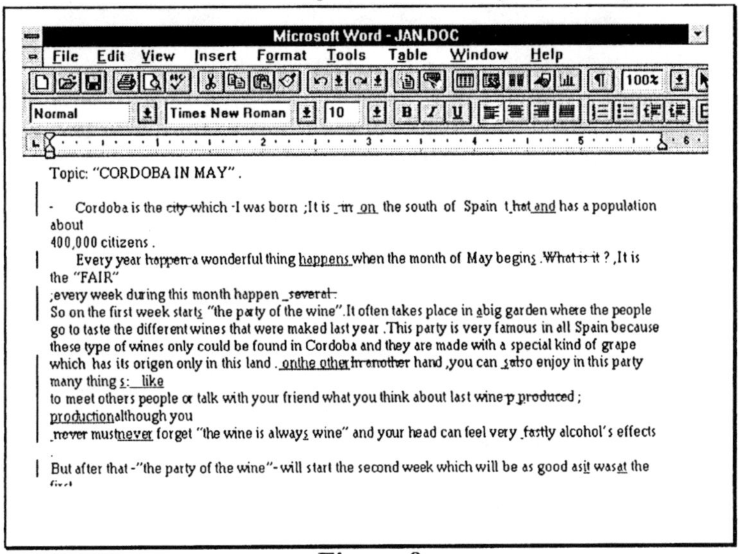

Figure 9

After critiquing the files are exchanged over the network so that each student receives their original text . At this stage the students can either accept or reject the corrections. When students are uncertain about the correctness of the revisions to their text they often ask the teacher to arbitrate. It is important not to simply give the student the 'correct' version. A teacher cannot always be available to support students. It is, therefore, vital that students learn how to find the 'correct' form on their own. In this situation, it is best to direct the student to obtain a concordance from an expert corpus so that the item in question may be compared with examples from authentic text. Let us suppose that a student has received the text shown in Figure 9. S/he has doubts about the revision of 'It is **in** the south of Spain' to 'It is **on** the south of Spain'. S/he uses *MicroConcord* concordancing software to obtain a concordance of 'the south' (see Figure 10). From this it can be seen that 'in the south' is the normal collocation for this usage. It can furthermore be observed from this concordance that native speakers of English sometimes spell 'south' beginning with a capital letter and sometimes beginning with a lower-case letter. (For further discussion on the use of concordancers in the foreign language class see Mills 1996b.)

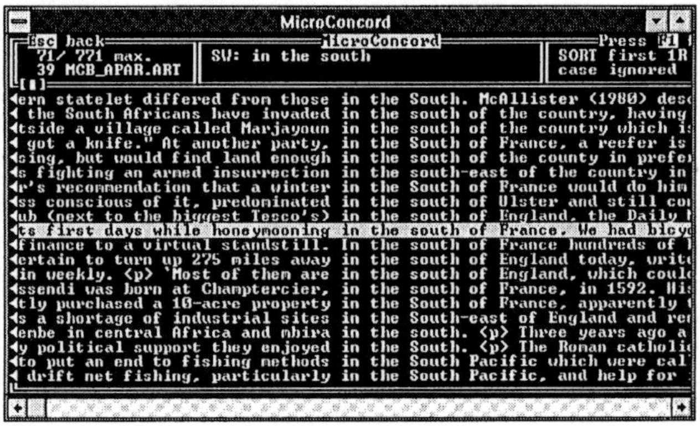

Figure 10

4. The Task Algorithm: Figure 11 shows how the various activities that comprise a lesson may be sequenced. CA-EAP is intended for classroom use with a teacher present. Students work at their own pace while reading expository pages and doing the drill tasks. However lock-step is necessary at various points during each lesson. For example, it is necessary to lock-step commencement of peer critiquing. It is necessary for the teacher to monitor students' progress and s/he may also wish to lock-step at other stages during the lesson, such as the commencement of the writing task.

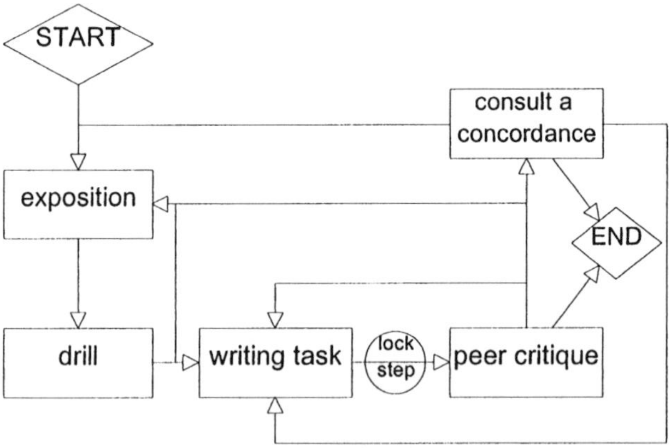

Figure 11

5. Discussion: CA-EAP has been found to have a number of strengths. It is robust; it is difficult to cause the system to crash. It is user friendly. Operation is on the whole fairly intuitive so that students and teachers rarely experience difficulty in using the system. It provides a variety of activities and activity types for each lesson. For much of the lesson, students are able to work at their own pace. On the whole, students report that they enjoy using the software and that they find the lessons helpful. Furthermore students like the anonymity that the virtual classroom provides. We have observed that our foreign students who attend the classes and use CA-EAP, demonstrate a great improvement in their academic writing. In fact, at the culmination of the course, they frequently display greater essay writing proficiency than our native speaker students who do not attend the classes.

On the other hand, there are some attributes with which we are not entirely satisfied. It has been observed that drill exercises don't always match the student's level of competence. In a class containing various levels of proficiency, some of the students may finish all the drill exercises quite quickly, whilst the less competent students require much more time. This can make it difficult to lock step at the commencement of writing activities. CA-EAP is not platform independent and requires *Qmark Presenter* to run. This means that, in its current state, CA-EAP cannot easily be made available to other institutions.

CA-EAP might be improved in a number of ways. Implementation in HTML with Java or Javascript applets would enable platform independence and facilitate distribution over a network. Alternatively the system could be compiled as a .EXE executable program. An intelligent tutoring system could be linked with the drill activities. This system could automatically adjust to student's level of competence for drill exercises and direct students to a help file after two failed attempts. An intelligent tutoring system could also be used in order to grammatically and semantically parse student input. This would facilitate more open ended drill activities in which students are required to type whole sentences rather than gap-fill or multiple choice responses. Another useful improvement would be to have the system automatically assign pseudonyms for peer critiquing.

Areas for future research and development include the integration intelligent tutoring and the development of drill exercises to teach certain aspects of literature review: summary, paraphrase, synthesis and referencing.

References:

Giltrow, J. (1990) *Academic Writing: How to Write Scholarly Prose* Broadview Press.

Jordan, R. R. (1997) *English for Academic Purposes: A Guide and Resource Book for Teachers* Cambridge: CUP.

MicroConcord Computer software. Oxford: OUP. IBM PC, XT, AT or PS/2 or compatible with minimum 175K RAM, hard disk and MS-DOS 2.11 or higher.

Mills, Jon (1996a) 'Computers in Applied Linguistics' *Solving Language Problems: From General to Applied Linguistics* ed. R.R.K. Hartmann Exeter Studies in Linguistics. Exeter: Exeter University Press. pp. 245-269. ISBN 0859894843.

Mills, Jon (1996b) 'Using a Concordancer with Advanced Level Students of EFL' EUROCALL94 - Technology Enhanced Language Learning in Theory and Practice, Pädagogiche Hochschule Karlsruhe, Germany, 15th-17th September 1994.

Mills, Jon (1997) 'Virtual Classroom Management and Communicative Writing Pedagogy' *Proceedings of 1996 European Writing Conferences: EARLI Special Interest Group Writing, Writing and Computers Association, University of Barcelona, 23-25 October 1996.* Barcelona: Universitat de Barcelona, Universitat Autònima de Barcelona. CD-ROM. ISBN 84-88795-36X.

Question Mark Designer Version 3.10 Computer software. N.p.: Question Mark Computing Ltd. (1996).

FINDING JOYS IN WRITING: A WEB-BASED EFL WRITING COURSE

Haruo Nishinoh
Doshisha University, Kyoto, Japan

Abstract: *In this paper I will examine the usability of a WWW system in college essay writing classes. In my classes of 1998, a small-scale WWW system was used to provide a bulletin board, computer manuals, and students' portfolios. The system enabled them to browse through and comment on their friends' essays while it gave students incentives to read and write. It also gave the teacher the ease to manage the class and to handle students' writings. Pros and cons of the usage of computers will also be discussed.*

1. Introduction: In Japan the study of English has been integrated in the school curricula in almost 99% of secondary (junior high and senior high) schools. The emphasis of English education has been placed upon learning grammar and reading by translation. This is in part due to the college entrance examination in which English plays an important role. However, historically speaking, this is in part due to the translation based foreign culture import started in Meiji Restoration in the mid 19th century. For Japan this has been one of the most important strategies of westernisation and industrialisation. Although there have been attempts since the late 1980s to communication based teaching methods, foreign language education remains fundamentally grounded in translation.

Just as reading has been based on translation, so has writing been based on translating Japanese passages into English. The purpose of translation is the reconfirmation of the knowledge of grammar, vocabulary and idiomatic expressions. In writing classes, students are rarely asked to express themselves in English, and when they are, it is often given as a part of drills called 'Jiyu Eisakubun', or free English composition. Nowadays many colleges and universities, especially private institutions, do not ask for writing skills as essential requisite qualifications at the entrance examinations. Due partly to the lack of further motivation and partly to the insufficiency of class hours, it is sometimes the case that college students' competence in English culminates at the entrance examination and then wanes as years go by.

English is a required subject for the first two years in most colleges and universities in Japan, and so it is in almost all the departments and faculties at Doshisha. At Doshisha, we offer approximately 550 English classes a week. With a few exceptions, students take two classes in English for two years. Most of the classes meet once a week. The majority (52%) of the classes are reading classes. Except for some advanced courses, relatively large class size (approximately 40 for reading and listening, and 30 for oral communication based courses) makes it difficult to integrate writing into the class activities. Currently 13 classes (both conventional and CAI/CALL; 2% of the English classes) are focusing on writing. These classes are offered as the electives for the second year students.

2. CAI/CALL Classes at Doshisha: Doshisha has a long history in English CAI/CALL education. We started English CAI classes in a computer laboratory in 1988. At present there are 10 CAI classes of which 8 are focused on writing. I have explored the possibility of using computers in English classes since 1992, and for the past two years I have been concentrating on WWW based writing classes. It is my view that the benefits of the use of computers can be best enjoyed in writing classes. In computer based writing classes students exercise their integrated skills in English, especially reading and writing, to the maximum. The WWW system, with its ease of disseminating information worldwide, will also give an ideal opportunity to the students to exercise their capability to write to the world, when Japan needs to express itself openly in international contexts.

3. Students' background: I had two sophomore writing classes in the fall semester of 1998, the last semester of our academic year. Each class had 25 students. Students' previous experience on computers varied widely, but very few had undergone extensive computer training before college. Although they all took another CAI reading class in the previous semester, most of the students did not even know how to type. This is because no instruction was given in using the computers other than on the drill machines. In order to function fully in my classes, students had to be active with computers. They had to be able to use computers skilfully as tools; as word processors, search tools, and hyper-media authoring tools. However, at the beginning we had to start with typing exercises.

4. Computer facilities: The classes were held in a computer lab, which was designed for general use. All the computers in this room were networked to a Campus Wide Information System, and were configured identically with Windows 95 as an operating system. Private directories were provided on a primary Web server for those faculty members who wished to create their home pages, but I found the NT server in our department far easier to use. This was chiefly because of the physical accessibility and the ease of network configuration of students' files and directories. I created two directories for my classes in the user area, and in each of them I put students' individual directories. A set of common ID and password protected the class directories from the outside access.

5. Software and use of network: In the classes I first asked students to use Microsoft Word for writing, but soon realised that this did not really help the students' learning process. This was because students soon became too much dependent on the automatic correction and spell checking functions. Therefore, we switched to Netscape with its composer function. One other software we frequently used was FTP Explorer. This software enables a file transfer by a simple drag-and-drop with a mouse.

I used the WWW system mainly as a bulletin board and for students' portfolios. At the beginning of the semester, I uploaded the syllabus and the class schedule. The date of each session was linked to a detailed instruction page. It was my weekly routine to create the page and upload it on to the network. On this page were posted the tasks and instructions for students' class activities for that week. The details of their homework assignments were also posted there. I also created manual pages in order to show how to use computers and software, and linked them to the instruction pages. During the class, when students completed the pages, they uploaded them to their individual directories on the server. Soon after, individual directories served as the students' portfolios.

6. Working in the class: Class activities consisted of typing, reading, research, writing and revising. The topic of the essays shifted from narrative self-introduction for the first essay, to self-reflective journals, and finally to expository team projects. At the beginning of the semester I had to dedicate two sessions exclusively to the introduction of computers and network functions. Since few students were skilled in typing, I had to start with the instruction for keyboarding. Initially at each session, half an hour was spent for typing training. I recorded the typing speed of each student. Students liked this, for it was the only scale by which their progress of any kind was 'visibly' — and objectively — measured.

6.1. The first project: Students started with simple sentences, as I introduced some related expressions and essential vocabulary. The first page they created was their self-introduction page, which was to become the top page of their home page. I asked them to include four sets of information: first, about themselves and their hometown; second, their academic interest and future goals; third, their club and extra curricular activities; and fourth, their hobbies and special interests. The four parts were written as components and later they were combined together to form an essay.

Although many of the students had read the syllabus and had known that this was a writing course, they were not quite ready to write anything. At the beginning of the semester I asked them how often and how much they wrote at all. Most of them replied they did not write at all on regular basis, even in Japanese. They did not even keep a diary. Most of them handed in some papers for the courses in the previous semester, but they said that no one properly taught them how to write. A few of them replied that they were accustomed to writing e-mail to their friends. In general, college students have very little training in writing, nor are they used to expressing themselves openly. Overcoming the initial psychological barrier and getting themselves on the track is the most important thing to do.

As they became skilled in typing, most of the students started to enjoy writing. We spent approximately four weeks completing the first essay. In the meantime I taught them how the WWW system functions and showed them the basic skills in searching for and finding the information they were looking for. I asked them to add relevant links to their departments and the faculties they belonged to, to the towns where they were from, etc. While they were doing this, they started to get involved in creating hyper-linked documents. For the first time they started to have fun in creative writing and, at the same time, they felt that they were fully in control of the incoming and outgoing information over the computer networks. The ease of editing and revising of the document was something new to them, and because of this they liked to write with computers.

I corrected their papers on weekly basis. I printed out their essays and with a marker underlined the passages where rewriting was necessary, adding comments on the content. Actual corrections of words and phrases were kept to a minimum. I asked the students to find out where and why they had the markings. I graded everything and every version they handed in.

6.2. The second project: After this self-introduction page, we wanted to move on to something more analytic and expository, but students found it quite difficult to find a topic to write on. In order to explore their interests, I asked them to write a series of journal entries, two to three a week, in order to keep track of what they did, what they found, what they thought and how they reacted — in short, how they were related to the society in general.

Although I expected them to find some topic in a social context, some of the students could only find personal interests. Generally students' interest in social affair is very limited. Newspapers and news magazines are readily available on campus in the library, but the majority of the students do not bother to read them through. However, for these students and, of course, for more willing students, the WWW functioned as a window to what was happening in the world. I created a list of URLs of relevant news sites for the students.

6.3. The final project: The final project was a team project. The purpose of this project was to tackle a theme that students could not handle individually. I asked each student to go through brainstorming to give ideas for the final project. After this, students who found they had the similar interests formed teams of up to four members so as to give their idea a more specific and concrete shape. Each team was to draw a plan, do research, present, and finally complete the Web-based documents. Some students wanted to work individually, so about twelve teams were formed in each class. Each team was asked to draw up a plan on paper and make a presentation of it to the class. The purpose of this presentation was to collect suggestions from the audience and introduce competitiveness among the students. It took approximately five weeks to complete this project.

The outcome was quite a remarkable one. One team did research on their hometown, Minamikawachi, a town near Osaka, introducing the past emperors' tombs and important archaeological remains around the town. With pictures they took and maps they drew they presented this in very well designed Web pages.

Another team created a home page for the Yomiuri Giants, a professional baseball team. In doing so, they added their own analyses of the team's performance. They critically evaluated each player on the team and assessed their contributions to the team. What was unique with this group was that they located relevant numerical data on the Internet, gathered them and processed them into visual form with spreadsheet software, thus making their points very clear in a graphic form.

Another team created a home page on the campus cafeterias. They knew that it would become very popular if they provided the detailed information as to when and where the cafeterias were less crowded during the lunch hours, and what were the 'hot' items in each cafeteria. To gather the details, they made a survey on this project. They asked for students' views on each cafeteria; its menus, services and its regulations. They also asked for cafeteria employees' views on the manners of student customers. In their pages they have analysed the gathered results. Using simple tools they drew elaborate layouts of each cafeteria, which provided convenient visual guides. Thus their pages became very appealing and persuasive.

Generally, when they worked together, students tended to be more active and interested in social issues. This seemed to be the result of the series of arguments and discussions they went through in the course of creating the pages. Sharing of ideas and working together produced a better outcome. On the whole, those students who worked together produced appealing pages, but those who worked alone were not as successful — there were fewer pages and less appealing ideas.

7. Evaluation and students' response: The final grade was given mostly by my evaluation of students' essays and partly by students' peer reviews. When the introduction page and journal pages were completed, I asked the students to give peer review of their friends' writings. Students sat in pairs and I asked them to evaluate each other's pages. Evaluation was done on the readability of the contents, 'clickability' of the links, and correctness of English. They were also asked to give comments that would help improve the quality of the pages. Punctuation was also checked. Each student reviewed at least two others' pages and later revised their own according to their friends' advice.

Similarly, all the team projects were evaluated by all classmates, too. The result was gathered and to this was added my own evaluation and grading. For me, evaluation of the team projects was a perplexing one. This was because I could not tell who was responsible for which part of the pages. Some students who were knowledgeable about computers seemed to have worked as engineers to create such tricks as framed pages and clickable maps. Some worked on graphics. Of course, there were those who took the initiative in the overall scheme and wrote large part of the documents. I soon abandoned the idea of giving each student a separate evaluation. I treated a team as a whole, giving each member of the team the same score. This final score was added to the ones from the other pages previously handed in, and each of the students received his/her individual final grade.

The class survey at the end of the semester shows that students were generally satisfied with the class. Students' contentment was firstly on their improvement of typing skills rather than on the improvement of their English. Secondly, they found it fun to handle the Web-based documents. They were also satisfied with what they wrote and the amount they wrote. Many of them pointed out that for the first time they found joy in expressing themselves in English and some came to have confidence in writing in English. Most of them unanimously pointed out that creating Web-based documents was more enjoyable than writing on paper.

8. How computers help students: From what I have experienced, I would like to point out some of the advantages of using computer facilities for the students.

Firstly and most importantly, computers help students' writing processes, brainstorming, outlining, sentence and paragraph writing and especially editing and revising. The ease of rewriting rids the students of the discomfort of rewriting and encourages their willingness to write.

Secondly, networked computers allow students to freely browse through and comment on their friends' works. Students soon become conscious that their writings are being read not only by teachers but also by their peers.

Thirdly, networked computers allow students access to materials they need. This includes not only newspapers and magazine articles on-line, but also conventional materials in the library through the library catalogue database.

Fourthly, creating HTML documents gives the students opportunities to enrich their writings. This is done by using pictures, drawings, and other digitally processed materials in the documents. Furthermore, creating links to relevant online sources gives authenticity and depth to their writings. Thus, either directed or voluntarily done, these HTML functions make students' writings more appealing and persuasive.

9. How computers help teachers: There are some advantages to teachers also, in using computers.

Firstly, computers, above everything, make it easier for teachers to save students' works. This is done by copying the whole directory into another with a drag of the mouse. The saved files make it easy to keep track of students' revising process.

Secondly, computers allow teachers and students to communicate asynchronously with each other. In my classes teacher-to-student communication was carried out by both e-mail and bulletin board, and student-to-student communication was done by e-mail. This feature is quite important and convenient in a large institution like Doshisha.

Thirdly, by delivering instructions and materials through computer networks, teachers' burden of handing out classroom materials can be greatly lessened.

Fourthly, by creating the documents in an initially closed, protected directory, students enjoyed the security and privacy. This is also necessary when the students handle copyrighted materials.

Fifthly, accumulated students' writings can be used for further analyses. Although crude in quality, a collection of students' writings forms a learner corpus of Japanese students. An analysis of their writings will give us suggestions regarding the nature of what they write and for guidance of their English usage.

10. Some drawbacks and solutions: Lastly, however, I have to point out that computer-based writing class has some drawbacks.

First of all, there are always some students who are not fit to use computers. Most students, even when they did not know that they were going to use computers, overcame difficulties, but there are some who seem to be just unable to bear the 'virtuality' of computing. These students drop out at an early stage.

Secondly, there is the problem of plagiarism. Any digital material is very easy to copy. In 1998 classes, despite my repeated warnings, two students handed in copied materials, one copied from a printed magazine and the other directly from an Internet page. The former admitted that she did so, and rewrote the essay, but the latter was adamant that his writing was original. I had to fail him, for I searched the Web and located the exact document from which he copied his page.

Thirdly, for a novice user of the Internet, it is difficult to find useful materials to read. In order to raise the students' consciousness of social affairs, a selected collection of topical essays is needed. Most of the students look for the Internet to find some. However, what they retrieve is not always worth reading, for there are so many worthless personal views and opinions now posted on the Internet. A novice user cannot discriminate useful materials from useless ones.

Fourthly, it is often difficult to keep track of what students read. The materials that are obtained via the Internet are evanescent and ephemeral in nature. Unless they are not wisely printed out or properly bookmarked, it is hard to encounter the same materials again.

Fifthly, in computer classes, where students tend not to write down on paper, enriching their vocabulary and instructing them in the correct usage of English can often be difficult.

One possible solution to the above problems will be to create an article archive into which teachers store useful essays and news articles. This is relatively easy to do when the college or university subscribes to such commercial database like LEXIS-NEXIS. In order to supply necessary vocabulary and to provide the examples of correct usage, lists of appropriate words and phrases should be developed. Drill-type exercises may work well for this purpose.

I find my students, with their grammar-translation background, are ready for writing. With some improvement in methodological and technical details, we should be able to awaken the students' enthusiasm and boost their language skills to a higher level.

CREATING HYPERMEDIA LEARNING ENVIRONMENTS: SOME GUIDELINES FOR LEARNER-CENTRED DESIGN

Mark Peterson
Japan Advanced Institute of Science and Technology, Japan

Abstract
This paper will propose a provisional set of design guidelines applicable to the creation of hypermedia based language learning environments. These guidelines will draw on the findings of research from a number of fields, in an attempt to assist language educators in the task of creating activities for distributed learning environments.

Introduction: The emergence of the internet as a potential learning environment has had a great impact on many areas of education and language education has been no exception to this trend. Over the past few years increasing numbers of language educators have attempted to create network mediated learning activities (Peterson 1998 a). However at present, there remains relatively little domain specific information to assist the language educator in the task of hypermedia design (Hemard 1997). This paper will draw on the findings of relevant research drawn from the areas of cognitive science, ESL pedagogy, instructional design (ID), human-computer interaction (HCI) and SLA in order to assist educators in the task of designing to facilitate L2 knowledge representation and construction.

Cognitive Science and Hypermedia Design: Cognitive learning theory provides educators with a number of insights that may guide the process of creating hypermedia CALL environments. Although a consensus has yet to emerge, many proponents of cognitive views of learning stress that language learning is a complex cognitive process that centres on the processing of information (Ellis 1990). Cognitive learning theory emphasises the importance of creating learning environments that engage learners (Jonassen 1997) and facilitate the difficult process of cognitive restructuring (O'Malley et al 1987). From this perspective, cognitive overhead must be reduced in order for new schema to be assimilated and for the proceduralisation of new knowledge to take place (Bialystock 1988). Moreover a further factor may make cognitive views of learning an important influence on hypermedia CALL. Plass (1998: 38) has observed that in the context of interface design, cognitive views of learning are the only perspectives that put learner needs and learning tasks at the forefront of the design process. Plass (1998) recommends that the language learning interface must be deigned to support the cognitive processes involved in SLA. From the perspective of cognitive learning theory, hypermedia based language learning activities should therefore be designed to help learners manage cognitive load while at the same time provide opportunities for cognitive restructuring.

Pedagogy, SLA Research and Hypermedia Design. Two main developments in the field of ESL pedagogy are relevant to the development of hypermedia learning environments. The contemporary focus on the importance of needs analysis has been noted by a number of authors (Johnson 1989, Munby 1978). In the authors view educators should conduct a through needs analysis of before embarking on any web site development project Peterson (1998 b). As the results of such an analysis will enable the individual site designer to more effectively identify and address specific learner needs. Recent trends in language teaching pedagogy (influenced in part by developments in SLA research) further stress the issues of learning styles and developing learners' proficiency Omaggio (1986). These perspectives emphasise the provision of authentic meaning based communicative tasks, that provide access to a range of learning activities compatible with a variety of learning styles (Peterson 1998 a).
Drawing on the findings of recent SLA research, Chappelle (1998) has made the following recommendations that may be used to inform the design of hypermedia learning environments:

1) The linguistic characteristics of TL input need to be made salient. This may be achieved through the use of colour or alternatively highlighting.

2) Offer modifications of linguistic input. Chappelle (1998: 26) proposes that modification of input may be facilitated through the use of repetition, simplification, decreased speed, the use of reference materials and change of input mode.

3) Provide opportunities for learners to produce comprehensible output. Speech recognition software may be used to enhance interaction between the learner and the software. An alternative would be to incorporate into a site text based internet chat rooms, such as the MOO Schmooze University.

4) Create affordances that enable learners to identify their errors. Designers may incorporate error indexes into a hypermedia web site.

5) Provide means for learners to correct their output. Learners will require access to error specific help.

6) Support interaction between the learner and the software. Interaction may be facilitated by the use of speech recognition software, interactive online quizzes and bulletin boards.

7) Learning tasks must focus the learner's attention on achieving a communicative task. This approach could be supported by providing learners with access (within a hypermedia web site) to video or synchronous email conferencing software.

General Principles of Hypermedia Design: General principles applicable to hypermedia design include the brevity (Lynch 1998), clarity (Tufte 1990) and consistency (Shneiderman 1998). In terms of interface design, the following factors have been identified in the literature as being of primary importance:

***Colour*:** In hypermedia web sites colour is best used sparingly to draw attention to tasks (Brown 1986: 66). The use of colour can increase the information resolution of a computer screen (Tufte1990: 89), however the overuse of colour may cause visual clutter and confuse users (Apple 1992: 264). Shneiderman (1998) recommends that designers use no more than 4 to 7 colours in a display.

Incompatible colour combinations such as red/green, blue/yellow, green/blue and red/blue should be avoided (Hemard 1997:21). Blue and white backgrounds have been found to have the lowest user error rates (Shneiderman 1998). Designers should also be aware of such issues as colour blindness and popular expectations regarding colours.

Text: Designers are advised to use fonts specifically designed for low resolution computer screens; MS Sans-serif, MS Serif, Macintosh Geneva and New York are examples of these types of font. Consistency in font use (Lynch 1994) and the inclusion of a left margin in sites (Siegel 1996: 79) is perceived as facilitating on screen reading. Text is best viewed in logically arranged chunks (Shneiderman 1998), as long screens of text are difficult to read on computer screens. Hunter (1998) recommends keeping text lines short when possible and Hemard (1997: 22), notes that optimum line spacing should be 1.5 or a double line depending on text length. Blinking text, underlines and upper case characters are best avoided, as the overuse of these elements may reduce the prominence of important information (Berkeley 1996). Siegel (1996: 79) advises including a left margin on all screens that contain extensive amounts of text.

Structure: The literature emphasises the importance of providing consistently structured interfaces characterised by the use of hierarchy and sequentialisation.
The hypermedia interface should be designed to afford cognitive scaffolding (Jacobson & Archodidou), through the use of frames and tables. Graphic map s and images may be used to show interrelationships and concepts. Designers should note that the use of large graphic images may impose lengthy download times for some users (Peterson 1998 a). In structuring hypermedia learning environments designers may utilise the concept of progressive disclosure (Apple 1992: 35). The basis of this approach is the creation of simple choice options that provide access to more complex choices and information. In an example of this technique, a designer may limit the number links from a node in order to avoid overwhelming learners. In a variation of this concept, buttons may be created that display a number of alternative choices. Designing for progressive disclosure promotes exploratory learning by enabling learners to access a richer learning environment at their own pace.

Hypermedia learning environments should provide simple easy to understand navigational metaphors that are utilised consistently throughout a site. User friendly interfaces provide learners with simple error handling and informative feedback. An exit icon or return to home link should be included on all screens. Data entry procedures should be as simple possible. In large sites, the inclusion of a site based search engine facilitates navigation.

***Metacognition*:** Effective network based hypermedia learning activities are designed to encourage metacognition; the process of learners cognitive self monitoring (Gange & Dick 1983). Metacognition may be facilitated through the provision of on screen feedback mechanisms such as mailto links or bulletin boards.

***Rapid prototyping (Trip & Bechelmeyer 1990)*:** Designers are advised to pilot projects. The feedback gained from learners and fellow educators, will prove invaluable in enhancing the effectiveness of a hypermedia project.

***Audio and video*:** Designers area advised to use high quality audio and video relevant to the content of the site.

Conclusion. The guidelines proposed in this paper represent an attempt to assist the individual language educator in the task of hypermedia design. These guidelines are provisional and may be interpreted by the individual designer to meet their needs. Given the limited nature of research in this field, further research is needed in order to deepen understanding of the nature of network based language learning. Promising areas for future research include investigation of learners mental models (Hemard 1999), individual learner differences and the role of structure in hypermedia design (Hunter 1998). As authoring technology becomes increasingly accessible, the challenge for educators lies in utilising the potential of hypermedia to the benefit of learners.

References:

Apple Computer Inc. (1992). *Macintosh human interface guidelines*. Addison-Wesley.
Berkeley Digital Library Sunsite. (1996). Guidelines for web document style and design. Retrieved July 15, 1997 from the World Wide Web: http://sunsite.berkeley.edu/Web/guidelines.html
Bialystock, E. (1988). Psycholinguistic dimensions of second language proficiency. In M. Sharwood-Smith, & W. Rutherford, (Eds.), *Grammar and Second Language Teaching*. Massachusetts: Newbury House.
Brown, C. M. (1988). *Human-computer interface design guidelines*. New York: Ablex.
Chapelle, C. A. (1998). 'Multimedia CALL: Lessons to be learned from research on instructed SLA', *Language Learning & Technology* 2, (1), 22-34.
Ellis, R. (1990). *Instructed second language acquisition*. Oxford: Blackwell.
Gange, R. M., & Dick, W. (1983). 'Instructional psychology', *Annual Review of Psychology* 34, 261-295.
Hemard, D. P. (1997). 'Design principles and guidelines for authoring hypermedia learning applications'. *System 25* (1), 9-27.
Hemard, D. P. (1999). 'Knowledge representations in hypermedia CALL authoring: Conception and evaluation' *Computer Assisted Language Learning* 11, (3).

Hunter, L. (1998). 'Text nouveau visible structure in text presentation', *Computer Assisted Language Learning* 11 (4), 363-379.
Jacobson, M. J., & Archodidou, A. (in press). 'The Knowledge Mediator Framework: Toward the design of hypermedia tools for learning', In M. J. Jacobson, & R. J. Kozma (Eds.), *Innovations in science and mathematics education: Advanced designs for technologies of learning*. Mahwah, NJ: Erlbaum.
Johnson, R. K. (1989). (Ed.) *The second language curriculum*. Cambridge: Cambridge University Press.
Jonassen, D. H., (1996). *Computers in the classroom: Mindtools for critical thinking*. Ohio: Merrill.
Lynch, J. (1994). 'Visual design of the user interface: Part 2 graphics in the interface', *Journal of Biocommunication* 21 (2), 6-15.
Lynch. J. (1997). Web style guide. Retrieved March 10 1998 from the World wide web: http://info.med.yale.edu/caim/manual/contents.html
Munby, J. (1978). *Communicative syllabus design*. Cambridge: Cambridge University Press.
Omaggio, A. C. (1986). *Teaching language in context: Proficiency-oriented instruction*. Boston: Heinle and Heinle.
O'Malley, J. M., Chamot, A. U., Walker, C. (1987). 'Some applications of cognitive learning theory to second language acquisition', *Studies in Second Language Acquisition*.
Peterson, M. (1998 a). 'Creating hypermedia learning environments: Guidelines for designers' *Computer Assisted Language Learning* 11 (2), 115-124.
Peterson, M. (1998 b). 'The virtual learning environment: The design of a website for language learning'. *Computer Assisted Language Learning* 11 (4), 34 9-361.
Plass, J. L. (1998). 'Design and evaluation of the user interface of foreign language multimedia software a cognition approach', *Language Learning and Technology* 2 (1), 35-45.
Siegel, D. (1996). *Creating killer web sites: The art of third generation site design*. Indianapolis: Hayden Books.
Shneiderman, B. (1997). *Designing the user interface: Strategies for effective human-computer interaction*. Reading, Addison-Wesley.
Tufte, E. R. (1990). *Envisioning information*. Connecticut: Graphics Press.
Trip, S. D. & Bichelmeyer, B. (1990). 'Rapid prototyping: An alternative instructional design strategy', *Educational Technology Research and Development* 38 (1), 31-44.

RUSSIAN LANGUAGE LEARNING ON THE WEB

Stella Rock & Natalia Tronenko
University of Sussex, UK

Introduction: The importance of integrating individual CALL work with the total programme of language instruction, including the classroom, cannot be underestimated. Our current concern is to make language teaching more responsive to the needs of the recipients and to incorporate use of Internet resources into the teaching of language, literature and history courses available to students at Sussex University.

Our package is designed with attention to the specific educational context and its various activities are derived from needs and real problems experienced by the students. To maximise relevance the following factors were taken into account: students' motivation; learning styles; learning strategies; previous learning experience and course level.

1. Motivation. Our concern is to ensure that methodologies used for other language programmes are not simply transferred wholesale from one context to another. To maximise its impact and increase interest among students our package is designed with attention to their specific educational needs. We have had the freedom to devise activities which, after preliminary taster sessions of other language packages we considered important to concentrate on. In addition to maximum relevance to other courses, positive motivation is obtained through a stimulating layout and no sense of failure. The combination of these factors will ensure the consolidation of prior knowledge and facilitate learning of new concepts and phrases.

2. Learning Styles. Although student interaction and involvement in shared activities are considered to be important for the efficient use of CALL facilities, this method may not necessarily be suitable for all learners, since not all of them respond equally well to co-operative techniques. Some students may require more private opportunities before they feel comfortable about working closely in a team with others. Our package provides many activities for those who prefer to work individually and do not appreciate the value of competition.

3. Learning Strategies. The short-term goals of every lesson involving the use of this package are elaboration of the main four language skills: reading, writing, listening and speaking. The long-term goal is the development of independent techniques in processing literary texts. This package is a clear case of explicit instruction in cognitive processes that is guided by a specific curriculum and yet stimulates the construction of knowledge of processing strategies of the texts to which they are applied. On the one hand, the ready-made exercises gain in practical convenience and remain valuable as a tutor-led or independent supplementary activity; on the other hand, they could be adapted and made relevant to a specific teaching context: they may be tailored in such a way that one can use them for students of different proficiency and ability levels and for different types of sessions in or outside the classroom. In the classroom, the use of various strategies may be supported by teacher prompts. Using these web pages for self-study, students can work at their own pace and complete the tasks in their own time.

4. Proficiency Level. Many activities provided are designed in such a way that they can be used with either little or no teacher involvement. For example, intermediate and advanced students can tackle most of the grammar exercises independently, and students of any proficiency level are able to use historical or literary comments without guidance. However, more teacher prompting and assistance (e.g. specially designed work-sheets, cue cards and charts) is required for less experienced beginner and post-beginner level students tackling the exercises offered under the EXERCISES and VIDEO options.

CONCEPTION AND DESIGN

The *Russian Language Learning on the Web* project at Sussex sprang partly from the realisation that student IT skills, particularly amongst Humanities students, were fairly poor. After the creation of a *Russian Studies at Sussex* web page (http://www.sussex.ac.uk/Units/russian), and some initial seminars on Russian material currently available on the Web, we felt that learning by computer was a method that students respond enthusiastically to. The type of material available however was not adequate for our needs, and a number of technical problems accessing and using other university sites meant that creating our own interactive, web-based language learning package was the most viable option. We felt that using the package would not only reinforce conventional classroom learning, but also improve student proficiency of Internet use, an increasingly vital research skill.

The primary design criterion for the web pages was simplicity. Because we wanted a package that would build student confidence, to be used by students with little experience of the Internet as well as the proficient, designing a clear layout with a fixed menu was the first goal. With a minimum of on-screen instructions, the students should be able to work their way through the individual author options, which all offer the same choices: HISTORY, CRITICISM, TEXT, TRANSLATION, EXERCISES, GRAMMAR, AUDIO, and VIDEO.

From the HOME page, users can select a non-frames option if working with a browser that does not support frames. All Sussex computers are frames capable, but it was felt that the choice should be provided since students working from home might not have this option. The MORE button leads to pages directed primarily at teachers who want more information on the creation and design of the package, or who wish to make comments/suggestions on the material.

The basic frames format offers students a series of activity options centred on one work by a Russian author. To date, only one author, Pushkin, has been completed, since technical problems and the steep learning curve necessary to overcome them took up far more time than expected. The student selects an author, and the initial page provides brief information and several links to external biographical pages. They may then choose between the HISTORY or CRITICISM buttons which lead to essays in English, with hypertext links to external pages on relevant topics, or going straight to the TEXT Russian. The historical and literary criticism essays are written by Sussex faculty and postgraduates specially for the Project, and our intention is to translate them and offer the choice of reading them in Russian for more advanced students. The external links are deliberately limited, since we intend the students to approach the material in a focused fashion, and the frames format ensures that students can easily return to the author they are working with.

The Russian text contains numerous hypertext links to vocabulary and grammar points made in a separate frame at the bottom of the text page, and these points are reinforced by the interactive EXERCISES offered as a separate option. The GRAMMAR option is the only button (other than the AUTHORS and HOME) which remains constant and leads to the same shared page from every author option.

The students may also listen to an AUDIO version while reading a stressed version of the text. While the use of bold to indicate the stressed syllable is far from ideal, we were unable to find a commonly available stressed Cyrillic font. The Leeds font for example has not been installed on campus computers, and even if we managed to persuade the Computing Service to provide it, we felt that students working from home would be unlikely to overcome this difficulty. Other options, such as italics and colour made the text very difficult to read.

Choosing the TRANSLATION option allows learners to read a parallel text in English and Russian, in table format. We have tried various options with students — English and Russian in separate frames with scroll bars to move each version independently, and English only, but the fixed table version was the most popular. The translations are our own, and deliberately Nabokovian, sacrificing English style for the sake of clearly rendering the Russian original.

The VIDEO option currently under construction contains QuickTime video – for Pushkin, a dialogue between native speakers about the text and a short interview with a Russian child about Pushkin.

The Choice of Literary Texts. The package is literature based, designed to complement the Literature and History options offered at the University of Sussex. Our faculty takes an inter-disciplinary approach to Russian Studies, and it was felt that this should be reflected in the overall design. The choice of literary texts was determined by several factors: their brevity and simplicity (i.e. the nature and difficulty of the texts); historical and cultural context in which the texts are set and students' motivation to understand and remember their content. We selected literary works with interesting themes or historical relevance that would complement the set texts and topics. Authors from the second year literature course options *Russian Literature and Thought from Pushkin to the Symbolists* and *Writers and Revolution* were chosen — Pushkin, Gogol, Tolstoy and Blok, and texts with interesting themes or historical relevance that students would not necessarily be familiar with were selected. Thus the Pushkin story *The Blizzard* is not one usually studied by the second year students, but is set during the Napoleonic War, which is of immense significance in the history of nineteenth century Russia. Gogol's *One Night in May, or The Drowned Maiden* was chosen because of its use of folkloric imagery and themes, and Tolstoy's parable *The Candle* because of its insight into peasant life and mentality, as well as the author's 'post-crisis' period of literary creativity. Blok's *The Twelve,* possibly the best known of the four, was chosen because of its historical significance as an early literary response to the Revolution.

Initially, we took the full texts of the Pushkin and Tolstoy short stories (7 pages each). However, trial workshops with Sussex University students showed that if the texts are longer than 3 pages, they would rather print them out than read from the screen, which does not further our aim to encourage students to use the IT resources. For this reason, it has been decided to provide reading, listening, vocabulary and grammar exercises only for selected extracts from remaining literary works (those by Gogol' and Blok, and any others that we may add in future), but to supply historical and literary comments referring to the whole texts. As to the Pushkin and Tolstoy stories, we suggest dividing the texts and accompanying exercises into several parts to ensure their thorough, step-by-step analysis.

Our paper focuses mainly on the description of possible activities based on the Pushkin short story *The Blizzard*. Stylistically and syntactically, it stands out when compared with many of his other works. A 'sparing use of epithets, similes, and metaphors; a great reliance on verbs; brevity; an exact material frame of reference; and an emphasis on actions rather than feelings'[1] are characteristic of this text and the other four stories published as 'The Tales of Belkin'. 70 percent of the sentences in *The Blizzard* are simple sentences. 'Out of a total of 238 sentences, only in 20 to 25 is the basic subject-predicate-object order of words reversed to any marked degree. There is only one simile in the whole story. Epithets usually stand alone, rarely come in pairs, never in clusters of three or more. Close to a third of the vocabulary consists of verbs; the share of adjectives is less than 10 percent'.[2] It is expected that due to the aforementioned peculiarities of the chosen text students should find it easier to focus on problematic areas in their grammar

---

[1] A. Z. Lezhnev quoted in Paul Debreczeny, *The Other Pushkin* (Stanford University Press, California 1983) p. 94

[2] ibid. p. 94

and vocabulary, without being distracted by complex syntactic structures and experimental stylistic patterns.

Prerequisites for Using the Website. The layout of our website is simple and easy to use; it does not require explicit instruction, which will save a lot of precious time during the tutor-led sessions and encourage students to use the package individually. Nevertheless, there are the following prerequisites for using it:

1. Students must have prior experience of using Internet facilities.
Special interactive tutorials outside the curriculum are organised to ensure that all students studying Russian at Sussex are familiar with using computer facilities and word-processing in Cyrillic. Materials have been designed to explain and practice basic techniques.

2. CALL activities must be integrated into the language teaching curriculum.
Not all courses chosen by students involve the use of Internet, however, our aim is to encourage both students and lecturers teaching related subjects to incorporate it in the range of their activities; hence, the interdisciplinary approach that has been employed for the programme development. A special tutorial will be given to lecturers in the Autumn term 1999 to ensure that this medium becomes a familiar teaching instrument for them. Sufficient time needs to be provided for students to work on the computers, therefore students must have regular access to computing facilities during and outside of class time.

3. Opportunities for collaboration and peer support must be provided.
Using computer-based resources encourages student interaction and offers excellent opportunities for joint activities in pairs or groups. Such collaboration will ensure a balance between concentration on issues discussed and taught in the classroom and finding their own areas of interest.

Technical Issues. The primary aim of the project was to create the best possible resource for Sussex students, and how the site would look and sound to off-campus users was a secondary consideration. The way in which the Sussex student computers are configured caused us a number of problems which may not be relevant to all those present, but basically the issues we confronted are as follows:

1. Choice of font and Cyrillic encoding.
   As indicated above, there isn't a commonly available stressed font that we are aware of, so we have been unable to use stress marks. We opted for WIN encoding, and inserting the line <META HTTP-EQUIV='Content-Type' CONTENT='text/html; charset=windows-1251'> at the top of each page tells the browser to switch to Cyrillic fonts. FrontPage Editor, which we used to create the pages, does not show Cyrillic in HTML format, but otherwise was perfectly adequate.

We used Cuneiform Gold OCR software (a trial version is downloadable from the NET) to scan and recognise Cyrillic texts, which worked reasonably well.

2. Cyrillic also caused problems while we were creating the exercise pages. The exercises we designed were inspired by the freeware Hot Potatoes exercise authoring package by Half-baked Software, which can be found at http://web.uvic.ca/hrd/halfbaked/ Hot Potatoes doesn't support Cyrillic, and can only be used for Roman alphabet languages. We had to use multiple choice options rather than fill-in-the-blanks as we were unable to type in Cyrillic in HTML form text boxes. Campus computers use Netscape 4.06 on NT4, which has a bug preventing use of foreign scripts in these areas. Further details can be found at http://ourworld.compuserve.com/homepages/Paul_Gorodyansky/cwww_eng.htm # formsin4

3. The video page was created with the aid of our multimedia specialist at Sussex, who compressed and edited digital video footage using MediaCleaner Pro and Adobe Premiere, and created QuickTime files which we embedded on the page. The outstanding problem here is that the video clips degraded significantly when processed for the Web.
The original footage of the student dialogue was filmed in a room unsuited for the purpose, and there does not seem to be a technical remedy for the resulting poor sound quality. The sound of the interview clip is good, but the poor lighting while filming means that it appears almost black on screen. Limited funding gave us no option but to film the clips ourselves, without technical support, and we intend to replace them as soon as possible.

4. The audio page was more difficult. We experimented with WAV files, using JavaScript in an attempt to provide a variety of control options for the students, but finally opted for embedded RealAudio controls next to each paragraph. We also decided against using WAV files due to their size and therefore download time; although the primary audience is on the local network, the quality of RealAudio files is adequate for students and they begin playing faster — students do not have to wait for the files to fully download before they hear them.

Exercises. There are four groups of interactive exercises accompanying the literary text of a particular author. They are offered as two separate options: the EXERCISES option includes grammar, reading comprehension and vocabulary exercises, and the VIDEO option provides authentic material for listening comprehension. Grammar exercises are designed to assist students in tackling the most difficult grammar topics and are suitable for intermediate and advanced students. Reading comprehension, listening and vocabulary exercises can be used by students of all levels with either little or no teacher involvement for intermediate and advanced students, and with more prompting for less experienced students. All exercises under the EXERCISE option are supplied with feedback given in a separate frame at the bottom of the exercise page and provide the score reflecting students' progress in a specific activity. Grammar mistakes are analysed and presented in the form of comments on each particular example. Students may also look for grammar explanations relevant to the chosen exercise by clicking on the GRAMMAR button, if necessary. Reading comprehension exercises include explanatory commentaries in the case of a wrong answer. Vocabulary exercises allow several attempts to fill the gap with the missing word, and the number of attempts is taken into account for scoring. Listening exercises based on video recordings of contextually relevant interviews and dialogues can, if required, be accompanied with the scripts.

1. Reading Comprehension Exercises

The purposes of reading, its rate and focus were taken into account when writing comments and designing tasks. The aim is to teach students how to be active readers and make associations between their prior knowledge and content encountered in the text; and how to predict and summarise as they read. For example, when encountering a new word in the text, the reader can skip it, use context clues to infer its meaning, guess what the meaning might be, reread for additional clues to meaning, or, finally, if all else fails, click on the TRANSLATION button to bring up a parallel English/Russian text.

In order to increase the quality of reading comprehension and develop good reading skills students are advised to approach every text adapting their use of strategies to the demands of the text and situation. Active processing of the text is stimulated by offering students brief comments on selected vocabulary and grammar points as well as by providing outlines of historical context and literary criticism. Such techniques support cognitive actions, which is consistent with theoretical positions developed by Vygotsky (1978, 1986) and Meichenbaum.

Students are taught to mix their strategic actions with associations to prior learning experience in ways that permit fulfilment of their purpose, such as summarising the text, seeking information, or simply reading for pleasure. The use of strategies is supported by teacher prompts which would be of a different nature for students of a different proficiency level. With advanced students there is little external physical support. They are expected to work on their basic processing strategies (e.g., word-for-word and skimming); anticipate what might happen in a text; evaluate their expectations as reading proceeds; generate questions about the text; seek clarification when confused; identify main ideas; and attend selectively to certain parts of the material.

However, when less experienced students use the package, more prompting is offered by the teacher, and specially designed work-sheets, cue cards and charts may be used. Our hope is that a sensitive teacher could take a ready-made activity and adapt it in their teaching to make it relevant to their own teaching context.

Here are some practical examples. Tasks prior to reading may be specified as follows: What do students expect a particular text to be about? The tutor informs students that after they read some of the text, they should look back at their prediction to determine whether the ensuing text supported it. Further, subtasks are allocated among groups, separating planning and researching, drafting, revising and editing, so that comprehension becomes a shared activity involving organising and discussion. Students indicate when they need clarification about points made in the text, and other students respond, often by referring to text content that provided the relevant information. If online vocabulary comments do not cover certain unknown words, they are dealt with as they are encountered. Which strategies will be used and how they will be deployed will vary from text to text and with reader needs in processing those texts. Advanced students are expected to read actively: to anticipate automatically what might occur in the text, visualise events portrayed in the text, monitor their understanding of the material and use problem-solving strategies in interpreting the unknown word (e.g. by skipping a word with the expectation that its meaning might become more obvious with additional reading). If their attempts to understand the text are unsuccessful, they are advised to refer to the English-Russian TRANSLATION option in separate frames and look for the appropriate part of the translated text. Beginners are allowed to use dictionaries, read in word-by-word fashion and are recommended to refer to the parallel English-Russian translation. Later, students are invited to make interpretative comments about the text and to provide spontaneous reactions about its literary value. At the end of the session students are asked to examine their written predictions to see whether they needed revision to reflect what happened in text and to make the revision if necessary. Summaries are made both as reading proceeds and at the end of the session. If students are working on a longer text (e.g. the Pushkin or Tolstoy short story) their tutor may choose to divide the text into 3 parts and then introduce the aforementioned assignments.

Another possible activity is to divide participants into three groups; each of the groups will read and discuss one of three parts of the text; groups are then divided so as to be with members of other groups. Each participant reports what his/her text had said and listeners ask questions and take notes; finally, selected participants report back what they have heard/read to the class. Similar activities can be introduced for listening comprehension.

Most learners find reading in Russian problematic, since Russian stress is irregular. For this reason, an AUDIO option has been supplied with the stressed text, in which the vowels of stressed syllables are printed in bold type. Thus, if students wish to work on their pronunciation, they may switch over from the TEXT option to the AUDIO option to listen to the text and/or read it out loud.

2. Listening Comprehension

The content of the activity offered under the VIDEO option was chosen to catalyse discussion of issues pertinent to the particular author or text. Tutors introducing this exercise may combine communicative and interactive approaches (such as group-work and pair-work when all the four skills are taught in an integrated way) with more traditional ones, i.e. patterns involving extensive teacher-student interaction and little student-student interaction. In addition to the activities described in the Reading Comprehension section, listening to the short dialogues may be accompanied by formal instructions and standard comprehension questions and is supposed to stimulate a flurry of responses. Students may prepare for listening through discussion (e.g. using discussion sheets and/or an information gap activity); and competition is considered to be an important factor for encouraging students to listen.

3. Vocabulary Exercises

The vocabulary exercises are designed to test whether the students have familiarised themselves with the literary piece to an extent that they are able to fill the gaps with the missing words. Learners are expected to rely on both their understanding of the whole text and contextual cues of given sentences while tackling this task. They may have several attempts to find the appropriate word; and the more attempts are made, the lower is the score. This type of exercise is suitable for students of different proficiency levels: advanced students are invited to attempt the assignment without teacher prompts, whereas beginners will need to receive some guidance. Students may be asked to complete this task on a competitive basis.

4. Grammar Exercises

The grammar topics chosen for our package derive from the results of a questionnaire on the most problematic areas of Russian grammar. They include Participles, Gerunds, Verbs of Motion and Prepositions. All exercises use authentic sentences from a given literary piece, and the student task is to select the correct word form in a multiple choice activity. Both familiarity with the text and an understanding of appropriate grammar patterns will ensure successful completion of the task. Students are usually reluctant to do grammar tests during teaching sessions, but doing exercises on the computer seems less threatening; it allows learners to assess themselves independently, using the scoring system. The practical value of this type of exercise is reinforced by the introduction of detailed explanatory comments accompanying each incorrect answer. All grammar exercises are supplied with reference sections under the GRAMMAR option, which provide a brief outline of a relevant topic. This type of activity is designed mainly for advanced students, familiar with the basics of Russian grammar.

Conclusion: These web pages represent a potentially valuable way of increasing the effectiveness of teaching sessions by enhancing teacher responsiveness to student needs. Our initial, informal impression derived from the trial workshops was that the new model had been highly motivating and aroused lively and intense discussion. Our hope is that students are exposed to an approach which stimulates reflection as well as to content maximally relevant to their other courses. There are important benefits to students in using the new web pages, since they provide the necessary conditions for productive educational change. Our method does not lead to mechanical responding, but rather promotes the creative construction of meaning by students and teachers working together: it alters the roles of participants in significant ways, providing students with more independence.

Amongst the advantages of this package is its versatility: it is 'pre-packed' and can be used as it comes, but it also can be tailored according to the specific needs of learners and teaching techniques of a particular tutor. The package continues to evolve with every lesson and every tutor. Hence its higher motivation factor, since teaching materials will derive from real problems experienced by the students.

A SYNCHRONOUS LEARNING ENVIRONMENT TO SUPPORT DISTANCE LANGUAGE LEARNERS

Lesley Shield and Sue Hewer
Open University, UK

Abstract
The Open University has a current enrolment of approximately 8000 students of French, German and Spanish, all of whom study individually at home, at a distance from each other and from their tutors. While traditional methods of delivery — print, video- and audiocassettes and face-to-face tutorials — are still used, alternative methods, ranging from telephone conferencing to synchronous, Internet-based audio and audiographic conferencing, are being actively investigated. This paper describes the outcomes of the most recent Internet audio and audiographics conferencing trials during which learners were encouraged to participate in collaborative, active learning in groups. A task-based learning approach was adopted. Analysis of data collected during the trials is provided to illustrate how learning environments which allowed real-time and asynchronous exchanges between communities of learners and learners and tutors and learners were used in order to engage, motivate and support distance language learners.

1. Open and Distance Learning and Communications Technologies. With increasing access to communications technologies, there has been a corresponding growth of interest in various forms of Open and Distance Learning [ODL]. For the purposes of this discussion, we will define ODL in the Centre for Modern Languages [CML] as follows. To deal with *distance* first, CML students are at a distance from other students and from their tutor, with the exception of face-to-face tutorials, should they choose to attend these, and summer school. *Open*-ness is considered in terms of content, pace and time and place of learning.

Rapid technological change and economic pressures have caused campus universities to review course delivery mechanisms in order to ensure that all available resources are used as efficiently as possible and that financial savings are made wherever possible. This inevitably results in heightened interest in electronic delivery and tutoring across the sector, regardless of whether students are working entirely at a distance or essentially within a contact model. It is also inevitable that academics wish to explore possible uses for the new technologies not merely to meet the desires of educational administrators, but rather to improve the quality of the learning experience for students and to widen access to their courses.

The choice of modes of communication open to course designers in campus universities is now very wide. Alongside the traditional 'one-way' media (eg books, audio and video tape), the limited 'two-way' media (eg. lectures) and the full 'two-way' media (eg taught classes and seminars), there now exists a number of 'one-way' electronic media (eg on-line dictionaries), limited 'two-way' media (eg software programs which give feedback on student input) and full 'two-way' media which can be synchronous (eg audio conferences, on-line chat facilities and MOOs) or asynchronous (eg. e-mail and discussion lists). This choice of media will increasingly pose the question about the value of face-to-face meetings with students in lectures, classes and seminars, and, as potential students begin to get on-line at home, will challenge the concept of a campus university as we currently understand it.

2. The British Open University context: While the Open University [OU] has been grappling with the kind of issues that colleagues on 'traditional' campuses are now beginning to confront, for the immediate future, these issues will remain similar, but fundamentally different for all but the few campus universities which are currently experimenting with distance learning courses which fit into the OU's definition of distance learning as this is described above. This is especially true of courses in modern languages.

2.1.Language courses at the OU. Although face-to-face tutorials are offered in varying degrees for different courses and there is an expectation that students will attend summer school, essentially OU learners work alone, their base being their home or workplace. There is no requirement to attend a given number of face-to-face sessions and, if they opt not to do so, learners never meet their tutor, communicating by traditional mail, telephone or, increasingly, by e-mail. More importantly for language learners, if they do not attend these meetings, they will not have the opportunity to communicate in the target language with either their tutor or their fellow students.

3. Addressing the needs of the distance language learner. One of the aims of the Open University's language courses is:

> ...to give [you] plenty of practice in the four skills — reading, writing, speaking and listening — and to enable you to consolidate and develop your expertise in practical situations of a general nature. (Ouverture Study Guide:1994)

It is, therefore, considered important to provide opportunities for learners to interact orally with each other. For this reason, they are offered the chance to attend 18 hours of face-to-face tutorials per year. It has been found, however, that some learners, whether as a result of circumstance or location, are unable to attend these sessions so, in 1994, the Open University's Centre for Modern Languages began its investigations into the potential of various telecommunications facilities to promote language learning and to offer an alternative mode of delivery for those learners who cannot attend face-to-face meetings or who would prefer a different means of participating in synchronous oral/aural exchange.

3.1. Telephone tutorials: 1995-1996. In order to support those language learners unable or unwilling to attend face-to-face tutorials, it was decided to trial the possibilities offered by telephone conferencing and to provide a series of telephone tutorials to four groups of learners from remote areas of the UK. The groups consisted of 6-8 learners and a tutor. Telephone tutorials, planned in advance by the tutor, usually comprised four activities, which were similar to those presented during face-to-face tutorials. Learners received the programme in advance of the conference. The lack of visual cues and body language resulted inevitably in a highly managed learning environment where risk taking and spontaneity, important factors in the development of expertise in the spoken language, were difficult to achieve. Lessons learned from the first year of the telephone tutorials informed the second round of the trials and activities were then designed which required more general preparation and fewer 'prepared speeches'.

3.2. Telephone and E-mail: 1996-1997. Research has suggested that text-chat 'rehearsal' in preparation for face-to-face 'performance' appears to improve the quality of that performance (Chun 1994, Warschauer et al. 1995, Stevens & Hewer 1998). Given improvements in learner performance in the second phase of the telephone tutorials, the positive feedback received from these learners in terms of increased motivation, a decrease of their feelings of isolation and improvements in their pronunciation, it was decided to investigate the medium further, this time with the inclusion of e-mail to allow 'practice' before the audio conference. This work formed the first phase of the On-Line Language Learning project [OL3]. Group sizes were much the same as for the telephone tutorial project. However, a task-based approach to the activities was adopted. Each activity involved a 'kick-off' telephone conference followed by a 2 -3 week period in which learners exchanged e-mail with each other and with their tutors, and culminated in a final telephone conference. Similar improvements in learner performance were observed, but, this time, there were fewer 'read' responses than when e-mail was not used as a 'rehearsal' tool.

3.3. Voice-over-Internet and audiographics — plugging gaps in the existing learning environment. Telephone conferences must be arranged in advance, can be costly and do not permit learners to meet between scheduled sessions. Furthermore, although some telephone conferencing systems allow for larger groups to be split in two, using different channels, it is not possible for many small groups to use work together at the same time in a telephone conferencing environment. Improvements in voice-over-Internet technology means that, using an Internet-based virtual learning environment [VLE], it has now become possible to offer more flexibility (in terms of time, frequency and group composition) than does a telephone conference; not only can learners arrange to meet each other online between scheduled events at any convenient time for the cost of a local telephone call, applications using a 'rooms' metaphor support small group work. In 1997, then, it was decided to investigate the possibility of using Internet-based tools to offer distance language learners a richer, more flexible learning environment than had, until then, been available. It was, however, considered essential to provide learners with the best possible learning experience and to adopt the available technologies to the pedagogy rather than the pedagogy to the technology, so a two-stage approach was taken to address the problem:

1. Learner needs were identified and analysed
2. Available technologies were investigated and evaluated with reference to the needs of the learners.

4. Learner needs: Existing OU language courses are evaluated by students every year. One of the most striking aspects of these evaluations has been the high number of requests for more speaking and listening practice to improve confidence and fluency in communicating in the target language. It was this need that had informed the initial telephone conferencing trials, since the 'traditional' methods of delivery more strongly support the development of accurate than fluent production. In the remainder of this paper, we will describe the theoretical basis upon which the design of learning activities for the audio- and audiographics conferencing trials were based. Finally, we will present an analysis of qualitative data obtained from recent sets of trials, in the light of identified student needs and task design.

4.1. Fluency and accuracy in language learning. One way in which to analyse language learning tasks is to examine the extent to which they encourage the development of accuracy or fluency. This is not to imply that the two are opposites, nor that they are opposite ends of the same spectrum. They are complementary; it is not possible to use language without 'knowing' some of the language in terms of form and lexis. On the other hand, for most learners, there is not much point in acquiring knowledge about a language without the opportunity to develop fluency in its use.

Brumfit (1984:51) suggests '...the emphasis in making the accuracy/fluency distinction is on the mental state of the learner'. If the learner is engaged in a task in order to demonstrate or develop knowledge of the language, the focus of the task is on *accuracy*. If the intention is to convey meaning, and to do so in the same way as in the first language, the learner is engaged on a task in which, despite imperfections in terms of structure and vocabulary, and comparatively halting delivery, the focus of the activity is *fluency*.

Discussing the application of this distinction to the planning of teaching, Brumfit concludes (1984:131):

> accuracy will tend to be closely related to the syllabus, will tend to be teacher-dominated, and will tend to be form-based. Fluency must be student-dominated, meaning-based and relatively unpredictable towards the syllabus.

Given this definition of accuracy and the purpose of accuracy-focused activities, it is comparatively easy both to design appropriate tasks and to determine the characteristic behaviours that learners engaged on such tasks are likely to exhibit. It is less easy to do either with regard to fluency.

4.2. Skill-related fluency: Fluency is sometimes taken as referring simply to speaking skills because non-linguists tend to use the adjective 'fluent' to describe someone who speaks a foreign language with ease. It is not too difficult to begin to list the kinds of behaviours which the non-linguist would identify with the 'fluent' speaker, and it is likely that implicit in the list would be behaviours related to the interpretation of incoming language as well as the production of language. Brumfit, discussing the roles of fluency and accuracy in group work rejects the breakdown of language into skills and prefers the following 'isolable' activities:

> conversation or discussion;
> comprehension (either of speech or writing);
> extended writing. (ibid p. 70)

He acknowledges that a fourth activity 'extended speaking' can be added, but that this rarely engaged in by native speakers and can, therefore, be treated separately.

By 'comprehension' in connection with speech, Brumfit intends the learner listening to a spoken text, such as a story, rather than the kind of comprehension involved in conversation or discussion. His focus on the intentions of the learner again enables him to differentiate between fluency-focused comprehension in which the learner reads or listens to a text for the sake of the content and accuracy-focused comprehension in which learners listen in order to respond to the teacher's questions rather than in engaging with the text and pursuing their own interests in it. The listener's intention is all important whether the spoken text is delivered personally by a teacher, or by audio or video tape, or as a sound file on computer, possibly attached to an e-mail message.

On the other hand, the difference between traditional and electronic written text production affects the role of writing as a fluency activity. When Brumfit posited his argument, electronic 'writing' was not undertaken by many language learners. Brumfit believed that fluency activity was problematic in writing because of the tendency of native speakers to monitor their writing more than their speech, not least because writing has a degree of permanency not shared by the spoken word and because written documents could not, at that time, be readily changed in response to feedback from an interlocutor. Given the high value placed by literate societies on the quality of the written word, in addition to its comparative permanence, it is unsurprising that accuracy was the primary focus of writing activities. However, writing is not what it used to be. Native speakers tend not to monitor their writing in e-mail messages in the same way that they did messages on paper. As well as being saved and/or printed out, e-mail messages can be deleted, lending them a lack of permanence and encouraging the use of the kind of production strategies normally associated with speech. Indeed, the kind of discourse structure found in e-mail messages tends more to resemble spoken than traditional written discourse. Because of the ability to edit e-mail and word-processed documents, a two-stage approach to writing becomes possible a focus on fluency coming first, followed by formal monitoring and a focus on accuracy. The fact, then, that all written text produced electronically for asynchronous communication remains provisional, until declared permanent or redundant by the originator, brings writing into the range of activities appropriate for the development of fluency. It enables task designers to set up multi-skill activities which closely resemble 'real world' activities and which tend to channel learners' efforts into behaviours associated with interpreting and creating meaning, rather than with getting the form right.

Whilst e-mail and word-processed documents are closely related to their traditional counterparts, on-line synchronous text chat is quite different and is even more likely to produce speech-like written text (see Chun 1994, Warschauer et al 1994, Burdeau 1997, Warschauer 1998). Unlike e-mail production, there is no real opportunity to monitor input. While text chat exchanges do tend to be slower than oral exchanges they also require learners to respond in real time, 'thus providing them with instantaneous impetus to be understood in a written format, without relying on non-verbal crutches.' (Jeney 1997), a point also made by Turbee (1996).

4.3. Characteristics of Fluency-Orientated Tasks. Taking into account various factors related to fluency, in particular the views of Brumfit and the advice offered by Sidwell (1993), ten characteristics of a fluency task are proposed (Table 1). It is likely that such tasks will cause learners to exhibit behaviours of the sort outlined in Table 2 and are much more likely to provide adequate opportunities for the development of fluency if they are properly contextualised and involve placing the learner in a recognised role. Certain features of task design are also likely to promote such behaviours (Table 3).

i.	There should be no prior specification of the linguistic code by teacher or student;
ii.	There should be no attempt on the part of the task designer to 'drill' specific structures or vocabulary except as required by the student to convey meaning;
iii.	The carrying out of the task should be student-dominated;
iv.	The task should be meaning-based;
v.	Tutor explanations should match those implied in the task design;
vi.	The objectives of the task should always be distinct from the formation of accurate language;
vii.	The intervention of the tutor should always be as interlocutor within the context of the task, rather than as manager/assessor;
viii.	It is essential that there is the potential for unpredictability in the task as the context develops so that participants have a reason to read and/or listen, as well as to create their own spoken and/or written output;
ix.	Tasks should always include genuine information and/or opinion gaps to provide real reasons for listening, reading, speaking and writing;
x.	Procedures to deal with error correction should be non-intrusive and should never be allowed to inhibit the student whilst the task is in progress. The procedure(s) and the reasons for them should be explained carefully to students.

Table 1. Characteristics of a fluency-orientated task

In a fluency-orientated task:	
(i)	students will have a primary regard to the comprehension, creation and transmission of meaning, consistent with their current level of achievement in the target language;
(ii)	monitoring of output should be less apparent than in accuracy-orientated tasks when students are engaged in synchronous communication and when using on-line asynchronous tools (eg e-mail);
(iii).	students will operate in the same way as they would in the mother-tongue as they engage in the task (eg bring into play existing problem-solving skills);
(iv)	the language produced should have been processed by the student, not by the tutor;
(v)	students will respond to the changing context as the task develops by improvising, paraphrasing, engaging in repair activities and re-organising incoming and outgoing information;
(vi)	comprehension should be constructed by the reader/listener and never received via an intermediary such as the tutor;
(vii)	the content of utterances should be defined by the speaker/writer;
(viii)	students should display an appropriate level of linguistic 'risk-taking' to enable them to participate as fully as possible in the task given their current level of expertise in the use of the target language.

Table 2. Behaviours likely to be exhibited by learners involved in a fluency-related task

- Collaboration and/or conflict (for example, working in a sub-group to plan a case against that being prepared by a second sub-group).
- Providing information genuinely required by other participants
- Undertaking meaningful transactions
- Personal responses, provided that the motivation is strong enough to provoke participation

Table 3: Possible features of tasks likely to promote behaviours which characterise fluency.

5. The Trials. During the course of 1998-1999, four major sets of trials were run with OU learners of French and German. Two used voice-over-Internet conferencing (the FLUENT project), one with a hybrid solution involving voice-over Internet conferencing and a separate shared, electronic whiteboard with textchat (OL3-2), and the most recent using a purpose-built, integrated audiographics client (OL3-3). (Table 4). Learning activities for all trials adhered closely to the outline above. (Table 5).

Course	FLUENT 1 Oct 98- Feb 99	FLUENT 2 Mar 99 - Jun 99	OL3-1 Nov 98- Jan 99	OL3-2 July 99
German 1	24 students	24 students	n/a	n/a
French 2	n/a	n/a	12 students	6 students
French 3	20 students	16 students	n/a	n/a

Table 4: Composition and timing of voice-over-Internet and audiographics trials: 1998-1999.

FLUENT: German. In pairs, students designed a questionnaire to ascertain how health-conscious their colleagues were. Over a period lasting 3 weeks, they tested their questionnaires on the members of another group, revised the questionnaire on the basis of the test, administered it to their peers and reported back on their findings in a final plenary session.

FLUENT: French. In small groups, students worked together over a period of 4 weeks to design a new invention. At the end of the period, the groups came together in a plenary session and described their invention to their peers who had to guess its purpose from the description.

OL3-2. Learners were provided with a situation - a bypass is to be built around a French village - and, in groups, assigned roles in which they would argue for, or against the bypass in a plenary session which would take the form of a village debate. They prepared their roles over a 3 week period and the activity culminated with learners participating in a plenary session during which they used voice-over-Internet conferencing to discuss the issues, while employing a separate electronic whiteboard to illustrate various alternative solutions.

OL3-3. Again, learners participated in a role-play, in the roles of organic farmers or those who support genetically modified food. They were required, in role, to debate the case for or against genetic modification and to vote about the future of farms in the area. Learners used a specially-developed, integrated client which included both audio and whiteboard modules within a single application (Figure 1).

Table 5: Examples of learning activities used for voice-over-Internet & audiographics trials during 1998-99.

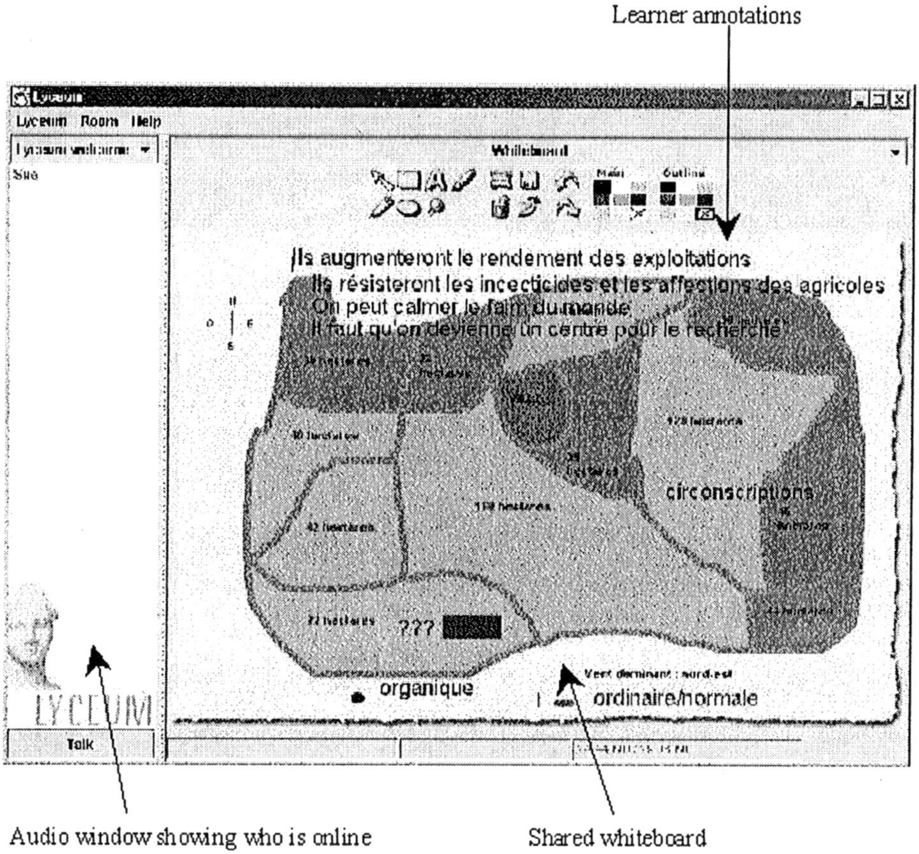

Figure 1. Example of a task being performed using the integrated audiographics client.

5.1. Feedback on VLEs from students. As noted above, students have regularly requested increased opportunities to practise syncrhonous speaking and listening skills. The projects described here aimed to meet such requests by offering meaningful, engaging and motivating tasks to encourage students to work collaboratively. Questionnaires were distributed to students at the end of each learning activity asking them to evaluate their learning experience.

While we are aware that the overall number of students involved in these trials was small, it is interesting, nevertheless, to note that the types of feedback provided is very similar regardless of project (Table 6). Responses fell into three main categories:

1. taking part in the trials made learners feel less isolated in their learning, in other words, they emphasised the importance of a learning community.

2. learners enjoyed having the opportunity to participate in learning activities which allowed them to use the target language in a meaningful and purposeful way.
3. learners believed their performance improved.

The additon of graphics to the VLE was well-received in spite of some technical hitches in the case of the integrated clients.

FLUENT	'gave individuals & groups the opportunity to develop it as they wished and encouraged discussion before the session'
French	'Feeling part of a team '
	'gave me the opportunity to talk to a group of people most of whom I had never met before, in a purposeful way with each other'
	'I particularly enjoyed communicating with other people who I have not ever met especially through the medium of German.'
German	'I like the contact with other students, and the growing companionship with them, the feeling of support.'
	'I have noticed an improvement in my oral German already.'
	'...it is not as easy as when in a real German situation, but better than any other class situation.'
OL3-2	'Spoke plenty of French and covered a lot of possibilities for story-lines, especially during individual group sessions'
	'We used e-mail a lot...it was excellent practice in writing French that someone else would actually be reading'
	'It builds up a feeling of belonging to something real and reduces isolation'
	'I have very much enjoyed taking part in the project so far - not only have I 'met' *new* people, but using the technology that we have so far has been exciting for me'
OL3-3	'many thanks for the opportunity to take part in an exciting venture. I think that this project is excellent and could fill a big gap for many students'
	'It was an excellent opportunity to use previously learned language. It demonstrated to me where I felt confident and where I felt unsure. I also realised areas where I had difficulty with pronunciation. Hearing it in your head is one thing. Saying it is quite another.'
	'I found it of much more benefit than say , discussing grammar points'
	' it helps to feel you are not struggling alone'

Table 6: Learner and tutor feedback on their learning experiences using voice-over-Internet and audiographics for distance language learning.

6. Conclusion: Qualitative analysis of data obtained from the FLUENT and OL3 projects revealed that both tutors and learners saw VLEs of this type as adding greatly to the (distance) language learning experience. Learners emphasise the importance of learning community and stress the motivating effect of using the target language to talk with others they have never met. Further, like learners using text chat (Healy Beauvois 1998) they believe that their performance in the target language has improved.

While there remains much to be done in terms of quantitative analysis of linguistic data before we can make any suggestions about the effect of these VLEs on actual learner performance, results of the trials so far, have been very encouraging, with participants being motivated and engaged by their experience:

> I have been very happy to take part in the project and I can see the day when this system will be common place. The potential to support distance teaching is enormous. (Tutor for FLUENT).

References:

Brumfit, C. (1984) Communicative Methodology in Language Teaching: the roles of fluency and accuracy UK:CUP

Burdeau, I. (1997) *Virtual Classrooms, Virtual Schools*, Unpublished dissertation for the MA in Media and Language Learning, University of Brighton, Available: http://www.burdeau.clara.net/ma/virtual.htm.

Chun, D.M (1994) 'Using computer networking to facilitate the acquisition of interactive competence', *System*, 22 (1), pp. 17-31.

Healy Beauvois, M. (1998) 'E-Talk: Computer-Assisted Classroom Discussion — Attitudes and Motivation', in (Eds) J. Swaffar, S. Romano., P. Markley, & K. Arens (Eds) (1998) *Language Learning Online: Theory and Practice in the ESL and L2 Computer Classroom*, Labyrinth Publications, Austin, Texas. pp. 99-120.

Jeney, C. (1997) *Chat! Synchronous Computer Mediated Communications* , Available: http://www.public.asu.edu/~starbuck/chat.htm.

Ouverture Course Team (1994) *Ouverture Study Guide*, UK, Open University.

Sidwell, D. (1993) *A toolkit for talking: strategies for independent communication,* CILT, UK.

Stevens, A. & Hewer, S. (1998) 'From policy to practice and back', *Proceedings of 1st LEVERAGE conference*, Cambridge 7-8 January, Available: http://greco.dit.upm.es/~leverage/conf1/hewer.htm.

Turbee, L. (1996) 'MOOing in a Foreign Language: how, why and who?' Paper presented at the Information Technology Education Connection's *International Virtual Conference/Exhibition on Schooling and the Information Superhighway,* Available: http://web.syr.edu/~lmturbee/itechtm.html.

Warschauer, M., Turbee, L & Roberts, B. (1994) 'Computer Learning Networks and Student Empowerment' *NFLRC Research Notes #10*, University of Hawaii.

A TASK-BASED APPROACH TO USING MOO FOR COLLABORATIVE LANGUAGE LEARNING

Lesley Shield
Open University, UK

Markus J.Weininger
Universidade Federal de Santa Catarina, Brazil

Lawrence B.Davies
Nanzan University, Japan

Abstract
Research suggests that a major reason for the popularity of computer mediated communications in L1 writing classes is that they offer great potential for '...collaborative scaffolding of shared knowledge in the construction of new ideas...' (Warschauer 1998) and increased opportunities for peer review and reflection. The authors of this paper argue that this is equally true for L2 learners. With Shneiderman (1998), they suggest that learners are motivated by participating in learning events which encourage them to work together towards producing an outcome which is available to an audience wider than that afforded by their peers and facilitators. This, they suggest, is an aspect of using MOO which is often overlooked but easily harnessed. They present examples involving learners in a task-based approach to language learning where the emphasis is on the development of autonomous and active learning communities who take responsibility for their own and their peers' learning

1. Introduction: The scenario is familiar: the teacher assigns a task. Learners work, usually individually or, sometimes, with a partner or in small groups, to complete the assignment which is then assessed according to specific criteria. This is far from the reality of real world tasks, yet is still widespread in language teaching. The learner's audience is never a single entity, such as the teacher, nor even a small group of immediate peers. Operating 'in the real world' the learner's task is complicated by the myriad perspectives of the disparate audience.

Recent research suggests that a major reason for the popularity of computer mediated communications [human:human communication where the computer acts as a bridge for interaction, as opposed to the human:computer interaction of CALL] in L1 writing classes is that they offer great potential for '...collaborative scaffolding of shared knowledge in the construction of new ideas...' (Warschauer 1998) and increased opportunities for peer review and reflection. We argue that this is equally true for L2 learners. This, we suggest, is an aspect of MOO (Multi-user domain, Object Oriented —

a programmable, multi-user database program with permanent rather than transient objects) that is often overlooked, but which can be easily harnessed by taking a task-based approach to learning activities within the learning environment. Furthermore, we assert that although working in a *text-based* environment, regular users of MOO may develop more than their reading/writing skills.

2. MOOs as Learning Environments. With Shneiderman (1997), we believe learners are highly motivated by participating in learning events which are meaningful to them and which encourage them to work together towards producing an outcome available to a wide audience. Harris (1996) emphasises the potential of MOO to expose learners to this sort of disparate audience, while McCallum et al (1997) refer to the socialising function of such applications. Unlike Papert's individual 'microworlds', they claim, multi-user CMC is:

> ...characterised by social interaction ...it is hard to overstate the importance of affective motivation in language and literacy learning. That is, the best kind of learning often occurs when students discover the pleasure of meaningful personal response through diversion and performances.... Environments such as MOO provide for such motivation in that they can involve discussions that are important to students...

We further believe the social nature of MOOs can promote both collaboration [mutual creation of outcomes through dialogue, negotiation, tinkering and play] and co-operation [the individual efforts of each member of the group produces outcomes with different textures and moods in different sections of the work] between learners.

Oren (1996), too, refers to the importance of the social nature of MOO:

> On-line communication in a group setting creates a social environment which may foster learning and instruction.

while Swaffar (1998) points out that 'networked environments' provide an excellent setting for small groupwork because, in theory, they allow all participants an equal voice and an equal chance to practise L2. She contrasts this with the 'real life' classroom, where strong personalities can dominate activities, excluding less confident or shyer learners. Empowerment of this sort is also seen as important by learners, as shown in the following extract from a MOO log (Figure 1).

Razor is a long-term MOO user. English is not his first language.

```
Razor says, "I personally feel this is a world within a world...:)"
Lesley asks, "Hmm?"
Razor says, "I mean, I see so many people just saying anything that comes to
their heads...irl...I'm sure they'd think first."
Lesley asks, "So, do you think this environment somehow disinhibits people?
Do  you think it helps shy people, for example?"
Razor says, "I'd say YES...it does."
...
Razor says, "I feel people keep coming back here because places such as these
help breaking their hesitation."
Lesley nods.
Lesley asks, "And that's valuable?"
Razor says, "to a certain level...yes."
Lesley asks, "Because?"
Razor says, "because if they're shy, they'll never ask...and thus never learn."
Lesley asks, "Ah... so, because MOO breaks down barriers, shy students feel more
comfortable about asking questions?"
Razor says, "I'd say yes...."
```

Figure 1. A young user's view of MOO and the shy language learner

Increased 'learner talk' within CMC environments is widely documented (eg Chun 1994, 1998, Warschauer et al. 1994, Burdeau 1997, Warschauer 1998) and Healy Beauvois (1998:101) points out this is a feature of which learners themselves are aware:

> In the category of linguistic benefits, the unanimous student perception of increased use of the target language constituted the most important finding.

2. MOO and Language Learning

2.1. Peer review and reflection. The importance of CMC to L1 writing classes has been widely documented (eg. Jordan-Henley & Maid 1995, Harris 1996, Chun 1994, 1998, Warschauer 1998, Holmes & Holmvik 1998). MOO-based composition and rhetoric classes are not uncommon and examples of these may be found at Diversity University MOO, Lingua MOO and MediaMOO, sometimes involving groups of learners on the same campus, and sometimes distributed groups of learners. In all cases, MOO is used as a tool by which learners present their work to an audience. They are then subject to peer review and can use the logs from MOO sessions as a reflective tool.

Although the emphasis in the literature about writing has been upon the use of MOO by L1 learners, it can be, and is, used by L2 learners and professionals for their learning and in their work, as illustrated in the short extract from a MOO log which follows (Figure 2).

Ana and Markus, who live several hundred kilometres apart, are preparing a teacher training workshop they are going to run.

```
Ana [Guest] says, "How about thinking about the title when we finish. I always
find it easier that way."

 ------- Markus pastes info to the screen ---------

Demonstrar as participantes como se acessa e utiliza o SchMOOze, quais os
recursos disponiveis, num espaco virtual em que pessoas se encontram para
discutir temas de interesse comum.

Discutir as possibilidades e limitaes pedaggicas do recurso.

------- Markus stops pasting ---------

Ana [Guest] says, "I like this part."

------- Markus pastes info to the screen ---------

Demonstrar as participantes como se acessa e utiliza a schMOOze University
(universidade virtual em Syracuse, NY), quais os recursos disponiveis, num
espaco virtual em que pessoas se encontram para discutir temas de interesse
comum.

Discutir as possibilidades e limitacoes pedagogicas do recurso.

------- Markus stops pasting ---------

Markus asks, "Can we let this?"
Ana [Guest] jumps up and down and exclaims, "Yeees!!!"
Markus will paste it then back to Eudora where he's composing the mail for SENAC
Ana [Guest] says, "OK."
You frantically ask, "Conteudo: ????"
Markus says, "Conteudo: ????."
Markus asks, "what do they want us to put there..?"
Markus asks, "Like :Apresentacao online com uma visita guiada e a possibilidade
de interagir em tempo real?"
Ana [Guest] asks, "I don't know what SENAc means by that. The content would be
the MOO itself, don't u think?"
```

Figure 2. Example of MOO being used for collaborative planning and editing

Here, we see MOO used collaboratively to define the content of a presentation. Later in the discussion, it becomes clear that the log of the session is being saved by Markus who will send it to Ana as an *aide-memoire* as to what was agreed:

> Markus says, 'Yeah... I mail it [the logfile] to you too, then you can always print it and hand it in as hardcopy if e-mail fakes...'

Furthermore, this logfile will be presented to the workshop audience as an example of how MOO can be used for the collaborative design of a workshop, thus providing Markus and Ana, as well as a wider audience, with the opportunity to reflect on and review both its linguistic content and the potential MOO provides for collaboration.

Turner (1996) reports that her ESL learners often considered the language used for room descriptions at Schmooze to be too advanced for their linguistic level. She adds, however, that as time went on and learners began to write descriptions for their own personae and rooms, these became increasingly more complex as they observed and reflected on existing descriptions which proved to be a motivating factor for them. The task of writing descriptions for their own characters and rooms was also popular, in that it was meaningful to them and the product would be seen by a diverse audience of MOO users.

Within the virtual learning environment that is Schmooze University, the Graffiti Wall object provides learners with the opportunity to express their thoughts to a wide audience. Since the Graffiti Wall is a public object, any user of the MOO can read what is written there and add to its content. Peer review of comments here is frequently and often harshly critical of both topic and linguistic content. Despite the likelihood of such criticism, even the most retiring of learners continue to visit and add to this object.

2.2. Register and Fluency

Much has been written about the register encountered in CMC. It is claimed:

> A large body of literature agrees in principle that the English used in CmC is neither standard spoken English nor standard written English... (Lundstrom, 1995)

and:

> ...they share characteristics of spoken and written language, computer 'conversations'... They enable the spontaneous responses of speech and the reflective, iterative responses of writing... (Swaffar 1998:2)

Burdeau (1997:np) identifies several ways in which synchronous CMC (which he calls CMHC) diverges from 'standard English' (Figure 3).

The generally poor spelling found in synchronous CMHC, often the result of sacrificing clarity for speed.

Poor punctuation (often capital letters and full stops are omitted), again, this is generally due the desire to increase speed of communication.

The use of abbreviations, such as "btw (by the way), "i c " (I see), "r u" (are you), "c u" (see you), "lol" (laughing out loud), "imho" " (in my humble opinion) or "bbl" (be back later) for reasons of economy.

The use of capitals and asterisks to denote stress and intonation, for example: Frizzy says, "NO, none of *those* types." (NETEACH session 7-A, 12/97)

The use of "emoticons", such as :-), ;-), :-((smiling, winking and frowning, respectively) to give paralinguistic clues.

Figure 3. Principle differences between 'standard English and the language of synchronous CMC (Burdeau 1997)

He identifies three main types of linguistic community which occur within CMC environments (Table 1).

Community	**Participants**	**Characteristics**
Chat	Young, typically university students & teenagers	All the characteristics shown in Figure 3
Professional	Typically older, research students, teachers, writers, professionals	'Fairly frequent use of emoticons, asterisks and capital letters to signal non-verbal cues, facial expressions, stress and intonation. Overall, the use of English, at least in terms of form, is fairly close to what one might call "standard spoken English"'
Non-native speakers	Non-native speakers	'...contains frequent errors of spelling, punctuation, grammar and vocabulary. Does **not** (typically) contain the features mentioned earlier which can be said to be specific to synchronous CMHC. While some users in these environments make use of emoticons, asterisks and capitalised words, it is not...very common'.

Table 1: Burdeau's linguistic communities within CMC environments (Burdeau 1997:np)

We would agree with this classification, but would add that these communities are not discreet; a single MOO user may well be a member of one or all of these communities, varying register according to context. Returning to the example given in Figure 2, although the context reveals the protagonists fall into Burdeau's **Professional** community, both are non-native speakers of English who work with young CMC users. An examination of their discourse reveals linguistic examples which fall into all three of Burdeau's categories, even within this short extract (Table 2):

Community	Example	Characteristics
Chat:	**Yeees!!!** Don't **u** think	Exclamation marks, abbreviation
Professional:	**How about** thinking about the title when we are finished?	Reference to task in hand, **but**, notc that the informal **How about** as opposed to the more formal **Perhaps we might consider**… which might be expected in written form.
NNS:	Can we **let** this?	Lexical error

Table 2: Examples of different register
Such variation gives emphasis to Burdeau's claim:

> …it would seem that it difficult, if not impossible, to make blanket statements about the 'quality' of language found in synchronous CMHC…

According to Turner (1996), one of the most immediate benefits of MOO to the language learner is that it allows practice in the target language. As we have already noted, text-based CMC environments seem to encourage increased 'learner talk' Research into the effect of text-based CMC on L2 production (eg Chun 1994, Stevens & Hewer 1998) suggests that there may be consequences not only in terms of improved keyboarding skills, but also improvement learners' spoken performance by offering a means for 'rehearsal' before a scheduled learning event. Although Warschauer (1998) remarks that any such conclusion can only be tentative, there is evidence that fluency and confidence in the spoken L2 certainly increase (Chun, 1994, Stevens & Hewer, 1998, Warschauer et al 1994, Jeney 1997, Healy Beauvois 1998).

In the case of MOO, evidence from informal interviews, at least, appears to support the widespread belief that MOO is, as Oren (1995) puts it, 'more than writing'. For example, a Chinese EFL teacher, when asked what he considered to be the benefits of MOO, replied:

> `I think it a good place for my students to practise speaking, reading and writing` (MOO log, 12th July 1999).

It is surely noteworthy that this teacher unconsciously and immediately referred to the 'speaking' practice — probably a reference to the synchronous nature of MOO which requires users to respond in real-time to their interlocutors rather than to actual speaking — afforded by MOO. It is also interesting to observe that one of the authors of this paper responded to a question about the effect of MOOing on his own L2 performance as follows:

> ...enables you to have permanent contact with NSs [native speakers]. As language is a social phenomenon, exposure to a social group that is part of that language and culture) gives me the chance to deepen cultural knowledge, achieve greater fluency, expand vocabulary and reinforce conscious and unconsciously syntactic particularities of the target language that start to twinkle down into my active use. This is an opportunity I wouldn't have easily (and even less continuously) without MOOing – living in Brazil.
> (Weininger 1999, personal communication)

2.3. MOO and language learning: a task-based approach

As we have seen, the 'quality' of language encountered in MOO is unpredictable. Razor, a young Pakistani MOO user remarked,

> ... theoretically, it should be that they [language learners using MOO] actually learn and improve on their language skills right?... but I don't see that happening too much around here.

This comment appears to support Swaffar (1998:4):

> Not only must the quantity of student production in a computer network be greater to validate it as a unique learning environment, but the quality of this production must also be.

but, when questioned further, Razor's answers showed that he sees MOO as a vehicle to empower shyer learners and to provide them with a tool with the primary aim of increasing their fluency (see Figure 1).

For learners whose aim is not necessarily to increase fluency and confidence, it **is** possible to take part in 'drill and practice' sessions — there is, for example, a 'Grammar Maze' in Schmooze which requires learners to work their way through a randomised multiple choice grammar test, progression through the 'maze' being governed by choosing the correct response to each question. There is even a 'scavenger hunt' whose aim is to acquaint new users with the MOO. While this could be undertaken jointly and collaboratively, most users choose to solve the clues alone.

MOO is, however, as McCallum (1997:np) point out a socialising technology:

> Involvement in a MOO is indeed far from the solitary nature of completing a workbook page, or a skill and drill software application.

An analysis of the sorts of activities MOO users engage in (Table 3), reveals that many promote collaboration and reflection/peer review. Furthermore, their outcomes are public and available beyond the immediate user(s) who was involved. Interestingly, it is the 'professional' community whose activity-types appear to fulfil these criteria most frequently, perhaps because they tend to use MOO for professional as well as social purposes.

Community	**Activity**	**Collaborative**	**Reflection /Review**	**Public Outcome**
Chat	Chat	Yes	Logs	Interlocutor/s
	'Graffiti Wall'	Sometimes	Yes	Yes
	Writing descriptions of character & rooms	Not usually	Yes	Yes
	Extending the MOO	Not usually	Yes	Yes
	MOO-based games	Sometimes	No	No
Professional	Chat	Yes	Logs	Interlocutor/s
	Professional discussion groups	Yes (in theory)	Yes	Yes
	Online conferences	Yes	Yes	Yes
	Writing/revising academic papers	Yes	Yes	Yes
	Preparing joint presentations/learning events	Yes	Yes	Yes
	MOO-based classes/presenations	Sometimes	Yes	Yes
NNS	Chat	Yes	Logs	Interlocutor/s
	'Graffiti Wall'	Sometimes	Yes	Yes
	Writing descriptions of character & rooms	Yes	Yes	Yes
	Extending the MOO	Yes	Yes	Yes
	MOO-based games	Sometimes	No	No
	MOO-based language drills	No	No	No
	MOO-based learning events	Sometimes	Sometimes	Sometimes

Table 3: Typical activities of MOO-based communities

It is this sort of task that we consider to be the most appropriate to the MOO environment, since it is this sort of task which encourages socialisation and thus an increase of confidence and fluency in L2. Furthermore, a task-based approach to activities within MOO reveals many 'real' tasks which can be easily adapted to the language learner and which have public outcomes which are, therefore, meaningful to and motivating for the learner.

3. Conclusion: The potential of MOO as a learning environment is largely underestimated by those who wish to implement language drills or try to replicate the teacher-controlled and teacher-centred classroom. It can be developed much further. It offers learners the opportunity to socialise in L2, communicating in an autonomous and authentic way, and to engage in meaningful, purposeful and productively challenging tasks.. Working on the tasks in collaboration with peers and external (target language) communication partners, learners participate in learning events that provide an L2 experience which is contextualised, more efficient and more motivating, thus increasing their confidence and fluency in using L2. In addition, there is more qualitatively new potential for an improvement of social, cultural and linguistic competence than any 'closed-shop' language learning material or teaching limited to the traditional language classroom can ever strive for.

References:

Burdeau, I. (1997) *Virtual Classrooms, Virtual Schools*, Unpublished dissertation for the MA in Media and Language Learning, University of Brighton, Available: http://www.burdeau.clara.net/ma/virtual.htm

Chun, D. M (1994) 'Using computer networking to facilitate the acquisition of interactive competence', *System*, 22 (1), pp. 17-31.

Chun, D.M. (1998) 'Using Computer-Assisted Class Discussion to Facilitate the Acquisition of Interactive Competence', in (Eds) J. Swaffar et al., pp. 57-80.

Harris, L. (1996) 'Writing Spaces: Using MOOs to teach Composition and Literature', *Kairos,* 1(2), Available: http://english.ttu.edu/kairos/1.2/coverweb/Harris/contents.htm.

Healy Beauvois, M. (1998) 'E-Talk: Computer-Assisted Classroom Discussion – Attitudes and Motivation', in (Eds) J. Swaffar et al., pp. 99-120.

Holmes, C. & Holmvik, J. R. (Eds) (1998) *High Wired: On the Design, Use and Theory of Educational MOOs*, Ann Arbor, University of Michigan Press.

Jordan-Henley, J. & Maid, B. M. (1995) 'MOOving along the Information Superhighway: Writing Centers in Cyberspace', *Wtiting Lab Newsletter,* 19 (5), pp. 1-6, Also available: http://www2.rscc.cc.tn.us/~jordan_jj/OWL/MOOving.html

Lundstrom, P. (1995) *Synchronous Computer-Mediated Communication: Will Internet Talkers Improve the Communicative Competence of ESL/EFL Students?* Unpublished Master's thesis, The University of Hawaii, Manoa, Available: ftp.hawaii.edu/outgoing/phxrsng/masters/paper.

McCallum, R. D., McGrath, O. G. & Rusch, J. B. (199?) *Instructional Applications of Internet Technology: Teacher training in the Language and Literacy MOO*, Available: http: www.readingonline.org/electronic/moo/.

Oren, A. (1996) 'MOOing is more than writing', *Kairos,* 1(2), Available: http://english.ttu.edu/kairos/1.2/coverweb/avigail.html.

Papert, S. (1980) *Mindstorms: Children, Computers, and Powerful Ideas*, Brighton, England, The Harvester Press Ltd.

Shneiderman, B. (1997) Relate-Create-Donate: A teaching/learning philosophy for the cyber-generation, *Computers & Education*, 31(1), pp. 25-39, Also available: ftp://ftp.cs.umd.edu/pub/hcil/Reports-Abstracts-Bibliography/97-17html/97-17.html.

Stevens, A. & Hewer, S. (1998) 'From policy to practice and back', *Proceedings of 1st LEVERAGE conference*, Cambridge 7-8 January, Available: http://greco.dit.upm.es/~leverage/conf1/hewer.htm.

Swaffar, J. (1998) Introduction in (Eds) J.Swaffar et al., pp 1-16.

J.Swaffar, Romano, S., Markley, P. & Arens, K. (Eds) (1998) *Language Learning Online: Theory and Practice in the ESL and L2 Computer Classroom*, Labyrinth Publications, Austin, Texas.

Turbee, L. (1996) MOOing in a Foreign Language: how why and who? Paper presented at the *Information Technology Education Connection's International Virtual Conference/Exhibition on Schooling and the Information Superhighway*, Available: http://home.twcny.rr.com/lonnieturbee/itechtm.html.
Turner, J. (1996) *Using Text-based Virtual Reality in the Classroom – A Narrative*, Available: http://elicos.qut.edu.au/moo/mpaper.html.
Warschauer, M. (1998) *Interaction, Negotiation and Computer-Mediated Learning*, Available: http://www.insa-lyon.fr/Departements/CDRL/interaction.html.
Warschauer, M., Turbee, L & Roberts, B. (1994) 'Computer Learning Networks and Student Empowerment' *NFLRC Research Notes #10*, University of Hawaii.
Weininger, M. J. (1999) Personal communication.

MOOs
Diversity University, telnet 206.212.27.32:8888.
Lingua MOO, telnet lingua.utdallas.edu:8888.
Media MOO, telnet mediamoo.cc.gatech.edu:8888.
Schmooze University, telnet schmooze.hunter.cuny.edu:8888.

EXPLORING TIME-RELATED VARIABLES IN A COMPUTER-BASED READING TEST

Tetsuhito Shizuka
Kansai University, Japan

Abstract
This study concerns several time-related behavioural variables recorded in college-level Japanese ESL students taking a computer-based multiple-choice sentence comprehension test. The variables were explored in hope that analysis might shed light on aspects of test-taker ability and item characteristics not revealed by the resultant number-correct score alone. The test was composed of 50 items, each consisting of one stimulus sentence followed by a multiple-choice question on that sentence. Each sentence was presented word-by-word on a computer display at a subject-determined pace. When a key was hit at the end of the sentence, four options appeared, overwriting the sentence. When one was chosen, a second button appeared allowing the subject to indicate his/her confidence level (1/2/3) regarding the choice just made. Immediate feedback on the correctness of the response was given after each item, with advice encouraging faster or slower reading depending on the correctness of the response. Major findings included:

1. *A quicker response to an item indicated a response more likely to be correct.*
2. *A quicker response indicated a higher confidence rating.*
3. *A higher confidence rating was associated with a response more likely to be correct.*
4. *Confidence rating did not take up much of test taking time, indicating marginal interference in the main task.*

1. Introduction: I am now engaged in a Ph. D. research project to develop a computer-administered sentence reading test to measure L2 general reading proficiency of EFL Japanese learners of English (Shizuka 1998a). The purpose of this paper is to describe a preliminary version of the test and report on insights obtained through analyzing time-related variables.

2. The Study

2.1 Subjects: The subjects participated in the reported phase of the study was 74 students enrolled in English reading course at Kansai University, Japan. They sat for the test as a class requirement.

2.2 Description of the test: The computer program for presenting the items was created as a HyperCard (Version 2.3J) stack for use on Macintosh computers (Shizuka 1998c). This computer-based sentence comprehension test will hereafter be referred to as the

SCT. After the test-taker types in their identification information, the following instruction appears (in Japanese, the test-takers' L1).

1. This is a test for measuring speed and accuracy with which you read English sentences.
2. There are 40 items in all, each of which consists of one isolated sentence followed by a multiple-choice question.
1. First, a sentence will be presented word-by-word as you hit the enter key. Since the inter-key latencies will be recorded as a measure of your reading speed, and will influence your score, try to reach the end of the sentence as quickly as possible once you begin.

The instruction above corresponds to Figure 1. The sentence is presented in what is known as the stationary window condition (Just et al. 1982), the words in a sentence being presented successively in the center of the screen. The time duration spent on reading the sentence is recorded in 'tics', one sixtieth of a second, and reading speed in words per minute is simultaneously computed and recorded for each item.

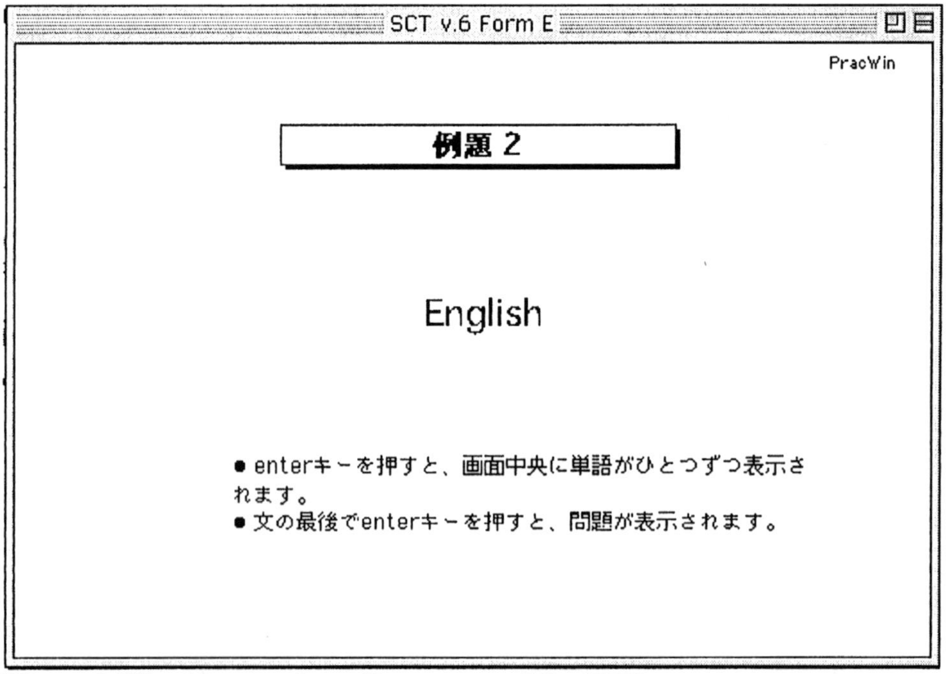

Figure 1. Word-by-word reading screen of the SCT

2. When you hit the key on the last word of the sentence, a multiple-choice question will appear, overwriting the sentence. The time you take to choose the best choice will NOT influence your score, so there is no need to hurry once in this phase.

The four options are related to the sentence in terms of meaning, one of which is correct. The details of the item development was described elsewhere (Shizuka). This phase appears as in Figure 2.

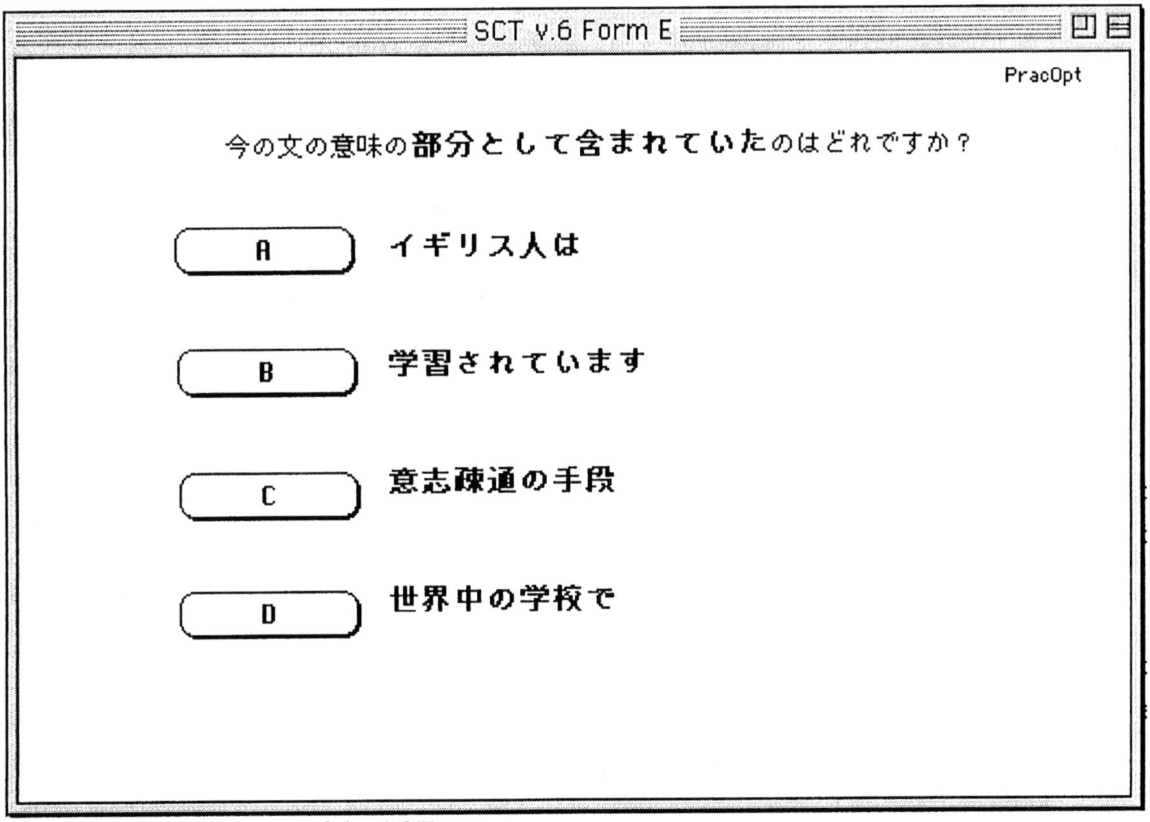

Figure 2. Options screen of the SCT

3. When you choose one answer, you are prompted to choose one of the three confidence levels you have in the choice you just made: high confidence (Confidence level 3), medium confidence (Confidence level 2), and low confidence (Confidence level 1), as follows (Figure 3).

4. The confidence level you choose for each option will be used in scoring the item in such a way that a correct response made with a higher confidence is awarded more highly than that made with a lower confidence, and conversely, an incorrect response

made with a higher confidence is penalized more severely than that made with a lower confidence.

With this explanation, the actual conversion table (Table 1) is also presented. The SCT terminates automatically when all the items are finished.

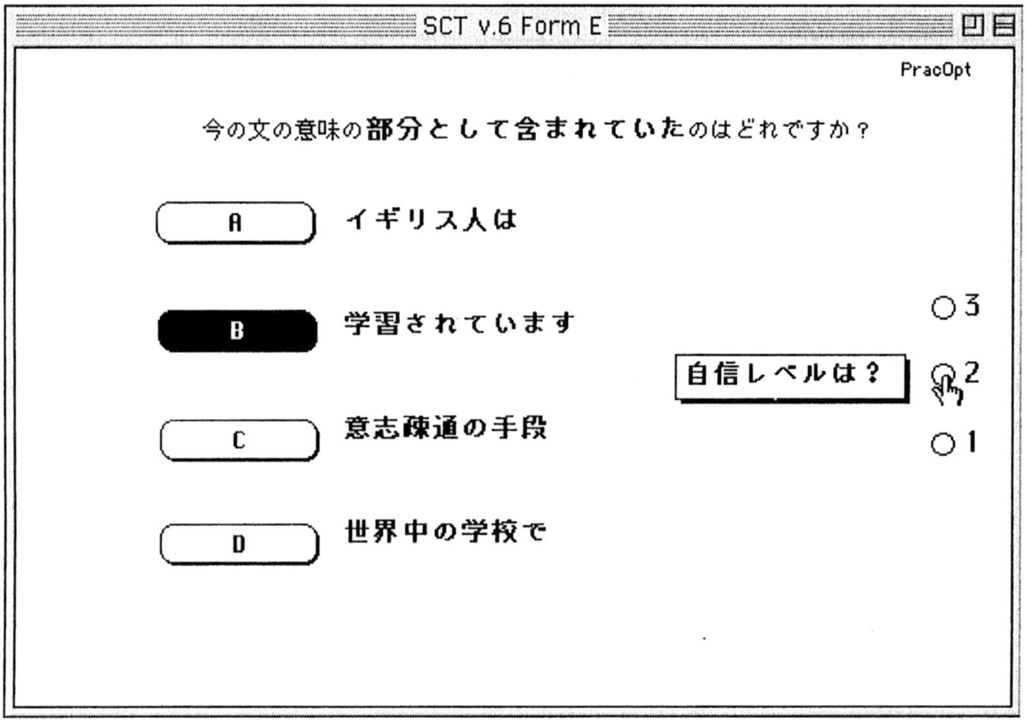

Figure 3. Confidence rating screen of SCT

Table 1. Conversion table for combining the response correctness and the confidence ratings

Correctness of the choice made	Confidence level at which the choice was made	Resultant score
1 (correct)	3 (high)	5
1 (correct)	2 (medium)	4
1 (correct)	1 (low)	3
0 (incorrect)	1 (low)	2
0 (incorrect)	2 (medium)	1
0 (incorrect)	3 (high)	0

2.3 Variables: Main variables collected were as follows, the ones with an asterisk are related to time factor, which are of particular interest in this paper.

WPM*: speed at which each sentence was read, in words per minute
ChoiceTime: time spent choosing the most plausible option, in seconds
Res*: response for each item coded as 1 (correct) or 0 (incorrect)
ConfTime*: time spent choosing the perceived confidence level, in seconds
Conf: confidence level chosen for each item
TestTime*: time spent on entire test, in seconds

2.4 Hypotheses: The following reasoning was made and hypotheses formulated:

WPM and Res: When a person attempts 50 items, a relatively large WPM value should mean that the person found the item relatively easy to read, and a relatively small WPM value should indicate that the person found the sentence relatively difficult to read. Therefore, there should be a tendency that faster read items are more correctly responded items (Hypothesis 1A).

Previous research indicates that reading speed increases when a reader becomes more proficient. Therefore, a person's mean WPM should correlate positively with his/her mean Res, an indicator of overall reading ability (Hypothesis 1B).

ChoiceTime and Res: A smaller ChoiceTime value should indicate that the item was found relatively easy, and a larger ChoiceTime value should indicate the opposite. Therefore, when averaged across all persons, correctly responded items should correspond to smaller mean ChoiceTime than incorrectly responded items (Hypothesis 2).

ChoiceTime and Conf: Confidence rating procedure is often criticized for potential unwarranted rating, which will magnify measurement error. If the examinee is consistent in confidence rating, a smaller ChoiceTime value should correspond to a higher Conf, and a larger ChoiceTime value to a lower Conf (Hypothesis 3).

Conf and Res: If confidence is consistently rated, there should be a tendency that a higher Conf corresponds to a higher Res, and a lower Conf to a lower Res. Thus, it is predicted that the mean Res should increase in the order of Conf 1, Conf 2, and Conf 3 (Hypothesis 4).

ConfTime and TestTime: One may wonder if confidence rating procedure may impose additional burden to test-takers, who are already under pressure for the main task, solving the items. To obtain some indirect evidence on the extent to which confidence rating procedure take up test-takers' cognitive resources, ConfTime was recorded and examined in relation to TestTime. It was hoped that ConfTime would be small enough to be regarded negligible relative to TestTime.

3. Results

Hypothesis 1A

For each of the 74 persons, 50 WPM values produced were classified into those that subsequently led to correct responses (1_WPM) and those that led to an incorrect responses (0_WPM). The descriptive statistics are shown in Table. Although the mean value for 1_WPM was larger than 0_WPM, as predicted, the difference did not reach statistical significance (t=1.63, p=.053). Thus, Hypothesis 1A was not supported.

Table 2. Descriptive statistics of WPM that led to correct/incorrect responses

	N	Mean	SD	Max	Min
1_WPM	74	86.53	46.20	362.79	35.83
0_WPM	74	84.31	42.56	291.22	35.04

Hypothesis 1B

The Res is plotted against WPM in Figure 4.

Apparently, there is no clear relationship between the two variables, which is confirmed by the non-significant correlation coefficient of r=-.046 (n. s.). The slightly negative value seems to be largely influence by one outlier who produced a large WPM of 311.26 but a small Res of .26. Thus Hypothesis 1B was not supported.

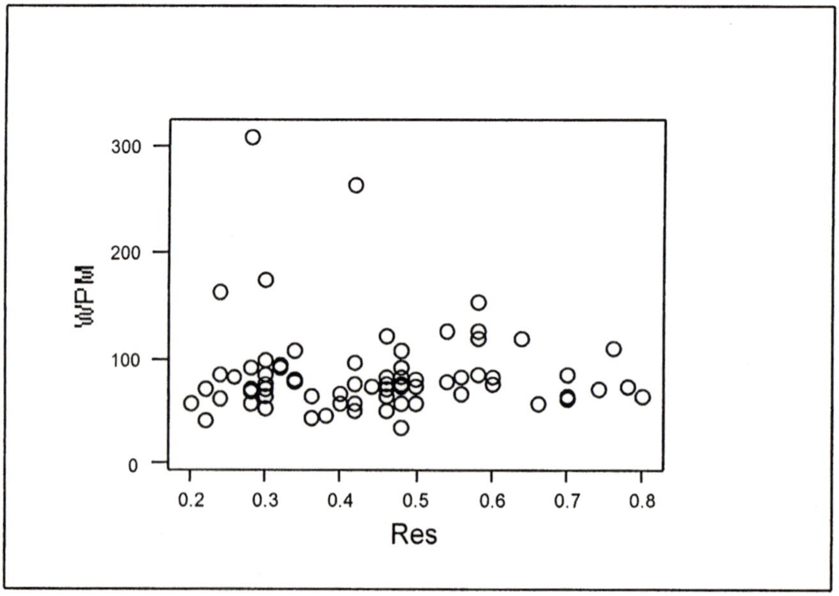

Figure 4. WPM plotted against Res

Hypothesis 2: ChoiceTime and Res

For each of the 74 persons, 50 ChoiceTime values produced were classified into those that subsequently led to correct responses (1_ChoiceTime) and those that led to an incorrect responses (0_ChoiceTime). The descriptive statistics are shown in Table. As predicted, the 1_ChoiceTime was smaller than 0_ChoiceTime, which a t-test revealed was significant at p=.0001. Thus, Hypothesis 2 was supported.

Table 3. ChoiceTime that led to correct and incorrect responses

	N	Mean	SD	Max	Min
1_ChoiceTime	74	11.28	5.96	34.09	2.73
0_ChoiceTime	74	13.32	6.61	31.54	2.43

Hypothesis 3: ChoiceTime and Conf

For each of the 74 persons, 50 ChoiceTime values were classified into those followed by the confidence rating of 1 (1C_ChoiceTime), those followed by Conf 2 (2C_ChoiceTime), and those accompanied by Conf 3 (3C_ChoiceTime). The results of an ANOVA together with descriptive statistics are shown in Table 4 .

Table 4. Analysis of Variance on ChoiceTime by 3 levels of Conf

```
Source       DF          SS         MS          F          p
C143          2      2091.5     1045.7      20.83      0.000
Error       215     10795.4       50.2
Total       217     12886.8
                                         Individual 95% CIs For Mean
                                         Based on Pooled StDev
Conf          N        Mean      StDev  ----+---------+---------+------
  1          72      15.727      9.461                      (----*-----)
  2          73      12.725      6.927            (----*-----)
  3          73       8.187      3.699   (----*-----)
                                        ----+---------+---------+-------
Pooled StDev =     7.086                 9.0      12.0      15.0
```

As can be seen, the mean ChoiceTime value increased in the predicted order and the difference was significant (p=.000). Tukey's pairwise comparison confirmed that 1C_ChoiceTime was larger than 2C_ChoiceTime, which in turn was larger than 3C_ChoiceTime, both at p<.05 level. Thus, Hypothesis 3 was supported.

Hypothesis 4

In the same way as above, Res values by each person was classified into three groups by the preceding Conf value: 1C_Res, 2C_Res, and 3C_Res. Table shows the results of a one-way ANOVA and the descriptive statistics.

Table 5. Analysis of Variance on Res by 3 Levels of Conf

Source	DF	SS	MS	F	p
C146	2	3.9939	1.9969	54.93	0.000
Error	215	7.8161	0.0364		
Total	217	11.8100			

```
                                       Individual 95% CIs For Mean
                                       Based on Pooled StDev
Conf      N      Mean      StDev  ----+---------+---------+-------
   1     72    0.3012     0.1567 (---*---)
   2     73    0.4102     0.1766      (--*---)
   3     73    0.6270     0.2306               (--*---)
                                  ----+---------+---------+-------
Pooled StDev =  0.1907              0.36      0.48      0.60
```

Again, the means were ordered as hypothesized. The difference between the adjacent levels were significant at $p<.05$ according to Tukey's pairwise comparions. Thus, Hypothesis 4 was supported.

ConfTime and TestTime

ConfTime (that is, per item), the sum of mean ConfTime, and TestTime is tabulated in Table 6.

Table 6. Descriptive statistics of ConfTime and TestTime

	N	Mean	SD	Max	Min
ConfTime	74	1.94	0.60	4.70	1.07
Sum of ConfTime	74	97.00	30.00	235.00	53.5
TestTime	74	1869.2	489.1	3066.7	587.6

It can be seen that on the average, the test-takers spent approximately 2 seconds per item on assessing their own confidence. In the entire test, this adds up to approximately one and a half minutes, which accounted for about 5 % of the whole test time.

4. Discussion. Three out of five hypotheses were supported. The results that did not turn out as predicted were both those related with WPM, the reading speed at which the item sentence were read. Although the result concerning Hypothesis 1 was at least in the predicted direction and almost reached statistical significance, the relationship between WPM and Res in general revealed by the scatter plot (Figure 4) and its correlation coefficient in the negative completely rejected our hypothesis.

The most plausible reason for this unexpected result seems to lie, on second thought, not in the true lack of relationship between these variables but in the lack of precision in measuring reading speed in the specific SCT used in this study.

When conducting and supervising the test-taking session, I noticed that the stack's response to the test-taker's key hits in the sentence reading phase was often unbearably slow. The impression was that however quickly you hit the key, the appearance of the words did not catch up. This was not noticed in the stack development phase because the stack was written and tried on the latest Apple Macintosh G3 in my office. However, when put to use on older machines in the computer lab, the key response turned out to be so slow as to invalidate the reading speed data. It seems that Scripts need to be changed before we can discuss with more certainty whether or not the meaningful relationship between reading speed and the other variables.

5. Conclusion. This study explored the relationship between several time-related variables collected in a computer-based sentence reading test.Apa r t from those concerning reading speed data, the existence of predicted relationships were confirmed. The results indicate that time-related data, which can only be recorded on a computer-based test, can provide valuable information on the validity of non-time-related data, such as confidence rating and response correctness. If, in a future study, time-related data are shown to contain valuable information about the test-takers' ability that is not revealed by non-time related data alone, it might be worthwhile to explore an optimal way of incorporating time-related variables in arriving at the best estimate of the test-takers' reading proficiency.

References:

Just, M. A. & Carpenter, P. A. & Woolley, J. D. (1982) 'Paradigms and processes in reading comprehension', *Journal of Experimental Psychology: General* 111 (2) :228-238.

Shizuka, T. (1998a). 'Measuring EFL Proficiency in the Moving-Window Paradigm on the Computer', *Language Testing Update* spring: 52-53.

Shizuka, T. (1998b) 'Writing Multiple-choice Items for Measuring Sentence Comprehension', *Research Reports Fukushima National College of Technology* 38: 84-91.

Shizuka, T. (1998c) 'The Effects of Stimulus Presentation Mode, Question Type, and Reading Speed Incorporation on the Reliability/Validity of a Computer-based Sentence Reading Test', *JACET Bulletin* 29: 155-172.

LANGUAGE LEARNING VIA E-MAIL — AUTONOMY THROUGH COLLABORATION

Kirsten Söntgens
University of Central England in Birmingham, UK

Language teaching in Higher Education in the United Kingdom has changed considerably over the past decades. Conditions in Higher Education have made the introduction of autonomous learning possible. The ever-increasing range of language provision and the growing role of media and information technologies in language teaching seem to have become linked to Autonomous Language Learning. This link has supported the growth of self-access language learning. Computer software for language learning is an example of a technology which claims to promote autonomy simply by offering the possibility of self-study. Research has shown, however, that there is no necessary link between learning a language in a self-access facility and the development of autonomy as there is a danger that students become more dependant on the materials and technology that support this situational autonomy (Benson & Voller 1997).

However Brian Tomlinson has shown how self-access materials can be developed to facilitate autonomous learning. His so-called 'access-self activities' provide the learner with the opportunity to choose when and what to work on and at his/her own pace, be open-ended (variety of acceptable responses), provide opportunities for personal development and learner discoveries. He describes his approach to autonomous language learning as humanistic, clearly going beyond situational autonomy (Tomlinson 1997).

We can not therefore be content simply to promote self-access; we must be concerned with how autonomous language learning works and what its influences are. There are influences that are rooted in the communicative approach to language teaching, which has nowadays become prevalent in many Institutions of Higher Education. These are learner-centredness, authenticity, language use with a purpose, open-endedness of tasks and materials, negotiation, collaborative group work and individuality. These concepts, if developed beyond their current boundaries, are also central to autonomous language learning.

Learner autonomy is not a permanent state the learner reaches once and for all. Instead we need to provide language learning environments that promote learner autonomy and e-mail tandem learning is, in my view, one of them. Certain aspects of language learning autonomy can be fostered through e-mail tandem learning, mainly those of collaboration and reflectivity.

Tandem learning can be described as a situation where learners come together both as foreign language learners and native speaker experts at the same time. In e-mail tandems the mode of communication is writing, although e-mails often display an informal style and register not dissimilar to oral interaction. However, the asynchronous form of e-mails provide the participants with the opportunity to analyse and look back at their own and their partners' writing, in order not only to support each other's learning (collaborative element of autonomous learning), but to reflect on the learning process, as a vital element in becoming a 'more autonomous' learner.

Tandem learning is characterised by the principles of learner autonomy and reciprocity. Reciprocity is described by Bobst & Krohn as

> *'das gleichberechtigte Geben und Nehmen zwischen Partnern' (Bobst & Krohn 1993).*

Giving and taking in equal shares is seen to facilitate tandem learning and as such can be described as the collaborative element of autonomous learning. Edith Esch names this criterion 'shareability' and describes it as a system for learners to share activities and/or problems and difficulties (Esch 1996). The establishment of social relations in e-mail tandem learning as a means of anchoring ones language learning must also be stressed.

In e-mail tandem learning there are two or more participants whose native language the partner is learning. The aim is to learn from each other through the active negotiation of the communication as partners have to make decisions with regard to the subject matter, the frequency and the rules of the exchange. In e-mail tandem learning the partners have to take responsibility for their own as well as each other's learning. Individual needs and learning styles have to be brought in line with those of the partners. In evaluating this aspect I looked at the distribution of messages, the use of L1 and L2 and support structures amongst partners.

E-mail tandem learning will not only bring closer the 'real world' of the country whose language the participants are studying, but it is truly authentic as participants will act as native speaker models for language and cultural acquisition. Language will be used to communicate a purpose and not simply for language practice.

Using the criteria above I will attempt to show to what degree the participants of the three email projects have moved towards becoming autonomous language learners. As autonomy is not a state one reaches once and for all I will show the opportunities the participants had to become 'more or less' autonomous.

The Projects: 3 different projects involving the medium of e-mail for communication have taken place at Bolton Institute of Higher Education. The first project of e-mail tandems took place in the winter semester of 1997, followed by the second one in the winter of 1998. The third project is a discussion forum that took place in the summer semester of 1999. A further collaborative e-mail project has been planned for the winter term of 1999.

I will first briefly summarise the results of the first project which have been disseminated at Eurocall 98 in detail. Further information about this project can be found on my webpage at http://www.acs.bolton.ac.uk/~ks1.

The second project will then be described in detail highlighting the differences between the first and the second project. I will finish with the third project, which can be described as a collaborative e-mail discussion list.

The First E-mail Tandems: The first e-mail tandem learning project took place in the winter semester of 1997/8 in conjunction with out long-standing Socrates partner the Hochschule für Technik, Wirtschaft und Kultur (HTWK) in Leipzig/Germany. Two co-ordinators monitored the e-mail exchanges throughout the project. Evaluation took place through the use of questionnaires, interviews and the analysis of the actual correspondence, as participants from Bolton were asked to send a copy of their e-mails to the co-ordinator. 18 e-mail tandems started in October 1997. Participants were required to be available for 1 semester, write regularly and use the foreign and native languages in equal amounts. They also had to decide on the subject matter and negotiate the rules of the exchange, especially with regard to correcting each other. Integration of the e-mail tandem learning into the existing curriculum at BIHE was achieved via an assessed oral seminar presentation that gave the students the opportunity to disseminate the work of their tandems. The actual writing during the e-mail exchanges was not assessed.

Out of 18 partnerships 4 never got started. Despite efforts from the co-ordinators these 'dysfunctional' partnerships could not be revived. In another two partnerships new partners were allocated after initial problems. The number of messages sent varied between 4 and more than 10 messages during the 10-week period. Uneven distribution of messages between partners was found in the less successful partnerships, while the active partnerships showed an equal distribution of messages and languages used. Not all partnerships were successful in negotiating the rules of the exchanges, finding the right way and amount of corrections was perceived as most difficult. Most students at least offered some sort of help to their respective partners. Some students clearly felt uncomfortable in their role as native speaker expert.

The lack of control of the partnership was especially evident in the case of negotiating the topic or subject matter of the exchange. Responses from participants ranged from wanting to relinquish all responsibility to genuinely shared responsibility.

On the whole though it can be said that the principle of reciprocity was adhered to, only one partnership totally ignored each other's need to be able to benefit from each other as native speaker models and saw the e-mail exchange as a practice exercise in writing in L2.

The students' perception of e-mail tandems was on the whole positive. 3 participants found the tandems very useful, 5 found them useful and 2 found them not useful. They felt that they had gained more confidence in using German away from the normal classroom setting through authentic communication with a native speaker.
Perceived benefits were primarily seen in the area of language learning rather than inter-cultural learning. The problems most frequently mentioned by students were technical problems, no or infrequent messages from their partners and no common interests.

Conclusion drawn for the second round of e-mail tandem learning: It is quite clear from the first round of e-mail tandems that learners need help in becoming more autonomous, as they do not automatically become autonomous simply by being placed in a self-study situation. The following changes were therefore implemented for 1998.

The concept of 'double-dating or double tandems' has been introduced not only to reduce the failure rate of partnerships but also to stress that e-mail tandem learning is a collaborative effort in an autonomous learning setting.

As autonomous learners via e-mail who are meant to take charge of their own as well as their partner's learning students have only partly been successful. As reported above 'subject matter autonomy' proved to be a problem especially in terms of selecting an appropriate topic for the seminar presentation. To alleviate this problem for the next set of e-mail tandems participants had to sign up for a specific project, which will provide the framework for the exchange. This project work will then be presented together by all partners during the face-to-face meeting in Leipzig, which has been made possible through funding from the DAAD.

Participants of the first round of e-mail tandems also found it difficult to control the partnership. The negotiation or reflective component of autonomous language learning only functioned well in some of the partnerships. The participants clearly need some 'learner training' (Little 1995) in terms of negotiating the rules of the partnerships and how to critically reflect on each other's learning. An introductory session on learning via e-mail was again conducted at the start of the second e-mail tandem project. The principles of learning in tandem were discussed and students were shown various strategies of communicating with and helping each other so that students could choose appropriate strategies that fitted their needs (theirs and their partners).

The Second E-mail Tandem Learning Project: The organisational and evaluation procedures remained the same for the second round of e-mail tandems. Two co-ordinators set up and monitored the scheme throughout the usual 10-week period. Evaluation took place via questionnaires and informal interviews with participants and through the analysis of the e-mail correspondence. Integration into the existing curriculum was achieved by means of a common seminar presentation at the face-to-face meeting in Leipzig.

As described above to facilitate the collaborative element of e-mail tandem learning it was decided to set up so-called 'double-tandems' consisting of 2 students each from Bolton and Leipzig. They were 'paired up' according to the choice of topic made, which was to give them the overall framework of their discussion and final seminar presentation. 24 participants were thus put into 6 'double tandems' of 4 people each. One 'double tandem' never got moving. Other groups had inactive elements, i.e. one partner out of four was not corresponding. Altogether 6/7 students out of 24 must be described as inactive.

It became quickly apparent that the mode of 'double tandems' had advantages and disadvantages. The major advantage identified was that discussion could still take place even if one partner was inactive thus preventing 'dysfunctional' tandems. On the other hand there were organisational problems in that participants found it more difficult to organise the writing to more than one partner. Problems encountered were in the area of whom to correct, when and how to address the different partners.

Monitoring the correspondence via copies of all e-mails was mainly restricted to e-mails from Bolton students, although some of the students from Leipzig also send copies to me.

Principles of Shareability, Authenticity, Reflectivity: I will first of all look at how students perceived the idea of 'double tandems' to facilitate the collaborative aspects of autonomous language learning. The view on this aspect was divided. I have found some evidence in the e-mail corpus sent that some groups recognised the potential of 'exploiting' all partners:

> *Zum Beispiel H.: Es würde mich sehr freuen, wenn Du mir auch einiges über dein Heimatland und deine Beweggründe, warum du dich entschieden hast in Bolton zu studieren, schreibst.*
>
> *Genauso interessiert es mich, wie du J., Dein Jahr in Deutschland empfunden hast.* (student K.)

Some others ask for help or offered help and encouragement to group members thus recognising the dependency on each other in order to make the exchange a success:

> *Kannst du bitte meine Fehler korrigieren. So ungefähr 5 Fehler jedes Mal korrigieren. Das würde mir sehr helfen. Ich korregiere einige Sachen für dich.*
> *'As I drived home' sollte 'As I drove home' sein, weil 'drive' in der Vergangenheit 'drove' ist'. [...] (student E.)*

It was originally left to the 'double-tandems' to sort out whom, when and how to correct each other. It became quickly apparent that this approach did not work for most groups. Participants did not want to 'publicly correct' any of the partners. Instead they preferred to have one of the partners allocated for corrections, whom they then corrected in separate emails.

> *Thank you for your long message. I'll address to you only the corrections of your first message. I have rewritten the sentences that needed correcting.* (student N.)

Some participants unfortunately then continued writing to just one partner. The wish to have a close and more personal relationship with just one partner was named as one reason for this approach:

> *It is, in my opinion, better to write to only one person. It is closer.* (student questionnaire)

The social anchoring of learning in a personal relationship with a partner was obviously perceived as more important than the potential benefits of enhanced group discussion. One student named as the main benefit of the scheme 'that a friendship had developed' (student questionnaire).

There were also instances in which participants wrote to both their respective partners in Leipzig, but left out their second English partner (group 3). I guess that they were less interested in learning from another native speaker. This seems to be supported by answers in the student questionnaire that stressed, just like the first time, that language learning took precedence over inter-cultural learning.

Although we tried to provide a learning environment conducive to the development of collaborative forms of autonomous learning, individual learning styles, preferences and needs cannot be left out of the equation. The following example illustrates how different attitudes about language learning can affect the communication adversely:

> *Na gut, ich weiss, dass ich meine größten Schwierigkeiten mit der englischen Grammatik habe. Da kannst du mich auf jeden Fehler hinweisen. Sei ruhig pingelig, ich verkrafte das schon.* (student M.)

The student in question applied 'his' approach (correction of all grammatical errors) to the partner's messages and corrected most, if not all, of her mistakes. This is her reaction in the student questionnaire:

> *I can write a bit more although he made me have an even greater lack of confidence by correcting every word — some words were only machine errors.* (student J.)

The incompatibility of the two individual learning styles made collaborative group work almost impossible. Both students did not possess the ability to change their approach in order to accommodate their partner's needs. They have failed to reflect on the learning process and have missed the opportunity afforded to them to become 'more autonomous'.

The authenticity of the e-mail exchanges was shown in the conversations of various groups and most obviously during the face-to-face presentations in Leipzig. The following extract from student R's contribution shows that he has realised the unique potential of communicating with native speakers and fellow British students alike:

> *I would really appreciate if the Germans could tell me whether or not they feel truly European after 7 years of the Maastricht treaty [...]'*
> *S., do you know of any websites dealing with the European Union?*

Student R. realised that he can only get this kind of information from native speakers who can provide insights into the topics to be discussed he could not otherwise have obtained in a classroom setting. The general topic areas, in this case 'Europe' were only meant to provide a general framework for the discussion, but not meant to be restrictive in any way. It was up to the various group members to determine in which direction the discussion was heading, depending on individual needs and preferences.

The majority of students thought that working on a specific topic helped the discussion (5), only one student thought it was limiting the discussion. The face-to-face presentations in Leipzig confirm that assessment. The possibility of meeting one's partners face-to-face was clearly motivating for the students. Not all participants met in Leipzig, as the study-trip took place during the inter-semester break and some students were not available. The individual groups met first to get to know each other and to prepare and co-ordinate their presentations, the second session was then dedicated to the actual presentations. Each group member presented their side of the topic, e.g. the status of foreigners in Germany and the U.K. in general and their personal experience with foreigners in Bolton and Leipzig. This was followed up by a general discussion of everybody present. During the initial presentation students used their L2 during the subsequent discussion they could choose L1 or L2. Each mini-discussion took about 30 minutes each and was a truly authentic multi-lingual exchange.

The students' questionnaires revealed that students did appreciate the general learning potentials of e-mail tandem partnerships. 7/8 enjoyed taking part, the most frequent reasons given were 'learning with native speakers' and 'learning without the teacher' thus stressing the principles of authenticity and communication with a purpose rather than practising language for its own sake. The collaborative aspects of 'double tandems' were not perceived so positively by the participants as 6/8 did not find working in groups of 4 helpful. Although I generally found an equal distribution of messages and languages in the e-mails copied to me (principle of reciprocity), the German students said in the students' questionnaire that they preferred to write in L2 to gain maximum benefit from the e-mail tandem learning.

Conclusions drawn from the second round of e-mail tandem learning: It was the aim of the project to provide conditions conducive to develop language learning autonomy. 'Double tandems' were set up with 2 participants from each institution to foster group discussion and facilitate collaborative efforts to control and manage the e-mail tandem learning. As shown in the above examples some participants were successful in conducting a fruitful group discussion via e-mail. The perception of the students though points to the lack of a personal relationship previously experienced in 'single tandems'. This must lead us to the conclusion that the social anchoring of language learning is perceived as paramount to the success of autonomous language learning via e-mail.

The principle of authenticity can be accommodated well in e-mail tandem learning. Communicating with native speakers whose language the partners are learning will bring the 'real world' of the foreign country much closer to the learners. Together with their partners learners can participate in 'real' conversations, practising skills they were able to put into practice during the face-to-face meeting in Leipzig. This is described by Koschmann et al as 'calling upon students to engage in the same activities in their learning that they will be called upon to perform in eventual practice (Koschmann et al 1996).

Reflecting on the learning process in order to control and monitor an asynchronous communication via e-mail still needs further 'learner training'. As shown above taking control of one's own learning needs to be done in relation to the partners' learning taking account of each other's learning styles and preferences. Not all the participants were totally aware that their partners were meant to learn from them as native speaker models. Those students insisting on using L2 only denied their partners opportunities to learn form them.

The nature of e-mail should be conducive to reflection on the learning process as participants end up with a database of real life communication they could utilise for their learning. I observed though that most students did not prepare their e-mail messages at home, but replied rather spontaneously to messages received from their partners, treating it very much as an oral conversation rather than a reflective medium. In future tutorials with participants have to make this aspect much clearer. Learner training of this kind does already take place during normal classes in that groups of students analyse a text with a view to deciding what they personally could learn from a specific text. This approach then needs to be transported to future collaborative learner via e-mail.

Discussion Forum via E-mail: A discussion forum via e-mail took place during the summer semester of 1999. Participants of the 'double tandems' project were asked to sign up to the electronic discussion forum called 'Deutschland in Europa' (Germany in Europe). For students from Bolton the aim was to provide an opportunity to discuss matters related to the seminar they were doing as part of their BaHons German course with students from Germany. Despite the personal contacts made in Leipzig no German students actually signed up, limiting discussions to 8 students from Bolton. Although the forum was originally envisaged as being conducted in English and German with obvious benefits for all students it was now decided to conduct the discussions in the foreign language only (collaborative group work in writing in L2). As with previous projects the forum was monitored by myself (analysis of e-mail messages and student questionnaire). The work done by students was assessed as part of their coursework mark for the seminar. Students had to submit a portfolio of e-mails at the end of the project. A minimum of 10 messages was required. Students were assessed according to the principles of collaboration and reflectivity rather than purely on language skills.

8 students took part, one dropped out of the seminar and one submitted only one message. The other six students took an active part in the discussion. I was interested to find out if and how students initiated discussions through the introduction of new topics, if and how they reacted to other students, if and how they provided help for the other students, how well their were informed about and involved with the topic (principle of collaboration). In terms of reflectivity I looked at how they composed the messages and if they looked back at their own and other participants previous messages.

After an initially slow start the six students involved had very lively discussions about issues centred around the topic of the seminar. Some topics of the forum were directly related to the subject matter discussed in the seminar. Students thus used the forum to clarify issues or discuss them further. The topic discussed most was the war in Kosovo. But there were also instances where entirely new topics were introduced by the students (comparison of school and exam systems in Europe) or current news related to European matters were discussed (blockade by British truck drivers).

Two students performed exceptionally well in the forum. Their contributions show a good understanding and involvement with the topic. They tried not to discuss topics on a purely abstract level, but bring them down to a personal level, i.e. discuss how issues have a personal bearing for them, thereby making learning more relevant for them (e.g. effects of a particular school/examination system on their career prospects). Both students prepared their messages at home, taking great care, not only with sentence construction and use of language, but also with the way they reacted to other students. They frequently tried to involve the other students in the discussion through thanking them for their contributions, by answering questions or directly addressing other members of the forum. For example one student conducted a mini-survey:

> *Wer denkt, dass ein größeres Europa, ungefähr 21 bis 30 Mitglieder, besser sein wird? Und warum? Welche Vorteile und/oder Nachteile siehst du?* (student R.)

Three students wrote their contributions at home, the other participants wrote spontaneously with their writing displaying all the obvious features of high number of mistakes and colloquial use of language. Although they succeeded in collaborating with the other group members (principle of collaboration) they did not spend the time to look back at their partners' contributions in more detail in order to analyse and reflect on the learning process (principle of reflectivity).

One student commented that improvement in writing in the foreign language was greatly diminished due to the lack of native speaker participation. Although this is certainly true, students did not realise that their writing in L2 should nevertheless serve as a model, so that learning from each other is made possible. An example of language development within the forum is student E.'s list of 'Austrian equivalents' to German words, she had learnt during a stay in Austria. Some examples of reflecting on their own learning was also evident in the messages from the forum:

> *Die Aufnahme (kann mir jemand sagen, ob das Wort richtig ist?) [...]*
> (Student E.) (reflection on language development)
>
> *Ich denke, daß dieser E-mail Dailog besser geht als die vorherigen E-mails? Was denkt ihr?* (student R.) (reflection on learning via e-mail)

Compared with the two previous e-mail tandem learning projects, I personally agree with the view voiced by the above student, that the e-mail discussion forum has been the most successful 'dialogue' between students in being the one that has facilitated collaborative and reflective elements of autonomous language learning most. Students have clearly demonstrated more features of collaboration and reflectivity during the discussion forum than during the e-mail tandems. This might be attributed to the fact that this is the third project in which students (most of them took part in all three projects) are asked to collaborate via the medium of e-mail on a topic directly related to their studies and have by now become more familiar with forms of collaborative group work. I do believe that by making available to learners a variety of learning environments conducive to reflective and collaborative group work they will move towards becoming 'more autonomous language learners'.

References:

Apfelbaum, Birgit *Erzählen im Tandem. Sprachlernaktivitäten und die Konstruktion eines Diskursmusters in der Fremdsprache*, Tübingen 1993.

Benson, P. & Voller, P. (Ed) *Autonomy and Independence in Language Learning*, Longman 1997.

Bobst, H. & Krohn, D. 'Erfahrungen aus einem "Landeskunde-Tandem"' in: *Zielsprache Deutsch,* 1993, 25:4, 213-220.

Brammert, Helmut & Little, David (Ed) *Leitfaden für das Sprachenlernen im Tandem über das Internet*, Bochum 1996.

Brammerts, Helmut 'International E-Mail Tandem Network' in: Warschauer, Mark *Virtual Connections. Online Activities and Projects for Networking Language Learners.* Amsterdam 1991.

Calvert, M. 'Working in tandem: peddling an old idea' in: *Language Learning Journal 6/1992,* 17-19.

Esch, E. 'Promoting learner autonomy: Criteria for the selection of appropriate methods' in: Pemberton, R. *Taking Control — Autonomy in Language Learning,* 35-48, Hong Kong University Press 1996.

Koschmann, T. *CSCL: Theory and Practice of an Emerging Paradigm*, Lawrence Erlbaum 1996.
Little, D. *Learner Autonomy 1: Definitions, Issues and Problems*, Dublin 1995.
Little, D. 'Freedom to learn and compulsion to interact: Promoting learner autonomy through the use of information systems and information technologies'.
in: Pemberton, R. *Taking Control — Autonomy in Language Learning,* 203-218, Hong Kong University Press 1996.
Little, D. & Ushioda E. 'Designing, implementing and evaluating a project in tandem language learning via e-mail' in: *ReCALL 10/1998*, 95-102.
Murray, D. *Conversation for Action: The Computer Terminal as a Medium of Communication*, Amsterdam 1991.
Ushioda, E. *Learner Autonomy 5: The Role of Motivation*, Dublin 1996.
Pemberton, R. et all *Taking Control — Autonomy in Language Learning*, Hong Kong University Press 1996.
Tomlinson, B. 'Self-access materials' In: Benson, P. & Voller, P. (Ed) *Autonomy and Independence in Language Learning*, Longman 1997.
Weskamp, R. 'Selbstevaluation: Ein zentraler Aspekt schülerorientierten Fremdsprachenunterrichts', in: *fsu*, 1996 40/49 406-411.
Warschauer, Mark (Ed) *Virtual Connections. Online Activities and Projects for Networking Language Learners*, Hawai 1995.
Wolff, Jürgen Ein Tandem für jede Gelegenheit? in: *Die neueren Sprachen*, 4/93, 374-385.
Woodin, J. 'Email tandem learning and the communicative curriculum' in: *ReCall 9/1997*, 22-33.
The CTI Centre for Modern Languages, University of Hull.

USING CASE-BASED REASONING TO HELP IN COMPUTER ASSISTED LANGUAGE LEARNING

Nicole Tourigny, Laurence Capus
Université Laval, Canada

Abstract
Case-Based Reasoning (CBR) uses past solutions to solve current problems. However, CBR is not often used in Computer Assisted Language Learning (CALL) systems. In this paper, we explore some reasons for using the CBR approach so that computer systems designers specialising in CALL will be more aware of this type of reasoning. These reasons are drawn from both a literature survey and our work. We first explain how Computer Assisted Language (CAL) systems can benefit from the CBR approach by referring to the literature. Next, we describe our GARUCAS project to illustrate how CALL systems could take advantage of past experiences to help their learners. This project aims at developing a CBR tool to help one learn to summarise French texts. Given a text to summarise, this system will use previous similar texts in order to make a new summary by reusing and adapting, if necessary, the same summarisation methods. The retrieval process is currently being implemented. Results obtained up to now show that examples can be classified according to their similarity with the new situation. This system will allow the learner to benefit from both theoretical and practical instructional methods.

1. Introduction: Case-Based Reasoning (CBR) uses past solutions to solve current problems (Kolodner 1993). Thus, CBR systems can be seen as Knowledge-Based Systems (KBS) with a particular analogical mode of reasoning that uses past experiences to solve problems. Where our human memories are limited concerning the amount of information we can recall and simultaneously process, CBR systems are able to efficiently process an enormous quantity of data (Kolodner 1993). Therefore, given the parameters of a problem, the system is capable of searching its knowledge base in order to find past experiences or cases that most closely match the current problem. Such CBR systems have proven to be effective in providing desired results in numerous fields (Marir and Watson 1994; Kolodner 1993; Watson 1997).

CBR has been used in several Computer-Assisted Learning (CAL) systems (Weber and Schult 1998; Khan and Yip 1996). Many of them served to test the design practices and pedagogical principles involved, as well as to show how CBR offers an alternative to conventional rule-based and other artificial intelligence methods (Khan and Yip 1996). CBR can be of great service in CAL systems where learning is based on examples, especially when it is difficult, even impossible, to build a conceptual model in a given field (Weber and Schult 1998). In fact, these authors reported that the most successful tutoring systems have been developed in domains not covered by complete theories, like programming and chess playing, where learners are often introduced to the domain by means of examples. However, a recent literature survey that we conducted showed that CBR was not often used in Computer Assisted Language Learning (CALL) systems.

In this paper, we explore some reasons for using the CBR approach so that computer systems designers specialising in CALL will be more aware of this type of reasoning. These reasons are drawn from a literature survey and our work. CALL systems could take advantage of past experiences to help their learners. In the following, we first give a short overview of CBR technology and review the three components of a CAL system. Next, we examine some reasons why CBR has been used in CAL systems. Finally, we will summarise our research work concerning the GARUCAS project, which aims at developing a CBR tool to help one learn summarisation techniques. Given a text to summarise, this system will use previous similar summarising contexts in order to make a new summary by reusing and adapting, if necessary, the same summarisation methods.

2. What Is Case-Based Reasoning (CBR)? For a long time, the human intellect has been a source of inspiration in the solution of problems. Based on the processes of the human memory, CBR technology is a product of such inspiration. In fact, past situations are often called upon to solve a problem (Kolodner and Leake 1996). Thus, proven solutions from the past can be applied, taking into account the degree of similarity between preceding situations and the current circumstances. This method of reasoning is interesting because it is based on real-world observations.

In order to automate an application, domain knowledge must first be modelled according to its requirements. Secondly, a reasoning mode must be implemented so that this knowledge may be accessible to users looking for the solutions to their particular problems. In a CBR system, this knowledge or expertise is represented as cases, each one consisting of a problem situation and its solution. This knowledge base is called a case base. As indicated in Figure 1, the reasoning is generally implemented with four RE-processes (Aamodt and Plaza 1996).

When a problem is presented, the system will REtrieve from its case base the most closely corresponding cases, usually following an index, and compare them to the data provided upon entry. The system indexes its cases on the basis of characteristics that are pertinent to the retrieval process, or in other words, those that help determine the degree of similarity between the two cases. The next process consists of deciding which case will be chosen, and the solution of that case will be REused. In some CBR systems, these processes can be only partially automated because some decisions may require information unknown to the system. As a rule, the designers of such systems try to assist users by providing them with elements of a solution wherein the adaptations are explained in such a way as to serve in subsequent problem-solving situations. The result obtained can also be REvised if it is found to be unsatisfactory. To conclude the problem-solving cycle, the system must REtain this new element of knowledge by adding it to the base in the form of a new case in order to be able to access it later for use in similar situations. On the basis of this description of CBR, it is possible to assess the relevance of its use in solving problems.

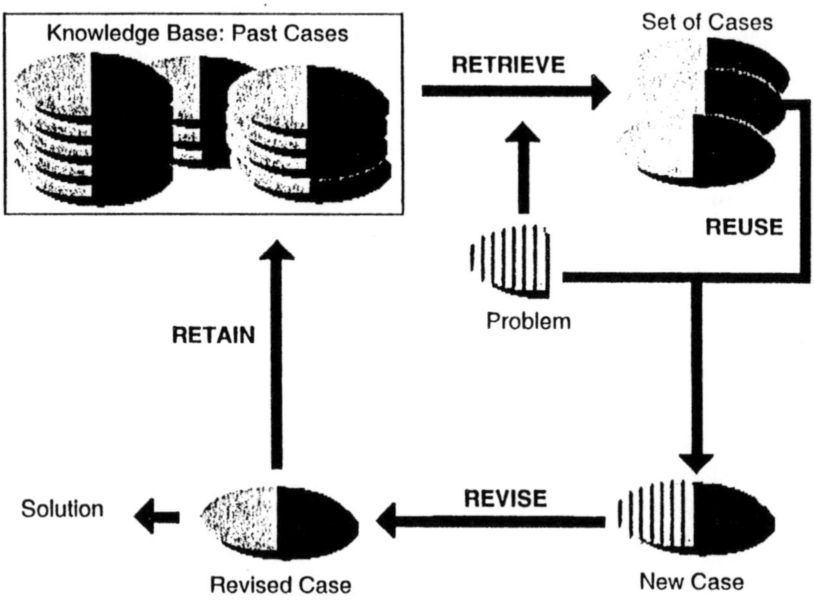

Figure 1. The four CBR processes

3. Computer Assisted Learning (CAL) Systems: The use of artificial intelligence is becoming increasingly common in computer applications in various fields such as education, administration, etc. Its most advanced application is certainly that of Expert Systems (ES), also more generally referred to as Knowledge-Based Systems (KBS). KBS uses domain-specific knowledge to solve problems. The solutions obtained are essentially the same as those an expert in the field might find when confronted with the same problem (Gonzalez and Dankel 1993). KBS is also characterised by the reasoning modes used (deduction, induction, analogy, etc.), the tasks achieved (classification, diagnosis, planning, forecasting, etc.), and by the manner in which the knowledge is represented (rule-based, model-based, case-based, etc.). In these systems, explicitly represented knowledge is used by the reasoning process in order to make intelligent decisions.

CAL systems are considered 'intelligent' if they can make decisions themselves; it means that they do not require that every decision be made by the system's designer (Khan and Yip 1996). For example, a tutoring system with summary expertise coupled with a reasoning capacity can make decisions on how best to select pertinent examples, according to a given context. An intelligent CAL must have two important characteristics (Weber and Schult 1998). The first is a capacity to generate problem solutions automatically by using its domain knowledge. This allows the system to analyse complex and uncommon problem solutions as well as to identify and explain errors. The second is based on the capacity to represent learner information and to use it in order to individually adapt the learning process.

According to Wenger (1987) and Khan and Yip (1996), an intelligent CAL system has three main, and relatively distinct, components: the domain expert, the learner, and the tutor. Each of them can have a varying degree of intelligence depending on how she/he solves problems.

- The ***domain expert model*** contains all the domain knowledge used to solve problems relating to this domain. This is the learner's subject matter, and can be represented with different modes such as rules, models, cases, etc. The expert module can use various reasoning modes to solve problems.
- The ***learner model*** is used to take the important characteristics of the learner into account: what the learner knows or does not know, the style of learning, etc.
- The ***tutor model*** (the pedagogical component or the teacher) contains the knowledge concerning how the subject matter is presented to the learner. It takes information from the learner model into account in order to present instructional material. For instance, a tutor model may help to decide what instructional material is to be presented to the learner and how it will be done: examples, explanations, questions, etc. According to Khan and Yip (1996), most traditional CAL systems are pre-programmed or allow only a few variations in the pedagogical component.

4. Why Use CBR in CAL Applications? Each of the three components of a CAL system can make use of CBR techniques. Expertise needed for a specific component is recorded in terms of past experiences as cases. Problems are solved by retrieving old solutions that proved to be correct or by adapting them to fit the new situation. Many reasons can justify a CBR component. When knowledge in the field exists in the form of cases, it is preferable to opt for the CBR model (Kolodner 1993). The acquisition of knowledge can be simplified because it is based on reports of past experiences (Xia *et al.* 1997). CBR systems can also be useful as teaching tools. Moreover, psychologists agree that people learn more quickly and easily from derived situations, using examples and drawing on idea associations (Kolodner 1993). With time, uninitiated users will be able to interpret the solutions (Meyer and Flanagan 1992) which result from expert data. CBR is a methodology often employed in CAL systems to organise a set of examples or cases in a structured network (Khan and Yip 1996). For instance, Aleven and Ashley (1992) proposed a CBR tutorial to help generate examples in the legal argumentation domain. Their experiment showed that system-created examples were clearer and more concise than the ones produced by traditional methods.

The domain expert module can use CBR to find solutions to problems arising in the expertise domain. When a solution is needed, the CBR component searches the case base for a similar situation and retrieves the solution that was applied. This solution can be reused and/or revised depending on the new situation. For instance, a CBR summariser will use similar past experiences in summarisation to help to write summaries of new texts (Capus and Tourigny 1998). Another example is the work of Aluísio and Oliveira (1995) which used a CBR expert module to help non-native English users to produce introductions for scientific papers.

CBR can also be used to model the learner and the teacher. This aspect is documented in Khan and Yip (1996). They identified fourteen fundamental pedagogic principles that influenced the design of CBR CAL systems. According to the survey they made, the CBR technology is often used to describe cognitive aspects during the learning/teaching process. Past experiences of the learner and the teacher can be put in a knowledge base and the system will analyse them in the course of a learning/teaching session. The knowledge can relate to lesson plans, choice of problems to present, learning styles, material presentation methods, interpretations about the learner's level of understanding, pedagogical strategies, etc. CBR thus enables CAL systems to make use of previous decisions concerning the learner or the teacher by adapting those solutions to the current problem.

5. GARUCAS: Using CBR to Help Learning French Summarisation: GARUCAS is the name of a project (and the resulting system) consisting in modelling a tutor system for learning French text summarisation by using examples. To summarise a new text, the system retrieves a similar example of summarisation from its knowledge base and reuses the same methods to produce a new summary. A new example is then created and will serve in future similar situations. Our learning hypothesis is that one can learn to summarise by observing an expert carry out this task in similar situations (Capus and Tourigny 1998). Examples are intended to illustrate how rules can be applied to produce a summary. This way, one can learn which rules to apply and what their effects are. Thus, the learner can follow the summary process step by step.

5.1 Architecture: The architecture of the proposed system is composed of three major parts (Figure 2). A *summarisation module* uses the four CBR processes to produce new summaries by using similar examples. They are stored in a *case base* and each case corresponds to a summarising example. Two kinds of cases are necessary to demonstrate summarisation: some contain examples which allow one to identify essential items in original texts (identification rules based on information extraction and selection processes) while others describe rules defined by Kintsch and van Dijk (1978) for generating final versions (condensation rules). The third part, called the *assisted learning module*, employs information provided by the summarisation module to explain to human learners how the summarisation task was performed. The examples are selected using a similarity function. The learner's problem is compared with each case in the case base according to features characterising the summarisation process: input (type of text, subject matter, text structure, learner's knowledge, etc.), purpose (summary function, summarisation context, etc.) and output (learner's preferences for summary presentation, style of summary, etc.). These features were discussed in Sparck Jones and Endres-Niggemeyer (1995).

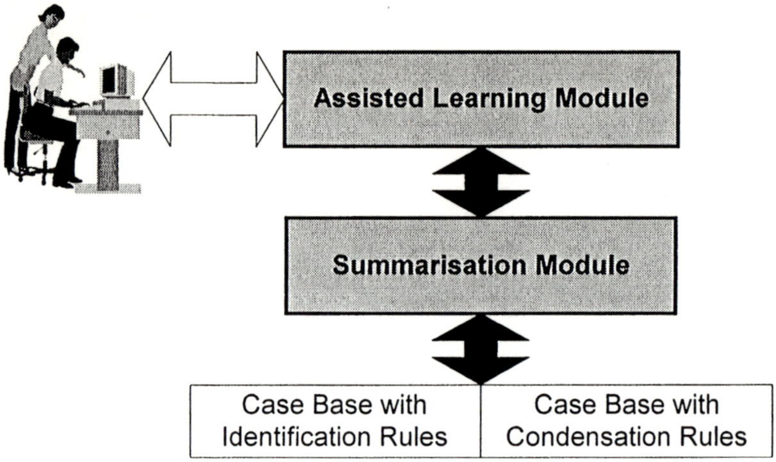

Figure 2. The GARUCAS Architecture

One can see the link with a CAL system as described in the preceding section. The summarisation module plays the role of the domain expert in summarisation. This is the component responsible for producing the summaries. The assisted learning module represents the tutor that identifies the learner's parameters (the learner model) by asking questions at the beginning of the session. The tutor can explain the summarisation process based on the learner's answers. For the moment, the emphasis is put on the CBR expert module because of its paramount importance in the learning cycle using examples.

5.2 How and When to Learn with the CBR Component in GARUCAS? Users learn by considering relevant examples selected by similarity. In a general manner, the assisted learning module explains to learners how the summarisation module accomplishes its task. Our approach offers three degrees of learning activity. First, one can observe the system as it summarises texts in similar situations. Given a text to summarise, the system retrieves similar contexts of summarisation and explains to the learner how the summaries were produced in these similar examples. Thus, the learner can learn from the explanatory retrieval process of the CBR component: the system guides the learner through the manner in which the rules were applied to produce the summary. The explanations will increase the learner's comprehension in order to prevent misunderstanding. Next, one can also observe the reuse and revise steps of the CBR component as the system summarises the learner's text. The tutor explains how to apply in the new situation the method used to identify essential information that was previously used in the similar case. Afterwards, the obtained result is revised, using examples of condensation rules to produce a coherent version. The observer will learn by watching the expert using the reuse and revise processes to generate a new summary using the old method. Finally, the learner can elaborate a summary and the system will advise her/him by providing examples of similar situations. In brief, the tutor system allows one to learn how to identify essential information in texts and also how to apply condensation rules to produce a coherent summary.

Considering this tutorial model, one can identify several underlying pedagogic principles. The following discussion refers to pedagogical principles concerning case-based techniques as demonstrated by Khan and Yip (1996). According to their fifth[1] principle, the system proposed by the GARUCAS project is a situated learning/task-centred instruction: the summary skill that is taught is situated in a task where knowledge is normally applied. The learner thus learns how to summarise by observing an expert of the domain. Specific summarisation domain experiences are recorded in a case base and serve as examples to illustrate how to perform the task. Thus, the system demonstrates a kind of story-based teaching method (Principle 1). Moreover, the sequence of rules needed to transform a source text into a summary can be regarded as a kind of story. The system proposes a meaningful instruction (Principle 3): examples of previously summarised texts are retrieved based on similarity, and this will help the learner to develop a cognitive structure of the summarisation domain. We can also refer to principle 8 (instructional congruence/felicity conditions) which stipulates that a conducive selection of examples will ensure the realisation of intended instructional goals and prevent misunderstanding. For instance, at the retrieval step, by explaining to the learner how the rules were applied in a similar case, the system reinforces the summarisation theory with concrete examples which will increase the learner's understanding. The learner can also learn to summarise by observing the system as it revises the case. At this step, the tutor will explain why the previous method needs revision before being applied to the new case.

In brief, GARUCAS uses a CBR expert module to produce summaries. For each step of the CBR process, the tutor system explains how the expert works. By observing the expert and by watching the rules being applied, the learner will assimilate the summarising process.

Conclusion: In this paper, we explored some reasons for using the CBR approach so that computer systems designers specialising in CALL will be more aware of this type of reasoning. As pointed out by some authors, CBR systems can be of great service, especially when it is difficult to build a conceptual model. They can also serve to illustrate theory by means of relevant examples. CALL systems could take advantage of past experiences in each of their three components, namely the expert, the learner and the tutor. The GARUCAS system presented in this paper uses CBR to help in learning summarisation techniques. Given a text to summarise, this system uses previous similar texts in order to make a new summary by reusing and adapting, if necessary, the same summarisation methods. Thus, the learner will benefit from both theoretical and practical instructional methods by observing a 'specialist' performing the summarisation task on similar examples. Other research works show that CBR could help to implement an

---

[1] The principle numbers are from Khan and Yip (1996).

intelligent tutor module taking into account appropriate aspects of the learner model (Khan and Yip 1996).

At the present time, we have modelled some summarisation examples from short children stories and we are now prototyping the system presented in this paper. The retrieval process is being implemented using the Prolog language. Examples are retrieved according to the learner' knowledge level (value scale), the plot units of the story related to the principal character — based on Lehnert's work (Lehnert 1981) — and the summary presentation (text or frame). Results obtained up to now show that examples can be classified according to their similarity with the new situation.

Acknowledgements
This work has been supported by the National Science and Engineering Research Council of Canada. We would like to express our gratitude to David Stafford for his help in verifying the English version.

References:

Aamodt, A., and E., Plaza (1996). 'Case-based Reasoning: Foundational Issues, Methodological Variations, and System Approaches', *AI Communications*, 7(1), 39-59.
Aleven, V., and Ashley, K. D. (1992). 'Automated Generation of Examples for a Tutorial in Case-Based Argumentation', *Proceedings, Second International Conference on Intelligent Tutoring Systems (ITS 92)*, C. Frasson, G. Gauthier and G. I. McCalla (Eds.), Springer-Verlag, Berlin, Germany, 575-584.
Aluísio, S.M., and Oliveira Jr., O.M. (1995). 'A Case-Based Approach for Developing Writing Tools Aimed at Non-native English Users', *Lectures Notes in Artificial Intelligence 1010, Case-Based Reasoning: Research and Development, First International Conference, ICCBR-95, Sesimbra, Portugal, October 1995, Proceedings*, M. Veloso et A. Aamodt (Eds.), Springer, New-York (NY), 121-132.
Capus, L., and Tourigny N. (1998). 'Learning Summarization by Using Similarities', *Computer Assisted Learning Language (CALL)*, 11(5), 475-488.
Gonzalez, A.J., and Dankel, D.D. (1993). *The Engineering of Knowledge-based Systems. Theory and Practice*, Prentice Hall, Englewood Cliffs, New Jersey.
Khan, T., and Yip, Y. J. (1996). 'Pedagogic principles of case-based CAL', *Journal of Computer Assisted Learning*, 12, 172-192.
Kintsch, W., and van Dijk, T.A. (1978). 'Toward a Model of Text Comprehension and Production', *Psychological Review*, 85(5), September, 363-394.
Kolodner, J. L. (1993). *Case-based Reasoning*, Morgan Kaufmann Publishers Inc., San Mateo, California.
Kolodner, J. L., and Leake, D. B. (1996). 'A Tutorial Introduction to Case-based Reasoning', *Case-Based Reasoning Experiences, Lessons, & Futures Directions*, D. B. Leake, (Ed.) AAAI Press/The MIT Press, Menlo Park, California, 31-65.
Lehnert, W.G. (1981). 'Plot Units and Narrative Summarization', *Cognitive Science*, 4, 293-331.
Marir, F., and Watson, I. (1994). 'Case-based Reasoning: A Categorised Bibliography', *The Knowledge Engineering Review*, 9(3).
Meyer, C. R., and Flanagan, D. C. (1992). 'Application of Case-based Reasoning: Concepts to the WEPP Soil Erosion Model', *AI Applications*, 6(3), 63-71.
Sparck Jones, K., and Endres-Niggemeyer, B. (1995). 'Introduction: Automatic Summarizing', *Information Processing & Management*, (31)5, 625-630.
Watson, I. (1997). *Applying Case-Based Reasoning, Techniques for Enterprise Systems*, Morgan Kaufmann Publishers Inc., San Francisco, California.

Weber, G., and Schult, T. J. (1998). 'CBR for Tutoring and Help Systems', *Lecture Notes in AI 1400, Case-Based Reasoning Technology, From Foundations to Applications*, M. Lenz, B. Bartsch-Spörl, H.-D. Burkhard, S. Weiss (Eds.), Springer, Berlin, 255-272.
Wenger, E. (1987). *Artificial Intelligence and Tutoring Systems*, Morgan Kaufmann, Los Altos (California).
Xia, Q., Rao, M., Henricksson, C., and Farzadeh, H. (1997). 'Case-based Reasoning for Intelligent Fault Diagnosis and Decision Making in Pulp Processes', *Pulp & Paper Canada*, 98(2), 26-30.

EXPANDING A MULTIMEDIA APPLICATION FOR A WIDER RANGE OF USERS

Michio Tsutsui, Masashi Kato, and Bradley Mohr
University of Washington, USA

1. Introduction: Since the communicative approach was introduced, a number of methods have been attempted in teaching conversational skills. Among them, one method which is commonly employed in many language classrooms is role-playing using model dialogues. This activity, although effective if properly executed, has several problems. For example, students are often not prepared for effective practice in class. The major reasons for this are that assigned dialogues are too long and/or too difficult, having many new linguistic items, being unfocused in terms of function, and are not related to students' real lives. Another problem is that classes are often too large, and the class time is too short for every student to practice role-plays effectively. Furthermore, even prepared students cannot perform well in classrooms because they have not prepared themselves in simulated situations before they come to class.

In order to solve these problems and make role-playing work effectively, the University of Washington's Technical Japanese Program developed an interactive multimedia language learning program called *Nihongo Partner*. Using multimedia and other computer technologies, this program provides simulated conversation situations which enable students to practice model dialogues as if they were talking with real human beings. In addition, instructors can create model dialogues suitable for their classes and integrate them into the program on their own.

Nihongo Partner (or NP in short) consists of four components, the NP Learner Interface, the NP Library, the NP Author, and the NP Database Tool. The NP Learner Interface provides an environment in which students can practice assigned dialogues and master them with minimum effort by following the guided practice steps provided in three sessions: the Presentation Session, the Repeat-After-Me Session, and the Interaction Session. In these sessions, students can view and learn the linguistic and socio-cultural points of given dialogues, repeat each line of one or both speakers until they can deliver them effortlessly, and finally practice the dialogues with a speaker on the computer screen. They can also record their voice to self-check their performance.

Dialogues for this program are stored in the NP Library in the form of QuickTime movie files and Segment Description Files. These files contain dialogue texts and their English translations, as well as other information for controlling the video presentation and managing the library. Acceptable media for storing these items are any mass storage devices, including large-volume magnetic disks, CD-ROMs, and servers.

The NP Author enables instructors to integrate video dialogues they have created into the program with minimum technical knowledge and resources. Once the video dialogues have been transformed to the proper video segment files and loaded in the NP Library, the NP Database Tool handles library maintenance.

Nihongo Partner has been developed on Macintosh computers because some crucial technologies which support this program — such as QuickTime — were not available for PCs when the project began. Consequently, the most recently released version (Version 4) runs only on Macintosh computers. Another limitation of this version is that the program has to be installed on local computers, and the video segments must reside on local storage devices. In terms of the language limitation, Version 4 is designed with Japanese as the target language and English as the assisting language.

Although *Nihongo Partner* is a highly usable program as it is, we the development team see its larger potential if its capabilities are expanded in certain areas. In the following sections, we will first discuss some needed expansions to *Nihongo Partner*'s capabilities, and then, the available technologies which enable such expansion. The final section will mention some implications when the planned expansion has been implemented.

2. Needs for expanding NP's capabilities. Through our NP promotional activities, we have recognised two areas where needs for capability expansion are crucial and urgent. They are cross-platform capability and multi-language capability.

Cross-platform capability

For the historical reason mentioned earlier, *Nihongo Partner* has been able to run only on Macintosh computers. However, through conference presentations and workshops on NP, it has become clear that there is a large population of potential NP users who work in PC environments. As a matter of fact, a great number of institutions currently use Windows operating systems exclusively. Thus, the NP development team's top priority is to add the capability to run on both Macintosh and Windows.

Multi-language capability

Another area of expansion we recognise to be crucial is multi-language capability. This realisation also came from our promotional activities, where we heard inquiries about plans to develop similar programs for languages other than Japanese. In fact, it is our belief that the theories and premises NP is based on are valid cross-linguistically and that programs like NP will be useful in learning other languages.[1] From the developer's point

---

[1] The development of NP is based on three premises: (1) Activities that involve real communication promote learning; (2) Low personal anxiety and low classroom anxiety are more conducive to second language learning; and (3) Mastering meaningful model dialogues with a

of view, however, it is more reasonable to develop a single program applicable to multiple languages rather than to develop a separate program for each different language. This is an attractive approach from an administrative point of view, too, because it is much more economical and efficient to install and maintain a single program which serves multiple language programs than to do the same thing with different software programs for different language programs.

In addition to the above two areas, we have also realised that given the rapid expansion of the Internet, it is important to include some remote access capability and administrative capability in NP so that students can enjoy the power of NP when they are away from their institutions.

Remote access capability
Computers continue to be more affordable, and an increasing number of people use personal computers at home. In addition, connecting to the Internet is becoming more available and inexpensive. In fact, the Internet has been penetrating many aspects of our daily lives. Considering these changes in the use of computers and the Internet, we believe that remote access capability will soon become an important element in the field of language learning as well. That is, if the Internet connects students' institutions and their homes, the students will be able to do the exercises they do at language labs now without being there. This remote access capability is invaluable for students who cannot afford to go to a language lab during regular business hours and for those who do not feel comfortable doing oral drills when other students are around.[2] This capability is also valuable for institutions with limited facilities to serve a large number of students. It is an even more critical need for working professionals who want to learn foreign languages, because this capability can free them from geographical and time constraints and allow them to practice conversations from their office or home, or even while they are away on a business trip.

Administrative capability
In order for the remote access capability mentioned above to function fully, we foresee that NP will need some administrative capability as well. For example, the program will need to have an authentication system so that program resources will not be used by unauthorised individuals. NP will also need access record management capability so that it can record when and for how long each student has logged into the system and what tasks he/she has performed. This capability enables instructors to monitor students' performance and progress. A note function that allows the teacher and students to

---

focused function promotes acquisition of communicative skills. (See Tsutsui, M., M. Kato, and B. Mohr (1998)).

[2] Matsuda (1999) reports that quite a few students in her class preferred not to use the recording function of NP because they felt uncomfortable recording their voice when other students were around.

communicate within the NP system might also be necessary. In addition, a system maintenance function will be important in case of a system failure.

3. Technological potential. In order to meet the need to expand of NP's current capabilities as discussed above, some new technologies are necessary. Fortunately, since the *Nihongo Partner* project began in 1993, several important technologies which can be utilised for NP expansion have developed. These include advancements in Apple's QuickTime media technologies, the emergence of Java and XML, and the rapid explosion of the Internet.

QuickTime

From its inception, *Nihongo Partner* has been built upon QuickTime as one of its foundation technology. At the time, QuickTime was a Macintosh-only multimedia technology, but since then it has expanded to the Windows operating systems. QuickTime movie files are completely cross-platform; a movie created on a Macintosh can be played on a Windows 95/98/NT computer without any conversion. This expansion provides *Nihongo Partner* with an excellent opportunity to expand its reach without having to make obsolete any existing content.

With the release of QuickTime 4 in the summer of 1999, QuickTime has become fully 'Internet savvy'. This new version of QuickTime supports streaming of video content over the Internet, so it is unnecessary to download a video file before playing it. In addition, QuickTime now supports a wider variety of video and graphic formats, including the most popular formats on Microsoft Windows. Java support is also included as a core part of the latest QuickTime release.

Java

Java is a programming language from Sun Microsystems that provides a consistent platform for cross-platform, Internet-enabled application development. Applications written using Java are, by their nature, cross-platform. A Java program written on a Macintosh can easily be run on a Windows computer with little or no modification and vice versa.

In addition to easing cross-platform development, Java has several other important features. Most important for language education purposes is its ability to handle any language and script system. A single string of characters in a Java program can contain English, Japanese, Arabic, or any other set of characters. Provided that the computer on which the program is running provides fonts and other support, the Java program will work in these languages as well.

Java has its roots in networked computing, providing an additional advantage to developing in Java. Developing an 'Internet enabled' application in Java is dramatically easier than in most other programming languages.

Internet
The explosion of the Internet has provided a myriad of opportunities. The capability to provide richly interactive multimedia content at extremely low cost to students located virtually anywhere would have been impossible just a few years ago.

Today, fast, full-time connections to the Internet are becoming much more prevalent. Just a few years ago, the typical Internet connection was a part-time dial-up connection at relatively slow speed. With the increasing popularity of Cable modems and Digital Subscriber Line (DSL) services, many potential students have fulltime high-speed Internet access in their homes. Similarly, most educational institutions and corporations now have fast Internet connectivity.

Fast, full-time Internet access enables applications that would not have been possible otherwise. For example, students may view full-motion video with high-quality sound over the Internet just as they would from a CD-ROM. Similarly, it is possible to centralise software management functions on a remote server, enabling an instructor to track each student's progress without intervention.

XML
Extensible Markup Language (XML) is a superset of HTML, the language of the World Wide Web. Virtually any type of information may be expressed in XML, including content designed to be viewed by users as well as information passed among applications 'behind the scenes'. XML has the advantage that it is a well-defined format, yet it is fully extensible for the particular needs of a given application. For example, *Nihongo Partner*'s Segment Description Files (SDFs) are a perfect application of XML. As mentioned earlier, each SDF includes the text and translation of a dialogue segment as well as timing information for the associated video clips. In prior versions of *Nihongo Partner*, these files were in a proprietary format that made them difficult to read and write and made it especially difficult to add or modify the format without extensive modifications to *Nihongo Partner* itself. Using XML, these files may be written and read using standard routines.

The combination of these technologies enables the creation of a new, more broadly focused *Nihongo Partner* that provides the capabilities mentioned earlier:[3]

(1) *Cross-Platform Capability*
Java is at the heart of *Nihongo Partner*'s new cross-platform capability. By writing NP in Java, full cross-platform compatibility is assured with minimal effort. QuickTime's new

---

[3] The current development version of *Nihongo Partner* (Version 5) has not yet met all of our objectives. The transition to Java is complete, bringing with it cross-platform capability and basic multi-language capability. However, the current version is largely a direct translation of the existing Macintosh-based *Nihongo Partner*, so it does not yet take full advantage of the Internet, nor does it include the rich set of administrative tools we envision.

cross-platform capabilities are also essential, as is the link between QuickTime and Java provided in QuickTime 4.

(2) *Multi-language Capability*
Again, Java's core support for multiple languages, including double-byte languages such as Japanese and Chinese, makes it much easier for a Java *Nihongo Partner* to support a virtually unlimited number of languages.

(3) *Internet Capability*
QuickTime and Java both enable a rich Internet experience with minimal development effort. Dramatic advances in the speed and pervasiveness of the Internet make this capability much more usable.

(4) *Administration Capability*
Java's network architecture, combined with the Internet of today, make it possible for students' and instructors' computers to communicate about students' progress, instructional materials, etc. Using XML for these communications enables a wide variety of rich interactions between student and instructor, thus helping to bridge the gap between students who use the program in a lab setting and those who do so at home or work.

4. Concluding remarks — Implications of *Nihongo Partner*'s new capabilities.
The new capabilities of *Nihongo Partner* discussed above have some important implications regarding language learning in the future. First, the Internet-capable NP has the potential to change the present scene in language labs dramatically. With the convenience that NP provides, practising dialogues at home with NP might well become common practice for students instead of practising at language labs. Second, if instructors and administrators find this change beneficial, their duties will involve more remote teaching, and the settings of language labs and/or computer labs will be geared toward this mode of instruction rather than local use. Eventually, these changes may promote the offering of distance language learning courses.

NP with multi-language capability, on the other hand, is expected to affect users differently. Unlike the use of conventional language software, the use of multi-language-capable NP, once installed, is likely to encourage other language programs at the same institution to use it. The use of the same software across different language programs will promote cross-departmental co-operation in improving the use of the technology and developing new teaching resources and management systems.

Finally, the Java version of NP with cross-platform capability will set a model of language software development by demonstrating the power and benefit of using Java, which can involve virtually any personal computer users as potential users.

References:

Tsutsui, M., M. Kato, and B. Mohr. 1998. Closing the Gap between Practice Environments and Reality: An Interactive Multimedia Program for Oral Communication Training in Japanese. (Part 1. Theory; Part 2. Practice) *Computer Assisted Language Learning — An International Journal*, 11:2, 115-151.

Matsuda, I. 1999. *Implementation of Interactive Multimedia Program 'Nihongo Partner'* Unpublished paper presented at the 9th Virginia Japanese Pedagogy Workshop, Georgetown University, Washington, D.C.

CONCORDANCING AND LEARNER AUTONOMY: AN EXPERIMENT WITH FIRST AND SECOND YEAR UNDERGRADUATES

Jeremy Whistle
University College Northampton, UK

Introduction: The experiment described in this paper is also the subject of an article to appear this month in a special issue of *ReCALL* (Whistle 1999). I do not want to repeat what I said in the article except where it is absolutely necessary. Instead, I propose to address today those issues which I could only touch upon in my article and to develop the discussion beyond the scope of the article. Above all, I want to look at some of the practical problems of getting students to use CALL in an autonomous way and, based upon my experiences this year, suggest a path of action for the future. I hope also to situate concordancing within a coherent framework of language teaching.

Using a concordancer: Because concordancing is crucial to my experiment, I will say a little about concordancers, partly for anyone who may not be familiar with them, and partly to illustrate why I have found them indispensable. Although most concordancers will also produce word-frequency lists, I am primarily interested in the concordancer's ability to search large numbers of texts incredibly quickly for examples of real language usage. Quite a good description of the process is provided by Flowerdew (1993):

> Concordancing is a means of accessing a corpus of text to show how any given word or phrase in the text is used in the immediate contexts in which it appears. By grouping the uses of a particular word or phrase on the computer screen or in printed form, the concordancer shows the patterns in which the word or phrase is typically used.

Taking these patterns as the starting point, one can ask questions about meaning or structures and, one hopes, find answers. If anyone is unfamiliar with a computer concordance, here is what one looks like: (OHP)

```
ite Duras était quelqu'un qui espérait toujours que la vie serait plus intéressan
able. Cela dit, je continue à espérer que cela n'est pas leur position définitive.
 Conseil de l'Europe. Il faut espérer que le système européen pourra garder son ef
t modestes. Les organisateurs espèrent simplement que la fête débordera du stade e
 qu'il faut incontestablement espérer que se mette en place une confédération mond
 un 'France Info étranger'. J'espère simplement que dans dix ans, cette radio exis
```

As you can see, this one is based on the phrase 'espérer que'. This particular example came about because I had just read in a book which I was using with my students that, and here I quote, 'verbs in subordinate clauses dependent on *espérer* are always indicative'. This did not tie up with my own experience. In fact, just recently I heard on France-Inter the presenter say: 'Il faut espérer qu'elle (i.e. la campagne publicitaire) soit efficace' but this is of course purely anecdotal and not the stuff to impress students. In addition, it is oral and therefore open to accusations of being a typical error of hyper-correction or performance. What I felt I needed was written proof to support my view that this statement was not true. In four seconds I searched 276 files totalling 364188 words and found the six examples given above. While they are not enough to formulate a general theory explaining the mood of verbs after the verb *espérer,* the fact that one sixth of the examples in my corpus was in the subjunctive gives the lie to the rule enunciated and suggests to me that one needs to be more circumspect when presenting rules. What the concordancer cannot do is explain why the subjunctive is used once here after 'il faut espérer que...', as also in my oral example, but not in the other case. The concordance is the starting point, not the end. This, then, is an example of a concordance being used to test a grammatical rule.

Another example is the following which set out to test a lexical point. As part of my teaching is within a European Business degree, I have frequently to talk about marketing. I tend, like most French people I have met, to use the word 'le marketing' although I know very well that the term 'la mercatique' exists. It struck me one day that I could perform a search in order to discover how far 'la mercatique' might have replaced 'le marketing'. The results were interesting: (OHP)

```
? S'appuyer sur les techniques marketing classiques et profiter de l'intérêt crois
va devenir un outil central du marketing relationnel . A l'échelle mondiale, les d
lus modernes de management, de marketing et d'organisation industrielle. Bernard
ramme de cinq cours européens (marketing, droit communautaire, économie, projet
 MBA bilingue en management et marketing touristique a été créé. Il s'adresse en
a formation avec des arguments marketing . Ils appliquent tout naturellement sur l
atrice Larcher, responsable du marketing chez Arianespace, la société française qu
r ISL Worldwide, le partenaire marketing de la Fédération internationale de footba
ule. Denis Weill, directeur du marketing, explique : Jacqueline est totalement dis
directrice de la stratégie, du marketing et de la communication d'EDF internationa
 doivent rien à l'argent ni au marketing et tout à l'amour de l'art . Les valeurs
 aux hamburgers Spécialiste en mercatique, un jeune français, Pierre Truchet, s'es
```

As you can see, there are eleven examples of 'marketing' to one of 'mercatique' so I shall continue to use the former knowing that I am doing what the natives do. One extension of this was a second concordance, this time combining 'marketing' and 'commercialisation', which I used with a final year class in order to alert them to the lack of symmetry between English and French in the meanings of apparently similar words.

An obvious question that these examples raise is: how representative are they? Any concordance is ultimately only as valid as the corpus it is based on. I will say more about the corpus I used later because the question is an important one which I would like to address when I have said more about my learning groups and the experiment I undertook with them. The examples above clarify, I hope, exactly what a concordance is in case anyone was unfamiliar with concordancing.

Using the Concordancer with Students: Using concordances for one's own purposes is one thing. Using them with students is another. My starting point was the frustration that I feel each time I am confronted by my students' inability not just to use but actually to **see** grammatical structures. I will admit that for a long time I was fairly skeptical about formal grammar teaching, at least where it is essentially exercise based. My objections are basically: (OHP)

1) it leads to simplifications when we have to teach our students to cope with complexity
2) it tends to treat forms in isolation and not in opposition to other forms
3) it involves decontextualisation which effectively excludes precisely those discourse features which, alone, can often explain why a specific word or structure is used.

I do believe in the teaching of concepts but have always thought that the most effective way of learning was from structured exposure through listening and reading. The concepts allow the students to make sense, semantically and grammatically, of what they are hearing and reading. To this extent I sympathised with Krashen's 'input hypothesis' (Krashen 1985).

> [W]e acquire language in an amazingly simple way — when we understand messages. We have tried everything else — learning grammar rules, memorizing vocabulary, using expensive machinery, forms of group therapy etc. What has escaped us all these years, however, is the one essential ingredient: comprehensible input.

There are those who challenge this but it does in large part correspond to my own experience of learning French and other languages.

I have always believed that it is impossible to develop beyond a certain point in a foreign language without a core grammatical competence, at a minimum that which used to be taught for the old 'O'-level. One only has to observe the occasional mature student, 15 or 20 years after taking 'O' or 'A'-level, in a class of 18/19 year old whose 'A'-level is barely a couple of months old. However slow and hesitant the mature students may be at the beginning, by the end of the first year they have begun to outstrip the others, in all skills including the spoken. Many, if not most, of the rest are handicapped by what I can only describe as 'grammar-blindness'. Because in the first crucial years of language learning, essentially up to GCSE, they are not taught to see things such as gender, number, tense, subject, object, word order, they become blind to them. Apparently, if you rear kittens in an environment in which there are only horizontal lines and then put them in a cage with vertical bars, they cannot see the bars and walk into them. Presumably because walking into bars hurts, the kittens quickly learn to put their head on one side. Because there is no pain involved in not seeing grammar, our students remain unaware of its existence. As a result, in Krashen's terms, there is no input and therefore there is no learning. The students have reached a plateau from which there is no advance.

In spite of my skepticism, I tried putting in place a revision grammar syllabus going back to the absolute basics. This was in part because I was under pressure to come into line with colleagues in other languages and also because my institution requires detailed schemes of work to be given out at the beginning of the year. Unfortunately, it was like trying to teach choral singing to the tone-deaf. There remained an irreducible number of students who gained nothing and for whom, to take one example, use of the relative pronouns 'qui' and 'que' remained totally arbitrary. I put this down, in part, to the passive role that the grammar classes imposed on the students. I had not intended them to remain passive. I had always hoped for questions but when these came they were always from the mature students. Not only did the non-mature students for the most part not ask questions, they positively resented my answering the mature students' questions, complaining that I was wasting class time on unnecessary complications. It was at this stage of frustration that I decided to build on my own experience of using a concordancer and introduce it as a language learning tool with my first and second year students. I thought that, through having to search texts for forms and provide explanations, they would not only become more active participants in their language learning but, crucially, they would begin to see the surface features of language and progressively lose their blindness. The general conceptual framework was that of discovery learning or, more specifically, to quote Johns, 'data-driven learning' (Johns 1991a & 1991b):

> [T]he language learner is also, essentially, a research worker whose learning needs to be driven by access to linguistic data — hence the term [...] The use of the concordancer can have a considerable influence on the process of language learning, stimulating enquiry and speculation on the part of the learner, and helping the learner also to develop the ability to see patterning in the target language and to form generalisations to account for that patterning. (1991a:2)

The framework is important for another reason and one that takes us back to the title. The changes that I have referred to mean that one has to teach students more than one used to in order to bring them to a level where they can read with reasonable accuracy. Yet, at the same time the teaching hours have over the years been progressively reduced. Whereas ten years ago, first year students had six hours of French, they now have four. It is therefore even more important that they can use their non-timetabled time to extend their knowledge of the language. They need in fact to become autonomous learners. Yet without the concepts and the core grammatical knowledge, this is not possible. My purpose was therefore to give my students a method for making sense of the surface features of French and perceiving the forms underlying them and, at the same time, a resource for private study. My hope was that, over time, when they came up against problems that they could not resolve with the usual reference tools, they would use the concordancer to look for examples in the corpus and interrogate these. The concordancer and the corpus would thus become a shared resource of the 'French community'.

The Practical Issues: The first two issues to resolve were what to use as a concordancer and what to use as a corpus. The latter was the easier. I was already using the corpus referred to already derived mainly but not exclusively from the French Ministry of Foreign Affairs website[1] and primarily the articles from *Label-France*. These texts had been chosen because of their French focus and because the language is essentially conservative. A teaching corpus is not the same as a research corpus. Its purpose is to provide normative examples and not to test the limits of the given language. Journalistic texts were largely excluded because they contain all manner of stylistic problems that act as barriers to students' understanding. First and second year undergraduates need a linguistic model or models on which they can base their own French confident that they have wide acceptance. Examiners and employers tend after all to be linguistically conservative. Making the corpus available to students raised however the copyright question. Fortunately, clearance was given by the French Embassy in London, provided the source of the texts was acknowledged, which was another very good reason for using *Label-France*.

The choice of the concordancer was more problematic or would have been if I had had any money to buy one. I use *WordSmith Tools*[2] for research purposes but, like the author, I feel it is too complex for students to use except perhaps at postgraduate level. The *Longman Mini-Concordancer*[3] was another possibility. However, both cost money and I did not have any. *Micro-concord*[4] is available now for free download from its author's website but had two major disadvantages. The first was its DOS interface which makes it relatively user-unfriendly, at least by modern standards, and the fact that it only reads texts in ASCII (or DOS) as opposed to ANSI (or Windows) form. This may not matter with texts in English but is of crucial importance when dealing with texts in a

---

[1] http://www.france.diplomatie.fr/

[2] *WordSmith Tools*, 1993, written by Tim Johns and published by Oxford University Press
cf http://www4.oup.co.uk/isbn/0-19-459283-9
or http://www.liv.ac.uk/~ms2928/index.htm

[3] Longman Mini-Concordancer, 1989, Longman

[4] cf http://www.liv.ac.uk/~ms2928/index.htm

foreign language. It means that all your accented characters behave in a bizarre way, as in the following example: (OHP)

> C'est Ó partir des annÚes trente que le tourisme devient un phÚnomÞne de masse.

The results are to say the least disconcerting. Imagine instructing students to enter an upper case 'u' acute every time they want a lower case 'e' acute.

Practical and financial considerations forced me to develop for student use a program which I had written for my own research purposes. This was a basic concordancer without the frequency-count facility that more sophisticated programs have. The advantage of my program, for which I coined the name *KWIC-CONCORD,* was that it had been written specially to search for words containing accented characters in ASCII, ANSI and HTML formats. It allowed a search to be performed on single or multiple files, on a whole directory or subdirectory or on a whole disk. It is, in Tribble and Jones' (1990) taxonomy, a streaming concordancer in that it reads texts line-by-line (actually in 31k chunks) and produces concordanced text to screen and, if required, to disk. It also matched Stevens (1995) parameters:

> A concordancer for use with students must be fast and responsive. It must load quickly [...] Sorts on output should be instantaneous and permitted both one-over and proximally left and right of the key word[...] Loading and querying should be interruptable at any point, and the user should be able to work with the portion of the corpus or concordance processed up to that point [...] (pp.3-4)

Although streaming can never be as comprehensive as text-indexing, it is faster and on modern machines almost as fast as in-memory concordancing. The main modification made to the program before using it with students was to port it from DOS to Windows 3.1. The advantages at the time were perceived as mainly cosmetic.

Putting Theory into Practice: I could confidently assume that none of the students would have used a concordancer before so I decided to leave nothing to chance and devised detailed worksheets (OHP/Appendix). These were designed to take students through the process stage-by-stage, beginning with finding the corpus files on the hard-disk. The most complicated part is the stage where the search strings have to be entered. A full instruction manual as well as a set of guidelines were also produced to help students manage the software. First reactions seemed promising. Students found their way around the Windows Program Manager screen, found the program group and the icon and got the program running. With the worksheets, they entered the words and began searching. The problems arose when they started analysing the results of the searches. The difficulty was that these could only be viewed on screen, scrolling up and down as necessary. Some students could not really cope with this. Also, if the search took longer than anticipated, the results were lost at the end of the session before they could be analysed. Gradually, from observation of the students, other shortcomings of the software became apparent. These led to a continuing process of software development in parallel with the classes, which were timetabled fortnightly.

What were the problems that arose with the software? One significant one was that, in writing the program, I had to perceive language as a computer does, as a string of characters. A space is no different from any other character, except for the few which are reserved for use as line feeds, carriage returns, etc. For the computer, words only become words if the boundaries are explicitly marked. To search for 'qui' it was therefore necessary to enter it as '\qui\'. If the slashes were omitted then the search would come up with everything from 'quinconce' to 'maquisard'. I had no problem with this procedure since I had begun to think like a computer. However, from the students' point of view it was counter-intuitive. If they left a slash off or put the wrong one in, then the results were unpredictable. Early on then in the experiment, it proved necessary to include an interpreter to translate human concepts into machine concepts.

Other modifications were prompted by the specific difficulties thrown up by working in a language other than English. Nearly all the literature on concordancing is based on practice in English, mainly in English as a Foreign Language. English lacks many things such as accents. Changes in French verb stems, usually permutations of 'e', 'é' or 'è', require a search for 'espérer' to include both 'espér' and 'espèr'. German (addition of umlaut) and Spanish (use of grave to indicate the tonic accent) present similar problems. Other difficulties are caused by the highly inflected nature of the other languages. To search for an adjective in English, one has only to enter one form. However, romance languages can have a separate masculine and feminine singular and plural forms making four in all. German too has a number of inflected forms. A simple solution is to use a standard DOS wildcard such as '?' or '*'. Thus, a search for 'français*' will find all forms of the adjective and nothing else. Try searching for 'blanc*' and you will get, in addition to the desired adjectival forms, 'blanchâtre', 'blanchir' (and all its inflections), 'blanchissage', blanchisseur', etc. With verbs, the situation becomes even more complicated. The form 'esp?r*' will find all forms of the verb (plus 'espérance' but this is not too much of a problem since it is predictable and the program allows one to enter a list of words to exclude). A search however for all the forms of the imperfect of 'être' based on 'ét*' will in addition to finding 'étant' and 'été' (including of course 'été(s)' meaning 'summer') also find totally unrelated forms ranging from 'établi' via 'étranger' to 'étudiés'. (OHP) My corpus produced a total of 2590 responses of which only 377 were forms of the imperfect. Most of the unwanted forms are difficult if not impossible to predict and therefore exclude.

The simplest solution, and the one first adopted, was simply to enter each word separately. However, in the case of the imperfect, this produced five separate files which made follow-up analysis difficult. This required the addition of an option allowing results to be saved to a single file. Ultimately, it proved desirable to introduce two new search procedures based on the use of special characters. The slash '/' allows a search for incremental endings. Thus the single form 'blanc/he,s' will find all masculine and feminine singular and plural forms and nothing else. The combination 'esp?r* qu/e' will find all forms of 'espérer' (and admittedly 'espérance') before both 'qu′' and 'que'. The sign '+' allows searches for a stem plus endings. Thus the single form 'ét+ais,ait,ions, iez,aient' will find these and nothing else. (OHP) While making the program more flexible, these changes did however make it more complicated. In addition, the progress of development was faster than that of updating the manual so students were not always able to use the new features.

Other features that were incorporated were: the ability to print or copy to memory the concordance results; to sort them and save/copy/print them in sorted form; to delete unwanted forms (eg 'été' meaning 'summer' instead of 'been'); to delete the results files on exit to avoid cluttering up the hard disks; and finally to perform word counts. Another modification was to review all text that appeared on screen to make it more user-friendly to non-specialists. This meant replacing, for example, the phrase 'source files' by 'files to search' and 'target directory' by 'save results to...'.

Ultimately, though, however much effort one puts into the software, it cannot guard against hardware problems or students' lack of forethought. If the software is copied daily from a central server and something goes wrong in the process, this can sabotage a session with students. If the printers are not working or the printer switches point to the wrong number, students can become quickly frustrated and blame the activity. If they do not bring a floppy with them to save the results to, they cannot work on them afterwards.

What were the outcomes?: Feedback at the end of the Autumn Term indicated that the students did not enjoy the computer work and especially the concordancing. This was especially true of the weaker students. This was in marked contrast to the previous year when reaction to the computer had been generally favourable. The most obvious new variable was the concordancer. However, from a careful reading of the feedback returns, other factors became apparent and one of these was frequency. There is a general feeling in the field that the computer should not be timetabled too often. One session every three weeks, it seems, maintains interest whereas once a fortnight kills it. Lack of familiarity with computers is another factor which is often quoted in the research. A few students could not find the corpus texts because they were not familiar with directories and sub-directories. Some students had difficulty in typing the keywords in accurately, more so in the early stages when they had to enter the slashes. Some would keep 'losing' the program, usually when they clicked outside the program window on the background Program Manager screen, and start from scratch again. This would have been less of a problem with windows 95 and NT and did not happen with the other programs which filled the whole screen.

The main problem, however, that the experiment threw up was the inability of many students to process the results. A first year activity based on noun endings and gender worked well with most students making the right connections. So did one focusing on the environment surrounding, and especially preceding, the words 'France' and 'Paris' and contrasting the results with English. This was designed to focus on use of determiners. Searching on 'elle' and 'lui' with a second year group as part of revision of personal pronouns merely highlighted the fact that if students have no clear idea of the difference between subject and object they cannot make sense of the pronouns. Another exercise with the same group investigating the subjunctive showed that their interpretation of the data was mediated through their existing misunderstandings resulting in various distortions of the evidence. In many respects, the experiment reinforces what is known about most self-access language learning. If the student has a good conceptual basis, he or she will be able to learn, in other words teach him or herself, the language.

What Lessons Can One Learn?: Where does this leave concordancing as a class-based activity and how far can it encourage autonomy? Some of the practical lessons are obvious: (OHP)

1) the hardware must be reliable
2) the program must be intuitive in conception and user-friendly in practice
3) there must be adequate supporting documentation
4) do not use students as guinea pigs in the development of software
5) students must be familiar and relaxed with the computer
6) searching in a foreign language introduces difficulties that do not arise with English.

The pedagogic lessons are less easy to define. One which is however reasonably obvious is that students must be given an adequate grounding in the methodology. To get students to move from a passive to an active role requires time and effort. When asked at the beginning of the year in a questionnaire how they thought they learned grammar best, 87% of Year 1 and 85% of Year 2 students thought it was by having things explained by the teacher, while only 27% of Year 1 and 35% of Year 2 thought it was by working things out for themselves. Students also need to become familiar with concordances and with the problems of working with truncated text segments. More important, they need to become confident that they can formulate their own rules. In the same questionnaire, 87% of Year 1 and 92% of Year 2 students thought that grammar was best learnt by doing exercises.

At a tactical level, I propose in future to introduce prepared concordances early in the year as part of my class teaching in order that students become accustomed to the format and the kind of questions that must be asked. I shall also ask students to prepare concordances on specific keywords as part of their homework, after they have had one or more training sessions during the 'skills week' that will be part of the course year in future. Only in the second term do I propose to timetable concordancing as part of the IT teaching strand and expect students to have formulated rules by the end of the lesson. This, however, will not of itself suffice. The whole context in which grammar is taught must, in my view, be rethought.

Change must take place at a strategic and not just at a tactical level. For many years, I taught very little formal grammar, preferring to work with texts as a basis for comprehension, summary and translation. This meant that any discussion of grammar was embedded in the comprehension of the text and had to take into account textual and contextual features, including aspects of discourse such as the target public and intended purpose of the text. This was lost when I reluctantly, and against my better judgement, started 'teaching grammar'. In future, rather than present rules to students in a predetermined sequence, I intend to let the texts that I use generate the grammar. Circumstances require me to produce a scheme of work but this will be suitably vague and include headings such as 'Basic concepts', 'The verb group', 'The noun group', etc. spread over several weeks. It will not contain headings such as 'The present tense', etc. Tenses will be treated globally, if progressively, two or more at a time. Concordances will be based, selectively, on the texts, supplemented by examples from the corpus as and when necessary. Because concordances force one to focus much more on the words, the approach has to be fundamentally lexical rather than syntactic or morphological. The position in the sentence (or syntagm or collocation) and the endings are properties of the word and not features of an abstract grammatical system. The meaning of the word is not composed of a number of semantic features but determined by the context. To sum up with one word, the approach that is required must be 'lexico-grammatical'.

Only if this approach is adopted from the beginning and carried through consistently can I hope to encourage in my students the attitude and skills that will enable them to take charge of their own learning and become autonomous. In this way, they may achieve levels of performance that are at present beyond them as a consequence of their lack of prior linguistic knowledge and the ever-reducing hours of contact that we have with them.

References:

Flowerdew John, (1993), 'Concordancing in Language Learning', *Perspectives*, 5/2, pp. 87-101
Johns Tim, (1991a), 'Should you be Persuaded: Two Examples of Data-driven Learning', in Johns Tim & King Philip (eds), (1991), *Classroom Concordancing: ELR Journal vol. 4*, University of Birmingham, pp. 1-13
Johns Tim, (1991b), 'From Printout to Handout: Grammar and Vocabulary Teaching in the Context of Data-driven Learning', in Johns Tim & King Philip (eds), (1991), *Classroom Concordancing: ELR Journal vol. 4*, University of Birmingham, pp. 27-45
Krashen Stephen (1985), *The Input Hypothesis: Issues and Implications*, Longman
Stevens Vance, (1995), 'Concordancing with Language Learners: Why? When? What?', *CAELL Journal*, vol. 6, no. 2, pp.2-10
Tribble Chris & Jones Glyn (1990), *Concordances in the Classroom*, Longman
Whistle Jeremy (1999), 'Concordancing with students using an 'off-the-Web' corpus', (forthcoming).

APPENDIX

FRENCH: LANGUAGE: LEVEL 1

Activity number: 1a

Directory/Files	c:\french\french.txt\fr_dip\label\19
Language structure	noun and noun group
Word to search for:	France
Procedure:	
Select files	1) click the yellow folder icon 'source files' 2) click the drive control box and then click 'C' to change drive 3) click the appropriate directory to change to '...\label\19' 4) click the little triangle in the 'Files of type' box and then click '*.txt' 5) hold down the shift key with your left hand and then, with your right hand, click first the top name in the files list box and then the bottom name to highlight all the files 6) click 'Ok'
Select target directory	1) click the white folder icon ('target directory') 2) click the drive box and then click 'C' to change drive 3) click 'french' 4) click the 'Create new directory' box 5) in the box that appears, enter the word 'temp' 6) press 'Enter' 7) click 'Ok'
Select strings	1) click the keyboard icon ('enter strings') 2) when the new window has appeared, enter the word 'France' in the top text box 3) click the 'Case sensitive' circle 4) click 'Ok'
Perform search	1) click the 'Save to File' box under the 'Search' button 2) click 'Search'
View results	1) click the monitor icon ('view target files') 2) in the files list box click 'dumpfile.001' and then click 'Ok' 3) use the 'Pause/Continue' and 'Up' and 'Down' buttons to control the movement of the text
Analysis	look at the words that immediately precede the word 'France' how many are there in total? what types of word are they? can you identify any pattern(s)? translate the word 'France' and those words which belong with it into English
Conclusions	what differences in construction are there between the two languages?
Rule	formulate a basic rule when using the word 'France' in French